National Trust

Handbook 2011

The complete guide for
members and visitors.
1 January to 31 December 2011

For much more about
National Trust places, visit
www.nationaltrust.org.uk

Everything you can do with the National Trust

Contents

Visit

Membership

People and places, clockwise from top left: **the Manor garden, Avebury, Wiltshire; the harbour at Boscastle, Cornwall; Hill Top, Cumbria; The Crown Bar in Belfast, County Antrim; National Trust campsite at Wasdale Head, Cumbria; Kedleston Hall, Derbyshire; Bodiam Castle, East Sussex; Welsh mountain sheep at Hafod y Llan, Snowdonia, Wales.** *Previous page, clockwise from top left:* **St Michael's Mount, Cornwall; tern on the Farne Islands, Northumberland; Max Gate, Dorset; fungus at Devil's Dyke, South Downs, West Sussex; Brownsea Island, Dorset.** *Cover:* **Lanhydrock, Cornwall.**

2011

Spring into action

It's the time of year when nature puts on its greatest show, so wrap up warm and head off to the great outdoors. Walk into wild landscapes and look out for luminous trees, bright with young new leaves, and woodland floors bursting with colour and scent, or rise and shine with a 'dawn chorus walk'.

Colour bursts

For stunning spring displays try:
208
Calke Abbey, Derbyshire. Experience a shower of spring flowers in the woodlands. Look out for dainty bluebells and yellow archangel.
338
Colby Woodland Garden, Pembrokeshire. Spot wonders beneath your feet. Take to the woodland and discover carpets of bluebells and an abundance of camellias.
369
Rowallane Garden, County Down, Northern Ireland. See the much-admired collection of rhododendrons bursting into bloom.

New experiences

Join a modern-day treasure hunt and try geocaching, using GPS technology on your phone or Sat Nav. Top spots are the Clent Hills, near Birmingham, the Long Mynd, Shropshire Hills, Upper Wharfedale and Malham Tarn, Yorkshire Dales, and Tyntesfield, near Bristol.

The Weir

Charlecote Park

Summer days

Make the most of hazy blue skies and the longer days of summer by getting out into the fresh air with friends and family. Race up windswept hills, just right for kite flying and bird spotting. Have a seaside adventure, uncovering hidden coves and secret bays. Play hide and seek in pretty gardens and wildflower meadows. Or, relax and unwind in wide, open spaces, ideal for a bit of alfresco dining.

Here comes the sun

For a shot of summer colour don't miss:
145
Sissinghurst Castle, Kent. Don't miss the scent-drenched rose garden, the colourful lime walk and the famous grey, green and white garden.
235
Biddulph Grange Garden, Staffordshire. Discover upside-down trees, rockwork, a formal Italian garden, Egyptian Court and a tranquil Chinese garden.
316
Cragside, Northumberland. Take in a splash of Victorian colour on the dahlia walk, where more than 700 flowers bloom in fiery hues.

Shore thing

Catch a wave – try Sandy Mouth near Bude in Cornwall, Rhossili in South Wales or Compton Bay on the Isle of Wight.

A taste of autumn

As summer gives way to autumn, take a stroll and celebrate the arrival of the new season. Explore gardens and parks ablaze with Technicolor displays and let the views take your breath away. Enjoy the unmistakable 'crunch' of leaves underfoot, spot trees bursting with delicious fruit and experience all the drama of a deer rut. Indulge your friends, family and your taste buds in tea-rooms and restaurants, sharing mouth-watering treats full of the rich colours and aromas of the season.

In the shade

Some of the best places to visit this autumn:

40
Dyrham Park, Gloucestershire. Take a peep out of the windows of this lavish baroque mansion and you might catch a glimpse of dramatic deer battles in the colourful parkland.

60
Lanhydrock, Cornwall. After the ultimate 'upstairs/downstairs' experience in the Victorian house, take a stroll, lit by scarlet acers and yellow tulip trees, down to the River Fowey.

175
Anglesey Abbey, Gardens and Lode Mill, Cambridgeshire. Discover a house packed with treasures, then explore the working watermill and enjoy walks dominated by trees in hues of crimson, topaz and every shade of gold.

Two-wheeled adventures

Get on your bike at the Blickling Estate, Norfolk; Ashridge Estate, Buckinghamshire; Barrington Court and Montacute House, Somerset; or Box Hill, Surrey.

Stourhead

Roseberry Topping

Winter wonderlands

Explore stunning houses dressed with all the trimmings of Christmas, warm up with mulled wine and crackling log fires and pick up stocking fillers at festive markets. Join in with a spot of carol singing or enjoy a visit from Santa Claus. From country house Christmases to ancient abbeys, join us and discover the spirit of this special season. Wrap up and head out to spectacular estates, glorious gardens and rolling countryside. Stroll among snowdrops or make it a great big family adventure with snowballs and snowmen.

Blow away the cobwebs

For a refreshing winter day out visit:

105
Bodiam Castle, East Sussex. Experience life in a medieval castle, complete with a moat and impressive towers. Climb the spiral staircases and enjoy views across the Rother Valley.

270
Dunham Massey, Cheshire. Enjoy the 2.83-hectare (seven-acre) Winter Garden – the largest of its kind in the UK – with more than 700 different plant species and a further 1,600 shrubs.

298
Fountains Abbey and Studley Royal Water Garden, North Yorkshire. Explore the dramatic 12th-century abbey ruins, before enjoying the water garden's tranquil lakes, canals and temples.

Take a guided tour

There are more than 200 free downloadable walks on our website, including some of the most iconic sites in the UK. Find out more at **www.nationaltrust.org.uk/walks**

Using your Handbook

This *Handbook* gives details of the many National Trust places you can visit, including opening arrangements for 2011 from the start of January to the end of December, and available facilities. Property entries are arranged by area (see map on page 391) and are ordered alphabetically. Maps for each area appear on pages 392 to 404, and these show properties with a charge for entry, together with a selection of coast and countryside places plus three Historic House Hotels. Maps also show main population centres.

To find places within a particular county/administrative area, please refer to the index on page 405. County names are included in the postal address of individual entries.

A simple grid reference is given in each entry. These refer first to the number of the appropriate map in this Handbook, then to the grid square, for example ② D7.

Property features are indicated by symbols. The key to the symbols is on the inside front cover.

Ordnance Survey (Landranger series or OSNI for Northern Ireland) grid references are given at the beginning of the 'Getting here' section.

Information regarding access is shown using symbols. For the key to the Access symbols, please see the inside front cover.

Date at which the place (or first part of the place) was acquired by the National Trust.

Hinton Ampner

Bramdean, near Alresford,
Hampshire SO24 0LA

Map ② D7   🏠 ✳ 🔔 🍴 1986

Getting here: 133:SU895356. Beside A3, at Hindhead, near crossroads with A287. Note: when A3 tunnel opens (in the summer) access will be via Hazel Grove roundabout, just south of the tunnel. **Bus**: Stagecoach 18 or 19; 71 from Haslemere. No service Sundays or public holidays. Haslemere ≈ to Aldershot ≈. Coach National Express 30 London to Portsmouth stops at Hindhead.

Finding out more: 01428 604040 (wardens). 01428 608771 (café) or hindhead@nationaltrust.org.uk

Access for all: Café Grounds

For information on prices please telephone 0844 800 1895 or visit **www.nationaltrust.org.uk**

Opening arrangements

The information is given in table format, intended to show at a glance when places or parts of places are open and when they are closed.

A grey dot indicates that the place or facility is **closed** on those days.

Black type indicates that the place or facility is **open** on those days.

Opening period in date order.

Opening times.

Special notes or important information relating to opening arrangements.

Hinton Ampner		M	T	W	T	F	S	S
Garden, shop and tea-room								
19 Feb–30 Oct	10–5	M	T	W	T	.	S	S
31 Oct–30 Nov	10–5	M	T	W	.	.	S	S
House								
~~19 Feb–30 Oct~~	11–5	M	T	W	T	.	S	S
31 Oct–30 Nov	11–5	M	T	W	.	.	S	S
House, garden, shop and tea-room								
3 Dec–11 Dec	11–4	M	T	W	T	F	S	S
9 Dec–9 Dec	11–7	.	.	.	.	F	.	.

Open Good Friday. Last entry to property 4:30, last entry to house 4:40. 9 December open to 7. Last entry for December opening 3:45.

Please note the following points about this year's *Handbook*:

- areas are shown in hectares (1 hectare = 2.47 acres) with the acres equivalent in brackets. Short distances are shown in yards (1 yard = 0.91 metre); longer distances are measured in miles. Heights are shown in metres.

- although opening times and arrangements vary considerably from place to place and from year to year, most houses will be open during the period 1 March to 31 October inclusive, usually on three or more days per week between about noon and 5pm.

Please note that, unless otherwise stated in the property entry, last admission is 30 minutes before the stated closing time.

- we make every effort to ensure that property opening times and available facilities are as published, but very occasionally it is essential to change these at short notice. Always check the current *Handbook* for details and, if making a special journey, please telephone in advance for confirmation. You can also check our website **www.nationaltrust.org.uk**

- when telephoning a property, please remember that we can provide a better service if you call on a weekday morning, on a day when the property is open. Alternatively, call our Membership Department on 0844 800 1895, seven days a week (9 to 5:30 Monday to Friday, 9 to 4 at weekends and Bank Holidays).

Extra copies of the National Trust *Handbook* are available to buy, while stocks last.

Top ten places to get to without a car

Corfe Castle, Dorset (page 34). What better way to reach this dramatic ruin than by steam train from Norden park and ride?

Prior Park Landscape Garden, Somerset (page 72). Save your energy for the Bath Skyline Walk by taking the frequent buses from Bath railway station to this glorious park.

River Wey and Godalming Navigations and Dapdune Wharf, Surrey (page 140). Five railway stations provide easy access to this unique waterway and its 15½ miles of splendid walking along the towpath.

Peckover House and Garden, Cambridgeshire (page 194). Half-hourly buses from Peterborough railway station and close to King's Lynn station run to Wisbech for this Georgian merchant's house.

Belton House, Lincolnshire (page 207). A half-hourly bus (except Sunday) links Grantham railway station and this Restoration jewel featured in the BBC's *Pride and Prejudice*.

Hill Top, Cumbria (page 278). The Windermere Cross Lakes Experience makes it easy to reach Hilltop by connecting bus and boat from Windermere railway station using a single ticket.

Beningbrough Hall and Gardens, North Yorkshire (page 295). It is an idyllic 10-mile level pedal or walk beside the River Ouse along NCN65 from York to this Georgian mansion.

Gibside, Tyne & Wear (page 320). Make a walk or bike ride part of the pleasure of a day at this Georgian landscape park, just half a mile from the Derwent Walk/NCN14.

Powis Castle and Garden, Powys (page 348). Most of the mile-long walk from Welshpool's High Street is through castle parkland.

Downhill Demesne and Hezlett House, County Londonderry (page 363). The stunning clifftop views and gardens can be easily reached by buses between Londonderry and Coleraine, or by bike on NCN93.

Top ten places for tea and cakes

Trelissick Garden, Cornwall (page 85). After a day exploring this constantly evolving garden, reward your efforts with a spot of tea in the 19th-century converted barn.

Stowe Landscape Gardens, Buckinghamshire (page 150). Work up an appetite visiting the 40-plus temples and monuments in this Georgian gem, a delight to visit all year.

Wimpole Estate, Cambridgeshire (page 201). Choose from one of the tea or lunch spots close to the house or in nearby Wimpole Home Farm, with its adventure playground.

Canons Ashby, Northamptonshire (page 209). Whether it is the gardens, history or the Elizabethan house that interest you, a visit to the tea-room is sure to be welcome.

Croome, Worcestershire (page 242). Discover the 18th-century pleasure gardens then travel back in time to the 1940s and experience homemade delights with a difference.

Dunham Massey, Cheshire (page 270). This mansion with a working waterwheel is also well known for its cream teas and menus made from fresh local produce.

Nunnington Hall, North Yorkshire (page 305). Enjoy art exhibitions or riverside walks, before taking tea at this manor house – which also has its own organic walled garden.

Wallington, Northumberland (page 326). Savour the delights of this impressive, yet friendly, house with its remarkable collections, then tuck into local produce in the café.

Plas Newydd Country House and Gardens, Anglesey (page 346). Stunning house, breathtaking views, a museum, famous paintings – there's so much to enjoy. The icing on the cake is the charming tea-room.

Springhill, County Londonderry (page 370). After exploring this beguiling 17th-century 'Plantation' house, its walled gardens and parkland, relax in the Servant's Hall tea-room.

For enquiries contact 0844 800 1895

South West

Gently curving hillside at Prior Park Landscape Garden sweeps down to the Palladian Bridge nestling in the valley, with the City of Bath beyond

Outdoors in the South West

Miles of coastline, expanses of woodland, moors, farmland and downland – it's no wonder the glorious South West exudes a powerful magnetism. The distinctive landscape, so unspoilt and so beautiful, offers a huge variety of places to visit and activities to enjoy.

Below:
catching the
surf at Godrevy,
St Ives Bay,
Cornwall

What makes it so special?

Most people will say that what they love best about the South West is the coast. The Trust protects 370 miles (36 per cent) of the coastline in Devon and Cornwall, and wherever you are in the two far western counties you are never more than 25 miles from the sea: from the great sandy surfing beaches of the north coast to the high rocky headlands, rock pools, coves and tidal inlets of the south coast. Around all this runs the incomparable South West Coast Path, linking everywhere and providing unparalleled access on foot to all the lonely shores and soaring cliffs. Totalling 630 miles, it is the longest national trail in the country.

The Trust cares for more than 50,000 hectares (123,550 acres) of countryside in the South West. As well as the peninsula of Devon and Cornwall, there is Gloucestershire in the north, Somerset and Wiltshire, then Dorset further south, with spectacular stretches of coastline, chalk downland, high moorland, historic landscapes and beautiful rolling countryside. The northern Cotswolds boasts many lovely villages, some of which, such as Sherborne, are partly owned by the Trust – which also owns uplands, farmland and ancient woodland.

Go fossil hunting or pool-dipping

Devon and Cornwall are rightly famous for their surfing beaches, such as Godrevy and Croyde. But there are many other attractions. Kynance Cove on the Lizard has been famous since Victorian times for its fantastic rocks and botanical rarities; Wembury, close to Plymouth Sound, has fabulous rock pools and many popular children's events; and Carnewas overlooks the famous beauty spot of Bedruthan Steps. Popular family beaches include Woolacombe and South Milton Sands in Devon; Crantock, Gunwalloe and Porthcurno in Cornwall.

While in Dorset anyone with an interest in nature and prehistory will be drawn to the Purbeck Estate, which boasts one of Britain's best beaches at Studland, two National Nature Reserves, and is home to the richest ten square miles of wild flowers in the country.

The Jurassic Coast, stretching all the way along the Dorset and East Devon coast, is a World Heritage Site and covers Purbeck, Burton Bradstock and Golden Cap, and Branscombe. The landscape is wonderfully varied, ranging from heathland, dunes and a mile-long stretch of sand, to shingle and sandstone cliffs – perfect for picnics, walking and fossil hunting.

Above:
the Golden Cap Estate, Dorset
Below:
the remains of Wheal Coates mine near St Agnes, Cornwall

So much fascinating history

There is so much to explore in the old mining areas of Cornwall and West Devon, now a World Heritage Site. Visit the many ruined engine houses preserved by the Trust, some of which, like Wheal Trewavas overlooking Mount's Bay and the Crowns at Botallack near St Just, seem to defy gravity, clinging to the cliff edge just above the sea. In Botallack Count House's Workshop you can while away hours examining fascinating displays on mining history.

In this long-settled peninsula there are many mysterious sites to discover, including ancient settlements and field systems in West Penwith, cliff castles, such as the Dodman and the Rumps, and prehistoric sites, of which Lanyon Quoit is just one.

Many of the more recent developments are just as fascinating, such as the military fortifications at Froward Point, near Brixham, and St Anthony Head, and then there are the oddities, such as the driftwood hut of the poet-parson R. S. Hawker on the Morwenstow cliffs beyond Bude, the castellated lookout at Mayon Cliff above Sennen and the candy-striped Gribbin daymark near Fowey (open for climbing to the top on most summer Sundays).

Outdoors in the South West

The historic landscape of the Dorset Downs includes magnificent Iron Age hill forts, such as Hod Hill, Eggardon and Lambert's Castle. Make sure you don't miss North Somerset's Cheddar cliffs. Cheddar, Britain's largest gorge, was carved by melt-water from the last Ice Age and has been forming and changing over the past two million years. Not far away is dramatic Brean Down. This extends a mile and a half into the Bristol Channel and has truly breathtaking views, as well as abundant wildlife and fascinating history – including a Roman Temple, Napoleonic era fort and Second World War gun battery.

If you would like to delve a bit more deeply into this rich history, see page 15 for details of how to obtain one of the many leaflets available covering the Trust's coast and countryside.

Above:
golden sand and rock pools make a tempting combination at Poldhu Cove on Cornwall's Lizard Peninsula

Right:
stormy skies over Blackmore Vale, as seen from the Iron Age hill fort at Hod Hill, near Blandford, Dorset
Above right:
children playing amongst the trees at Studland, Dorset

Glorious wildlife

The many years we have spent on pioneering nature conservation work have paid off handsomely, for our coast and countryside sites in Devon and Cornwall now boast an abundance of wildlife. Walk along the Rosemergy and Bosigran cliffs near Zennor in West Penwith, between Bolt Head and Bolt Tail in South Devon, or from Kynance to Mullion on the Lizard, and appreciate the swathes of wild flowers which carpet the grazed clifftops in spring and summer.

The Cornish chough – a truly emblematic bird – has returned to breed in Cornwall, making its home on the grazed cliffs of West Penwith, Mount's Bay and the Lizard. If you visit Lizard Point, be sure to stop by the 'Chough Watchpoint' next door to the café at fledging time in early summer. Or if you go cycling along the old railway line in Plym Bridge Woods near Plymouth (a downloadable cycle guide is available from our website), you can stop off on Cann Viaduct at the Peregrine Falcon Watchpoint and take a close look at the breeding falcons' nest sites in a disused quarry.

On the Exmoor coast of North Devon and Somerset, in West Penwith and around Chapel Porth in Cornwall the glorious rolling heathland provides a rich habitat for birds and insects. Ashclyst Forest on the Killerton Estate and Lydford Gorge are great spots for bats and butterflies (as are the Lanhydrock and Arlington estates), and there are numerous other sites, including areas of Dartmoor, such as Hembury, where the Trust's protective grazing regimes have encouraged rare butterflies to flourish.

One high-summer sight not to be missed in the fields of West Pentire, near Crantock in North Cornwall, is the astonishing display of vivid arable flowers, including poppies and corn marigolds, along with Venus's looking glass and weasel's snout.

While over in Wiltshire, some of the most important areas of chalk grassland in the country can be found at Calstone Coombes, Cherhill Down and Whitesheet Hill. Calstone and Cherhill Down also have a wide range of wildlife, including 25 varieties of breeding butterfly, while Fontmell and Melbury Downs in North Dorset boast a wealth of wild flowers.

As well as Studland, one of the richest areas for flora and fauna in Dorset is Brownsea Island in Poole Harbour. It has an immensely diverse range of wildlife and habitats, and is one of the few places in the country where there are red squirrels. Two of Dorset's largest remaining expanses of heathland are near Corfe Castle and at Holt Heath, near Kingston Lacy. These are important breeding sites for heathland birds, as well as being home to sand lizards, snakes, dragonflies, grasshoppers, crickets, moths, beetles and butterflies.

At Minchinhampton and Rodborough Commons in Gloucestershire there are rare butterflies and wild flowers, including thirteen recorded species of orchid, while Holnicote Estate in Somerset boasts sixteen species of bat, and Collard Hill in the same county is home to the rare large blue butterfly.

Open for everyone to enjoy

Although the South West Coast Path is primarily for walkers, the Trust has provided many specially adapted or graded paths and viewpoints suitable for wheelchair users, such as those at Glebe Cliff by Tintagel, Loe Pool near Helston, Snapes Point and Bolberry Down near Salcombe, Cadsonbury on the River Lynher near Callington, and Branscombe and Salcombe Hill in East Devon.

Further east, Burrow Mump in Somerset has stunning views across the Levels and Moors to the River Parrett and Glastonbury Tor. There are also 87 miles of footpaths, bridleways and cycle paths running across the beautiful Holnicote Estate – perfect for exploring the open moors and deep-sided valleys in the heart of Exmoor National Park. Take a picnic to Horner Wood, with its magnificent pollarded oaks and heathland grazed by red deer, or climb to Exmoor's highest point on Dunkery Beacon and enjoy the views along the coast. The Sherborne Estate, in the Cotswolds, has stunning water meadows, as does Eyebridge on the Kingston Lacy Estate in Dorset.

One walk not to be missed is the Bath Skyline. Skirting the city, this six-mile walk passes through woodlands and wildflower meadows. There are many excellent kite-flying and picnic spots, as well as quiet corners for those after some peace. Leigh Woods, on Bristol's doorstep, is another unique experience. A National Nature Reserve with numerous waymarked trails and paths, it even has an all-ability orienteering trail.

Outdoors in the South West

Below:
Warden Jemma Lowin with young visitors at Morte Point, Devon

My favourite place
'Morte Point'

A place for me that has it all,
An easy walk from an ice-cream stall!
A downhill stroll on short springy turf,
Views of Lundy and white-pounding surf.

A fern-covered spring for those that
    know where,
And seals below if you make time to stare.
A hilly coast path that's great for a run,
And sharp jagged rocks that soak up the sun.

Crumbling old walls lie crowned with dry grass,
With sheep nibbling quietly, unaware of
    the past.
For echoing voices tell of poverty and strife,
Of wrecked ships and plunder all caused by
    false lights.

And slopes that are dented from artillery fire
Speak of the days when war made life dire.
Whilst memorial gates hint at
    Victorian grandeur,
Sailing parties, and picnics and
    family adventure.

That's my favourite place summed up in a song
So come down and see it and don't leave it
    too long!

Jemma Lowin
Warden, Morte, North Devon

My favourite walk
My favourite walk is on May Hill, the Gloucestershire icon next to the border with Herefordshire.

Starting from May Hill Common you walk through acid heathland of bilberry and heather. A backward glance gives you far-reaching views to the Black Mountains in Wales. As you approach the top of the hill you come to the famous ring of Scots pine planted to commemorate the golden jubilee of Queen Victoria. These trees give May Hill its distinctive silhouette.

From the summit there is the most spectacular 360-degree panorama. From here you can see the horseshoe of the River Severn, the Malverns, and the Cotswold escarpment.

Sir Edward Elgar is said to have walked here and appreciated the views, while every May Day Morris dancers celebrate here and most likely gave the hill its name.

Passing one of the many small ponds – home to rare plants and palmate newts – you follow the path down the hill. Walking through the neighbouring plantation of coast redwoods you find yourself back on the common.

Local folklore tells of a cavern under the hill containing buried treasure; today the treasure is the hill itself.

Jerry Green
Gardener in Charge, Westbury Court Garden, Gloucestershire

Below: **May Hill, Gloucestershire**

Coast and countryside guides

To help you make the most of your time and to discover more about the places you visit, there are nearly 40 in-depth map/guide leaflets covering the coast and countryside owned by the Trust in Cornwall and Devon. For a full list, contact the shops at Trerice in Cornwall, or Arlington Court in Devon.

There are also many downloadable walks, cycle routes and orienteering guides on the Trust's website – **www.nationaltrust.org.uk/walks** For more information on the coast and countryside in Cornwall, Devon, Dorset, Gloucestershire, Somerset and Wiltshire (and what you can do there) visit our website.

Coastal car parks in the West Country

The Trust owns numerous coastal car parks in Cornwall, Devon and Dorset, most of which are simply inconspicuous parking spots providing access to lovely remote coves, cliffs and headlands – undisturbed homes to a host of birds, bugs and butterflies. Some of the Trust's car parks are the gateways to more popular destinations, where you will find facilities such as beach cafés and toilets.

Dorset

Cogden, West Dorset	SY 503 883
Stonebarrow Hill	SY 383 933
Langdon Hill	SY 413 931
Burton Bradstock	SY 491 888
Ringstead Bay	SY 760 822
Spyway	SY 996 785
Studland	SZ 036 835

Devon

Barna Barrow, Countisbury	SS 753 497
Countisbury	SS 747 497
Combe Park, Hillsford Bridge	SS 740 477
Woody Bay	SS 676 486
Hunter's Inn, Heddon Valley	SS 655 481
Trentishoe Down	SS 635 480
Trentishoe Down	SS 628 479
Torrs Walk, Ilfracombe	SS 512 476
Baggy Point, Croyde	SS 433 396
Brownsham, Hartland	SS 285 259
East Titchberry, Hartland	SS 244 270
Wembury Beach	SX 517 484
Stoke	SX 556 465
Ringmore	SX 649 457
South Milton Sands	SX 677 415
Bolberry Down	SX 689 384
East Soar	SX 713 376
Snapes Point	SX 739 404
Mill Bay	SX 742 381
Prawle Point	SX 775 354
Little Dartmouth	SX 874 492
Higher Brownstone	SX 905 510
Coleton Camp	SX 909 513
Scabbacombe	SX 912 523
Man Sands	SX 913 531
Salcombe Hill	SY 139 882
Branscombe	SY 197 887

Cornwall

Morwenstow	SS 205 154
Duckpool	SS 202 117
Sandy Mouth	SS 203 100
Northcott Mouth	SS 204 084
Strangles Beach	SX 134 952
Glebe Cliff, Tintagel	SX 050 884
Port Quin	SW 972 805
Lundy Bay	SW 953 796
Lead Mines, Pentireglaze	SW 942 799
Pentire Farm	SW 935 803
Park Head	SW 853 707
Carnewas (for Bedruthan Steps)	SW 850 690
Crantock	SW 789 607
Treago Mill (for Polly Joke)	SW 778 601
Holywell Bay	SW 767 586
St Agnes Head	SW 699 512
St Agnes Beacon	SW 704 503
Wheal Coates	SW 703 500
Chapel Porth	SW 697 495
Basset's Cove	SW 638 440
Reskajeage Downs	SW 623 430
Deadman's Cove	SW 625 432
Derrick Cove	SW 620 429
Hudder Down	SW 612 428
Fishing Cove	SW 599 427
Godrevy	SW 582 432
Carn Galver	SW 422 364
Levant	SW 368 345
Botallack	SW 366 334
Cape Cornwall	SW 353 318
Bollowall	SW 354 314
Porth Nanven (Cot Valley)	SW 358 308
Rinsey	SW 593 272
Highburrow (Loe Bar west)	SW 635 249
Penrose (Loe Pool west)	SW 639 259
Degibna Chapel (Loe Pool east)	SW 653 252
Chyvarloe (Loe Bar east)	SW 653 235
Gunwalloe Church Cove	SW 660 207
Predannack	SW 669 162
Kynance Cove	SW 688 132
Lizard Point	SW 703 116
Poltesco	SW 725 157
Bosveal (for Durgan)	SW 775 276
Trelissick	SW 836 397
St Anthony Head	SW 847 313
Porth Farm (Towan Beach)	SW 867 329
Pendower Beach	SW 897 384
Carne Beach	SW 905 384
Nare Head	SW 922 380
Penare (Dodman Point)	SW 998 404
Lamledra (Vault Beach)	SW 011 411
Coombe Farm	SX 110 512
Pencarrow Head	SX 150 513
Frogmore	SX 157 517
Lansallos	SX 174 518
Hendersick	SX 236 520
Bodigga	SX 273 543
Cotehele Quay	SX 424 682

A la Ronde

Summer Lane, Exmouth, Devon EX8 5BD

Map (1) G7 1991

'**Excellent. The guides at A la Ronde are some of the most helpful and friendly we've met. Great with kids.**'
Mrs Satchwell, York

This unique sixteen-sided house, described by Lucinda Lambton as having 'a magical strangeness that one might dream of only as a child', was built for two spinster cousins, Jane and Mary Parminter, on their return from a European grand tour in the late 18th century. It contains many objects and mementoes of their travels, and the extraordinary interior decoration includes a feather frieze from many species of birds, including game birds, fowl, jays and parrots, laboriously stuck down with isinglass. A fragile shell-encrusted gallery, said to contain nearly 25,000 shells, can be viewed in entirety on closed-circuit television. **Note**: small and fragile rooms. Lockers for large/bulky bags. Non-flash photography permitted.

Exploring
  – Be amazed and inspired by the decorative wow factor!
  – Discovery Room with dressing up, silhouette and shell activities.
  – Wildlife brass rubbing and spotter sheets in the grounds.
  – Enjoy free garden games – croquet, snakes and ladders and more.
  – New art exhibition and sale of work every two weeks.
  – Follow us on Facebook!

Eating and shopping: buy local and regional products in the shop. Plant sales. Licensed tea-room, home-cooked lunches and afternoon teas using local, regional produce. Special diets catered for. Outside seating with stunning views. Get a drink or ice-cream in the shop. Picnic area.

Making the most of your day: full programme of events and exhibitions, school holiday craft activities. Self-guided themed tours and family trail in house. Stunning views over Exe estuary and panorama showing places of interest. **Dogs**: welcome, on leads, in car park and orchard picnic area.

Access for all: 🅿️ 🚻 ♿ 🏠 🛗 🖥️ 🪜 ⬅️
House 🚹🚹 Tea-room ♿ Grounds ➡️

Getting here: 192:SY004834. **Foot**: East Devon Way borders A la Ronde. South West Coast Path within 2 miles. **Cycle**: cycle racks at A la Ronde. Reduced admission for visitors arriving by green transport. **Bus**: Stagecoach in Devon 57/58 Exeter to Exmouth/Budleigh Salterton to within ½ mile. **Train**: Lympstone village 1¼ miles; Exmouth 2 miles. **Road**: 2 miles north of Exmouth on A376. **Parking**: free. Coaches must be booked. Caravans and trailers telephone in advance.

You may also enjoy: Overbeck's, near Salcombe, another house with amazing collections of curios and glorious coastal views.

Finding out more: 01395 265514 (office). 01395 255918 (shop). 01395 278552 (tea-room) or alaronde@nationaltrust.org.uk

A la Ronde		M	T	W	T	F	S	S
12 Feb–20 Feb	11–5	M	T	W	·	·	S	S
26 Feb–6 Mar	11–5	·	·	·	·	·	S	S
12 Mar–29 Jun	11–5	M	T	W	·	·	S	S
1 Jul–2 Sep	11–5	M	T	W	·	F	S	S
3 Sep–30 Oct	11–5	M	T	W	·	·	S	S
5 Nov–18 Dec	12–4	·	·	·	·	·	S	S

Open Good Friday. 12 February to 30 October: shop, tea-room and grounds open as house, but shop and grounds 10:30 to 5:30, tea-room 10:30 to 5. Last admission to house 4. 5 November to 18 December: shop, tea-room and grounds open as house but shop and grounds 11:30 to 4:30, tea-room 11:30 to 4. The house is shown 'put to bed'. Guided tours only showing closed season conservation work. Last tour 3:15.

Detail of a diamond-shaped window at A la Ronde, Devon

Antony

Torpoint, Cornwall PL11 2QA

Map ① E8 🏠🏡❄️♣️🏛️ 1961

Still the home of the Carew Pole family after hundreds of years, this beautiful early 18th-century mansion contains fine collections of paintings, furniture and textiles. The grounds, landscaped by Repton, sweep down towards the Lynher estuary and include formal gardens with topiary, a knot garden, modern sculptures and the National Collection of Daylilies. The Woodland Garden has outstanding rhododendrons, azaleas, magnolias and camellias. The magic of Antony was recognised by Walt Disney when it was chosen recently as the set for the film *Alice in Wonderland*, directed by Tim Burton. **Note**: members free to Woodland Garden (not National Trust) only when house is open.

The Yew Walk at Antony, Cornwall

Exploring
- Spot the locations used in Disney's *Alice in Wonderland* movie.
- Soak up the unique atmosphere of a family home.
- Hunt for the modern sculpture installed throughout the gardens.
- Smell the delicious sea air and seasonal plant scents.
- Sit on the terrace and enjoy breathtaking river views.
- Hear amazing stories about the Carew Pole ancestors.

Eating and shopping: enjoy light snacks in our self-service tea-room. Shop offers a good range of souvenirs and gifts.

Making the most of your day: varied year-round family events programme and activities.

Access for all:
House 🦽♿ Tea-room ♿ Grounds ♿➡️♿

Getting here: 201:SX418564. **Cycle**: NCN27, 2 miles. **Ferry**: Torpoint 2 miles. **Bus**: First 81 from Plymouth (passing close Plymouth ⊠) alight Great Park Estate, ¼ mile.

Train: Plymouth 6 miles via vehicle ferry. **Road**: 6 miles west of Plymouth via Torpoint car ferry, 2 miles north-west of Torpoint, north of A374, 16 miles south-east of Liskeard, 15 miles east of Looe. **Parking**: free, 250 yards.

You may also enjoy: Saltram, a beautiful Georgian mansion and parkland, only a short distance away in Plymouth.

Finding out more: 01752 812191 or antony@nationaltrust.org.uk

Antony		M	T	W	T	F	S	S
House								
29 Mar–26 May	1–5	·	T	W	T	·	·	·
29 May–30 Oct	1–5	·	T	W	T	·	·	S
Garden, shop and tea-room								
29 Mar–26 May	11–5	·	T	W	T	·	·	·
28 May–30 Oct	11–5	·	T	W	T	·	S	S
Woodland Garden								
1 Mar–30 Oct	11–5		T	W	T	·	S	S

Also open Sundays 17 April, 24 April (Easter) and 1 May, plus Bank Holiday Mondays and Good Friday. Bath Pond House interior can only be seen, by written application to the Property Manager, on days house is open. At peak times, timed tickets for entry to the house will be in operation.

Arlington Court and the National Trust Carriage Museum

Arlington, near Barnstaple, Devon EX31 4LP

Map ① F5  1949

Arlington Court is an unexpected jewel: a complete family estate. The intimate Regency house contains treasures for all tastes, from model ships to shells, all collected by the Chichesters. Offering incident and contrast, the 19th-century picturesque garden is a perfect place to explore, picnic or play. The walled kitchen garden provides fruit and vegetables for the tea-room and flowers for the house. The tranquil estate, abundant with wildlife, includes an ancient heronry. The Carriage Museum, in the stables, has a vehicle for every occasion from cradle to grave. Our working horses and stables keep the story alive.

Arlington Court, Devon: an intimate Regency house

Exploring
- Delve into a house full of treasures and secrets.
- Discover the romance of travel in a bygone age.
- Explore three gardens in one: kitchen, flower and pleasure grounds.
- Experience the sights, sounds and smells of our working stables.
- Spy on our lesser horseshoe bats with the bat-cam.
- Stretch your legs searching for rare breeds on the estate.

Eating and shopping: buy jams and preserves made locally from Arlington-grown produce. Taste local, seasonal fruit and vegetables in our tea-room, which serves gluten-free options every day. Stay longer in one of the estate's holiday cottages.

Making the most of your day: daily harnessing demonstrations and rummage through a Victorian's luggage in our Explorer Room. Events: from children's crafts to living history tours. Waymarked estate walks and bird hide with binoculars to borrow. **Dogs**: on leads, in garden, Carriage Museum and the wider estate.

Access for all:
House Carriage Museum
Grounds

Getting here: 180:SS611405. **Bus**: TW Coaches 309 Barnstaple to Lynton, infrequent. **Train**: Barnstaple 8 miles (1 mile from bus station). **Road**: 8 miles north of Barnstaple on A39. Use A399 from South Molton if travelling from the east. **Parking**: free, 150 yards. Coaches access car park at second entrance. An area will be marked off if prior warning is given.

You may also enjoy: Dunster Castle, near Minehead. For carriages, visit Charlecote Park in Warwickshire.

Finding out more: 01271 850296 or arlingtoncourt@nationaltrust.org.uk

Arlington Court		M	T	W	T	F	S	S
House, Carriage Museum and bat-cam								
19 Feb–27 Feb	11–3	M	T	W	T	F	S	S
5 Mar–6 Mar	11–3	.	.	.	.	.	S	S
12 Mar–30 Oct	11–5	M	T	W	T	F	S	S
5 Nov–18 Dec	11–3	.	.	.	.	.	S	S
Shop, tea-room and garden								
1 Jan–3 Jan	11–3	M	.	.	.	.	S	S
19 Feb–27 Feb	11–3	M	T	W	T	F	S	S
5 Mar–6 Mar	11–3	.	.	.	.	.	S	S
12 Mar–30 Oct	10:30–5	M	T	W	T	F	S	S
5 Nov–18 Dec	11–3	.	.	.	.	.	S	S
19 Dec–31 Dec	11–3	M	T	W	T	F	S	.

Limited access to house and Carriage Museum in February, 5 and 6 March, November and December. Shop and tea-room closed 24 and 25 December. Grounds open dawn till dusk, all year.

Entry is still possible at most places up to 30 minutes before closing

Ashleworth Tithe Barn

Ashleworth, Gloucestershire GL19 4JA

Map ① J2   1956

The barn, with its immense stone-tiled roof, is picturesquely situated close to the banks of the River Severn. **Note**: no toilet.

Access for all: Building 🏛

Getting here: 162:SO818252. 6 miles north of Gloucester, south-east of Ashleworth.

Finding out more: 01452 814213 or ashleworth@nationaltrust.org.uk

Ashleworth Tithe Barn		M	T	W	T	F	S	S
2 Jan–31 Dec	Dawn–dusk	·	·	·	·	·	**S**	**S**
Other times by appointment.								

Children enjoy an unusual seat on one of the ancient stones at Avebury, Wiltshire

Avebury

near Marlborough, Wiltshire

Map ① K4

In the 1930s, the pretty village of Avebury, partially encompassed by the stone circle of this World Heritage Site, was witness to the excavations of archaeologist Alexander Keiller. In re-erecting many of the stones, Keiller uncovered the true wonder of one of the most important megalithic monuments in Europe. His fascinating finds are on display in the 17th-century threshing barn and stables galleries of the Alexander Keiller Museum, where interactive displays and activities for children bring the landscape to life. The Manor, with notable Queen Anne alterations and Edwardian renovation, sits amongst tranquil gardens surrounded by topiary and garden 'rooms'. **Note**: English Heritage holds guardianship of Avebury Stone Circle, owned and managed by the National Trust.

Exploring
- Wander amidst the largest stone circle in the world.
- Discover Avebury's past secrets in our unique onsite museum.
- Explore the many prehistoric monuments of the World Heritage Site.
- Listen for voices of the past in the manor house.
- Don't miss the hidden gem of the tranquil Manor gardens.

Eating and shopping: local, seasonal food at Circles, the only Trust vegetarian restaurant! Children's meals, homemade cakes and picnic food are also available. Buy a memento of your visit at the shop. Don't miss the Wessex range of locally sourced giftware.

Making the most of your day: come and spend a day at Avebury with world-renowned experts in archaeology on the Avebury team. Don't miss our calendar of lectures and events, from archaeology to wildlife walks. **Dogs**: on leads are welcome.

Access for all:
Building 🚶♿ Manor house 🚶♿
Stone circle and gardens 🚶♿➡

Getting here: 173:SU102699. **Foot**: Ridgeway National Trail. **Cycle**: NCN4 and 45.
Bus: Stagecoach in Swindon 49 Swindon to Trowbridge; Wiltshire and Dorset 96 Swindon to Pewsey. Both pass close Swindon 🚍. **Train**: Pewsey 10 miles; Swindon 11 miles.
Road: 6 miles west of Marlborough, 1 mile north of the Bath road (A4) on A4361 and B4003. **Parking**: pay and display, 500 yards (off A4361). National Trust and English Heritage members free. Parking during the Summer Solstice in late June may be limited. Telephone estate office before travelling. Overnight parking prohibited.

You may also enjoy: Dyrham Park and Lacock Abbey.

Finding out more: 01672 539250 or avebury@nationaltrust.org.uk. National Trust Estate Office, High Street, Avebury, Wiltshire SN8 1RF

Avebury		M	T	W	T	F	S	S
Stone circle								
Open all year	Dawn–dusk	M	T	W	T	F	S	S
Museum								
1 Apr–31 Oct	10–6	M	T	W	T	F	S	S
1 Nov–31 Dec	10–4	M	T	W	T	F	S	S
Shop and Circles restaurant								
1 Apr–31 Oct	10–6	M	T	W	T	F	S	S
1 Nov–31 Dec	10–4	M	T	W	T	F	S	S

Museum, shop and restaurant closed 24 to 26 December. Manor house and gardens: for opening times and any restrictions on access, visit our website or telephone property.

Barrington Court

Barrington, near Ilminster, Somerset TA19 0NQ

Map ① 16 🏛🏠♣♧⛱🏠🍸 1907

'**Officially my favourite Trust property ever!
…a wonderful atmosphere, as if there has only been happiness and contentment here.**'
K. Welch, Evesham, Worcestershire

Echoes of the past haunt this now empty Tudor manor house, so lovingly restored in the 1920s by Sir Arthur Lyle. Old farm buildings host a pottery and woodcarver, both of whom sell their wares. What were once cow yards, pens

and fields have been transformed into fragrant and delightful flower gardens, their design influenced by Gertrude Jekyll. The stone-walled kitchen garden produces a variety of wonderful fruit and vegetables, which can be enjoyed in the restaurant, while the orchards provide the apples for our own cider and apple juice. This is a place to relax and refresh the senses.

Exploring
- Search out echoes of the past in the Court House.
- Indulge yourself with high quality, home-grown and handmade food.
- Come on a painting course led by an expert.
- Savour the fragrance of the flowers in the White Garden.
- Ask a professional potter how he makes those wonderful bowls.
- Take a circular walk over the hill to Shepton Beauchamp.

Brightly coloured azaleas at Barrington Court, Somerset

Eating and shopping: eat freshly cooked vegetables straight from the gardens. Drink our own South Somerset-produced cider or apple juice. Sit outside and have a pasty and cup of tea. Browse in the shop – buy a present for someone special.

Making the most of your day: we are well known for our love of, and support for, good food and drink through the Wassail (17 January), quality food fairs and our Strode House Restaurant. **Dogs**: assistance dogs only in the gardens. Shaded parking available.

Access for all:
Building **Grounds**

Getting here: 193:ST396182. In Barrington village, 5 miles north-east of Ilminster. **Foot**: numerous public footpaths. **Cycle**: NCN30. Cycle hire available in Langport (01458 250350). **Bus**: Stagecoach 632/3 Ilminster to Martock, with connections on 30 from Taunton. **Train**: Crewkerne, 7 miles. **Road**: on B3168. Signposted from A358 (Ilminster to Taunton) or A303 (Hayes End roundabout). **Sat Nav**: incorrectly directs visitors to a rear entrance – please follow brown tourist signs. **Parking**: free, 30 yards.

You may also enjoy: Montacute House, a stunning Elizabethan mansion, just eight miles away.

Finding out more: 01460 242614 (Infoline). 01460 241938 or barringtoncourt@nationaltrust.org.uk

Barrington Court		M	T	W	T	F	S	S
Strode House Restaurant								
26 Feb–31 Mar	11–5	**M**	**T**	·	**T**	**F**	**S**	**S**
1 Apr–30 Sep	12–3	**M**	**T**	·	**T**	**F**	·	·
2 Apr–2 Oct	12–5	·	·	·	·	·	**S**	**S**
3 Oct–1 Nov	11–5	**M**	**T**	·	**T**	**F**	**S**	**S**
Beagles Café								
1 Apr–30 Sep	11–5	**M**	**T**	·	**T**	**F**	**S**	**S**
1 Oct–30 Oct	11–5	·	·	·	·	·	**S**	**S**
House, gardens and shop								
26 Feb–1 Nov	11–5	**M**	**T**	·	**T**	**F**	**S**	**S**

1 April to 30 September: restaurant open for lunches only weekdays, for lunches and teas weekends. Café may close in poor weather (October). Bookings for Strode House Restaurant accepted up to 24 hours prior to visit. On Bank Holiday weekends we operate on a first-come, first-served basis (not bookable).

Bath Assembly Rooms

Bennett Street, Bath, Somerset BA1 2QH

Map (1) J4   1931

Elegant colonnade at the Bath Assembly Rooms, Somerset

The Assembly Rooms were at the heart of fashionable Georgian society, the perfect venue for entertainment. When completed in 1771, they were described as 'the most noble and elegant of any in the kingdom'. The Fashion Museum (Bath and North East Somerset Council) is on lower ground floor. **Note**: limited visitor access during functions.

Exploring
- Holiday activities for families, on a fashion theme.
- Enjoy the summer exhibition in the Ball Room.
- New museum displays and exhibitions, visit www.fashionmuseum.co.uk.
- For concerts and music festivals, visit www.bathfestivals.org.uk.

Eating and shopping: café open nearly every day: coffee, light lunch or tea. Browse the extensive gift shop and renowned fashion bookshop. Savour an ice-cream in the garden café this summer.

Making the most of your day: stop for coffee, browse the bookshop and enjoy the latest fashion exhibition.

Access for all:
Building ☐☐☐☐ Grounds ☐

Getting here: 156:ST749653.
Cycle: NCN4, ¼ mile. **Bus**: from Bath Spa ≢ and surrounding areas.
Train: Bath Spa ¾ mile. **Road**: north of Milsom Street, east of the Circus.
Parking: city-centre car parks (pay and display), nearest Charlotte Street (not National Trust), charge including members. Very little on-street parking, park and ride recommended.

Finding out more: 01225 477789 or bathassemblyrooms@nationaltrust.org.uk

Bath Assembly Rooms		M	T	W	T	S	S
1 Jan–28 Feb	10:30–5	M	T	W	T	S	S
1 Mar–31 Oct	10:30–6	M	T	W	T	S	S
1 Nov–31 Dec	10:30–5	M	T	W	T	S	S

Last admission one hour before closing. Closed when in use for booked functions and on 25 and 26 December.
*Access to all rooms guaranteed in August until 4:30, at other times some rooms may be closed (visitors should telephone in advance).

Blaise Hamlet

Henbury, Bristol BS10 7QY

Map ① I3   🏠🏠 1943

A delightful hamlet of nine picturesque cottages. Designed by John Nash in 1809 to accommodate Blaise Estate pensioners.
Note: access to green only; cottages not open. No toilet.

Getting here: 172:ST559789. 4 miles north of central Bristol.

Finding out more: 01275 461900 or blaisehamlet@nationaltrust.org.uk

Blaise Hamlet	Open every day all year

Bolberry Down

near Salcombe, Devon

Map ① F9   1938

Dramatic clifftop with far-reaching views. Bolberry Down has levelled circular trails through a breathtaking coastal landscape.
Note: no toilet. Hotel and inn (not National Trust).

Access for all: ☐☐

Getting here: SX689383. Between Hope Cove and Salcombe. Take the A381 towards Salcombe and turn right at Malborough. Go through the village and look out for a right-hand turn signposted Bolberry. **Sat Nav**: use TQ7 3DY.

Finding out more: 01752 346585 or bolberrydown@nationaltrust.org.uk.
The Stables, Saltram House, Plymouth, Devon PL7 1UH

Bolberry Down	Open every day all year

Boscastle

Cornwall PL35 0HD

Map ① D7   1955

Much of the land in and around Boscastle is owned by the National Trust. This includes the cliffs of Penally Point and Willapark, which guard the sinuous harbour entrance, Forrabury Stitches, high above the village and divided into ancient 'stitchmeal' cultivation plots, as well as the lovely Valency Valley. **Note**: toilet by main car park (neither National Trust).

Exploring
- Wander through the village and down to the picturesque harbour.
- Stroll along the Valency Valley to Minster church.
- Follow the coast path and discover Forrabury church.

Fishing boats aground at low tide in the harbour at Boscastle, Cornwall

Eating and shopping: browse in the shop by the lower harbour. Visit the adjoining café and enjoy the courtyard seating area.

Making the most of your day: children's quiz/trail. Look out for family events in school holidays. **Dogs**: welcome in café courtyard.

Access for all: 🚾♿🔊📷 Grounds 🚶

Getting here: 190:SX097914. **Bus**: Western Greyhound 595 from Bude, 594 from Wadebridge (connections with 555 at Wadebridge for Bodmin Parkway ⭤).
Road: 5 miles north of Camelford, 3 miles north-east of Tintagel on B3263. **Parking**: pay and display, 100 yards (not National Trust). Charge including members.

Finding out more: 01840 250353 or boscastle@nationaltrust.org.uk

Boscastle		M	T	W	T	F	S	S
Open all year		**M**	**T**	**W**	**T**	**F**	**S**	**S**
Shop, café and National Trust info								
12 Feb–27 Mar	10:30–4	**M**	**T**	**W**	**T**	**F**	**S**	**S**
28 Mar–30 Oct	10–5	**M**	**T**	**W**	**T**	**F**	**S**	**S**
31 Oct–13 Nov	10:30–4	**M**	**T**	**W**	**T**	**F**	**S**	**S**
18 Nov–20 Nov	10:30–4	·	·	·	·	**F**	**S**	**S**
10 Dec–18 Dec	10:30–4	·	·	·	·	·	**S**	**S**
26 Dec–30 Dec	10:30–4	**M**	**T**	**W**	**T**	**F**	·	·

Shop sometimes open later than 5 in high season.

Bradley

Newton Abbot, Devon TQ12 6BN

Map ① G8 🏛🌳♨ 1938

Unspoilt and fascinating medieval manor house, still a relaxed family home, in a green haven of riverside meadows and woodland. **Note**: no toilet, shop or refreshments. Parking from 1:30.

Access for all: 🅿♿🔊📷🔅📷
Building 🚶♿ Grounds 🚶♿➡

Getting here: 202:SX848709. ½ mile from Newton Abbot town centre. From Totnes, gate lodge is on left just past Ogwell roundabout. **Sat Nav**: does not lead to Bradley.

Finding out more: 01803 661907 or bradley@nationaltrust.org.uk

Bradley		M	T	W	T	F	S	S
5 Apr–29 Sep	2–5	·	**T**	**W**	**T**	·	·	·

4 to 27 October open weekdays by prior appointment. Telephone at least one day in advance.

Branscombe: the Old Bakery, Manor Mill and Forge

Branscombe, Seaton, Devon EX12 3DB

Map ① H7    1965

Nestling in a valley that reaches down to the sea, these thatched buildings date back more than 200 years. Visit the working forge and mill, then enjoy a traditional cream tea in the Old Bakery. Explore the beach or woodlands – there are plenty of paths to choose from. **Note**: toilets at bakery and village hall.

Exploring	–	Visit the Old Forge and watch the blacksmith in action.
	–	Enjoy open fires and a bit of baking history.
	–	Discover the restored water-powered Manor Mill along the millstream.
	–	Find out about the history of this old seaside community.

Eating and shopping: quality ironwork on sale – candlestick holders to log burners. Delicious homemade soups, ploughman's and sandwiches served all day.

Making the most of your day: cycling along bridleways or walking along an extensive network of paths is the perfect way to enjoy this area. **Dogs**: on leads in garden and information room of Old Bakery only.

Access for all: Building   Manor Mill   Grounds

Getting here: 192:SY198887. **Foot**: South West Coast Path within ¾ mile. **Cycle**: public bridleway from Great Seaside to Beer gives shared access for cyclists. **Bus**: Stagecoach Devon Honiton to Sidmouth; Axe Valley Mini Travel Sidmouth to Branscombe and Axminster to Seaton and Seaton to Branscombe; then Axe Valley 899 Sidmouth to Seaton, alight at Branscombe. **Train**: Honiton 8 miles. **Road**: off A3052, signposted Branscombe village.

Water-powered Manor Mill at Branscombe, Devon

Parking: small car park next to Old Forge (donations welcome); also car park next to village hall (not National Trust; donations in well).

Finding out more: 01752 346585 (South and East Devon Countryside Office). 01297 680333/680481 (Old Bakery/Old Forge) or branscombe@nationaltrust.org.uk. South and East Devon Countryside Office, The Stables, Saltram House, Plymouth, Devon PL7 1UH

Branscombe		M	T	W	T	F	S	S
Branscombe								
Open all year		M	T	W	T	F	S	S
Old Bakery								
1 Apr–31 Jul	10:30–5	·	·	W	T	F	S	S
1 Aug–31 Aug	10:30–5	M	T	W	T	F	S	S
1 Sep–30 Oct	10:30–5	·	·	W	T	F	S	S
Manor Mill								
17 Apr–26 Jun	2–5	·	·	·	·	·	·	S
3 Jul–31 Aug	2–5	·	·	·	W	·	·	S
4 Sep–30 Oct	2–5	·	·	·	·	·	·	S
Old Forge								
Open all year	*	M	T	W	T	F	S	S

Old Forge: telephone 01297 680481 for opening times.

Brean Down

Brean, North Somerset

Map ① H4   1954

One of the most striking landmarks of the Somerset coastline, Brean Down projects dramatically into the Bristol Channel. Offering magnificent views for miles around, it is rich in wildlife and history; an ideal place to explore. The Palmerston Fort, built 1865, provides a unique insight into Brean's past. **Note**: steep climbs and cliffs; please stay on main paths. Dangerous beach (not National Trust).

Exploring
- Enjoy the bracing steep climb to the Fort.
- See the gun magazines on most Saturday and Sunday afternoons.
- Learn at the Fort and Down exhibition.

Eating and shopping: brand new café and shop opening in March, or settle down for a long, lazy picnic.

Making the most of your day: there are circular walks for all abilities. **Dogs**: on leads only.

Access for all: 🚻 Building 🦽

Getting here: 182:ST290590. **Bus**: First 112 Highbridge to Weston-super-Mare (passing close Highbridge ≋ and close Weston-super-Mare ≋), alight Brean, 1¾ miles. **Train**: Highbridge 8½ miles. **Road**: between Weston-super-Mare and Burnham-on-Sea, 8 miles from exit 22 of M5. **Parking**: 200 yards, at Brean Down Cove Café at the bottom of Brean Down. The higher Down is a steep climb from the car park and the Fort is approximately 1½ miles further.

Finding out more: 01934 844518 or breandown@nationaltrust.org.uk

Brean Down		M	T	W	T	F	S	S
Cliffs								
Open all year		M	T	W	T	F	S	S
Café and shop								
7 Mar–30 Oct	10–5	M	T	W	T	F	S	S
5 Nov–18 Dec	10–5	M	·	·	T	F	S	S

Brean Down, Somerset: an ideal place to explore

Brownsea Island

Poole Harbour, Poole, Dorset BH13 7EE

Map ① K7      1962

Brownsea Island is dramatically located in Poole Harbour, with spectacular views across to the Purbeck Hills. Thriving natural habitats – including woodland, heathland and a lagoon – create a haven for wildlife, such as the rare red squirrel and a wide variety of birds. Visitors will be fascinated by the island's rich history, for as well as boasting daffodil farming and pottery works, it was the birthplace of the Scouting and Guiding movement. So whether you love wildlife or just want to escape from the stresses of modern life, Brownsea is the perfect place to explore and enjoy throughout the year. **Note**: part of island leased to Dorset Wildlife Trust, 01202 709445. No public access to castle.

Exploring
- Get wild about wildlife with a family Tracker Pack.
- Visit the Outdoor Centre and scout stone.
- Look out for pottery remains on the seashore.
- Enjoy peace, tranquillity and breathtaking coastal views.
- Watch avocets, terns and godwits on the lagoon.
- Find out more about Brownsea Island in the Visitor Centre.

Eating and shopping: enjoy stunning views and delicious food in the Villano Café. Browse in the shop for Brownsea Island gifts. Take home a Brownsea Island Red Squirrel souvenir.

Making the most of your day: seasonal family activities and trails. Wildlife walks and talks. Brownsea open-air theatre. Daily introductory walks and guided tractor trailer tours for less mobile visitors (bookable). **Dogs**: island is a nature reserve, so assistance dogs only.

Access for all: 🚻 👂🔊 🦻 📷 🔈 🅿
Building 🦽♿🦼 Grounds 🚶➡🦼

Getting here: 195:SZ032878. In Poole Harbour, access by ferry. **Foot**: close to start/end of South West Coast Path at Shell Bay. **Ferry**: half-hourly boat service from 10 (not National Trust) from Poole Quay (01202 631828 or 01929 462383) and Sandbanks (01929 462383). Wheelchair users are advised to contact ferry operators. **Bus**: Wiltshire and Dorset 50 Bournemouth to Swanage, alight Sandbanks; 52 Poole to Sandbanks. Buses from surrounding areas to Poole Bridge, a few yards from Poole ferry. **Train**: Poole ½ mile to Poole Quay; Branksome or Parkstone, both 3½ miles to Sandbanks.

You may also enjoy: Corfe Castle and Studland Beach.

Finding out more: 01202 707744 or brownseaisland@nationaltrust.org.uk

Brownsea Island	M	T	W	T	F	S	S
Boat service*							
19 Feb–27 Mar	10–4						S	S
Full boat service from Poole Quay and Sandbanks							
2 Apr–30 Oct	10–5	M	T	W	T	F	S	S
Limited opening for booked groups only							
31 Oct–31 Dec	10–4	M	T	W	T	F	S	S

*Winter weekend opening by boat (National Trust) from Sandbanks only. Telephone or visit website for information. Shop and Villano Café close 15 minutes before island. For group bookings telephone 01202 492161.

Spot red squirrels on Brownsea Island, Dorset

Buckland Abbey

Yelverton, Devon PL20 6EY

Map ① E8  1948

'**If Buckland Abbey doesn't give you a love of history and desire to find out more, nothing will. Absolutely fantastic**.'
Lesley Boxall, Swindon

Buckland Abbey was home to Cistercian monks, who built the Abbey and the incredible Great Barn and farmed the then vast estate. The Abbey was later converted into a home by Sir Richard Grenville and then bought by Sir Francis Drake. It now has a combination of furnished rooms and interactive galleries which tell the story of how these two men changed the shape of the house and the fate of the country. Discover the Buckland estate, the meadows, the orchards and the late spring bluebells. Enjoy the peace and tranquillity of the Tavy Valley and the far-reaching views. **Note**: the Abbey is presented in association with Plymouth City Museum.

Exploring
– Witness 700 years of history and change in the Abbey.
– Enjoy the peaceful estate on one of our four walks.
– Try on a Tudor costume. What will suit you?
– Take up the challenge of our letterbox trail!
– See the famous Drake's Drum and learn the legend.
– Full programme of events, from concerts to living history.

Eating and shopping: 14th-century Refectory Restaurant serving freshly cooked local produce. Enjoy your picnic in the beautiful grounds. Browse for that special gift or plant in our shop. Restaurant available for private function hire.

Making the most of your day: events include guided walks, in-depth tours and living history. Craft fairs (entrance fee including members), concerts and family fun through the year. Christmas event in December.

Members may have to pay on special events days

The kitchen at Buckland Abbey in Devon is brought to life

Dogs: for conservation and wildlife reasons only assistance dogs allowed.

Access for all: 🅿️🚗♿🚻🚹♿📷🖼️🎒👓🔊

Abbey 🐕♿♿ **Reception, shop, restaurant** ♿♿

Grounds 🐕♿♿➡️

Getting here: 201:SX487667. **Cycle**: Drake's Trail, NCN27, 2 miles. **Bus**: Holsworthy 55 from Yelverton (with connections from Plymouth ➡️), Monday to Saturday; First 48 from Plymouth Sundays. **Train**: Plymouth 11 miles. **Road**: 6 miles south of Tavistock, 11 miles north of Plymouth: turn off A386 ¼ mile south of Yelverton. **Parking**: free, 164 yards.

You may also enjoy: Saltram, Cotehele, Lydford Gorge and Antony.

Finding out more: 01822 853607 or bucklandabbey@nationaltrust.org.uk

Buckland Abbey		M	T	W	T	F	S	S
18 Feb–27 Feb	11–4:30	M	T	W	T	·	S	S
4 Mar–6 Mar	11–4:30	·	·	·	·	F	S	S
12 Mar–30 Oct	10:30–5:30	M	T	W	T	F	S	S
4 Nov–11 Dec	11–4:30	·	·	·	·	F	S	S
16 Dec–23 Dec	11–4:30	M	T	W	T	F	S	S

Last admission 45 minutes before closing. Some areas may occasionally be closed to visitors due to private functions.

Carnewas and Bedruthan Steps

Bedruthan, St Eval, Wadebridge, Cornwall PL27 7UW

Map ① C8   🏛️ | 1930 |

This is one of the most popular destinations on the Cornish coast. Spectacular clifftop views stretch across Bedruthan beach (not National Trust). The Trust has rebuilt the steep cliff staircase to the beach, but visitors need to be aware of the risk of being cut off by the tide. **Note**: it is unsafe to bathe at any time. Toilet not always available.

Exploring – Enjoy magnificent walks along the coast path towards Park Head.
– Discover more in *Coast of Cornwall* leaflet, number six.

Eating and shopping: browse in the National Trust shop. Treat yourself in the popular café (National Trust-approved concession). Relax in the clifftop tea garden, adjoining the café.

Making the most of your day: children's quiz/trail, walks leaflet and information panel. Occasional family events, including treasure hunts and rock pooling. **Dogs**: allowed.

Access for all: 🅿️♿🚻🚹🖼️

Bedruthan Steps, Cornwall

Getting here: 200:SW849692. **Foot**: ¾ mile of South West Coast Path on property. **Bus**: Western Greyhound 556, Newquay to Padstow ≅. **Train**: Newquay 7 miles. **Road**: just off B3276 from Newquay to Padstow, 6 miles south-west of Padstow. **Parking**: seasonal charge for non-members.

Finding out more: 01637 860563 or carnewas@nationaltrust.org.uk

Carnewas and Bedruthan Steps		M	T	W	T	F	S	S
Open all year		M	T	W	T	F	S	S
Shop								
11 Feb–27 Feb	10:30–3:30	M	T	W	T	F	S	S
5 Mar–6 Mar	10:30–3:30						S	S
12 Mar–30 Oct	10:30–5	M	T	W	T	F	S	S
Café								
11 Feb–20 May	11–4	M	T	W	T	F	S	S
21 May–30 Sep	10:30–5	M	T	W	T	F	S	S
1 Oct–30 Oct	11–4	M	T	W	T	F	S	S
5 Nov–18 Dec	11–4						S	S
26 Dec–30 Dec	11–4	M	T	W	T	F		

Cliff staircase closed from 1 November to 1 March. For café enquiries telephone 01637 860701.

Castle Drogo

Drewsteignton, near Exeter, Devon EX6 6PB

Map ① F7

Inside this remarkable granite building, set above the Teign Gorge, is a surprisingly warm and comfortable family home. Commissioned by retail tycoon Julius Drewe, and designed by Sir Edwin Lutyens, the castle harks back to a romantic past, while its brilliant design heralds the modern era. Behind the imposing façade, poignant family keepsakes sit alongside 17th-century tapestries. The dramatic Dartmoor setting can be appreciated from the delightful formal garden and walks into a rhododendron valley. Tours and activities are arranged throughout the year. Our visitor centre, shop and café specialise in local produce. **Note**: approach lane is narrow with tight corners. Extreme moorland weather may be experienced.

Exploring
- Within the austere granite castle, discover unexpected family comforts.
- Explore the Arts and Crafts-inspired garden.
- Enjoy the estate's changing landscapes, from moorland to woodland.
- Visit the woodchip boiler and discover Drogo's green initiatives.
- Follow in Mr Drewe's footsteps along the gorge edge.
- Explore the Dartmoor orchard and wildflower meadow area.

Eating and shopping: café – local produce, open-air seating and play area. Try the delicious Drogo breakfasts from 8:30 every morning. Shop – local products and plants inspired by Drogo garden. Café available for corporate and private functions and parties.

Making the most of your day: events throughout the year. Enjoy a guided tour or activity, available most days. Waymarked walks through the garden and surrounding countryside. Quizzes and trails. Play croquet on dry summer days. **Dogs**: welcome on leads throughout the countryside and informal garden areas.

Access for all: 🅿️♿🏠🚾♿♿📷♿♿♿
Building ♿♿♿ Grounds ♿♿♿➡️

The chapel at the south end of Castle Drogo, Devon

Getting here: 191:SX721900. **Foot**: Two Moors Way. **Bus**: Dartline Service 173 Exeter to Moretonhampstead (passing Exeter Central ⊞) Monday to Saturday. Camel Coaches 274 from Okehampton ⊞, Sunday and Bank Holiday Mondays, May to September. **Train**: Yeoford 8 miles. **Road**: 5 miles south of A30 Exeter to Okehampton. Take A382 Whiddon Down to Moretonhampstead road; turn off at Sandy Park. **Parking**: free, 400 yards. Tight corners and narrow lanes.

You may also enjoy: Finch Foundry, Lydford Gorge and Coleton Fishacre.

Finding out more: 01647 433306 or castledrogo@nationaltrust.org.uk

Castle Drogo		M	T	W	T	F	S	S
Visitor centre, café, shop and garden								
2 Jan–11 Mar	11–4	M	T	W	T	F	S	S
12 Mar–30 Oct	9–5:30	M	T	W	T	F	S	S
31 Oct–31 Dec	11–5	M	T	W	T	F	S	S
Castle								
19 Feb–27 Feb	11–4	M	T	W	T	F	S	S
12 Mar–30 Oct	11–5	M	T	W	T	F	S	S
5 Nov–11 Dec	11–4:30	·	·	·	·	·	S	S
17 Dec–23 Dec	11–4:30	M	T	W	T	F	S	S

Castle: also open 5 to 6 March (times as February). Café: open all year; opens 8:30, 12 March to 30 October. Please visit website or telephone to check winter opening times. Closing time dusk if earlier. Closed 24 to 26 December.

Cheddar Gorge

The Cliffs, Cheddar, Somerset

Map ① I4

Cheddar Gorge is one of England's most iconic and spectacular landscapes. Diverse flora and fauna, including the Cheddar pink. **Note**: new information centre and shop opening in Cheddar, providing information and interpretation about the site as well as the local area. Downloadable walks available.

Getting here: ST468543. 8 miles north-west of Wells, signposted off the M5, A371 Axbridge to Wells road and A38 Burnham to Bristol road.

Finding out more: 01934 844518 or cheddargorge@nationaltrust.org.uk

Cheddar Gorge		M	T	W	T	F	S	S
Cliffs								
Open all year		M	T	W	T	F	S	S
Information centre and shop								
7 Mar–30 Oct	10–5	M	T	W	T	F	S	S
5 Nov–18 Dec	10–5	·	·	·	·	·	S	S

Chedworth Roman Villa

Yanworth, near Cheltenham, Gloucestershire GL54 3LJ

Map ① K2   1924

Fun at Chedworth Roman Villa, Gloucestershire

Nestling in a wooded combe in the heart of the Cotswolds and surrounded by beautiful woodland walks are the remains of one of the largest Roman villas in the country. With Heritage Lottery Fund support we are embarking on an exciting programme of redevelopment this season. Site access, interpretation and conservation are all being improved. During the work the water shrine and north bathhouse will remain open and there will be site tours to explain the building work in progress, plus an exhibition about the project. A unique chance to see conservation in action at a major archaeological site. **Note**: no access to main mosaics this season (site reopens fully spring 2012). Parking limited.

Exploring — Discover a Roman water shrine and bathhouse.
— Find out about life in 4th-century Roman Britain.
— Learn all about our exciting redevelopment project.
— Experience Roman life at our living history events.
— Enjoy stunning Cotswold scenery and wonderful wildlife.

Eating and shopping: relocated Roman retail experience this season during the project. Range of Roman-themed gifts and plants. Selection of Roman/archaeological books and classic Roman novels. Light snacks and drinks available in tea tent at weekends and school holidays.

Making the most of your day: Romano-British costumed interpretation on certain days throughout the season. Children's Tracker Packs plus drop-in mosaic-making sessions, trails and quizzes during school holidays. **Dogs**: assistance dogs only.

Access for all: ☐☐☐☐☐ Temporary reception/shop ☐☐ Museum ☐ Grounds ☐

Getting here: 163:SP053135.
Train: Cheltenham Spa 14 miles. **Road**: 3 miles north-west of Fossebridge on Cirencester to Northleach road (A429); approach from A429 via Yanworth or from A436 via Withington (coaches must approach from Fossebridge). **Parking**: two car parks. Villa car park, 15 yards from entrance (very limited number of spaces this season due to building works); overflow car park (April to September), 250 yards from entrance. Extra parking in nearby field for gladiator and Roman soldier events.

You may also enjoy: Lodge Park, Sherborne Park Estate, Crickley Hill, Haresfield Beacon, Snowshill Manor and Hidcote.

Finding out more: 01242 890256 or chedworth@nationaltrust.org.uk

Chedworth Roman Villa		M	T	W	T	F	S	S
2 Mar–26 Mar	10–4	·	·	W	T	F	S	S
27 Mar–30 Oct	10–5	·	·	W	T	F	S	S

Open Bank Holiday Mondays. Tea tent open weekends and school holidays.

The Church House

Widecombe-in-the-Moor, Newton Abbot, Devon TQ13 7TA

Map ① F7   1933

One of the finest examples of a 16th-century Church House, originally used for parish festivities or 'ales'. **Note**: used by the local community. Please check with National Trust shop next door to see if you can visit. No toilet.

Access for all: ☐☐☐
Church House ☐☐ Shop ☐☐

Getting here: 191:SX718768. In centre of Widecombe, north of Ashburton, west of Bovey Tracey. On B3387 about 12 miles from A38, Bovey Tracey. 270 bus runs daily in August.

Finding out more: 01364 621321 or churchhouse@nationaltrust.org.uk

The Church House		M	T	W	T	F	S	S
Shop/information centre								
12 Feb–23 Dec	10:30–4*	M	T	W	T	F	S	S

The Church House is open to visitors when not in use as a village hall; telephone shop to check opening times.
*Shop/information centre closing time dependent on weather, but never before 4.

Clevedon Court

Tickenham Road, Clevedon, North Somerset BS21 6QU

Map ① I4   1961

Home to the lords of the manor of Clevedon for centuries, the core of the house is a remarkable survival from the medieval period. The house was purchased by Abraham Elton in 1709 and it is still the much-loved family home of his descendants today. **Note**: the Elton family opens and manages the property for the National Trust.

Clevedon Court, Somerset: a much-loved family home

Exploring
— Be delighted by the fascinating collection of Nailsea glass.
— Look at striking examples of Eltonware pottery.
— Explore the delightful terraced garden.

Eating and shopping: quench your thirst at the tea kiosk (not National Trust).

Making the most of your day: family guide and children's quiz/trail.

Access for all: ⛗ ♿ ♿ 🖼 ♿ ⠿ ⟁
Building 🏠 Grounds 🏠

Getting here: 172:ST423716. **Bus**: First 361 Clevedon to Bristol. **Train**: Yatton 3 miles. **Road**: 1½ miles east of Clevedon, on Bristol road (B3130), signposted from M5 exit 20. **Parking**: free, 50 yards. Unsuitable for trailer caravans or motor caravans. Alternative parking 100 yards east of entrance in cul-de-sac.

Finding out more: 01275 872257 or clevedoncourt@nationaltrust.org.uk

Clevedon Court		M	T	W	T	F	S	S
3 Apr–29 Sep	2–5			W	T			S

Open Bank Holiday Mondays. Car park opens 1:15. House entry by timed ticket, on a first-come, first-served basis. Tea kiosk: telephone for opening arrangements.

Clouds Hill

Wareham, Dorset BH20 7NQ

Map ① J7 | 1937 |

This tiny isolated brick and tile cottage in the heart of Dorset was the peaceful retreat of T. E. Lawrence ('Lawrence of Arabia'). The austere rooms are much as he left them and reflect his complex personality and close links with the Middle East, as detailed in a fascinating exhibition. **Note**: no toilet.

Exploring
— 'Lawrence Trail', three-mile circular walk, organised by Purbeck Council.
— Follow the trail to a perfect hilltop picnic spot.

Eating and shopping: the small shop features Lawrence memorabilia and books.

Making the most of your day: visit www.purbeck.gov.uk for information on 'Lawrence Trail'. **Dogs**: in the grounds on leads only.

Access for all: ⠿ Building 🏠 Grounds 🏠

Getting here: 194:SY824909. **Train**: Wool 3½ miles; Moreton 3½ miles. **Road**: 1 mile north of Bovington Tank Museum, 9 miles east of Dorchester, 1½ miles east of Waddock crossroads (B3390), 4 miles south of A35 Poole to Dorchester. **Parking**: free in small car park, 50 yards. No coaches (only minibuses) or trailer caravans.

Finding out more: 01929 405616 or cloudshill@nationaltrust.org.uk

Clouds Hill		M	T	W	T	F	S	S
16 Mar–30 Oct	11–5			W	T	F	S	S

Open Bank Holiday Mondays. Closes at dusk if earlier: no electric light.

Clouds Hill in Dorset, which T. E. Lawrence bought in 1929 as a refuge and a place to spend his retirement

Coleridge Cottage

35 Lime Street, Nether Stowey, Bridgwater,
Somerset TA5 1NQ

Map (1) H5   🏠 1909

Discover the former home of Samuel Taylor
Coleridge, who lived in the cottage for three
years from 1797. It was here that he wrote
The Rime of the Ancient Mariner, Frost at Midnight
and *Kubla Khan*. Mementoes of the poet
can be seen throughout the cottage.
Note: property is managed by
Dunster Castle.

Exploring
   — See the cottage of this great
      Romantic poet.
   — Write poetry with a quill in
      Coleridge's bedroom.
   — Walk along the
      Coleridge Way on the
      nearby Quantock Hills.

Eating and shopping: several pubs in Nether
Stowey (not National Trust).

Making the most of your day: children's trail
for cottage. Displays and poetry books in
reading room.

Access for all: ⏺⏺ 🔍 Building ♿

Getting here: 181:ST191399. **Bus**: First
14 Bridgwater to Williton (passing close
Bridgwater ≷). **Train**: Bridgwater 8 miles.
Road: at west end of Lime Street, opposite
Ancient Mariner pub, 8 miles west of
Bridgwater. **Parking**: pub car park
opposite, or village car park, 500 yards
(not National Trust).

Finding out more: 01278 732662 or
coleridgecottage@nationaltrust.org.uk

Coleridge Cottage	M	T	W	T	F	S	S

For opening arrangements please telephone 01643 821314
(Dunster Castle's Infoline) or visit website.

Coleton Fishacre

Brownstone Road, Kingswear, Devon TQ6 0EQ

Map (1) G9   🏠 ❀ 🏛 🏠 1982

**'Wonderful! This must be the most beautiful
property and garden we have ever visited.
When can we move in?!'**
Mrs Ashman, Cambridge

Coleton Fishacre, Devon: imbued with 1920s elegance

Travel back in time to the Jazz Age at the
holiday home of the D'Oyly Carte family.
You can lose yourself in the magical 12-hectare
(30-acre) garden: viewpoints give enticing
glimpses out to sea, paths weave through
glades past tranquil ponds, and tender plants
from the Mediterranean, South Africa and New
Zealand thrive in the moist and sheltered valley.
This most evocative of holiday homes, built in
the Arts and Crafts style, is imbued with 1920s'
elegance. A light, joyful atmosphere fills the
rooms and music plays, echoing the family's
Gilbert and Sullivan connections. **Note**: narrow
busy approach lane, reversing required –
especially around busiest time (1 to 2:30).

Exploring
   — Soak up the gorgeous Art
      Deco style in the house.
   — Play the Blüthner piano in
      the Saloon.
   — Explore the network of
      pathways through the
      valley garden.

Exploring
- Relax by the ponds or in the gazebo.
- Walk the coast path, parking at Coleton Camp or Brownstone.
- Seemly Hut open, with garden and Pudcombe Cove information.

Eating and shopping: fabulous 'Taste of the West' award-winning licensed tea-room. Try a famous Coleton cream tea. Shop features items with an Art Deco/Jazz Age influence. Unusual shrubs and garden furniture in the plant centre.

Making the most of your day: new 'behind the scenes' areas. Guided garden walks every afternoon. Quizzes and trails for both house and garden. Jazz events and open-air theatre. **Dogs**: dogs under control welcome in garden on designated dog route (map available at reception).

Access for all: ⬛⬛⬛⬛⬛⬛⬛⬛⬛⬛ Building ⬛⬛⬛ Grounds ⬛➡⬛

Getting here: 202:SX910508. **Foot**: South West Coast Path within ¾ mile.
Bus: Stagecoach in Devon 120 Paignton to Kingswear; otherwise Stagecoach in Devon 22/4 Brixham to Kingswear (with connections from Paignton). On all, alight ¾ mile south-west of Hillhead, 1½ miles walk to garden. **Train**: Paignton 8 miles; Kingswear (Dartmouth Steam Railway and Riverboat Company) 2¼ miles by footpath, 2¾ miles by road. **Road**: 3 miles from Kingswear; take Lower Ferry road, turn off at toll house (take care in narrow lanes). 6 miles from Brixham, take A3022 to Kingswear, turn left at toll house. Narrow entrance and drive. **Parking**: free, 20 yards. For visitors to house and garden only. Coaches must book.

You may also enjoy: Greenway, the holiday home of Agatha Christie, on the River Dart.

Finding out more: 01803 752466 or coletonfishacre@nationaltrust.org.uk

Coleton Fishacre		M	T	W	T	F	S	S
5 Mar–30 Oct	10:30–5	M	T	W	·	·	S	S
5 Nov–18 Dec	11–4	·	·	·	·	·	S	S
Open Good Friday.								

Compton Castle

Marldon, Paignton, Devon TQ3 1TA

Map ① G8 ⬛✝⬛⬛ 1951

A rare survivor, this medieval fortress with high curtain walls, towers and two portcullis gates, set in a landscape of rolling hills and orchards, is a bewitching mixture of romance and history. Home for nearly 600 years to the Gilbert family, including Sir Humphrey Gilbert, half-brother to Sir Walter Ralegh. **Note**: credit cards not accepted. Few rooms open. Restricted access for those with limited mobility.

Exploring
- Feed your imagination among machicolations, spiral staircases and squints.
- Discover Sir Humphrey Gilbert, Elizabethan adventurer and explorer.
- Enjoy the lovely rose, knot and herb gardens.

Eating and shopping: refreshments available at Castle Barton restaurant (not National Trust). Table-top shop selling souvenirs, guidebooks, postcards and local produce. Seasonal plants for sale.

Making the most of your day: house, squirrel and garden trails. Walks with the gardener throughout the season and on National Gardens Scheme garden day. **Dogs**: assistance dogs only.

Access for all: ⬛⬛⬛⬛⬛ Building ⬛⬛ Grounds ⬛⬛

The north front of Compton Castle, Devon

Getting here: 202:SX865648. **Bus**: Country Bus 7 Marldon to Paignton ⟁; 111 Dartmouth to Torquay (passing Totnes ⟁), on both alight Marldon, 1½ miles. **Train**: Torquay 3 miles. Newton Abbot 6 miles. **Road**: at Compton, 5 miles west of Torquay, 1½ miles north of Marldon. Signposted off A380 to Marldon (not suitable for coaches) or turn south from A381 Totnes road at Ipplepen – 2 miles to Compton. **Parking**: free, 30 yards. Additional parking at Castle Barton opposite entrance, 100 yards. Access for coaches via Ipplepen, not Marldon. Coaches may park at bus turning area opposite, 125 yards.

Finding out more: 01803 661906 or comptoncastle@nationaltrust.org.uk

Compton Castle		M	T	W	T	F	S	S
4 Apr–31 Oct	10:30–4:30	**M**	·	**W**	**T**	·	·	·

Corfe Castle

The Square, Corfe Castle, Wareham, Dorset BH20 5EZ

Map ① K7   1982

One of Britain's most majestic ruins and once a controlling gateway through the Purbeck Hills, the castle boasts breathtaking views and several waymarked walks. The demolition of the castle in 1646 by the Parliamentarians marked the end of a rich history as both fortress and royal residence. With its fallen walls and secret places, it is a place to explore, a giant playground for children of all ages. The crumbling ruins and subtle invasion by plants and animals, along with its almost ethereal quality as light and weather change, all contribute to the unique atmosphere of Corfe Castle. **Note**: steep, uneven slopes, steps and sudden drops.

Exploring
– Uncover the secrets of Dorset's iconic medieval monument.
– Discover how royalty, warfare and nature have shaped the castle.
– Spot the 'murder holes' and count the arrow loops.

Corfe Castle, Dorset, was demolished by Parliamentarians in 1646

Exploring
– Guided tours are often available through the main season.
– Try a self-guided walk around the surrounding Purbeck countryside.
– Visit the pretty village, with its medieval church tower.

Eating and shopping: delightful licensed 18th-century tea-room, with tea garden. Enjoy a traditional Dorset cream tea with local clotted cream. Treat yourself to a light lunch and homemade pudding. Locally made gifts in our shop in the village square.

Making the most of your day: open-air theatre and cinema. Enid Blyton's birthday celebration (11 August). Family and general tours. Castle Quests during school holidays. Living History events and jester fun days. **Dogs**: welcome on a short lead.

Access for all: [icons] Grounds [icons]

Getting here: 195:SY959824. **Bus**: Wiltshire and Dorset 40 Poole to Swanage (passing Wareham ☰). **Train**: Wareham 4½ miles. Corfe Castle (Swanage Steam Railway) a few minutes walk (park and ride from Norden station). **Road**: on A351 Wareham to Swanage road. **Parking**: pay and display at Castle View, off A351 (800 yards walk uphill to castle). Members free. Norden park and ride (all-day parking, ½ mile walk to castle) and West Street in village (pay and display), neither National Trust.

You may also enjoy: Kingston Lacy, built by the Bankes family after the castle was destroyed.

Finding out more: 01929 481294 (Infoline). 01929 480921 (shop) or corfecastle@nationaltrust.org.uk

Corfe Castle		M	T	W	T	F	S	S
1 Jan–28 Feb	10–4	M	T	W	T	F	S	S
1 Mar–31 Mar	10–5	M	T	W	T	F	S	S
1 Apr–30 Sep	10–6	M	T	W	T	F	S	S
1 Oct–31 Oct	10–5	M	T	W	T	F	S	S
1 Nov–31 Dec	10–4	M	T	W	T	F	S	S

Tea-room: closed for refurbishment 4 to 15 January (01929 481332). Shop and tea-room close at 5:30 April to September. Property completely closed 25 and 26 December, also closed one day in March for staff training (visit website for actual date). High winds can cause closure of all or parts of castle.

Cornish Mines and Engines

See East Pool Mine, page 41.

Cotehele

St Dominick, near Saltash, Cornwall PL12 6TA

Map ① E8
1947

A Tudor house with many stories and legends, festooned with tapestries and adorned with textiles, arms and armour, pewter, brass and old oak furniture; a magical experience where little has changed over the years. Outside, explore the formally planted terraces, or lose yourself in the Valley Garden, which includes a medieval stewpond and dovecote. Seek tranquillity in the Upper Garden or visit the two orchards planted with local apples and cherries. Cotehele Quay is the home of the restored Tamar sailing barge *Shamrock* and gateway to a wider estate. The Discovery Centre tells the story of the Tamar Valley.

Exploring
 – New: house open on school holiday Fridays.
 – Climb the 18th-century Prospect Tower folly, with fantastic views.
 – Explore the Quay's Discovery Centre, open daily.
 – Relax in the garden and Mother Orchard.
 – Walk miles of footpaths exploring wildlife and industrial ruins.
 – Discover England's oldest domestic clock, still in its original position.

Eating and shopping: buy Cornish food, gifts and local plants in our shop. Enjoy local produce in the Barn Restaurant and The Edgcumbe bistro on the Quay. Browse the exquisite arts and crafts in Cotehele Gallery. Stay in one of nine holiday cottages.

Making the most of your day: meet our housekeeping team and learn how they look after the house. Join in with our gardeners. Lots of family events throughout the year. **Dogs**: welcome on the estate (assistance dogs only in the formal garden).

Access for all:

Building **Grounds**

Getting here: 201:SX422685. **Cycle**: NCN27, 8 miles. Hilly route from Tavistock to Cotehele. **Ferry**: Calstock can be reached from Plymouth by water (contact Plymouth Boat Cruises Ltd, 01752 822797) and from Calstock local river passenger ferry operates during summer subject to tides (01822 833331). **Bus**: DAC 79A Tavistock to Callington (passing Gunnislake ⇌), selected journeys to Cotehele car park. **Train**: Calstock, 1½ miles (signposted from station). **Road**: on west bank of the Tamar, 1 mile west of Calstock by steep footpath (6 miles by road), 8 miles south-west of Tavistock, 14 miles from Plymouth via Saltash Bridge; 2 miles east of St Dominick, 4 miles from Gunnislake (turn at St Ann's Chapel). Coaches only by prior arrangement. **Parking**: free. Parking charge on quay.

You may also enjoy: Cotehele Mill, Buckland Abbey, Lydford Gorge and Antony.

Ancient charm at Cotehele, Cornwall

Finding out more: 01579 351346. 01579 352711 (restaurant). 01579 352717 (tea-room) or cotehele@nationaltrust.org.uk

Cotehele		M	T	W	T	F	S	S
House								
12 Mar–30 Oct	11–4:30	M	T	W	T	.	S	S
Hall of House and garland								
14 Nov–31 Dec	11–4	M	T	W	T	F	S	S
Garden and estate								
Open all year	Dawn–dusk	M	T	W	T	F	S	S
Barn Restaurant, shop, plant sales and gallery								
12 Feb–11 Mar	11–4	M	T	W	T	F	S	S
12 Mar–30 Oct	11–5	M	T	W	T	F	S	S
31 Oct–31 Dec	11–4	M	T	W	T	F	S	S
The Edgcumbe								
8 Jan–11 Mar	11–4	M	T	W	T	F	S	S
12 Mar–30 Oct	11–5	M	T	W	T	F	S	S
31 Oct–31 Dec	11–4	M	T	W	T	F	S	S

House open Good Friday and special opening on Fridays in the school holidays. Barn Restaurant opens 10:30 12 March to 30 October. Hall of house, The Edgcumbe, Barn Restaurant, shop and gallery closed on 25 and 26 December. For evening opening at The Edgcumbe please telephone for availability.

Cotehele Mill

St Dominick, near Saltash, Cornwall PL12 6TA

Map ① E8   1947

This working mill is an atmospheric reminder of the recent past when corn was ground here for the local community. A range of outbuildings includes a traditional furniture maker and a potter, along with re-creations of wheelwright's, saddler's and blacksmith's workshops.
Note: no toilets or parking (park at the Quay).

Exploring
- Watch the mill grinding (Tuesdays and Thursdays) and buy flour.
- Find out more about the new hydro-power scheme.
- Jump on the shuttle bus to Cotehele House and Quay.
- Stay in one of the mill's two holiday cottages.

Eating and shopping: buy Cotehele flour here or at the main shop. Walk to the Quay for a pasty or ice-cream. Enjoy local produce in The Edgcumbe Arms.

The Yew Tree Walk at The Courts Garden, Wiltshire: English country style at its best

Making the most of your day: tours every day at 3. Family trails. **Dogs**: welcome, but assistance dogs only in the workshops.

Access for all: 🖼️🦻🚾🖥️♿
Building 🔼 Grounds ♿

Getting here: 201:SX417682. **Cycle**: NCN27, 8 miles. Hilly route from Tavistock to Cotehele. **Ferry**: Calstock can be reached from Plymouth by water (contact Plymouth Boat Cruises Ltd, 01752 822797) and from Calstock local river passenger ferry operates during summer subject to tides (01822 833331). **Bus**: DAC 79A Tavistock to Callington (passing Gunnislake ➔), selected journeys to Cotehele car park. **Train**: Calstock, 1½ miles (signposted from station). **Road**: on west bank of the Tamar, 1 mile west of Calstock by steep footpath (6 miles by road), 8 miles south-west of Tavistock, 14 miles from Plymouth via Saltash Bridge; 2 miles east of St Dominick, 4 miles from Gunnislake (turn at St Ann's Chapel). Coaches by prior arrangement only. **Parking**: no parking, except by prior arrangement for visitors with disabilities. All other visitors must park at Cotehele Quay and walk ½ mile through the woods.

Finding out more: 01579 350606. 01579 351346 (property office) or cotehele@nationaltrust.org.uk

Cotehele Mill		M	T	W	T	F	S	S
12 Mar–30 Sep	11–5	M	T	W	T	F	S	S
1 Oct–30 Oct	11–4:30	M	T	W	T	F	S	S

The Courts Garden

Holt, near Bradford-on-Avon,
Wiltshire BA14 6RR

Map ① J4   ✽ 1943

Full of variety, this charming garden shows the English country style at its best. Peaceful water gardens and herbaceous borders, with organically shaped topiary, demonstrate an imaginative use of colour and planting, creating unexpected vistas. Stroll through the arboretum with its wonderful species of trees and naturally planted spring bulbs.

Exploring – Relax in our tranquil garden, with topiary and colourful borders.
– Productive small vegetable garden and orchard.
– Arboretum with naturalised bulbs.
– Orchard room display area.

Eating and shopping: tea-room serving coffee, lunches and afternoon tea (not National Trust). Plants for sale, some grown on the property.

Making the most of your day: events programme, guided tours (booking essential) and children's trail. Cross-country walk to Great Chalfield Manor and Garden (please check open days and times). **Dogs**: assistance dogs only.

Access for all:
Garden

Getting here: 173:ST861618. **Cycle**: NCN254, 1¼ miles. **Bus**: Faresaver 237 Trowbridge to Melksham (passing close Trowbridge ≷). **Train**: Bradford-on-Avon 2½ miles; Trowbridge 3 miles. **Road**: 3 miles south-west of Melksham, 2½ miles east of Bradford-on-Avon, on south side of B3107. Follow signs to Holt. **Parking**: free (not National Trust), 80 yards, in village hall car park opposite, on north side of B3107. Additional parking, when signed, at Tollgate Inn and at Manor Farm (for coaches and cars), both on the B3107 towards Bath. No visitor parking on village streets.

Finding out more: 01225 782875 or courtsgarden@nationaltrust.org.uk

The Courts Garden	M	T	W	T	F	S	S
12 Feb–6 Mar						S	S
12 Mar–30 Oct	M	T		T	F	S	S

11–5:30 (both date ranges)

Tea-room open as garden. Out of season by appointment only.

Crickley Hill

Birdlip, Gloucestershire

Map ① K2   1935

Crickley Hill sits high on the Cotswold escarpment overlooking Gloucester and Cheltenham with far-reaching views toward the Welsh hills. **Note**: partly owned and managed by Gloucestershire County Council. Parking charge applies to all visitors (including members).

Access for all:

Getting here: 179:SO930165. Approximately 3½ miles from Gloucester and 2½ miles from Cheltenham on the A417.

Finding out more: 01452 814213 or crickley@nationaltrust.org.uk

Crickley Hill	Open every day all year

Information point (not National Trust) 1 April to 30 September afternoons only.

Dunster Castle

Dunster, near Minehead, Somerset TA24 6SL

Map ① G5   1976

Dramatically sited on top of a wooded hill, a castle has existed here since at least Norman times, with an impressive medieval gatehouse and ruined tower giving a reminder of its turbulent history. Home of the Luttrell family for more than 600 years, the present building was remodelled in 1868–72 by Antony Salvin. The fine oak staircase and plasterwork ceiling he adapted can still be seen. Visitors can relax on the sunny sheltered south terrace, which is home to a variety of subtropical plants. Panoramic views over the surrounding countryside and moorland complete the experience.

Exploring
 – Enjoy breathtaking views across Exmoor and the Bristol Channel.
 – Admire beautiful plasterwork ceilings, carved staircase and unique leather hangings.
 – Play the piano, enjoy snooker or handle a shotgun.
 – Linger over croquet or boules on the lawn.
 – Explore the subtropical river gardens, magnificent stables and nearby watermill.

Eating and shopping: our 17th-century stables shop has local and original gifts. Visit Dunster village or the working watermill for more shops and places to eat.

Making the most of your day: there is a range of family trails to help you explore the castle and gardens. Behind the scenes tours and re-enactments, many costumed, run throughout the season. **Dogs**: welcome in parkland and garden on leads.

Access for all:
Castle   Stables
Grounds

Getting here: 181:SS995435. **Cycle**: cycle lane from Minehead along A39. **Bus**: First 398 Tiverton to Minehead; also 28 Taunton to Minehead (passing Taunton), alight Dunster Steep, ½ mile. **Train**: Dunster (West Somerset Railway) 1 mile. **Road**: in Dunster, 3 miles south-east of Minehead. National Trust car park approached direct from A39. **Parking**: 300 yards, shuttle bus to entrance available.

You may also enjoy: take a ride around Arlington Court in a carriage from the National Trust's carriage collection.

Finding out more: 01643 823004 (Infoline). 01643 821314 or dunstercastle@nationaltrust.org.uk

Dunster Castle		M	T	W	T	F	S	S
Garden and park								
1 Jan–11 Mar	11–4	M	T	W	T	F	S	S
12 Mar–30 Oct	10–5	M	T	W	T	F	S	S
31 Oct–31 Dec	11–4	M	T	W	T	F	S	S
Castle								
12 Mar–8 Apr	11–5	M	T	W	.	F	S	S
9 Apr–24 Apr	11–5	M	T	W	T	F	S	S
25 Apr–15 Jul	11–5	M	T	W	.	F	S	S
16 Jul–26 Aug	11–5	M	T	W	T	F	S	S
27 Aug–30 Oct	11–5	M	T	W	.	F	S	S
Shop								
1 Jan–30 Jan	11–4	.	.	.	.	.	S	S
31 Jan–31 Dec*	11–4	M	T	W	T	F	S	S

Last entry to Castle at 4 from 12 March to 15 July and 5 September to 30 October. *Shop opens 10 to 5, 12 March to 30 October, closed 25 and 26 December.

Dunster Working Watermill

Mill Lane, Dunster, near Minehead, Somerset TA24 6SW

Map ① G5   🏠   1976

A restored working 18th-century watermill built on the site of a mill mentioned in the Domesday survey of 1086. **Note**: the mill is a private business, admission charge (including members).

Access for all: 🏠 Building ♿👥

Getting here: 181:SS995435. On River Avill, beneath Castle Tor.

Finding out more: 01643 821759 (mill). 01643 821314 (Dunster Castle) or dunstercastle@nationaltrust.org.uk

Dunster Working Watermill		M	T	W	T	F	S	S
Mill								
2 Apr–30 Oct	11–4:30	M	T	W	T	F	S	S
Tea-room								
2 Apr–30 Oct	10:30–4:45	M	T	W	T	F	S	S

Dunster Castle in Somerset is dramatically sited on a wooded hilltop and offers panoramic views

The east front of Dyrham Park, South Gloucestershire, on a beautiful autumn day

Dyrham Park

Dyrham, near Bath,
South Gloucestershire SN14 8ER

Map (1) J4    1961

Dyrham Park is a treasure to enjoy; set in a dramatic deer park on the edge of the stunning Cotswold escarpment, near the World Heritage Site City of Bath. Discover the beautiful late 17th-century home of William Blathwayt, a hard-working civil servant who thrived during the political upheaval of three monarchs. Explore how fashions changed over the centuries, from the original 17th-century Dutch-inspired interiors and formal gardens, to the very different style of Victorian country squire Colonel Blathwayt. The elegant garden is a more recent restoration, recreating the spirit of what had been lost.

Exploring
- Follow the park trails.
- Family fun in the Old Lodge play area.
- Discover the park and garden Tracker Packs.
- Step out on a guided park and garden walk.
- Look out for the historic deer.

Eating and shopping: local venison, perry pears and seasonal produce are used in menu recipes. Quench your thirst in the tea garden, with snack kiosk. Look out for the plant sales and a selection of local produce in the shop.

Making the most of your day: open-air theatre in the summer, guided tours of the house, park and garden, Perry Pear Day and plenty more. **Dogs**: exercise area at the far end of the car park.

Access for all: 🅿️♿🚻🔊🖐️💺🖼️♿📷🅰️
Building 🅰️♿ Grounds ♿➡️

Getting here: 172:ST743757. **Foot**: Cotswold Way passes property. **Cycle**: Avon and Wiltshire cycleways. **Bus**: telephone the property for latest details. **Train**: Bath Spa 8 miles. **Road**: 8 miles north of Bath, 12 miles east of Bristol; approached from Bath to Stroud road (A46), 2 miles south of Tormarton interchange with M4, exit 18. **Sat Nav**: use SN14 8HY. **Parking**: free, 500 yards.

You may also enjoy: don't miss Prior Park Landscape Garden in nearby Bath.

Finding out more: 0117 937 2501 or dyrhampark@nationaltrust.org.uk

Dyrham Park		M	T	W	T	F	S	S
House*								
19 Feb–28 Jun	11–5	M	T	.	.	F	S	S
1 Jul–30 Aug	11–5	M	T	W	T	F	S	S
2 Sep–30 Oct	11–5	M	T	.	.	F	S	S
5 Nov–18 Dec	11–4	.	.	.	.	.	S	S
Garden, shop and tea-room								
19 Feb–28 Jun	10–5	M	T	.	.	F	S	S
1 Jul–30 Aug	10–5	M	T	W	T	F	S	S
2 Sep–30 Oct	10–5	M	T	.	.	F	S	S
5 Nov–18 Dec	10–5	.	.	.	.	.	S	S
Park**								
Open all year	10–5	M	T	W	T	F	S	S

Open Bank Holiday Mondays and Good Friday. Last admission one hour before closing. *Limited offer in the house 19 February to 11 March, Wednesdays and Thursdays in July and August and 5 November to 18 December. **Park closed 25 December. Whole property closed until 1 on 7 and 14 September, 9 and 23 November and 7 December for park maintenance.

East Pool Mine

Pool, near Redruth, Cornwall TR15 3ED

Map ① C9 🏛 ⬆ 1967

At the very heart of the Cornish Mining World Heritage Site sit these two great beam engines, originally powered by high-pressure steam boilers introduced by local hero Richard Trevithick. Preserved in their towering engine houses, they are a reminder of Cornwall's days as a world-famous centre of industry, engineering and innovation. Our pumping engine is one of the largest surviving Cornish beam engines in the world, and our restored winding engine can be seen in action daily. So come and enjoy our film, displays, models and knowledgeable guides, and discover the whole dramatic story of Cornish mining. **Note**: Trevithick Cottage is nearby at Penponds (open April to October, Wednesday 2 to 5).

Exploring
- Brand-new displays, family activities and trails for 2011.
- Discover the massive 52-ton beam in Taylor's engine house.
- See the 1887 Michell's winding engine in action every day.
- Experience the dizzying view inside a 36-metre-high chimney.
- Watch the atmospheric film about the history of Cornish mining.
- Find out more about the Cornish Mining World Heritage Site.

Eating and shopping: comprehensive selection of mining and local history books for sale. Spoil yourself with local fudge and chocolate from the Lizard. Local rocks, minerals and Cornish tin available from our shop.

Making the most of your day: guided tours of the whole site. Regular films about the history of the mine and the Cornish World Heritage Site. Many specialist events and family days throughout the year.

Access for all: 🦷 🚻 🛗 🎦 👓 📷
Taylor's engine house 🔼 Michell's engine house 🦽
Visitor centre and shop 🦽 🦽 ➡

Getting here: 203:SW672415. At Pool, 2 miles west of Redruth on either side of A3047 midway between Redruth and Camborne. **Cycle**: NCN3, ½ mile. **Bus**: First 14/18 Penzance/St Ives to Truro (passing Camborne and Redruth 🚉). **Train**: Redruth 2 miles; Camborne 2 miles. **Road**: signposted from A30 Camborne East and Redruth junctions. Site reached through Morrisons' car park. **Parking**: free at Morrisons' superstore, 50 yards. Secondary car park (not National Trust) outside Michell's engine house off A3047.

You may also enjoy: the clifftop Levant Mine and Beam Engine.

Finding out more: 01209 315027 or eastpool@nationaltrust.org.uk. Trevithick Road, Pool, Cornwall TR15 3NP

East Pool Mine		M	T	W	T	F	S	S
1 Apr–30 Jun	11–5	M	·	W	T	F	·	S
1 Jul–31 Aug	11–5	M	·	W	T	F	S	S
1 Sep–30 Oct	11–5	M	·	W	T	F	·	S

November to end March by arrangement only.

East Pool Mine, near Redruth, Cornwall

Finch Foundry

Sticklepath, Okehampton, Devon EX20 2NW

Map (1) F7 🏠 🍴 ♿ 1994

Set amid beautiful Dartmoor countryside in the village of Sticklepath, this last remaining water-powered forge in England gives a unique insight into village life in the 19th century. In its heyday the foundry made 400 tools a day, including sickles, scythes and shovels for West Country farmers and miners. **Note**: narrow entrance to car park. Height restrictions apply.

Exploring
- Demonstrations and tours of the machinery every hour.
- Watch the large waterwheels driving the tilt hammer and grindstone.
- Learn about the lives of the foundry owners and workers.
- See Tom Pearse's summerhouse, of Widecombe Fair fame.

Waterwheel used to power the machinery at Finch Foundry, Devon

Eating and shopping: local blacksmiths' items and plants on sale in the shop. Try delicious local ice-cream at the tea-room.

Making the most of your day: family activities, vintage vehicle rallies and moorland walks. **Dogs**: welcome in all areas except tea-room, shop and foundry during demonstrations.

Access for all: 🔲🔲🔲🔲 ··
Foundry 🔲 Upstairs gallery 🔲

Getting here: 191:SX641940. In the centre of Sticklepath village. **Foot**: on the 180-mile Tarka Trail. **Cycle**: on West Devon Cycle Route. **Bus**: Western Greyhound 510 Exeter to Okehampton (passing Exeter Central ⊠), First X9, Carmel Coaches 179 Okehampton to Moretonhampstead. **Train**: Okehampton (Sunday, June to September only) 4½ miles. **Road**: 4 miles east of Okehampton off A30. **Parking**: free. Not suitable for coaches and high vehicles. Access is narrow and low.

Finding out more: 01837 840046 or finchfoundry@nationaltrust.org.uk

Finch Foundry		M	T	W	T	F	S	S
12 Mar–30 Oct	11–5	**M**		**W**	**T**	**F**	**S**	**S**

Foundry and shop open for St Clement's Day (patron saint of blacksmiths) in November.

Fyne Court

Broomfield, Bridgwater, Somerset TA5 2EQ

Map (1) H5 🏠 ❀ ♿ 🐾 🍴 1967

A real hidden Somerset gem. The former pleasure grounds of the partly demolished home of pioneer 19th-century electrician Andrew Crosse. Spend a magical time walking through the woodland garden and the delightful meadows on the wider estate, then play one of a variety of games on offer in the courtyard.

Exploring
- Walk through an enchanting landscape with folly and boathouse.

Fyne Court, Somerset: a hidden gem

Exploring
- Learn about the scientist Andrew Crosse, 'thunder and lightning man'.
- Pick up a walks leaflet and follow our nature trails.
- Headquarters of the Quantock Hills Area of Outstanding Natural Beauty.

Eating and shopping: tea-room now open selling delicious homemade lunches, cream teas and cakes.

Making the most of your day: exciting seasonal events programme. Listen to birdsong in spring, go wild in the woods and take part in our family activities. **Dogs**: under close control on estate.

Access for all: ⬛⬛⬛⬛ Grounds ⬛⬛

Getting here: 182:ST222321. 6 miles north of Taunton; 6 miles south-west of Bridgwater. **Train**: Taunton 6 miles, Bridgwater 6 miles. **Parking**: 150 yards.

Finding out more: 01823 451587 or fynecourt@nationaltrust.org.uk

Fyne Court		M	T	W	T	F	S	S
3 Jan–23 Dec	9–5	M	T	W	T	F		
8 Jan–18 Dec	10–5						S	S
Tea-room								
3 Mar–30 Oct	10:30–4	M			T	F	S	S

Gates locked at 5. Tea-room open Bank Holidays.

Glastonbury Tor

near Glastonbury, Somerset

Map ① I5   ✚ ⬛ 1933

Dramatic Tor, topped by 15th-century tower, offering spectacular views across three counties. Excavation has revealed plans of two superimposed churches. **Note**: no toilet.

Exploring
- Climb the Tor for spectacular views over three counties.
- Walk the public footpaths across the Tor.

Eating and shopping: enjoy the perfect picnic.

Access for all: ⬛ Grounds ⬛

Getting here: 182/183:ST512386.

Finding out more: 01934 844518 or glastonburytor@nationaltrust.org.uk

Glastonbury Tor	Open every day all year

Glendurgan Garden

Mawnan Smith, near Falmouth, Cornwall TR11 5JZ

Map ① C9 ⬛⬛⬛⬛⬛ 1962

Lose yourself in the three valleys of Glendurgan Garden – full of fun, natural beauty and amazing plants. Discover giant rhubarb plants in the jungle-like lower valley and spiky arid plants basking in the sunny upper slopes. Wander through the garden down to the beautiful hamlet of Durgan on the Helford River: a place to watch birds and boats, skim stones and build sandcastles. Find a boat-seat, gigantic tulip trees and ponds teeming with wildlife. Learn about the Fox family who created this 'small peace [sic] of heaven on earth'.

Exploring
- Get lost in the 176-year-old cherry laurel maze.
- Become airborne on the 'Giant's Stride' swing.
- Explore three beautiful valleys leading to the Helford River.
- Discover weird and wonderful plants from all around the world.
- Find tranquillity among the many native wild flowers and wildlife.
- Challenge yourselves to a stone-skimming competition on Durgan beach.

Eating and shopping: treat yourself to delicious home-cooked locally sourced food. Indulge in an irresistible cream tea or slice of cake. Sample the best of Cornish produce from our shop. Find a living souvenir of Glendurgan from the plant sales.

Making the most of your day: a variety of special events for families and keen gardeners takes place throughout the year. Information room in Durgan village with stories about the Helford River and its wildlife. **Dogs**: assistance dogs only.

Access for all: 🅿♿🚾♿🛗🔍💻⊙

Getting here: 204:SW772277. 4 miles south-west of Falmouth. **Foot**: South West Coast Path within ¾ mile. **Ferry**: link between Helford Passage (1½-mile walk from Durgan) and Helford village on south side of Helford River. **Bus**: First 35 Falmouth to Helston. **Train**: Penmere 4 miles. **Road**: 4 miles south-west of Falmouth, ½ mile south-west of Mawnan Smith, on road to Helford Passage. **Parking**: free. Car park gates locked at 5:30.

You may also enjoy: Trelissick, with its stunning views over the sea and river, plus its fantastic plant collection.

Finding out more: 01326 252020 (during opening hours). 01872 862090 (out of hours). 01326 250247 (tea-house) or glendurgan@nationaltrust.org.uk

Glendurgan Garden		M	T	W	T	F	S	S
12 Feb–29 Oct	10:30–5:30		T	W	T	F	S	
1 Aug–31 Aug	10:30–5:30	M	T	W	T	F	S	

Open Bank Holiday Mondays.

Visitors enjoy the challenge of the laurel maze at Glendurgan Garden, Cornwall

Members may have to pay on special events days

Godolphin

Godolphin Cross, Helston, Cornwall TR13 9RE

Map ① B9  2000

The haunting garden at Godolphin, Cornwall

Beautiful and romantic historic house and garden, where time has stood still, giving the house, garden and surrounding estate buildings a haunting air of antiquity and peace. The garden is largely unchanged since the 16th century. Archaeologically rich estate walks. **Note**: major conservation work underway. House will not be open until July.

Exploring
– Enjoy the peace and calm of the ancient garden.
– New family trails and behind-the-scenes tours.
– Explore surrounding countryside with lots of archaeological features.

Eating and shopping: enjoy tea, coffee, biscuits, sandwiches and cakes in the Piggery. Small souvenirs, postcards and walks booklets on sale.

Making the most of your day: food fair, family activities, hard-hat tours of building conservation work in action, guided walks. Bring a picnic – borrow a blanket from the Piggery and picnic anywhere. **Dogs**: welcome in the garden on short leads, and under control throughout the estate.

Access for all: 🅿️♿🚾 Garden ♿

Getting here: 203:SW599321. **Bus**: First 39 Camborne to Helston (passing close Camborne ⭋). **Train**: Camborne 9 miles. **Road**: from Helston take A394 to Sithney Common, turn right onto B3302 to Leedstown, turn left and follow signs. From Hayle take B3302 to Leedstown, turn right and follow signs. From west, take B3280 through Goldsithney and turn right at Townshend. **Parking**: free. Coach access from Townshend.

Finding out more: 01736 763194 or godolphin@nationaltrust.org.uk

Godolphin		M	T	W	T	F	S	S
Garden								
12 Mar–30 Oct	10–4	M	T	W	T	F	S	S
Estate								
Open all year		M	T	W	T	F	S	S
House								
2 Jul–8 Jul	10–4	M	T	W	T	F	S	S
3 Sep–9 Sep	10–4	M	T	W	T	F	S	S
1 Oct–7 Oct	10–4	M	T	W	T	F	S	S

'Hard-hat' tours will be available on a regular basis early in the season. **Tickets cannot be booked in advance and sell out quickly.**

Godrevy

Gwithian, near Hayle, Cornwall TR27 5ED

Map ① B9 1939

Awe-inspiring expanse of sandy beaches around St Ives Bay. Wild cliffs, rich in wildlife and archaeology, with popular café. **Note**: beware of cliff edges, unstable cliffs and incoming tides. Toilet not always available.

Access for all: 🚾 Grounds ♿

Getting here: 203:SW582430. Hayle 5 miles. Just off the B3301 north of Gwithian village.

Finding out more: 01208 265212 or godrevy@nationaltrust.org.uk

Godrevy	Open every day all year

Café open daily in main season; weekends out of season (visit www.godrevycafe.co.uk or telephone 01736 757999).

Great Chalfield Manor and Garden

near Melksham, Wiltshire SN12 8NH

Map (1) J4  1943

This beautiful medieval manor sits in peaceful countryside. Cross the upper moat, passing barns, gatehouse and delightful parish church to enjoy fine oriel windows and the soldiers, griffons and monkey adorning the rooftops. Romantic gardens offer terraces, topiary houses, gazebo, lily pond, roses and views across the spring-fed fishpond. **Note**: home to donor family tenants who manage it for the National Trust.

Exploring
- Explore gardens designed by Alfred Parsons, replanted by the family.
- Elegant architecture and Edwardian restoration completed for the donor.
- Enjoy stone looking-masks, furniture, tapestries and Tropnell's Cartulary.
- Beautiful adjacent parish church (not National Trust), donations welcome.

Eating and shopping: enjoy tea/coffee in the Motor House (not National Trust). Buy plants grown on site from the gardens and orchards. Pick up a guidebook and postcards of the manor.

Making the most of your day: spot woodpeckers or nesting swallows. Enjoy history posters and slide show of the garden in the Edwardian Motor House. Walk to nearby Courts Garden (check opening) for lunch or tea.

Access for all: 🅿️ 🅳 ♿ 🖼️ 🎵 ∴
Manor ♿ Garden ♿ ➡️

Getting here: 173:ST860631. **Foot**: 1-mile walk by public footpath from The Courts Garden (National Trust), Holt. **Cycle**: NCN254. On the Wiltshire Cycleway. **Bus**: Libra Travel 11 Bradford-on-Avon to Holt.

Train: Bradford-on-Avon, 3 miles.
Road: 3 miles south-west of Melksham off B3107 via Broughton Gifford Common (follow sign for Broughton Gifford, take care in narrow lane). Coaches must approach from north (via Broughton Gifford); lanes from south too narrow. **Parking**: free, 100 yards, on grass verge outside manor gates.

Finding out more: 01225 782239 or greatchalfieldmanor@nationaltrust.org.uk

Great Chalfield Manor		M	T	W	T	F	S	S
Manor								
3 Apr–30 Oct	*			T	W	T		S
Garden								
5 Apr–27 Oct	11–5			T	W	T		
3 Apr–30 Oct	2–5							S

*Admission to manor house by guided tour only (not bookable). Tuesday to Thursday: tours at 11, 12, 2, 3 and 4. Sunday: tours at 2, 3 and 4. Tours take 45 minutes and numbers are limited. Visitors arriving during a tour can visit the adjoining parish church and garden first. Group visits welcome on Friday and Saturday (not Bank Holidays) by written arrangement with the donor family tenant, Mrs Robert Floyd (charge applies).

The west wing of the beautiful medieval Great Chalfield Manor, Wiltshire

Dittisham on the Dart estuary as seen from Greenway, Devon: Agatha Christie's holiday home

Greenway

Greenway Road, Galmpton, near Brixham,
Devon TQ5 0ES

Map ① G8  2000

'A rare opportunity to be part of a wonderful experience. We felt like Agatha Christie was here with us!'
Miss T. Ogby, Plymouth

This is an extraordinary glimpse into the private holiday home of the famous and much-loved author Agatha Christie and her family. The relaxed and atmospheric house is set in the 1950s, and contains many of the family's collections, including archaeology, Tunbridgeware, silver, botanical china and books. Outside you can explore the large and romantic woodland garden, with a restored vinery and peach house, wild edges and rare plantings, which drifts down the hillside towards the sparkling Dart estuary. Please consider 'green ways' to get here, to relieve pressure on lanes: for example cycling, walking or ferries from Dartmouth, Torquay and Brixham. **Note**: cars must be booked. Timed entry system: tickets cannot be booked and sell out quickly.

Exploring
- Enjoy the adventure of arriving by ferry at Greenway Quay.
- Use our touch screens to learn about writing and archaeology.
- Explore the garden and estate on a network of walks.
- Discover 'Ralegh's Boathouse' on the Dart.
- Stay in the Lodge or holiday apartment in the house.
- Theatre, literary and garden events; resident local artists.

Eating and shopping: licensed Barn Café specialising in local produce. Greenway House Kitchen serving delicious award-winning lunches and afternoon teas. Shop specialising in Agatha Christie books and other memorabilia. Local products, works of art and plant sales.

Making the most of your day: daily guided garden tours in the afternoon. Regular events include art exhibitions and artists in residence. Open-air theatre. Family: croquet, clock golf, trails, quizzes and Tracker Packs. **Dogs**: on short leads in the garden.

Access for all: 🚗♿️🔣♿️🔣📄📶♿️🅰️
Greenway house ♿️ Boathouse ♿️ Garden ♿️➡️

Getting here: 202:SX876548. **Foot**: Dart Valley Trail from Kingswear or Dartmouth. Greenway walk from Brixham. **Ferry**: ferry from Dartmouth (use Dartmouth park and ride only), Totnes (tidal, Steamer Quay) Brixham and Torquay. Contact Greenway Ferry service on 0845 489 0418 or www.greenwayferry.co.uk for all information (individuals and groups), or visit the ticket office in Dartmouth, opposite National Trust shop. Allow at least six hours' parking, from whichever destination you travel. Please note there is a steep uphill 800-yard walk from Greenway Quay to visitor reception (transport available if required). **Bus**: daily Greenway Charabanc, vintage bus, from Torquay and Brixham park and ride (details from 0845 489 0418, www.greenwayferry.co.uk). **Train**: Paignton 4½ miles, Churston 2 miles. Catch a steam train or bus: contact Dartmouth Steam Railway and Riverboat Company on 01803 834488/555872 or www.dartmouthrailriver.co.uk. Steam trains to the English Riviera: Torbay Express www.torbayexpress.co.uk. **Parking**: limited booked parking only, early sell-outs possible. We recommend you book three days in advance on 01803 842382 between 10 and 4 or on www.nationaltrust.org.uk/greenway. Unbooked cars will be turned away. No parking on Greenway Road or in Galmpton village. Groups by road: midi-coaches only, limited to one per day (booked only).

You may also enjoy: Coleton Fishacre close by: magnificent garden with sea views and Arts and Crafts-style house.

Finding out more: 01803 842382 or greenway@nationaltrust.org.uk

Greenway		M	T	W	T	F	S	S
5 Mar–30 Oct	10:30–5	·	·	**W**	**T**	**F**	**S**	**S**
12 Apr–26 Apr	10:30–5	·	**T**	·	·	·	·	·
26 Jul–30 Aug	10:30–5	·	**T**	·	·	·	·	·

Limited timed tickets to the house allocated upon arrival. On busy days there may be a delay during which time you are welcome to enjoy the garden, boathouse, café, gallery and shop. **Also open Tuesdays 31 May and 25 October 10:30 to 5.**

Hailes Abbey

near Winchcombe, Cheltenham, Gloucestershire GL54 5PB

Map ① K1 ✝🏛 1937

Once a Cistercian abbey, founded in 1246 by Richard of Cornwall and dissolved Christmas Eve 1539, Hailes never housed large numbers of monks but had extensive and elaborate buildings. It was financed by pilgrims visiting its renowned relic, 'the Holy Blood of Hailes' – allegedly a phial of Christ's blood. **Note**: financed, managed and maintained by English Heritage (0117 975 0700, www.english-heritage.org.uk/hailes).

Exploring
- Explore the ruins of this 13th-century Cistercian abbey.
- Interpretation panels guide you around the abbey buildings.
- Sculptures, stonework and other finds are displayed in the museum.
- The adjacent parish church has medieval wall-paintings.

Eating and shopping: browse in the shop. Choose a treat from the refreshments. Settle down for a picnic in the grounds.

Access for all: 🔣 Building ♿️

Getting here: 150:SP050300. **Foot**: Cotswold Way within ¾ mile. **Bus**: Castleways 606 Cheltenham to Willersey, alight Greet, 1¾ miles by footpath. **Train**: Cheltenham 10 miles. **Road**: 2 miles north-east of Winchcombe, 1 mile east of Broadway road (B4632, originally A46). **Parking**: free (not National Trust).

Finding out more: 01242 602398 or hailesabbey@nationaltrust.org.uk

Hailes Abbey		M	T	W	T	F	S	S
1 Apr–30 Jun	10–5	**M**	**T**	**W**	**T**	**F**	**S**	**S**
1 Jul–31 Aug	10–6	**M**	**T**	**W**	**T**	**F**	**S**	**S**
1 Sep–30 Sep	10–5	**M**	**T**	**W**	**T**	**F**	**S**	**S**
1 Oct–31 Oct	10–4	**M**	**T**	**W**	**T**	**F**	**S**	**S**

Opening times subject to change. Please confirm with the property.

Thomas Hardy was born in this small cob and thatch cottage in Dorset

Hardy Country

near Dorchester, Dorset

Map (1) J7 1940

Hardy Country in Dorset is home to Thomas Hardy's Birthplace and his later home, Max Gate. In the small cob and thatch cottage where he was born, Hardy wrote his early novels. He later designed Max Gate and lived there from 1885 until his death in 1928. **Note**: no toilet.

Exploring
 — Be delighted by the charming cottage garden at Hardy's Birthplace.
 — Visit Thomas Hardy's home.

Eating and shopping: we apologise but no catering is available at either place. Buy Thomas Hardy books, postcards and small gifts at Hardy's Birthplace.

Making the most of your day: programme of events runs at both properties throughout the season.

Access for all:
Hardy's Birthplace   Max Gate

Getting here: Hardy's Birthplace: 194:SY728925. Max Gate: 194:SY704899. **Train**: Dorchester South 4 miles; Dorchester West 4 miles. **Road**: Hardy's Birthplace: 3 miles north-east of Dorchester, ½ mile south of A35. From Kingston Maurward roundabout follow signs to Stinsford and Higher Bockhampton. Max Gate: from Dorchester follow A352 Wareham road to roundabout named Max Gate (at junction of A35 Dorchester bypass). Turn left and left again into cul-de-sac outside house. **Parking**: Hardy's Birthplace: free (not National Trust), 600 yards. Max Gate: free (not National Trust), 50 yards. Drop-off point.

Finding out more: 01305 262366 (Hardy's Birthplace) or hardycountry@nationaltrust.org.uk

Hardy Country		M	T	W	T	F	S	S
Hardy's Birthplace								
16 Mar–30 Oct	11–5			·	W	T	F	S	S

Open Bank Holiday Mondays. **Max Gate: due to ongoing projects please telephone 01297 489481 before visiting.**

Hardy Monument

Black Down, Portesham, Dorset

Closed this year.

Heddon Valley

Parracombe, Barnstaple, Devon EX31 4PY

Map (1) F5

The West Exmoor coast, favourite landscape of the Romantic poets, offers not only the Heddon Valley, but also Woody Bay and the Hangman Hills to explore. There are spectacular coastal and woodland walks, as well as an information centre, car park and gift shop in Heddon Valley itself.

Exploring
– Enjoy the South West Coast Path and dramatic sea cliffs.
– Enjoy circular walks with our new walks leaflet.
– Discover the fantastic birdlife of Woody Bay.
– Don't miss the majestic Hangman Hills.

Eating and shopping: outdoor wear, Exmoor products and great gifts in the shop. Delicious local ice-cream with flavours to suit all tastes.

Heddon's Mouth near Lynton, Devon

Making the most of your day: free family activity packs and all-terrain buggies to borrow at the Heddon Valley shop. The whole family can learn about and enjoy the nature and history of the valley. **Dogs**: welcome.

Access for all:

Getting here: 180:SS655481. **Foot**: South West Coast Path within ¾ mile. **Bus**: TW Coaches 309, 310 Barnstaple to Lynton (passing close Barnstaple ≥), alight just north of Parracombe, then 2 miles. **Road**: halfway between Combe Martin and Lynton, off A39 at Hunter's Inn. **Parking**: 50 yards.

Finding out more: 01598 763402 or heddonvalley@nationaltrust.org.uk

Heddon Valley		M	T	W	T	F	S	S
Countryside								
Open all year		M	T	W	T	F	S	S
Shop								
12 Mar–29 Apr	11–4:30	M	T	W	T	F	S	S
30 Apr–2 Oct	10:30–5:30	M	T	W	T	F	S	S
3 Oct–30 Oct	11–4:30	M	T	W	T	F	S	S

Heelis

Kemble Drive, Swindon, Wiltshire SN2 2NA

Map (1) K3

The National Trust's award-winning central office is a remarkable example of innovative and sustainable building construction, which uses timber from our woodlands and wool from Herdwick sheep grazed on Trust farmlands – making Heelis a unique working environment.

Exploring
– Tours every Friday, except Bank Holidays (small charge for non-members).

Eating and shopping: café serves a range of delicious local food. There is plenty of choice in our spacious, airy shop.

Making the most of your day: a virtual tour of Heelis is available at reception every day during normal opening hours.

Frost on the stylised topiary birds in the White Garden at Hidcote, Gloucestershire

Access for all: ♿🚻♿🔾🔾♿ Building ♿⬍

Getting here: 173:SU141850. On Swindon's historic railway site, next door to Swindon Designer Outlet. **Foot**: from town centre follow finger post signs through tunnel beneath railway line to Swindon Designer Outlet. **Bus**: Thamesdown Transport and Stagecoach, 13 and 14, alight Rodbourne Road, then 200 yards. **Train**: Swindon, ¾ mile, from station, turn right along Station Road, follow signs to Designer Outlet through second tunnel under railway line. **Road**: off B4289 (Kemble Drive). From M4 junction 16 follow signs for Swindon Designer Outlet Centre North car park. Park and ride from Wroughton. **Parking**: parking (not National Trust), 100 yards (pay and display). Heelis operates a green travel policy, visitor parking facilities are limited and must be booked with reception.

Finding out more: 01793 817400 or heelisreception@nationaltrust.org.uk

Heelis

Admission to offices by booked guided tour only. Heelis, shop and café open daily throughout year, with the exception of 1 January, Easter Sunday, 25 and 26 December.

Hidcote

Hidcote Bartrim, near Chipping Campden, Gloucestershire GL55 6LR

Map ① L1   ✤ 🔔 ▼ 1947

Memories don't get any better than this. Relax and unwind in one of the country's great gardens and experience for yourself the fulfilment of a quiet American's English fantasy. You'll never forget the exquisite garden rooms, each with its own unique character. Discover rare shrubs and trees, herbaceous borders and unusual plants from around the world. The garden changes in harmony with the seasons, from vibrant spring bulbs to autumn's spectacular Red Border. Nestled in the Cotswolds with sweeping views across the Vale of Evesham, a visit to Hidcote is inspirational at any time of year.

Exploring   – Enjoy a game of croquet on the Theatre Lawn.
　　　　　　　– Share a picnic with family or friends in the Wilderness.

Exploring
- Capture the spirit of Lawrence Johnston in our new planthouse.
- Discover great views on one of the many public footpaths.
- Be inspired by breathtaking garden design and planting.
- Children will love our new garden activity sheets.

Eating and shopping: enjoy a delicious meal in our new Garden Restaurant and conservatory, with seasonal menus inspired by our fresh kitchen garden produce. Browse the largest plant centre in the National Trust and buy exclusive Hidcote souvenirs in the shop.

Making the most of your day: daily introductory talks, programme of exclusive evening Head Gardener tours, open-air theatre, themed family trails and workshops.

Access for all: 🅿️🅿️♿️♿️♿️🔲👁️📷
Visitor reception ♿️👁️ **Grounds** ♿️➡️♿️👁️

Getting here: 151:SP176429. **Foot**: 1½ miles by public footpath from Mickleton (route is uphill and steep). **Cycle**: NCN5, 1¼ miles. **Train**: Honeybourne 4½ miles. **Road**: close to Mickleton village, 4 miles north-east of Chipping Campden, 1 mile east of B4632 (originally A46), off B4081. Coaches are only allowed to approach Chipping Campden by designated routes and drop off passengers at the approved stop in the High Street, but are not permitted to use the High Street as a through route to Hidcote. **Parking**: free, 100 yards. Coaches must book – space limited.

You may also enjoy: the small organic garden at Snowshill Manor.

Finding out more: 01386 438333 or hidcote@nationaltrust.org.uk

Hidcote		M	T	W	T	F	S	S
19 Mar–29 Jun	10–6	M	T	W	·	·	S	S
2 Jul–31 Aug	10–6	M	T	W	T	F	S	S
3 Sep–28 Sep	10–6	M	T	W	·	·	S	S
1 Oct–6 Nov	10–5	M	T	W	·	·	S	S
7 Nov–21 Dec	11–4	M	T	W	·	·	S	S
Barn Café and plant sales additional opening								
14 Apr–1 Jul	11–4	·	·	·	T	F	·	·

Open Good Friday. All facilities close at the same time as last admission (one hour before closing).

Holnicote Estate

Selworthy, Minehead, Somerset TA24 8TJ

Map ① G5 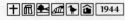 1944

This stunning estate, within Exmoor National Park, offers breathtaking views and spectacular coastline. Miles of footpaths through unspoilt rural landscapes, woods, moors, farmland and villages. **Note**: toilets at Bossington and Horner (National Trust), and Allerford and Selworthy (not National Trust).

Exploring
- Climb to the highest point on Exmoor.
- Cob and thatch cottages in unspoilt villages.

Eating and shopping: shop and café opening at Selworthy at Easter.

Making the most of your day: visit Exmoor Falconry Centre and the West Somerset Rural Life Museum. Witness the wild red deer rut. **Dogs**: on leads only.

Access for all: ♿️ **Grounds** ♿️♿️

Getting here: 181:SS920469. **Foot**: 3¾ miles of South West Coast Path; Coleridge Way; Macmillan Way. **Bus**: Quantock 39 Minehead to Porlock, 300 Taunton to Minehead to Lynmouth, alight Holnicote, ½ mile. **Train**: Minehead (West Somerset Railway) 5 miles. **Road**: off A39 Minehead to Porlock, 3 miles west of Minehead. **Parking**: free at Allerford, North Hill, Dunkery, Webbers Post and Selworthy. Parking (pay and display) at Horner and Bossington. Only Horner car park is suitable for coaches.

Finding out more: 01643 862452 or holnicote@nationaltrust.org.uk

Holnicote Estate		M	T	W	T	F	S	S
Countryside								
1 Jan–31 Dec		M	T	W	T	F	S	S
Selworthy shop								
20 Apr–30 Oct	10–4	·	·	W	T	F	S	S
Selworthy café								
2 Mar–30 Oct	10–5	M	T	W	T	F	S	S

Horton Court

Horton, near Chipping Sodbury,
South Gloucestershire BS37 6QR

Closed this year.

Jurassic Coast

Dorset

Map ① H-J7   1961

England's only natural World Heritage Site,
this stunning swathe of Jurassic coastline
traces almost 185 million years of the Earth's
history, creating a unique 'walk through time'.
The National Trust is embracing every possible
opportunity to make sure that everyone
who comes into contact with us has an
unforgettable experience.

Exploring – Explore the 95 miles of
unspoilt cliffs and beaches.
– Safely search for fossils on
the beach.

Getting here: visit www.nationaltrust.org.uk
for transport details. **Parking**: pay and display
car parks at various points.

Finding out more: 01297 489481 or
jurassiccoast@nationaltrust.org.uk

Jurassic Coast	Open every day all year

Killerton

Broadclyst, Exeter, Devon EX5 3LE

Map ① G6

Would you give away your family home for
your political beliefs? Sir Richard Acland did
just this with his estate, at 2,590 hectares
(6,400 acres) one of the largest the Trust has
acquired (includes 20 farms and 200-plus
cottages). Killerton House, built in 1778–9,
brings to life generations of the Aclands, one
of Devon's oldest families. 'Dressing up,
dressing down', this year's historic fashion
exhibition, explores the numerous changes
of dress required daily. The gem of Killerton,
beautiful all year round, is the garden created
by John Veitch – with rhododendrons,
magnolias and rare trees surrounded by rolling
Devon countryside.

Exploring – Feel at home in the relaxed
atmosphere of the house.
– Escape into the garden,
with majestic trees and
sloping lawns.
– Discover the
rustic summerhouse –
the Bear's Hut.
– Have fun or discover more
at one of our events.
– Meander through the
ancient parkland, woods and
Devon countryside.
– Enjoy 'Dressing up, dressing
down': an exhibition of
historic fashion.

Looking over the clifftop of the Jurassic Coast towards Golden Cap, Dorset

The house at Killerton, Devon: home to many generations of the Acland family

Eating and shopping: buy Killerton cider, chutney, flour or honey in the shop. Plant centre with peat-free plants. Two tea-rooms using local produce and Killerton estate flour. Stay in one of Killerton's four thatched holiday cottages.

Making the most of your day: discover 'Killerton's Characters'. Try on replica costumes. Browse in the second-hand bookshop. For families: Tracker Packs, play area, Discovery Centre (school holidays), trails. Waymarked walks and orienteering routes. **Dogs**: welcome on leads in park and estate walks only. Dog bowls and posts available.

Access for all: ⬚⬚⬚⬚⬚⬚⬚⬚⬚⬚
⬚ House ⬚⬚⬚ Shop ⬚⬚⬚
Grounds ⬚⬚⬚

Getting here: 192:SS973001. **Cycle**: NCN52. **Bus**: Stagecoach in Devon 1/A/B Exeter to Tiverton, alight Killerton Turn ¾ mile. **Train**: Pinhoe, not Sunday, 4½ miles; Whimple, 6 miles; Exeter Central and St David's, both 7 miles. **Road**: off Exeter to Cullompton road (B3181); from M5 northbound, exit 30 via Pinhoe and Broadclyst; from M5 southbound, exit 28. **Parking**: free, 280 yards.

You may also enjoy: Knightshayes Court. On the Killerton Estate: Broadclyst village, Marker's Cottage, Clyston Mill, Ashclyst Forest.

Finding out more: 01392 881345 or killerton@nationaltrust.org.uk

Killerton		M	T	W	T	F	S	S
Park and garden								
2 Jan–31 Dec	10:30–7	M	T	W	T	F	S	S
House								
12 Feb–11 Mar	12–4	M	T	W	T	F	S	S
12 Mar–31 Oct	11–5	M	T	W	T	F	S	S
3 Dec–23 Dec	2–4	M	T	W	T	F	S	S
Tea-room								
2 Jan–6 Feb	11–5						S	S
12 Feb–31 Dec	11–5	M	T	W	T	F	S	S
Shop and plant sales								
2 Jan–6 Feb	11–5						S	S
12 Feb–31 Oct	11–5:30	M	T	W	T	F	S	S
1 Nov–31 Dec	11–5	M	T	W	T	F	S	S

Orchard tea-room and shop close at 3 on 24 December and all day 25 and 26 December. In winter, shop and Orchard tea-room may not open in bad weather.

Killerton: Budlake Old Post Office

Broadclyst, Killerton, Exeter, Devon EX5 3LW

Map ① G7   ⬚ ⬚ 1944

Close to Killerton, this small thatched cottage was the village post office, serving Killerton House and the local community, until the 1950s. The cottage has a delightful cottage garden including rose borders, herb and vegetable plots. **Note**: nearest toilets at Killerton.

Exploring
- Discover the double-seated privy and pigsty.
- Listen to reminiscences of life in the post office.
- Step back in time amid the 1950s memorabilia.
- Imagine doing washing in the Victorian wash-house.

Eating and shopping: visit nearby Killerton for tea-rooms, shop and plants.

Making the most of your day: footpath to Killerton along old carriage drive. **Dogs**: on leads in garden only.

Access for all: Building 🚶 Grounds 🚶

Getting here: 192:SS973001. **Cycle**: NCN52. **Bus**: Stagecoach in Devon 1/A/B Exeter to Tiverton Parkway ➤ (passing close Exeter Central ➤), alight Killerton Turn ¾ mile. **Train**: Pinhoe, not Sunday, 4½ miles; Whimple, 6 miles; Exeter Central and St David's, both 7 miles. **Road**: off Exeter to Cullompton road (B3181); from M5 northbound, exit 30 via Pinhoe and Broadclyst; from M5 southbound, exit 28. **Parking**: limited parking. Ample parking for cars and coaches at Killerton, 800 yards.

Finding out more: 01392 881690 or budlakepostoffice@nationaltrust.org.uk

Budlake Old Post Office		M	T	W	T	F	S	S
3 Apr–31 Oct	2–5	**M**	**T**	·	·	·	·	**S**

Last admission 10 minutes before closing.

Killerton: Clyston Mill

Broadclyst, Exeter, Devon EX5 3EW

Map ① G7   🏠 1944

Historic water-powered corn mill in a picturesque setting by the River Clyst, surrounded by farmland and orchards. Corn is still ground here to make flour, keeping alive traditional skills. Discover more about what life would have been like for the miller, with hands-on activities and interpretation. **Note**: nearest parking and toilets in Broadclyst.

Exploring
- Wander through Broadclyst's old churchyard to visit the mill.
- Working mill: watch the flour being ground.
- See where the mill boy slept.
- Picnic by the river and listen to the birds.

Eating and shopping: buy a bag of Clyston Mill flour. Visit Killerton for produce made from Clyston Mill flour.

Making the most of your day: children's trail and hands-on activities. **Dogs**: welcome on a lead.

Access for all: Building 🚶 Grounds 🚶

Getting here: 192:SX981973. **Foot**: from village car park, walk towards church and follow signs through churchyard. **Cycle**: NCN52. **Bus**: Stagecoach in Devon 1/A/B Exeter to Tiverton Parkway ➤ (passing close Exeter Central ➤), alight Broadclyst village. **Train**: Pinhoe, not Sunday, 4½ miles; Whimple, 6 miles; Exeter Central and St David's, both 7 miles. **Road**: off Exeter to Cullompton Road (B3181) in village of Broadclyst. **Parking**: free (not National Trust), 450 yards.

Finding out more: 01392 462425 or clystonmill@nationaltrust.org.uk

Clyston Mill		M	T	W	T	F	S	S
3 Apr–31 Oct	2–5	**M**	**T**	·	·	·	·	**S**

Clyston Mill on the Killerton Estate, Devon

Killerton: Marker's Cottage

Townend, Broadclyst, Exeter, Devon EX5 3HX

Map ① G7 🏠 🚻 1944

An intriguing medieval cob cottage with a thatched roof and smoke-blackened timbers. Discover the fascinating history of the cottage, including the unusual painted decorative screen showing St Andrew. A cross passage opens out onto a garden with a contemporary cob summerhouse and blacksmith's workshop. **Note**: nearest parking and toilets in Broadclyst.

The Hall at Marker's Cottage, Devon

Exploring
- Find the painting of St Andrew and his boat.
- Be a history detective and follow the cottage's timeline.
- Discover the art of pargeting.
- Spot the dead rat.

Eating and shopping: visit nearby Killerton for tea-rooms, shop and plant centre.

Making the most of your day: handling collection and trail. Follow the Broadclyst village trail.

Access for all: 🅳 Building 🔲 Grounds 🅱

Getting here: 192:SX985973. **Cycle**: NCN52. **Bus**: Stagecoach in Devon 1/A/B Exeter to Tiverton Parkway 🚆 (passing close Exeter Central 🚆). **Train**: Pinhoe, not Sunday, 2½ miles; Whimple, 4½ miles; Exeter Central and St David's, both 6 miles. **Road**: in village

of Broadclyst. From village car park turn left, then right and right again onto Townend. Marker's Cottage is second cottage on left. **Parking**: free (not National Trust), 250 yards.

Finding out more: 01392 461546 or markerscottage@nationaltrust.org.uk

Marker's Cottage		M	T	W	T	F	S	S
3 Apr–31 Oct	2–5	**M**	**T**	.	.	.	.	**S**

King John's Hunting Lodge

The Square, Axbridge, Somerset BS26 2AP

Map ① I4 🏠 1968

This early Tudor timber-framed wool merchant's house (*circa* 1500) provides a fascinating insight into local history. Its strong medieval character is enhanced by the appearance of arcaded stalls opening onto the street on the ground floor (recreated by the National Trust during the building's restoration). **Note**: run as a local history museum by Axbridge and District Museum Trust (small entry charge).

Exploring
- Find out about local history in the museum.

Eating and shopping: visit the shop in museum (not National Trust).

Making the most of your day: occasional tours of historic Axbridge start from the museum.

Access for all: 🅰 Building 🔲

Getting here: 182:ST431545. In the Square, on corner of High Street. **Bus**: First 126 Weston-super-Mare to Wells (passing close Weston-super-Mare 🚆). **Train**: Worle 8 miles. **Parking**: 100 yards (not National Trust).

Finding out more: 01934 732012 or kingjohns@nationaltrust.org.uk

King John's Hunting Lodge		M	T	W	T	F	S	S
1 Apr–30 Sep	1–4	**M**	**T**	**W**	**T**	**F**	**S**	**S**

Kingston Lacy

Wimborne Minster, Dorset BH21 4EA

Map ① K7    1982

Home of the Bankes family for more than 300 years, this striking 17th-century house is noted for its lavish interiors. The outstanding art collection includes paintings by Rubens, Van Dyck, Titian and Tintoretto, with the largest private collection of Egyptian artefacts in the UK. Outside, stroll across the beautiful lawns towards the restored Japanese tea garden. There are several waymarked walks through the surrounding parkland, with its fine herd of North Devon cattle, and the 3,443-hectare (8,500-acre) estate is dominated by the Iron Age hillfort of Badbury Rings, home to fourteen varieties of orchid.

The park stretches beyond the house at Kingston Lacy, Dorset

Exploring
 — Outstanding art collection, including works by Rubens and Titian.
 — View the restored Tintoretto in the Dining Room.
 — Explore the Edwardian Japanese Gardens.
 — Stroll through the Cedar Walk, Lime Walk and Nursery Wood.
 — Seek out the Egyptian obelisk and sarcophagus.
 — Enjoy Eyebridge riverside walk (hard, level surface) and Badbury Rings.

Eating and shopping: be sure to sample our prize-winning scones. Try our beef, from the Kingston Lacy North Devon herd. Treat yourself to regional and local foods and wines. Take home some National Trust-grown plants.

Making the most of your day: 'Putting the House to Bed' tours in November, bookings only. Throughout the year: farmers' markets, open-air theatre, tractor trailer tours, children's crafts and 'Above and Below Stairs'days.
Dogs: on leads in restaurant courtyard, park and woodlands only.

Access for all:  Building ⓖ Grounds

Getting here: 195:ST980019. **Bus**: Wilts & Dorset 13 from Bournemouth, 3 from Poole (passing Bournemouth ≋ and close Poole ≋), alight Wimborne Square, change onto Nordcat Service 88 Wimborne Minster to QE School. Fridays and Saturdays limited Nordcat Service 28 from Wimborne Square to Kingston Lacy. **Train**: Poole 8½ miles. **Road**: on B3082 Blandford to Wimborne road, 1½ miles west of Wimborne Minster. **Sat Nav**: data unreliable, follow B3082. **Parking**: free. Charge at Badbury Rings on point-to-point race days.

You may also enjoy: White Mill, Corfe Castle, Hardy's Cottage, Max Gate and Studland.

Finding out more: 01202 883402 or kingstonlacy@nationaltrust.org.uk

Kingston Lacy		M	T	W	T	F	S	S
House								
12 Mar–30 Oct	11–5	·	·	W	T	F	S	S
Garden, park, shop and restaurant								
3 Jan–11 Mar	10:30–4	M	T	W	T	F	S	S
12 Mar–30 Oct	10:30–6	M	T	W	T	F	S	S
31 Oct–23 Dec	10:30–4	M	T	W	T	F	S	S

Open Bank Holiday Mondays. Timed tickets may operate on Bank Holiday Sundays and Mondays. Last admission to house one hour before closing. Garden, park, shop and restaurant closed 24, 25, 26 and 31 December; open 27 to 30 December. Shop and restaurant close 30 minutes earlier.

Knightshayes Court

Bolham, Tiverton, Devon EX16 7RQ

Map ① G6  1973

'**Wonderful. I adored it all**.'
Sarah Young, Cullompton, Devon

Feeding the chickens at Knightshayes Court, Devon

One of the finest surviving Gothic Revival houses, built in the lush landscape of mid-Devon, Knightshayes Court is a rare example of the work of the eccentric and inspired architect William Burges. Built for the grandson of pioneer lace-maker John Heathcoat in 1869, the house is an exciting architectural experience, with extraordinary 'medieval' romantic interiors, rich decoration and ceramics. The restored and fully productive organic kitchen garden is a treat for everyone who enjoys local produce. The vast garden, which was the Heathcoat Amory family's great passion, is renowned for its rare trees, shrubs and seasonal colours. **Note**: no photography in house. House and garden access may be restricted February, November and December.

Exploring
– Enjoy the wonderfully re-created 'Burges Bedroom'.
– Relax in the peaceful and glorious garden.
– Discover the Seven Deadly Sins in the Billiard Room.
– Search for the Talbot dogs in the house and garden.
– Explore the celebrated 'Garden in the Wood'.
– Discover how to grow your own in the kitchen garden.

Eating and shopping: enjoy organic kitchen garden produce in the restaurant. Opening hours may vary in October, but light refreshments are always available. Exceptionally well-stocked plant centre. Gift shop. Produce for sale in kitchen garden.

Making the most of your day: daily introductory talks in the house and introductory garden walks. Programme of open-air, family, Christmas, gardening and restaurant events. Picnics in parkland only.

Dogs: on leads in woodland and park.

Access for all: ▣▣▣▣▣▣▣▣▣▣▣
House ▣▣▣ Restaurant ▣ Gardens ▣▣

Getting here: 181:SS960151. **Cycle**: NCN3.
Bus: First 398 Tiverton to Minehead, alight Bolham, then ¾ mile. Otherwise Stagecoach in Devon 1 from Tiverton Parkway ☎; 55/A/B Exeter to Tiverton (passing close Exeter Central ☎), alighting Tiverton 1¾ miles. **Train**: Tiverton Parkway 8 miles. **Road**: 7 miles from M5 exit 27 (A361); 2 miles north of Tiverton; turn right off Tiverton to Bampton road (A396) at Bolham. **Sat Nav**: turn off on reaching Tiverton and follow signs. **Parking**: free.

You may also enjoy: Killerton.

Finding out more: 01884 254665 (office). 01884 257381 (visitor reception) or knightshayes@nationaltrust.org.uk

Knightshayes Court		M	T	W	T	F	S	S
House								
5 Mar–6 Mar	11–4						S	S
12 Mar–30 Oct	11–5	M	T	W	T		S	S
5 Nov–18 Dec	11–4						S	S
26 Dec–31 Dec	11–3	M	T	W	T		S	
House, garden, shop, plant centre and restaurant								
19 Feb–27 Feb	11–4	M	T	W	T		S	S
19 Dec–22 Dec	11–3	M	T	W	T			
Garden, shop, plant centre and restaurant								
3 Mar–6 Mar	11–4					T	F	S	S
12 Mar–30 Oct	11–5	M	T	W	T	F	S	S
3 Nov–18 Dec	11–4					T	F	S	S
26 Dec–31 Dec	11–3	M	T	W	T	F	S	

House: closed Fridays (excluding Good Friday); limited access in February, November and December (19 to 22 and 26 to 31 December – Great Hall and Smoking Room only open); house closed 11 December. Whole property closed 24 and 25 December.

Help the Trust with Gift Aid on Entry for non-members

Lacock Abbey, Fox Talbot Museum and Village

Lacock, near Chippenham, Wiltshire SN15 2LG

Map ① K4  1944

Set in rural Wiltshire, Lacock village is famous for its picturesque streets, historic buildings and its more recent role as a television and film location. The Abbey, located at the heart of the village within its own woodland grounds, is a quirky country house of various architectural styles, built upon the foundations of a former nunnery. Visitors can experience the atmosphere of the medieval rooms and cloister court, giving a sense of the Abbey's monastic past. The museum celebrates the achievements of former Lacock resident William Henry Fox Talbot, famous for his contributions to the invention of photography.

Exploring
– Discover the history of the Abbey and newly opened rooms.
– Enjoy the grounds' spring bulbs, summer borders and greenhouse.
– Wander the historic village streets, enjoying shopping and a meal.
– See wonderful exhibitions in the upper gallery of the museum.
– Experience Lacock life with a stay in our holiday cottage.
– Visit the location of films like *Harry Potter* and *Cranford*.

Eating and shopping: find locally made products in the recently expanded National Trust village shop. Browse the museum shop and take home a plant. Pick up your next read in the Abbey's second-hand bookshop. Enjoy food outlets and shops in the village.

Making the most of your day: a full programme of events runs throughout the year, including family fun days, themed activities, open-air theatre, exhibitions and walks. **Dogs**: welcome in the Abbey grounds in winter only.

Access for all: [icons]
Abbey [icons] Museum [icons]
Grounds [icons]

Getting here: 173:ST919684. **Foot**: surrounding network of footpaths, including route beside Wiltshire & Berkshire Canal. **Cycle**: NCN4, 1 mile. **Bus**: Faresaver X34/First 234 Chippenham to Frome (passing Melksham ▨, close Chippenham ▨ and close Trowbridge ▨). **Train**: Melksham 3 miles; Chippenham 3½ miles. **Road**: 3 miles south of Chippenham. M4 exit 17, signposted to Chippenham (A350). Follow A350 (signposted Poole/Warminster) until you reach Lacock, following signs leading to main car park. **Parking**: 220 yards (pay and display). No visitor parking on village streets.

You may also enjoy: The Courts Garden at Holt – six miles from Lacock.

Finding out more: 01249 730459 or lacockabbey@nationaltrust.org.uk

Lacock Abbey		M	T	W	T	F	S	S
Cloisters, grounds, museum, exhibition and museum shop								
2 Jan–18 Feb	11–4	M	T	W	T	F	S	S
19 Feb–30 Oct	10:30–5:30	M	T	W	T	F	S	S
31 Oct–31 Dec*	11–4	M	T	W	T	F	S	S
Abbey rooms								
2 Jan–13 Feb	12–4						S	S
19 Feb–30 Oct	11–5	M		W	T	F	S	S
5 Nov–31 Dec*	12–4						S	S
High Street shop								
2 Jan–18 Feb	11–4	M	T	W	T	F	S	S
19 Feb–30 Oct	10–5:30	M	T	W	T	F	S	S
31 Oct–31 Dec*	11–4	M	T	W	T	F	S	S
Village**								
Open all year		M	T	W	T	F	S	S

*All (excluding village) closed 1 January, 25 and 26 December.
**Village businesses open at various times.

Romantic Lacock Abbey, Wiltshire

Lanhydrock

Bodmin, Cornwall PL30 5AD

Map ① D8  1953

Lanhydrock is the perfect country house and estate, with the feel of a wealthy but unpretentious family home. Follow in the footsteps of generations of the Robartes family, walking in the 17th-century Long Gallery among the rare book collection under the remarkable plasterwork ceiling. After a devastating fire in 1881 the house was refurbished in the high-Victorian style, with the latest mod cons. Boasting the best in country-house design and planning, the kitchens, nurseries and servants' quarters offer a thrilling glimpse into life 'below stairs', while the spacious dining room and bedrooms are truly and deeply elegant.

Exploring
- There are 50 rooms to explore – allow plenty of time!
- Play the Steinway piano in the Long Gallery.
- Look out for our newly opened museum and second-hand bookshop.
- Explore the extensive garden and estate, colourful all the year.
- Discover the network of woodland, park and riverside paths.
- Don't miss our picnic area and adventure playground.

Eating and shopping: we serve local seasonal food in our friendly licensed restaurants. Go Cornish and have an Oggie pasty and cream tea. Local food and gifts available in the shop. Plant centre in car park outside the tariff area.

Making the most of your day: open-air theatre, garden tours and children's activities throughout the year. **Dogs**: welcome on leads in park and woods.

Access for all: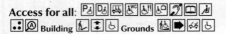
Building ⬛⬛⬛ Grounds ⬛⬛⬛⬛

The Long Gallery at Lanhydrock, Cornwall

Getting here: 200:SX088636. **Cycle**: NCN3, runs past entrance. **Train**: Bodmin Parkway 1¾ miles via original carriage-drive to house, signposted in station car park; 3 miles by road. **Road**: 2½ miles south-east of Bodmin. Follow signposts from either A30, A38 Bodmin to Liskeard or take B3268 off A390 at Lostwithiel. **Parking**: free, 600 yards.

You may also enjoy: Trerice and Cotehele.

Finding out more: 01208 265950 or lanhydrock@nationaltrust.org.uk

Lanhydrock		M	T	W	T	F	S	S
House								
26 Feb–31 Mar	11–5	·	T	W	T	F	S	S
1 Apr–30 Sep	11–5:30	·	T	W	T	F	S	S
1 Oct–30 Oct	11–5	·	T	W	T	F	S	S
Garden								
Open all year	10–6	M	T	W	T	F	S	S
Shop and refreshments								
1 Jan–13 Feb	11–4	·	·	·	·	·	S	S
19 Feb–31 Mar	11–5	M	T	W	T	F	S	S
1 Apr–30 Sep	11–5:30	M	T	W	T	F	S	S
1 Oct–30 Oct	11–5	M	T	W	T	F	S	S
31 Oct–31 Dec	11–4	M	T	W	T	F	S	S
Plant centre								
19 Feb–30 Oct	11–5	·	T	W	T	F	S	S

House open Bank Holiday Mondays and Mondays during state school holidays. Plant centre also open Mondays April to September to 5:30 and Mondays in October. Refreshments open 10:30, 26 February to 30 October. Closed 25 and 26 December. Shop and refreshments are inside the tariff area.

Lawrence House

9 Castle Street, Launceston, Cornwall PL15 8BA

Map (1) E7   1964

Built in 1753, Lawrence House is leased to Launceston Town Council and used as a local museum and civic centre.

Access for all: [wc] [symbols] **Building** [symbols] **Garden** [symbol]

Getting here: 201:SX330848. 1 mile approximately north of the A30 in the oldest part of Launceston.

Finding out more: 01566 773277 or lawrencehouse@nationaltrust.org.uk

Lawrence House			M	T	W	T	F	S	S
4 Apr–28 Oct	10:30–4:30	**M**	**T**	**W**	**T**	**F**			

Open by appointment at other times for groups or individuals for study.

Leigh Woods

Leigh Woods, near Bristol, Avon

Map (1) I4    1909

A beautiful haven on Bristol's doorstep, Leigh Woods is a tranquil and diverse woodland with wonderful views over the city, Avon Gorge and downs. Perfect for walking or cycling, there is a good network of paths including a 1¼-mile easy-access trail and links to the National Cycle Network. **Note:** no toilets. An off-road cycle route will be developed this year.

Exploring
– Look out for red Devon cattle grazing part of site.
– Let off steam in the natural play area.
– Track down many rare species, including whitebeam trees.
– Discover Stokeleigh Camp Iron Age hill fort.

Eating and shopping: picnics welcome as there are no catering facilities.

Making the most of your day: look out for the new natural play area. Explore the permanent orienteering course (to get a map please contact the property). **Dogs:** welcome, look out for signs letting you know if cattle are on site.

Getting here: 172:ST555730. 2 miles south-west of Bristol city centre. **Foot:** River Avon Trail from Pill to Bristol links with a footpath up Nightingale Valley. **Cycle:** blue trail that runs through the wood connects with NCN41. **Bus:** 357, 358 and 358 Bristol to Portishead (use Beggar Bush Lane stop and Valley Road to get into wood). **Train:** Clifton Down [symbol] 2½ miles, Bristol Temple Meads 3 miles. **Road:** 2 miles south-west of Bristol off A369 Bristol to Portishead road; from Bristol access via Clifton Suspension Bridge; from M5 at J19 take A369. **Parking:** roadside parking on North Road off A369. Alternatively use Forestry Commission car park, signed off A369.

Finding out more: 0117 973 1645 or leighwoods@nationaltrust.org.uk. Reserve Office, Valley Road, Leigh Woods, Bristol, Avon BS8 3PZ

Leigh Woods	Open every day all year

Levant Mine and Beam Engine

Trewellard, Pendeen, near St Just, Cornwall TR19 7SX

Map (1) A9   1967

Part of Cornwall and West Devon Mining World Heritage Site, this is the only Cornish beam engine anywhere in the world that is still in steam on its original mine site. The famous Levant engine is housed in a small engine house perched on the edge of the cliffs. Restored after 60 idle years by a group of volunteers known as the 'Greasy Gang', it is a thrilling experience for young and old alike to see this old engine in action, with its evocative sounds and smells.

The remains of Levant Mine, including its iconic beam engine house, on the cliffs of West Penwith in Cornwall

Exploring
- A film tells the story of Levant Mine.
- Take a short underground tour through the miners' dry tunnel.
- A cliff walk takes you to Botallack Mine.
- View historical displays at the Botallack Count House Workshop.
- Close by is Geevor Mine and museum (not National Trust).

Eating and shopping: vending machine available for drinks. Small shop with mining-related goods and books.

Making the most of your day: experience Levant through a guided tour or a self-guided family trail. Follow a biodiversity trail along the cliffs to Geevor (Tracker Packs available for children). Associated buildings also open. **Dogs**: welcome.

Access for all: 🅿️♿📷👁️📷 Building ♿

Getting here: 203:SW368346. **Foot**: South West Coast Path passes entrance. **Bus**: First 10/A Penzance ≷ to St Just. **Train**: Penzance 7 miles. **Road**: 1 mile west of Pendeen, on B3306 St Just to St Ives road. **Parking**: free, 100 yards. Not suitable for coaches. Limited parking for coaches at Geevor Mine, ½ mile walk to Levant mine.

You may also enjoy: East Pool Mine, Botallack Count House, St Michael's Mount and Trengwainton Garden.

Finding out more: 01736 786156 or levant@nationaltrust.org.uk

Levant Beam Engine		M	T	W	T	F	S	S
Steaming								
1 Apr–22 May	11–5			W		F		S
24 May–30 Sep	11–5		T	W	T	F		S
5 Oct–28 Oct	11–5			W		F		
Not steaming								
7 Jan–25 Mar	11–4					F		
4 Nov–30 Dec	11–4					F		

Open Bank Holiday Sundays and Mondays.

Little Clarendon

Dinton, Salisbury, Wiltshire SP3 5DZ

Map ① K5   🏠 ✚ 1940

Late 15th-century stone house and curious chapel adjoining. **Note**: no toilet.

Access for all: 👁️ Building ♿

Getting here: 184:SU015316. ¼ mile east of Dinton Church, close to post office; take B3089 from Salisbury to Dinton.

Finding out more: 01985 843600 or littleclarendon@nationaltrust.org.uk

Little Clarendon		M	T	W	T	F	S	S
25 Apr	2–5	M						
2 May	2–5	M						
30 May	2–5	M						
29 Aug	2–5	M						

Members may have to pay on special events days

The Lizard and Kynance Cove

The Lizard, near Helston, Cornwall

Map ① C10  1935

Lizard Point, Britain's most southerly point, offers dramatic cliff walks, wild flowers and geological features. Marconi's historic wireless experiments are celebrated at The Lizard Wireless Station and the Marconi Centre at Poldhu. Two miles north lies Kynance Cove, considered one of the most beautiful beaches in the world. **Note**: Kynance car park toilets closed in winter (cove toilets open all year). Some sheer cliffs.

Exploring — At the Point, watch Cornish choughs fledge and fly.
— Take a kayak out at Mullion Cove.
— Take to the waves and learn to surf at Poldhu.
— Take a picnic and explore the creeks around the Helford.

Eating and shopping: café at Kynance Cove (March to October), ice-cream in Kynance car park (peak season only), café at Lizard Point (March to October) – all Trust-approved concessions. Seasonal café at Poldhu (not National Trust).

Making the most of your day: visit in May and June to see the wild flowers at their best – you may even spot basking sharks. Go surfing at Poldhu or kayak at Mullion. **Dogs**: seasonal dog bans on some beaches, including Kynance.

Access for all: P WC Kynance Cove ➡

Getting here: 203:SW688133. Lizard Point and Kynance: off the A3083 from Helston. Mullion and Poldhu: signposted. Helford and Gillan: signposted off the main road to St Keverne, B3293, from Helston. **Foot**: South West Coast Path runs around Lizard peninsula. **Ferry**: foot ferry from Helford Passage to the south side of the river to reach Helford village and walks around Frenchman's Creek. **Bus**: Western Greyhound 537 Redruth ≆ to Helston to Lizard, then walk to Kynance Cove ½ mile, to Lizard Point 1 mile. **Road**: Lizard Point and Kynance: A3083 from Helston to Lizard town. Mullion and Poldhu: signposted. Helford and Gillan: take road signposted St Keverne B3293 until you see signs from Helford. **Parking**: at Kynance and Lizard Point (charge Easter to November). Additional parking (not National Trust) in Lizard town, from where a footpath leads to Lizard Point. No caravans or trailers. Limited parking around Helford (council car park) and Gillan.

Finding out more: 01326 561407 or lizard@nationaltrust.org.uk

The Lizard	Open every day all year

Telephone for opening times of the Lizard Wireless Station at Bass Point and the Marconi Centre at Poldhu.

The sandy beach at Kynance Cove, on The Lizard in Cornwall

Lodge Park and Sherborne Estate

Lodge Park, Aldsworth, near Cheltenham, Gloucestershire GL54 3PP

Map (1) K/L2 1983

17th-century grandstand created in 1634 by John 'Crump' Dutton inspired by his passion for gambling, banqueting and entertaining. The National Trust's first restoration project relying on archaeological evidence. Enjoy the impressive views of the deer course and park (designed by Charles Bridgeman in the 1720s). **Note**: may close for weddings. Repairs may require scaffolding. Toilet at Lodge Park only.

Lodge Park, Gloucestershire

Exploring
- England's only surviving 17th-century deer course and grandstand.
- Dramatic views from the grandstand of Charles Bridgeman's landscape.
- Explore the windswept and romantic countryside.
- Plenty of space for picnics and ball games.

Eating and shopping: small National Trust shop. Hot and cold drinks available, including local apple juice, as well as ice-cream and sandwiches.

Making the most of your day: open-air theatre during the summer. Walks around the surrounding Sherborne Estate. Christmas concert at Lodge Park. **Dogs**: welcome under close control.

Access for all: Building

Getting here: 163:SP146123. **Bus**: Swanbrook 853 Oxford to Gloucester (passing Gloucester and close Oxford). 1½-mile walk to Lodge Park from bus stop or 1 mile Sherborne; also 833 Cheltenham to Northleach. **Road**: 3 miles east of Northleach; approach from A40 only. **Parking**: estate walks parking at Ewe Pen Barn car park, 163:SP158143, and water meadows, 163:SP175154 (off A40 towards Sherborne). Donation of £1 will help our conservation work on the estate.

Finding out more: 01451 844130 or lodgepark@nationaltrust.org.uk

Lodge Park and Sherborne Estate		M	T	W	T	F	S	S
11 Mar–30 Oct	11–4	·	·	·	·	**F**	**S**	**S**
17 Dec–18 Dec	11–4	·	·	·	·	·	**S**	**S**

Open Bank Holiday Mondays. Property occasionally closes for weddings (telephone to confirm opening times). Sherborne Park Estate open all year (access from Ewe Pen car park).

Loughwood Meeting House

Dalwood, Axminster, Devon EX13 7DU

Map (1) H7 1969

Set in the beautiful East Devon countryside, this atmospheric 17th-century thatched Baptist meeting house is dug into the hillside. **Note**: no toilet.

Access for all: Building

Getting here: 192/193:SY253993. 4 miles west of Axminster, 1 mile south of Dalwood, 1 mile north-west of Kilmington.

Finding out more: 01752 346585 or loughwood@nationaltrust.org.uk. South and East Devon Countryside Office, The Stables, Saltram House, Plymouth, Devon PL7 1UH

Loughwood Meeting House		M	T	W	T	F	S	S
Open all year	11–4	**M**	**T**	**W**	**T**	**F**	**S**	**S**

Services held twice yearly. Details at Meeting House.

Landing Bay on Lundy Island in the Bristol Channel, Devon, as seen from the air

Lundy

Bristol Channel, Devon EX39 2LY

Map ① D5  1969

Undisturbed by cars, the island encompasses a small village with an inn and Victorian church, and the 13th-century Marisco Castle. For nature-lovers there is a variety of wildlife, flora and fauna. Designated the first Marine Conservation Area, Lundy offers opportunities for diving and seal watching. **Note**: Lundy is financed, administered and maintained by the Landmark Trust. Holiday cottages available to rent.

Exploring
 – A unique island experience.
 – Sail from Ilfracombe or Bideford on board MS *Oldenburg*.
 – Peaceful and remote – a world apart.

Eating and shopping: Marisco Tavern serves hot and cold food and drinks. Island shop sells souvenirs, Lundy stamps, snacks and ice-creams.

Making the most of your day: there is a wealth of things to do, including walking, letterboxing, birdwatching and discovering the varied wildlife. **Dogs**: assistance dogs only permitted on Lundy.

Access for all: 🅿♿♿♿
Building 🔆 Grounds ♿

Getting here: 180:SS130450. In the Bristol Channel 11 miles north of Hartland Point, 25 miles west of Ilfracombe, 30 miles south of Tenby. **Cycle**: NCN31 (Bideford). **Ferry**: sea passages from Bideford or Ilfracombe according to tides up to four days a week, end of March to end October. Landing fee included when travelling on MS *Oldenburg*. **Bus**: First 3 Barnstaple to Ilfracombe, First 1, 2 Barnstaple to Bideford ☒. **Train**: Barnstaple: 8½ miles to Bideford, 12 miles to Ilfracombe. **Sat Nav**: postcode for Ilfracombe booking office is EX34 9EQ and for Bideford office is EX39 2EY. **Parking**: at Bideford or Ilfracombe for ferries (pay and display).

Finding out more: 01271 863636 or lundy@nationaltrust.org.uk. The Lundy Shore Office, The Quay, Bideford, Devon EX39 2LY

Lundy
MS *Oldenburg* sails from Bideford or Ilfracombe up to four times a week from the end of March until the end of October carrying both day and staying passengers. A helicopter service operates from Hartland Point from November to mid-March, Mondays and Fridays only, for staying visitors.

Lydford Gorge

Lydford, near Tavistock, Devon EX20 4BH

Map (1) F7   📧 1947

'**Lydford Gorge is the most beautiful place in the world. Something for all the family.**'
Mrs Long, Bristol

This lush oak-wooded steep-sided river gorge (the deepest in the South West), with its natural beauty, fascinating history and many legends, can be explored through a variety of exhilarating short or long walks. Around every corner the River Lyd plunges, tumbles, swirls and gently meanders as it travels through the gorge. Throughout the seasons there is an abundance of wildlife and plants to see, from woodland birds to wild garlic (you can smell it too) in the spring and fungi in the autumn. **Note:** strenuous walking, rugged terrain, vertical drops. Unsuitable for visitors with heart complaints or walking difficulties.

Exploring
- Discover the magical 30-metre-high Whitelady Waterfall.
- Walk out over the bubbling Devil's Cauldron.
- Watch woodland birds from the bird hide.
- See the water tumble through Tunnel Falls.
- Learn about the myths of the Gubbins and Whitelady Waterfall.
- Keep a look out for the woodland sculptures.

Eating and shopping: browse in the shop and plant centre. Wildlife books and outdoor clothing in the shop. Enjoy Devon cream teas at one of two tea-rooms. Add to your picnic with takeaway drinks and food.

Making the most of your day: school holiday and family events, wildlife-themed activities, wild food area, children's play area, bird hide. **Dogs**: welcome on leads.

Access for all: 📷🚻♿🅿📷📷📷∴ⓐ
Buildings 🏠 Gorge ♿

Getting here: 191/201:SX509845. **Foot**: as road directions or via Blackdown Moor from Mary Tavy. **Cycle**: NCN27 and 31. Close to three cycle routes: Devon Coast to Coast, West Devon Way and Plym Valley. **Bus**: Holsworthy 118 Tavistock to Barnstaple, bus stop at main entrance and waterfall entrance to gorge. **Road**: 7 miles south of A30. Halfway between Okehampton and Tavistock, 1 mile west off A386 opposite Dartmoor Inn; main entrance at west end of Lydford village; waterfall entrance near Manor Farm. **Parking**: free.

You may also enjoy: the last working water-powered forge: Finch Foundry in Sticklepath near Okehampton.

Finding out more: 01822 820320 or lydfordgorge@nationaltrust.org.uk

Lydford Gorge		M	T	W	T	F	S	S
Gorge, shop and tea-rooms								
12 Mar–2 Oct	10–5	M	T	W	T	F	S	S
3 Oct–30 Oct	10–4	M	T	W	T	F	S	S
Shop and tea-room								
21 Feb–27 Feb	10:30–4	M	T	W	T	F	S	S
5 Nov–24 Dec	10:30–4						S	S
Walks to the Whitelady Waterfall								
2 Jan–11 Mar	10:30–3:30	M	T	W	T	F	S	S
31 Oct–31 Dec	10:30–3:30	M	T	W	T	F	S	S

Parts of gorge closed in January, February, November and December due to weather conditions, higher river levels, reduced daylight hours and maintenance work. Shop also open 17 to 24 December.

The wooden bridge at Lydford Gorge, Devon

The east front of Lytes Cary Manor in Somerset, with its colourful herbaceous border of summer flowers

Lytes Cary Manor

near Charlton Mackrell, Somerton,
Somerset TA11 7HU

Map (1) I5 　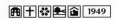 　1949

This intimate manor house was the former home of medieval herbalist Henry Lyte; here visitors can learn about his famous 16th-century plant directory, *Lytes Herbal*. The manor spans many years with its 14th-century chapel and 15th-century Great Hall. In the 20th century it was rescued from dereliction by Sir Walter Jenner. Its Arts and Crafts-style garden is a combination of outdoor rooms, topiary, statues and herbaceous borders. Explore the walks through the wider estate and riverside and discover many features typical of farmed lowland England, including ancient hedges, rare arable weeds and farmland birds.

Exploring
- Explore the intimate manor house and chapel.
- Stroll around the Arts and Crafts garden.
- Admire the topiary, statues and herbaceous borders of the garden.
- Walk the wider estate with waymarked tracks.
- Discover the estate with children's Tracker Packs and trails.
- Play croquet on the lawn – equipment is available to hire.

Eating and shopping: enjoy light refreshments at our 'Simple Foods' kiosk. Be inspired by our large range of plants for sale. Visit our well-stocked garden sundries and gift shop.

Making the most of your day: many events, including dawn chorus walks and croquet days. Family-themed events throughout the summer, visit website for details. **Dogs**: on leads on estate walks only.

Access for all: ⃞ ⃞ ⃞ ⃞ ⃞ ⃞ ⃞
Building ⃞ ⃞ Grounds ⃞ ⃞

Getting here: 183:ST529269. **Bus**: First 377 Wells to Yeovil, 54/A/B/C Taunton to Yeovil (passing close Taunton ≠). Both pass within ¾ mile Yeovil Pen Mill ≠. Alight Kingsdon, 1 mile. **Train**: Yeovil Pen Mill 8½ miles; Castle Cary 9 miles; Yeovil Junction 10 miles. **Road**: near village of Kingsdon, off A372. Signposted from Podimore roundabout where A303 meets A37. **Parking**: free, 40 yards. Coaches by prior arrangement only.

You may also enjoy: Montacute House, Tintinhull Garden, Barrington Court, plus Stourhead.

Finding out more: 01458 224471 or lytescarymanor@nationaltrust.org.uk

Lytes Cary Manor		M	T	W	T	F	S	S
House, garden, shop and catering								
12 Mar–30 Oct	11–5	M	T	W	.	F	S	S
Estate walks								
Open all year	Dawn–dusk	M	T	W	T	F	S	S

Open Good Friday and Bank Holiday Mondays.
Closes dusk if earlier.

Max Gate

See Hardy Country, page 49.

Mompesson House

The Close, Salisbury, Wiltshire SP1 2EL

Map ① K5   1952

When walking into the celebrated Cathedral Close in Salisbury, visitors step back into a past world, and on entering Mompesson House, featured in the award-winning film *Sense and Sensibility*, the feeling of leaving the modern world behind is deepened. The tranquil atmosphere is enhanced by the magnificent plasterwork, fine period furniture and graceful oak staircase, which are the main features of this perfectly proportioned Queen Anne house. In addition, the Turnbull collection of 18th-century drinking glasses is of national importance. The delightful walled garden has a pergola and traditionally planted herbaceous borders.

Exploring
- Perch on the window seats to admire the fine plasterwork.
- Children, seek out all the human faces in the mouldings.
- In cooler weather, sit in the Library by the fire.
- Treat yourself to a delicious cream tea in the garden.
- View the exceptional Turnbull collection of 18th-century drinking glasses.
- Fantasise about living in this townhouse in the 18th century.

Eating and shopping: locally baked scones and cakes served in the tea-room. Light lunches and teas can be eaten in the garden. Salisbury National Trust shop is only 60 yards away. Catalogue of Turnbull Glass Collection available for sale.

Making the most of your day: regular croquet sessions on the lawn for people of every age

and ability. Hands-on craft sessions. Music includes pianists playing our 1790s Broadwood square piano and Northumbrian Pipers sessions.

Access for all: [icons]
Building [icons] Grounds [icons]

Getting here: 184:SU142297. On north side of Choristers' Green in the Cathedral Close, near High Street Gate. **Bus**: Wilts & Dorset buses from surrounding area. **Train**: Salisbury ½ mile. **Road**: park and ride on all main routes into city. **Parking**: 260 yards in city centre (not National Trust, pay and display). Coach parking in Central car park. Coach drop-off point 100 yards at St Ann's Gate.

You may also enjoy: Mottisfont Abbey.

Finding out more: 01722 420980 (Infoline). 01722 335659 or mompessonhouse@nationaltrust.org.uk

Mompesson House		M	T	W	T	F	S	S
12 Mar–30 Oct	11–5	M	T	W	.	.	S	S
Open Good Friday.								

The main façade at Mompesson House, Wiltshire

Montacute House

Montacute, Somerset TA15 6XP

Map (1) I6   🏛️✳️♠️🏠⚓🔔🍴 1931

Montacute House is a magnificent, glittering mansion, built in the late 16th century for Sir Edward Phelips. There are many Renaissance features, and the Long Gallery, the longest of its kind in England, displays more than 60 of the finest Tudor and Elizabethan portraits from the National Portrait Gallery collection. The state rooms display a fine range of period furniture and textiles, including samplers from the Goodhart collection. Montacute's formal gardens are perfect for a stroll and include a collection of roses, mixed borders and famous wobbly hedges. Waymarked walks lead around the wider estate, which encompasses St Michael's Hill.

The east front of Montacute House, Somerset

Access for all: 🅿️♿🚾♿♿♿∴🅰️
Building 🏠♿♿ Grounds ♿➡️♿

Exploring
- Trails and Tracker Packs available to enhance family visits.
- Varied and exciting events programme, including farmers' markets.
- Parkland with walks for countryside and nature lovers.
- Many seating areas around the property to relax in.
- Excellent printed information easily accessible in each room.
- Stroll the famous West Drive, used in many feature films.

Eating and shopping: tasty local home-cooked food available in the Courtyard Café. Large, well-stocked gift shop and plant sales. Children's menu and lunch boxes available. A whole range of delicious fresh coffee and hot chocolate.

Making the most of your day: many events, including farmers' markets, open-air theatre and craft fairs, also many free family activity days. Licensed for weddings and private functions. **Dogs**: all year under control in parkland. On leads in garden November to March.

Getting here: 183/193:ST499172. **Foot**: Leyland Trail and Monarch Trail both pass through Montacute Park. **Cycle**: NCN30 passes Montacute village. **Bus**: South West Coaches 81 Yeovil Bus Station to South Petherton (passing within ¾ mile Yeovil Pen Mill ☰). **Train**: Yeovil Pen Mill 5½ miles; Yeovil Junction 7 miles (bus to Yeovil Bus Station); Crewkerne 7 miles. **Road**: in Montacute village, 4 miles west of Yeovil, on south side of A3088, 3 miles east of A303; signposted. **Parking**: free. Limited parking for coaches.

You may also enjoy: Barrington Court, Lytes Cary Manor, Tintinhull Garden and Stourhead.

Finding out more: 01935 823289 or montacute@nationaltrust.org.uk

Montacute House		M	T	W	T	F	S	S
House								
12 Mar–30 Oct	11–5	M	·	W	T	F	S	S
Garden, café and shop								
5 Jan–11 Mar	11–4	·	·	W	T	F	S	S
12 Mar–30 Oct	11–5:30	M	·	W	T	F	S	S
2 Nov–31 Dec	11–4	·	·	W	T	F	S	S
Parkland								
2 Jan–31 Dec	5–9	M	T	W	T	F	S	S

House and all facilities open the first four Tuesdays in August. Whole property closed 24 to 27 December.

Newark Park

Ozleworth, Wotton-under-Edge,
Gloucestershire GL12 7PZ

Map (1) J3　🏠🌸♿🍽🏠 1949

From its Tudor origins to today, Newark Park
contains elements reflecting 450 years of
history. The atmospheric house is lived in and
is furnished with an eclectic mix of old and
modern. Outside, the wild romantic garden
and landscape, with fantastic views to the
distant Mendips, are breathtaking.

Exploring　– Discover fascinating stories
about those who lived in
the house.
– Enjoy spectacular unspoilt
countryside.
– Marvel at the view.
– Relax in the wild,
romantic garden.

Eating and shopping: browse in the
intimate shop. Be tempted by the plant stall.
Enjoy a cup of tea.

Making the most of your day: waymarked
countryside walks and footpath link to the
Cotswold Way. Family events and children's
house and garden quiz. Croquet set for hire.
Picnics welcome in garden (rugs for hire).
Dogs: on leads in grounds only.

The atmospheric Newark Park, Gloucestershire

Access for all: 🔲🔲🔲🔲🔲
Building 🔲🔲 Grounds 🔲

Getting here: 172:ST786934. **Foot**: Cotswold
Way passes property. **Bus**: First 310 Bristol to
Thomley, then connecting First 311 Thomley to
Dursley, alight Wotton-under-Edge, 1¾ mile.
Train: Stroud 10 miles. **Road**: 1½ miles east
of Wotton-under-Edge, 1¾ miles south of
junction of A4135 and B4058, follow signs for
Ozleworth. House signposted from main road.
Parking: free, 100 yards. Coaches by prior
arrangement only.

Finding out more: 01793 817666 (Infoline).
01453 842644 or
newarkpark@nationaltrust.org.uk

Newark Park		M	T	W	T	F	S	S
2 Mar–26 May	11–5		·	**W**	**T**	·	·	·
1 Jun–30 Oct	11–5		·	**W**	**T**	·	**S**	**S**

Open May and August Bank Holiday Mondays and
Good Friday, 11 to 5. Open Easter Saturday and Sunday,
11 to 5, closes dusk if earlier.

Overbeck's

Sharpitor, Salcombe, Devon TQ8 8LW

Map (1) F9　🏠🌸🍽🏛 1937

'**Amazing views and garden. We arrived by
ferry and walked up, well worth the effort.
A real hidden treasure.**'
Mrs J. Davies, St Albans

One of the most fascinating and exotic gardens
in the South West; explore the banana garden,
meander through the towering purple echiums
or just relax beneath palms and soak up the
spectacular panorama across miles of beautiful
coastline and estuary. Continue your journey
of discovery into the Edwardian house of Otto
Overbeck to see his amazing invention – the
rejuvenator – hear the giant (1890s) music box
and prepare to be intrigued by his collections.
The perfect day out for families who enjoy
exploring, or the keen gardener who wants to
be inspired and excited. **Note**: the grounds are
very steep in places.

The Edwardian Overbeck's in Devon is surrounded by a fascinating garden full of exotic plants

Exploring
- Find out more by enjoying one of our family trails.
- Join our garden tours and discover how we garden organically.
- Discover the abundance of rare and exotic plants.
- Hunt for Fred, the friendly ghost in the museum.
- Listen to the melodious sounds of the Victorian music box.
- Pick up a walks leaflet and enjoy even more views.

Eating and shopping: enjoy local crab in a freshly prepared sandwich. Kick off those boots and relax by a warming fire. Book a luxury picnic hamper to make the day complete. Take home a bar of South Devon chilli chocolate or dip.

Making the most of your day: garden tours: learn more about our organic exotic garden. Listen to the rare polyphon play its melodies. Find Fred, the friendly ghost. Children's trails available all season. **Dogs**: assistance dogs only.

Access for all: 🅿️ 🅳 🔊 🏠 🖼️ 💺 ⌨️ 🅰️
Building 🏠♿ Grounds 🚶♿

Getting here: 202:SX728374. **Foot**: South West Coast Path within ⅔ mile. **Ferry**: from Salcombe to South Sands, then ½ mile strenuous walk (uphill). **Bus**: Stagecoach in Devon X64, Sunday and Bank Holidays only; Tally Ho! 164, 606 from Totnes ≊. From all alight Salcombe, 1½ miles. **Road**: 1½ miles south-west of Salcombe, signposted from Malborough and Salcombe (narrow approach road). Roads leading to Overbeck's are steep and single track and not suitable for coaches over 25 seats or large vehicles. Or park and walk from East Soar, turn right in Malborough following the signs for Soar then follow signs for East Soar car park and walk (2 miles) to Overbeck's to get your free cup of tea. **Sat Nav**: warning, continue towards Salcombe ignoring Sat Nav in Malborough and follow the brown signs thereafter. **Parking**: small car park reserved for visitors to Overbeck's, 150 yards. Charge for non-members (refundable on paid admission). Parking along driveway. Care must be taken on steep narrow ascent to entrance. Not suitable for motorhomes/large vehicles (telephone for advice). Extra parking at East Soar car park (see road information).

You may also enjoy: A la Ronde, Coleton Fishacre, Greenway, Saltram, Salcombe: Thurlestone to Torcross.

Finding out more: 01548 842893 or overbecks@nationaltrust.org.uk

Overbeck's		M	T	W	T	F	S	S
Garden								
1 Jan–12 Mar	11–4	M	T	W	T	·	S	S
31 Oct–31 Dec	11–4	M	T	W	T	·	S	S
Tea-room								
1 Jan–6 Mar	11–3	·	·	·	·	·	S	S
12 Feb–20 Feb	11–3	M	T	W	T	F	S	S
5 Nov–31 Dec	11–3	·	·	·	·	·	S	S
Garden, museum, tea-room and shop								
12 Mar–16 Apr	11–5	M	T	W	T	·	S	S
17 Apr–3 Sep	11–5	M	T	W	T	F	S	S
4 Sep–22 Oct	11–5	M	T	W	T	·	S	S
23 Oct–30 Oct	11–5	M	T	W	T	F	S	S

Tea-room closes 4:15 March to October. Property closed 24 and 25 December.

Penrose Estate: Gunwalloe and Loe Pool

near Helston, Cornwall TR13 0RD

Map (1) B10  1974

Loe Bar separates Cornwall's largest freshwater pool, The Loe, from the sea. At Gunwalloe, beautiful beaches frame a medieval church. **Note**: cliff edges and coast path subject to erosion. Seasonal dog ban on Gunwalloe Church Cove. Seasonal refreshments kiosk at Gunwalloe. 'Outdoor gym' alongside Loe path.

Access for all: P D Penrose parkland

Getting here: 203:SW639259. 2 miles south-west of Helston.

Finding out more: 01326 561407 or southwestcornwall@nationaltrust.org.uk

Penrose Estate	Open every day all year
Beach refreshments kiosk (not National Trust) at Gunwalloe during peak summer season.	

Philipps House and Dinton Park

Dinton, Salisbury, Wiltshire SP3 5HH

Map (1) K5 1943

Neo-Grecian house with fine Regency furniture, designed by Jeffry Wyatville for William Wyndham, 1820. Excellent parkland walks throughout the year. **Note**: no toilet.

Access for all: Building Grounds

Getting here: 184:SU004319. 9 miles west of Salisbury, on north side of B3089; Tisbury 5 miles.

Finding out more: 01722 716663 or philippshouse@nationaltrust.org.uk

Philipps House and Dinton Park	M	T	W	T	F	S	S
House							
16 Apr–29 Oct	10–1						S	
18 Apr–31 Oct	1–5	M						
Park							
Open all year		M	T	W	T	F	S	S

Priest's House

Muchelney, Langport, Somerset TA10 0DQ

Map (1) I6 1911

This medieval hall-house, built in 1308 for the parish priest, has been little altered since the early 17th century. **Note**: house is tenanted. No toilet.

Access for all: Building

Getting here: 193:ST429250. 1 mile south of Langport.

Finding out more: 01458 253771 or priestshouse@nationaltrust.org.uk

Priest's House		M	T	W	T	F	S	S
13 Mar–26 Sep	2–5	M						S
Admission by guided tour, last tour 4:30.								

Prior Park Landscape Garden

Ralph Allen Drive, Bath, Somerset BA2 5AH

Map (1) J4 1993

One of only four Palladian bridges of this design in the world can be crossed at Prior Park, which was created in the 18th century by local entrepreneur Ralph Allen, with advice from 'Capability' Brown and the poet Alexander Pope. The garden is set in a sweeping valley where visitors can enjoy magnificent views of Bath. Restoration of the 'Wilderness' has reinstated the Serpentine Lake, Cascade and Cabinet. A five-minute walk leads to the Bath Skyline, a six-mile circular route encompassing beautiful woodlands and meadows, an Iron Age hill fort, Roman settlements, 18th-century follies and spectacular views. **Note**: mansion not accessible. There are steep slopes, steps and uneven paths in the garden.

Exploring
- A green tourism site with disabled parking only.
- Beautiful and intimate 18th-century garden.
- Fabulous views of the city of Bath.
- Restored Wilderness area.
- One of only four Palladian bridges in the world.
- Free family activity packs.

Eating and shopping: refresh yourself at our tea kiosk by the lakes.

Making the most of your day: free family activity packs throughout the year. Open-air events programme. Guided tours of the Wilderness. **Dogs**: on leads only.

Access for all: ♿🅿♿🚻♿ :• Ⓐ
Grounds 🏞🏞

Getting here: 172:ST760633. Prior Park is a green tourism site; there is only disabled car parking (please telephone to book), but public transport runs regularly (every 30 minutes) to and from the park. Please telephone for leaflet

or download from the website. **Foot**: 1 mile uphill (very steep) walk from railway station. To rear of railway station cross river, pass Widcombe shopping parade, turn right onto Prior Park Road at White Hart pub, proceed up steep hill, garden on left. Kennet & Avon canal path ¾ mile. **Cycle**: NCN4, ¾ mile. **Bus**: First 1, Bath to Combe Down. Pick up on Dorchester Street by the bus station. City Sightseeing Skyline Tour open-top tour bus runs to the garden (last stop on tour) every 20 minutes in summer, every hour in winter (11 to 5). Pick up from railway station and Abbey. £1 off for members. Ticket valid for 24 hours. **Train**: Bath Spa 1 mile. **Road**: no brown signs. **Parking**: no onsite parking – Prior Park is a green tourism site. Please park in the city and follow the directions above.

You may also enjoy: the Bath Skyline, Dyrham Park, The Courts, Lacock and Stourhead.

Finding out more: 01225 833422 or priorpark@nationaltrust.org.uk

Prior Park Landscape Garden		M	T	W	T	F	S	S
Garden								
1 Jan–6 Feb	11–5:30	·	·	·	·	·	S	S
12 Feb–30 Oct	11–5:30	M	T	W	T	F	S	S
5 Nov–31 Dec	11–5:30	·	·	·	·	·	S	S
Tea kiosk								
12 Feb–26 Jun	11:30–5	·	·	·	·	·	S	S
2 Jul–2 Oct	11:30–5	M	T	W	T	F	S	S
8 Oct–30 Oct	11:30–5	·	·	·	·	·	S	S

Last admission one hour before closing. Closed 25 December. Closes dusk if earlier than 5:30. Tea kiosk also open school holidays, events and Bank Holidays.

Looking through the columns of the Palladian Bridge at Prior Park Landscape Garden, Somerset

Purbeck Countryside

Purbeck, near Corfe Castle, Dorset

Map ① K7
 1976

From the dinosaur-era Purbeck limestones to the recent sand dunes of Studland, nowhere else packs such a variety of habitats into such a small area. As a result, Purbeck is the richest place for plant life in Britain. Discover these landscapes through 37 miles of paths and bridleways.

Exploring
— Waymarked off-road family cycle route between Hartland and Studland.
— Ridgetop walk from Old Harry to Creech Arch via Corfe.
— Relax and take in the heathland wildlife at Middlebere.
— Rock climbing on the cliffs west of Swanage.

Old Harry Rocks on the Purbeck estate, Dorset

Eating and shopping: look out for the shops and cafés at Studland beach and Corfe Castle village. Throughout Purbeck there are other suitable facilities to start or finish your visit.

Making the most of your day: enjoy the 'best view in the kingdom' at the viewpoint by Purbeck Golf Club. Horse riding over Ballard Down and Godlingston Heath from Studland Stables. Discover carving at Burngate Stone Centre.

Dogs: welcome under close control, some restrictions may apply (see signs).

Getting here: OL15:SY9615. **Foot**: South West Coast Path begins at Shell Bay, Studland; many other footpaths. **Cycle**: NCN2 between Hartland and Studland, plus bridleways. **Ferry**: Sandbanks car ferry for access to Studland. **Bus**: Wareham to Swanage Wilts and Dorset 40 for walks to Hartland Moor, Corfe Castle and Spyway. Bournemouth to Swanage Wilts and Dorset 50 for Studland Beach and Nature Reserve and Ballard Down. **Train**: Wareham 3 miles from Hartland Moor. Bournemouth ⭳ has connecting bus service to Studland. **Road**: access to most of Purbeck countryside from A351 Wareham to Swanage, B3351 Studland road and B3069 to Langton Matravers. **Parking**: free parking at Durnford Drove, Langton and Slepe road verges for Hartland Moor. Pay and display (free to members) at Castle View by Corfe Castle; Studland beaches. Visit website for other parking in the area.

Finding out more: 01929 450259 or purbeck@nationaltrust.org.uk. Purbeck Office, Studland, Swanage, Dorset BH19 3AX

Purbeck Countryside	Open every day all year

Bird hides at Studland and Hartland open all year.

St Anthony Head

Portscatho, Cornwall TR2 5EY

Map ① C9 1959

Overlooking the spectacular entrance to the Fal Estuary. Excellent coastal and sheltered creekside walks. Remains of defensive fortifications. Bird hide. **Note**: toilets by main car park.

Access for all: Grounds 🦽

Getting here: 204:SW847313. South of St Mawes.

Finding out more: 01208 265212 or stanthonyhead@nationaltrust.org.uk

St Anthony Head	Open every day all year

We welcome dogs assisting visitors with disabilities

Low tide reveals the causeway leading to St Michael's Mount, off Marazion in Cornwall

St Michael's Mount

Marazion, Cornwall TR17 0HT

Map ① B9  1954

Still home to the St Aubyn family (which runs and maintains it in partnership with the Trust) as well as to a small community, this iconic rocky island is crowned by a medieval church and castle – the oldest buildings dating from the 12th century. Immerse yourself in history, wonder at the architecture and discover the legend of Jack the Giant Killer. Look down on the subtropical terraced garden and enjoy breathtaking views of spectacular Mount's Bay.

If the weather is favourable, take a short evocative boat trip to the island, or at low tide enjoy the walk across the causeway. **Note**: steep climb to the castle up an uneven, cobbled pathway. Narrow passageways in castle.

Exploring
- Enjoy the adventure of getting here – by foot or boat.
- Find the giant's heart in the path to castle.
- Discover the amazing plaster frieze showing medieval hunting scenes.
- See the model of the Mount made from champagne corks!
- Explore the exotic subtropical garden.
- Guided tours of the castle in the winter months.

Eating and shopping: Island Café: (licensed) enjoy a cream tea or a Cornish pasty. Sail Loft Restaurant (licensed): local food freshly produced and sustainably sourced. National Trust shop: contemporary gifts, Cornish produce and art. The Island Shop offers local gifts and artwork.

Making the most of your day: children's quiz for castle and garden. Live music most Sundays during summer. Garden tours (by arrangement). Sunday church services: Whitsun to end September. Winter guided tours. **Dogs**: assistance dogs only in castle and gardens.

Access for all: Castle 🦽 Village 🚾

Getting here: 203:SW515298. Off coast at Marazion (from where there is access on foot over the causeway at low tide). **Foot**: South West Coast Path within ¾ mile. Access to Mount on foot at low tide only. **Cycle**: NCN3, ¾ mile. **Ferry**: small boats make the crossing at high tide. Occasionally, the boats don't run if the weather is very poor (please telephone if in doubt). **Bus**: First 2/A/B Penzance to Helston; 17B Penzance to St Ives. All pass Penzance ⭍. **Train**: Penzance 3 miles. **Road**: ½ mile south of A394 at Marazion. **Parking**: ample parking in Marazion opposite St Michael's Mount (not National Trust, fee payable including members).

You may also enjoy: Godolphin, Trengwainton Garden and Levant Mine.

Finding out more: 01736 710507/710265 (general enquiries/tide information). 01736 711067 (shop). 01736 710748 (restaurant) or stmichaelsmount@nationaltrust.org.uk

St Michael's Mount		M	T	W	T	F	S	S
Castle								
27 Mar–30 Jun	10:30–5	M	T	W	T	F		S
1 Jul–31 Aug	10:30–5:30	M	T	W	T	F		S
1 Sep–30 Oct	10:30–5	M	T	W	T	F		S
Garden								
18 Apr–30 Jun	10:30–5	M	T	W	T	F		
1 Jul–26 Aug	10:30–5:30				T	F		
1 Sep–30 Sep	10:30–5				T	F		

Last admission 45 minutes before castle closing (enough time should be allowed for travel from the mainland). Castle winter opening: Tuesday and Friday, entry by guided tour only, 11 and 2 (subject to weather conditions). Telephone in advance.

Saltram

Plympton, Plymouth, Devon PL7 1UH

Map ① F8 🏠🏡♠♣♥♦🍷 1957

Still a largely undiscovered treasure, and the result of centuries of sophistication and extravagance, Saltram is the perfect family day out: close to Plymouth and yet in a world of its own. Home to the Parker family for nearly 300 years, the house with its original contents provides a fascinating insight into country-estate life throughout the centuries. Fine Robert Adam interiors and beautiful collections bring the 'age of elegance' to life at Saltram. Learn about some of the fascinating characters and family stories, including the correspondence between Frances, the first Countess, and Jane Austen.

Exploring
– Escape the Plymouth hustle and bustle in this green haven.
– Be blown away by the grandeur of the impressive Saloon.
– Visit the Western Apartments, newly opened to visitors.
– Transform yourself into a Georgian with the dressing-up clothes.
– Hunt out the romantic follies in the magnificent garden.
– Ride your bike or fly a kite in the parkland.

Eating and shopping: enjoy the local and seasonal food in the Park Restaurant, which is available for special occasions and private functions. Browse the gift and garden shops. Visit the Chapel Gallery for local arts and crafts.

Making the most of your day: varied year-round events programme, open-air theatre, craft fairs, costumed Georgian evenings. Special events for families include Wizard School, held in the cellars, and Pirates and Princesses Day. **Dogs**: on leads on designated paths only.

Saltram		M	T	W	T	F	S	S
Park								
Open all year	Dawn–dusk	M	T	W	T	F	S	S
House								
13 Feb–20 Feb	12–4:30	·	·	·	·	·	S	S
12 Mar–30 Oct	12–4:30	M	T	W	T	·	S	S
Park Restaurant								
1 Jan–10 Mar	10:30–4	M	T	W	T	·	S	S
12 Mar–30 Oct	10:30–5	M	T	W	T	F	S	S
31 Oct–31 Dec	10:30–4	M	T	W	T	F	S	S
Garden, shops and gallery								
2 Jan–10 Mar	11–4	M	T	W	T	·	S	S
12 Mar–30 Oct	11–5	M	T	W	T	F	S	S
31 Oct–31 Dec	11–4	M	T	W	T	F	S	S

Last admission to house 45 minutes before closing. Parts of house open for special Christmas events, visit website for details. Garden, gallery and shops closed 24 to 26 December. Park Restaurant closed 25 and 26 December. Chapel Gallery opening hours may vary during the winter, please telephone to check.

Giltwood sofa attributed to Thomas Chippendale in the Saloon at Saltram, Devon

Access for all: [icons]
House [icons] Restaurant [icons] Grounds [icons]

Getting here: 201:SX520557. 3½ miles east of Plymouth city centre. **Foot**: South West Coast Path within 4 miles. **Cycle**: NCN27. **Bus**: Plymouth Citybus 20 from Plymouth, alight Merafield Road, ½ mile. **Train**: Plymouth 3½ miles. **Road**: 3½ miles east of Plymouth city centre. Travelling south (from Exeter): leave A38, 3 miles north of Plymouth. Exit is signed Plymouth City Centre/Plympton/Kingsbridge. At roundabout take centre lane, then 3rd exit for Plymouth. Take right-hand lane and follow brown signs. Travelling north (from Liskeard): leave A38 at Plympton exit. At roundabout take first exit for Plympton, then as before. **Sat Nav**: please add Merafield Road to the address. **Parking**: free, 50 yards.

You may also enjoy: Antony, still home to the Carew Pole family.

Shute Barton

Shute, near Axminster, Devon EX13 7PT

Map (1) H7   [icons] 1959

A fascinating medieval manor house, with a later Tudor gatehouse and battlemented turrets, set in pretty grounds. **Note**: limited opening. Shute has been converted into National Trust holiday apartments.

Access for all: Building [icon]

Getting here: 177/193:SY253974. 3 miles south-west of Axminster, 2 miles north of Colyton on Honiton to Colyton road (B3161).

Finding out more: 01752 346585 or shutebarton@nationaltrust.org.uk. South and East Devon Countryside Office, The Stables, Saltram House, Plymouth, Devon PL7 1UH

Shute Barton		M	T	W	T	F	S	S
14 May–15 May	11–5	·	·	·	·	·	S	S
18 Jun–19 Jun	11–5	·	·	·	·	·	S	S
17 Sep–18 Sep	11–5	·	·	·	·	·	S	S
15 Oct–16 Oct	11–5	·	·	·	·	·	S	S

Entrance by guided tours only (last tour 4:30).

Snowshill Manor and Garden

Snowshill, near Broadway,
Gloucestershire WR12 7JU

Map (1) K1   🏛️ ❄️ 🏠 | 1951 |

Snowshill Manor, Gloucestershire, contains
thousands of treasures

'A beautiful place with hours of interest
and rooms full of intriguing objects.
Not to be missed.'
Mrs C. J. White, Witham

Charles Wade was a treasure-seeker who loved
buying and restoring beautifully made objects.
His family motto was 'Let nothing perish', and
he spent his inherited wealth doing just that,
amassing a spectacular collection of everyday
and extraordinary objects from across the
globe. He restored the ancient Cotswold manor
house specifically to display these unlikely
treasures. Laid out with creative flair, just as Mr
Wade intended, the Manor is literally packed to
the rafters with thousands of unusual objects
– from tiny toys to splendid suits of Samurai
armour. The Manor is surrounded by an equally
characterful hand-crafted terraced garden built
on the hillside.

Exploring
- Be fascinated by the story of
  collector Charles Wade.
- Be amazed by his vast and
  astonishing collection.
- Be intrigued by stunning
  examples of craftsmanship.
- Relax in the 'outdoor rooms'
  of the peaceful hillside garden.
- Have a go at one of our
  children's trails.

Eating and shopping: enjoy a delicious
home-cooked lunch in the restaurant. Try one
of our legendary cream teas or homemade
cakes on the terrace. Treat yourself to local
produce in our gift shop. Pick up a bargain in
the second-hand bookshop.

Making the most of your day: monthly
Snowshill Secrets Explorer Tours. Children's
trails indoors and around garden. Archaeology
weekend 23 and 24 July. Apple weekend

22 and 23 October. Winter weekend events in
November and December. **Dogs**: assistance
dogs only in garden and Manor (good walks
from car park).

Access for all: 🅿️ ♿ 🚻 ♿ ♿ 📷 📺 ⠿ ♿
Manor ♿ Garden ♿ ♿

Getting here: 150:SP096339. **Foot**: Cotswold
Way within ¾ mile. **Bus**: Castleways 559,
Evesham to Broadway, then 2½ miles uphill.
Train: Moreton-in-Marsh 7 miles, Evesham
8 miles. **Road**: 2½ miles south-west of
Broadway; turn from A44 Broadway bypass
into Broadway village; at green turn right uphill
to Snowshill. **Parking**: free, 500 yards. Walk
from car park to Manor and garden along
undulating country path. Transfer available.

You may also enjoy: the Wade Costume Collection at Berrington Hall in Herefordshire (by prior appointment only).

Finding out more: 01386 852410 or snowshillmanor@nationaltrust.org.uk

Snowshill Manor and Garden		M	T	W	T	F	S	S
Manor								
1 Apr–3 Jul	12–5		·	W	T	F	S	S
4 Jul–29 Aug	11:30–4:30	M	·	W	T	F	S	S
31 Aug–30 Oct	12–5		·	W	T	F	S	S
Garden, shop and restaurant								
1 Apr–3 Jul	11–5:30		·	W	T	F	S	S
4 Jul–29 Aug	11–5	M	·	W	T	F	S	S
31 Aug–30 Oct	11–5:30		·	W	T	F	S	S
5 Nov–11 Dec	12–4		·	·	·	·	S	S
Priest's House								
1 Apr–3 Jul	11–5		·	W	T	F	S	S
4 Jul–29 Aug	11–4:30	M	·	W	T	F	S	S
31 Aug–30 Oct	11–5		·	W	T	F	S	S

Admission by timed ticket. Tickets issued at reception on a first-come, first-served basis and cannot be booked in advance. Tickets often run out at peak times; please arrive early. Last admission: Manor 4; garden 5 (summer Manor 3:30; garden 4:30). Open Bank Holidays between March and October (August 29 Bank Holiday open 11 to 5:30).

Stembridge Tower Mill

High Ham, Somerset TA10 9DJ

Map (1) I5 1969

Built in 1822, this is the last remaining thatched windmill in England – the last survivor of five in the area. **Note**: holiday cottage on site, please respect the tenants' privacy. No toilet. Parking limited.

Getting here: 182:ST432305. 2 miles north of Langport, ½ mile east of High Ham.

Finding out more: 01935 823289 or stembridgemill@nationaltrust.org.uk

Stembridge Tower Mill		M	T	W	T	F	S	S
12 Mar–25 Sep	11–5	M	T	W	T	F	S	S

Interior open 10 April, 12 June and 20 August, 12 to 5.

South Milton Sands

South Milton Sands, Thurlestone, Devon

Map (1) F9 1980

Long sandy beach and dunes. Great rock-pooling and kayaking. Beach house café.

Access for all:  Beach house

Getting here: SX677414. 4 miles outside Kingsbridge. From Kingsbridge take the A381 towards Salcombe. Turn right to South Milton village, then turn left (signposted) to the beach.

Finding out more: 01752 346585 or southmiltonsands@nationaltrust.org.uk. South Devon Countryside Office, The Stables, Saltram House, Plymouth, Devon PL7 3UH

South Milton Sands	Open every day all year

Café open in summer and at various times out of season, weather dependent (telephone 01548 560844).

Stoke-sub-Hamdon Priory

North Street, Stoke-sub-Hamdon, Somerset TA14 6QP

Map (1) I6 1946

The priests who lived here served the Chapel of St Nicholas (now destroyed). The Great Hall is open to visitors. **Note**: no toilet.

Access for all: Grounds

Getting here: 193:ST473175. 2 miles west of Montacute between Yeovil and Ilminster.

Finding out more: 01935 823289 or stokehamdonpriory@nationaltrust.org.uk

Stoke-sub-Hamdon Priory		M	T	W	T	F	S	S
1 Mar–30 Sep	11–5	M	T	W	T	F	S	S

Closes dusk if earlier. Great Hall only open.

Stonehenge Landscape

near Amesbury, Wiltshire

Map (1) K5   1927

Within the Stonehenge World Heritage Site, the Trust manages 827 hectares (2,100 acres) of downland surrounding the famous stone circle. On the ridges all around Stonehenge are fine Bronze Age round barrows, the resting places of the privileged. The shallow banks of Stonehenge's Great Cursus enclosure are 5,500 years old, pre-dating the stone circle. The massive henge of Durrington Walls, 4,500 years ago the site of feasting and huge gatherings, encloses a natural valley. Large areas of arable land are being restored as chalk grassland, habitat for a diverse range of insects, birds and wild flowers. **Note**: Stone Circle managed by English Heritage (admission free to members).

Exploring
- Explore the monuments on foot with our downloadable walk leaflets.
- Check out our events, walks and workshops before you visit.

Exploring
- Family activity archaeology trail downloadable from our website.
- Listen for skylarks and keep an eye out for hares.
- Enjoy a picnic while admiring the Stonehenge views.

Eating and shopping: catering kiosk at the Stone Circle (not National Trust).

Making the most of your day: walks and workshops available throughout the year – visit our website to find out more. **Dogs**: welcome under close control (assistance dogs only at Stone Circle).

Access for all: 🅿️♿ 🚻

Getting here: 184:SU120420. 2 miles west of Amesbury. **Bus**: Stonehenge Tour bus Salisbury ➡ to Stonehenge. **Train**: Salisbury 9½ miles. **Road**: Stonehenge car park 2 miles west of Amesbury, on A344. **Parking**: 50 yards (not National Trust). Charge may apply between June and October (Trust members free).

You may also enjoy: Figsbury Ring, Cley Hill near Warminster and Avebury.

Finding out more: 01980 664780 or stonehenge@nationaltrust.org.uk. 3 Stonehenge Cottages, King Barrows, Amesbury, Wiltshire SP4 7DD

Stonehenge Landscape	Open every day all year

King Barrows, part of the magical Stonehenge Landscape, Wiltshire: a World Heritage Site

Members may have to pay on special events days

Stourhead

near Mere, Wiltshire

Map (1) J5

Autumn colours at Stourhead, Wiltshire

The jewel in the Stourhead crown has to be the world-famous 18th-century landscape garden. A magnificent lake shimmering with reflections of classical temples, mystical grottoes and rare and exotic trees. Secrets of the Hoare family history are revealed at Stourhead House (orginally the family holiday home!) with the chance to discover the unique Regency library, collections of Chippendale furniture and inspirational paintings, all set amid 'picnic perfect' lawns and parkland. The lake and house are at the heart of a 1,072-hectare (2,650-acre) estate where chalk downs, ancient woods and farmland are managed for people and wildlife to enjoy.

Exploring
- Step back in time with our Richard Colt Hoare exhibition.
- Climb 205 steps to the top of King Alfred's Tower.
- Families can become nature detectives with our Tracker Packs.
- Discover secrets of the garden on a fascinating free tour.
- Enjoy a walk in the woods and over chalk downs.
- Pack a picnic and relax on the Stourhead House lawns.

Eating and shopping: take home a Stourhead memento from our shop and plant centre. Taste local, seasonal dishes in our award-winning restaurant. Visit the farm shop, art gallery, drink or dine in the Spread Eagle Inn. Enjoy tea, coffee and ices from the ice-cream parlour.

Making the most of your day: many exciting events, from climbing trees and guided walks to behind-the-scenes glimpses and fresh-air workouts. **Dogs**: welcome to the landscape garden between November and February, on short fixed leads.

Access for all: ⃞⃞⃞⃞⃞⃞⃞⃞⃞⃞
Building ⃞⃞⃞ Grounds ⃞⃞⃞⃞

Getting here: 183:ST780340. 3 miles north-west of Mere. **Cycle**: Wiltshire Cycle Way runs through estate. **Bus**: Frome Minibuses 82 Warminster to Mere; First 58/158 Shaftesbury to Wincanton (passing Gillingham ☒), alight Zeals, 1¼ mile. **Train**: Gillingham 6½ miles; Bruton 7 miles. **Road**: at Stourton, off B3092, 3 miles north-west of Mere (A303), 8 miles south of Frome (A361). King Alfred's Tower: 3½ miles by road from main car park. **Parking**: 400 yards. Shuttle transfer (main season only) to house and garden entrances. King Alfred's Tower: designated parking 50 yards.

You may also enjoy: Montacute House: just down the A303, a glittering Elizabethan mansion with National Portrait Gallery exhibition.

Finding out more: 01747 841152 or stourhead@nationaltrust.org.uk. Stourhead Estate Office, Stourton, Warminster, Wiltshire BA12 6QD

Stourhead		M	T	W	T	F	S	S
Garden								
1 Jan–31 Dec	9–6	M	T	W	T	F	S	S
House								
19 Feb–6 Mar*	11–3						S	S
12 Mar–19 Jul	11–5	M	T			F	S	S
22 Jul–6 Sep	11–5	M	T	W	T	F	S	S
9 Sep–11 Oct	11–5	M	T			F	S	S
14 Oct–6 Nov	11–5	M	T	W	T	F	S	S
2 Dec–18 Dec**	11–3					F	S	S
King Alfred's Tower								
12 Mar–30 Oct	11–5	M	T			F	S	S
Restaurant and shop								
1 Jan–31 Dec	10–5	M	T	W	T	F	S	S
Farm shop								
1 Jan–31 Dec	10–5	M	T	W	T	F	S	S

Garden and tower close dusk if earlier. Garden, house, tower, shop and restaurant closed 25 December. *Special opening of some areas of the house with chance to see and take part in conservation. **House will be decorated for Christmas. **Restaurant, shop and farm shop hours vary according to season**.

Building sandcastles on the beach at Studland, Dorset

Studland Beach and Nature Reserve

Studland, near Swanage, Dorset

Map ① K7  1982

A glorious slice of natural coastline in Purbeck featuring a four-mile stretch of golden, sandy beach, with gently shelving bathing waters and views of Old Harry Rocks and the Isle of Wight. Ideal for water sports and includes the most popular naturist beach in Britain. The heathland behind the beach is a haven for native wildlife and features all six British reptiles. Designated trails through the sand dunes and woodlands allow for exploration and spotting of deer, insects and bird life as well as a wealth of wild flowers. Studland was the inspiration for Toytown in Enid Blyton's *Noddy*. **Note**: Shell Bay toilets are low-water flush, only other toilets at Knoll Beach and Middle Beach.

Exploring
– The start of the South West Coast Path.
– Try the summer watersports, including boat hire, kayaking and windsurfing.
– Picnic in the dunes watching the activities in Poole Bay.
– Discover the bird life on Little Sea in the winter.
– Rent a wooden beach hut.
– Enjoy a BBQ in the designated beach areas.

Eating and shopping: bucket and spades, fishing nets and wetsuits to buy. Indoor and open-air seating with a spectacular sea view. Local Purbeck ice-creams and daily seasonal specials. Serving local meat dishes from the wider estate.

Making the most of your day: wide range of events year round, including children's trails, wildlife guided walks, food events and Discovery Centre. Coastal change interpretation hut open all year. **Dogs**: restrictions apply 1 May to 30 September.

Access for all: Grounds

Getting here: 195:SZ036835. **Foot**: 5 miles of South West Coast Path. **Ferry**: car ferry from Sandbanks, Poole, to Shell Bay. **Bus**: Wilts and Dorset 50 Bournemouth to Swanage to Shell Bay and Studland. **Train**: Branksome or Parkstone, both 3½ miles to Shell Bay (via vehicle ferry) or Wareham 12 miles. **Parking**: at Shell Bay and South Beach, 9 to 11; Knoll Beach and Middle Beach, 9 to 8 or dusk if earlier. Prices vary through season. Most car parks are pay and display (members stickers must be displayed).

You may also enjoy: Corfe Castle and Brownsea Island.

Finding out more: 01929 450259 or studlandbeach@nationaltrust.org.uk. Purbeck Estate Office, Studland, Swanage, Dorset BH19 3AX

Studland Beach		M	T	W	T	F	S	S
Shop and café								
1 Jan–25 Mar	10–4	M	T	W	T	F	S	S
26 Mar–1 Jul	9:30–5*	M	T	W	T	F	S	S
2 Jul–4 Sep	9–6	M	T	W	T	F	S	S
5 Sep–30 Oct	9:30–5*	M	T	W	T	F	S	S
31 Oct–31 Dec	10–4	M	T	W	T	F	S	S

*Shop and café open one hour later at weekends. Shop and café opening hours may be longer in fine weather and shorter in poor weather. Visitor centre, shop and café closed 25 December. **Car parks can be very full in peak season.**

Exploring
– Discover Victorian postal memorabilia and 19th-century samplers.
– A tranquil cottage garden offers respite from the busy street.
– Experience the glow of the open fire on wintry days.
– Enjoy the traditionally made rag rugs and quilts.

Eating and shopping: visit our small shop.

Making the most of your day: children's trail.

Access for all:
Building Grounds

Getting here: 200:SX056884. In centre of village. **Foot**: South West Coast Path within ¾ mile. **Bus**: Western Greyhound 594 St Columb Major to Boscastle via Wadebridge (connections with 555 at Wadebridge from Bodmin Parkway). **Parking**: no parking on site. Numerous pay and display car parks in village (not National Trust).

Finding out more: 01840 770024 or tintageloldpo@nationaltrust.org.uk

Tintagel Old Post Office		M	T	W	T	F	S	S
19 Feb–27 Feb	11–4	M	T	W	T	F	S	S
12 Mar–1 Apr	11–4	M	T	W	T	F	S	S
2 Apr–30 Sep	10:30–5:30	M	T	W	T	F	S	S
1 Oct–6 Nov	11–4	M	T	W	T	F	S	S

Tintagel Old Post Office

Fore Street, Tintagel, Cornwall PL34 0DB

Map ① D7   1903

Nestling among the modern buildings of Tintagel high street, this unusual and atmospheric 14th-century yeoman's farmhouse, with a famously wavy roof, beckons the curious to explore. The name dates from the Victorian period when it briefly held a licence to be the letter-receiving station for the district. **Note**: nearest toilet in Trevena Square (not National Trust).

The hall inside the Old Post Office at Tintagel, Cornwall

Tintinhull Garden

Farm Street, Tintinhull, Yeovil, Somerset BA22 8PZ

Map ① l6   🎴🏠🔔 1953

Created last century around an attractive 17th-century manor house (available as a holiday let), which has two ground-floor rooms open to visitors, the garden is one of the most harmonious small gardens in Britain. It features secluded lawns, pools and colourful borders.

A quiet corner of Tintinhull Garden, Somerset

There is also an attractive kitchen garden (the produce is used in the kitchens at nearby Montacute House), woodland walk and orchard to explore. In the courtyard is a fascinating exhibition completed by the Tintinhull Historical Society. Even the car park is set among picturesque orchards where sheep graze contentedly.

Exploring
- Sit by the tranquil pools and just enjoy.
- Discover interesting facts about Tintinhull in the village exhibition.
- Be enchanted by the bird-feeding area.
- Relax on the newly upholstered sofa in the garden room.
- Tintinhull House is a beautiful holiday let that sleeps eight.
- You can even get married here.

Eating and shopping: small, pretty tea-room serving delicious cakes and cream teas. Sit outside and enjoy your food in the sunshine. Take home a plant or a postcard, available in reception.

Making the most of your day: summer family activities. Pick up an explorer sheet from the exhibition and explore the beautiful villlage of Tintinhull.

Access for all: 🅿️ D🎴 ♿WC ♿ 🖼️ 👓 🐾
Building ♿♿ Gardens ♿➡️♿

Getting here: 183:ST503198. **Bus**: First 52 Yeovil Bus Station to Martock (passing within ¾ mile Yeovil Pen Mill 🚉). **Train**: Yeovil Pen Mill 5½ miles; Yeovil Junction 7 miles (bus to Yeovil Bus Station). **Road**: 5 miles north-west of Yeovil, ½ mile south of A303, on east outskirts of Tintinhull. Follow road signs to Tintinhull village. **Parking**: free, 150 yards.

You may also enjoy: Montacute House, Lytes Cary, Barrington Court and Stourhead.

Finding out more: 01935 823289 or tintinhull@nationaltrust.org.uk

Tintinhull Garden		M	T	W	T	F	S	S
12 Mar–30 Oct	11–5			W	T	F	S	S

Closes dusk if earlier. Open Bank Holiday Mondays.

Spring blooms at the constantly evolving Trelissick Garden, Cornwall

Treasurer's House

Martock, Somerset TA12 6JL

Map (1) I6 | 1971 |

Medieval house with Great Hall, completed 1293 – with kitchen added in the 15th century. Solar Block contains an unusual wall-painting. **Note**: no toilet (nearest opposite church in village).

Access for all: Building 🏛 Grounds 🏛🏛

Getting here: 193:ST462191. 1 mile north-west of A303, between Ilminster and Ilchester.

Finding out more: 01935 825015 or treasurersmartock@nationaltrust.org.uk

Treasurer's House		M	T	W	T	F	S	S
13 Mar–27 Sep	2–5	**M**	**T**	·	·	·	·	**S**

Trelissick Garden

Feock, near Truro, Cornwall TR3 6QL

Map (1) C9 ·1955

This modern garden was created within shelter belts planted 200 years ago. It is constantly evolving, with new planting and fresh ideas. Trelissick has seen trees grow to maturity, the tide ebbing and flowing, but has become a dynamic, forward-looking estate. The iconic Water Tower was built for irrigation and fire-control; now the lavatories are flushed with rainwater stored underground in modern reservoirs. Heat is extracted from kitchen appliances and the sun to provide hot water and heating. The River Fal is now more than just a beautiful setting for Trelissick; many visitors arrive by boat each summer.

Exploring – Discover not one but four summerhouses dotted around the garden.

Exploring
- Turn cartwheels on the tennis lawn (avoiding the ha-ha)!
- Find the perfect place to picnic in the sheltered garden.
- Explore the magical *Cryptomeria* tree on the main lawn.
- Get close to nature on the riverside woodland walks.
- Relax in the spacious parkland overlooking the River Fal.

Eating and shopping: taste Cornish produce indoors or out at Crofters Restaurant. Find the perfect souvenir in our shop and plant sales. Discover work from Cornish artists and craftspeople in the gallery. Stay longer: Trelissick's five holiday cottages include the Water Tower.

Making the most of your day: open-air theatre in summer, exhibitions and shows held in the stables by local groups, extensive calendar of events for all the family.
Dogs: welcome on the woodland walks only.

Access for all: 🅿♿🚻📶🔵🎦💿
Grounds 🔵♿➡🚶♿

Getting here: 204:SW837396. **Cycle**: NCN3. **Ferry**: link from Falmouth, Truro and St Mawes: Enterprise boats 01326 374241, K&S Cruisers 01326 211056, Newman's Cruises/Tolverne Ferries 01872 580309. Please note there is a steep uphill walk from the ferry pontoon to the garden entrance building. **Bus**: First 93 Truro to Feock. **Train**: Truro 5 miles; Perranwell, 4 miles. **Road**: 5 miles south of Truro, on B3289 above King Harry ferry. **Parking**: 50 yards, £3.50 for non-members.

You may also enjoy: Glendurgan Garden – a valley garden of natural beauty leading down to the Helford River.

Finding out more: 01872 862090 or trelissick@nationaltrust.org.uk

Trelissick Garden		M	T	W	T	F	S	S
2 Jan–11 Feb	11–4	M	T	W	T	F	S	S
12 Feb–30 Oct	10:30–5:30	M	T	W	T	F	S	S
31 Oct–23 Dec	11–4	M	T	W	T	F	S	S
27 Dec–31 Dec	11–4		T	W	T	F	S	

Restaurant opens 30 minutes earlier than stated times above. Garden closes dusk if earlier. Copeland China Collection open Thursdays, May and September, 2 to 4.

Trengwainton Garden

Madron, near Penzance, Cornwall TR20 8RZ

Map ① B9   ✿🏠 1961

With plants from around the globe scattered throughout this ten-hectare (25-acre) garden, there is something to inspire around every corner. Champion magnolias and vibrant rhododendrons make way for lush banana plants and soaring echiums. Unusually, the restored walled kitchen garden was built to the dimensions of Noah's Ark, and is today used to demonstrate contemporary varieties of fruit and vegetables. A colourfully bordered stream leads up to a shady pond and sunny terrace, with stunning views across Mount's Bay.

Exploring
- Be inspired by some great kitchen garden ideas.
- Imagine dinosaurs as you explore the giant tree fern glades.
- Enthuse the children with our family trail.
- Find your bearings in the amazing view from the toposcope.
- Wander along wooded paths or picnic on grassy spaces.

Eating and shopping: enjoy some retail therapy in the shop and plant centre. Indulge yourself with our range of Cornish products. Sample mouth-watering cakes in the tea-room (National Trust-approved concession). Enjoy light meals with ingredients sourced from the kitchen garden.

Making the most of your day: programme of events and activities for all the family throughout the year. **Dogs**: on leads welcome, except in the tea-room and its garden.

Access for all: 🅿♿♿🚻📶🎦🔵📶
Tea-room ♿ **Shop/reception** ♿
Grounds ♿➡♿

Azaleas and rhododendrons line the path to a bridge at Trengwainton Garden, Cornwall

Getting here: 203:SW445315. **Foot**: from Penzance via Heamoor village. **Cycle**: NCN3, 2½ miles. **Bus**: First 10/A Penzance to St Just (passing Penzance ≊). **Train**: Penzance 2 miles. **Road**: 2 miles north-west of Penzance, ½ mile west of Heamoor off Penzance to Morvah road (B3312), ½ mile off St Just road (A3071). **Parking**: free, 150 yards.

You may also enjoy: Levant Mine and Beam Engine and Glendurgan Garden.

Finding out more: 01736 363148 or trengwainton@nationaltrust.org.uk

Trengwainton Garden		M	T	W	T	F	S	S
13 Feb–30 Oct	10:30–5	M	T	W	T	·	·	S

Open Good Friday. Tea-room opens 10. Last admission 15 minutes before closing.

Trerice

Kestle Mill, near Newquay, Cornwall TR8 4PG

Map ① C8   🏠 🏡 ✿ 🏛 ▼ 1953

An intimate Elizabethan manor and a Cornish gem, Trerice remains little changed by the advances in building fashions over the centuries, thanks to long periods under absentee owners. Today the renowned stillness and tranquillity of Trerice, much prized by visitors, is occasionally pierced by the curious lilts of Tudor music or shouts of excitement from the Bowling Green (surely you will want to try a game of kayling or slapcock?), bringing back some of the bustle and noise that must have typified its time as a busy manor house.

Exploring —
- Handle replica artefacts and armour and make a brass rubbing.
- Discover the beautiful architecture and fine plaster ceilings.
- Enjoy the tranquillity of the informal garden and Cornish orchard.
- Try the Tudor open-air games of kayling and slapcock.

Eating and shopping: relax in the Barn Kitchen tea-room or tea garden. Try some Tudor recipes or our famous lemon meringue pie. Visit our shop for children's armour, books on Tudor life and historic Cornwall and buy local produce from the area.

Making the most of your day: look out for Tudor-themed family and adult workshops, family trails and special Living History days. **Dogs**: welcome in the car park only.

Access for all: ⚕♿🚻♿♿⚕⎕🎵⠿Ⓐ
House ♿⚕ Garden ♿♿➡♿

Getting here: 200:SW841585. **Cycle**: NCN32. **Bus**: Western Greyhound 527 Newquay ≋ to St Austell ≋, alight Kestle Mill, ¾ mile. **Train**: Quintrell Downs, 1½ miles. **Road**: 3 miles south-east of Newquay via A392 and A3058 signed from Quintrell Downs (turn right at Kestle Mill), or signed from A30 at Summercourt via A3058. **Sat Nav**: instructions via Kestle Mill A3058. **Parking**: free, 300 yards. Coach access only via Kestle Mill 1 mile.

You may also enjoy: Trelissick Garden or Godolphin.

Finding out more: 01637 875404 or trerice@nationaltrust.org.uk

Trerice		M	T	W	T	F	S	S
House								
5 Mar–30 Oct	11–5	M	T	W	T	F	S	S
Great Hall only								
4 Nov–18 Dec	11–4					F	S	S
Garden, shop and tea-room								
5 Mar–30 Oct	10:30–5	M	T	W	T	F	S	S
4 Nov–18 Dec	11–4					F	S	S

Having fun in the orchard at Trerice, Cornwall: a place of timeless charm

Tyntesfield

Wraxall, Bristol, Somerset BS48 1NX

Map ① I4  2002

The wraps are off! Unveiled for 2011, this extraordinary Victorian estate is ready to explore all year round. Come and see the progress we've made on our groundbreaking conservation project. Tyntesfield's house, chapel, gardens and woodland make for an inspiring day of fresh air and discovery. This year Tyntesfield's new Home Farm visitor centre is open for the first time too – with a restaurant, shop, exhibition space and family play area, free to visit every day.

Tyntesfield, Somerset: an extraordinary Victorian estate

Exploring
– Enjoy family fun at Home Farm play area.
– Stroll through the woodland for stunning views of the valley.
– See fascinating objects from the Trust's largest collection.
– Take home fresh produce from our working kitchen gardens.
– Have a seat and relax in the rose garden gazebos.

Eating and shopping: Home Farm visitor centre's restaurant, café and shop are open daily. There are local products and produce – including ingredients grown on the estate. The nearby plant centre brings together old varieties and the second-hand bookshop is open for browsing.

Making the most of your day: explore the story of four generations of family fortunes. Find out all about the people that called Tyntesfield home. **Dogs**: welcome on the estate walks. Assistance dogs only in formal gardens.

Access for all: 🅿️♿♿♿♿🖼️👓♿
Building ♿♿♿ **Grounds** ♿♿

Getting here: ST502724. 7 miles south-west of Bristol. **Bus**: First 361 Bristol to Clevedon stops on B3128 at entrance. First 354 Bristol to Nailsea stops on B3130 at foot of drive.

Train: Nailsea and Backwell 1½ miles. **Road**: on B3128. 7 miles south-west of Bristol; M5 southbound exit 19 via A369 (towards Bristol), B3129, B3128. M5 northbound exit 20, B3130 (towards Bristol), B3128. Brown signs from exit 19 and 20 of M5. For a Tyntesfield Travel Map, please contact the property. **Parking**: at visitor centre – transfer to house and gardens available daily.

You may also enjoy: Clevedon Court, Dyrham Park and Prior Park Landscape Garden.

Finding out more: 0844 800 4966 (Infoline). 01275 461900 or tyntesfield@nationaltrust.org.uk

Tyntesfield		M	T	W	T	F	S	S
Restaurant, shop and café								
28 Feb–31 Dec	10:30–4:30	M	T	W	T	F	S	S
Shop								
1 Apr–30 Sep	10–5:30	M	T	W	T	F	S	S
Gardens and estate*								
28 Feb–31 Dec	10–6	M	T	W	T	F	S	S
House and chapel								
28 Feb–30 Oct	11–5	M	T	W	·	·	S	S
5 Nov–27 Nov	11–3	·	·	·	·	·	S	S

Gardens and estate close dusk if earlier than 6. Gardens, estate, shop, restaurant and café closed 25 December. House open Good Friday. House Christmas events 3 and 4, 10 and 11, 17 and 18 December. Last admission to house one hour before closing (tickets available until 15 minutes before last admission, to allow time for transfer to house). *Closes 5, January, February, November and December, or dusk if earlier. Closed 25 December.

Watersmeet

Watersmeet Road, Lynmouth, Devon EX35 6NT

Map (1) F5   🏠🏛🏊⛵🏠🍴 1955

A haven for wildlife with waterfalls and excellent walking, where the lush valleys of the East Lyn and Hoar Oak Water tumble together. At the heart of this area sits Watersmeet House, a 19th-century fishing lodge, which is a tea garden, shop and information point. **Note**: deep gorge with steep walk down to house.

Exploring
— Treat yourself to a delicious cream tea in the garden.
— Explore this walkers' paradise with our local walks leaflet.
— Walk dramatic sea-cliffs, from Countisbury to Foreland Point.
— Enjoy fishing the best salmon river in England.

Eating and shopping: enjoy local and seasonal food in Watersmeet's riverside setting. Local produce, walking gear and gifts available in the shop.

Making the most of your day: buy the *Exmoor Coast of Devon* walks leaflet to help you explore and enjoy the beautiful coast and countryside of West Exmoor. Family and nature events througout the season. **Dogs**: allowed in the tea garden.

Access for all: 🚻♿🅿 Building 🏢 Grounds 🏞

Getting here: 180:SS744487. **Foot**: South West Coast Path within ¾ mile. **Bus**: TW Coaches 309, 310 from Barnstaple (passing close Barnstaple ≷), Quantock 300 from Minehead; Filers 300 from Ilfracombe. On all, alight Lynmouth, then walk through National Trust gorge. **Road**: 1½ miles east of Lynmouth, in valley on east side of Lynmouth to Barnstaple road (A39). **Parking**: pay and display (not National Trust), 500 yards, with steep walk down to house. Free National Trust car parks at Combepark, Hillsford Bridge and Countisbury.

Finding out more: 01598 753348 or watersmeet@nationaltrust.org.uk

Watersmeet	M	T	W	T	F	S	S
Countryside							
Open all year	M	T	W	T	F	S	S
Tea-room and tea garden							
12 Mar–29 Apr	10:30–4:30	M	T	W	T	F	S	S
30 Apr–2 Oct	10:30–5	M	T	W	T	F	S	S
3 Oct–30 Oct	10:30–4:30	M	T	W	T	F	S	S

Watersmeet House shop opens 30 minutes after tea-room and tea garden.

Waterfalls on the Hoar Oak Water at Watersmeet in Devon

Entry is still possible at most places up to 30 minutes before closing

Wembury

Wembury Beach, Wembury, Devon PL9 0HP

Map ① F9  1939

A coastal village with a small, pretty beach and a charming 19th-century mill, which is now a tea-room. With beautiful views, excellent rock-pooling and a great starting point for coastal and inland walks, Wembury, near the Yealm estuary, is a popular place to visit.

Exploring — Join a rock-pool ramble discovering life under the sea.
— Enjoy miles of coastal trails.
— Simply relax and enjoy the beautiful sunsets.
— Treat yourself to a cream tea at the Old Mill.

Eating and shopping: morning coffees, homemade cakes, soups, pasties and ice-creams. Local arts and crafts. Beach shop sells everything from spades and wetsuits to windbreaks. Deckchairs, body boards and wetsuits for hire at weekends and school holidays.

Making the most of your day: discover a wide variety of activities at Wembury, including rock-pooling (01752 862538), sailing, surfing, kayaking, walking and horse riding (visit www.oldmillwembury.co.uk for more details). **Dogs**: welcome on coast path. Restricted from beach 1 May to 30 September.

Access for all: ♿ WC 🚻 Old Mill Café 🔊
Marine Centre ♿ Wembury Beach 🔊

Getting here: 201:SX517484. **Foot**: South West Coast Path runs through. **Ferry**: seasonal ferries to Noss Mayo and Bantham. **Bus**: First 48 Plymouth to Wembury, Monday to Saturday (limited Sunday service). For Wembury Point: City Bus 49 Plymouth to Heybrook Bay, via Wembury Point, limited service. Check with Traveline 0871 200 2233. **Train**: Plymouth 10 miles. **Road**: for Wembury Point and beach follow the A379 from Plymouth, then turn right at Elburton, follow the signs to Wembury. At Wembury follow the road until you see

Marine vegetation and lichen surround the rock pools at Wembury Point, near Plymouth, Devon

Wembury primary school and turn left where you see a brown sign for the café. **Parking**: free (charge for non-members). Manned during busy times.

Finding out more: 01752 346585 (South Devon Coast and Countryside Office). 01752 862314 (Old Mill Café) or wembury@nationaltrust.org.uk. South and East Devon Countryside Office, The Stables, Saltram House, Plymouth, Devon PL7 1UH

Wembury		M	T	W	T	F	S	S
Beach								
Open all year		M	T	W	T	F	S	S
Old Mill Café								
1 Jan–2 Jan	11–3						S	S
19 Feb–27 Feb	10:30–5	M	T	W	T	F	S	S
2 Apr–30 Oct	10:30–5	M	T	W	T	F	S	S
26 Dec–31 Dec	11–3	M	T	W	T	F	S	

Café opening hours may be longer in fine weather and shorter in poorer weather. Visit www.oldmillwembury.co.uk for more information.

Westbury College Gatehouse

College Road, Westbury-on-Trym,
Bristol BS9 3EH

Map (1) I3 | 1907

15th-century gatehouse to the 13th-century College of Priests – where the 14th-century theological reformer John Wyclif lived.
Note: access by key. No toilet.

Access for all: **Building**

Getting here: 172:ST572775. 3 miles north of the centre of Bristol.

Finding out more: 01275 461900 or westburycollege@nationaltrust.org.uk

Westbury College Gatehouse
Access (Monday to Friday) by key to be collected by appointment from the Parish Office, Church Road, Westbury-on-Trym, Bristol BS9 4AG. 0117 950 8644 (mornings only).

Westbury Court Garden

Westbury-on-Severn, Gloucestershire GL14 1PD

Map (1) J2 | 1967

Originally laid out between 1696 and 1705, this is the only restored Dutch water garden in the country. Visitors can explore canals, clipped hedges and working 17th-century vegetable plots and discover many old varieties of fruit trees.

Exploring

- See the gardening style of the late 18th century.
- The huge tulip tree flowers at the end of June.
- One of the oldest holm oaks in the country.
- Historic fruit and vegetables grown and sold throughout the year.
- Footpath access to the River Severn.
- Lovely picnicking spot.

Neptune gazes across the water from his plinth in the T-canal at Westbury Court Garden in Gloucestershire

We welcome dogs assisting visitors with disabilities

Making the most of your day: evening garden tours, Easter Egg trails, Apple Day.

Access for all: 🚹♿📷📖∴
Grounds 🚹♿

Getting here: 162:SO718138. **Foot**: River Severn footpath runs from garden to river. **Bus**: Stagecoach in South Wales 73 Gloucester 🚆 to Chepstow; Stagecoach in Wye and Dean 30/31 Gloucester 🚆 to Coleford. **Train**: Gloucester 9 miles. **Road**: 9 miles south-west of Gloucester on A48. **Parking**: free, 300 yards.

You may also enjoy: Ashleworth Tithe Barn, The Kymin, May Hill and The Weir.

Finding out more: 01452 760461 or westburycourt@nationaltrust.org.uk

Westbury Court Garden		M	T	W	T	F	S	S
9 Mar–30 Jun	10–5	·	·	**W**	**T**	**F**	**S**	**S**
1 Jul–31 Aug	10–5	**M**	**T**	**W**	**T**	**F**	**S**	**S**
1 Sep–30 Oct	10–5	·	·	**W**	**T**	**F**	**S**	**S**

Open Bank Holiday Mondays. Open other times by appointment.

Westwood Manor, Wiltshire: small but perfectly formed

Westwood Manor

Westwood, near Bradford-on-Avon, Wiltshire BA15 2AF

Map ① J4 1960

This beautiful small manor house, built over three centuries, has late Gothic and Jacobean windows, decorative plasterwork and two important keyboard instruments. There is some fine period furniture, 17th- and 18th-century tapestries and a modern topiary garden. **Note**: administered for the National Trust by the tenant. No toilet.

Exploring	–	Enjoy an elegant manor house with a friendly, domestic atmosphere.
	–	The country's earliest Italian keyboard instrument in playing order.
	–	A variety of woods, colours and textiles in the furniture.

| Exploring | – | Sit in the peaceful green garden surrounded by yew topiary. |

Eating and shopping: buy a CD of atmospheric musical recordings of the recently restored virginal and spinet.

Making the most of your day: children's quizzes for five to eight year olds, plus eight and aboves. House unsuitable for under-fives.

Access for all: 🚹∴🅰
Manor 🚹♿ Garden 🚹

Getting here: 173:ST812590. 1½ miles south-west of Bradford-on-Avon, in Westwood village, beside the church. **Cycle**: NCN254, ¾ mile. **Bus**: Libra 94, Bodmans 96 Bath 🚆 to Trowbridge (passing close Trowbridge 🚆). **Train**: Avoncliff, 1 mile; Bradford-on-Avon 1½ miles. **Road**: Westwood village is signposted off Bradford-on-Avon to Rode road (B3109). Turn left opposite the New Inn pub towards the church. **Parking**: free, 90 yards.

Finding out more: 01225 863374 or westwoodmanor@nationaltrust.org.uk

Westwood Manor		M	T	W	T	F	S	S
3 Apr–28 Sep	2–5	·	**T**	**W**	·	·	·	**S**

Small groups at other times by written application with stamped addressed envelope.

White Mill

Sturminster Marshall, near Wimborne Minster, Dorset BH21 4BX

Map (1) K6 🏠🖼️🔩 1982

Corn mill with original wooden machinery in a peaceful riverside setting.

Access for all: 🅿️♿♿🔊
Building ♿♿ Grounds ♿

Getting here: 195:ST958006. On the River Stour in the parish of Shapwick, close to Sturminster Marshall.

Finding out more: 01258 858051 or whitemill@nationaltrust.org.uk

White Mill		M	T	W	T	F	S	S
26 Mar–30 Oct	12–5	·	·	·	·	·	S	S

Admission by guided tour. Open Bank Holiday Mondays: 12 to 5, last tour 4.

The pond at Woodchester Park, Gloucestershire

Woodchester Park

Nympsfield, near Stonehouse, Gloucestershire GL10 3TS

Map (1) J3 📱♣️♿ 1994

The tranquil wooded valley contains a 'lost landscape'; remains of an 18th- and 19th-century landscape park with a chain of five lakes. The restoration of this landscape is an ongoing project. Waymarked trails (steep in places) lead through picturesque scenery, passing an unfinished Victorian mansion (not National Trust). **Note**: toilet not always available. Parking is £2 (no change given from ticket machine).

Exploring – Don't miss Woodchester Mansion Open Days (01453 861541).

Making the most of your day: follow the waymarked trails through the valley. **Dogs**: under close control, on leads where requested.

Access for all: Grounds ♿

Getting here: 162:SO797012. 4 miles south-west of Stroud. **Foot**: Cotswold Way within ¾ mile. **Bus**: Cotswold Green 35 Stroud to Nympsfield (passing close Stroud 🚆). **Train**: Stroud 5 miles. **Road**: off B4066 Stroud to Dursley road. **Parking**: £2 (pay and display). Accessible from Nympsfield road, 300 yards from junction with B4066. Last admission to car park one hour before dusk.

Finding out more: 01452 814213 or woodchesterpark@nationaltrust.org.uk. The Ebworth Centre, The Camp, Stroud, Gloucestershire GL6 7ES

Woodchester Park		M	T	W	T	F	S	S
Open all year	Dawn–dusk	M	T	W	T	F	S	S

South and
South East

**Visitors enjoy a vertiginous view of
Louis Laguerre's 'Pandora's Box', on
the ceiling above the Grand Staircase
at Petworth House**

Outdoors in the South and South East

The South and South East of England is one of the country's most densely populated areas, however thanks to the National Trust and similar organisations, it still boasts extensive and beautiful green spaces and miles of dramatic coastline – perfect places to enjoy some fun out of doors.

Top:
the tranquil River Wey Navigations, Surrey
Above:
dunes and crunchy white sand at East Head, West Sussex

When you visit Surrey why not set yourself the challenge of cycling up the steep slopes of Box Hill? Once at the top, you can treat yourself to a visit to the exciting Discovery Zone in our visitor centre. Or if you prefer something a little less demanding, then hire a boat and take in the delights of the River Wey. Surrey also boasts some of the region's best views. Follow the footpaths up Leith Hill and climb to the top of the Gothic tower, and you may be able to see St Paul's Cathedral away to the north, while to the south you can enjoy the panorama stretching from the Weald to the English Channel. Amazingly, on a clear day, thirteen counties are visible!

If a day at the beach is your idea of heaven then East Head, at the mouth of Chichester Harbour in West Sussex, is ideal. Relax and soak up the sun or gather a group together for a friendly game of cricket. West Sussex also boasts the perfect site for kite flying – for the vast open space of Devil's Dyke attracts people from far and wide to indulge in this favourite English pastime.

Kent is well known for its woodlands. Many of these were devastated by the great storm of 1987; however more than 20 years on, places such as Toys Hill, near Westerham, are thriving. In fact they actually contain more types of flora and fauna than before. Petts Wood and Hawkwood are oases of calm amid the urban sprawl of south-east London. The quiet charm of this spacious woodland and working farm provides a tranquil spot to walk or simply to escape the bustle of everyday London life.

Rock pools and secret bays

The inspiring coastline of East Sussex is a magnificent sight. The guardians of the South Downs, the Seven Sisters, stretch between Birling Gap and Cuckmere Haven, and all the way along them there are glistening rock pools and secret bays carved out by the sea just waiting to be explored.

The most southerly point of the region is the Isle of Wight. Here much of the finest countryside and coastline is owned by the National Trust, including the magnificent chalk downs of Ventnor, Tennyson Down and the Needles Headland. The protection this ownership gives means that the natural beauty and rich wildlife of this popular holiday island, including its famous red squirrels, will continue to survive and thrive for future generations to enjoy.

Get out and about

In Hampshire, local residents and visitors alike enjoy many of the areas of countryside cared for by the Trust, including Selborne Hill, Ludshott Common, Waggoners Wells and The Chase – all great places for walking and enjoying the flora and fauna.

To the north of the region there are many popular beauty spots in the Chilterns, including Watlington Hill, West Wycombe Hill, Coombe Hill and Ivinghoe Beacon along the Chiltern escarpment. If you are looking for an action-packed day, the Ashridge Estate, which covers more than 2,000 hectares (5,000 acres) of outstanding Chilterns countryside, attracts tens of thousands of visitors who flock to enjoy its fine walks, picnic areas and cycling routes. There is also a lively Discovery Room in the Bridgewater Monument Visitor Centre, with updates on wildlife, events and activities.

In Oxfordshire don't miss the famous White Horse at Uffington – the oldest chalk figure in the country. It is set amid a landscape that is peppered with ancient sites and monuments, including Dragon's Hill where St George was reputed to have slain the dragon, and the famous neolithic burial chamber known, somewhat enigmatically, as Wayland's Smithy. The nearby villages and agricultural estates of Buscot and Coleshill are definitely worth exploring, and have a range of pleasant circular walks.

Above: enjoying the beach and Compton Downs on the Isle of Wight

With a little help from livestock

Around the region the National Trust relies on livestock to help look after our amazing landscapes. Hindhead Common in Surrey is home to Exmoor ponies, while pigs are a favourite of visitors to Woolbeding in West Sussex, and cows stroll leisurely all along the Surrey Hills. In the wild heaths of the New Forest the historic method of grazing animals on common land continues into the 21st century, ensuring that it remains a unique landscape.

Spectacular wildlife

The summer spectacle of the Adonis blue butterflies on Denbies Hillside, Surrey, or Cissbury Ring, West Sussex, is a sight not to be missed. For another wildlife treat, head down to the beach at East Head and see if you can spot the seals. While in the Chilterns, the successful reintroduction of red kites means that these magnificent birds are now a common sight across an ever-widening area.

Outdoors in the South and South East

'Spring is the most dramatic time of the year on Tennyson Down, with the strong smell of nature in the air and dramatic sunshine that reflects off the sea and floods the cliffs and coastline with light. It's one of my favourite spots in the world.'

Tony Tutton
Property Manager, Isle of Wight

Tales of times past

There is also an array of unique places with fascinating stories of times past and our ancestors. Saddlescombe Farm near Devil's Dyke in West Sussex is just one. This ancient farmstead was once home to the Knights Templar, and visitors can find out about its fascinating 1,000 years of history during public open days in spring and autumn – alternatively it is possible to arrange special guided tours. Another place full of historical interest is Runnymede on the banks of the River Thames. The Magna Carta was signed here in 1215, and the warden organises occasional guided walks – the ideal opportunity to discover more. Or why not book yourself onto a guided tour of Reigate Fort in Surrey, once used to defend us from invasion?

Fun in the open air

Besides visiting and exploring our many countryside places, do take advantage of the extensive programme of open-air events organised by the Trust. There is something for everyone – from bug hunts to rock-pooling, and hurdle-making to bat watching. Of particular interest to those with children is the vibrant programme of family events and activities the Trust runs across its countryside properties – from the Newtown Nature Reserve in the Isle of Wight all the way across the Surrey Hills.

Don't miss...

Saddlescombe Farm Open Days, Sussex: telephone 01273 857712 or see the What's On section of the regional newsletter for details.

Guided tours of Reigate Fort, Surrey: discover this fascinating building, which was once used to defend us from invasion. To book special guided tours or study days telephone 01342 843225.

Admiring the view from Wingate Hill, Surrey, towards Gatton Park in the distance

My favourite walk

There is nothing more enjoyable than strolling through the historic parkland of Gatton and glimpsing its diverse history.

Gatton Park was landscaped in the mid-18th century by the renowned Lancelot 'Capability' Brown. Today, 200 years on, his work still has the ability to impress – whether it be the broad view or details such as the tree-framed vistas and series of ponds winding their way down the valley to the large lake.

Highlights along this two-mile circular walk include the stone circle placed in the park by the Jerusalem Trust to commemorate the turn of the millennium, spotting the spire of St Andrew's Church, which dates from the 16th century, and the view of the lake from Nut Wood.

Andrew Wright
Countryside Manager, Surrey Hills

www.nationaltrust.org.uk/coastandcountryside

Alfriston Clergy House

The Tye, Alfriston, Polegate,
East Sussex BN26 5TL

Map ② H8   🏠🌼 │ 1896 │

This rare 14th-century Wealden 'hall house' was the first building to be acquired by the National Trust, in 1896. The thatched, timber-framed house is in an idyllic setting, with views across the River Cuckmere and surrounded by a delightful, tranquil cottage garden featuring a magnificent Judas tree. **Note**: no toilet, nearest in village car park.

Exploring
- Admire the first house the National Trust saved.
- Enjoy the tranquillity of our English cottage garden.
- Discover the chalk and sour milk floor in the hall.
- Soak up the atmosphere of this 600-year-old house.

Eating and shopping: browse in the shop for a souvenir of your visit.

Making the most of your day: children's quizzes and trails. Varied events programme all year. Short circular walks and longer distance hikes over South Downs. Situated in the interesting and historic medieval village of Alfriston.

Access for all: 🖼️ ⠿ 📷
Building 👟 Grounds 👟♿

Getting here: 189:TQ521029. **Foot**: South Downs Way within ¾ mile. **Cycle**: NCN2. **Bus**: Countryliner 125 from Lewes, Renown 126 from Eastbourne and Seaford (pass close Lewes ⮕ and Seaford ⮕). **Train**: Berwick 2½ miles. **Road**: 4 miles north-east of Seaford, just east of B2108, in Alfriston village, adjoining The Tye and St Andrew's church. **Parking**: 500 yards at other end of village (not National Trust).

Finding out more: 01323 870001 or alfriston@nationaltrust.org.uk

The tranquil garden at Alfriston Clergy House, East Sussex

Alfriston Clergy House		M	T	W	T	F	S	S
26 Feb–9 Mar	11–4	M	T	W	·	·	S	S
12 Mar–31 Jul	10:30–5	M	T	W	·	·	S	S
1 Aug–28 Aug	10:30–5	M	T	W	·	F	S	S
29 Aug–30 Oct	10:30–5	M	T	W	·	·	S	S
31 Oct–18 Dec	11–4	M	T	W	·	·	S	S

Open Good Friday. Special Friday openings in August.
Please note new opening days.

Ascott

Wing, near Leighton Buzzard,
Buckinghamshire LU7 0PS

Map ② E3   🏠🌼 │ 1949 │

This half-timbered Jacobean farmhouse, transformed by the de Rothschilds towards the end of the 19th century, now houses an exceptional collection of paintings, fine furniture and superb oriental porcelain. The extensive gardens are an attractive mix of formal and natural, with specimen trees and shrubs and some unusual features.

Exploring
- See one of the best small picture collections in Britain.
- Tell the time by the unusual topiary sundial.
- Relax in the Dutch Garden admiring the Eros Fountain.

Access for all: 📱♿🎧⠿📷
Building 👟♿🅿 Grounds 👟♿➡

Getting here: 165:SP891230. **Bus**: Arriva 100 Aylesbury to Milton Keynes (passing close Aylesbury ⮕ and Leighton Buzzard ⮕). **Train**: Leighton Buzzard 2 miles.

Road: ½ mile east of Wing, 2 miles south-west of Leighton Buzzard, on south side of A418.
Parking: free, 220 yards, and coach parking.

Finding out more: 01296 688242 or ascott@nationaltrust.org.uk

Ascott		M	T	W	T	F	S	S
22 Mar–24 Apr	2–6	·	T	W	T	F	S	S
25 Apr–2 May*	2–6	M	T	W	T	F	S	S
3 May–31 May	2–6	·	T	W	T	·	·	·
30 May ·	2–6	M	·	·	·	·	·	·
1 Jun–28 Jul	2–6	·	T	W	T	·	·	·
2 Aug–9 Sep·	2–6	·	T	W	T	F	S	S
29 Aug*	2–6	M	·	·	·	·	·	·

Open Bank Holiday Mondays and Good Friday. Last admission one hour before closing. ***Gardens open in aid of National Gardens Scheme on Mondays 2 May and 29 August (charge including members).**

Ashdown House

Lambourn, Newbury, Berkshire RG17 8RE

Map ② C5   🏚️ ❄️ ♿ 1956

This extraordinary building with a doll's-house appearance nestles in a beautiful valley on the Berkshire Downs, surrounded by woodland. **Note**: no toilet. The house is tenanted. Access limited to staircase and roof (100 steps). Opening restrictions may apply from August due to building conservation work.

Access for all: ♿🔍📷🖼️📖
Building 🏚️ Grounds ♿

Getting here: 174:SU282820. 2½ miles south of Ashbury, 3½ miles north of Lambourn, on west side of B4000.

Finding out more: 01494 755569 (Infoline). 01793 762209 or ashdownhouse@nationaltrust.org.uk

Ashdown House		M	T	W	T	F	S	S
2 Apr–29 Oct	2–5	·	·	W	·	·	S	·
Woodland								
1 Jan–31 Dec	Dawn–dusk	M	T	W	T	·	S	S

Admission by guided tour to house at 2:15, 3:15 and 4:15 (numbers limited). Woodland walks open every day except Fridays.

Ashridge Estate

Visitor Centre, Moneybury Hill, Ringshall, Berkhamsted, Hertfordshire HP4 1LT

Map ② E3   🏚️❌🏛️♿ 1926

This magnificent and varied countryside estate runs across the borders of Hertfordshire and Buckinghamshire, along the main ridge of the Chiltern Hills. There are more than 2,000 hectares (4,942 acres) of woodlands, commons and chalk downland supporting a rich variety of wildlife and offering splendid walks through outstanding scenery. The focal point is the Bridgewater Monument, erected in 1832 to the Duke of Bridgewater. Ivinghoe Beacon provides wonderful views of the surrounding landscape, inhabited from pre-history to the current day. Ideas for walks and family days out can be found at the Visitor Centre. **Note**: toilet only available when Visitor Centre open.

Exploring — Escape to fresh air and freedom.
— Discover more about local wildlife at our lively Visitor Centre.
— Acres of breathtaking scenery, from ancient woodland to chalk downland.
— Experience a landscape rich in history and archaeology.
— Climb the Bridgewater Monument for wonderful panoramic views.

Golden hues on the Ashridge Estate, Hertfordshire

Eating and shopping: local maps, books and products available to purchase in the National Trust shop. Treat yourself to delicious homemade food (National Trust-approved concession).

Making the most of your day: the Visitor Centre provides information on local facilities, walks and events. Children will enjoy the Discovery Room and our self-guided family trails. **Dogs**: must be under close control (deer roam freely).

Access for all:
Visitor Centre 🦽 Grounds

Getting here: 181:SP970131. **Foot**: 2¾ miles of the Ridgeway on property. Visitor Centre can be reached by a short detour from the Ridgeway Walk. **Bus**: Visitor Centre and Monument: Arriva 30/31 or Red Rose Travel 387 from Tring ≋, alight Monument Drive or Aldbury ½ mile on foot (steep climb). Ivinghoe Beacon: Arriva 61 Aylesbury to Luton (passing close Aylesbury ≋ and Luton ≋). **Train**: Visitor Centre and Monument: Tring ≋, 1¾ miles; Ivinghoe Beacon: Cheddington ≋ 3½ miles. **Road**: Visitor Centre and Monument: between Northchurch and Dagnall, just off B4506. **Parking**: free.

You may also enjoy: Pitstone Windmill, Hughenden, Stowe Landscape Gardens and Dunstable Downs.

Finding out more: 01494 755557 (Infoline). 01442 851227 or ashridge@nationaltrust.org.uk

Ashridge Estate		M	T	W	T	F	S	S
Estate								
Open all year	Dawn–dusk	M	T	W	T	F	S	S
Visitor Centre and shop*								
14 Feb–18 Dec	10–5	M	T	W	T	F	S	S
Bridgewater Monument (weather dependent)								
9 Apr–30 Oct	12–4:30	·	·	·	·	·	S	S
Brownlow Café**								
1 Jan–31 Mar	8–4	M	T	W	T	F	S	S
1 Apr–15 Oct	8–6	M	T	W	T	F	S	S
16 Oct–31 Dec	8–4	M	T	W	T	F	S	S

*Visitor Centre, shop and café may close at dusk if earlier than the published closing time. **Café closed 25 and 26 December. Toilet opening as café.

Lower Basildon, Reading, Berkshire RG8 9NR

Map ② D5   🏠 ❄ ♠ ⚑ 🔔 🍴 1978

Stately grandeur at Basildon Park, Berkshire

This impressive Georgian mansion, surrounded by glorious parkland, was lovingly rescued from ruin by Lord and Lady Iliffe in the mid-1950s, when they restored the elegant interior and scoured the country salvaging 18th-century architectural fixtures and fittings. They filled their comfortable new home with fine paintings, fabrics and furniture, which can still be enjoyed by visitors today. There are waymarked trails through the historic parkland and gravel paths around the gardens to be explored. Don't miss our newly opened 1950s kitchen. **Note**: main show rooms are on the first floor – 21 steps up from ground level.

Exploring
– Be inspired by the remarkable restoration of Basildon Park.
– Discover the magic of the Shell Room.

Exploring
- Relax in the gardens and on the croquet lawn.
- Burn off some energy on the parkland trails.
- Drink in the beauty of our parkland views.

Eating and shopping: enjoy traditional English fare in our tea-room. Treat yourself to afternoon tea, with homemade cakes and scones. Don't miss the plant sale area and gift shop. Browse in our second-hand bookshop.

Making the most of your day: introductory talks, waymarked trails and picnic tables. Family-friendly events and activities, toys on the croquet lawn. Exciting events programme. **Dogs**: welcome in grounds, on leads only.

Access for all: [icons] Building [icons] Grounds [icons]

Getting here: 175:SU611782. **Bus**: Thames Travel 133 Reading ≋ to Goring & Streatley ≋, alight Lower Basildon (Park Wall Lane), ½ mile. **Train**: Pangbourne 2½ miles; Goring & Streatley 3 miles. **Road**: between Pangbourne and Streatley, 7 miles north-west of Reading, on west side of A329; leave M4 at exit 12 and follow signs for Beale Park (not National Trust) through Pangbourne, then brown National Trust signs to Basildon Park. **Sat Nav**: please use main entrance from A329. **Parking**: free, 400 yards from mansion (buggy transfer service available).

You may also enjoy: Greys Court and The Vyne. Or, for something completely different, Sandham Memorial Chapel.

Finding out more: 0118 984 3040 or basildonpark@nationaltrust.org.uk

Basildon Park		M	T	W	T	F	S	S
Ground floor exhibition area, tea-room, shop and grounds								
9 Feb–7 Mar	10–4	M	·	W	T	F	S	S
9 Mar–31 Oct	10–5	M	·	W	T	F	S	S
2 Nov–19 Dec	10–4	M	·	W	T	F	S	S
House (main show rooms)								
9 Mar–31 Oct	11–5	M	·	W	T	F	S	S
1 Dec–19 Dec	11–4	M	·	W	T	F	S	S

Open Bank Holiday Mondays. **House opens 11 for guided tours only, free-flow from 12**. Monday: entry by guided tour only (except Bank Holidays). Timed tickets may apply.

Bateman's

Bateman's Lane, Burwash,
East Sussex TN19 7DS

Map (2) H7

'**There is a wonderful feeling of tranquillity and expectation of things to come. Super restaurant!**'
Mr and Mrs C. W. Dennay,
Alresford, Hampshire

'That's She! The Only She! Make an honest woman of her – quick!' was how Rudyard Kipling and his wife, Carrie, felt the first time they saw Bateman's. Surrounded by the wooded landscape of the Sussex Weald, this 17th-century house, with its mullioned windows and oak beams, provided a much needed sanctuary for this world-famous writer. The rooms, described by him as 'untouched and unfaked', remain much as he left them, with oriental rugs and artefacts reflecting his strong association with the East. Bateman's is very much a family home, but impressive none the less. **Note**: the garden, shop and tea-room are open free of charge in November and December.

Exploring
- Soak up the atmosphere in Kipling's book-lined study.
- Enjoy the serenity of the Formal Garden.
- Walk by the river as it flows through the meadow.
- Watch the watermill grind flour most Wednesday and Saturday afternoons.
- Experience 'Kipling Country', with a walk through the valley.
- Discover Kipling's 1928 Rolls-Royce Phantom 1.

Eating and shopping: buy Kipling books and souvenirs in the shop. Eat in the tea-room, with its wonderful garden setting. Relax and have fun in the picturesque Picnic Glen.

Bateman's in East Sussex: this Jacobean house was the home of Rudyard Kipling from 1902 to 1936

Making the most of your day: programme of events, family fun days, storytelling, re-enactment weekends, garden/countryside walks. Virtual tour of watermill and first floor of house. Children's quizzes and trails. **Dogs**: on leads in car park only. Dog crèche available.

Access for all: 🅿️🐕♿🚾🔼🔽🎞️📺🎵👁️🅰️
Building 🔼🔼♿ Grounds 🔼➡️♿

Getting here: 199:TQ671238. Burwash, East Sussex, TN19 7DS. **Bus**: Renown 318 Uckfield to Etchingham ≷. **Train**: Etchingham 3 miles. **Road**: ½ mile south of Burwash. A265 west from Burwash, first turning on left. **Parking**: free, 30 yards. Coaches: tight left turn into first bay.

You may also enjoy: Scotney Castle, a Victorian country house and romantic garden with a 14th-century ruin.

Finding out more: 01435 882302 or batemans@nationaltrust.org.uk

Bateman's		M	T	W	T	F	S	S
Garden, shop and tea-room								
26 Feb–6 Mar	11–4	·	·	·	·	·	S	S
12 Mar–30 Oct*	10–5	M	T	W	·	·	S	S
31 Oct–21 Dec	11–4	M	T	W	·	·	S	S
House								
12 Mar–30 Oct	11–5	M	T	W	·	·	S	S
3 Dec–18 Dec	11:30–3:30	·	·	·	·	·	S	S

Open Good Friday: 10 to 5. *Shop and garden close 5:30, 12 March to 30 October. The mill grinds corn most Wednesdays and Saturdays at 2. House: downstairs rooms decorated for traditional Edwardian Christmas on 3 and 4, 10 and 11, and 17 and 18 December, 11:30 to 3:30.

Bembridge Windmill

High Street, Bembridge, Isle of Wight PO35 5SQ

Map ② D9   ✖️ 🚆 1961

This tiny gem, the only surviving windmill on the Isle of Wight, is one of its most iconic images. Built around 1700, it last operated in 1913 but still has most of its original machinery intact. Climb to the top and follow the milling process back down its four floors. **Note**: no toilet. This year the mill celebrates 50 years of ownership by the National Trust.

Exploring
– See how the windmill worked with our working model.
– Feel the wooden machinery worn smooth by the years.
– Watch a short film to discover the milling process.
– Enjoy the views that inspired J. M. W. Turner.

Eating and shopping: treat yourself with ice-creams or drinks in the kiosk. Buy a souvenir as a reminder of your visit.

Making the most of your day: children's I-Spy trail sheet. The start of the Culver Trail. Take a guided tour of nearby Bembridge Fort (limited availability, booking essential on 01983 741020).

Access for all: 🏠📷🖼️📋📷📷 Building 🏛️

Getting here: 196:SZ639874. On the bend where the High Street becomes Mill Road, B3395. **Cycle:** NCN67, ½ mile. **Ferry:** Ryde (Wightlink Ltd) 6 miles (0871 376 1000); East Cowes (Red Funnel) 13 miles (0844 844 9988). **Bus:** Southern Vectis 14 from Ryde Esplanade ≋ to within ½ mile; 10 Newport to Sandown to within ¼ mile. **Train:** Brading 2 miles by footpath. **Road:** ½ mile south of Bembridge on B3395. **Parking:** free (not National Trust), 100 yards in lay-by.

Finding out more: 01983 873945 or bembridgemill@nationaltrust.org.uk

Bembridge Windmill		M	T	W	T	F	S	S
12 Mar–30 Oct	11–5	M	T	W	T	F	S	S

Closes dusk if earlier. Conducted school groups and special visits March to end October by written appointment.

The Seven Sisters, East Sussex: crisp white cliffs

Birling Gap and the Seven Sisters

near Eastbourne, East Sussex

Map ② H9 1931

Stretching between Birling Gap and Cuckmere Haven are the gleaming white cliffs of the Seven Sisters, eroded continuously by the sea. They are an impressive sight, both from the cliff tops and from the beach below. There are some lovely walks across rolling downland with spectacular views out to sea.

Exploring
- Explore 202 hectares (500 acres) of Trust open-access land.
- Variety of walks; access to South Downs Way (steep paths).
- Range of events and activites through the year, including rock-pooling.
- Pick up a Tracker Pack to help you explore.

Eating and shopping: treat yourself to fish and chips by the sea – just one of a range of hot snacks available throughout the day.

Making the most of your day: close to Cuckmere Haven and Alfriston Clergy House.

Getting here: 189:TQ554961. **Foot:** on the South Downs Way between Exceat and Eastbourne. **Bus:** 13X varying times throughout the year (www.buses.co.uk). **Train:** Eastbourne ≋ 6 miles, Seaford ≋ 7 miles. **Road:** 5 miles approximately west of Eastbourne and 6 miles east of Seaford, south of A259 and East Dean village. **Parking:** at Birling Gap, £2 for half day, £4 for whole day (pay and display). No lorries. Coaches £5 for half day, £10 for whole day (pay and display).

Finding out more: 01323 423197 or birlinggap@nationaltrust.org.uk. Birling Gap Café, Birling Gap, East Dean, near Eastbourne, East Sussex BN20 0AB

Birling Gap and the Seven Sisters		M	T	W	T	F	S	S
Countryside								
Open all year		M	T	W	T	F	S	S
Café								
1 Jan–28 Feb	10–4	M	T	W	T	F	S	S
1 Mar–30 Jun	10–5	M	T	W	T	F	S	S
1 Jul–31 Aug	10–6	M	T	W	T	F	S	S
1 Sep–31 Oct	10–5	M	T	W	T	F	S	S
1 Nov–31 Dec	10–4	M	T	W	T	F	S	S

Café closed 24 and 25 December.

Boarstall Duck Decoy

Boarstall, near Bicester,
Buckinghamshire HP18 9UX

Map ② D3 1980

One of the few surviving 17th-century duck decoys in working order – on a picturesque lake with a nature reserve walk.

Access for all: Exhibition hall 🏢♿ Grounds ♿

Getting here: 164/165:SP624151. Midway between Bicester and Thame, 2 miles west of Brill. Entrance through farm.

Finding out more: 01280 822850 or boarstalldecoy@nationaltrust.org.uk

Boarstall Duck Decoy		M	T	W	T	F	S	S
2 Apr–28 Aug	10–4						S	S
6 Apr–24 Aug	3:30–6			W				
Open Bank Holiday Mondays, 10 to 4.								

Boarstall Tower

Boarstall, near Bicester,
Buckinghamshire HP18 9UX

Map ② D3 1943

Enjoy a guided tour of this 14th-century moated gatehouse, once part of a fortified manor house set in beautiful gardens. **Note**: property is tenanted.

Access for all: 🚻♿ Building ♿ Grounds ➡️

Getting here: 164/165:SP624141. Midway between Bicester and Thame, 2 miles west of Brill.

Finding out more: 01280 822850 or boarstalltower@nationaltrust.org.uk

Boarstall Tower		M	T	W	T	F	S	S
4 May–28 Sep	2–5			W				
Also open 11 to 5 on 23, 25 and 30 April, 2, 28 and 30 May, 27 and 29 August.								

Bodiam Castle

Bodiam, near Robertsbridge,
East Sussex TN32 5UA

Map ② I7 1926

One of the most famous and evocative castles in Britain, Bodiam was built in 1385 as both a defence and a comfortable home. The exterior is virtually complete and the ramparts rise dramatically above the moat. Enough of the interior survives to give an impression of castle life. There are spiral staircases and battlements to explore, and wonderful views of the Rother Valley from the top of the towers. In the impressive gatehouse is the castle's original wooden portcullis, an extremely rare example of its kind. **Note**: only onsite toilets are in car park. Bodiam Castle is often used by educational groups during term.

Exploring
- Explore the courtyard and battlements and imagine medieval castle life.
- Costumed historical interpreters in courtyard daily from April to October.
- Discover Bodiam's story through a film and exhibition.
- Children's discovery challenges available, plus seasonal trails and events.

The dramatic towers of Bodiam Castle, East Sussex

Exploring – Climb the towers for wonderful views of the Rother Valley.
– See the original portcullis, probably the oldest in England.

Eating and shopping: the shop has a range of exciting gifts and produce. Try our Bodiam wine and local honey, plus much more. The Wharf tea-room serves seasonal, local food cooked onsite. Ice-creams, snacks and drinks available from castle kiosk (seasonal).

Making the most of your day: exciting events programme throughout the year – from the mid-February challenge to Santa's Christmas Grotto. Also evening events and medieval-themed weekends. Activities for all the family daily throughout August. **Dogs**: welcome on leads in grounds only.

Access for all: ⃞⃞⃞⃞⃞⃞⃞⃞⃞⃞ ⃞⃞ Castle ⃞⃞⃞⃞ Grounds ⃞⃞⃞⃞

Getting here: 199:TQ785256. **Foot**: on the Sussex Border path. **Ferry**: Bodiam Ferry (seasonal) from Newenden Bridge (A28). **Bus**: Stagecoach in Hastings 349 Hastings ➤ to Hawkhurst. **Train**: steam railway (seasonal) from Tenterden ¼ mile; Robertsbridge 5 miles; Battle 10 miles. **Road**: 3 miles south of Hawkhurst, 3 miles east of A21 Hurst Green midway between Tunbridge Wells and Hastings. **Parking**: 400 yards, £2. Coaches £5.

You may also enjoy: Bateman's – the beautiful home of Rudyard Kipling; or Winchelsea – medieval town planning at its best.

Finding out more: 01580 830196 or bodiamcastle@nationaltrust.org.uk

Bodiam Castle		M	T	W	T	F	S	S
8 Jan–6 Feb	11–4						S	S
12 Feb–30 Oct*	10:30–5	M	T	W	T	F	S	S
2 Nov–18 Dec	11–4			W	T	F	S	S

*12 February to 30 October, gift shop and tea-room close at 5 most days but at 5:30 during school summer holidays.

Box Hill

The Old Fort, Box Hill Road, Box Hill, Tadworth, Surrey KT20 7LB

Map ② F6

Far-reaching views at Box Hill, Surrey

A great place to visit whatever you are looking for: stunning countryside, wildlife, history, far-reaching views, a place for fun or quiet contemplation. The busy shop, servery and Discovery Zone on the hilltop are in contrast to the peaceful woodlands off the beaten path.

Exploring – Visit the new Discovery Zone and 'Bee' amazed.
– New mountain bike hire facilities – explore Box Hill by bike.
– Many guided walks, including impromptu tours – see noticeboard for details.
– Natural play trail and new guided walks.

Eating and shopping: homemade sandwiches and cakes, including famous 'Rider's Revival' flapjack. Try our gluten-free, dairy-free and fat-free options. Treat your children to a delicious lunch box. Visit our shop for a special gift or pick up a jar of local honey.

Making the most of your day: children's quiz/trail. Special Christmas shopping day, Friday 16 December. Suitable for school groups. Education room/centre. **Dogs**: under close control where sheep grazing.

Access for all: Building 🚶♿ Grounds ➡

Getting here: 187:TQ171519. **Foot**: 1 mile of North Downs Way from Stepping Stones to South Scarp; 1 mile of Thames Down link footpath at Mickleham Downs; 1 mile from Dorking station (½ mile from Boxhill 🚃). Many rights of way lead to Box Hill summit. **Bus**: Sunray Travel 516 Leatherhead 🚃 to Dorking to Box Hill east car park (not Sundays or Bank Hols); Arriva 465 Kingston to Dorking to foot of Box Hill, 1½ miles to summit. **Train**: Boxhill, ½ mile, and Westhumble 1½ miles. **Road**: 1 mile north of Dorking, 2½ miles south of Leatherhead on A24. **Parking**: £3 (pay and display or RinGo by mobile). Coaches must **not** use zig-zag road from Burford Bridge on west side of hill (weight restriction) – approach from east side of hill B2032 or B2033; car/coach parks at summit.

Finding out more: 01306 885502 or boxhill@nationaltrust.org.uk

Box Hill		M	T	W	T	F	S	S
Countryside								
Open all year		M	T	W	T	F	S	S
Servery								
1 Jan–26 Mar	10–4	M	T	W	T	F	S	S
27 Mar–29 Oct	9–5	M	T	W	T	F	S	S
30 Oct–31 Dec	10–4	M	T	W	T	F	S	S
Shop/Discovery Zone								
1 Jan–26 Mar	11–4	M	T	W	T	F	S	S
27 Mar–29 Oct	11–5	M	T	W	T	F	S	S
30 Oct–31 Dec	11–4	M	T	W	T	F	S	S

Shop, Discovery Zone and servery closed 25 December. In summer, the servery may be open for longer, weather permitting.

Bradenham Village

near High Wycombe, Buckinghamshire

Map ② E4   1956

Scenic village with cottages clustered around a village green. 17th-century manor house (not open) and church provide impressive backdrop. **Note**: designated parking at the village green above the cricket pavilion. Contact property to arrange group garden tours.

Access for all: Grounds ♿

Getting here: 165:SU825970. 4 miles north-west of High Wycombe, off A4010.

Finding out more: 01494 755573 or bradenham@nationaltrust.org.uk

Bradenham Village	Open every day all year
Contact property for garden tours.	

Brighstone Shop and Museum

North Street, Brighstone, Isle of Wight PO30 4AX

Map ② C9 🏠 1989

National Trust shop in a row of traditional thatched cottages adjoining the small village museum. **Note**: nearest toilet in public car park, 100 yards.

Access for all: ♿📷♿ Building 🚶

Getting here: 196:SZ428828. Next to post office, just off B3399 in Brighstone.

Finding out more: 01983 740689 or brighstone@nationaltrust.org.uk

Brighstone Shop and Museum		M	T	W	T	F	S	S
3 Jan–21 Apr	10–1	M	T	W	T	F	S	
22 Apr–27 May	10–4	M	T	W	T	F	S	
28 May–24 Sep	10–5	M	T	W	T	F	S	
29 May–25 Sep	12–5							S
26 Sep–23 Dec	10–4	M	T	W	T	F	S	
24 Dec–31 Dec	10–1				T	F	S	

Buckingham Chantry Chapel

Market Hill, Buckingham,
Buckinghamshire MK18 1JX

Map ② D2   1912

Peruse second-hand books while enjoying a coffee in this atmospheric 15th-century chapel, restored by Gilbert Scott in 1875. **Note**: also available to hire for functions and events.

Access for all: 🔲 Building 👟

Getting here: 152/165:SP693340. On Market Hill, opposite post office.

Finding out more: 01280 822850 or buckinghamchantry@nationaltrust.org.uk

Buckingham Chantry Chapel		M	T	W	T	F	S	S
4 Jan–17 Dec	10–2		T			F	S	

Available for hire. Closed 25 December.

The Buscot and Coleshill Estates

Coleshill, near Swindon, Wiltshire

Map ② B4    1956

These countryside estates on the western borders of Oxfordshire include the attractive, unspoilt villages of Buscot and Coleshill, each with a thriving village shop and tea-room. There are circular walks of differing lengths and a series of footpaths criss-crossing the estates. **Note**: toilets in Coleshill estate office yard and next to Buscot village shop and tea-room.

Exploring
- Enjoy countryside walks across Coleshill Park.
- From Buscot enjoy access to the River Thames.

Exploring
- See the Iron Age hill fort at Badbury Hill.
- Visit the restored watermill and see the milling process.

Eating and shopping: Buscot tea-rooms offer lunches and afternoon tea. The Radnor Arms uses locally sourced produce and has a wide range of ales including its own micro brewery. The Coleshill shop and tea-room also offer locally sourced produce.

Making the most of your day: range of guided walks throughout the year. **Dogs**: on leads only.

Getting here: SU239973. **Cycle**: NCN45, 10 miles. Regional Route 40: Oxfordshire Cycleway. **Bus**: Stagecoach in Swindon 64 Swindon to Carterton (passing close Swindon ➤), alight Highworth, 2 miles. **Train**: Swindon 10 miles. **Road**: Coleshill village on B4019 between Faringdon and Highworth. Buscot village on A417 between Faringdon and Lechlade. **Parking**: at Buscot village and Badbury Clump; for Coleshill at Estate Office.

Finding out more: 01793 762209 or buscotandcoleshill@nationaltrust.org.uk. Coleshill Estate Office, Coleshill, Swindon, Wiltshire SN6 7PT

The Buscot and Coleshill Estates	Open every day all year

Mill open second Sunday of the month: April to October, 2 to 5.

Buscot Old Parsonage

Buscot, Faringdon, Oxfordshire SN7 8DQ

Map ② C4   1949

Early 18th-century house with small walled garden, situated on the banks of the River Thames. **Note**: no toilet. Property is opened by the tenants.

Access for all: Building 👟

Getting here: 163:SU231973. 2 miles from Lechlade, 4 miles from Faringdon on A417.

Finding out more: 01793 762209 or buscot@nationaltrust.org.uk

Buscot Old Parsonage		M	T	W	T	F	S	S
6 Apr–26 Oct	2–6	·	·	**W**	·	·	·	·

Admission by written appointment with the tenant. Please mark envelope 'National Trust booking'.

Buscot Park

Estate Office, Buscot Park, Faringdon, Oxfordshire SN7 8BU

Map ② C4    1949

Family home of Lord Faringdon, who continues to care for the property as well as the family art collection, the Faringdon Collection, which is displayed in the house. Consequently, despite the grandeur of their scale, both the house and grounds remain intimate and idiosyncratic and very much a family home. They also continue to change and develop – nothing is preserved in aspic here! Outside, a water feature, Faux Fall, by David Harber. Inside, contemporary glassware by Colin Reid and Sally Fawkes. **Note**: administered on behalf of the National Trust by Lord Faringdon.

Exploring
- Explore one of England's finest water gardens.
- Discover the Faringdon Collection of Art.
- Enjoy the scents of the Four Seasons Walled Garden.
- Marvel at Burne-Jones's *Legend of the Briar Rose*.
- Revisit your childhood in the Swinging Garden.
- **New**: seventeen life-size terracotta warriors from China.

Eating and shopping: savour a delicious homemade tea (not National Trust). Pick up some local honey, fudge and cider. Buy plants and kitchen garden produce, when available. Treat yourself to an ice-cream and enjoy a picnic.

Making the most of your day: occasional events in grounds and theatre (available for hire). **Dogs**: allowed in the Paddock area only.

Access for all: ▣▣▣▣▣▣▣▣
Building ▣ Grounds ▣▣▣▣

Getting here: 163:SU239973. **Foot**: 4 miles by footpath from Faringdon, 3¼ miles from Lechlade. **Bus**: Stagecoach 65/66 Oxford/Swindon to Faringdon. Stagecoach in Swindon 64 Swindon to Carterton (passing close Swindon ≋), alight Lechlade, 3¼ miles. **Train**: Oxford 18 miles, Swindon 10 miles. **Road**: between Faringdon and Lechlade on south side of A417. **Parking**: free.

You may also enjoy: Buscot and Coleshill Estate and Buscot Parsonage.

Finding out more: 01367 240932 (Infoline). 01367 240786 or estbuscot@aol.com. www.buscotpark.com

Buscot Park		M	T	W	T	F	S	S
House, grounds and tea-room[*]								
1 Apr–30 Sep	2–6	·	·	**W**	**T**	**F**	·	·
Grounds only								
4 Apr–27 Sep	2–6	**M**	**T**	·	·	·	·	·

Open Bank Holiday Mondays. Last admission to house one hour before closing. ***House, grounds and tea-room weekend opening**: 9 and 10, 23 and 24 April; 30 April and 1, 14 and 15, 28 and 29 May; 11 and 12, 25 and 26 June; 9 and 10, 23 and 24 July; 13 and 14, 27 and 28 August; 10 and 11, 24 and 25 September, 2 to 6 **(tea-room 2:30 to 5:30)**.

The Water Garden at Buscot Park, Oxfordshire

Chartwell

Mapleton Road, Westerham, Kent TN16 1PS

Map (2) G6   1946

Stylish dining at Chartwell, Kent

Bought by Sir Winston Churchill for its magnificent views over the Weald of Kent, Chartwell was his home and the place from which he drew inspiration from 1924 until the end of his life. The rooms remain much as they were when he lived here, with pictures, books and personal mementoes evoking the career and wide-ranging interests of this great statesman. The hillside gardens reflect Churchill's love of the landscape and nature. They include the lakes he created, Lady Churchill's Rose Garden and the kitchen garden. Many of Churchill's paintings can be seen in the studio.

Exploring
- Explore the Churchills' stunning family home.
- Enjoy wandering through the beautiful, tranquil garden.
- Spot the black swans on Sir Winston's lake.
- Take a walk around the surrounding Wealden countryside.
- Watch the gardeners at work in the productive kitchen garden.

Eating and shopping: large, popular restaurant with regular special events. Enjoy fresh produce from the Chartwell kitchen garden. Beautiful shop stocking Churchill memorabilia and interesting local ranges. Kiosk serving light bites, drinks and snacks on busy days.

Making the most of your day: year-round events programme, free talks and tours on selected days, daily studio talks, children's trails and activities, walk sheets available from car park. **Dogs**: on short leads in gardens only.

Access for all: ⊞♿♨♨♨♨♨♨♨ ♨♿ **Building** ♨♨♨ **Shop and restaurant** ♨♨
Grounds ♨♨♨

Getting here: 188:TQ455515. **Foot**: Greensand Way passes through car park. **Bus**: Southdown PSV 236 Westerham to East Grinstead to within ½ mile. SelKent 246 from Bromley North (passing close Bromley South ≷); Go Coach 401 from Sevenoaks (passing close ≷), both Sundays and Bank Holidays only. **Train**: Edenbridge 4 miles; Edenbridge Town 4½ miles; Oxted 5 miles; Sevenoaks 6½ miles. **Road**: 2 miles south of Westerham, fork left off B2026 after 1½ miles; leave M25 at exit 5 or 6. **Parking**: 250 yards (pay and display). Year-round opening (except 25 December) for countryside access; gates locked 5:30 March to October, 4:30 November to 31 December.

You may also enjoy: Emmetts Garden and Quebec House.

Finding out more: 01732 868381 or chartwell@nationaltrust.org.uk

Chartwell		M	T	W	T	F	S	S
House								
12 Mar–30 Oct	11–5		·	W	T	F	S	S
5 Jul–23 Aug	11–5		T	W	T	F	S	S
Garden, exhibition, shop and restaurant								
1 Jan–11 Mar	11–4		·	W	T	F	S	S
Garden, exhibition, studio, shop and restaurant								
12 Mar–30 Oct	10:45–5		·	W	T	F	S	S
5 Jul–23 Aug	10:45–5		T	W	T	F	S	S
2 Nov–11 Dec	11–4		·	W	T	F	S	S
14 Dec–31 Dec	11–4	M	T	W	T	F	S	S
Catering kiosk								
1 Jul–29 Aug	11–4	M	T	W	T	F	S	S
Car park*								
Open all year	9–5	M	T	W	T	F	S	S

*Car park closes at 4 from 1 January to 11 March and 2 November to 31 December, or dusk if earlier; also closed 25 December. Admission to house by timed ticket, which should be purchased immediately on arrival (not bookable) as these can sell out on busy days. Open Bank Holiday Mondays. Last admission 45 minutes before house closes. Garden, exhibition and studio open in winter, weather and conditions permitting. Closed 24 and 25 December. Closes 3:30 Saturday 3 September.

Chastleton House

Chastleton, near Moreton-in-Marsh,
Oxfordshire GL56 0SU

Map (2) C3 1991

A rare gem of a Jacobean country house,
Chastleton House was built between 1607
and 1612 by a prosperous wool merchant as
an impressive statement of wealth and
power. Owned by the same increasingly
impoverished family until 1991, the house
remained essentially unchanged for nearly
400 years as the interiors and contents
gradually succumbed to the ravages of
time. With virtually no intrusion from the
21st century, this fascinating place exudes
an informal and timeless atmosphere in a
gloriously unspoilt setting. There is no shop
or tea-room, so you can truly believe you
have stepped back in time.

Exploring
- Discover rooms full of rare objects without ropes or barriers.
- Enjoy the garden, with Jacobean topiary and a vegetable plot.
- See a kitchen ceiling last cleaned in 1612.
- Learn family history through exhibitions of everyday items and costume.
- See rare 17th-century wall coverings still in place.

Eating and shopping: picnics welcome
in car park.

Making the most of your day: free family
Explorer packs; seasonal concerts; garden
party; family events during school holidays;
private views each Wednesday and themed
events on last Saturday of each month during
open season. **Dogs**: allowed on leads in field
opposite house.

Access for all: [symbols]
Building [symbols] Garden [symbols]

Getting here: 163:SP248291.

Train: Moreton-in-Marsh 4 miles. **Road**: 6 miles
from Stow-on-the-Wold. Approach only from
A436 between A44 (west of Chipping Norton)
and Stow. **Sat Nav**: follow brown signs, not Sat
Nav directions, into Chastleton village from the
A44. **Parking**: free, 270 yards. Return walk to
car park includes a short but steep hill. Sensible
shoes recommended. Disabled parking in
stableyard next to house (signposted from
main car park).

You may also enjoy: Snowshill Manor and
Charlecote Park.

Finding out more: 01494 755560 (Infoline).
01608 674981 or
chastleton@nationaltrust.org.uk

Chastleton House		M	T	W	T	F	S	S
12 Mar–31 Mar	1–4	·	·	W	T	F	S	·
1 Apr–30 Sep	1–5	·	·	W	T	F	S	·
1 Oct–29 Oct	1–4	·	·	W	T	F	S	·

Admission by timed ticket (180 available each open
afternoon). Ticket office opens at 12:30. Last admission
one hour before closing. Visitor numbers are limited to
conserve the fragile house (at busy times entry cannot be
guaranteed). Groups of ten plus must book (01608 674981).

Unusual topiary shapes at Chastleton House, Oxfordshire

Clandon Park

West Clandon, Guildford, Surrey GU4 7RQ

Map ② F6  1956

Clandon Park was built *circa* 1730 for the 2nd Lord Onslow by Venetian architect Giacomo Leoni. One of the country's most complete examples of a Palladian mansion, it contains a superb collection of 18th-century furniture, porcelain and textiles, much of which was acquired in the 1920s by connoisseur Mrs Gubbay. While the wider parkland is still in the hands of the Onslow family, the mansion is set in intimate gardens which are home to a Maori meeting house, brought back from New Zealand in 1892. The Onslow family is unique in providing three Speakers of the House of Commons. **Note**: the Queen's Royal Surrey Regiment Museum is based at Clandon Park.

Exploring
- Be awed by the stunning two-storey white marble hall.
- Enjoy the informal gardens, including the secluded sunken Dutch Garden.
- Take in a wealth of ceramics, tapestries and furniture.
- Discover the Maori meeting house – unique in the UK.
- Come on a Wednesday to learn more about 'Clandon Uncovered'.
- Enjoy a children's trail around the house or garden.

Eating and shopping: visit our shop in the 19th-century kitchen. Enjoy a meal in the vaulted undercroft restaurant (approved concession).

Making the most of your day: events include conservation demonstrations, behind-the-scenes tours, children's activities, re-enactors, art exhibtions and much more.

Access for all: ⓟ🅳🅳♿🅆🅲🔼🔽🅰📷👓🅰

Building 🚶♿🔽 Grounds 🚶♿

Getting here: 186:TQ042512. **Foot**: follow the drive to reception. **Bus**: Countryliner 479 Guildford to Epsom (passing Leatherhead 🚉, close Guildford 🚉). Countryliner 463 Guildford to Woking 🚉. **Train**: Clandon 1 mile – turn left when leaving the station. **Road**: at West Clandon on A247, 3 miles east of Guildford; if using A3 follow signposts to Ripley to join A247 via B2215. **Sat Nav**: may be incorrect – make sure you enter from A247. **Parking**: free, 300 yards.

You may also enjoy: nearby Hatchlands Park, a beautiful mansion set in stunning Repton parkland.

Finding out more: 01483 222482 (office). 01483 222502 (restaurant) or clandonpark@nationaltrust.org.uk

Clandon Park			M	T	W	T	F	S	S
House, garden, museum, shop and restaurant									
13 Mar–30 Oct	11–5			T	W	T			S
Shop and restaurant									
1 Nov–1 Dec	12–4			T	W	T			S
4 Dec–22 Dec*	12–4		M	T	W	T			S
Queen's Royal Surrey Regiment Museum									
1 Nov–22 Dec	12–4			T	W	T			S

Open Bank Holiday Mondays, Good Friday and Easter Saturday. Shop, restaurant and museum open for Waking Up the House (Sunday 27 February and 6 March) and Putting the House to Bed (Sunday 6, 13 and 20 November). *Restaurant open for lunch and dinner (booking essential). Lift availability restricted (booking essential).

Clandon Park, Surrey: Palladian perfection

Claremont Landscape Garden

Portsmouth Road, Esher, Surrey KT10 9JG

Map ② F6   ❖ 1949

The Belvedere built by Vanbrugh in 1715 on the mount at Claremont Landscape Garden, Surrey

Claremont is a beautiful garden surrounding a small lake and featuring an unusual grass amphitheatre. The garden's creation and development has involved great names in garden history, including Sir John Vanbrugh, Charles Bridgeman, William Kent and 'Capability' Brown. In 1726 it was described as 'the noblest of any in Europe' and the garden today is of national importance. Visitors walking round the lake will see the island and pavilion, grotto and many viewpoints and vistas. There are hidden features to enjoy as well as wider estate walks and a new children's play area.

Exploring
- Camellia Terrace is a mass of blooms, December to May.
- Don't miss the rhododendrons and azaleas flowering late spring.
- Marvel at the stunning autumn colour.
- Enjoy the constant changing views around the lake.
- Children will love their exciting play area.
- Special children's trails and activities during school holidays.

Eating and shopping: licensed tea-room serving cakes, cream teas, soup, sandwiches and hot lunches. Made daily on the premises (high chairs, children's menu and baby-food heating facilities available).

Making the most of your day: open-air theatre events in July. Children's craft workshops, storytelling and trails during school holidays. Guided walks April to October. Full yearly programme of walks, talks and activities. **Dogs**: allowed between 1 November and 31 March only (on short leads).

Access for all: 🅿️♿🚻♿🍴♿👁️♿
Grounds ♿➡️

Getting here: 187:TQ128631. **Bus**: Abellio Surrey 515/A Kingston to Guildford (passing close Esher ☰). **Train**: Esher 2 miles.
Road: 1 mile south of centre of Esher, on east side of A307 (no access from Esher bypass).
Parking: free, at entrance.

You may also enjoy: The Homewood, a 20th-century Modernist house and garden.

Finding out more: 01372 467806 or claremont@nationaltrust.org.uk

Claremont Landscape Garden		M	T	W	T	F	S	S
Garden								
1 Jan–30 Jan	10–4	·	T	W	T	F	S	S
1 Feb–31 Mar	10–5	·	T	W	T	F	S	S
1 Apr–31 Oct	10–6	M	T	W	T	F	S	S
1 Nov–31 Dec	10–4	·	T	W	T	F	S	S
Tea-room and shop								
1 Jan–30 Jan	10–3	·	T	W	T	F	S	S
1 Feb–31 Mar	10–4	·	T	W	T	F	S	S
1 Apr–31 Oct	10–5	M	T	W	T	F	S	S
1 Nov–23 Dec	10–3	·	T	W	T	F	S	S
26 Dec–31 Dec	10–3	M	T	W	T	F	S	·

Closed Mondays November to April but open Monday 21 February and Bank Holiday Mondays, including 3 January and 26 December. Closed 25 December. Belvedere Tower open 1 January 11 to 2 and first weekend each month April to October 2 to 5. Late night openings 4, 11, 18, 25 June until 9. May close early on events days in July and in bad weather, especially high winds (telephone before visit).

Claydon

Middle Claydon, near Buckingham,
Buckinghamshire MK18 2EY

Map ② D3  1956

In the 1750s at his family seat in
Buckinghamshire, Sir Ralph Verney set out
to create a country house of extraordinary
grandeur that would dazzle his wealthy
neighbours and outdo his political rivals.
Thirty years on he was facing financial ruin.
Today the interiors that remain are among the
most ambitious and lavish ever created in the
18th century. Claydon has been continually
occupied by the Verney family for more
than 550 years; the place is a testament to
their fascinating fluctuating fortunes, from
their close involvement in the English Civil
War to the family connection with Florence
Nightingale. **Note**: the gardens are maintained
by the Verney family, additional entry charges
apply (including members).

Exploring
- New: enjoy 'talking portraits', bringing Claydon alive.
- New: from the Verney archive, 17th-century heroes and villains.
- New: Florence Nightingale Centenary Garden (run by the Verney family).
- New: we've removed the ropes from our extravagantly decorated rooms.
- New: virtual tours of upstairs rooms for visitors with disabilities.
- Wander along walks through picturesque parkland and around the lakes.

Eating and shopping: visit our new shop.
Browse in our second-hand bookshop.
Courtyard craft shops and galleries (not
National Trust). Relax in the Carriage House
restaurant/tea-room (not National Trust).
Vegetables for sale from kitchen garden,
when in season.

Making the most of your day: family activity
worksheets. **Dogs**: welcome in the park on leads.

Access for all: ⬛⬛⬛⬛⬛⬛⬛⬛⬛
Building ⬛⬛⬛ Grounds ⬛⬛➡

Getting here: 165:SP720253. In
Middle Claydon 13 miles north-west of
Aylesbury, 4 miles south-west of Winslow.
Foot: Bernwood Jubilee Way. **Cycle**: NCN51.
Road: signposted from A413 and A41 (M40
exit 9, 12 miles); entrance by north drive only.
Parking: free.

You may also enjoy: Waddesdon Manor and
Stowe Landscape Gardens, with its new visitor
centre opening in the summer.

Finding out more: 01494 755561 (Infoline).
01296 730349 or
claydon@nationaltrust.org.uk

Claydon		M	T	W	T	F	S	S
House								
12 Mar–2 Nov	11–5	M	T	W	·	·	S	S
Tea-room, church and bookshop								
12 Mar–2 Nov	11–5	M	T	W	·	·	S	S
Garden, restaurant and shops								
12 Mar–2 Nov	12–5	M	T	W	·	·	S	S

Open Good Friday.

View through the Saloon at Claydon, Buckinghamshire

Cliveden, Buckinghamshire, has been visited by virtually every monarch since George I

Cliveden

Taplow, Maidenhead, Buckinghamshire SL6 0JA

Map ② E5   1942

A country retreat on a grand scale, Cliveden's magnificent gardens and breathtaking views have been admired for centuries. Visited by virtually every British monarch since George I, in the early 20th century it became home to Waldorf and Nancy Astor. As the glittering hub of society, numerous parties and political gatherings were hosted here and later Cliveden became infamously associated with the Profumo Affair. Today, the whole family can experience the relaxed grandeur of Cliveden and enjoy exploring the beautiful gardens and woodlands. The house is a hotel, and tours of part of the interior are available on certain days. **Note**: no toilet in woodlands. Mooring charge on Cliveden Reach (including members).

Exploring
– Don't get lost in the new maze (opens May)!
– Be inspired by stunning seasonal floral displays.

Exploring
– Admire the famous parterre, beautifully restored with colourful bedding.
– Stretch your legs with a riverside or woodland walk.
– Let imaginations run wild in the storybook-themed play area.
– Discover more through our full events programme and guided walks.

Eating and shopping: enjoy home-cooked lunches and snacks at The Orangery. Morning coffee and afternoon tea served in new coffee shop. Kiosk in car park sells light refreshments. Picnic areas available. Wide selection of products and plants for sale in the gift shop.

Making the most of your day: don't miss the introductory film *Cliveden: Camelot on Thames*. Take a relaxing boat trip on the River Thames (additional charge, call for schedule). **Dogs**: welcome under close control in the woodlands only.

Access for all: [symbols]
Cliveden House (hotel) [symbols] Garden [symbols]

Getting here: 175:SU915851. **Train**: Taplow (not Sunday) 2½ miles; Burnham 3 miles. **Travel to Cliveden by 'green transport' and receive a £1 voucher to spend in the National Trust shop or café. Visit website for details. Road**: 2 miles north of Taplow; leave M4 at exit 7 onto A4, or M40 at exit 4 onto A404 to Marlow and follow brown signs. Entrance by main gates opposite Feathers Inn. **Sat Nav**: enter Cliveden Road and SL1 8NS. **Parking**: free.

You may also enjoy: Hughenden Manor, and the elegant mansion of Basildon Park.

Finding out more: 01494 755562 (Infoline). 01628 605069 or cliveden@nationaltrust.org.uk

The restored Darnley Mausoleum at Cobham Wood, Kent

Finding out more: 01474 816764 or cobham@nationaltrust.org.uk

Cliveden		M	T	W	T	F	S	S
Estate, garden and shop								
19 Feb–30 Oct	10–5:30	M	T	W	T	F	S	S
31 Oct–31 Dec*	10–4	M	T	W	T	F	S	S
Woodlands								
1 Jan–18 Feb	10–4	M	T	W	T	F	S	S
19 Feb–30 Oct	10–5:30	M	T	W	T	F	S	S
31 Oct–31 Dec*	10–4	M	T	W	T	F	S	S
Coffee shop								
19 Feb–30 Oct	10–5	M	T	W	T	F	S	S
31 Oct–23 Dec	10–3:30	M	T	W	T	F	S	S
The Orangery (café)								
19 Feb–30 Oct	10–5	M	T	W	T	F	S	S
5 Nov–18 Dec	10–3:30	.	.	.	.	.	S	S
House (part), chapel								
3 Apr–27 Oct	3–5:30	.	.	.	T	.	.	S

*Shop closed 24 to 31 December. Garden, woodlands and coffee shop closed 24 to 26 December. Admission to house is limited and by timed ticket only from the information centre. Some areas of formal garden may be closed for private events or when ground conditions are poor.

Cobham Wood and Mausoleum
Visit website for opening information.

Cobham Wood and Mausoleum

South Lodge Barn, Lodge Lane, Cobham, Kent DA12 3BS

Map ② H5   2011

Acquisition of the wonderfully restored Darnley Mausoleum and the tranquil surrounding woodland will, hopefully, be completed this year. Please visit our website for more information.

Dorneywood Garden

Dorneywood, Dorney Wood Road, Burnham, Buckinghamshire SL1 8PY

Map ② E5   1942

1930s-style garden, with herbaceous borders, rose garden, cottage garden and lily pond. **Note**: upkeep funded by Dorneywood Trust, at no cost to National Trust or public. **No photography**.

Access for all: Grounds ♿ ▶

Getting here: 175:SU938848. On Dorney Wood Road, south-west of Burnham Beeches, 1½ miles north of Burnham village, 2 miles east of Cliveden.

Finding out more: dorneywood@nationaltrust.org.uk

Dorneywood Garden		M	T	W	T	F	S	S
In aid of National Gardens Scheme*								
19 Apr–20 Apr	2–5	.	T	W	.	.	.	.
15 Jun	2–5	.	.	W	.	.	.	.
30 Jul	2–5	.	.	.	.	.	S	.
In aid of Dorneywood Trust*								
11 Jun	2–5	.	.	.	.	.	S	.

Admission by appointment only (email for tickets, giving at least two weeks' notice). *Charge including members.

Emmetts Garden

Ide Hill, Sevenoaks, Kent TN14 6BA

Map (2) H6 1965

Charming Emmetts – an Edwardian estate owned by Frederic Lubbock – was a plantsman's passion and a much-loved family home. Influenced by William Robinson, the delightful garden was laid out in the late 19th century and contains many exotic and rare trees and shrubs from across the world. Explore the rose and rock gardens, take in the spectacular views and enjoy glorious shows of spring flowers and shrubs, followed by vibrant autumn colours.

Exploring
- Stunning rock garden returned to its original design.
- Charming formal rose garden.
- Unique collection of exotic shrubs.
- Beautiful woodland and spectacular views.

Eating and shopping: stable tea-room, with delicious homemade cakes. Enchanting tack room shop. Plants available to buy.

Making the most of your day: year-round events programme, guided tours on selected days, children's activities, walks sheets for surrounding countryside. **Dogs**: on short leads only.

Access for all:
Grounds

Getting here: 188:TQ477524. **Foot**: from Ide Hill (½ mile). Weardale walk from Chartwell (3 miles) – guide leaflet available. **Bus**: Nu-Venture 404 from Sevenoaks, Monday to Friday only, alight Ide Hill, 1½ miles. **Train**: Sevenoaks 4½ miles; Penshurst 5½ miles. **Road**: 1½ miles south of A25 on Sundridge to Ide Hill road, 1½ miles north of Ide Hill off B2042, leave M25 exit 5, then 4 miles. **Parking**: free, 100 yards.

You may also enjoy: Chartwell and Quebec House nearby.

Finding out more: 01732 751509 (Infoline). 01732 868381 or emmetts@nationaltrust.org.uk. Chartwell Office, Mapleton Road, Westerham, Kent TN16 1PS

Emmetts Garden		M	T	W	T	F	S	S
12 Mar–30 Oct	11–5	**M**	**T**	**W**	·	·	**S**	**S**

Open Bank Holiday Mondays and Good Friday.
Last admission 45 minutes before closing.

Swathes of stunning bluebells at Emmetts Garden in Kent

Country charm in the kitchen at Greys Court, Oxfordshire: an intimate family home

Great Coxwell Barn

Great Coxwell, Faringdon, Oxfordshire SN7 7LZ

Map ② C4 1956

Former monastic barn was a favourite of William Morris, who would regularly bring his guests to wonder at the structure. **Note**: no toilet, narrow access lanes.

Access for all: 🅟♿

Getting here: 163:SU269940. 2 miles south-west of Faringdon between A420 and B4019.

Finding out more: 01793 762209 or greatcoxwellbarn@nationaltrust.org.uk

Great Coxwell Barn		M	T	W	T	F	S	S
Open all year	Dawn–dusk	M	T	W	T	F	S	S

Greys Court

Rotherfield Greys, Henley-on-Thames, Oxfordshire RG9 4PG

Map ② D5 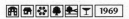 1969

An intimate family home and peaceful estate set in the rolling hills of the Chilterns. This picturesque 16th-century mansion and tranquil gardens were home to the Brunner family until recent years. The house exudes a welcoming atmosphere, with a well-stocked kitchen and homely living rooms. The series of walled gardens is a colourful patchwork of interest set amid medieval ruins. Other buildings from earlier eras include the Great Tower from the 12th century and a rare Tudor donkey wheel, in use until the early 20th century.

Exploring
— Soak up the atmosphere of a real family home.
— Stroll around the enchanting gardens.
— Burn off some energy in the beech woodlands.
— Find out how the donkey drew water from the well.

Exploring – Follow your food from plot to plate.

Eating and shopping: treat yourself to a light lunch or tea and cake in the tea-room. Buy a memento for your garden from the plant stall. Browse in our newly opened shop. Pick up seasonal organic produce from the gardens (when available).

Making the most of your day: programme of open-air events and garden days. Wider estate walk, taking in the interesting ice-house. Family activities, including explorer packs and garden and house trails. **Dogs**: on the estate walk only.

Access for all: ⛴ ⛴ ♿ 🐕 📷
House 🏠 Tea-room ♿ Grounds ♿

Getting here: 175:SU725834.
Cycle: on Oxfordshire cycleway.
Train: Henley-on-Thames 3 miles.
Road: west of Henley-on-Thames. From Nettlebed mini-roundabout on A4130 take B481 and property is signed to the left after approximately 3 miles. There is also a direct (unsigned) route from Henley-on-Thames town centre. Follow signs to Badgemore Golf Club towards Peppard, approximately 3 miles out of Henley. **Parking**: free, 220 yards.

You may also enjoy: on a grander scale: Basildon Park and the magnificent gardens of Cliveden.

Finding out more: 01494 755564 (Infoline). 01491 628529 or greyscourt@nationaltrust.org.uk

Greys Court		M	T	W	T	F	S	S
House*								
1 Apr–30 Oct	1–5			W	T	F	S	S
Garden								
1 Apr–30 Oct	11–5			W	T	F	S	S
Tea-room								
1 Apr–30 Oct	11–4:30			W	T	F	S	S
Shop								
1 Apr–30 Oct	11–5			W	T	F	S	S

Open Bank Holiday Mondays. Closed Good Friday. On village fête day, 4 September, special opening arrangements apply (charge including members), contact property for details. *All visitors require a timed ticket to visit the house, including members, available from the ticket office from 11 on the day. (Limited number of tickets available for house daily – they may run out on busy days, especially at weekends and Bank Holidays.)

Ham House and Garden

Ham Street, Ham, Richmond-upon-Thames, Surrey TW10 7RS

Map ② F5 🏛 ❀ 🔔 🍽 1948

'**An amazing place. Strong sense of history, yet fun and welcoming. The garden is paradise in densely urbanised south-west London**.'
Simon Dixon, Kingston-upon-Thames

A 400-year-old treasure trove waiting to be discovered and one of a series of grand houses and palaces alongside the River Thames. Ham House and Garden is an unusually complete survival of the 17th century that impressed in its day and continues to do so today. Rich in history and atmosphere, Ham is largely the vision of Elizabeth Murray, Countess of Dysart, who was deeply embroiled in the politics of the English Civil War and subsequent restoration of the monarchy. Discover the fine interiors and historic gardens that make Ham an unusual and fascinating place to visit.
Note: for conservation reasons, some rooms have low light levels.

Stunning symmetry at Ham House and Garden, Surrey

Exploring
— Discover our outstanding collections of furniture and textiles.
— Learn about 17th-century global trade.
— Relax in our historic gardens, including a kitchen garden.
— Taste delicious home-grown produce in the Orangery Café.
— Explore the unique wilderness visitors voted 'Favourite piece of Ham'.
— Find out about blockbusters that have been filmed here.

Eating and shopping: taste our freshly home-cooked dishes or a delicious home-baked cake. Find local and unusual gifts in our shop.

Making the most of your day: regular free garden tours, confirm in advance. Interactive discovery room, family garden trails, treasure map to the house. Programme of events throughout the year; check *What's On* leaflet or website. **Dogs**: assistance dogs only.

Access for all: 🅿♿🚻♿♿🔊🖼🛏📷📖Ⓐ
Building 🔣♿♿♿ Grounds 🔣➡♿♿

Getting here: 176:TQ172732. On south bank of Thames, west of A307, between Richmond and Kingston; Ham gate exit of Richmond Park. **Foot**: Thames Path passes main entrance. 1½ miles from Richmond, 3 miles from Kingston. **Cycle**: NCN4. Ferry access from Twickenham. **Ferry**: seasonal foot/bike ferry across River Thames from Twickenham towpath (by Marble Hill House – English Heritage) to Ham House and Garden. **Bus**: TfL371 Richmond to Kingston, alight Ham Street by Royal Oak pub, then ½-mile walk (follow signposts). 65 Ealing Broadway to Kingston, alight Sandpits Road stop on Petersham Road by Ham Polo Ground, ¾-mile walk along historic avenues (both pass Richmond ≋ and Kingston) – 020 7222 1234. **Train**: Richmond 1½ miles by footpath, 2 miles by road. **Underground**: District Line Richmond 1½ miles by footpath, 2 miles by road. **Road**: on south bank of the Thames, west of A307, between Richmond and Kingston; Ham gate exit of Richmond Park, readily accessible from M3, M4 and M25. **Parking**: free, 400 yards (not National Trust).

Japanese lacquer cabinet on a Dutch gilt stand in the Long Gallery at Ham House and Garden, Surrey

You may also enjoy: Osterley Park and House – an extravagant 18th-century mansion.

Finding out more: 020 8940 1950 or hamhouse@nationaltrust.org.uk

Ham House and Garden		M	T	W	T	F	S	S
Garden, shop and café								
1 Jan–11 Feb	11–4	M	T	W	T	F	S	S
12 Feb–30 Oct	11–5	M	T	W	T	F	S	S
31 Oct–18 Dec	11–4	M	T	W	T	F	S	S
House tours, selected rooms only*								
12 Feb–31 Mar	11:30–3:30	M	T	W	T		S	S
31 Oct–29 Nov	11:30–3	M	T				S	S
House								
2 Apr–30 Oct**	12–4	M	T	W	T		S	S

*Guided tours of selected rooms only (40 minutes duration), no free-flow (tours start every 30 minutes), entry, by timed ticket only (maximum 20 tickets a tour). Book on arrival (not bookable in advance). Normal admission charges apply.
**Free-flow visit only. House open Good Friday 12 to 4. Special Christmas openings 3 and 4, 10 and 11, 17 and 18 December (telephone for opening times). Please note: some rooms occasionally close for essential conservation work; we may also have to close the property at short notice. For specific information visit the website or telephone.

Hartwell House Hotel, Restaurant and Spa

Oxford Road, near Aylesbury,
Buckinghamshire HP17 8NR

Map ② E3  2008

The most famous resident of this elegant Grade I listed stately home (held on long lease from The Ernest Cook Trust) was Louis XVIII, the exiled King of France, who lived here with his Queen and members of his court for five years from 1809. Only one hour from central London, the magnificent grounds include a romantic ruined church, lake, bridge and 36 hectares (90 acres) of parkland.

The house and gardens are already accessible to the public as a hotel, and welcome guests to stay, to dine in the restaurants and to have afternoon tea (booking strongly advised). Contact hotel direct for best available offer. **Note**: all paying guests to the hotel are welcome to walk in the garden and park. Children above the age of six are welcome.

Finding out more: 01296 747444. 01296 747450 (fax) or info@hartwell-house.com www.hartwell-house.com

The historic Hartwell House: a hotel in Buckinghamshire

Hatchlands Park

East Clandon, Guildford, Surrey GU4 7RT

Map ② F6 1945

Hatchlands Park was built in the 1750s for Admiral Boscawen, hero of the Battle of Louisburg. Robert Adam ceilings decorate the house, featuring appropriately nautical motifs. Today the mansion is a family home, containing tenant Alec Cobbe's superb collection of paintings. Six rooms also display the Cobbe Collection, Europe's largest collection of keyboard instruments associated with famous composers such as J. C. Bach, Chopin and Elgar. The mansion is set in informal grounds, with one small parterre garden designed by Gertrude Jekyll. The surrounding parkland provides a number of waymarked walks in a tranquil and beautiful setting.

Exploring
- An intimate mansion with an exemplary collection.
- Listen to the instruments with an audio guide (charge applies).
- More than 161 hectares (400 acres) of parkland to explore.
- Explore the stunning bluebell wood in April and May.
- Fun trails and activities for children both inside and out.
- Join a guided tour of the mansion on Thursdays.

Eating and shopping: homely tea-room (Trust-approved concession) in the original kitchen. Visit the friendly shop for a memento of your visit.

Making the most of your day: walk in the parkland, come for a 'Conservation in Action' demonstration or a Cobbe Collection Trust concert (telephone 01483 211474 or visit www.cobbecollection.co.uk). **Dogs**: welcome under close control in designated parkland areas only.

Access for all: ⬚⬚⬚⬚⬚⬚⬚⬚⬚
Building ⬚⬚⬚ **Grounds** ⬚⬚⬚

Getting here: 187:TQ063516. **Bus**: Countryliner 478/9 Guildford to Leatherhead (passing Leatherhead ⊒ and close Guildford ⊒). **Train**: Clandon 2 miles, Horsley 2½ miles. **Road**: entry off the A246 between Guildford and Leatherhead. **Sat Nav**: please follow brown signs to main entrance on the A246. **Parking**: free, 300 yards.

You may also enjoy: nearby Clandon Park, another 18th-century property.

Finding out more: 01483 222482 or hatchlands@nationaltrust.org.uk

Hatchlands Park		M	T	W	T	F	S	S
Park walks*								
1 Apr–30 Oct	11–6	M	T	W	T	F	S	S
House and garden								
3 Apr–30 Oct	2–5:30		T	W	T			S
Tea-room**								
3 Apr–30 Oct	11–5		T	W	T		S	S
Shop**								
3 Apr–30 Oct	12–5:30		T	W	T		S	S

*Park walks open from 10, 9 April to 8 May. **Saturdays: shop and tea-room open 12 to 4:30. Open Bank Holiday Mondays. Fridays in August, house, shop and tea-room open usual times. Timed tickets may be used on Bank Holidays and busy periods. Parkland: self-drive mobility scooter available (telephone to book).

Hatchlands Park, Surrey: a family home

Hindhead Commons and the Devil's Punch Bowl

London Road, Hindhead, Surrey GU26 6AB

Map ② E7   1906

This summer, following the opening of the A3 tunnel at Hindhead, the reunited landscape will be a reality at last as the overground A3 is buried. Exciting new views will be created and you will be able to hear yourself think for the first time in 100 years. **Note**: some disruption likely when tunnel opens. Trust car park and old A3 subject to change.

Exploring
– New views from café and old A3.
– See both portals of new A3 tunnel from viewing platforms.
– New self-guided trail from café into the Punch Bowl.

Eating and shopping: treat yourself to 'all-day' breakfast from 9 to 2:30. Lunches with two daily specials until 2:30. Homemade cakes, including delicious shortbread, and sandwiches throughout the day. Seating inside or out. Plenty of peace and quiet from the summer!

Making the most of your day: extensive programme of guided walks – contact the wardens for details. Maps, books and walks about the locality on sale from the Devil's Punch Bowl café. Souvenir postcards. **Dogs**: allowed (under very close control during bird-nesting season, March to October).

Access for all: 🅿️ ⛑ ♿ Café ♿ Grounds ♿ ➡️

Getting here: 133:SU895356. Beside A3, at Hindhead, near crossroads with A287. Note: when A3 tunnel opens (in the summer) access will be via Hazel Grove roundabout, just south of the tunnel. **Bus**: Stagecoach 18 or 19; 71 from Haslemere. No service Sundays or public holidays, Haslemere ⊒ to Aldershot ⊒. Coach National Express 30 London to Portsmouth stops at Hindhead. The service will

View to the South Downs from Surrey

operate until the tunnel opens, thereafter, please contact National Express on 0871 7818 181 or www.nationalexpress.com for further information. **Train**: Haslemere 3 miles. **Parking**: £2.50 (pay and display or RinGo pay by mobile). No lorries. Coach parties by arrangement.

Finding out more: 01428 604040 (wardens). 01428 608771 (café) or hindhead@nationaltrust.org.uk

Hindhead Commons		M	T	W	T	F	S	S
Countryside								
Open all year		M	T	W	T	F	S	S
Café								
1 Jan–26 Mar	9–4	M	T	W	T	F	S	S
27 Mar–29 Oct	9–5	M	T	W	T	F	S	S
30 Oct–31 Dec	9–4	M	T	W	T	F	S	S
Café closed 25 December.								

Hinton Ampner

Bramdean, near Alresford,
Hampshire SO24 0LA

Map ② D7 🏠 ❖ 🔔 🍴 | 1986 |

The vision of one man, Hinton Ampner is best known for its magnificent garden with stunning views to the south. The elegant country house was remodelled by Ralph Dutton, the 8th and last Lord Sherborne, in 1960 after a devastating fire, and contains his collection of Georgian and Regency furniture, Italian pictures and objets d'art. The gardens were also laid out by Ralph Dutton and are widely acknowledged as a masterpiece of 20th-century design, mixing formal and informal planting, providing year-round interest.

Exploring	– Admire elegant interiors and fine furnishings.
	– Visit the upstairs rooms.
	– Stroll through different areas of the formal gardens.
	– Wander through the walled garden.
	– Enjoy fine views of the South Downs.

Eating and shopping: enjoy homemade cakes and dishes made with produce from the walled garden in the tea-room. Browse the shop and plants for sale. Property plants and produce on sale, when available.

Making the most of your day: our gardeners are always on hand to chat and answer your questions. Free guided walk in the garden on Tuesdays.

Access for all: 🅿️♿ 🚾 ♿ 🐕 ♿ ⦿ ⦿
Building ♿ 🅱️ Grounds ♿ ➡️ 🅱️

Getting here: 185:SU597275. Midway between Winchester (M3) and Petersfield (A3) on the A272. **Bus**: Stagecoach in Hampshire 67 Winchester to Petersfield (passing close Winchester ➡ and passing Petersfield ➡). **Train**: Winchester 9 miles; Alresford (Mid-Hants Railway) 4 miles.

The view through the columned arch into the drawing room at Hinton Ampner, Hampshire

Road: on A272, 1 mile west of Bramdean village, 8 miles east of Winchester, leave M3 at exit 9 and follow signs to Petersfield. **Sat Nav**: please use entrance off the A272 not via village road as directed by Sat Nav. **Parking**: free. Special entrance for coaches – map indicating where coaches can park sent with confirmation of booking.

You may also enjoy: Uppark, Winchester City Mill and Mottisfont.

Finding out more: 01962 771305 or hintonampner@nationaltrust.org.uk

Hinton Ampner		M	T	W	T	F	S	S
Garden, shop and tea-room								
19 Feb–30 Oct	10–5	M	T	W	T		S	S
31 Oct–30 Nov	10–5	M	T	W			S	S
House								
19 Feb–30 Oct	11–5	M	T	W	T		S	S
31 Oct–30 Nov	11–5	M	T	W			S	S
House, garden, shop and tea-room								
3 Dec–11 Dec	11–4	M	T	W	T	F	S	S
9 Dec	11–7					F		

Open Good Friday. Last entry to property 4:30, last entry to house 4:40. 9 December open to 7. Last entry for December opening 3:45.

The Homewood

Portsmouth Road, Esher, Surrey KT10 9JL

Map ② F6 🏠 ❀ 1999

Twentieth-century house and garden designed by the architect Patrick Gwynne reflecting the style and ethos of the Modern Movement. **Note**: administered by a tenant. No toilet.

Access for all: 🚶 ⦙⦙ 📷 **Building** 🔱 🔱
Grounds 🔱 ➡

Getting here: 187:TQ130635. **Access is via minibus from Claremont Landscape Garden only**.

Finding out more: 01372 476424 or thehomewood@nationaltrust.org.uk

The Homewood

Entrance by booked guided tours only. Open first and third Friday and the second and fourth Saturday of every month April to October. Five guided tours (45 minutes approximately), 10:30, 11:30, 12:30, 2 and 3. Garden open day Wednesday 12 October.

Hughenden Manor

High Wycombe, Buckinghamshire HP14 4LA

Map ② E4 🏠🌸♿🐾♨️🍽️ 1947

'**A lovely warm home atmosphere**.'
W. Bynorth, Ickenham

Discover the country hideaway and colourful private life of Benjamin Disraeli, the most unlikely Victorian Prime Minister. Follow in his footsteps: stroll through his German forest, relax in his elegant garden, and imagine dining with Queen Victoria in the atmospheric manor. Uncover the top secret Second World War story of Operation Hillside, for which unconventional artists painted bombing maps for missions, including the famous Dambusters raid. Experience Sergeant Hadfield's wartime living room. Then get tips for growing your own vegetables in our walled garden. Our new Ice House bunker has hands-on activities for all ages. **Note**: limited electric light.

Exploring
- Get to know Queen Victoria's favourite Prime Minister.
- Discover why Hughenden was top of Hitler's hit list.
- Travel back in time in our new 1940s living room.
- Delve into our new interactive Ice House bunker.
- Explore the newly flourishing walled garden.
- Stroll in the Chilterns countryside, with woodlands and chalk stream.

Eating and shopping: enjoy home-grown produce in many of our dishes. Browse in the glorious gift shop. Pick up an old treasure in our second-hand bookshop. Choose a plant from our volunteer-run stall.

Making the most of your day: varied events programme, woodland trails, introductory film, morning guided tour of manor at 11:20 in peak season. Children's hands-on activities and I-Spy sheets. **Dogs**: welcome under close control in park and woodland.

Access for all: 🅿️♿🔤♨️🏛️📷📦🎦📶📷
Building 🏛️♿♿♿ Grounds 🏛️♿

Getting here: 165:SU866955. **Foot**: 1½ miles from High Wycombe. **Bus**: Arriva 300 High Wycombe to Aylesbury (passing close High Wycombe ☰). Note: long, steep walk to house entrance. **Train**: High Wycombe 2 miles. **Road**: 1½ miles north of High Wycombe; on west side of the Great Missenden road (A4128). From M40 exit 4, take A404 towards High Wycombe, follow signs to Eden shopping centre, then take A4128 towards Great Missenden. Follow brown signs. **Parking**: free, 200 yards. Waiting possible at peak times; parking for only one coach; overflow car park, 400 yards.

You may also enjoy: on a grand scale: Waddesdon Manor, West Wycombe Park and Cliveden.

The dining room at Hughenden Manor, Buckinghamshire

Finding out more: 01494 755565 (Infoline).
01494 755573 or
hughenden@nationaltrust.org.uk

Hughenden Manor		M	T	W	T	F	S	S
Garden, shop and restaurant								
19 Feb–28 Feb	11–4	M	T	W	T	F	S	S
1 Mar–31 Oct	11–5:30	M	T	W	T	F	S	S
1 Nov–31 Dec	11–4	M	T	W	T	F	S	S
House								
19 Feb–28 Feb	11–3	M	T	W	T	F	S	S
1 Mar–31 Oct	12–5	M	T	W	T	F	S	S
1 Nov–31 Dec	11–3	M	T	W	T	F	S	S
Park								
Open all year		M	T	W	T	F	S	S

Admission by timed ticket on Bank Holidays and other
busy days. Occasional early closing for special events and
weddings. Admission by guided tour only on weekdays
during February and November. Special Christmas opening
during December. Closed 25 December.

The romantic 14th-century Ightham Mote in Kent

Ightham Mote

Mote Road, Ivy Hatch, Sevenoaks,
Kent TN15 0NT

Map (2) H6   🏠✝❀♟🏚 1985

'**An oasis of tranquillity and beauty.
Thank goodness for Mr Robinson and
the National Trust**.'
Suzie Sinden, Brendon, Devon

Lose yourself in this romantic moated manor
house, described by David Starkey as 'one of
the most beautiful and interesting of English
country houses'. Built nearly 700 years ago,
this house has seen many changes and been
owned by medieval knights, courtiers to
Henry VIII and high-society Victorians.
Highlights include the picturesque courtyard,
Great Hall, crypt, Tudor painted ceiling,
Grade I listed dog kennel and the private
apartments of Charles Henry Robinson, who
gave Ightham Mote to the National Trust in
1985. The building is surrounded by peaceful
gardens with an orchard, water features,
lakes and woodland walks. **Note**: very
steep slope from reception (lower drop-off
point available).

Exploring
– Enjoy a free introductory talk.
– See the Tudor royal
emblems and 18th-century
Chinese wallpaper.
– Join a free garden tour and
discover South Lake.
– Learn about the Trust's largest
ever conservation project.
– See for miles from
the top of the tower
(weather-permitting).

Eating and shopping: shop for gifts, local
produce and a wide variety of shrubs and
herbaceous plants. Enjoy locally sourced
food in the Mote Restaurant or attend one
of our events.

Making the most of your day: there are plenty of quizzes, activities and events to keep the children busy. Enjoy one of the many walks around the estate. **Dogs**: welcome on leads on estate walks only.

Access for all: [icons] Building [icons] Grounds [icons]

Getting here: 188:TQ584535. Between Sevenoaks and Borough Green 1¾ miles south of A25. **Bus**: Nu-Venture 404 from Sevenoaks ⬛, calls Thursday and Friday only, on other days alight Ivy Hatch, ¾ mile. Autocar 222 Tonbridge to Borough Green, alight Fairlawne estate north of Shipbourne, ½ mile by footpath. Arriva 306/8 Sevenoaks ⬛ to Gravesend, alight Ightham Common, 1½ miles. **Train**: Borough Green and Wrotham 3 miles; Hildenborough 4 miles; Sevenoaks 6 miles. **Road**: 6 miles north of Tonbridge on A227; 6 miles south of Sevenoaks on A25; 16 miles west of Maidstone on A20/A25. **Parking**: free, 200 yards.

You may also enjoy: Knole, Chartwell, Emmetts Garden, Old Soar Manor, Quebec House and Toys Hill.

Finding out more: 01732 810378 (extension 100) or ighthammote@nationaltrust.org.uk

Ightham Mote		M	T	W	T	F	S	S
House*								
5 Mar–30 Oct	11–5	M			T	F	S	S
1 Jun–31 Aug	11–5	M		W	T	F	S	S
3 Nov–18 Dec	11–3				T	F	S	S
Shop, restaurant and garden**								
5 Feb–27 Feb	11–3						S	S
5 Mar–30 Oct	10:30–5	M			T	F	S	S
1 Jun–31 Aug	10:30–5	M		W	T	F	S	S
3 Nov–18 Dec	11–3				T	F	S	S
Restaurant								
27 Dec–31 Dec	11–3		T	W	T	F	S	
Estate								
Open all year	Dawn–dusk	M	T	W	T	F	S	S

Shop: for additional opening times telephone 01732 811203. Restaurant: to enquire about opening times, book themed evenings, functions and Christmas lunch telephone 01732 811314. *November and December, 11 to 3: partial gardens, courtyard, library, ground-floor access, visitor reception and conservation exhibition. Dressed for Christmas. **Restaurant may not fully open when private function taking place. February weekends: restaurant, part of gardens, shop, visitor reception and conservation exhibition.

King's Head

King's Head Passage,
Market Square, Aylesbury,
Buckinghamshire HP20 2RW

Map ② E3

Set in the heart of this historic market town, the King's Head is one of England's best-preserved coaching inns. Dating back to 1455, the building has many fascinating architectural features, including rare stained-glass windows, exposed wattle and daub and the original stabling for the inn.

| **Exploring** | – Visit The Farmers' Bar for local beer and fine foods. |
| | – The Tourist Information Centre provides local information. |

Eating and shopping: award-winning Farmers' Bar, run by local Chiltern Brewery, provides excellent local food and fine ales.

Access for all: [icons]
Building [icon] Grounds [icon]

Getting here: 165:SP818137. At top of Market Square in the centre of Aylesbury. **Foot**: access through cobbled lane near the war memorial. **Bus**: from surrounding areas. **Train**: Aylesbury 400 yards. **Sat Nav**: will bring you into Aylesbury, but not the King's Head. **Parking**: no onsite parking. Car parks in town centre (not National Trust).

Finding out more: 01296 381501 or kingshead@nationaltrust.org.uk

King's Head

Farmers' Bar open all year round – normal pub opening hours apply.

Knole

Sevenoaks, Kent TN15 0RP

Map ② H6 1946

'**Knole encapsulates everything a great day out should be – the place is beautiful and the welcome warm and sincere**.'
Mrs N. Warrener, Crowborough, East Sussex

Knole has been shown off to visitors for the past 500 years. Thirteen show rooms remain much as they were in the 18th century, when they were laid out to impress visitors with the Sackvilles' wealth. The birthplace and childhood home of Vita Sackville-West, who went on to create the gardens at Sissinghurst, Knole was also the setting for Virgina Woolf's novel *Orlando*. The house includes world-renowned Stuart furniture, important paintings and the prototype of the famous Knole settee. Knole is set at the heart of the only remaining medieval deer park in Kent (sika and fallow deer roam freely). **Note**: wheelchair access impossible beyond Great Hall (virtual reality tour available). Possible work in show rooms.

Exploring
  – Visit the newly opened Orangery and visitor centre.
  – Explore Lord Sackville's private garden (Tuesdays, April to September).
  – Discover more with the family courtyard guide 'Speaking Stones'.
  – Significant conservation project being undertaken in the show rooms.
  – Explore the deer park, a Site of Special Scientific Interest.
  – See the October deer rut on a special guided walk.

Eating and shopping: treat yourself to some local produce in the Knole shop. Browse through a large selection of books, gifts and children's pocket money toys. Enjoy a delicious home-cooked lunch or afternoon cream tea in the original 'Brew House' tea-room.

Making the most of your day: guided park walks and school holiday family trails and activities. Housekeeping days, evening candlelit tours, Christmas workshops and carol concerts. Annual plant and book stall.
Dogs: welcome on leads and in the park only.

Access for all: [icons] House [icons] Grounds [icons]

Getting here: 188:TQ532543. **Foot**: park entrance at south end of Sevenoaks town centre, opposite St Nicholas's church.
Bus: from surrounding area to Sevenoaks, ¾-mile walk. **Train**: Sevenoaks 1½ miles.
Road: leave M25 at exit 5 (A21). Park entrance in Sevenoaks town centre off A225 Tonbridge Road (opposite St Nicholas's church).
Sat Nav: some Sat Nav systems may not direct you to Knole. **Parking**: 60 yards, £4 for non-members. Parking available when house, shop, tea-room or garden are open, otherwise parking available in nearby town centre. Vehicle gates open 10:15 and locked at 6.

The elegant Orangery at Knole, Kent

Members may have to pay on special events days

You may also enjoy: Sissinghurst Castle Garden, the creation of Vita Sackville-West and her husband, Harold Nicolson.

Finding out more: 01732 450608 (Infoline). 01732 462100 or knole@nationaltrust.org.uk

Knole	M	T	W	T	F	S	S
House							
12 Mar–30 Oct	12–4	·	·	·	W	T	F	S	S
Shop, tea-room, visitor centre, Orangery and courtyards							
5 Mar–6 Mar	11–4	·	·	·	·	·	S	S
12 Mar–3 Apr	10:30–5	·	·	W	T	F	S	S
5 Apr–2 Oct	10:30–5	·	T	W	T	F	S	S
5 Oct–30 Oct	10:30–5	·	·	W	T	F	S	S
2 Nov–23 Dec	11–4	·	·	W	T	F	S	S
Garden							
5 Apr–27 Sep	11–4	·	T	·	·	·	·

Open Bank Holiday Mondays. Garden open Tuesdays only between April and September. As this is a private garden, seating is limited and plants are not labelled. Vehicles not admitted when whole of property is closed. Park open daily for pedestrians.

Lamb House

West Street, Rye, East Sussex TN31 7ES

Map ② J8 1950

Fine brick-fronted house with literary associations – both Henry James and E. F. Benson lived here. Surprisingly large town garden. **Note**: administered and largely maintained on the National Trust's behalf by a tenant. No toilets.

Access for all: ⦂ Building 🔏 Grounds 🔏

Getting here: 198:TQ920202. In West Street, facing west end of church.

Finding out more: 01580 762334 or lambhouse@nationaltrust.org.uk

Lamb House	M	T	W	T	F	S	S
15 Mar–22 Oct	2–6	·	T	·	·	S	·

Leith Hill

Leith Hill, near Coldharbour village, Dorking, Surrey

Map ② F7 1923

Climb the spiral staircase and, at more than 1,000 feet, become the highest person in south-east England. Enjoy panoramic views and see how many landmarks can be spotted with the aid of the telescope. Follow the circular nature trail and then reward yourself with refreshments from the tea servery. **Note**: no toilet. Henman basecamp (for recreational, corporate, conservation working groups). Etherley Farm Campsite 01306 621423.

Exploring
 – New 360-degree panoramic leaflet/quiz available from tower.
 – Child entry includes panoramic leaflet/quiz, pencil and telescope token.
 – New guide to Rhododendron Wood available from car-park noticeboard.

Eating and shopping: light refreshments sold from tower (opening hours only).

Making the most of your day: programme of guided walks and activities, including children's fun afternoons throughout the year. Two circular waymarked nature trails, with accompanying leaflet available from tower and Rhododendron Wood noticeboards. **Dogs**: under close control in Rhododendron Wood.

Access for all: Tower 🔏

Getting here: 187:TQ139432. 1 mile south-west of Coldharbour village. **Foot**: comprehensive network of rights of way, including the Greensand Way National Trail. **Cycle**: many rights of way. **Bus**: Arriva 21 Guildford to Dorking (passing close Guildford ≋ and passing Chilworth ≋ and Dorking), alight Holmbury St Mary, 2½ miles, not on Sunday or public holidays. **Train**: Holmwood, not Sunday, 2½ miles; Dorking 5½ miles.

The 18th-century Gothic Leith Hill Tower in Surrey

Road: 1 mile south-west of Coldharbour A29/B2126. **Parking**: free in designated areas along road at foot of the hill (some steep gradients to tower). No direct vehicle access to summit. Rhododendron Wood £2.50 per car.

Finding out more: 01306 712711 or leithhill@nationaltrust.org.uk

Leith Hill		M	T	W	T	F	S	S
Countryside								
Open all year		M	T	W	T	F	S	S
Tower								
1 Jan–26 Mar	10–3:30	·	·	·	·	·	S	S
22 Feb–25 Feb	10–3:30	·	T	W	T	F	·	··
27 Mar–29 Oct	10–5	·	·	·	·	F	S	S
31 May–3 Jun	10–5	·	T	W	T	·	·	·
2 Aug–4 Sep	10–5	·	T	W	T	F	S	S
25 Oct–28 Oct	10–5	·	T	W	T	F	·	·
30 Oct–31 Dec	10–3:30	·	·	·	·	·	S	S

Open Bank Holidays, except 25 December (tower).
Now open half-term weeks, except Monday
(unless Bank Holiday).

Long Crendon Courthouse

Long Crendon, Aylesbury,
Buckinghamshire HP18 9AN

Map ② D4   🏠 1900

This building is a fine example of early timber-frame construction. The ground floor (now tenanted) was the village poor house. **Note**: extremely steep stairs. Village exhibition on display. No toilet.

Access for all: Building ⬆

Getting here: 165:SP698091. Next to the parish church at the end of High Street.

Finding out more: 01280 822850 or longcrendon@nationaltrust.org.uk

Long Crendon Courthouse		M	T	W	T	F	S	S
2 Apr–25 Sep	11–6	·	·	·	·	·	S	S
6 Apr–28 Sep	2–6	·	·	W	·	·	·	·

Open Bank Holiday Mondays, 11 to 6.

Monk's House

Rodmell, Lewes, East Sussex BN7 3HF

Map ② G8   🏠 ✿ 1980

18th-century weatherboarded cottage, novelist Virginia Woolf's country retreat – featuring the room where she created her best-known works. **Note**: administered and largely maintained on the National Trust's behalf by a tenant.

Access for all: 🅿 Building ⬆ Grounds ⬆ ♿

Getting here: 198:TQ421063. In Rodmell village, near church, 4 miles south of Lewes.

Finding out more: 01323 870001 or monkshouse@nationaltrust.org.uk

Monk's House		M	T	W	T	F	S	S
2 Apr–29 Oct	2–5:30	·	·	W	·	·	S	·

Mottisfont

Mottisfont, near Romsey, Hampshire SO51 OLP

Map ② C7  1957

At the heart of this tranquil rural estate is Mottisfont, set in glorious grounds alongside the fast-flowing River Test. There are many layers of history for the visitor to explore, including the Gothic remains of the original 13th-century Augustinian priory. In the mid-20th century the final private owner, society hostess and patron of the arts Maud Russell, used the Abbey as a base for her racy and intriguing life. The River Test is one of the finest chalk streams in the world, and the walled gardens house the National Collection of old-fashioned roses. **Note**: during the rose season in June weekday and/or evening visits are recommended.

Exploring
- New art gallery opens this year.
- See Rex Whistler's *trompe l'oeil* design in the drawing room.
- Winter garden, 60,000 spring bulbs, late summer borders, autumn colour.
- Picnic on the lawn, under our majestic plane trees.
- Build dens, run, jump or enjoy our creative play space.
- Explore Mottisfont's wider estate by bike or on foot.

Eating and shopping: taste Mottisfont's locally sourced home-made food, including 'cake of the month'. Cool down in the Angel Ice-cream Parlour, serving a delicious choice of local ice-creams. Browse and buy in our Coach House shop. Find a bargain in the second-hand bookshop.

Making the most of your day: a comprehensive events programme runs throughout the year. Enjoy our popular open-air theatre, guided walks and talks, and throughout the school holidays take part in activity days and trails. **Dogs**: welcome in designated areas and the estate walk.

Access for all: 🅿️♿🦽🚾👶🖼️🎨💻🔈🅰️
Building ♿♿ **Grounds** ♿➡️

Getting here: 185:SU327270. In Test Valley between Romsey and Stockbridge. **Foot**: on Hampshire's long-distance path, Testway. Clarendon Way 2 miles north. **Cycle**: on Testway. **Train**: Dunbridge 1½ miles. **Road**: signposted off A3057 Romsey to Stockbridge, 4½ miles north of Romsey. Also signposted off B3087 Romsey to Broughton. **Parking**: free.

You may also enjoy: a visit to The Vyne.

Finding out more: 01794 340757 or mottisfont@nationaltrust.org.uk

Mottisfont		M	T	W	T	F	S	S
Garden, shop and café								
1 Jan–20 Feb	10–5	M	·	·	·	F	S	S
4 Nov–19 Dec	10–5	M	·	·	·	F	S	S
26 Dec–31 Dec	10–5	M	T	W	T	F	S	·
Garden, shop, café and house*								
21 Feb–31 Oct	10–5	M	T	W	T	F	S	S

Closes dusk if earlier. *House opens 11. **Late opening (except house and café) to 8 on 10 to 12, 17 to 19 and 24 to 26 June for roses in the Walled Garden.**

Mottisfont, Hampshire, is set in glorious grounds alongside the River Test

Mottistone Manor Garden

Mottistone, Isle of Wight PO30 4EA

Map ② C9 ❄🏊🏛🏠 1965

Set in a sheltered valley this magical garden is full of surprises, with shrub-filled banks, hidden pathways and colourful herbaceous borders. Surrounding an attractive Elizabethan manor house this 20th-century garden is experimenting with a Mediterranean-style planting scheme to take advantage of its southerly location. Other surprises include a young olive grove, a small organic kitchen garden and a traditional tea garden set alongside The Shack, a unique cabin retreat designed as their summer drawing office by architects John Seely (2nd Lord Mottistone) and Paul Paget. There are also delightful walks across the adjoining Mottistone Estate. **Note**: manor house is only open one day a year.

Exploring
- Enjoy this hillside garden throughout the seasons.
- Relish the informality – a bit on the wild side.
- Discover our resident flowerpot people.
- Explore the garden with a family discovery trail.
- Venture inside The Shack, a unique 1930s garden cabin.
- Extend your visit with a walk to the Long Stone.

Eating and shopping: browse in our gift shop. Take home a plant from the plant stall. Snap up a second-hand book bargain. Relax in the tea garden (not National Trust).

Making the most of your day: programme of family events and garden tours. Flowerpot trail and estate walks. **Dogs**: welcome on leads only.

Access for all: 🅿️♿🚻♿♿📷📷🎧🅰️
Grounds ♿♿➡♿

Rose borders at Mottistone Manor Garden, Isle of Wight

Getting here: 196:SZ406838. **Foot**: 1 mile north of coastal path; 1 mile south of Tennyson Trail. **Cycle**: NCN67. On the 'Round the Island' cycle route. **Ferry**: Yarmouth (Wightlink Ltd) 5 miles (0871 376 1000); East Cowes (Red Funnel) 16 miles (0844 844 9988). **Bus**: Southern Vectis 7 Newport to Alum Bay. **Road**: at Mottistone, between Brighstone and Brook on B3399. **Parking**: free, 50 yards.

You may also enjoy: The Needles Old Battery, Newtown Old Town Hall, Bembridge Windmill and Brighstone Shop and Museum.

Finding out more: 01983 741302 or mottistonemanor@nationaltrust.org.uk

Mottistone Manor Garden		M	T	W	T	F	S	S
13 Mar–27 Oct	11–5	**M**	**T**	**W**	**T**	·	·	**S**

Closes dusk if earlier. House open Bank Holiday Monday 30 May only, 2 to 5. Additional charges apply. Guided tours for members on that day 9:30 to 12 by timed ticket (available on the day). Late night opening: Wednesday 22 June, garden open until 9.

The Needles Old Battery and New Battery

West High Down, Alum Bay,
Isle of Wight PO39 OJH

Map ② C9  1975

Perched high above the Needles, amid acres of unspoilt countryside, is the Needles Old Battery, a Victorian fort built in 1862 and used throughout both world wars. The Parade Ground has two original guns and the Fort's fascinating military history is brought to life with a series of vivid cartoons by acclaimed comic book artist Geoff Campion. An underground tunnel leads to a searchlight emplacement with dramatic views over the Needles rocks. The New Battery, further up the headland, has an exhibition on the secret British rocket tests carried out there during the Cold War. **Note**: steep paths and uneven surfaces. Spiral staircase to tunnel. Toilet at Old Battery only.

Exploring
— Enjoy dramatic sea views from the clifftop walk.
— Discover the rooms where soldiers worked with gunpowder.
— Explore the site with a family activity pack.
— See the Needles from our wheelchair-friendly viewing platform.
— Don't miss one of our most unusual tea-rooms.
— Discover recently revealed secrets of Britain's rocket test programme.

Eating and shopping: enjoy homemade food in our clifftop tea-room. Treat yourself to a souvenir in the guardroom shop. Drinks and ice-creams available at the New Battery kiosk.

Making the most of your day: programme of family events. Family activity packs, children's quiz and soldier trail. Clifftop walks to Tennyson Monument and beyond.
Dogs: welcome on leads only.

Access for all: 🅿️ 🚻 ♿ 📷 🖥️ ♿ 📷
Building ♿♿♿ Grounds ♿♿♿

Getting here: 196:SZ300848. **Foot**: access on foot only from Alum Bay ¾ mile along a well-surfaced private road, Highdown National Trust car park 2 miles across the Downs, Freshwater Bay 3½ miles across the Downs. **Cycle**: NCN67, ½ mile 'Round the Island' route. **Ferry**: Yarmouth (Wightlink Ltd) 5 miles (0871 376 1000); East Cowes (Red Funnel) 16 miles (0844 844 9988). **Bus**: Southern Vectis 7 Newport to Alum Bay, then ¾ mile. Southern Vectis 'Needles Tour' from Yarmouth and Alum Bay (March to October). Half-price fare for members on production of membership card. No bus or disabled vehicular access on 15 May. **Road**: Alum Bay west of Freshwater Bay (B3322). No bus or disabled vehicular access on 15 May. **Parking**: no onsite parking. Limited disabled parking by prior arrangement with property. Car park at Alum Bay (not National Trust; minimum charge £4), or in Freshwater Bay (Isle of Wight Council) or Highdown car park SZ325856 (National Trust) and walk over Downs.

You may also enjoy: Mottistone Manor Garden, Newtown Old Town Hall, Bembridge Windmill and Brighstone Shop and Museum.

Bird spotting at The Needles Old Battery, Isle of Wight

Finding out more: 01983 754772 or needlesoldbattery@nationaltrust.org.uk

The Needles Batteries		M	T	W	T	F	S	S
Tea-room								
8 Jan–27 Feb	11–3	·	·	·	·	·	S	S
Old Battery and tea-room								
12 Mar–30 Oct	10:30–5	M	T	W	T	F	S	S
Tea-room								
5 Nov–11 Dec	11–3	·	·	·	·	·	S	S
New Battery*								
12 Mar–30 Oct	11–4	·	T	·	·	·	S	S

Old Battery closes dusk if earlier. Property closes in high winds: telephone on day of visit to check. *Open other days where possible: please telephone to check. 25 June: Old Battery opens at 6:30 for Round the Island Yacht Race.

Newtown Old Town Hall

Newtown, Newport, Isle of Wight PO30 4PA

Map ② C9   🏛 1933

Tucked away in a tiny hamlet adjoining the National Nature Reserve, the 17th-century Old Town Hall is the only remaining evidence of Newtown's former importance. It's hard to believe that this tranquil corner of the island once held often turbulent elections before sending two Members to Parliament. **Note**: nearest toilet in car park.

Exploring
- Discover the surprising local and political history.
- Learn about the mysterious Ferguson Gang who saved the Hall.
- Enjoy regular art and photographic exhibitions.
- Take a delightful estuary walk.

Eating and shopping: treat yourself to a small memento of your visit.

Making the most of your day: children's quiz sheet. Programme of countryside family activities (bookable) run by the Newtown Warden from a nearby Visitor Point. Nature Reserve information, 01983 531622.

Access for all: 🚾♿📷📹📖♿ Building ♿

Getting here: 196:SZ424905. **Cycle**: NCN67, ½ mile. **Ferry**: Yarmouth (Wightlink Ltd) 5 miles (0871 376 1000); East Cowes (Red Funnel) 11 miles (0844 844 9988). **Bus**: Wightbus 35 from Newport; otherwise Southern Vectis 7 Newport to Yarmouth, alight Shalfleet, Barton's Corner, 1 mile. **Road**: Newtown is between Newport and Yarmouth, 1 mile north of A3054. **Parking**: free, 15 yards. Not suitable for coaches.

Finding out more: 01983 531785 or oldtownhall@nationaltrust.org.uk

Newtown Old Town Hall		M	T	W	T	F	S	S
13 Mar–30 Jun	2–5	·	T	W	T	·	·	S
3 Jul–31 Aug	2–5	M	T	W	T	·	·	S
1 Sep–27 Oct	2–5	·	T	W	T	·	·	S

Last admission 15 minutes before closing. Closes dusk if earlier than 5. Also open Bank Holiday Mondays.

Nymans

Handcross, Haywards Heath, West Sussex RH17 6EB

Map ② G7   1954

In the late 19th century an unusually creative family bought the Nymans estate, in the picturesque High Weald landscape of Sussex, to make a home in the country. Inspired by the setting and the soil, the Messels created one of the great gardens, with experimental designs and new plants from around the world. Here they entertained family and friends, enjoying relaxing times, strolling in the garden, playing, picnicking and walking in the woods. Enjoy Nymans in the way they did. We are reinventing Nymans for the 21st century by running the estate in a new, greener way. **Note**: now open seven days per week.

Exploring
- Experience beauty and seasonal colours all year.
- Learn about one of the Trust's greenest gardens.
- Discover intriguing ruins, summerhouses and the house filled with flowers.

The colourful summer borders in the Walled Garden at Nymans, West Sussex

Exploring
- Learn about creative family: Oliver Messel - designer; Lord Snowdon - photographer.
- Enjoy splendid views across the Sussex countryside.
- Savour delicious local food and buy unique local crafts.

Eating and shopping: large shop supporting local products. Garden centre and nursery sells plants propagated from the garden. New-look restaurant: open-air covered seating, serving home-cooked food. Refresh yourself at the garden catering buggy.

Making the most of your day: information point, trails and iPod audio guides. Mobility buggy tours of garden/woods. Bamboo jungle. Events include family activities, open-air theatre, gardening workshops, woodland wildlife walks. **Dogs**: welcome in the woodland only.

Access for all:
House **Garden**

Getting here: 187:TQ265294. 5 miles south of Crawley. **Foot**: 5 miles by footpath from Balcombe. **Cycle**: on the National Cycle Network route 20. **Bus**: Metrobus 273 Brighton to Crawley, 271 Haywards Heath to Crawley. Both stop outside Nymans. Both pass Crawley. **Train**: Balcombe 4 miles; Crawley 5 miles. **Road**: on B2114 at Handcross, just off London to Brighton M23/A23. **Parking**: free. Designated coach bays.

You may also enjoy: Standen's Arts and Crafts, the landscape garden at Sheffield Park and Devil's Dyke's countryside.

Finding out more: 01444 405250 or nymans@nationaltrust.org.uk

Nymans		M	T	W	T	F	S	S
Garden, woods, restaurant, shop and plant centre								
1 Jan–28 Feb	10–4	**M**	**T**	**W**	**T**	**F**	**S**	**S**
1 Mar–31 Oct	10–5	**M**	**T**	**W**	**T**	**F**	**S**	**S**
1 Nov–24 Dec	10–4	**M**	**T**	**W**	**T**	**F**	**S**	**S**
House								
2 Mar–31 Oct	11–3	**M**	·	**W**	**T**	**F**	**S**	**S**

Oakhurst Cottage

Hambledon, near Godalming, Surrey GU8 4HF

Map ② E7 1952

A restored and furnished simple labourer's dwelling, containing artefacts reflecting four centuries of continual occupation, with delightful cottage garden. **Note**: no toilet.

Access for all:

Getting here: 186:SU965380. Off A283 between Wormley and Chiddingfold.

Finding out more: 01798 342207 or oakhurstcottage@nationaltrust.org.uk

Oakhurst Cottage	M	T	W	T	F	S	S
6 Apr–30 Oct 2–5				W	T		S	S

Admission by guided tour and appointment only. Open Bank Holiday Mondays, 2 to 5. Please book, preferably at least three days in advance.

Old Soar Manor

Plaxtol, Borough Green, Kent TN15 0QX

Map ② H6 1947

Rare remaining structure of a late 13th-century knight's dwelling, including solar chamber, barrel-vaulted undercroft, chapel and garderobe. **Note**: no toilet.

Access for all: Building

Getting here: 188:TQ619541. 2 miles south of Borough Green (A25); approached via A227 and Plaxtol.

Finding out more: 01732 810378 (extension 100) or oldsoarmanor@nationaltrust.org.uk

Old Soar Manor	M	T	W	T	F	S	S
2 Apr–29 Sep 10–6	M	T	W	T		S	S

Owletts

The Street, Cobham, Gravesend, Kent DA12 3AP

Closed this year.

Petworth House and Park

Petworth, West Sussex GU28 0AE

Map ② E7 1947

The vast late 17th-century mansion is set in a beautiful 283-hectare (700-acre) deer park, landscaped by 'Capability' Brown and immortalised in Turner's paintings. The house contains the National Trust's finest collection of pictures, with numerous works by Turner, Van Dyck, Reynolds and Blake, ancient and Neo-classical sculpture, fine furniture and carvings by Grinling Gibbons. The servants' quarters contain fascinating kitchens (including a copper *batterie de cuisine* of more than 1,000 pieces) and other service rooms. On weekdays additional rooms in the house are open by kind permission of Lord and Lady Egremont.

Exploring
- Discover the National Trust's largest painting and sculpture collection.
- See the 'Leconfield Aphrodite', a sculpture from fourth century BC.
- Year-round horticultural interest in the Pleasure Ground.
- Explore the magnificent park, landscaped by 'Capability' Brown.
- Magnificent historic kitchens with 1,000 copper pots and moulds.
- Find the largest herd of fallow deer in England.

Petworth House and Park, West Sussex: the house contains the Trust's finest picture collection

Parking: 700 yards. Coaches can drop off at Church Lodge entrance and park in house car park. Petworth Park car park: £2 charge for non-members.

You may also enjoy: 18th-century Uppark House and Garden.

Finding out more: 01798 343929 (Infoline). 01798 342207 or petworth@nationaltrust.org.uk

Petworth House and Park		M	T	W	T	F	S	S
House								
12 Mar–2 Nov	11–5	M	T	W	·	·	S	S
Shop and restaurant								
12 Feb–9 Mar	10:30–3:30	M	T	W	·	·	S	S
12 Mar–2 Nov	11–5	M	T	W	·	·	S	S
9 Nov–18 Dec	10:30–3:30	·	·	W	T	F	S	S
Pleasure Ground								
12 Feb–9 Mar	10:30–3:30	M	T	W	·	·	S	S
12 Mar–2 Nov	11–6	M	T	W	·	·	S	S
9 Nov–18 Dec	10:30–3:30	·	·	W	T	F	S	S

Open Good Friday. **Extra rooms shown weekdays from 1:** Monday (not Bank Holiday Mondays), White and Gold Room and White Library; Tuesday and Wednesday, three bedrooms on first floor.

Eating and shopping: Audit Room Restaurant offers local and seasonal home-cooked food. Visit the National Trust shop, with its extensive gift selection. Look out for the plants and garden products for sale, also, hand-turned Petworth wood gifts.

Making the most of your day: extensive and varied event and exhibition programme, including open-air opera, tours and guided walks. **Dogs**: under close control in park only (not Pleasure Ground).

Access for all: ⊞ ⊞ ⊞ ⊞ ⊞ ⊞ ⊞ ⊞ ⊞ ⊞ ⊞ ⊞ ⊞ Building ⊞ ⊞ ⊞ ⊞

Getting here: 197:SU976218. In centre of Petworth. **Bus**: Stagecoach in the South Downs 1 Worthing to Midhurst (passing Pulborough ⊠); Compass 76 Horsham to Petworth (passing Horsham ⊠). **Train**: Pulborough 5¼ miles. **Road**: in centre of Petworth (A272/A283); both house and park car parks on A283; pedestrian access from Petworth town and A272. No vehicles in park.

Pitstone Windmill

Ivinghoe, Buckinghamshire

Map ② E3   ⊠ ⊞ 1937

A rare and striking example of an early form of windmill. **Note**: no toilet. Located at the end of a rough track.

Access for all: Building ⊞

Getting here: 181:SP945157. ½ mile south of Ivinghoe, 3 miles north-east of Tring, just west of the B488.

Finding out more: 01442 851227 or pitstonemill@nationaltrust.org.uk

Pitstone Windmill		M	T	W	T	F	S	S
29 May–28 Aug	2:30–6	·	·	·	·	·	·	S

Open Bank Holiday Mondays 30 May and 29 August. Due to staffing restrictions, property may not open as publicised (telephone to check).

One of the many stunning interiors at Polesden Lacey in Surrey

Polesden Lacey

Great Bookham, near Dorking, Surrey RH5 6BD

Map (2) F6 1942

An Edwardian country estate designed to be the perfect setting for a millionairess hostess to entice royalty, politicians and the best of Edwardian society for entertaining weekends in the country. The house, with its notably stunning interiors and collection, delightful gardens and superb views across the rolling Surrey hills is waiting to be explored. Immerse yourself in the lifestyle where nothing was too much trouble for your hostess, while discovering the secrets that Polesden Lacey has to tell from the parties it has seen. Wander through the beautiful walled garden, before strolling through the extensive grounds and landscape walks.

Exploring
- Newly opened areas of the house.
- Feel like one of Mrs Greville's house-party guests.
- Enjoy the stunning formal gardens, including the famous Rose Garden.

Exploring
- Take in the beautiful countryside on a landscape walk.
- Discover nature and history with family activities and play area.
- Enjoy the music and drama festival, 1 to 3 July.

Eating and shopping: savour home-cooked seasonal menus at our restaurant. Treat yourself to homemade cakes in our coffee shop. Unique shopping experience, including items from Surrey artists. Live the Polesden Lacey life in our holiday cottage.

Making the most of your day: welcome talks and guided tours, extensive events programme, including specialist tours and opening of the house weekends November to February. Shops and restaurant located outside the pay perimeter. **Dogs**: on leads in designated areas, under close control on landscape walks, estate and farmland.

Access for all: Building Grounds

Getting here: 187:TQ136522. **Foot**: North Downs Way within ¾ mile. **Bus**: Countryliner 479 Guildford to Epsom, alight Great Bookham, 1½ miles. **Train**: Boxhill and Westhumble 2 miles; Dorking 4 miles.

Road: 5 miles north-west of Dorking, 2 miles south of Great Bookham, off A246 Leatherhead to Guildford road. **Parking**: 200 yards (pay and display), 7:30 to dusk. £2.50 charge for non-members, redeemable against purchases over £10 in shops or restaurant or membership taken out at Polesden Lacey. No charges 1 to 23 December.

You may also enjoy: Clandon Park, Hatchlands Park and Box Hill.

Finding out more: 01372 458203 (Infoline). 01372 452048 or polesdenlacey@nationaltrust.org.uk

Polesden Lacey		M	T	W	T	F	S	S
House								
8 Jan–27 Feb*	11–4						S	S
2 Mar–30 Oct	11–5			W	T	F	S	S
5 Nov–27 Nov*	11–4						S	S
3 Dec–18 Dec	11–4						S	S
Gardens, restaurant, gift and garden shop, and coffee shop								
1 Jan–18 Feb	10–4	M	T	W	T	F	S	S
19 Feb–30 Oct**	10–5	M	T	W	T	F	S	S
31 Oct–31 Dec***	10–4	M	T	W	T	F	S	S
Car park								
1 Jan–31 Dec	7:30–6:30	M	T	W	T	F	S	S

Open Bank Holiday Mondays. *Weekends in January, February, November house entry by guided tour only. **Closed 15 March. ***Closed 24 and 25 December.

Priory Cottages

1 Mill Street, Steventon, Abingdon, Oxfordshire OX13 6SP

Map ② C5   1939

Former monastic buildings, now converted into two houses. Properties were gifted by the famous Ferguson's Gang. **Note**: Priory Cottage South only open. No toilet.

Getting here: 164:SU466914. 4 miles south of Abingdon.

Finding out more: 01793 762209 or priorycottages@nationaltrust.org.uk

Priory Cottages		M	T	W	T	F	S	S
7 Apr–29 Sep	2–6				T			

Admission by written appointment with the tenant.

Quebec House

Quebec Square, Westerham, Kent TN16 1TD

Map ② G6   1918

This Grade I-listed gabled house in the beautiful village of Westerham has features of significant architectural and historical interest. Quebec House was the childhood home of General James Wolfe and is full of family and military memorabilia. The coach house contains an exhibition about the 1759 Battle of Quebec.

Exploring
- Charming 16th-century family home.
- Pretty garden with newly created vegetable plot and herb beds.
- New exhibition telling the story of the Battle of Quebec.
- Look out for the fascinating architectural features.

Eating and shopping: enjoy tea, coffee and homemade cakes and biscuits. Delightful shop in the old coach house.

Making the most of your day: exciting events programme, including special talks, children's activities and family trails.

Access for all: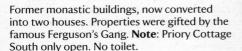
Building ⬚⬚⬚⬚ Grounds ⬚

The gabled façade of Quebec House in Kent

Getting here: 187:TQ449541. **Bus**: SelKent 246 from Bromley North ≣ (passing Bromley South ≣); Arriva 401 from Sevenoaks ≣ (also Tunbridge Wells ≣ Sundays). **Train**: Sevenoaks 4 miles; Oxted 4 miles. **Road**: at east end of village, on north side of A25, facing junction with B2026 Edenbridge road. M25 exit 5 or 6. **Parking**: 200 yards east of Quebec House on A25 (not National Trust). Visitors should follow footpath beside A25 to house.

Finding out more: 01732 868381 or quebechouse@nationaltrust.org.uk. Chartwell Office, Mapleton Road, Westerham, Kent TN16 1PS

Quebec House		M	T	W	T	F	S	S
House								
12 Mar–30 Oct	1–5	·	·	·	W	T	F	S	S
5 Nov–18 Dec	1–5	·	·	·	·	·	S	S
Garden and exhibition								
12 Mar–30 Oct	12–5	·	·	·	W	T	F	S	S

Open Bank Holiday Mondays.

The towpath at the River Wey Navigations, Surrey

River Wey and Godalming Navigations and Dapdune Wharf

Navigations Office and Dapdune Wharf, Wharf Road, Guildford, Surrey GU1 4RR

Map ② F6  1964

The Wey was one of the first British rivers to be made navigable, and opened to barge traffic in 1653. This 15½-mile waterway linked Guildford to Weybridge on the Thames, and then to London. The Godalming Navigation, opened in 1764, enabled barges to work a further four miles upriver. The award-winning visitor centre at Dapdune Wharf in Guildford tells the story of the Navigations and the people who lived and worked on them. Visitors can see where the huge Wey barges were built and climb aboard *Reliance*, one of three surviving barges. **Note**: mooring and fishing fees payable by all, including members.

Exploring
- Take a boat trip on our electric launch.
- Climb aboard *Reliance*, one of the last surviving Wey barges.
- Enjoy the peace and tranquillity of a towpath walk.
- Have a go at pond dipping in the creek.
- For schools: our river studies workshop.

Eating and shopping: small tea-room serves sandwiches, ice-cream and drinks. Small shop with plant sales. Picnic areas at Dapdune Wharf.

Making the most of your day: year-round events programme, with children-focused events at Dapdune and programme of guided walks along the towpath and beyond. Annual Guildford Festival Boat Gathering in July. Overnight moorings available. **Dogs**: on leads at Dapdune Wharf and lock areas; elsewhere under control.

Access for all: ⬛ Grounds ⬛

Getting here: 186:SU993502. **River**: visiting craft can enter from the Thames at Shepperton or slipways at Guildford or Pyrford. Visitor moorings available at Dapdune Wharf and along towpath side of Navigations. **Foot**: North Downs Way crosses Navigations south of Guildford. Easy access from town centre on foot via towpath. **Bus**: Arriva 28 Guildford to Epsom. Stagecoach 20 Guildford to Aldershot. Safeguard 4 Guildford to Park Barn (cricket ground), 100 yards. **Train**: Addlestone ≣, Byfleet and New Haw, Guildford, Farncombe and Godalming all close to the Navigations. **Road**: Dapdune Wharf is on Wharf Road to rear of Surrey County Cricket Ground, off Woodbridge Road (A322), Guildford. Access to rest of Navigations from A3 and M25. **Parking**: free, 10 yards at Dapdune Wharf. Parking for the Navigations in Godalming town centre, Catteshall Road bridge. Dapdune Wharf: Bowers Lane (Guildford), Send village, Newark Lane (B367) and New Haw Lock.

You may also enjoy: Shalford Mill, an evocative example of an earlier industrial age.

Finding out more: 01483 561389 or riverwey@nationaltrust.org.uk

Dapdune Wharf			M	T	W	T	F	S	S
Dapdune Wharf									
26 Mar–30 Oct	11–5		M	·	·	T	F	S	S
30 May–5 Jun	11–5		M	T	W	T	F	S	S
1 Aug–31 Aug	11–5		M	T	W	T	F	S	S
24 Oct–30 Oct	11–5		M	T	W	T	F	S	S

River trips 11 to 4 (conditions permitting). Access to towpath during daylight hours all year.

Runnymede

near Old Windsor, Surrey

Map ② F5   1931

Runnymede is a famous historical site which witnessed, in 1215, King John's sealing of Magna Carta. Set within the beautiful natural landscape are various memorials by Maufe, Jellicoe and Lutyens. The memorials commemorate moments in world history and provide the perfect countryside setting in which to remember and reflect. **Note**: toilet only available when tea-room is open. Mooring/fishing fees payable, including members.

Runnymede, Surrey: natural beauty and great history

Exploring
- Reflect on world history at the memorials.
- Stroll along the River Thames path.
- Wander through the historic meadows.
- Explore the ancient woodlands.

Eating and shopping: tea-room (not National Trust). Runnymede Art Gallery open all year. For upcoming artists and exhibitions visit www.runnymedegallery.com. River boat trips available from Runnymede; contact French Brothers for more information, visit www.frenchbrothers.co.uk.

Making the most of your day: guided walks throughout the year and Easter Egg Trail event on Easter Monday. **Dogs**: under close control or on leads near livestock.

Access for all: 🚾 ⊡ ♿
Building 🏛 Grounds 👫 ♿

Getting here: 176:TQ007720. By River Thames, 2 miles west of Runnymede Bridge. **Foot**: 1¼ miles of Thames Path, National Trail. **Cycle**: 1¼ miles of Thames Path. **Bus**: First 71 Windsor Heathrow, alight 'Bells of Ouzeley'. **Train**: Egham ≅, 1¼ miles from memorials. **Road**: by River Thames, 2 miles west of Runnymede Bridge, on south side of A308 (M25, exit 13), 6 miles east of Windsor. **Parking**: pay and display. Limited space for coaches on hard-standing. Riverside grass/seasonal car park closed when wet.

Finding out more: 01784 432891 or runnymede@nationaltrust.org.uk. Runnymede Estate Office, North Lodge, Windsor Road, Old Windsor, Berkshire SL4 2JL

Runnymede		M	T	W	T	F	S	S
Countryside								
Open all year		M	T	W	T	F	S	S
Memorials car park (hard-standing)								
2 Jan–1 Apr	8:30–5	M	T	W	T	F	S	S
2 Apr–30 Sep	8:30–7	M	T	W	T	F	S	S
1 Oct–31 Dec	8:30–5	M	T	W	T	F	S	S
Riverside car park (grass/seasonal)								
2 Apr–30 Sep	10–7	M	T	W	T	F	S	S

Car parks may close at dusk if earlier. Car parks closed 25 and 26 December. Riverside grass car park open when ground and weather conditions permit.

St John's Jerusalem

Sutton-at-Hone, Dartford, Kent DA4 9HQ

Map ② H5 [✝] [✿] [1943]

This 13th-century chapel, surrounded by a tranquil moated garden, was part of the former Commandery of the Knights Hospitallers. **Note**: occupied as a private residence, maintained and managed by a tenant on National Trust's behalf.

Access for all: [••] Chapel [♿] Grounds [♿]

Getting here: 177:TQ558703. 3 miles south of Dartford at Sutton-at-Hone.

Finding out more: 01732 810378 (c/o Ightham Mote) or stjohnsjerusalem@nationaltrust.org.uk

St John's Jerusalem		M	T	W	T	F	S	S
6 Apr–28 Sep	2–6	·	·	W	·	·	·	·
5 Oct–26 Oct	2–4	·	·	W	·	·	·	·

Exterior of Sandham Memorial Chapel, Hampshire

Sandham Memorial Chapel

Harts Lane, Burghclere, near Newbury, Hampshire RG20 9JT

Map ② C6 [✝] [✿] [1947]

Modest red-brick building housing an unexpected treasure – an outstanding series of large-scale paintings by acclaimed artist Stanley Spencer. Inspired by his experiences as a First World War medical orderly and soldier, and peppered with personal and unexpected details, these paintings are considered to be among his finest achievements. **Note**: no toilet. No credit card facilities.

Exploring – Revel in the details of this extraordinary work of art.
– Wander through the orchard to spot wild flowers.

Exploring – Enjoy the surroundings, with walks and views to Watership Down.

Eating and shopping: a selection of books and postcards are available for purchase.

Making the most of your day: bring a picnic and enjoy the garden. Reference folders, children's quiz and handling kit available. No artificial lighting, so bright days are best for viewing. **Dogs**: in grounds only on leads.

Access for all: [♿] [📷] [♿] [••] [🏢]
Building [♿] [♿] Grounds [♿] [♿]

Getting here: 174:SU463608. **Bus**: Cango C21/2 'demand-responsive' service from Newbury (telephone 0845 602 4135 to book). **Train**: Newbury approximately 4 miles. **Road**: 4 miles south of Newbury, ½ mile east of A34. From M4, follow A34, then brown signs. From A339 (Basingstoke to Newbury) follow brown signs and white National Trust signs. Exit A34 at Tothill services. **Parking**: no onsite parking. Parking in public lay-by opposite chapel, or village car park ¼ mile.

Finding out more: 01635 278394 or sandham@nationaltrust.org.uk

Sandham Memorial Chapel		M	T	W	T	F	S	S
5 Mar–27 Mar	11–3	·	·	·	·	·	S	S
30 Mar–2 Oct	11–5	·	·	W	T	F	S	S
5 Oct–30 Oct	11–3	·	·	W	T	F	S	S
5 Nov–18 Dec	11–3	·	·	·	·	·	S	S

Open Bank Holiday Mondays, 11 to 5. Open other times by appointment. Groups of more than ten must book to avoid queuing.

We welcome dogs assisting visitors with disabilities

Scotney Castle

Lamberhurst, Tunbridge Wells, Kent TN3 8JN

Map (2) I7  1970

'**We lost ourselves in this stunning magical place and were sad to leave. We will definitely be back for more!**'
The Beard Family, Australia

Scotney is not one but two houses. At the top of the hill is the new house, designed by Anthony Salvin in Elizabethan style and built in 1837 for Edward Hussey III, who took the 'Picturesque' style as his inspiration. At the bottom of the valley are the romantic ruins of a medieval castle and moat. This is the focal point of the celebrated gardens featuring spectacular displays of rhododendrons, azaleas and kalmia in May/June with trees and shrubs providing autumnal colour. The estate is open all year, offering a variety of walks through beautiful parkland, woodland and farmland.

Exploring
— Voted among the top ten best English gardens to visit.
— Superb display of rhododendrons and azaleas.
— Explore the beautiful 315-hectare (780-acre) estate, with woodland and parkland.
— The only National Trust-owned working hop farm.
— Garden and estate designated a Site of Special Scientific Interest.
— Discover the fantastic rooms in the country mansion.

Eating and shopping: Coach House tea-room serves delicious sandwiches, glorious cream teas, plus hot and cold lunches. Buy an ice-cream from the shop/tea-room. Seek out Scotney ale, Scotney honey and peat-free plants for sale. New estate explorer for purchase with lovely walks.

Making the most of your day: a wide range of activities and events throughout the year – including open-air theatre, music, lecture lunches and great family activities. Estate and wildlife walks – a full events programme is available. **Dogs**: welcome on leads around estate, but assistance dogs only in the garden.

Access for all: ⊞⊞⊞⊞⊞⊞⊞⊞⊞⊞
House ⊞⊞ Grounds ⊞➡⊞

Getting here: 188:TQ688353. **Foot**: links to local footpath network. **Cycle**: NCN18, 3 miles. **Bus**: Trust/East Sussex County Council-run Tunbridge Wells service (telephone for details). **Train**: Wadhurst 5½ miles. **Road**: signposted from A21 at Lamberhurst. **Parking**: 130 yards. Limited parking, cannot be guaranteed at busy times. Grass car park may be closed when wet.

You may also enjoy: Bateman's, Bodiam Castle and Sissinghurst Castle.

Finding out more: 01892 893820 (Infoline). 01892 893868 or scotneycastle@nationaltrust.org.uk

Scotney Castle		M	T	W	T	F	S	S
Garden*								
23 Feb–30 Oct	11–5:30			W	T	F	S	S
5 Nov–18 Dec	11–5						S	S
House								
23 Feb–30 Oct	11–5			W	T	F	S	S
3 Dec–18 Dec	11–4						S	S
Old Castle								
23 Feb–30 Oct	11–3			W	T	F	S	S
Estate walks								
Open all year		M	T	W	T	F	S	S
Shop and tea-room								
23 Feb–30 Oct	11–5:30			W	T	F	S	S
5 Nov–18 Dec	11–4						S	S

Open Bank Holiday Mondays and Good Friday. Last admission one hour before closing. Timed tickets for the house are limited and may sell out on busy days. Guided tours of the house only during December opening. Garden and estate may close during high winds. *Closes dusk if earlier.

Ruins of the 14th-century moated Scotney Castle, Kent

Shalford Mill

Shalford, near Guildford, Surrey GU4 8BS

Map ② E6   🏚 🚬 1932

Large timber-framed watermill on the River Tillingbourne with well-preserved machinery – almost unaltered since ceasing operations in 1914. **Note**: no toilet. No parking. Regular guided tours.

Access for all: VT .. Building 🧎

Getting here: 186:TQ001476. 1½ miles south of Guildford on A281 opposite Seahorse Inn.

Finding out more: 01483 561389 or shalfordmill@nationaltrust.org.uk

Shalford Mill		M	T	W	T	F	S	S
3 Apr–30 Oct	11–5			**W**				**S**

Also open Saturday, Sunday and Monday on Bank Holiday weekends and Saturday and Sunday on National Mills Weekend (early May) and Heritage Open Weekend (September). Guided tours for groups by arrangement, except Wednesday and Sunday.

Sheffield Park and Garden

Sheffield Park, East Sussex TN22 3QX

Map ② G7   ❄ 🌿 1954

This magnificent informal landscape garden was laid out in the 18th century by 'Capability' Brown and further developed in the early years of the 20th century by its owner, Arthur G. Soames. The original four lakes form the centrepiece. There are dramatic shows of daffodils and bluebells in spring, and the rhododendrons and azaleas are spectacular in early summer. Autumn brings stunning colours from the many rare trees and shrubs, and winter walks can be enjoyed in this garden for all seasons. Visitors can now also explore South Park, 107 hectares (265 acres) of historic parkland, with stunning views.

Exploring
- Don't miss the 'What's in the garden' board.
- Enjoy a cricket match on our historic cricket pitch.

Sheffield Park and Garden, East Sussex: a magnificent informal landscape garden

Help the Trust with Gift Aid on Entry for non-members

Exploring
- Enjoy the mirror-like reflections in the lakes.
- Explore our 'Parkland Playful Places' – new parkland family trail.
- Go on a tour, Tuesdays and Thursdays in May/October.
- Take home a locally produced souvenir from our shop.

Eating and shopping: enjoy refreshments from the catering buggy or from the tea-room (not National Trust). Local products available in our shop. Browse through our plants for sale, sourced from National Trust properties.

Making the most of your day: special events throughout the year (telephone or visit website for details). Family activities available for garden and parkland – just pop into our reception to find out more.
Dogs: allowed under close control in parkland (assistance dogs only in garden). Please observe restrictions.

Access for all: ⬛♿🚾♿♿🚗📷♿🔊⬛📷
Reception ♿♿ Garden ♿➡♿♿

Getting here: 198:TQ415240. **Bus**: Bluebell Railway link (Metrobus 473) from near East Grinstead ≋ to Kingscote ≋, Countryliner 121 from close Lewes ≋ (Saturday only), 246 from Uckfield (Monday, Wednesday, Friday only). **Train**: Sheffield Park (Bluebell Railway) ¾ mile; Uckfield 6 miles; Haywards Heath 7 miles. **Road**: midway between East Grinstead and Lewes, 5 miles north-west of Uckfield, on east side of A275 (between A272 and A22). **Parking**: free.

You may also enjoy: Standen, Alfriston Clergy House, Bateman's or Nymans.

Finding out more: 01825 790231 or sheffieldpark@nationaltrust.org.uk

Sheffield Park and Garden		M	T	W	T	F	S	S
Garden								
1 Jan–13 Feb	10:30–4	M	T	W	T	F	S	S
14 Feb–31 Oct	10:30–5:30	M	T	W	T	F	S	S
1 Nov–31 Dec	10:30–4	M	T	W	T	F	S	S
Parkland								
Open all year	Dawn–dusk	M	T	W	T	F	S	S

Garden closed 25 December. Last admission one hour before closing. Closes dusk if earlier (see board on entry).

The White Garden, Sissinghurst Castle, Kent

Sissinghurst Castle

Sissinghurst Castle, Biddenden Road, near Cranbrook, Kent TN17 2AB

Map ② I7 🏠🏠🎧♣♿🏠🔔 1967

'**The castle and garden and views and history – it's all just amazing!**'
Mrs Newton, Winchester

Sissinghurst is more than a garden. It is a garden in the ruin of an Elizabethan house, set in the middle of its own woods, streams and farmland and with long views on all sides across the fields and meadows of the Kentish landscape. When Harold Nicolson, the writer and diplomat, and Vita Sackville-West, poet, novelist and gardener, first came here in 1930, Sissinghurst was dripping in its own inheritance; it had been a medieval manor house and was visited by Queen Elizabeth in the 16th century before falling into ruins and being mistreated for nearly 300 years.

Exploring
- Visit our beautiful, romantic garden – full of colour all season.

Exploring
- Explore the estate, a haven for Wealden wildlife.
- Visit our working vegetable garden between May and September.
- Enjoy home-grown food in the Granary Restaurant.
- Climb the steps of the tower and enjoy the view.
- Shop at the farmers' market – second Monday of every month.

Eating and shopping: fruit and vegetables grown on our 1.4-hectare (3½-acre) vegetable garden are used in our restaurant and coffee shop. Meat and eggs are produced by our tenant farmer, John. The gift shop sells local products and crafts.

Making the most of your day: look out for late night summer opening in the garden and afternoon events. **Dogs**: the woods are glorious for dog walks. Assistance dogs only in garden.

Access for all: 🅿🅳♿🚻🦽🖐🐕📷📹🎨 👁🅰 Building 🦽♿🐾 Grounds 🦽♿➡

Getting here: 188:TQ810380. **Foot**: from Sissinghurst village, past church to footpath on left, signposted to Sissinghurst Castle (can get muddy). **Cycle**: NCN18, 8 miles. **Bus**: Arriva 5 Maidstone to Hawkhurst (passing Staplehurst 🚆), alight Sissinghurst, 1¼ miles. **Train**: Staplehurst 5 miles. **Road**: 2 miles north-east of Cranbrook, 1 mile east of Sissinghurst village on Biddenden Road, off A262. **Parking**: 315 yards, £2.

You may also enjoy: Smallhythe Place, Knole, Scotney Castle, Bateman's and Bodiam Castle.

Finding out more: 01580 710701 (Infoline). 01580 710700 or sissinghurst@nationaltrust.org.uk

Sissinghurst Castle		M	T	W	T	F	S	S
Garden, shop and restaurant								
12 Mar–30 Oct	10:30–5	M	T	·	·	F	S	S
Vegetable garden								
7 May–30 Sep	10:30–5	M	T	·	·	F	S	S
Estate								
Open all year	Dawn–dusk	M	T	W	T	F	S	S

Closes dusk if earlier. Special late night opening, 10:30 to 8: Friday 27 May, 3 June, 10 June, 17 June and 24 June.

Smallhythe Place

Smallhythe, Tenterden, Kent TN30 7NG

Map ② I7   1939

The half-timbered house, built in the early 16th century when Smallhythe was a thriving shipbuilding yard, was the home of the Victorian actress Ellen Terry from 1899 to 1928, and contains her fascinating theatre collection. The cottage grounds include her rose garden, orchard, nuttery and the working Barn Theatre.

Exploring
- Fabulous new costume exhibition with Ellen's famous beetle-wing dress.
- Pick up an events programme at the wonderful Barn Theatre.
- Discover Smallhythe's shipbuilding heritage through our fascinating exhibition.
- Explore Ellen Terry's informal cottage garden, a tranquil retreat.

Eating and shopping: try local ale and cider at the Barn Theatre tea-room. Look out for garden produce for sale in the autumn. Our tea-room now has weatherproof sides, so you can stay sheltered and remain dry in bad weather.

Making the most of your day: enjoy our unique open-air theatre, indoor plays and music in the Barn Theatre. Experience family fun days, including children's theatre. Visit Smallhythe Music and Beer Festival in September. **Dogs**: allowed on leads in grounds.

Access for all: 🦽📷📹🎨👁🅰 Building 🦽♿ Grounds ♿➡

Getting here: 189:TQ893300. **Bus**: Coastal Coaches 312 Rye 🚆 to Tenterden. **Train**: Rye 8 miles; Appledore 8 miles; Headcorn 10 miles. **Road**: 2 miles south of Tenterden, on east side of Rye road (B2082). **Parking**: free (not National Trust), 50 yards. Coaches park at Chapel Down Winery, 500 yards.

South Foreland Lighthouse

The Front, St Margaret's Bay, Dover, Kent CT15 6HP

Map ② K6 🏠🚽🏊🚂🏠  1989

This distinctive, historic landmark with unrivalled views is well worth the walk along the White Cliffs. The building has a fascinating tale to tell: a beacon of safety guiding ships past the infamous Goodwin Sands; the first lighthouse powered by electricity and the site of the first international radio transmission. **Note**: no access for cars.

Exploring	– Guided tours for all visitors. – Discover the challenges of navigating the Strait of Dover. – Learn about the pioneering scientific experiments of Marconi and Faraday. – Astonishing 360-degree views of the Kent countryside and English Channel.

Eating and shopping: small shop selling bottled water, confectionery, gifts and souvenirs.

Making the most of your day: children's events during school holidays. Guided walks programme throughout the year, in conjunction with The White Cliffs of Dover, a two-mile walk away. **Dogs**: allowed in the grounds.

Access for all: 🔲🚶♿📷
Building 🔲 Grounds 🔲

Getting here: 179:TR359433. **No vehicular access. Foot**: on public footpaths 2½ miles from Dover, 1 mile from St Margaret's. **Cycle**: NCN1, ½ mile. **Bus**: Stagecoach in East Kent Diamond 15; Canterbury via Dover to Deal, alight Bay Hill 1 mile (via Lighthouse Road). **Train**: Martin Mill 2½ miles; Dover Priory 3½ miles by footpath.

Smallhythe Place, Kent: Ellen Terry's home

Finding out more: 01580 762334 or smallhytheplace@nationaltrust.org.uk

Smallhythe Place		M	T	W	T	F	S	S
House								
26 Feb–30 Oct	11–5	M	T	W			S	S
3 Dec–18 Dec	12–3						S	S
Tea-room								
26 Feb–30 Oct	12–4	M	T	W			S	S

Open Good Friday. Last admission 4:30 or dusk if earlier. Seasonally dressed downstairs rooms in the house open the three weekends before Christmas.

The distinctive South Foreland Lighthouse, Kent

Parking: **no onsite parking**. Parking at The White Cliffs of Dover (National Trust), then walk along clifftops to lighthouse (2 miles approximately) or at St Margaret's village/bay (1 mile approximately).

Finding out more: 01304 852463 or southforeland@nationaltrust.org.uk

South Foreland Lighthouse		M	T	W	T	F	S	S
11 Mar–10 Apr	11–5:30	M				F	S	S
11 Apr–1 May	11–5:30	M	T	W	T	F	S	S
2 May–29 May	11–5:30	M				F	S	S
30 May–5 Jun	11–5:30	M	T	W	T	F	S	S
6 Jun–24 Jul	11–5:30	M				F	S	S
25 Jul–4 Sep	11–5:30	M	T	W	T	F	S	S
5 Sep–23 Oct	11–5:30	M				F	S	S
24 Oct–31 Oct	11–5:30	M	T	W	T	F	S	S

Admission by guided tour, last tour 5. Open by arrangement during closed period for booked groups only.

Sprivers Garden

Horsmonden, Kent TN12 8DR

Closed this year.

Standen

West Hoathly Road, East Grinstead, West Sussex RH19 4NE

Map ② G7 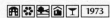 1973

Late Victorian family home brought vividly to life in this gem of the Arts and Crafts Movement. Standen is hidden at the end of a quiet Sussex lane with breathtaking views over the High Weald and Weirwood Reservoir. The design of the house is a monument to the combined genius of architect Philip Webb and his friend William Morris. All the big names of the Arts and Crafts period are represented, including ceramics by William De Morgan and metalwork by W. A. S. Benson. The beautiful hillside gardens provide year-round interest; the woodlands, a number of easily accessible walks.

Exploring
- Experience being a guest in this Victorian family's home.
- Explore the Sussex countryside through our picturesque woodland walks.
- Enjoy many designs of Morris and Co. throughout the house.
- Study and play with learning resources for all ages.
- New: see our garden grow as the restoration gets underway.
- New: enjoy the smells and sounds of a Victorian kitchen.

Eating and shopping: discover our unique shop with gifts inspired by William Morris. Enjoy delicious meals, or grab a snack, in the Barn Restaurant. Fresh produce from the barrow in our kitchen garden. Add colour to your garden from our plant sales area.

Making the most of your day: open-air theatre, guided walks, children's school holiday activity days, regular temporary exhibitions and workshops, introductory talks, conservation demonstrations, lecture lunches, special Christmas programme of festive events and activities. **Dogs**: welcome on leads in designated areas, including the extensive woodland walks.

Standen in West Sussex was designed by Philip Webb in the Arts and Crafts style

Access for all: P D WC 🦽 📖 ♿ ∴ Ⓐ
Building 🦽♿♿ Grounds 🦽♿ ➡

Getting here: 187:TQ389356. **Cycle**: NCN21, 1¼ miles. **Bus**: Metrobus 84 East Grinstead ▓ to Crawley (passing Three Bridges ▓), alight at the end of our drive (just north of Saint Hill), ½ mile, or at Saint Hill, then ¾ mile by footpath. **Train**: East Grinstead 2 miles; Kingscote (Bluebell Railway) 2 miles. **Road**: 2 miles south of East Grinstead, signposted from town centre and B2110 (Turners Hill Road). **Parking**: free, 200 yards.

You may also enjoy: Red House – William Morris's own home, also built by his friend, Philip Webb.

Finding out more: 01342 323029 or standen@nationaltrust.org.uk

Standen		M	T	W	T	F	S	S
19 Feb–6 Mar	11–4:30						S	S
12 Mar–10 Apr	11–4:30			W	T	F	S	S
11 Apr–25 Apr	11–4:30	M		W	T	F	S	S
27 Apr–24 Jul	11–4:30			W	T	F	S	S
25 Jul–4 Sep	11–4:30	M		W	T	F	S	S
7 Sep–23 Oct	11–4:30			W	T	F	S	S
24 Oct–30 Oct	11–4:30	M		W	T	F	S	S
5 Nov–18 Dec	11–3						S	S
19 Dec–21 Dec	11–3	M	T	W				

Open Bank Holiday Mondays. Bank Holidays and event days: queuing on approach possible. **On open days the shop and restaurant close at 5, garden at 5:30** (at 3 from 5 November to 21 December).

Stoneacre

Otham, Maidstone, Kent ME15 8RS

Map ② I6 🏚 ❀

15th-century half-timbered yeoman's house, featuring a great hall and surrounded by harmonious garden, orchard and meadows. **Note**: occupied as private residence and administered on the National Trust's behalf by tenants. No toilet.

Access for all: P D ∴
Building 🦽♿ Grounds ➡

Getting here: 188:TQ800535. At north end of Otham village, 3 miles south-east of Maidstone, 1 mile south of A20.

Finding out more: 01622 863247 or stoneacre@nationaltrust.org.uk

Stoneacre		M	T	W	T	F	S	S
19 Mar–1 Oct	11–5:30						S	

Open Bank Holiday Mondays. Last admission one hour before closing. Coach bookings welcome.

View across the Octagon Lake at Stowe Landscape Gardens in Buckinghamshire

Stowe Landscape Gardens

Buckingham, Buckinghamshire MK18 5DQ

Map ② D2  1990

'The family had so much fun discovering wildlife and hidden corners of this beautiful place.'
Heidi Stevens, Oxford

One of the most remarkable creations of Georgian England, Stowe was created by a family once so powerful they were richer than the king. The scale, grandeur and beauty of Stowe has inspired writers, philosophers, artists, politicians and members of the public from the 18th century to the present day. Since the National Trust acquired the gardens, an ambitious programme of restoration has ensured that over 40 temples and monuments remain, gracing an inspiring backdrop of lakes and valleys with an endless variety of walks and trails, a delight to explore at any time of year. **Note**: new visitor centre opening summer, visit website for details. Stowe House (not National Trust).

Exploring
 — Enjoy the plant world's changing seasons in 18th-century grandeur.
 — Play hide and seek in temples with hidden mythical meanings.

Exploring
 — Enjoy lakeside walks, wooded valleys and open vistas.
 — Guided tours to unravel the secrets and surprises of Stowe.
 — New from summer – land train between visitor centre and gardens.

Eating and shopping: enjoy homemade delights in the tea-room before finding the perfect present in the gift shop. Or pick your own picnic spot among temples, lakes and valleys. Mobile food buggy offering snacks and drinks will be out and about.

Making the most of your day: take a guided walk to learn about Stowe's history or pick up a family activity pack at reception. For special events throughout the year visit the website. **Dogs**: welcome on leads.

Access for all:
Building Grounds

Getting here: 152:SP665366. **Foot**: 3 miles from Buckingham along Stowe Avenue and along bridleway through parkland. **Bus**: nearest buses serve Buckingham (3 miles), then taxi. **Train**: Bicester North 9 miles; Milton Keynes Central 14 miles. **Road**: 3 miles north-west of Buckingham via Stowe Avenue, off A422 Buckingham to Banbury road. Motorway access from M40 (exits 9 to 11) and M1 (exits 13 or 15a). **Sat Nav**: use MK18 5DQ, then after new visitor centre opens use MK18 5EQ. **Parking**: free, 200 yards.

You may also enjoy: intriguing Claydon and magnificent Waddesdon Manor.

Finding out more: 01280 822850 (weekdays). 01280 818825 (weekends). 01280 818166/818229 (Stowe House) or stowegarden@nationaltrust.org.uk

Stowe Landscape Gardens		M	T	W	T	F	S	S
Gardens, shop and tea-room*								
2 Jan–27 Feb	10:30–4						S	S
2 Mar–30 Oct	10:30–5:30			W	T	F	S	S
5 Nov–18 Dec	10:30–4						S	S
Shop only special Christmas opening								
9 Nov–23 Dec	11–3			W	T	F		
Parkland								
Open all year	Dawn–dusk	M	T	W	T	F	S	S

Open Bank Holiday Mondays and Monday and Tuesday during half-terms. Last entry 90 minutes before closing or dusk if earlier. **Closed Saturday 28 May.** *Tea-room closes 30 minutes before gardens and shop. May close in severe weather conditions.

Eating and shopping: our shop stocks a range of local food products, including honey, jams and pickles. This complements the restaurant which serves seasonal homemade dishes with local breads and cheeses. Freshly baked cakes and scones from our own kitchen are a speciality.

Making the most of your day: to enhance your visit there are introductory talks on the house, free garden history tours every Thursday and a 'Plant of the Month' to look out for. **Dogs:** on leads on woodland walk only. Please note: no shaded parking.

Uppark House and Garden

South Harting, Petersfield, West Sussex GU31 5QR

Map (2) E8   🏠 ❄ ♿ 🍴 1954

Uniquely placed on the South Downs and restored to its former glory after a major fire in 1989, Uppark is home to a famous Grand Tour collection within an elegant Georgian interior. Discover the world of Sir Harry, Lady Emma Hamilton and the dairymaid who married her master. The complete servants' quarters in the basement are shown as they were in Victorian days, when H. G. Wells's mother was housekeeper. The garden is adorned with wonderfully scented shrubs and fine specimen trees, all planted within a naturalistic framework.

Exploring
- Complete 18th-century doll's house.
- Fascinating servants' tunnels to explore.
- Woodland walk with eco seat.
- House and garden trails and toy box for the children.
- Lecture lunch programme in March and December.
- Garden tours and welcome talks.

Uppark House and Garden, West Sussex: a view of the Saloon, showing the ornate gilt ceiling and chandelier

Access for all: [icons]
House [icons]
Shop and restaurant [icons]
Gardens [icons]

Getting here: 197:SU775177. **Foot**: South Downs Way within ¾ mile. **Bus**: Countryliner 54 Petersfield ≈ to Chichester ≈ (bus stop is 500 yards from property, via a steep hill). **Train**: Petersfield 5½ miles. **Road**: 5 miles south-east of Petersfield on B2146, 1½ miles south of South Harting. **Parking**: free, 300 yards.

You may also enjoy: Petworth House and Park and Hinton Ampner.

Finding out more: 01730 825857 (Infoline). 01730 825415 or uppark@nationaltrust.org.uk

Uppark House and Garden		M	T	W	T	F	S	S
House								
20 Mar–30 Oct	12:30–4:30	**M**	**T**	**W**	**T**		·	**S**
Garden, shop and restaurant								
20 Mar–30 Oct	12:30–4:30	**M**	**T**	**W**	**T**		·	**S**
House, garden, shop and restaurant								
20 Nov–18 Dec	11–3						·	**S**

Open Good Friday. Bank Holiday Mondays and Bank Holiday Sundays: garden, shop and restaurant open 11 to 5 and house 11:30 to 4:30. Open Sundays from 20 November to 18 December. Also open Saturday 10 December. Garden tours every Thursday from April to October. Print Room open first Wednesday of each month (times as house).

The Vyne, Hampshire, was built as a great Tudor 'power house' and was visited by King Henry VIII several times

The Vyne

Vyne Road, Sherborne St John, Basingstoke, Hampshire RG24 9HL

Map (2) D6

Originally built as a great Tudor 'power house', The Vyne was visited by King Henry VIII on at least three occasions and later became a family home, cherished by the Chute family for more than 350 years. Dramatic improvements and changes over the centuries have made The Vyne a fascinating microcosm of changing fads and fashions. The house is filled with an eclectic mix of fine furniture, portraits, textiles and sculpture. The attractive gardens and grounds feature an ornamental lake, delightful woodlands and flourishing wetlands, a haven for wildlife and waterfowl which can be observed from the bird hide.

Exploring
– Discover 500 years of history in one family home.
– Stroll through the tranquil grounds and gardens.
– Don't miss the Tudor chapel visited by Henry VIII.
– Find out about the restoration of our Walled Garden.
– Explore our woodlands and wetlands, a rich haven for wildlife.

Eating and shopping: visit the Coach House shop for gifts and local produce. Plants and garden-related products in our tea garden.

Delicious home-cooked food available in the Tudor Brewhouse restaurant. New refreshment kiosk in the car park.

Making the most of your day: free children's activities. Waymarked woodland walks. Changing displays within house. Exciting garden projects and tours. Comprehensive events programme runs thoughout the year. Enjoy open-air theatre, Tudor Weekend and Orchard Day. **Dogs**: welcome in car park and woodlands. Assistance dogs only in house and gardens.

Access for all: 🅿♿🚻🚼👁🔈📷🖼♿ 👁🔊 Building ♿🚶 Grounds ♿🚶

Getting here: 175/186:SU639576.
Cycle: NCN23, 1 mile. **Bus**: Stagecoach in Hampshire numbers 14 and 15 from Basingstoke (passing Basingstoke ≥). No Sunday service. **Train**: Bramley 2½ miles; Basingstoke 4 miles. **Road**: 4 miles north of Basingstoke between Bramley and Sherborne St John. From Basingstoke Ring Road A339, follow North Hampshire Hospital signs until Brown property signs. Follow A340 Aldermaston Road towards Tadley. Right turn into Morgaston Road. Right turn into car park. **Sat Nav**: will not deliver you to the main car park, instead follow National Trust brown signs. **Parking**: free, 40 yards. ⅓-mile walk through gardens from visitor reception to house entrance.

You may also enjoy: other fine houses and gardens: Mottisfont and Basildon Park. Something completely different: Sandham Memorial Chapel.

Finding out more: 01256 883858 or thevyne@nationaltrust.org.uk

The Vyne		M	T	W	T	F	S	S
House, gardens, shop and restaurant								
19 Feb–3 Mar	11–3	M	T	W	T		S	S
5 Mar–30 Oct	11–5	M	T	W	T		S	S
5 Nov–29 Nov	11–3	M	T				S	S
Christmas house (part), gardens, shop and restaurant								
3 Dec–22 Dec	11–3	M	T	W	T		S	S

House, gardens, shop and restaurant open Good Friday and Bank Holiday Mondays, 11 to 5. House: please note, no handrail on the 18th-century staircase, therefore access to first floor can be restrictive. Low light levels to be expected on overcast days. Also note: areas of house and gardens may be closed from November to early March for essential conservation work; reduced entry fees apply during winter.

Waddesdon Manor

Waddesdon, near Aylesbury, Buckinghamshire HP18 0JH

Map ② D3  1957

This Renaissance-style château was built by Baron Ferdinand de Rothschild to display his outstanding collection of art treasures and to entertain the fashionable world. The 45 rooms on view combine the highest quality French furniture and decorative arts from the 18th century with superb English portraits and Dutch Old Masters. The Victorian garden is considered one of the finest in Britain with its parterre, seasonal displays, fountains and statuary. At its heart lies the aviary, stocked with species once part of Baron Ferdinand's collection. Visit the new contemporary art gallery in the Coach House at the Stables. **Note**: managed by a Rothschild family charitable trust. House entrance by timed tickets only.

Aerial view of Waddesdon Manor, Buckinghamshire

Exploring
- See one of the finest collections of Sèvres porcelain.
- Marvel at Marie-Antoinette's writing desk.
- Discover contemporary sculptures in the gardens.
- Relax in the rose garden, aviary glade and parterre.
- Enjoy the wildlife interpretation trail and woodland playground.
- Visit the new contemporary art gallery at the Stables.

Eating and shopping: enjoy a meal in one of the two licensed restaurants (not National Trust). Have a snack or drink at the Summerhouse. Browse and buy in the shops and plant centre. Visit the old-fashioned sweet shop at the Stables.

Making the most of your day: family events and free activities, children's quiz/trail, wine tastings, Christmas opening and events, garden workshops, plant centre. Visit www.waddesdon.org.uk for more information. **Dogs**: assistance dogs only.

Access for all: 🅿️🅳🚌🚾🚻👶🖼️🎨📷
Building 👤🔆🔳 Grounds 👤➡️

Getting here: 165:SP740169. **Bus**: Arriva 16 from Aylesbury (passing close Aylesbury ▆). **Train**: Aylesbury Vale Parkway 4 miles; Aylesbury 6 miles; Haddenham & Thame Parkway 9 miles. **Road**: access via Waddesdon village, 6 miles north-west of Aylesbury on A41; M40 (westbound) exit 6 or 7 via Thame and Long Crendon or M40 (eastbound) exit 9 via Bicester. **Parking**: free.

You may also enjoy: Claydon, Cliveden, Hughenden Manor, King's Head and Stowe Landscape Gardens.

Finding out more: 01296 653226 or waddesdonmanor@nationaltrust.org.uk

Waddesdon Manor		M	T	W	T	F	S	S
Gardens, aviary, woodland playground, shops, restaurants								
8 Jan–27 Mar	10–5	·	·	·	·	·	S	S
30 Mar–31 Dec	10–5	·	·	W	T	F	S	S
26 Apr	10–5	·	T	·	·	·	·	·
House and wine cellars								
30 Mar–28 Oct	12–4	·	·	W	T	F	·	
2 Apr–30 Oct	11–4	·	·	·	·	·	S	S
26 Apr	12–4	·	T	·	·	·	·	·
16 Nov–31 Dec	11–4	·	·	W	T	F	S	S
19 Dec–20 Dec	12–4	M	T	·	·	·	·	·
Bachelors' Wing								
30 Mar–28 Oct	12–4	·	·	W	T	F	·	

Open Bank Holiday Mondays. Last recommended admission to house one hour before closing. Sculpture in garden uncovered week before Easter, weather permitting. Property open Monday and Tuesday 19 and 20 December. Property closed 24 to 26 December. All visitors require a timed ticket to visit the house, including members, available from the ticket office or online at www.waddesdon.org.uk (limited number of tickets available for house daily – they may sell out on busy days, especially at weekends and throughout December).

Wakehurst Place

Ardingly, Haywards Heath,
West Sussex RH17 6TN

Map ② G7

The National Trust's most visited property. Open throughout the year, Wakehurst is the country estate of the Royal Botanic Gardens, Kew. This beautiful botanic garden is internationally significant, for both its collections and its vital scientific research and plant conservation. Enjoy visiting woodland and lakes, formal gardens, the Elizabethan house and Kew's Millennium Seed Bank. Wakehurst marked an international conservation milestone in 2010, conserving the seeds of 10 per cent of the world's plant species for the future, and now embarks on the target of conserving a quarter of the world's plant species by 2020. **Note**: funded and managed by the Royal Botanic Gardens, Kew (www.kew.org).

Exploring
- Journey through changing landscapes of garden, wetland and woodland.
- Discover and enjoy plants from all around the world.
- Explore the nature reserves.
- Watch science in action at the Millennium Seed Bank.
- Join a free guided tour.
- Be inspired as each season brings something new.

Eating and shopping: enjoy a lunch of seasonal and local produce at the Stables Café. Fresh homemade sandwiches and cakes at the Seed Café. Take home the perfect gift from the Kew-run shop. Enhance your own garden with something from the plant centre.

Making the most of your day: spring and autumn colour weekend events, Christmas celebrations. Children's trail. Kingfisher and badger-watching evenings. Loder Valley nature reserve with wetland and meadowland: admission limited to 50 people per day.

Kew's Millennium Seed Bank at Wakehurst Place, West Sussex

Dogs: assistance dogs only.

Access for all: ♿🚻♿🏠
Building ♿♿ Grounds ♿➡♿♿

Getting here: 187:TQ339314. **Foot**: footpath from Balcombe (4 miles). **Bus**: Metrobus 82 Haywards Heath to Crawley (passing Haywards Heath ➡ and Three Bridges ➡). **Train**: Haywards Heath 6 miles; East Grinstead 6 miles. **Road**: on B2028, 1 mile north of Ardingly; 3 miles south of Turners Hill. From M23 exit 10, take A264 towards East Grinstead. **Parking**: not National Trust, charges may apply.

You may also enjoy: the beauty of Nymans, the Arts and Crafts of Standen and Sheffield Park and Garden.

Finding out more: 01444 894066 or wakehurst@kew.org. www.kew.org

Wakehurst Place		M	T	W	T	F	S	S
1 Jan–28 Feb	10–4:30	M	T	W	T	F	S	S
1 Mar–31 Oct	10–6	M	T	W	T	F	S	S
1 Nov–31 Dec	10–4:30	M	T	W	T	F	S	S

Last admission to Seed Bank and house 90 minutes before closing. Closed 24 and 25 December. Shop closed Easter Sunday. Note: reciprocal organisations do not receive free entry.

West Green House Garden

West Green, Hartley Wintney, Hampshire RG27 8JB

Map ② D6 1957

A delightful series of walled gardens surrounds the charming 18th-century house. **Note**: lessee has agreed to open on a limited basis.

Access for all: ♿🏠 Grounds ♿♿

Getting here: 175:SU745564. 1 mile west of Hartley Wintney, 10 miles north-east of Basingstoke, 1 mile north of A30.

Finding out more: 01252 844611 or westgreenhouse@nationaltrust.org.uk

West Green House Garden		M	T	W	T	F	S	S
23 Apr–18 Sep	11–4:30	·	·	W	·	·	S	S

West Wycombe Park

West Wycombe, Buckinghamshire HP14 3AJ

Map ② E4 🏛️✥♠️ 1943

The fine Georgian landscape garden was created by infamous Sir Francis Dashwood, founder of the Dilettanti Society and Hellfire Club. The Palladian villa is among the most theatrical and Italianate in England. Lavishly decorated, it has featured in films and television series, including *Cranford* and *Foyle's War*. A breathtaking visit. **Note**: Hellfire Caves and café are privately owned.

West Wycombe Park, Buckinghamshire

Exploring	– Stroll round the beautiful lake, streams and temples.
	– Discover the stories behind the 2nd Baronet's notoriety.
	– Enjoy the sumptuous decor of the Dashwood family home.

Eating and shopping: refreshments at garden centre, library and village pubs (not National Trust). Browse among the quaint high street shops (not National Trust).

West Wycombe Park			M	T	W	T	F	S	S
Grounds only									
3 Apr–26 May	2–6		M	T	W	T			S
House and grounds									
29 May–31 Aug	2–6		M	T	W	T			S

Admission by guided tour only on weekdays, tours every 20 minutes (approximately). Last admission 45 minutes before closing.

Making the most of your day: fabulous guided tours of house on open weekdays. Hire an audio guide of park or try a family trail.

Access for all: 🅿️♿🚻📷
Building 🔼♿ Grounds ♿

Getting here: 175:SU828947.
Foot: circular walk links West Wycombe with Bradenham and Hughenden Manor. **Bus**: Arriva 40 High Wycombe to Thame, Red Rose 275 High Wycombe to Oxford; Magpie Travel 321 High Wycombe to Princes Risborough. **Train**: High Wycombe 2½ miles. **Road**: 2 miles west of High Wycombe. At west end of West Wycombe, south of the Oxford road (A40). **Parking**: 250 yards. Disabled parking adjacent to house.

Finding out more: 01494 755571 (Infoline). 01494 513569 or westwycombe@nationaltrust.org.uk

West Wycombe Village and Hill

West Wycombe, Buckinghamshire

Map ② E4 🏛️✝🏛️♿🚻 1934

Historic village with cottages and inns of architectural interest dating from 16th century. Far-reaching views from West Wycombe Hill. **Note**: church, mausoleum and caves are not National Trust. Nearest toilets in village.

Access for all: Grounds ♿

Getting here: 175:SU828946. 2 miles west of High Wycombe, on both sides of A40.

Finding out more: 01494 755573 or westwycombe@nationaltrust.org.uk

West Wycombe Village	Open every day all year

The White Cliffs of Dover

Langdon Cliffs, Upper Road, Dover, Kent CT16 1HJ

Map (2) K7 1968

There can be no doubt that The White Cliffs of Dover are one of this country's most spectacular natural features. They are an official icon of Britain and have been a symbol of hope and freedom for centuries. You can appreciate their beauty and enjoy their special appeal through the seasons by taking one of the dramatic clifftop walks, which offer unrivalled views of the busy English Channel and the French coast. While here, learn more about the fascinating military and penal history of The White Cliffs and savour the rare flora and fauna only found on this chalk grassland. **Note**: toilets only available when Visitor Centre open.

Exploring
- Spectacular cross-Channel panorama to France.
- View the world's busiest shipping lanes.
- Dramatic clifftop countryside walks.
- Search out rare chalk grassland flora and fauna.
- Explore the hidden wartime heritage of Hellfire Corner.
- Learn about life as a convict in the former prison.

Eating and shopping: browse in the shop for a great range of gifts to suit all ages, including local produce/items of interest and White Cliffs souvenirs. Enjoy seasonal light lunches and afternoon teas in the coffee shop with its unique cross-Channel views.

Making the most of your day: self-guided walks and Tracker Packs. Events and guided walks throughout the year, including Easter trails, spring plant fair and autumn Apple Fayre. **Dogs**: under close control at all times (stock grazing).

Access for all:
Visitor Centre **Grounds**

Getting here: 138:TR336422. **Foot**: signed pathways from the port, station and town centre. Located on the Saxon Shore Way path. **Cycle**: NCN1. **Bus**: Stagecoach in East Kent Diamond 15 Canterbury to Dover to Deal, alight Castle Hill then 1 mile (via Upper Road – no footpath). Also 15a, alight Dover Docks. **Train**: Dover Priory 2½ miles. **Road**: from A2/A258 Duke of York roundabout, take A258 towards Dover town centre. After 1 mile turn left into Upper Road. Entrance on right after 1 mile. From A20 go straight ahead at first four roundabouts. Turn left at second set of lights into Woolcomber Street. Turn right onto Castle Street at next lights. After ½ mile turn right into Upper Road. Entrance on right after 1 mile. **Sat Nav**: may direct you to Eastern Docks.

You may also enjoy: a visit to South Foreland Lighthouse, a pleasant two-mile walk away.

Finding out more: 01304 202756 or whitecliffs@nationaltrust.org.uk

The White Cliffs of Dover		M	T	W	T	F	S	S
Visitor Centre								
1 Jan–28 Feb	11–4	M	T	W	T	F	S	S
1 Mar–31 Oct	10–5	M	T	W	T	F	S	S
1 Nov–31 Dec	11–4	M	T	W	T	F	S	S
Car park								
1 Jan–28 Feb	8–5	M	T	W	T	F	S	S
1 Mar–31 Oct	8–6	M	T	W	T	F	S	S
1 Nov–31 Dec	8–5	M	T	W	T	F	S	S

Visitor Centre closed 24, 25 and 26 December. Car park closed 24 and 25 December.

The spectacular White Cliffs of Dover, Kent

White Horse Hill

Uffington, Oxfordshire

Map (2) C4 1979

The oldest chalk figure in the country and an Iron Age hill fort, two of many local ancient sites. **Note**: archaeological monuments under English Heritage guardianship. No toilet.

Access for all: P♿

Getting here: SU299863. South-west Oxfordshire, on the Ridgeway between Swindon and Wantage.

Finding out more: 01793 762209 or whitehorsehill@nationaltrust.org.uk

White Horse Hill	M	T	W	T	F	S	S
Countryside							
Open all year	**M**	**T**	**W**	**T**	**F**	**S**	**S**
National Trust information trailer*							
2 Apr–30 Oct	11–4	·	·	·	·	·	**S**	**S**

*Information trailer may be closed at short notice.

Hands-on fun at Winchester City Mill, Hampshire

Winchester City Mill

Bridge Street, Winchester, Hampshire SO23 0EJ

Map (2) D7  1929

The City Mill is a rare surviving example of an urban working corn mill, powered by the fast-flowing River Itchen, which can be seen passing under the mill, thrilling our visitors. Rebuilt in 1743 on a medieval mill site, it remained in use until the early 20th century. The National Trust recently undertook an ambitious restoration project, and the mill resumed grinding flour in March 2004. With hands-on activities for families and audio-visual displays about milling and the rich wildlife in the area, the City Mill is a lively and informative place for all ages to enjoy. **Note**: no toilet (public toilet 220 yards).

Exploring
- Discover a millennium of milling history.
- Enjoy our weekend milling demonstrations.
- Have a go at milling flour using hand querns.
- Watch CCTV footage of Winchester's resident otters.
- Escape to the nearby Winnall Moors Nature Reserve.
- Programme of baking demonstrations.

Eating and shopping: browse in our shop for gifts, books and local produce. Buy a bag of freshly milled wholemeal flour.

Making the most of your day: wide-ranging programme of events. Family activities and children's activities during school holidays. Regular milling demonstrations. Programme of baking demonstrations and workshops.

Access for all: ♿🅿️📷🏠🎵👁️🅰️ Building 🐕

Getting here: 185:SU487294. At foot of High Street, beside City Bridge. **Foot**: South Downs Way, King's Way, Itchen Way, Three Castles Path, Clarendon Way – all pass through or terminate at Winchester. **Bus**: from surrounding areas. **Train**: Winchester 1 mile. **Road**: junction 9 from north M3. Junction 10 from south M3. **Sat Nav**: do not use postcode. **Parking**: at Chesil car park, no onsite parking. Park and ride, St Catherine's to Winchester (from M3, exit 10).

You may also enjoy: Hinton Ampner, The Vyne, Sandham Memorial Chapel and Mottisfont.

Finding out more: 01962 870057 or winchestercitymill@nationaltrust.org.uk

Winchester City Mill		M	T	W	T	F	S	S
2 Jan–14 Feb	11–4	M	.	.	.	F	S	S
18 Feb–30 Nov	10–5	M	T	W	T	F	S	S
1 Dec–23 Dec	10:30–4	M	T	W	T	F	S	S

Open 1 January 11 to 4.

Winkworth Arboretum

Hascombe Road, Godalming, Surrey GU8 4AD

Map ② F7   1952

Established in the 20th century, this stunning natural landscape houses more than 1,000 different shrubs and trees, many of them rare. There is year-round colour, with the most impressive displays being in spring, when the magnolias, bluebells and azaleas flower, and autumn, when the colour of the foliage is stunning. In summer this tranquil place is ideal for the family to explore and picnic. **Note**: steep slopes and banks of lake and wetlands are only partially fenced.

Exploring
– Arboretum offers peace and tranquillity.
– Superb display of old English bluebells in springtime.
– Magnolias, cherry blossom and azaleas.
– Famed for stunning autumn colour.

Exploring
– Inspiring landscape and views.
– Award-winning collection: more than 1,000 different shrubs and trees.

Eating and shopping: delicious home-prepared light lunches. Afternoon teas with homemade cakes and biscuits. Visit our small, friendly tea-room.

Making the most of your day: programme of events, walks and talks throughout the year (send stamped addressed envelope for details). **Dogs**: welcome on leads.

Access for all: ⬚⬚⬚⬚⬚ Grounds ⬚⬚

Getting here: 169/170/186:SU990412. **Bus**: Arriva 42/44 Guildford to Cranleigh (passing close Godalming ⬚). **Train**: Godalming 2 miles. **Road**: near Hascombe, 2 miles south-east of Godalming on east side of B2130. **Parking**: free, 100 yards.

You may also enjoy: Claremont Landscape Garden.

Finding out more: 01483 208477 or winkwortharboretum@nationaltrust.org.uk

Winkworth Arboretum		M	T	W	T	F	S	S
Arboretum								
1 Jan–31 Mar	10–4	M	T	W	T	F	S	S
1 Apr–31 Oct	10–5	M	T	W	T	F	S	S
1 Nov–24 Dec	10–4	M	T	W	T	F	S	S
26 Dec–31 Dec	10–4	M	T	W	T	F	S	S
Tea-room								
1 Jan–27 Feb	11–4	.	.	.	.	.	S	S
2 Mar–31 Mar	11–4	.	.	W	T	F	S	S
1 Apr–30 Oct	11–5	.	.	W	T	F	S	S
2 Nov–27 Nov	11–4	.	.	W	T	F	S	S
3 Dec–18 Dec	11–4	.	.	.	.	.	S	S
26 Dec–31 Dec	11–4	M	T	W	T	F	S	.

Tea-room opens Bank Holiday Mondays and additional days during school holidays, when bluebells bloom and in autumn. Arboretum may be closed in bad weather (especially in high winds). Closed 25 December.

Winkworth Arboretum, Godalming, Surrey

Woolbeding Gardens

Midhurst, West Sussex GU29 9RR

Map ② E7/8   1956

Woolbeding is a 20th-century garden of two halves, with the colour-themed garden rooms surrounding the house, plus a woodland garden. A short walk over open pasture land provides views of the River Rother and leads to the fantasy garden, which includes a Chinese-style bridge, waterfall and stumpery.

Exploring   —   Be inspired by the colourful borders.
      —   Enjoy the diversity of the plant collection.
      —   Admire the birds fishing in the River Rother.

Exploring   —   Stroll across to the fantasy garden.

Access for all: 🅿️♿🚾♿
Reception ♿ Garden ♿ ➡️

Getting here: SU872227. **Foot**: local footpaths provide access to the village and gardens. **Bus**: Countryliner 91, 92 and 93 Petersfield ≋ to Midhurst. Stagecoach 70 Haslemere ≋ to Midhurst. **Train**: Petersfield ≋ 8¾ miles. Haslemere ≋ 8¾ miles. **Road**: no access by car. Access is by minibus only (booking essential). **Parking**: no onsite parking, apart from disabled parking (booking essential).

Finding out more: 01730 825415 or woolbedinggardens@nationaltrust. org.uk. South Harting, Petersfield, Hampshire GU31 5QR

Woolbeding Gardens		M	T	W	T	F	S	S
7 Apr–30 Sep	10:30–4:30	·	·	·	**T**	**F**	·	·

Woolbeding Gardens in West Sussex: created by Simon Sainsbury and Stewart Grimshaw

    We welcome dogs assisting visitors with disabilities

London

A surprisingly homely corner in Ernö Goldfinger's Modernist masterpiece, 2 Willow Road

Outdoors
in London

Despite being one of the world's major conurbations, London still contains numerous green and relatively tranquil areas. Many are fragments of the city's once extensive common land and have been saved thanks, in part, to the efforts of the National Trust.

The phenomenal growth of the capital over the centuries has meant that several Trust properties which once stood in open countryside, now fall within the Greater London area. Sutton House in Hackney, for example, was once part of a small village, yet has long since been surrounded by development, so that it now sits within a densely populated area. This has advantages, however, for it is ideally placed for carrying out the Trust's work with local communities and inner-city schools.

Above:
stately spires of lupins at Osterley Park and House, Middlesex

Welcome green haven
Another property which has been subsumed by the city is Osterley Park. This large estate was originally created as a retreat, where wealthy guests could be entertained away from the hustle and bustle of urban life. Since then, of course, the city has crept up on it, and instead of being a countryside property it now stands in the midst of suburbia – providing a welcome green haven for local residents and visitors.

Tranquil park and farmland
Osterley House was designed in 1761 by Robert Adam, the leading architect and interior designer of his day, and the dazzling interiors are impressive. A total of 145 hectares (359 acres) of park and farmland surround the mansion, and this land is a much-loved local amenity. At present the Trust is in the midst of a major project which will gradually restore the gardens to their former 18th-century splendour.

Pleasure for all
Visitors with walking difficulties will find a trip to Morden Hall Park or Osterley Park particularly rewarding. Both properties have extremely accessible paths: Osterley Park boasts numerous routes suitable for wheelchair users – encircling the lake as well as through the wider parkland – while Morden Hall Park's routes run through the rose garden and along the River Wandle.

An urban oasis
There is another unexpected oasis in South West London. Morden Hall Park is a picturesque and historic park with meadows, waterways and lovely old buildings. It also has an impressive rose garden, with more than 2,000 rose bushes, and is the perfect safe haven, whether you want to take the family for a picnic or a pleasant day out or go for a stroll or a jog.

Blewcoat School Gift Shop

23 Caxton Street, Westminster,
London SW1H 0PY

Map ② G5 🏠 | 1954 |

Built in 1709 as a school for poor children, this architectural gem now houses a shop selling attractive gifts. **Note**: no toilet.

Access for all: 🦽 Building 🦼

Getting here: 176:TQ295794. Near the junction of Caxton Street and Buckingham Gate.

Finding out more: 020 7222 2877 or blewcoat@nationaltrust.org.uk

Blewcoat School Gift Shop		M	T	W	T	F	S	S
3 Jan–30 Dec	10–5:30	**M**	**T**	**W**	**T**	**F**		
29 Oct–17 Dec	10–4							**S**
Closed Bank Holiday Mondays and Good Friday.								

Carlyle's House

24 Cheyne Row, Chelsea, London SW3 5HL

Map ② F5 🏠 ❀ | 1936 |

Preserved since 1895, this writer's house in the heart of one of London's most famous creative quarters tells the story of Thomas and Jane Carlyle. The couple moved here from their native Scotland in 1834 and became an unusual but much-loved celebrity couple of the 19th-century literary world.

Exploring
– Discover the writer who inspired Charles Dickens.
– Learn about the Carlyles' many other illustrious friends.
– Enjoy the evocative atmosphere in this Victorian literary shrine.
– New increased weekday opening times.

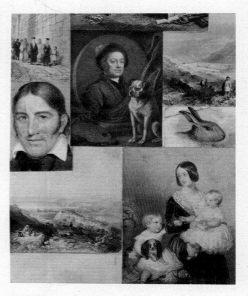

Detail of the prints on the découpage scrap screen, decorated by Jane Carlyle in 1849, in the drawing room at Carlyle's House in London

Making the most of your day: limited group tours available June, July and August 5 to 7 (minimum 10, maximum 20), by prior arrangement only. Learn more about the area's literary and artistic heritage.

Access for all: 🦽 🖼 👁 Building 🦼 Grounds 🦼

Getting here: 176:TQ272777. Off Oakley Street (between the King's Road and Albert Bridge), National Trust sign on corner of Upper Cheyne Row. Or off Cheyne Walk, National Trust sign on corner of Cheyne Row. **Foot**: Thames Path within ¾ mile. **Cycle**: NCN4. **Bus**: 11, 19, 22, 49, 319 to Carlyle Square then walk down Bramerton Street, turn right into Glebe Place. 170 to Albert Bridge. **Train**: Victoria 2 miles. **Underground**: Sloane Square (District and Circle lines) 1 mile; South Kensington (Piccadilly, District and Circle lines) 1 mile. **Parking**: no parking. Very limited street parking at nearby meters (pay and display).

Finding out more: 020 7352 7087 or carlyleshouse@nationaltrust.org.uk

Carlyle's House		M	T	W	T	F	S	S
5 Mar–30 Oct	11–5			**W**	**T**	**F**	**S**	**S**
Open Bank Holiday Mondays, 11 to 5.								

Eastbury Manor House

Eastbury Square, Barking, London IG11 9SN

Map ② G5 `1918`

Important brick-built Tudor gentry house, completed about 1573, little altered since. Early 17th-century wall-paintings showing fishing scenes and a cityscape grace the former Great Chamber. Evocative exposed timbers in attic, fine original spiral oak staircase in turret, soaring chimneys, cobbled courtyard, peaceful walled garden with bee boles. **Note**: managed by the London Borough of Barking and Dagenham (www.barking-dagenham.gov.uk).

Exploring
- Discover Eastbury through attic displays and fresh interpretation.
- Consider intriguing Gunpowder Plot connections (especially Saturday, 5 November).
- Marvel at the skills of the Tudor builders and craftsmen.
- Many events first and second Saturdays of month (visit website).

Eating and shopping: relax in our garden tea-room, or at tables outside. Enjoy hot and cold drinks, sandwiches and snacks. Drop in to our Old Buttery gift shop (not National Trust).

Making the most of your day: volunteer-led guided tours. Themed family days every first Saturday of the month – homemade cakes and tour guides in costume. School holiday activities. Candlelit tours (last Tuesday of the month). **Dogs**: in grounds only on leads.

Access for all: 🅿️♿🚻♿♿🎧📷🅥🚶♿📷♿
Building 🚶♿♿♿ Courtyard ♿♿ Grounds 🚶

Getting here: 177:TQ457838. In Eastbury Square, 750 yards walk south from Upney (District Line, follow brown signs). **Cycle**: LCN15 ¾ mile and local link. **Bus**: TfL 62, 287, 368. **Train**: Barking, 1½ miles, then

Underground to Upney. **Underground**: Upney (District Line). **Road**: ½ mile north of A13, signposted from A123 Ripple Road. **Parking**: free parking in street adjacent to property.

Finding out more: 020 8724 1002 or eastburymanor@nationaltrust.org.uk. www.barking-dagenham.gov.uk

Eastbury Manor House		M	T	W	T	F	S	S
House and grounds								
10 Jan–20 Dec	10–4			M	T			
Tea-room and shop								
10 Jan–20 Dec	10–3:30			M	T			

Also open every first and second Saturday of the month. Closed Bank Holiday Mondays, 1, 3 and 4 January and 26 and 27 December.

Fenton House

Hampstead Grove, Hampstead, London NW3 6SP

Map ② G4 `1952`

This charming 17th-century merchant's house has remained virtually unaltered during more than 300 years of continuous occupation, while the large garden is also remarkably unchanged since it was described in 1756 as 'pleasant… well planted with fruit-trees, and a kitchen garden, all inclos'd with a substantial brick wall'. Lady Katherine Binning bought the house in 1936 and filled it with her highly decorative collections of porcelain, Georgian furniture and 17th-century needlework. The sound of early keyboard instruments and the colours of early 20th-century drawings and paintings add to a captivating experience.

Exploring
- 'London's most enchanting country house' (*Country Life*).
- World-class collections of Oriental, European and English porcelain.
- Benton Fletcher Collection of early keyboard instruments, in playing condition.
- Delightful decorative schemes by John Fowler.

The Oriental Room at Fenton House in Hampstead

Exploring — Extensive walled garden with topiary hedges and fine mixed borders.
— Apple orchard and abundant displays of spring flowers.

Eating and shopping: interesting range of property-related cards, books and CDs to buy.

Making the most of your day: Easter Trail and Apple Day. Summer lunchtime and evening concerts, demonstration tours of instruments. To audition to play the early keyboard instruments, email property.

Access for all: ⚹⬚♿⬚⬚
Building ⬚⬚ Grounds ⬚⬚

Getting here: 176:TQ262860. On west side of Hampstead Grove. **Bus**: frequent local services (020 7222 1234). **Train**: Hampstead

Heath or Finchley Road and Frognal 1 mile. **Underground**: Hampstead (Northern Line), 328 yards. **Parking**: no onsite parking.

You may also enjoy: 2 Willow Road, Sutton House and Carlyle's House.

Finding out more: 01494 755563 (Infoline). 020 7435 3471 or fentonhouse@nationaltrust.org.uk. Fenton House, Windmill Hill, London NW3 6RT

Fenton House		M	T	W	T	F	S	S
5 Mar–30 Oct	11–5				**W**	**T**	**F**	**S**	**S**

Open Bank Holiday Mondays and Good Friday 11 to 5. Some Thursdays in June and July open at 2 due to lunchtime concerts. Please check dates with property office.

George Inn

The George Inn Yard, 77 Borough High Street, Southwark, London SE1 1NH

Map ② G5 ⬚⬚ 1937

Dating from the 17th century this public house, leased to a private company, is London's last remaining galleried inn. **Note**: telephone to book a table.

Getting here: 176:TQ326801. On east side of Borough High Street, near London Bridge ⬚.

Finding out more: 020 7407 2056 or georgeinn@nationaltrust.org.uk

George Inn		M	T	W	T	F	S	S
1 Jan–31 Dec	11–11	**M**	**T**	**W**	**T**	**F**	**S**	
2 Jan–18 Dec	12–10:30							**S**

Closed 25 and 26 December. Sunday opening hours also apply on Bank Holidays.

Ham House and Garden

See South and South East section, page 119.

Morden Hall Park

Morden Hall Road, Morden, London SM4 5JD

Map ② G5  1942

A green oasis in suburbia, giving visitors a glimpse back in time to a country estate with an industrial heart. This tranquil former deer park is one of the few remaining estates that lined the River Wandle during its industrial heyday. The river meanders through the park, creating a haven for wildlife, while snuff mills still survive – the western mill has been renovated and is now a centre for learning and community with an active education programme. The park is a much-loved rural idyll in a built-up area. **Note**: the Victorian stableyard is being renovated and will open later this year with enhanced visitor facilities.

Exploring
- Enjoy the two miles of paths around the park.
- Discover wetland wildlife and wildflower meadows.
- Relax in the rose garden, blooming from June to October.
- Learn how to grow your own with our engagement garden.
- Pick up a Family Explorer Pack for fun and discovery.
- Follow the Wandle Trail to Deen City Farm.

Eating and shopping: eat in the café, with a delightful riverside setting. Browse in the shop for our extensive range of gifts and cards. Visit our second-hand bookshop for bargain books. Stock up on gardening essentials in the garden centre (not National Trust).

Making the most of your day: selection of trails. Extensive events programme including walks, talks and open-air theatre. Snuff Mill open first and third Sunday from April to October. Thursday family activities in the school holidays. **Dogs**: on leads around buildings and mown grass; under close control elsewhere.

Access for all: ⓅⓈ☕♿♿📷 👓Ⓐ
Building 🔅🔅♿ Grounds 🔅➡

Getting here: 176:TQ261684. Near Morden town centre. **Foot**: Wandle Trail from Croydon or Carshalton to Wandsworth. **Cycle**: NCN20 passes through. **Bus**: frequent from surrounding areas (020 7222 1234). **Train**: Tramlink to Phipps Bridge stop, on park boundary ½ mile. **Underground**: Morden (Northern Line), then 500 yards walk along Aberconway Road. **Road**: off A24, and A297 south of Wimbledon, north of Sutton. **Parking**: free, 25 yards (not National Trust).

You may also enjoy: other London properties Carlyle's House, Chelsea or 2 Willow Road and Fenton House, Hampstead.

Finding out more: 020 8545 6850 or mordenhallpark@nationaltrust.org.uk

Morden Hall Park		M	T	W	T	F	S	S
Park								
Open all year		M	T	W	T	F	S	S
Estate and car park								
Open all year	8–6	M	T	W	T	F	S	S
Shop								
2 Jan–31 Dec	10–5	M	T	W	T	F	S	S
Café								
2 Jan–31 Mar	10–4:30	M	T	W	T	F	S	S
1 Apr–30 Sep	9–5	M	T	W	T	F	S	S
1 Oct–31 Dec	10–4:30	M	T	W	T	F	S	S
Bookshop								
3 Jan–23 Dec	11–3	M	T	W	T	F	·	·
2 Jan–18 Dec	12–4	·	·	·	·	·	S	S

Shop, café and bookshop closed 15 February. Shop and café closed 25 and 26 December. Snuff Mill open first and third Sunday April to October, 12 to 4.

The bridge over the River Wandle at Morden Hall Park

Osterley Park and House

Jersey Road, Isleworth, Middlesex TW7 4RB

Map ② F5  1949

With a spectacular mansion surrounded by gardens, park and farmland, Osterley is one of the last surviving country estates in London. Once described as 'the palace of palaces', Osterley was created in the late 18th century by architect and designer Robert Adam for the Child family to entertain and impress their friends and clients. Today you can explore the dazzling interior with handheld audio-visual guides, which bring the house to life in a completely new way. Outside the gardens are a delightful retreat from urban life and the park is perfect for picnics and leisurely strolls.

Exploring	— Atmospheric film in the Tudor stables brings Osterley to life.
	— Extravagant show rooms created by the great designer Robert Adam.
	— Explore servants' lives in the fascinating 'below stairs' area.
	— Dressing up and hands-on activities for children.
	— Beautiful gardens currently being restored to their 18th-century glory.
	— Varied events programme, including walks, tours and themed weeks.

Eating and shopping: enjoy home-cooked lunches and afternoon teas in the Stables Café. Browse in the National Trust gift shop. Farm shop with fresh vegetables and flowers.

Making the most of your day: family activities and trails for the house and garden. Walks around park and lake; free leaflet available. Cycling in park on shared paths. **Dogs**: allowed in park only (on leads unless indicated).

Access for all: ⬛⬛⬛⬛⬛⬛⬛⬛⬛⬛⬛
⬛⬛ House ⬛⬛ Café and shop ⬛⬛
Garden ⬛➡⬛⬛

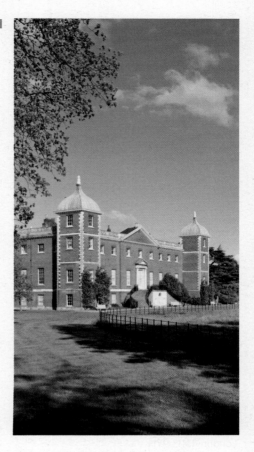

The imposing Osterley Park and House, Middlesex

Getting here: 176:TQ146780. **Cycle**: links to London Cycle Network. **Bus**: TfL H28 Hayes to Hounslow to Osterley, H91 Hounslow to Hammersmith to within 1 mile. **Train**: Isleworth 1½ miles. **Underground**: Osterley (Piccadilly Line) 1 mile. **Road**: on A4 between Hammersmith and Hounslow. Follow brown tourist signs on A4 between Gillette Corner and Osterley underground station; from west M4, exit 3 then follow A312/A4 towards central London. Main gates at junction with Thornbury and Jersey Roads. **Sat Nav**: enter Jersey Road and TW7 4RB. **Parking**: 400 yards. Booked coach parking free.

You may also enjoy: Ham House and Garden near Richmond-upon-Thames, and Cliveden near Maidenhead.

Finding out more: 020 8232 5050 or osterley@nationaltrust.org.uk

Osterley Park and House		M	T	W	T	F	S	S
House								
23 Feb–27 Mar*	12–3:30	·	·	W	T	F	S	S
30 Mar–30 Oct	12–4:30	·	·	W	T	F	S	S
5 Nov–27 Nov*	12–3:30	·	·	·	·	·	S	S
3 Dec–18 Dec	12–3:30	·	·	·	·	·	S	S
Park and car park								
1 Jan–31 Dec**	8–7:30	M	T	W	T	F	S	S
Café and shop								
23 Feb–30 Oct***	11–5	·	·	W	T	F	S	S
2 Nov–18 Dec	12–4	·	·	W	T	F	S	S
Garden								
26 Feb–6 Mar	12–3:30	·	·	·	·	·	S	S
9 Mar–30 Oct****	11–5	·	·	W	T	F	S	S
5 Nov–27 Nov	12–3:30	·	·	·	·	·	S	S

Open Good Friday and Bank Holiday Mondays. *Themed guided tours (Conservation in Action and Family Discovery) of selected rooms available every half hour from 12:15. Book on arrival, maximum 20 per tour, normal admission charges apply (members free). At times some rooms may be closed for essential conservation work. **Car park closed 1 January, 25 and 26 December. Park closes at 6 from 2 January to 27 March and 31 October to 31 December. ***Shop opens at 12, café closes at 4 from 23 February to 27 March. Additional kiosk selling teas/coffees/snacks open all week spring to autumn and weekends in winter. ****Garden closes at 4 from 9 to 27 March.

Rainham Hall

The Broadway, Rainham, Havering, London RM13 9YN

Map ② H5 1949

Charming Georgian house set in a peaceful, simple garden, with some surprising features, quality materials and fine craftmanship. Awaiting conservation. **Note**: no toilet.

Getting here: 177:TQ521821. 5 miles east of Barking. Just south of the church.

Finding out more: 020 7799 4552 or rainhamhall@nationaltrust.org.uk

Rainham Hall		M	T	W	T	F	S	S
2 Apr–29 Oct	2–5	·	·	·	·	·	S	·

Open Bank Holiday Mondays, April to October, 2 to 5. Open for May Day event and Rainham Christmas Fair.

Red House

Red House Lane, Bexleyheath, Kent DA6 8JF

Map ② H5 2003

'Fascinating guide, lovely friendly volunteers, and especially enjoyed the tea-room. Many thanks for a great day!'
J. Welsh, Winchester

The only house commissioned, created and lived in by William Morris, founder of the Arts and Crafts movement, Red House is a building of extraordinary architectural and social significance. When it was completed in 1860, it was described by Edward Burne-Jones as 'the beautifullest place on earth'. Only recently acquired by the Trust, the house is not fully furnished, but the original features and furniture by Morris and Philip Webb, stained glass and paintings by Burne-Jones, the bold architecture and a garden designed to 'clothe the house' add up to a fascinating and rewarding place to visit.

Exploring
- Booked guided tours daily, 11 to 1.
- Self-guided visits every afternoon from 1:30 (no booking required).
- Relax in the garden and play games on the lawn.
- Follow the leafy garden trail, perfect for children.
- Discover the original stables, with second-hand books and dried flowers.
- Teas, coffees, cake and light lunches every day.

Eating and shopping: Morris-related gifts – textiles, books, china, homeware. Second-hand bookshop in the old stables. Delicious light refreshments – all served with a smile.

Making the most of your day: Easter Fun, Arts and Crafts fair, open day, Apple Day in the orchard and carols at Christmas. Garden games, nature trail and picnicking in the orchard always available.
Dogs: assistance dogs only.

We welcome dogs assisting visitors with disabilities

Red House, Kent, designed by Philip Webb in 1859

Access for all: 🅿️♿🏠📷💻📺🎨
Building 🔼 Grounds ♿➡️

Getting here: 177:TQ481750. **Bus**: 89, 422, 486, B11 and B16 London Central; B12 and B15 Arriva Kent Thameside; B14 Metrobus; 96 Selkent. All stop at Upton Road. **Train**: Bexleyheath 🚉, ¾ mile. **Road**: M25 junction 2 to A2 for Bexleyheath. Exit at Danson interchange and follow A221 Bexleyheath. Turn left for parking at Danson Park or turn right onto Bean Road direct to Red House. **Parking**: no onsite parking (except disabled parking space, booking essential). Parking at Danson Park (approximately 1 mile). Charge at weekends and Bank Holidays.

You may also enjoy: Standen.

Finding out more: 020 8304 9878 or redhouse@nationaltrust.org.uk

Red House		M	T	W	T	F	S	S
2 Mar–30 Oct	11–5			W	T	F	S	S
4 Nov–18 Dec	11–5					F	S	S

Open Bank Holiday Mondays. Booked guided tours at 11, 11:30, 12, 12:30 and 1 (booking essential, 020 8304 9878). Self-guided viewing 1:30 until last entry at 4:15 (booking unnecessary).

'Roman' Bath

5 Strand Lane, London WC2

Map ② G5   🏛️ 1948

Remains of a bath – possibly Roman. Viewed through a grille all year, appointments required to see interior. **Note**: administered and maintained by Westminster City Council. No toilet.

Getting here: 176:TQ309809. Just west of Aldwych station (now closed), approach via Surrey Street.

Finding out more: 020 7641 5264 (bookings). 020 8232 5050 or romanbath@nationaltrust.org.uk

'Roman' Bath		M	T	W	T	F	S	S
6 Apr–19 Oct	1–4			W				

Admission by appointment only with Westminster County Council during office hours (020 7641 5264, 24-hours' notice). Bath visible through grille from pathway all year, 9 to dusk.

Sutton House

2 and 4 Homerton High Street, Hackney, London E9 6JQ

Map ② G4   🏠🔔☕ 1938

Built in 1535 by prominent courtier of Henry VIII, Sir Ralph Sadleir, Sutton House retains much of the atmosphere of a Tudor home despite some alterations by later occupants, including a succession of merchants, Huguenot silkweavers and squatters. With oak-panelled rooms, original carved fireplaces and a charming courtyard.

Exploring
 – Discover a hidden gem in the heart of East London.
 – Experience the sights and smells of a real Tudor kitchen.
 – Relax in our tranquil and stunning courtyard.
 – Enjoy our family treasure chests, representing our unusual residents.

Eating and shopping: charming, fully licensed tea-room. Browse in the second-hand bookshop. Small shop, stocking limited range of local and Trust goods.

Making the most of your day: lively and varied programme of events for all tastes and ages. Craft fairs, fantastic themed family days. Monthly Sunday guided tours, February to November. **Dogs**: assistance dogs only.

Access for all: Dᵢ | WC | 🚶 | 📷 | 📖 | 📋 | ∴ | Ⓐ
Building 🚶🚶🚶♿

Getting here: 176:TQ352851. At the corner of Isabella Road and Homerton High Street. **Cycle**: NCN1, 1¼ miles. **Bus**: frequent local services (020 7222 1234). **Train**: Hackney Central ¼ mile; Hackney Downs ½ mile. **Underground**: Bethnal Green (then 254, 106 or D6 to Hackney Central). **Parking**: no onsite parking. Limited metered parking on adjacent streets.

Finding out more: 020 8986 2264 or suttonhouse@nationaltrust.org.uk

Sutton House		M	T	W	T	F	S	S
Historic rooms								
3 Feb–16 Dec	10–4:30	·	·	·	**T**	**F**	·	·
5 Feb–18 Dec	12–4:30	·	·	·	·	·	**S**	**S**
25 Jul–31 Aug	10–4:30	**M**	**T**	**W**	·	·	·	·
Café, gallery and shops								
3 Feb–16 Dec	9–5	·	·	·	**T**	**F**	·	·
5 Feb–18 Dec	12–5	·	·	·	·	·	**S**	**S**
25 Jul–31 Aug	9–5	**M**	**T**	**W**	·	·	·	·

Open Bank Holiday Mondays and Good Friday. Property is regularly used by local community groups – the rooms will always be open as advertised, but please telephone in advance if you would like to visit the property during a quiet time.

2 Willow Road

Hampstead, London NW3 1TH

Map ② G5   🏛 | 1994

This unique Modernist home was designed by architect Ernö Goldfinger in 1939 for himself and his family. With surprising design details that were groundbreaking at the time and still feel fresh today, the house also contains the Goldfingers' impressive collection of modern art, intriguing personal possessions and innovative furniture. **Note**: nearest toilet at local pub.

Exploring
- Join a guided tour.
- Or explore on your own between 3 and 5.
- See a special exhibition about Goldfinger's designs for children.

The first-floor dining room at 2 Willow Road, Hampstead

Making the most of your day: London guided walks programme with evening events. Local attractions, including Fenton House. Many cafés, restaurants and pubs in Hampstead village. Children's playground and Hampstead Heath 21 yards. Children's quiz/trail.

Access for all: Pᵢ | 📷 | 📖 | 📋 | ∴ | Ⓐ   **Building** 🚶🚶

Getting here: 176:TQ270858. On corner of Willow Road and Downshire Hill. **Foot**: from Hampstead Underground, left down High Street and first left down Flask Walk (part pedestrianised). Turn right at the end into Willow Road and walk down the hill almost to end of road. **Bus**: frequent local services (020 7222 1234). **Train**: Hampstead Heath ¼ mile. **Underground**: Hampstead (Northern Line) ¼ mile. **Parking**: no onsite parking. Limited onstreet metered parking (free on Sundays). East Heath Road municipal car park, 100 yards, open intermittently (closed some Bank Holiday weekends due to local fair).

Finding out more: 01494 755570 (Infoline). 020 7435 6166 or 2willowroad@nationaltrust.org.uk

2 Willow Road		M	T	W	T	F	S	S
5 Mar–30 Oct	11–5	·	·	**W**	**T**	**F**	**S**	**S**

Entry by guided tour only at 11, 12, 1 and 2. Places on tours limited and available on a first-come first-served basis on the day. Non-guided viewing 3 to 5, with timed entry when busy. Introductory film shown at regular intervals. Wednesdays, Thursdays and Fridays are generally less busy.

East of England

Early morning mist hovers over the glassy waters of the lake on the Blickling Estate

Outdoors in the East of England

Above:
**wild fenland
at Wicken Fen,
Cambridgeshire**

The East of England is a region of surprising contrasts. Dramatic seascapes, breathtaking views over sweeping scenery, acres of parkland to explore, gardens in which to sit and watch life pass by – whatever mood you are in you'll find somewhere to match it.

Dotted along the roads of the region you will spot brown signs with a white acorn logo and a place name. If you follow these signs you will discover many pleasures. You could find a stately home set within beautiful parkland, a wild stretch of coast, an ancient fen abundant with wildlife, or even a tree cathedral.

The Trust cares for 11,000 hectares (27,000 acres) of land, of which almost half supports such a rich biological diversity that they are designated Sites of Special Scientific Interest.

Wicken Fen National Nature Reserve in Cambridgeshire, for example, is a haven for rare wildlife and virtually the last remnant of the extensive wild fenland that once covered much of the East of England. The 'Wicken Fen Vision' aims to create the largest nature reserve in the region, offering access to people and wildlife in an area increasingly under pressure from surrounding development.

So whether you are a serious 'twitcher' or just enjoy getting out into the countryside, regular visitors know that time spent in these wonderful places is time well spent.

Right:
**get on your bike
at Dunstable
Downs in
Bedfordshire**

Above: **the 1930s is brought to life at Blickling Hall**

Treasures on the coast

If you feel up to it you can explore more than 49 miles of coastline in the East of England.

The North Norfolk coast, as well as being home to several major colonies of common and grey seals, hosts more than 3,000 pairs of breeding Sandwich terns in the summer, while in the autumn and winter thousands of waders and waterfowl descend upon the marshes of Blakeney Freshes.

The Trust maintains this delicate mecca for people and wildlife for the benefit of future generations, successfully balancing access with conservation.

Further down the coast in Suffolk is Orford Ness, the once-secret military test site which is now an internationally important nature reserve and vital habitat for rare species. Unique is a term often overused, however Orford Ness is something special: with its rare flora and fauna, and unusual military architecture.

Natural habitats nearby include Dunwich Heath, a surviving fragment of the sandy heaths locally known as the 'Sandlings'. The heath is where the rare Dartford warbler returned to this part of the country, and is now home to a strong breeding population. When the heather and gorse are in full bloom you will struggle to find a more colourful breath of fresh air!

Ascending above the rhododendron canopy at Sheringham Park, visitors are treated to a magnificent sight; stretching away from you to the sea is a riot of colour and scents guaranteed to lift the tiredest of spirits.

The past comes to life

Ever thought you'd like to time travel and experience life as it may have been in the past? Well, various properties throughout the East of England offer just such an opportunity. So be sure to join us on a journey back to the dramatic periods that shaped our country and society.

At Sutton Hoo you could find yourself in the royal presence of King Raedwald as he recounts tales of the battles he fought to shape our nation. Alternatively get your hands dirty with a 1930s archaeologist – one of the amateur band who discovered Raedwald's ship burial.

Life above and below stairs is brought vividly to life at Blickling Hall. See if you would have preferred to shine shoes or clean a fire grate as one of the army of staff; or perhaps you would have liked to accompany the famous garden designer Norah Lindsay as she sketched out plans for the fashionably new double borders?

The dramatic years of the Second World War were a time of sacrifice and hardship, but it was also an age of unprecedented community spirit. Join in at Wimpole Hall and whisk yourself back to an era of powdered egg and rationing. Then take a turn with the Home Guard or learn how to 'make do and mend' – you could even take the opportunity to taste what many people lived on in the blackout.

With a multitude of historical events throughout the season at places such as Ickworth, Hatfield Forest, Shaw's Corner, Melford Hall and Oxburgh, you'll be able to fly through the centuries like a Time Lord!

Below: **Dunwich Heath in Suffolk is a great place to spot the scarce Dartford warbler**

Above: **climb to the top of Horsey Windpump in Norfolk for amazing views over Horsey Mere**

Bikes, beaches and adventures

A visit to a National Trust property is an ideal place to start your exploration of an area. Most of the places you'll visit with the Trust are set in, or near, historic, beautiful, bustling, tranquil or picturesque towns and villages.

On the Essex/Suffolk border, at the heart of 'Constable Country', Bridge Cottage is the perfect place for a breathtaking walk into the beautiful Dedham Vale.

Many other excellent walks are to be had on Dunstable Downs in Bedfordshire, which command outstanding views over the Vale of Aylesbury and along the Chiltern Ridge. A great starting point is the new Gateway Centre sitting atop the Downs and offering wonderful views. And if you log onto our website you'll find a host of walks to download to get you started.

If you take the opportunity to stay in one of the Trust's many holiday cottages, you'll find them a perfect base to explore the surrounding property, countryside or towns.

For the energetic souls among you who like to get out and explore on two wheels, there are miles of tracks, paths and accessible countryside. Hatfield Forest, Ickworth Park and Sheringham Park are best seen from a bike saddle in some people's opinion! You can even hire a bike at Blickling, if you are on holiday without your trusty metal steed. And if the weather is kind, why not just kick off your shoes and feel the sand between your toes as you wander along some of Britain's finest beaches?

My favourite place

Horsey is a hidden gateway to the Norfolk Broads which has changed little over the past 50 years and still retains an old-world charm and feeling of peace and tranquillity.

My first job in the morning is to make the long climb to the top of the magnificent windpump to open the balcony door. Even on the most depressing of days, I cannot stop myself pausing to view the spectacular Broadland landscape – populated solely by boats, birds and reedbeds.

This is not the part of the Norfolk Broads which has been manicured to please the eye of the visitor. Here the Broads are untouched and boast a natural raw beauty, with the wildlife taking centre stage and people being merely guests and awestruck observers.

The only noise I can hear is the pink-footed geese chattering away. They migrate to Horsey in their thousands to enjoy the protection the estate gives them, while feasting on the banquet that the sugar beet fields provide. On a good day I will spot one of the 30 cranes that have made their home at Horsey. For a creature which looks so uncomfortable on the ground, with its camel-like walk, it is a picture of elegance in flight.

Just before I make my way back down the steps to earn my daily bread, I always turn 180 degrees to take a look at the sand bank which protects us from the North Sea. This man-made structure is always in danger of being breached and reminds me that the land I stand on once belonged to the sea, and one day it may well be back to claim it.

Stuart Lake
Enterprises Supervisor,
Horsey Windpump

Anglesey Abbey, Gardens and Lode Mill

Quy Road, Lode, Cambridge, Cambridgeshire CB25 9EJ

Map ③ G7  1966

'**Very enjoyable – loved the combination of art and homely atmosphere**.'
Claire Robinson, St Albans

A passion for tradition and style inspired one man to transform a run-down country house and desolate landscape. Step into his elegant home and discover the luxuries enjoyed by guests. Experience the warmth and comfort and be amazed at rare and fabulous objects. Lord Fairhaven was a generous host, delighting in entertaining visitors and a life occupied with horse racing and shooting. The 46-hectare (114-acre) garden, with its working watermill, wildlife discovery area and statuary, offers inspiration and planting for all seasons. Explore the borders, meadow and avenues bursting with vibrant colour, delicious scent and the simple pleasures of nature.

Exploring
- Set out on an adventure with our family activity packs.
- Catch the chime of one of the 37 rare clocks.
- Transform yourself into a country gentleman with our dressing-up clothes.
- Be wowed by the Himalayan silver birches.
- Spy on nature from the wildlife watch hut.
- Unwind with a peaceful stroll through the gardens.

Eating and shopping: visit the plant centre and recreate the look. Dip into the shop for a bag of our specially ground Lode Mill flour. Try delicious home-cooked food, made with fresh local ingredients. Feel revitalised in the tranquil setting of Redwoods Restaurant.

Making the most of your day: exhibitions, activities and events all year round. Family trails and activity packs. Experience 1930s living and discover fascinating facts with the help of room cards and volunteer room guides. **Dogs**: assistance dogs only.

Access for all: 🅿️ 🚏 ♿ 🚹 🏛️ 📷 📺 🎢 ⦿ 🖐️
House ♿ 📷 Mill ♿ 📷 Grounds ♿ ➡️ 🚗 ♿

The wildflower meadow at Anglesey Abbey, Gardens and Lode Mill in Cambridgeshire

Getting here: 154:TL533622. **Foot**: Harcamlow Way from Cambridge. **Cycle**: NCN51, 1¼ miles. **Bus**: Stagecoach route 10 from Cambridge (frequent services link Cambridge ⧆ and bus station). Alight at Lode Crossroads stop. **Train**: Cambridge 6 miles. **Road**: 6 miles north-east of Cambridge on B1102. Signposted from A14, junction 35. **Parking**: free, 50 yards.

You may also enjoy: learn about 1930s life below stairs at Blickling Hall.

Finding out more: 01223 810080 or angleseyabbey@nationaltrust.org.uk

Anglesey Abbey		M	T	W	T	F	S	S
Garden, restaurant, shop and plant centre								
1 Jan–27 Feb	10:30–4:30	M	T	W	T	F	S	S
28 Feb–30 Oct	10:30–5:30	M	T	W	T	F	S	S
31 Oct–31 Dec	10:30–4:30	M	T	W	T	F	S	S
House								
2 Mar–30 Oct	11–5	·	·	W	T	F	S	S
Lode Mill								
1 Jan–27 Feb	11–3:30	·	·	W	T	F	S	S
2 Mar–30 Oct	11–4	·	·	W	T	F	S	S
2 Nov–31 Dec	11–3:30	·	·	W	T	F	S	S

House open Bank Holiday Mondays. Closed Christmas Eve, Christmas Day and Boxing Day. Some areas of the garden may be closed due to season. Snowdrop season 24 January to 27 February. Picture galleries only also open 1 to 16 January and 16 November to 31 December, 11 to 3:30.

Exploring
- Blakeney Point – internationally important for seabirds and seals.
- Follow the Norfolk Coast Path for great views and wildlife.
- Learn about marine life at Stiffkey, Morston and Blakeney.
- Guided walks (small charge) for schools and groups by arrangement.

Eating and shopping: refreshments and seafood stall (not National Trust) at Morston Quay. Seafood, including Morston mussels from local suppliers (not National Trust). Nearby pubs and hotels (not National Trust) offering locally themed menus.

Making the most of your day: learn more about this dynamic coastal environment – Information Centres at Morston Quay and at the Lifeboat House on Blakeney Point. Try one of our downloadable walks available via our website. **Dogs**: welcome, some restrictions apply (particularly Blakeney Point) from 1 April to mid-August.

Access for all: 🖥 Morston Quay Information Centre 🏛 Lifeboat House and toilets 🚻

Blakeney National Nature Reserve

Morston Quay, Quay Road, Morston, Norfolk NR25 7BH

Map ③ I3  1912

Wide open spaces and uninterrupted views of the natural and dynamic coastline make for an inspiring visit to Blakeney, at any time of the year. The moving tides, covering pristine saltmarsh or exposing the harbour, combined with the varying light of Norfolk's big skies, create an ever-changing scene. **Note**: nearest toilet at Morston Quay and Blakeney Quay (not National Trust).

Blakeney National Nature Reserve in Norfolk

Blickling Estate, Norfolk: the house is set in enchanting gardens within a landscape park

Getting here: 133:TG000460. **Foot**: Norfolk Coast Path passes property. **Cycle**: Regional route 30 runs along ridge above the coast. **Ferry**: to Blakeney Point (not National Trust). **Bus**: Norfolk Green 'Coast Hopper' 36 Cromer ⮞ to Hunstanton. **Train**: Sheringham 8 miles. **Road**: Morston Quay, Blakeney and Cley are all off A149 Cromer to Hunstanton road. **Sat Nav**: NR25 7BH. **Parking**: pay and display (members free) at Morston Quay and also at Blakeney Quay (administered by Blakeney Parish Council). Quayside car parks are liable to tidal flooding.

Finding out more: 01263 740241 or blakeneypoint@nationaltrust.org.uk. Norfolk Coast Office, Friary Farm, Cley Road, Blakeney, Norfolk NR25 7NW

Blakeney National Nature Reserve		M	T	W	T	F	S	S
Nature Reserve								
1 Jan–31 Dec		M	T	W	T	F	S	S
Lifeboat House (Blakeney Point)*								
4 Apr–30 Sep	Dawn–dusk	M	T	W	T	F	S	S

*Lifeboat House and toilets (Blakeney Point) open dawn to dusk. Refreshment kiosk (not National Trust) and Information Centre at Morston Quay open according to tides and weather.

Blickling Estate

Blickling, Norwich, Norfolk NR11 6NF

Map ③ J4

'The gardens were enchanting and thought-provoking, the house took us back to the periods it had seen.'
Edward Flaxman, Halesworth

Embark on a voyage of discovery and follow four centuries of history at Blickling, from the Boleyn family to the RAF and Second World War. Learn what life was like as a servant and hear the stories of the real people who kept Blickling going. Explore the Long Gallery, which holds the most important book collection in the National Trust. The estate is a treasure trove of romantic buildings, beautiful and extensive gardens and landscape park. From 400-year-old yew hedges and historic trees, to a hidden pyramid and glistening lake, there is something for everyone to enjoy throughout the year.

Exploring
- Experience the four seasons through the spectacular garden.
- Discover the splendour of a country house over four centuries.
- Magnificent library collection, with a regularly changing display of books.
- Listen to the actual voices of Blickling's servants.
- Enjoy the tranquillity of the lake (coarse fishing available).
- Follow Blickling's wartime history in the RAF Museum.

Eating and shopping: browse for that special gift in our East Wing shop. Enjoy local seasonal food in the restaurant and Courtyard Café. Plant centre and garden shop for the green fingered. Second-hand bookshop with bargains from 50p to £150.

Making the most of your day: house highlight tours (Mondays and Tuesdays at 1, 2 and 3, other days 10:45). Garden tours, RAF Museum, croquet, cycle hire and children's trails. Exhibitions throughout the year.
Dogs: welcome in park and woods, on leads at all times.

Access for all: ⓟ🅳♿🅆♿🍴⛲🎨🚲👓👂♿
Building 👫🅰♿🔂♿ Grounds ♿➡🔂♿

Getting here: 133:TG178286. **Foot**: Weavers' Way from Great Yarmouth and Cromer (Aylsham, 2 miles). **Cycle**: permitted path alongside Bure Valley Railway, Wroxham ≋ to Aylsham. **Bus**: Sanders 4, 41/43/44, First 50, Norfolk Green X5 Norwich to Holt/Sheringham (passing close Norwich ≋), alight Aylsham 1½ miles. **Train**: Aylsham (Bure Valley Railway from Hoveton and Wroxham ≋) 1¾ miles; North Walsham 8 miles. **Road**: 1½ miles north-west of Aylsham on B1354. Signposted off A140 Norwich (15 miles north) to Cromer (10 miles south) road. **Parking**: 400 yards, £2.50.

You may also enjoy: experience the luxurious 1930s lifestyle of Lord Fairhaven at Anglesey Abbey.

Finding out more: 01263 738030 or blickling@nationaltrust.org.uk

Blickling Estate		M	T	W	T	F	S	S
House								
19 Feb–24 Jul	11–5			W	T	F	S	S
25 Jul–11 Sep	11–5	M		W	T	F	S	S
14 Sep–30 Oct	11–5			W	T	F	S	S
Garden, shop, restaurant and bookshop								
1 Jan–18 Feb	11–4				T	F	S	S
19 Feb–30 Oct	10–5:30	M	T	W	T	F	S	S
2 Nov–31 Dec	11–4			W	T	F	S	S
Plant centre								
12 Mar–30 Oct	10–5:30	M	T	W	T	F	S	S
Cycle hire								
9 Apr–30 Oct	10–5:30						S	S
Park								
Open all year		M	T	W	T	F	S	S

House also open Monday 11, 18, 25 April, plus 2 and 30 May. Limited timed tours available on all other Mondays and Tuesdays 19 February to 30 October (spaces limited). Cycle hire available daily during Norfolk County Council school holidays. Closed 25 and 26 December.

Bourne Mill

Bourne Road, Colchester, Essex CO2 8RT

Map ③ I8   🏠 1936

A delightful piece of late Elizabethan playfulness. Built for banquets and converted into a mill, still with working waterwheel.
Note: no toilet. Limited parking in mill grounds.

Access for all: 🏠🚲👓 Building 👫 Grounds 👫🅰

Getting here: 168:TM006238. 1 mile south of centre of Colchester, on Bourne Road, off Mersea Road (B1025).

Finding out more: 01206 572422 or bournemill@nationaltrust.org.uk

Bourne Mill		M	T	W	T	F	S	S
5 Jun–26 Jun	2–5							S
30 Jun–28 Aug	2–5				T			S

Open Easter, May and August Bank Holidays, Sundays and Mondays.

Brancaster Estate

Harbour Way, Brancaster Staithe, Norfolk

Map ③ H3  1923

Famous for its mussels, the fishing village of Brancaster Staithe lies on the shores of the beautiful North Norfolk coast. Follow the history of the fishing industry at Brancaster Quay, visit Branodunum Scheduled Ancient Monument or be inspired at Brancaster beach. **Note**: nearest toilet (not National Trust) Brancaster beach. Scolt Head Island NNR managed by Natural England.

Exploring
- Enjoy the harbour and spectacular views across the saltmarsh.
- Follow the Norfolk Coast Path for great views and wildlife.
- Relax and picnic at Brancaster beach.
- Step back in time at the Roman fort of Branodunum.

Eating and shopping: try the fabulous Brancaster mussels or locally caught fresh fish. Quench your thirst at Brancaster Staithe's pubs (not National Trust).

Making the most of your day: visit our website and download one of our walks or sign up for a family adventure day or week at Brancaster Millennium Activity Centre during holiday periods. **Dogs**: welcome, some restrictions apply at Brancaster beach from May to mid-August.

Access for all: Grounds 🚻

Getting here: 132:TF800450. **Foot**: Norfolk Coast Path passes property. **Cycle**: Regional Route 30 runs along ridge above coast. **Bus**: Norfolk Green Coast Hopper 36 Sheringham ≋ to Hunstanton. **Road**: Brancaster Staithe is halfway between Wells and Hunstanton on A149. **Sat Nav**: use PE31 8AX. **Parking**: Beach Road, Brancaster (not National Trust). Charge including members. Limited parking at Brancaster Staithe, subject to tidal flooding.

A fishing boat at Brancaster Staithe in Norfolk

Finding out more: 01263 740241 or brancaster@nationaltrust.org.uk. Norfolk Coast Office, Friary Farm, Cley Road, Blakeney, Norfolk NR25 7NW

Brancaster Estate	Open every day all year

Brancaster Millennium Activity Centre

Dial House, Harbour Way, Brancaster Staithe, Norfolk PE31 8BW

Map ③ H3  1984

The 400-year-old Dial House was once a pub then later became a family home. It is now a residential activity centre for hundreds of schoolchildren, families and adults. Visitors experience and enjoy outdoor adventures, including sailing, kayaking, team-building, orienteering and more, while developing a better understanding of sustainable living. **Note**: contact the centre for activity programmes, prices and availability.

Exploring
- Enjoy memorable day or week-long adventures with your family.

Exploring
- Curious about sailing? Budding artist? Explore our varied adult courses.
- Discover our stunning coastline by kayak, bike, boat or foot.
- Share in our passion for the environment and sustainable living.

Eating and shopping: meals are prepared by our head cook, who uses locally sourced produce whenever possible (some of which is grown in our garden and looked after by our visitors). We have a small ethical gift shop for residents.

Making the most of your day: we offer adventure days/weeks for families during holiday periods, adult courses throughout the year and school day/residential weeks throughout term time. Please contact us for availability and choice. **Dogs**: please enquire within centre.

Access for all: [WC]
Brancaster Millennium Activity Centre [icons]

Getting here: 132: TF792444. **Foot**: Norfolk Coast Path passes property. **Cycle**: Regional Route 30 runs along ridge above the coast. **Bus**: Norfolk Green Coast Hopper 36 Sheringham [train] to Hunstanton. **Road**: on A149 coast road, halfway between Wells and Hunstanton. **Parking**: limited parking within Harbour Way, Brancaster Staithe.

Finding out more: 01485 210719 or brancaster@nationaltrust.org.uk

Brancaster Activity Centre	M	T	W	T	F	S	S
1 Jan–31 Dec	M	T	W	T	F	S	S

Please contact the centre for more information on residential group bookings, courses and activities.

Go wild at Brancaster Millennium Activity Centre, Norfolk

Coggeshall Grange Barn

Grange Hill, Coggeshall, Colchester, Essex CO6 1RE

Map (3) I8   [icons] 1989

One of Europe's oldest timber-framed buildings, the barn has an astonishing cathedral-like interior. Exhibition of local woodcarving and tools.

Access for all: [icons] Building [icon] Grounds [icon]

Getting here: 168:TL848223. Off A120 Coggeshall bypass; ¼ mile south from centre of Coggeshall, on B1024.

Finding out more: 01376 562226 or coggeshall@nationaltrust.org.uk

Coggeshall Grange Barn	M	T	W	T	F	S	S
22 Apr–9 Oct	1–5			W	T	F	S	S

Open Bank Holiday Mondays. May be closed some Saturdays for private functions.

Dunstable Downs, Chilterns Gateway Centre and Whipsnade Estate

Whipsnade Road, Dunstable, Bedfordshire LU6 2GY

Map (3) E8   [icons]  1928

Acres of space to enjoy with fabulous views over the Vale of Aylesbury and along the Chiltern Ridge. Dunstable Downs is an Area of Outstanding Natural Beauty and a kite-flying hotspot. Chalk grassland, rich in wildlife, provides prime walking country – spot the gliders soaring over the glorious landscape!

Fly kites and enjoy amazing views at Dunstable Downs, Bedfordshire: the highest point in the East of England

Note: Chilterns Gateway Centre is owned by Central Bedfordshire Council and managed by the National Trust.

Exploring
- Enjoy the views from the comfort of our visitor centre.
- Have fun flying kites from the top of Dunstable Downs.
- Walk across chalk grassland habitats and explore fascinating archaeological features.

Eating and shopping: try local foods, like the Bedfordshire Clanger, in the café. Explore the shop, which sells an excellent range of kites. Downs-based circular walks leaflets available from the visitor centre.

Making the most of your day: kite-flying all year round and annual kite festival. Waymarked routes, multi-user trail to Five Knolls and regular guided walks. Monthly farmers' market and wide programme of events. **Dogs**: under close control, on leads near livestock.

Access for all: 🅿️♿🚻♿♿🎨
Chilterns Gateway Centre ♿♿ Dunstable Downs ➡️

Getting here: 165/166:TL002189. **Foot**: from West Street and Tring Road, Dunstable. **Cycle**: bridleway from West Street, Dunstable, and Whipsnade. **Bus**: Arriva 60 from Luton, Centrebus 327 from Hemel Hempstead ≋ and Red Rose 343 from St Albans ≋, all Sundays only; otherwise Arriva 61 Aylesbury to Luton ≋ to within 1½ miles. **Train**: Luton 7 miles. Luton Airport Parkway 7 miles. **Road**: on B4541 west of Dunstable. **Sat Nav**: use LU6 2GY or LU6 2TA for older equipment. **Parking**: Dunstable Downs, off B4541 (£1.50); Bison Hill, off B4540; Whipsnade Tree Cathedral, B4540 (off village green); Whipsnade crossroads (Whipsnade Heath), junction of B4541 and B4540. Space for three coaches only at Dunstable, booking essential (no other coach facilities).

Finding out more: 01582 500920 or dunstabledowns@nationaltrust.org.uk

Dunstable Downs		M	T	W	T	F	S	S
Downs								
Open all year		M	T	W	T	F	S	S
Chilterns Gateway Centre								
1 Jan–11 Mar	10–4	M	T	W	T	F	S	S
12 Mar–30 Oct	10–5	M	T	W	T	F	S	S
31 Oct–31 Dec	10–4	M	T	W	T	F	S	S

Chilterns Gateway Centre closed 24 and 25 December. Centre closes dusk if earlier. Car park adjacent to Centre locked dusk in winter and 6 in summer.

Dunwich Heath: Coastal Centre and Beach

Dunwich, Saxmundham, Suffolk IP17 3DJ

Map ③ K6  1968

Tucked away on the Suffolk coast, Dunwich Heath offers you peace and quiet and a true sense of being at one with nature. A rare and precious habitat, the heath is home to special species such as the Dartford warbler, nightjar, woodlark, ant-lion, adder and much more. Quiet and serene, wild and dramatic, this is an inspiring visit, whatever the time of year. From July to September, the heath is alive with colour; a patchwork of pink and purple heather and coconut-scented yellow gorse is an unmissable experience. **Note**: parking restrictions may operate at times of extreme fire risk.

Exploring	– Follow a waymarked nature trail.
	– Inspiring walks linking beach and heath.
	– SeaWatch lookout – spot porpoises, seals and birds.
	– New children's trail.
	– See the scarce Dartford warbler.
	– Self-drive and chauffeured mobility vehicles.

Eating and shopping: award-winning tea-room, local produce, gluten-free choices, children's menu. Coastal-themed gifts in the shop. Holiday in our three clifftop flats or a village cottage. Eat outside and enjoy beautiful coastal views.

Making the most of your day: guided walks, family nature trails, Tracker Packs, smugglers' and history trails, tea-room events, sea-watching and wildlife identification charts and telescopes. Children's play area next to tea-room. **Dogs**: allowed, although restrictions apply (see notices).

Dunwich Beach, Suffolk, offers peace and quiet

Access for all: P D WC 🚻 📶 🖐
Tea-room and gift shop ♿ 👁
SeaWatch building ♿ 👁 **Grounds** ➡ ♿

Getting here: 156:TM476685. **Foot**: Suffolk Coast and Heaths Path and Sandlings Walk. **Cycle**: on Suffolk coastal cycle route. **Bus**: Coastlink from Darsham ₹ and Saxmundham (booking essential on 01728 833526). **Train**: Darsham 6 miles. **Road**: 1 mile south of Dunwich, signposted from A12. From Westleton/Dunwich road, 1 mile before Dunwich village turn right into Minsmere road. Then 1 mile to Dunwich Heath. **Parking**: 150 yards (pay and display, members free). Limited to three coaches.

You may also enjoy: the wild and remote former 'secret site' of Orford Ness offers a unique experience.

Finding out more: 01728 648501 or dunwichheath@nationaltrust.org.uk

Dunwich Heath		M	T	W	T	F	S	S
Heath								
Open all year		M	T	W	T	F	S	S
Tea-room and shop*								
2 Jan–6 Mar	10–4						S	S
9 Mar–10 Apr	10–4			W	T	F	S	S
11 Apr–1 May	10–5	M	T	W	T	F	S	S
4 May–10 Jul	10–5			W	T	F	S	S
11 Jul–18 Sep	10–5	M	T	W	T	F	S	S
21 Sep–18 Dec	10–4			W	T	F	S	S
26 Dec–31 Dec	10–4	M	T	W	T	F	S	

Open Bank Holiday Mondays. Open Monday to Sunday during local half-term holidays. *Tea-room and shop closing times vary.

Elizabethan House Museum

4 South Quay, Great Yarmouth,
Norfolk NR30 2QH

Map ③ K5 1943

An amazing 'hands-on' museum to enthrall all ages. This 16th-century quayside building reflects the life and times of the families who lived here from Tudor to Victorian times. Decide for yourself if the death of Charles I was plotted in the Conspiracy Room! **Note**: house is managed by Norfolk Museums and Archaeology Service.

Exploring	–	See how the Tudors lived in the 16th century.
	–	Discover Victorian life 'upstairs and downstairs'.
	–	Enjoy a stroll along Great Yarmouth's historic South Quay.

Hands-on fun at the Elizabethan House Museum, Norfolk

Eating and shopping: small shop on ground floor.

Making the most of your day: Tudor costumes to try on; activity-packed toy room for children and hands-on activities.

Access for all: ⬚⬚⬚⬚⬚ Building ⬚⬚

Getting here: 134:TG523073. On Great Yarmouth's historic South Quay. **Foot**: level walk from railway station along North Quay on to South Quay. **Cycle**: Regional Route 30 Great Yarmouth to Cromer. **Bus**: local services, plus services from surrounding areas. **Train**: Great

Yarmouth ½ miles. **Road**: from A47 take town centre signs, then follow brown Historic South Quay signs. From A12 follow brown signs. **Parking**: at the rear of the museum, operated by Borough Council (pay and display) Saturday and Sunday only. Other parking available near to the museum, town centre and historic quayside.

Finding out more: 01493 855746 or elizabethanhouse@nationaltrust.org.uk

Elizabethan House Museum		M	T	W	T	F	S	S
1 Apr–31 Oct	10–4	M	T	W	T	F	·	·
2 Apr–30 Oct	12–4	·	·	·	·	·	S	S

Felbrigg Hall, Gardens and Estate

Felbrigg, Norwich, Norfolk NR11 8PR

Map ③ J4 1969

'**Something very special in this ever-changing world**.'
Mr and Mrs Blakey, Suffolk

Once described as a hidden gem, the Hall is a place of surprises and delights, a mixture of opulence and homeliness where each room has something to feed the imagination. Outside, this 'bountiful estate' really lives up to its name. The decorative and productive walled garden is a gardener's delight, providing fruit and vegetables for the restaurant, flowers for the Hall and inspiration to visitors. The rolling landscape park with a lake, 211 hectares (520 acres) of woods and miles of waymarked trails is a great place to explore nature and wildlife or just to get away from it all.

Exploring	–	See the dining room laid for an 1860s dinner party.
	–	Don't miss the kitchen, the true 'engine-room' of the house.
	–	Look in the library, the 'internet' of the 18th century.
	–	Relax in the peace and quiet of the walled garden.

Felbrigg Hall, Gardens and Estate in Norfolk is a place of surprises and delights

Exploring — If you feel energetic, walk around the estate and woodlands.
— In the Cabinet, see the 'Grand Tour' in one room.

Eating and shopping: Carriages Brasserie, using seasonal produce from the walled garden and estate – enjoy our four-mile menu. Tea-room serving homemade cakes and snacks. Gift shop and plant sales. Browse the second-hand bookshop for that book you never thought you would find.

Making the most of your day: 'Garden Sleuths' trail. Easter and Hallowe'en children's trails. Chilli Fiesta 3 August, The Hall at Harvest 1 to 5 October and The Hall at Christmas 15, 16 and 17 December. **Dogs**: on leads in parkland when stock grazing, under close control in woodland.

Access for all: [icons]
Hall [icons] Shop and catering [icon]
Grounds [icons]

Getting here: 133:TG193394. **Foot**: Weavers' Way runs through property. **Cycle**: Regional Route 30, Great Yarmouth to Wells.

Train: Cromer or Roughton Road, both 2½ miles. **Road**: near Felbrigg village, 2 miles south-west of Cromer; entrance off B1436, signposted from A148 and A140. **Sat Nav**: gives poor directions, please follow 'brown signs'. **Parking**: 100 yards, £2 non-members.

You may also enjoy: Blickling Hall, built at the same time and by some of the same craftsmen.

Finding out more: 01263 837444 or felbrigg@nationaltrust.org.uk

Felbrigg Hall, Gardens and Estate		M	T	W	T	F	S	S
House								
5 Mar–30 Oct	11–5	M	T	W	.	.	S	S
16 Jul–7 Sep	11–5	M	T	W	T	F	S	S
Gardens, refreshments and shop								
5 Mar–30 Oct	11–5	M	T	W	T	F	S	S
3 Nov–18 Dec	11–3				T	F	S	S
29 Dec–31 Dec	11–3				T	F	S	
Refreshments, shop and bookshop								
1 Jan–27 Feb	11–3						S	S
Parkland								
Open all year	Dawn–dusk	M	T	W	T	F	S	S

Open Good Friday 11 to 5. Bookshop open as house.
On Thursdays and Fridays between 21 July and 2 September the house will be open to guided tours only.

Flatford: Bridge Cottage

Flatford, East Bergholt, Suffolk CO7 6UL

Map ③ I8   1943

In the heart of the beautiful Dedham Vale, the charming hamlet of Flatford is the location for some of John Constable's most famous pastoral paintings. Find out more about Constable at the exhibition in Bridge Cottage. Relax in the riverside tea-room and browse in the gift shop. **Note**: no public access to Flatford Mill.

Exploring
— Visit the sites of Constable's famous paintings.
— Discover more about Constable in Bridge Cottage.
— Escape on foot and explore the peaceful Dedham Vale.
— Take a boat or just relax beside the River Stour.

Eating and shopping: enjoy home-made food in the lovely riverside tea-room. Local gifts and Constable souvenirs in the thatched shop.

Making the most of your day: guided tours of Constable's painting locations, programme of longer rambles in the Dedham Vale, special tours of Flatford Mill buildings. Family activity trail.

Access for all: 🅿️♿🚻♿♿🅿️📷📿👀🖐🏷
Building ♿🅱 Grounds ♿♿🅱

Getting here: 168:TM075333. ½ mile south of East Bergholt. **Foot**: accessible from East Bergholt, Dedham and Manningtree. **Bus**: Network Colchester 93 Ipswich to Colchester (passing Ipswich ≋ and close Colchester Town ≋), Monday to Saturday alight East Bergholt, ¾ mile. **Train**: Manningtree 1¾ miles by footpath, 3½ miles by road. **Road**: Flatford is south of East Bergholt off the B1070. **Parking**: 200 yards, pay and display (not National Trust), charge including members.

Finding out more: 01206 298260 or flatfordbridgecottage@nationaltrust.org.uk

Flatford: Bridge Cottage		M	T	W	T	F	S	S
Bridge Cottage, shop and tea-room								
2 Jan–27 Feb	11–3:30	·	·	·	·	·	S	S
2 Mar–31 Mar	11–4	·	·	W	T	F	S	S
1 Apr–30 Apr	11–5	M	T	W	T	F	S	S
1 May–30 Sep	10:30–5:30	M	T	W	T	F	S	S
1 Oct–31 Oct	11–4:30	M	T	W	T	F	S	S
2 Nov–23 Dec	11–3:30	·	·	W	T	F	S	S
Information centre								
2 Jan–27 Mar	11–3:30	·	·	·	·	·	S	S
1 Apr–30 Sep	10–5	M	T	W	T	F	S	S
1 Oct–31 Oct	11–4:30	M	T	W	T	F	S	S
5 Nov–18 Dec	11–3:30	·	·	·	·	·	S	S

Open Bank Holiday Mondays. May close early in winter if weather is bad (October to March).

Visit the Constable exhibition at Bridge Cottage in Flatford, Suffolk

Hatfield Forest

near Bishop's Stortford, Essex

Map (3) G8 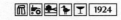 1924

No other forest on Earth evokes the atmosphere of a medieval hunting forest so completely. The ancient trees are like magnificent living sculptures, peaceful giants worn and fragile from centuries of seasons and use. Some of our extraordinary ancient trees are 1,200 years old! Just imagine what these trees have lived through and the stories they could tell. Whether you want somewhere for the children to let off steam, somewhere you can exercise to keep fit, or somewhere tranquil to walk where you can quietly reflect, you will be sure to find your own special place in Hatfield Forest.

Exploring	– Explore the hidden depths of the woods.
	– Space for children to run off energy.
	– Relax in beautiful surroundings.
	– Be inspired by the intricacies of the Shell House.
	– See the conservation team at work in the forest.
	– Marvel at the half a billion buttercups in spring.

Eating and shopping: delight in finding beautiful locally produced gifts in our shop.

Fallow deer graze at Hatfield Forest, Essex, where some trees are 1,200 years old

Discover the healthy option of Hatfield Forest venison. Enjoy seasonal, local food from the Forest Café. Buy our sustainable woodland products, from firewood to beanpoles.

Making the most of your day: full programme of family events. Tracker Packs and trail guides, Batricar and all-terrain pushchair available to help you explore the site. **Dogs**: on leads near livestock and lake (please note; dog-free zone also available).

Access for all: P♿ 👶 🦽 📷
Grounds ♿ ➡️ 🚶 ♿

Getting here: 167:TL547203. 4 miles east of Bishop's Stortford. **Foot**: Flitch Way from Braintree. Three Forests Way and Forest Way pass through the forest. **Cycle**: Flitch Way. **Bus**: Centrebus 7 Stansted to Mountfichet, alight Takeley Street (Green Man), then ½ mile. **Train**: Stansted Airport 3 miles. **Road**: from M11 exit 8, take B1256 towards Takeley. Signposted from B1256. **Parking**: cars £4.80, minibuses £6.50, coaches £25, school coaches £10.

You may also enjoy: Paycocke's, a stunning merchant's house, and Grange Barn, a 13th-century monastic building, both in Coggeshall.

Finding out more: 01279 874040 (Infoline). 01279 870678 or hatfieldforest@nationaltrust.org.uk. Hatfield Forest Estate Office, Takeley, Bishop's Stortford, Hertfordshire CM22 6NE

Hatfield Forest		M	T	W	T	F	S	S
Forest								
Open all year	Dawn–dusk	M	T	W	T	F	S	S
Shop								
1 Jan–6 Mar	10–3:30						S	S
12 Mar–30 Oct	10–5	M	T	W	T	F	S	S
5 Nov–31 Dec	10–3:30						S	S
Refreshments								
1 Jan–11 Mar	10–3:30				W	T	F	S	S
12 Mar–30 Oct	10–5	M	T	W	T	F	S	S
2 Nov–31 Dec	10–3:30				W	T	F	S	S
Elgins and Shell House car parks								
2 Jan–6 Mar	10–3:30							S
12 Mar–30 Oct	10–5	M	T	W	T	F	S	S
6 Nov–25 Dec	10–3:30							S

Elgins and Shell House car parks, refreshments and shop open daily during February and December school holidays, 10 to 3:30. Elgins and Shell House car park exits close 8. Shop closed 25 and 26 December.

Heigham Holmes

Martham Staithe, Ferrygate Lane,
Martham, Norfolk

Map ③ K5 1987

A remote island nature reserve with grazing marshes and ditches supporting wildlife special to this important and vast broadland landscape. **Note**: group visits only, by prior arrangement with Norfolk Coast Office. Access via floating swingbridge over River Thurne, by foot only. No toilet and limited parking.

Getting here: 134:TG445194. 1 mile north-west of Martham.

Finding out more: 01263 740241 or heighamholmes@nationaltrust.org.uk. Norfolk Coast Office, Friary Farm, Cley Road, Blakeney, Norfolk NR25 7NW

Heigham Holmes		M	T	W	T	F	S	S
1 Feb–30 Nov	10–2	.	**T**	**W**	**T**	.	.	.

Group visits only, by prior written arrangement via Norfolk Coast Office. Closed Bank Holidays.

Horsey Windpump

Horsey, Great Yarmouth, Norfolk NR29 4EF

Map ③ K4  1948

This striking windpump offers stunning views over Horsey Mere and this mysterious broadland landscape, full of exceptional wildlife. Surrounded by the Horsey Estate, you will find a great introduction to the Broads – whether you want to go for a walk, visit the beach or just enjoy a cup of tea. **Note**: the Horsey Estate is managed by the Buxton family, from whom it was acquired.

Exploring – Visit Horsey Staithe Stores to discover more about the area.
– Climb the windpump for unmissable views over Horsey Mere.

Climb to the top of Horsey Windpump, Norfolk

Exploring – Take a walk from the Broads to the beach.
– Discover the workings of this broadland drainage windpump.

Eating and shopping: enjoy a friendly welcome and light refreshments, including tea, coffee and ice-creams at our Horsey Staithe Stores (conveniently located next to Horsey Windpump) – also great for local gifts, souvenirs and books. Eat outside and relax before or after your walk.

Making the most of your day: friendly staff at Horsey Staithe Stores will help you make the most of your visit. Take a boat trip (not National Trust) across Horsey Mere during holiday periods. **Dogs**: welcome on leads around estate and near livestock.

Access for all:
Horsey Windpump
Horsey Staithe Stores Grounds

Getting here: 134:TG457223. 15 miles north of Great Yarmouth on B1159; 4 miles north-east of Martham. **Road**: off B1159 south of Horsey village. **Parking**: 50 yards, pay and display (members free).

Finding out more: 01263 740241 or horseywindpump@nationaltrust.org.uk. Norfolk Coast Office, Friary Farm, Cley Road, Blakeney, Norfolk NR25 7NW

Horsey Windpump		M	T	W	T	F	S	S
5 Mar–27 Mar	10–4:30	.	.	.	.	.	**S**	**S**
1 Apr–30 Oct	10–4:30	**M**	**T**	**W**	**T**	**F**	**S**	**S**

Open all Bank Holidays between 5 March and 30 October. Car park open all year, dawn to dusk.

Houghton Mill

Houghton, near Huntingdon, Cambridgeshire PE28 2AZ

Map (3) F6 1939

Situated in a stunning riverside setting and full of excellent hands-on activities for all the family, this five-storey historic building is the last working watermill on the Great Ouse. Flour is for sale, ground in the traditional way by water-powered mill stones. **Note**: milling demonstrations subject to river levels.

Exploring
- Milling demonstrations: Sundays and Bank Holiday Mondays, 1 to 5.
- Check our website for additional milling days.
- Wander or cycle through the neighbouring water meadows.
- Find out more with our new touchscreen display.

Eating and shopping: have a snack or try our famous Houghton scones in the delightful riverside tea-room. Spend some time browsing in the second-hand bookshop. Buy some of our freshly ground Houghton Mill wholemeal flour.

Making the most of your day: family events programme, including open-air theatre and hands-on baking days. Visit our website for children's summer holiday events. Follow the family Cat and Rat trail around the mill. **Dogs**: on leads in grounds only.

Access for all:
Building **Grounds**

Houghton Mill, Cambridgeshire, is still working

Getting here: 153:TL282720. **Foot**: Ouse Valley Way from Huntingdon and St Ives. **Cycle**: NCN51 from Huntingdon. **Bus**: Stagecoach in Huntingdon 55, Whippet 1A, Cambridge to Huntingdon (passing close Huntingdon). Cambridge guided busway. **Train**: Huntingdon 3½ miles. **Road**: in village of Houghton, signposted off A1123 Huntingdon to St Ives. **Parking**: 20 yards, £2 (pay and display). No access for large coaches (drop off in village square).

Finding out more: 01480 301494 or houghtonmill@nationaltrust.org.uk

Houghton Mill		M	T	W	T	F	S	S
Mill								
19 Mar–30 Oct	11–5	·	·	·	·	·	**S**	**S**
25 Apr–28 Sep	1–5	**M**	**T**	**W**	·	·	·	·
Tea-room								
19 Mar–30 Oct	11–5	·	·	·	·	·	**S**	**S**
25 Apr–28 Sep	11–5	**M**	**T**	**W**	·	·	·	·

Open Bank Holiday Mondays and Good Friday 11 to 5. Caravan and campsite: open March to October; managed by the Caravan Club (01480 466716). Groups and school parties at other times by arrangement. Car park closes 8 or dusk if earlier. **Toilets: as tea-room but closed Thursday and Friday**.

Ickworth

The Rotunda, Horringer, Bury St Edmunds, Suffolk IP29 5QE

Map (3) H7 1956

'There is so much to see and do, we keep returning as Ickworth is such a treasure trove of experiences.'
Mr George Donald, Black Notley, Essex

Step inside Ickworth and enjoy the story of the impressive central 'rotunda' and the 4th Earl of Bristol, who built this magnificent showcase to house his priceless treasures, collected on his tours around Europe in the 18th century. For 200 years the infamous and eccentric Hervey family continued to add to the treasures inside and out, creating the first and finest Italianate garden in England. Learn about the servants and workers who kept this country estate running and share their memories in the true

Visitors enjoying the beautiful Italianate gardens at Ickworth, Suffolk

story of 'upstairs-downstairs' domestic life in our innovative redisplaying of the basement servants' quarters.

Note: conference, dinner and weddings 01284 735957/www.ickworthwestwing.co.uk. Hotel 01284 735350.

Exploring —
- New: 'Ickworth Lives', representation of Edwardian technology and domestic life.
- View our collection of old masters, including Gainsborough and Titian.
- Share a day in the life of cook Mrs Sangster.
- Discover some of the finest collections of silver and miniatures.
- Creep amongst the ferns in the magical Victorian stumpery.
- Ask our gardeners about the historic walled garden restoration project.

Eating and shopping: full-service restaurant in the West Wing offers a delicious selection of seasonal dishes. Looking for the perfect gift? Ickworth wines and locally sourced products are available from the gift shop or visit our attractive plant and garden centre.

Making the most of your day: new 'Ickworth Lives' exhibition. Year-round events. Tours, trails and guides from West Wing reception. Ask about our wedding and conference facilities. Try out the cycle route, trim trail and play area. **Dogs**: welcome (on leads near livestock).

Access for all: ⛳🅿️♿🚻👶📷💻🎧
👓📷 House ♿♿🔊♿
West Wing ♿🔊♿ Grounds ♿♿➡️🐾

Getting here: 155:TL810610. **Foot**: 4½ miles via footpaths from Bury St Edmunds. **Bus**: Burtons 344/5 Bury St Edmunds to Haverhill (passing close Bury St Edmunds ⊠). **Train**: Bury St Edmunds 3 miles. **Road**: in Horringer, 3 miles south-west of Bury St Edmunds on west side of A143. **Parking**: 200 yards from West Wing visitor centre and house.

You may also enjoy: Wimpole Estate – Georgian architecture and sumptuous interiors on a grand scale.

Finding out more: 01284 735270 or ickworth@nationaltrust.org.uk

Ickworth		M	T	W	T	F	S	S
Park								
Open all year	8–8	M	T	W	T	F	S	S
House								
28 Feb–30 Oct	11–5	M	T	.	.	F	S	S
Gardens								
1 Jan–27 Feb	11–4	M	T	W	T	F	S	S
28 Feb–30 Oct*	10–5	M	T	W	T	F	S	S
31 Oct–31 Dec	11–4	M	T	W	T	F	S	S
Shop and restaurant*								
1 Jan–27 Feb	11–4	M	T	.	.	F	S	S
28 Feb–30 Oct	10–5	M	T	.	T	F	S	S
31 Oct–31 Dec	11–4	M	T	.	T	F	S	S

Open all Bank Holiday Mondays, Good Friday and 1 January. Property closed 24, 25 and 26 December. Park closes 8 or dusk if earlier. *Closed 14 April and 2 June for private functions and open every day during local school holidays.

Lavenham Guildhall

Market Place, Lavenham, Sudbury,
Suffolk CO10 9QZ

Map ③ I7   🏠 ✿ [1951]

'Truly a most absorbing building. It oozes history and magnifies the life and times of the past. Wonderful!'
Mr Hawks, Shefford, Bedfordshire

Set the scene for your day in the lovely village of Lavenham with a visit to us at the Guildhall of Corpus Christi. Lavenham is famed for its wealth of timber-framed buildings, which make it one of the best-preserved medieval villages in England. Step inside the Guildhall of Corpus Christi to experience one of the finest of these buildings. With us, you can understand the changing fortunes of Lavenham, from the boom times of the cloth industry to the poverty of the 19th century, before exploring the unique streets that have changed little in five centuries.

Exploring
- Learn about timber-framed construction and medieval guilds.
- Exhibits on cloth working, local railways and agriculture.

The Guildhall of Corpus Christi in the Market Place at Lavenham, Suffolk

Exploring
- See Ramesses, the mummified cat, discovered in a nearby roof.
- Tranquil walled garden with traditional dye plants.
- Summer programme of guided walks and talks.
- Don't miss Lavenham church, one of Suffolk's finest.

Eating and shopping: ploughman's lunches with local bread, regional cheeses and Norfolk ham. Mouthwatering cream teas, with the famous Guildhall scones. A wide range of local gifts, souvenirs, books and plants for sale in the shop.

Making the most of your day: guess the use of the mystery object from the museum's collections, follow children's trails around the house or try on children's Tudor dressing-up costumes. Programme of walks, talks and events.

Access for all: 🅿️♿🅱️💺🖼️🚶♿📷
Guildhall and garden ♿♿ Shop ♿ Tea-room ♿♿

Getting here: 155:TL916493. In Market Place, off the main High Street. **Foot**: 4 mile 'railway walk' links Lavenham with Long Melford. **Cycle**: South Suffolk Cycle Route A1. **Bus**: Chambers 753 Bury St Edmunds to Colchester (passes close Bury St Edmunds ≋ and Sudbury ≋). **Train**: Sudbury 7 miles. **Road**: A1141 and B1071. **Parking**: free (not National Trust) in front of the Guildhall.

You may also enjoy: Tudor architecture on a grander scale at Melford Hall.

Finding out more: 01787 247646 or lavenhamguildhall@nationaltrust.org.uk

Lavenham Guildhall		M	T	W	T	F	S	S
Shop								
8 Jan–27 Feb	11–4	·	·	·	·	·	S	S
3 Nov–23 Dec	11–4	·	·	·	T	F	S	S
Guildhall, tea-room and shop								
5 Mar–27 Mar	11–4	·	·	W	T	F	S	S
28 Mar–30 Oct	11–5	M	T	W	T	F	S	S
5 Nov–27 Nov	11–4	·	·	·	·	·	S	S
Tea-room								
3 Dec–18 Dec	11–4	·	·	·	·	·	S	S

Closed Good Friday. Parts of the Guildhall may be closed occasionally for community use.

Melford Hall

Long Melford, Sudbury, Suffolk CO10 9AA

Map ③ I7   1960

For almost five centuries the picturesque turrets of Melford Hall have dominated Long Melford's village green. Devastated by fire in 1942, the house was nurtured back to life by the Hyde Parker family and it remains their much-loved family home to this day. Their interior decoration and furnishings chart changing tastes and fashions over two centuries, but it is the stories of family life at Melford – from visits by their relation Beatrix Potter with her menagerie of animals, through to children sliding down the grand staircase on trays – that make this house more than just bricks and mortar.

The picturesque turrets of Melford Hall, Suffolk

Exploring
- Chat to our friendly volunteers and uncover Melford's stories.
- Discover 250 years of naval service and ancient captured treasure.
- See Beatrix Potter's Jemima Puddleduck toy and her bedroom.
- Relax on the family sofas in the Great Hall.
- Bring your visit alive with music, family toys and photos.
- Traditional games available in the garden.

Eating and shopping: delve deeper into Melford's history with our souvenir guidebook. Relax in the Old Kitchen for sandwiches, cream teas, cakes, tea and coffee. Browse our selection of souvenirs, gifts, second-hand books and plants in the Gatehouse shop.

Making the most of your day: wide programme of walks, talks and family events April to October. Children's treasure hunt in the house and garden trails. Some annual events in the park are not National Trust.

Access for all: 🅿️🔛🐕♿🔊🎧📷📹🅰️
Building 🔛🔛🐕♿ **Grounds** 🔛🔛

Getting here: 155:TL867462. **Foot**: Railway Walk linking Long Melford with Lavenham, 4 miles. **Bus**: Beestons/Chambers/Felix various services Mondays to Saturdays from Sudbury; Chambers 753 Monday to Saturday Bury St Edmunds to Colchester, all pass close Sudbury ➤. **Train**: Sudbury 4 miles. **Road**: in Long Melford off A134, 14 miles south of Bury St Edmunds, 3 miles north of Sudbury. **Parking**: free at Gatehouse car park, 200 yards. Access for coaches and other large vehicles by gated entrance 100 yards north of main gatehouse entrance. Further free parking in nearby Long Melford.

You may also enjoy: nearby Lavenham Guildhall: see Tudor wealth on a smaller scale.

Finding out more: 01787 376395 (Infoline). 01787 379228 or melford@nationaltrust.org.uk

Melford Hall		M	T	W	T	F	S	S
2 Apr–17 Apr	1:30–5						S	S
23 Apr–2 Oct	1:30–5			W	T	F	S	S
8 Oct–30 Oct	1:30–5						S	S

Also open on Bank Holiday Monday afternoons.
Closed Good Friday.

Orford Ness in Suffolk is the largest vegetated shingle spit in Europe

Orford Ness National Nature Reserve

Orford, Woodbridge, Suffolk

Map ③ K7  1993

Take a short boat trip to this wild and remote shingle spit, the largest in Europe. Follow trails through a stunning landscape and a history that will both delight and intrigue. Discover an internationally important nature reserve littered with debris and unusual, often forbidding, buildings from a sometimes disturbing past. **Note**: charge for ferry (including members). Steep, slippery steps. 'Pagodas' accessible on guided events only.

Exploring
- Explore this 'top-secret site' with our self-guiding booklet.
- Experience the wild, wide open spaces and the big skies.
- Children's trail – become a spy for the day!
- Come face to face with a nuclear bomb.

Eating and shopping: try some freshly caught fish for sale from the quay. Take home a flavour of the coast from local smokehouses.

Making the most of your day: guided tours and events (booked only). Crossings limited,

arrive early to avoid disappointment. Bring own food and drink (and suitable clothing). Sorry no cycling permitted. **Dogs**: assistance dogs only.

Access for all: ⬛⬛⬛⬛⬛
All buildings 🅰 **Grounds** 🅰 ➡

Getting here: 169:TM425495. **Foot**: Suffolk Coast Path runs nearby on mainland via Orford Quay. **Cycle**: NCN1, 1 mile. No cycling allowed onsite (no cycle parking). **Ferry**: only access to Ness via National Trust ferry *Octavia*. See opening arrangements. **Bus**: Far East Travel 71 from Woodbridge (passing Melton ➤). **Train**: Wickham Market 8 miles. **Road**: access from Orford Quay, Orford town 10 miles east of A12 (B1094/1095), 12 miles north-east of Woodbridge B1152/1084. **Parking**: in Quay Street, 150 yards, not National Trust (pay and display). Charge including members.

Finding out more: 01728 648024 (Infoline). 01394 450900 or orfordness@nationaltrust.org.uk. Quay Office, Orford Quay, Orford, Woodbridge, Suffolk IP12 2NU

Orford Ness		M	T	W	T	F	S	S
23 Apr–25 Jun	10–2						S	
28 Jun–1 Oct	10–2		T	W	T	F	S	
8 Oct–29 Oct	10–2						S	

The only access is by National Trust ferry from Orford Quay, with boats crossing regularly to the Ness between 10 and 2 only, the last ferry leaving the Ness at 5.

Oxburgh Hall

Oxborough, King's Lynn, Norfolk PE33 9PS

Map ③ H5 🏠✚❀☂ 1952

'**It was genuinely impressive and the guides as informative as ever. Loved the priest hole!**'
Mr Bradley, Wolverhampton

No one ever forgets their first sight of Oxburgh. A romantic, moated manor house, it was built by the Bedingfeld family in the 15th century and they have lived here ever since. Inside, the family's Catholic history is revealed, complete with a secret priest's hole which you can crawl inside. See the astonishing needlework by Mary, Queen of Scots, and the private chapel, built with reclaimed materials. Outside, you can enjoy panoramic views from the gatehouse roof and follow the woodcarving trails in the gardens and woodlands. The late winter drifts of snowdrops are not to be missed.

Exploring	— Marvel at the needlework by Mary, Queen of Scots.
	— Walk through the secret door in the library.
	— Wonder at the wealth of heraldry.
	— Climb the original spiral stairs to the gatehouse roof.
	— Be inspired in the kitchen garden and orchard.
	— Wander through the woodlands and meadow.

Eating and shopping: Old Kitchen tea-room; picnic tables in the car park. Well-stocked gift shop, including local Norfolk products. Browse in the second-hand bookshop. Plant sales for the green-fingered.

Making the most of your day: free garden tours every open day. Free children's trails in the house and garden. Year-round events programme. Woodland walks and nature trails. **Dogs**: assistance dogs only.

Access for all: 🅿️🔟♿🔟🔟🔟📷📖📺🔟
Hall 🔟🔟🔟 Chapel 🔟 Garden 🔟➡️🔟

You may also enjoy: Peckover House, a Georgian merchant's house and garden in Wisbech, 45 minutes away.

Finding out more: 01366 328258 or oxburghhall@nationaltrust.org.uk

Oxburgh Hall		M	T	W	T	F	S	S
House, garden, shop and tea-room								
26 Feb–9 Mar*	11–4	M	T	W	.	.	S	S
12 Mar–6 Apr	11–5	M	T	W	.	.	S	S
9 Apr–27 Apr	11–5	M	T	W	T	F	S	S
30 Apr–31 Jul	11–5	M	T	W	.	.	S	S
1 Aug–31 Aug	11–5	M	T	W	T	F	S	S
3 Sep–28 Sep	11–5	M	T	W	.	.	S	S
1 Oct–30 Oct	11–4	M	T	W	.	.	S	S
Garden, shop and tea-room								
8 Jan–20 Feb	11–4	.	.	.	.	.	S	S
1 Oct–30 Oct	11–5	M	T	W	.	.	S	S
5 Nov–18 Dec	11–4	.	.	.	.	.	S	S

*House: admission by timed tours only on weekdays during this period. House and garden open seven days a week during Easter school holidays, Whitsun week (30 May to 3 June) and throughout August. Chapel closes at 4 in October.

The romantic moated Oxburgh Hall in Norfolk

Paycocke's

25 West Street, Coggeshall, Colchester,
Essex CO6 1NS

Map ③ I8 1924

Marvel at the stunning woodcarving and
elaborate panelling inside this merchant's
house. Built around 1500 for Thomas Paycocke,
the house is a grand example of the wealth
generated by the cloth trade in the 16th
century. Outside, there is a beautiful and
tranquil cottage garden. **Note**: nearest toilet
at Grange Barn.

Exploring
– Discover the intriguing history
  of the house and
  past residents.
– Explore the sights and
  smells of the garden.
– Experience the atmosphere
  of this remarkable
  500-year-old building.
– Come and see the new
  exhibits as they develop.

Making the most of your day: children's trail
in the house and garden, children's activities
during events. Guided tours on request.
Dogs: in the garden only.

Access for all: [icons]
Building [icon] Grounds [icon]

Getting here: 168:TL848225. **Foot**: close
to Essex Way. **Bus**: First 70 Colchester
to Braintree (passing Marks Tey ≥).
Train: Kelvedon 2½ miles. **Road**: 5½ miles east
of Braintree. Signposted off A120. On south
side of West Street, 400 yards from centre of
Coggeshall, on road to Braintree next to the
Fleece Inn. **Parking**: Grange Barn (½ mile)
until 5. Very limited roadside parking.

Finding out more: 01376 561305 or
paycockes@nationaltrust.org.uk

Paycocke's		M	T	W	T	F	S	S
5 Mar–3 Apr	1–5						S	S
6 Apr–30 Oct	11–5			W	T	F	S	S
Open Bank Holiday Mondays.								

Peckover House and Garden

North Brink, Wisbech, Cambridgeshire PE13 1JR

Map ③ G5  1943

'**We really enjoyed our visit here today, it was
full of hidden treasures!**'
Mrs McLeish, Dersingham

Peckover House is a secret gem, an oasis
hidden away in an urban environment.
A classic Georgian merchant's town house,
it was lived in by the Peckover family for
150 years. The Peckovers were staunch
Quakers, which meant they had a very
simple lifestyle; yet at the same time they
ran a successful private bank. Both facets
of their life can be seen as you wander
through the house and gardens. The gardens
themselves are outstanding – 0.8 hectare
(two acres) of sensory delight, complete
with orangery, summerhouses, croquet
lawn and rose garden with more than
60 varieties of rose.

Exploring
– Learn about the Quaker
  history of the Peckover family.
– Examine the Cabinet of
  Curiosities – both old
  and new.
– Take a peek inside the
  unrestored butler's pantry.
– Admire the Rococo
  plasterwork in the drawing
  room and landing.
– See oranges growing in the
  orangery – where else!
– Appreciate the 'engine-room'
  of the garden – glasshouses,
  coldframes, compost area.

Eating and shopping: tea-room in the
thatched 17th-century barn, with a charming
courtyard seating area. The gift shop in
the old banking wing offers a range of local
products. Pick up a bargain in the second-hand
bookshop. Surplus plant sales for the
green-fingered.

The stunning garden at Peckover House in Cambridgeshire is full of sensory delights

Finding out more: 01945 583463 or peckover@nationaltrust.org.uk

Peckover House and Garden		M	T	W	T	F	S	S
Garden and tea-room								
19 Feb–6 Mar	12–4	.	.	.	.	.	S	S
12 Mar–6 Apr	12–5	M	T	W	.	.	S	S
9 Apr–27 Apr	12–5	M	T	W	T	F	S	S
30 Apr–30 Oct*	12–5	M	T	W	.	.	S	S
House								
12 Mar–6 Apr	1–5	M	T	W	.	.	S	S
9 Apr–27 Apr	1–5	M	T	W	T	F	S	S
30 Apr–30 Oct*	1–5	M	T	W	.	.	S	S
Whole property								
10 Dec–14 Dec	12–7	M	T	W	.	.	S	S

*Open all week during Whitsun (30 May to 3 June); open all week for Wisbech Rose Fair, 30 June and 1 July (garden and tea-room open 11); open all week for October half-term, 27 and 28 October. Special Christmas opening: 10 to 14 December, 12 to 7. We recommend visitors with disabilities telephone ahead of visit to discuss specific access needs.

Making the most of your day: play our Bechstein piano. Free garden tours most days, croquet in summer. Children's handling collection and trails. Behind-the-scenes tours on selected days. Octavia Hill's birthplace house is nearby. **Dogs**: assistance dogs only.

Access for all: [icons]
Main house [icon] Tea-room [icon] Garden [icons]

Getting here: 143:TF458097. **Foot**: from Chapel Road car park walk up passageway to left of W-Four restaurant, turn right by river. Peckover House is 164 yards on right. **Cycle**: NCN1, ¼ mile. **Bus**: First X1 Peterborough [rail] to Lowestoft; X1 and Norfolk Green 46 from King's Lynn (passing close King's Lynn [rail]). **Train**: March 9½ miles. **Road**: west of Wisbech town centre on north bank of River Nene (B1441). **Sat Nav**: to nearest car park PE13 1RG. **Parking**: free in town, nearest is Chapel Road (not National Trust), 273 yards. Limited Blue Badge parking on North Brink.

You may also enjoy: Oxburgh Hall, a medieval moated manor house 25 miles away in West Norfolk.

Ramsey Abbey Gatehouse

Abbey School, Ramsey, Huntingdon, Cambridgeshire PE17 1DH

Map ③ F6 [icon] 1952

This charming former gatehouse is all that remains of the once great Benedictine abbey at Ramsey. **Note**: on school grounds please respect school security. Exterior can be seen all year.

Access for all: [icon] Gatehouse [icon]
Grounds [icons]

Getting here: 142:TL291851. At south-east edge of Ramsey, at point where Chatteris road leaves B1096, 10 miles south-east of Peterborough.

Finding out more: 01480 301494 or ramseyabbey@nationaltrust.org.uk

Ramsey Abbey Gatehouse

Open 1 to 5 first Sunday of the month April to September. Tie in your visit with Ramsey Rural Museum and walled garden. Group visits by appointment on other weekends.

Rayleigh Mount

Rayleigh, Essex

Map (3) I10   1923

Enjoy amazing views at this medieval motte and bailey castle site, now abundant with wildlife. Adjacent windmill houses historical exhibition. **Note**: exhibition in windmill operated by Rochford District Council.

Access for all: Grounds 🔲

Getting here: 178:TQ805909. 100 yards from High Street, next to Mill Hall car park.

Finding out more: 01284 747500 or rayleighmount@nationaltrust.org.uk

Rayleigh Mount		M	T	W	T	F	S	S
Open all year	7–6	M	T	W	T	F	S	S

Mount closes at 2 on Saturdays and 5 in winter, other opening times may vary. For windmill exhibition opening times telephone 01702 318120.

St George's Guildhall

29 King Street, King's Lynn, Norfolk PE30 1HA

Map (3) H5   1951

The largest surviving medieval guildhall in England, with many original features. The guildhall is now a working theatre.

Access for all: Building 🔲
Grounds 🔲

Getting here: 132:TF616202. On west side of King Street close to the Tuesday Market Place.

Finding out more: 01553 765565 or stgeorgesguildhall@nationaltrust.org.uk

St George's Guildhall		M	T	W	T	F	S	S
Crofters coffee shop								
4 Jan–31 Dec	9:30–5	M	T	W	T	F	S	·
Riverside Restaurant								
4 Jan–31 Dec	12–2	M	T	W	T	F	S	·
4 Jan–31 Dec	6:30–9:30	M	T	W	T	F	S	·

Closed first Monday in January, Good Friday, Bank Holiday Mondays and 24 December. Guildhall by appointment only (48-hours notice required, telephone 01553 765565).

Shaw's Corner

Ayot St Lawrence, near Welwyn, Hertfordshire AL6 9BX

Map (3) F9   1944

Home to George Bernard Shaw for over 40 years, Shaw's Corner is a 1902 Arts and Crafts house set in a quintessentially English garden. It feels like Shaw has just left the room – his clothes are still in his wardrobe and his typewriter and glasses sit on his study desk. **Note**: access roads are very narrow.

Exploring
  – Discover Shaw's revolving writing hut in the garden.
  – See the 1938 Oscar for *Pygmalion*.
  – Enjoy a picnic in the garden or the orchard.
  – Get up close to some of Shaw's personal belongings.

Eating and shopping: pre-1950s varieties of plants for sale. Ice-creams and soft drinks to enjoy in the garden. Take time to browse in the second-hand bookshop.

The Arts and Crafts Shaw's Corner, Hertfordshire

Making the most of your day: open-air performances of George Bernard Shaw's plays each summer in the garden. Regular events including conservation days and family activity days.

Access for all: Building  Grounds

Getting here: 166:TL194167. **Cycle**: NCN12, 1 mile. **Bus**: Centrebus 304/Harpenden Taxis 904 from St Albans ≥, Sundays April to October only; Arriva 304 St Albans ≥ to Hitchin, alight Gustardwood, 1¼ miles. **Train**: Welwyn North 4½ miles; Welwyn Garden City 6 miles; Harpenden 5 miles;. **Road**: in the village of Ayot St Lawrence. A1(M) exit 4 or M1 exit 10. Signposted from B653 Welwyn Garden City to Luton road near Wheathampstead. Also from B656 at Codicote. **Parking**: free, 30 yards. Small car park, not suitable for very large vehicles, can be very busy at peak periods.

Finding out more: 01438 829221 (Infoline). 01438 820307 or shawscorner@nationaltrust.org.uk

Shaw's Corner		M	T	W	T	F	S	S
House								
12 Mar–30 Oct	1–5		·	**W**	**T**	**F**	**S**	**S**
Garden								
12 Mar–30 Oct	12–5:30		·	**W**	**T**	**F**	**S**	**S**

Open Bank Holiday Mondays and Good Friday. May close earlier when evening events occur.

Sheringham Park

Upper Sheringham, Norfolk

Map ③ J4 [icons] 1987

'**Lovely in all seasons, it draws me back again and again for its tranquillity, fabulous views and walks.**'
Julia Peters, Bodham

Sheringham Park and rhododendrons are often referred to in the same sentence. Not surprising with 80 different species on show. Flowers first appear in December, and the show gradually builds to a climax from mid-May into June. Many plants were brought

Visitors cycling in the Wild Garden at Sheringham Park in Norfolk

to Sheringham by plant collector Ernest Wilson in the early 20th century. The handkerchief tree, which grows at the edge of the wild garden, was found by Wilson in China. He discovered it working from a crude map on a scruffy piece of paper covering an area of 20,000 square miles with just an 'X' marking its location. **Note**: Sheringham Hall is privately occupied. April to September: limited access by written appointment with leaseholder.

Exploring
- Enjoy stunning coastal views, courtesy of landscape gardener Humphry Repton.
- Let your imagination run riot in our environmental art area.
- Climb 190 steps up our gazebo for superb parkland views.
- Take a relaxing walk, disturbed only by birdsong.
- Discover exciting wildlife facts with our children's Tracker Packs.
- Look for muntjac, roe or red deer in the park.

Eating and shopping: purchase a rhododendron to remind you of your visit.

Enjoy a cream tea from our refreshment kiosk. Visit our shop for a souvenir of Sheringham Park. Relax after a walk with a drink and ice-cream in the courtyard.

Making the most of your day: guided walks and events all year round. Wildlife trails for children during school holidays. Discover the history of the park in the exhibition barn. North Norfolk Railway nearby. **Dogs**: on leads near livestock and visitor facilities.

Access for all: 🅿️♿🚻👶🖼️🎨🚶🔵👁️ **Building** ♿🔵 **Grounds** ♿▶️♿

Getting here: 133:TG135420. **Foot**: on Norfolk Coast Path. **Cycle**: Regional Route 30 1½ miles south. **Bus**: First 50 from Norwich, Norfolk Green X6 from Cromer (passing close Cromer ≽), alight main entrance (both passing Sheringham ≽). Saunders Coaches (services 4 and 5) stop on request at main entrance to Park. **Train**: Sheringham 2 miles. **Road**: 2 miles south-west of Sheringham, 5 miles west of Cromer, 6 miles east of Holt. Main entrance at junction A148/B1157. **Parking**: 60 yards, £4.50 (pay and display). Coaches free (booking essential).

You may also enjoy: a walk around the Great Wood and lake at Felbrigg Hall, try the garden too.

Finding out more: 01263 820550 or sheringhampark@nationaltrust.org.uk. Visitor Centre, Wood Farm, Upper Sheringham, Norfolk NR26 8TL

Sheringham Park		M	T	W	T	F	S	S
Park								
Open all year		M	T	W	T	F	S	S
Visitor centre								
2 Jan–6 Mar	11–4	·	·	·	·	·	S	S
12 Mar–30 Sep	10–5	M	T	W	T	F	S	S
1 Oct–30 Oct	10–5	·	·	W	T	F	S	S
5 Nov–31 Dec	11–4	·	·	·	·	·	S	S
Refreshment kiosk								
12 Mar–30 Sep	10–5	M	T	W	T	F	S	S
1 Oct–30 Oct	10–5	·	·	W	T	F	S	S
5 Nov–31 Dec	11–3	·	·	·	·	·	S	S

Refreshment kiosk: 14 May to 19 June open 10 to 5. Visitor centre and refreshment kiosk: 19 to 27 February and 23 to 30 October open 10 to 5; 27 to 31 December open 11 to 3. Closed 25 and 26 December.

Sutton Hoo

Tranmer House, Sutton Hoo, Woodbridge, Suffolk IP12 3DJ

Map ③ J7 🏠🏛️🏊🏡🍽️  1998

'**A most wonderful time. Loved everything I saw. Very evocative of times gone by.'**
Cosette Harrington, Felixstowe

This hauntingly beautiful 91-hectare (255-acre) estate, with far-reaching views over the River Deben, is home to one of the greatest archaeological discoveries of all time. Walk around the ancient burial mounds and discover the incredible story of the ship burial of an Anglo-Saxon king and his treasured possessions. Come face to face with your ancestors and explore our award-winning exhibition, the full-size reconstruction of the burial chamber, stunning replica treasures and original finds from one of the mounds, including a prince's sword. Look inside the Edwardian house or enjoy the beautiful seasonal colours on our estate walks.

Exploring   –   Enjoy the beautiful period interiors of Mrs Pretty's country home.

Sutton Hoo, Suffolk: discover how the Anglo-Saxons lived and learn about the amazing ship burial discovery

Exploring — Meet a 1930s archaeologist and help them unearth the past.
— Take a guided tour of the royal burial mounds.
— Explore beautiful woodland and heathland walks with fine estuary views.
— Take time out to relax on sofas in the café.
— Stay for longer in one of our Edwardian holiday flats.

Eating and shopping: enjoy local, seasonal food in our licensed café and take time to enjoy sofas and games in our new chill-out area. Discover exclusive ceramics and jewellery in our gift shop. Browse through the books in our extensive second-hand bookshop.

Making the most of your day: family events, living history, exclusive behind-the-scenes tours and changing exhibitions. Wildlife/nature walks. Children's play area, quiz/trails, Tracker Packs and dressing-up box. **Dogs**: welcome on leads in park and café terrace area only.

Access for all: ⬛🅿️🅳♿🚻🛗🅿️🖼️🎦 ∴
Building ♿🅻 Grounds 🅻 ➡️ 🚬🅻

Getting here: 169:TM288487. **Foot**: 1¼ miles from Melton 🚊. **Bus**: First 63/4/5 Ipswich to Framlingham (passing Melton 🚊).
Train: Melton 1¼ miles, Woodbridge 3 miles.
Road: on B1083 Melton to Bawdsey. Follow signs from A12 north of Woodbridge.
Parking: 30 yards (pay and display when the exhibition is closed). Motorcycle parking area, cycle racks and free pannier lockers.

You may also enjoy: lovely walks and views at Flatford that inspired artist John Constable.

Finding out more: 01394 389700 or suttonhoo@nationaltrust.org.uk

Sutton Hoo		M	T	W	T	F	S	S
1 Jan–20 Feb	11–4						S	S
21 Feb–27 Feb	11–4	M	T	W	T	F	S	S
2 Mar–3 Apr	10:30–5			W	T	F	S	S
4 Apr–30 Oct	10:30–5	M	T	W	T	F	S	S
5 Nov–18 Dec	11–4						S	S
26 Dec–31 Dec	11–4	M	T	W	T	F	S	

Open Bank Holiday Mondays. Estate walks open daily all year, 9 to 6 (except for some Thursdays, November to end December).

Theatre Royal, Bury St Edmunds

Westgate Street, Bury St Edmunds, Suffolk IP33 1QR

Map ③ I7 🏠 1974

One of the country's most significant theatre buildings and the only surviving Regency playhouse in Britain, the recently restored Grade I-listed Theatre Royal in Bury St Edmunds offers visitors a unique and authentic experience of theatre-going in the early 19th century.

The stage at the Theatre Royal, Bury St Edmunds, Suffolk

Exploring — Unique year-round programme of professional period and contemporary productions.
— Highly entertaining guided tours provide a fascinating and lively introduction.
— Admire the beautiful interior, including the painted sky ceiling.

Eating and shopping: enjoy refreshments in spacious, modern surroundings. Browse in the theatre shop for gifts and souvenirs. Short walk to historic town centre and modern shopping arcade.

Making the most of your day: combine a guided tour with a matinée performance or one of our special heritage-themed events.

Access for all: [icons] Building [icons]

Getting here: 155:TL856637. **Bus**: from surrounding areas. **Train**: Bury St Edmunds ¾ mile. **Road**: on Westgate Street on south side of A134 from Sudbury (one-way system). **Parking**: nearest in Swan Lane, 546 yards. Limited parking in Westgate Street.

Finding out more: 01284 769505 or theatreroyal@nationaltrust.org.uk

Theatre Royal, Bury St Edmunds		M	T	W	T	F	S	S
1 Feb–29 Nov	2–4		**T**		**T**			
5 Feb–27 Nov	10:30–1						S	S

Closed during performances and at some other times for rehearsals or set up. Please telephone for changes in the schedule before you visit.

Whipsnade Tree Cathedral

Whipsnade Tree Cathedral, Whipsnade, Dunstable, Bedfordshire LU6 2LL

Map (3) E8 1960

This incredible tree cathedral was created after the First World War in a spirit of 'faith, hope and reconciliation'. **Note**: owned by the National Trust and administered by the Trustees of Whipsnade Tree Cathedral Fund.

Getting here: 165/166:TL008180. 4 miles south of Dunstable, off B4540. Free parking (spaces limited). Signposted off B4540.

Finding out more: 01582 872406 or whipsnadetc@nationaltrust.org.uk. Trustees c/o Chapel Farm, Whipsnade, Dunstable, Bedfordshire LU6 2LL

Whipsnade Tree Cathedral	Open every day all year

Car park: 1 January to 26 March, locked at 5; 27 March to 30 October, locked at 7; 31 October to 31 December, locked at 5.

Wicken Fen National Nature Reserve

Lode Lane, Wicken, Ely, Cambridgeshire CB7 5XP

Map (3) G6 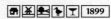 1899

'We came away relaxed and refreshed, the ancient landscape inviting us to forget the pace of modern life completely.'
Helene Felter, Ely

Wicken Fen, one of Europe's most important wetlands, supports an abundance of wildlife. There are more than 8,000 species, including a spectacular array of plants, birds and dragonflies. The raised boardwalk and lush grass droves allow easy access to a lost landscape of flowering meadows, sedge and reedbeds, where you may encounter rarities such as hen harriers, water voles and bitterns. The Wicken Fen Vision, an ambitious landscape-scale conservation project, is opening up new areas of land to explore. Our grazing herds of Highland cattle and Konik ponies are helping to create a diverse range of new habitats.

Exploring
- Step back in time to experience fenland as it was.
- Listen to the reeds as you enjoy a boat ride.
- Dip and discover the underwater world of pond creatures.
- See spectacular harriers hunting over the sedge fields at dusk.
- Imagine living as a fen worker in the Fen Cottage.
- Refresh your soul under huge inspiring skies.

Eating and shopping: our new-look shop specialises in local craft made for Wicken Fen and stocks a wide range of wildlife book titles. Try delicious home-cooked soup or 'Fen Docky', made with local seasonal produce. Enjoy cake – the perfect reward after your walk!

Making the most of your day: family events programme, all year. Trails for all, with nine wildlife observation hides. On summer weekends, visit Fen Cottage and the Dragonfly Centre, and enjoy boat trips on Wicken Lode. **Dogs**: on leads only.

Access for all: [icons] Building [icons] Grounds [icons]

Getting here: 154:TL563705. **Cycle**: NCN11 from Ely. **Bus**: Stagecoach in Cambridge 12 from Cambridge, Ely and Newmarket, alight Soham High Street, 3 miles, or X9, 9 Cambridge to Ely, alight Stretham, 6 miles. All pass Ely ≡. **Train**: Ely 9 miles. **Road**: south of Wicken (A1123), 3 miles west of Soham (A142), 9 miles south of Ely, 17 miles north-east of Cambridge via A10. **Parking**: 120 yards (pay and display for non-members).

You may also enjoy: a cycle ride or ramble through the Wicken Fen Vision to nearby Anglesey Abbey.

Finding out more: 01353 720274 or wickenfen@nationaltrust.org.uk

Wicken Fen		M	T	W	T	F	S	S
Reserve, Visitor Centre and shop								
Open all year	10–5	M	T	W	T	F	S	S
Café								
1 Jan–27 Feb	10–4:30	·	·	W	T	F	S	S
1 Mar–30 Oct	10–5	M	T	W	T	F	S	S
2 Nov–24 Dec	10–4:30	·	·	W	T	F	S	S
26 Dec–31 Dec	10–4:30	M	T	W	T	F	S	·
Fen Cottage								
26 Mar–24 Jul	2–5	·	·	·	·	·	S	S
27 Jul–31 Aug	11–5	·	·	W	·	·	S	S
3 Sep–30 Oct	2–5	·	·	·	·	·	S	S

Closed 25 December. Reserve and Visitor Centre close at dusk during winter months. Some paths may be closed in very wet conditions. Fen Cottage also open Bank Holiday Mondays.

Cyclists at Wicken Fen, Cambridgeshire

Willington Dovecote and Stables

Willington, Church End, near Bedford, Bedfordshire MK44 3PX

Map ③ F7   [icon] 1914

Enjoy the tranquil setting of these outstanding Tudor stone-built dovecote and stable buildings, built for Henry VIII's 1541 visit. **Note**: no toilet.

Access for all: [icon] Dovecote [icon] Stables [icons] Grounds [icons]

Getting here: 153:TL107499. In Willington village, off the A603.

Finding out more: 01480 301494 or willingtondovecote@nationaltrust.org.uk

---

Willington Dovecote and Stables
Open space accessible all year round. Buildings open last Sunday afternoon of month (April to September), 1 to 5. Admission also by appointment with the Voluntary Custodian, Mrs J. Endersby, 21 Chapel Lane, Willington MK44 3QG (01234 838278).

Wimpole Estate

Arrington, Royston, Cambridgeshire SG8 0BW

Map ③ G7   1976

A working estate still guided by the seasons, with an impressive mansion at its heart. Uncover the stories of the people who have shaped Wimpole; soak up the atmosphere; take in the spectacular views and find your own special place. Explore the hall, where intimate rooms contrast with some beautiful Georgian interiors. Stroll through the pleasure grounds to the walled garden, bursting with seasonal produce and glorious herbaceous borders. At Home Farm, contrast the traditional farmyard with the noisy modern piggery and cattle sheds.

Sheep from the Home Farm graze the parkland at Wimpole Hall in Cambridgeshire

Ask our Stockman about our rare breeds and learn more about your food and our farming. **Note**: members pay half price entry to Home Farm (under threes free).

Exploring
— Spot the tiny piglets escaping their sty.
— Ask our gardeners what and when to sow and grow.
— Enjoy the colourful pelargoniums in the parterre in July.
— 90 pints a day! Watch our Jersey cow being milked.
— Stroll to the serpentine lakes or through the shaded woodland.
— Let off steam in the adventure woodland at Home Farm.

Eating and shopping: taste delicious dishes made with produce from our walled garden. Buy local pottery, plants, gifts, rare-breed meat and more! Pick up a bargain in the second-hand bookshop. Plenty of gifts for children in the shop.

Making the most of your day: living history days, daily farm activities, free family trails and Tracker Packs, school holiday activities, open-air theatre, bat and wildlife walks, monthly seasonal larder and craft fair at Christmas. **Dogs**: welcome on leads in the park.

Access for all: 🅿 👤 🌡 🍴 🎫 🖼 📷 📖 🎦 🎵 ⓐ
Hall 👤♿ Farm ♿♿ Gardens ♿➡♿♿

Getting here: 154:TL336510. **Foot**: Wimpole Way from Cambridge, Harcamlow Way. **Cycle**: National Trust-permitted cycle path to entrance from Orwell (A603). **Bus**: Whippet 75 from Cambridge. Alight Arrington, then a 1-mile walk; return bus from Orwell, a 2-mile walk. **Train**: Shepreth 5 miles. Royston station with taxi service 8 miles. **Road**: 8 miles south-west of Cambridge (A603), 6 miles north of Royston (A1198). **Sat Nav**: access to estate is via A603, not A1198. **Parking**: 275 yards, £2.

You may also enjoy: going wild at Wicken Fen, with plenty of family events to discover.

Finding out more: 01223 206000 or wimpolehall@nationaltrust.org.uk

Wimpole Estate		M	T	W	T	F	S	S
Garden, restaurant, shop and bookshop								
1 Jan–16 Feb	11–4	M	T	W	.	.	S	S
19 Feb–30 Oct	10:30–5	M	T	W	T	F	S	S
31 Oct–24 Dec	11–4	M	T	W	.	.	S	S
Home Farm								
1 Jan–13 Feb	11–4	.	.	.	.	.	S	S
19 Feb–30 Oct	10:30–5	M	T	W	T	F	S	S
5 Nov–24 Dec	11–4	.	.	.	.	.	S	S
Hall								
19 Feb–20 Jul	11–5	M	T	W	.	.	S	S
23 Jul–1 Sep	11–5	M	T	W	T	.	S	S
3 Sep–30 Oct	11–5	M	T	W	.	.	S	S
Park								
Open all year	Dawn–dusk	M	T	W	T	F	S	S

Home Farm, garden, restaurant and shops: open daily 1 to 5 January and 27 to 31 December. Restaurant and shops: open 22 to 24 December 11 to 4. Stable shop and café: open 26 December. Hall: open Saturday to Thursday during local half-term, Easter and school summer holidays.

East Midlands

With its soaring windows and impressive
stonework, visiting Hardwick Hall
is a thrilling architectural experience

Outdoors in the East Midlands

The East Midlands is an area of breathtakingly diverse scenery, ranging from the heather-clad moors of the Peak District to the peaceful woods of Clumber Park in Nottinghamshire and the rolling parklands of its many historic properties in Derbyshire.

Drama abounds in this landscape, with soaring limestone cliffs, deep grassland gorges and tumbling streams. There are fantastic walking routes suitable for all abilities – with Dovedale, the Manifold Valley and Winnats Pass being rightly popular.

Perfect peaks, valleys and guided walks
The National Trust cares for about 14,970 hectares (37,000 acres) of land within the Peak District National Park, so there is plenty in this iconic landscape to explore. Enjoy a leisurely stroll around picturesque Ilam Park, or challenge yourself with a brisk walk to the top of Mam Tor, where you will be rewarded with amazing views.

The wild and dramatic heather moorlands of the Dark Peak, incised by deep wooded valleys such as Edale, offer important breeding grounds for birds, including the golden plover and short-eared owl.

At the Longshaw Estate it is impossible to resist a paddle in the tumbling stream at Padley Gorge – be sure to look out for the millstones scattered around offering clues to Longshaw's industrial past. Alternatively, why not follow one of our guided walks and find out more about the area from an expert guide?

Above:
Mam Tor, part of the Dark Peak Estate, Derbyshire
Right:
a family biking expedition at Clumber Park, Nottinghamshire

Above: **dramatic rocks and wild heathland on the Longshaw Estate in the Peak District**

Rare and special flora and fauna

We care for three National Nature Reserves at Dovedale, the plateau of Kinder Scout in the Peak District and Calke Park in Derbyshire.

Calke Park is home to some of the oldest trees in Europe, and the decaying wood of these trees provides a habitat for several endangered beetles. At Dovedale flower-rich grasslands support rare plants, including Jacob's ladder, and the large areas of woodland are home to many invertebrates, including at least seven nationally scarce beetles. Kinder Scout is an iconic part of the Peak District, with a dramatic landscape that is home to several upland breeding birds.

Always something to do

Whatever the time of year there is always something to do in the East Midlands countryside. Pick up a copy of the *Discover the Peak District* leaflet to find out just how many walks there are on offer and what events you can get involved in. Children will also keep themselves busy. There is always so much for them to do, from pond-dipping to butterfly hunting.

In the autumn and winter, when many National Trust properties close their doors, the parks and countryside are still open. So why not enjoy a winter walk and then warm up with a well-deserved hot drink at one of our cafés at Longshaw, Edale and Ilam?

Space to explore and relax in

For great activities and lots to see both indoors and out, our historic houses cannot be beaten.

At Belton House in Lincolnshire visitors can enjoy the beautiful landscape park with its attractive herd of deer, while those looking for an oasis of tranquillity can visit the restored boathouse. Calke Abbey offers great opportunities for a family adventure, including wildlife-themed Tracker Packs for children and a new wetland habitat to explore.

With picturesque parkland, peaceful woodland, open heath and a serpentine lake, Clumber Park has more than enough space to relax in and explore. There are more than 20 miles of open tracks, and whether you are keen on a gentle stroll around the lake or a more vigorous hike, Clumber is ideal. There are even bicycles available to hire, including those suitable for children, and there are many accessible pathways perfect for wheelchair users. Younger visitors can also let off steam in the Woodland Play Park.

The Peak District's Manifold Valley offers stunning unbroken views and wide open spaces

My favourite walk

When I reach the top of Wetton Hill from the Manifold Valley in the Peak District and take in the amazing view, it feels like I have a very special place all to myself.

From the tea-room at Wetton Mill I head up the path between the farmhouse and the National Trust holiday cottages, passing Nan Tor cave, once a shelter for neolithic hunters. The valley is full of traces of the people who lived here in those times, and as I reach the top of the ridge before Wetton Hill, the magnificent Thor's Cave appears in the distance, its entrance like a great eye watching me.

Wetton Hill is one of those places you never tire of – the seasons bring different wildlife every time you climb it. In spring the coconut smell of the gorse reminds me of suntan lotion on Spanish beaches, while in summer I listen out for the haunting call of the curlew. Come the autumn, little waxcap toadstools spread out across the hill like scattered smarties. And in winter, when the weather allows you to get to the top of the hill, you feel a long way from anywhere, though in reality, the pub at Wetton is just a fifteen-minute walk away!

Paul Mortimer
Projects Officer, Peak District

Belton House

Grantham, Lincolnshire NG32 2LS

Map ③ E4  1984

'Whenever we have friends staying, we bring them to Belton – we just love everything about it! Lots for families too.'
Trina Redfern, Lincoln

The 'perfect' English country-house estate, set in its own magnificent deer park, Belton was designed to impress. Built in the late 17th century for 'Young' Sir John Brownlow, its honey-coloured symmetry, opulent décor, fine furnishings, stunning silverware and gorgeous gardens provided the perfect setting for lavish hospitality and entertainment on a grand scale. Each generation left its mark, employing top designers, craftsmen and portrait painters. At the heart of society, the family enjoyed royal connections from William III to Edward VIII. Did they achieve perfection? Judge for yourself as you explore and discover many fascinating layers of Belton's history. **Note**: surfacing work may be underway on sections of the car park.

Exploring
- Explore magnificent parkland and discover a wealth of wildlife.
- Enjoy the seasonal delights of the garden and tranquil lakeshore.
- Burn off steam in Lincolnshire's largest adventure playground.
- Enjoy the Discovery Centre family activities (weekends, April to October).
- Step 'below stairs' – basements open Wednesday to Sunday (main season).
- Enjoy seasonal Family Fun trails.

Eating and shopping: find year-round inspiration in our plant and garden shop. Try Belton venison casserole and other local, seasonal dishes in our restaurant. Visit our gift shop or plant shop for seasonal inspiration and perfect presents. Local food producer showcases (selected weekends).

Making the most of your day: varied events programme, Easter and Hallowe'en trails, 'Paint the Garden', open-air theatre, Living History Weekends, Food Fayre, garden tours, Christmas Craft Market, wildlife explorers' Club (monthly). **Dogs**: on leads in parkland and stable yard only.

Access for all: 🅿️ 🔣 🔣 🔣 🔣 🔣 🔣 🔣 🔣 🔣 🔣
🔣 🔣 House 🔣 🔣 🔣 Grounds 🔣 ➡️ 🔣 🔣

Getting here: 130:SK930395. **Bus**: Stagecoach in Lincolnshire 1 Grantham to Lincoln; (passing close to Grantham ≊). **Train**: Grantham 3 miles. **Road**: 3 miles north-east of Grantham on A607 Grantham to Lincoln road, easily reached and signposted from A1. **Parking**: free, 250 yards.

You may also enjoy: on a smaller scale: Woolsthorpe Manor, Isaac Newton's birthplace, and Tattershall Castle.

The fountain at Belton House, Lincolnshire

Finding out more: 01476 566116 or belton@nationaltrust.org.uk

Belton House		M	T	W	T	F	S	S
House								
5 Mar–13 Mar	12:30–4	·	·	·	·	·	S	S
16 Mar–30 Oct	12:30–5	·	·	W	T	F	S	S
Basement								
5 Mar–30 Oct	11–3:30	M	T	W	T	F	S	S
Garden, park, restaurant and shop								
5 Feb–27 Feb	12–4	·	·	·	·	·	S	S
5 Mar–30 Oct	10:30–5:30	M	T	W	T	F	S	S
5 Nov–18 Dec	12–4	·	·	·	·	·	S	S
26 Dec–31 Dec	12–4	M	T	W	T	F	S	·
Adventure playground								
5 Mar–30 Oct	10:30–5:30	M	T	W	T	F	S	S

Open Bank Holiday Mondays (March to October). House conservation talks 11:30 most days; open for free-flow 12:30 (guided tours may replace free-flow some days). Timed tickets to house and basement likely at busy times. Basement may close occasionally for essential maintenance work (contact property for details). Bellmount Woods: open daily, access from separate car park. Please note: whole property likely to close early in poor weather or light conditions.

The grand south front of Calke Abbey, Derbyshire

Calke Abbey

Ticknall, Derby, Derbyshire DE73 7LE

Map ③ C4 1985

'We thoroughly enjoyed Calke. Excellent decision not to restore, making it a very different experience. Excellent food and helpful staff.'
Miss S. Mead, Droitwich Spa, Worcestershire

With peeling paintwork and overgrown courtyards Calke Abbey tells the story of the dramatic decline of a grand country-house estate. The house and stables are little restored, with many abandoned areas vividly portraying a period in the 20th century when numerous country houses did not survive to tell their story. Discover the tales of an eccentric family who amassed a vast collection of hidden treasures. Visit the beautiful, yet faded, walled gardens and explore the orangery, auricula theatre and kitchen gardens. Escape into the ancient and fragile habitats of Calke Park and its National Nature Reserve.

Note: all house and garden visitors require admission tickets (free for members).

Exploring — Discover Calke Abbey – the 'unstately home'.
— Follow the twists and turns of the Brewhouse Tunnel.
— Stroll in the beautiful walled garden and see the orangery.
— Explore Calke Park and its National Nature Reserve.
— Discover 'the old man of Calke', a 1,000-year-old oak.
— Have fun with Tracker Packs and our Discovery Trails.

Eating and shopping: restaurant serves freshly prepared local produce, including organically reared meat from the estate. Browse in the shop, full of wonderful gifts.

Buy local food in the Calke Pantry. Refreshments are available from the coffee shop kiosk at peak times.

Making the most of your day: enjoy the West Wing conservation tour. Discover our family events programme, available throughout the year. Tracker Packs, Discovery Trails and family activities in Squirt's Stable, weekends March to October. **Dogs**: welcome on leads in the park and stables only.

Access for all: ♿🚐🅦🔉🔦📷🎧📖📺⠿
Building 🔉📷🔉 Grounds 🔉📷➡

Getting here: 128:SK367226. 10 miles south of Derby. **Bus**: Arriva 61 Derby to Swadlincote, alight Ticknall, 1½ mile walk through park. **Train**: Derby 9½ miles; Burton-on-Trent 10 miles. **Road**: 10 miles south of Derby, on A514 at Ticknall between Swadlincote and Melbourne. Access from M42/A42 exit 13 and A50 Derby South. Entry via Ticknall main entrance only. **Parking**: per person park admission for all visitors (charges apply for non-members). Please note 3.6-metre height restriction at Middle Lodge arch. No shaded parking.

You may also enjoy: Staunton Harold Church, Kedleston Hall, Sudbury Hall and the Museum of Childhood.

Finding out more: 01332 863822 or calkeabbey@nationaltrust.org.uk

Calke Abbey		M	T	W	T	F	S	S
Calke Park National Nature Reserve								
Open all year	7:30–7:30	M	T	W	T	F	S	S
House								
26 Feb–30 Oct	12:30–5	M	T	W	·	·	S	S
Garden and stables								
26 Feb–20 Apr	11–5	M	T	W	·	·	S	S
21 Apr–30 Oct	11–5	M	T	W	T	F	S	S
Restaurant and shop								
2 Jan–25 Feb	10:30–4	M	T	W	T	F	S	S
26 Feb–30 Oct	10:30–5	M	T	W	T	F	S	S
31 Oct–24 Dec	10:30–4	M	T	W	T	F	S	S
West Wing conservation tour								
26 Feb–30 Oct	11–12:30	M	T	W	·	·	S	S

House open for West Wing conservation tours, 11 to 12:30 by timed ticket. Last admission 12. Admission to house by timed ticket for all visitors including members, delays may occur at peak times. Restaurant and shop closed 1 January and 25 and 26 December and closes at 4, January, February, November and December. Calke Park closed 7:30 or dusk if earlier. House and gardens open Good Friday.

Canons Ashby

Canons Ashby, Daventry, Northamptonshire NN11 3SD

Map ③ D7 🏠✝🏛♿♠  1981

'**A house I have passed by for many years, now I have found a jewel.**'
Mr Chilver, Spratton

Canons Ashby has been the family home of the Drydens since Elizabethan times and that family atmosphere remains today. The story of Canons Ashby, which has been little altered since the 19th century, is presented as if it were being seen through the eyes of Sir Henry Dryden, an eminent Victorian. The house is atmospheric and welcoming, while the delightful garden is being returned to its colourful Victorian style. A stroll in the wider parkland offers a glimpse of the earlier medieval history, while the church explores the story of the canons of Canons Ashby.

Exploring
- Enjoy the friendly home of the Dryden family.
- Relax in the newly restored gardens.
- Discover acres of historic parkland.
- Enjoy the delights of the garden tea-room.
- Follow a children's trail or grab a Tracker Pack.

Eating and shopping: browse in the shop for ideas for the home and garden. Enjoy freshly prepared food in the garden tea-room. Hundreds of second-hand books to discover.

Making the most of your day: many events throughout the year, including Victorian Country Gathering, guided walks, special aspects tours, family fun activities, Christmas market and Christmas Past. **Dogs**: on leads in Home Paddock, car park and parkland only.

Access for all: ♿🅦🔉🔦📷📖📺🎧⠿📷
Building 🔉🔉 Grounds 🔉🔉

Getting here: 152:SP577506. South of Daventry. **Foot**: on the Macmillan long-distance footpath. 3 miles on country lanes from Woodford Halse. **Cycle**: NCN70. **Bus**: to Woodford Halse, between Daventry and Banbury. **Train**: Banbury 10 miles. **Road**: easy access from either M40 exit 11, or M1 exit 16. From M1 take A45 (Daventry) and at Weedon crossroads turn left onto A5; 3 miles south turn right onto unclassified road through Litchborough and Adstone. From M40 at Banbury take A422 (Brackley) and after 2 miles turn left onto B4525; after 3 miles turn left onto unclassified road signposted to property. **Parking**: free, 200 yards.

You may also enjoy: Lyveden New Bield: an unfinished Elizabethan lodge set within a delightful historic landscape.

Finding out more: 01327 860044 or canonsashby@nationaltrust.org.uk

Canons Ashby		M	T	W	T	F	S	S
House, garden, tea-room, shop, church and park								
12 Feb–13 Feb	12–4*						S	S
19 Feb–27 Feb	12–4*	M	T	W			S	S
5 Mar–13 Mar	12–4*						S	S
14 Mar–20 Jul	11–5	M	T	W			S	S
23 Jul–4 Sep	11–5	M	T	W		F	S	S
5 Sep–2 Nov	11–5	M	T	W			S	S
5 Nov–18 Dec	12–4*						S	S

Open Good Friday 11 to 5. Closes dusk if earlier. *Tea-room, garden and church open at 11.

A kitchen maid at Canons Ashby, Northamptonshire

Clumber Park

Worksop, Nottinghamshire S80 3AZ

Map ③ D2　🏚✝♣♠🐾🚲🍴　1946

Clumber, once a family home to the Dukes of Newcastle, today offers families freedom to discover a ducal park while glimpsing its grand past. The woods, rolling countryside and lake are home to an amazing array of wildlife and provide a picturesque backdrop to a great day out. Whether you are looking for a place to stop-off on a long journey, somewhere to enjoy a gentle stroll followed by a relaxed picnic by the lake, or to play games then hire a bike and explore further afield, Clumber has got plenty of space for you to enjoy all year.

Exploring
- Be inspired to explore 1,537 hectares (3,800 acres).
- Discover 20 miles of cycle routes through spectacular scenery.
- Go wild at our new Discovery Centre.
- Hang out on the climbing forest in the play park.
- Unearth tastes of the past in the Walled Kitchen Garden.
- Take a trip onboard our tractor and trailer or ferryboat.

Eating and shopping: browse through a treasure trove of toys, gifts and souvenirs. Get inspiration and ideas at plant sales. Enjoy fresh, local, seasonal food and snacks in the café. Try our delicious local ice-cream, Clumber fudge or old-fashioned sweets.

Making the most of your day: year-round packed family events programme (visit www.nationaltrust.org.uk/clumberpark). Hands-on wildlife exhibitions and activities in the Discovery Centre. Family Tracker Packs. Cycle hire centre. **Dogs**: welcome, on leads in Walled Kitchen Garden, Pleasure Ground and grazing areas.

Access for all: 🅿♿🚻♿♿♿♿♿ ⓦ
Chapel ♿♿ Glasshouse ♿♿
Grounds ♿➡♿♿

Cycling at Clumber Park, Nottinghamshire

Getting here: 120:SK629752. **Cycle**: NCN6.
Bus: Stagecoach 'The Sherwood Arrow'
Worksop to Ollerton, alight Carburton,
¾ mile. **Train**: Worksop 4½ miles; Retford
6½ miles. **Road**: 4½ miles south-east of
Worksop, 6½ miles south-west of Retford,
1 mile from A1/A57, 11 miles from M1 exit 30.
Parking: throughout park. Main parking
200 yards from visitor facilities and 250 yards
from Walled Kitchen Garden.

You may also enjoy: Nottinghamshire's other
treasures: the fascinating Mr Straw's House
and The Workhouse, Southwell.

Finding out more: 01909 544917 or
clumberpark@nationaltrust.org.uk

Clumber Park		M	T	W	T	F	S	S
Park								
Open all year	Dawn–dusk	M	T	W	T	F	S	S
Café, shop, plant sales, play park and exhibition centre								
1 Jan–26 Mar	10–4	M	T	W	T	F	S	S
27 Mar–29 Oct	10–5	M	T	W	T	F	S	S
30 Oct–31 Dec	10–4	M	T	W	T	F	S	S
Cycle hire centre								
1 Jan–26 Mar	10–4	.	.	.	.	.	S	S
27 Mar–29 Oct	10–5	M	T	W	T	F	S	S
30 Oct–31 Dec	10–4	.	.	.	.	.	S	S
Walled Kitchen Garden								
12 Mar–26 Mar	10–4	M	T	W	T	F	S	S
27 Mar–2 Oct	10–5	M	T	W	T	F	S	S
3 Oct–30 Oct	10–4	M	T	W	T	F	S	S

27 March to 29 October: Saturday, Sunday and Bank
Holidays all facilities open 10 to 6. Discovery and Exhibition
Centre open from Easter. Last hiring of cycles two hours
before closing. Cycle Hire Centre also open midweek
November to March for school holidays and booked groups.
Chapel: 12 January to 28 March closed for conservation
cleaning. Park and all facilities closed 25 December.

Dark Peak

Edale, Hope Valley, Peak District,
Derbyshire S33 6RF

Map ③ B2

The estate stretches from the heather-clad
moors of Kinder to the gritstone tors of
Derwent Edge, from the peat bogs of Bleaklow
to the limestone crags of Winnats Pass.
The wild Pennine moorlands are of
international importance for their populations
of breeding birds and mosaic of habitats. Sites
of particular interest include Mam Tor, with
spectacular views, landslip and prehistoric
settlement, and the famous Snake Pass. Kinder
Scout, where the Mass Trespass of 1932 took
place, is the highest point for 50 miles.
The Trust also owns several farms and a
café in the beautiful Edale Valley.
Note: nearest toilet in adjacent villages
and at visitor centres at Ladybower
Reservoir, Edale, Castleton.

Exploring
- Follow one of the ancient routes aross wild moorland.
- Wander through the oak woods of the Derwent Valley.
- Explore the limestone caves and caverns of Winnats Pass.
- Climb Kinder Scout, the highest point in the Peak District.
- Discover the beautiful hay meadows in the Edale Valley.
- Learn about wildlife and history by booking on an event.

Eating and shopping: enjoy breakfast, lunch
or tea at Penny Pot Café in Edale. Stay at the
remote White Edge Lodge holiday cottage.
Camp and enjoy local food at Upper Booth
Farm, Edale. Discover more about our
moorlands at Edale Visitor Centre.

Making the most of your day: programme
of events throughout the year. New
downloadable walking trails, audio trails,
geocaching and podcasts from
www.nationaltrust.org.uk/peakdistrict.

Cyclists on the footpath at Mam Tor, part of the Dark Peak Estate, Derbyshire

Finding out more: 01433 670368 or darkpeak@nationaltrust.org.uk. Dark Peak Estate Office, Edale End, Hope Valley, Derbyshire S33 6RF

Dark Peak		M	T	W	T	F	S	S
Estate								
1 Jan–31 Dec		M	T	W	T	F	S	S
Penny Pot Café								
2 Jan–13 Mar	10–4:30						S	S
16 Mar–30 Oct	10–4:30			W	T	F	S	S
21 May–18 Sep	8:30–4:30						S	S
5 Nov–31 Dec	10–4						S	S

Five information shelters open all year: Lee Barn (110:SK096855) on Pennine Way near Jacob's Ladder; Dalehead (110: SK101843) in Edale; South Head Farm (SK060854) at Kinder; Edale End (SK161864) between Edale and Hope; Grindle Barns above Ladybower Reservoir (SK189895). Penny Pot Café closed 24, 25 and 26 December. Extended opening between Christmas and New Year (contact Penny Pot for details). For National Trust Peak District accommodation details visit www.nationaltrust.org.uk/peakdistrict

Various waymarked walks and information barns on the estate. **Dogs**: must be on a lead at all times from early March to end July.

Access for all: [icons] Penny Pot Café [icon]

Getting here: 110:SK100855. In the heart of the Peak District National Park. **Foot**: Pennine Way and many miles of waymarked footpaths. **Cycle**: Pennine Bridleway and many other routes. **Bus**: frequent from surrounding areas (Sheffield, Bakewell and Manchester) to Castleton, Edale and Hope Valley. **Train**: Edale is at the start of walks onto Kinder Scout and 3 miles from Mam Tor; Chinley is 3 miles from Kinder Scout western starting point; Hope is 3 miles from Losehill; Bamford 3 miles from Upper Derwent Valley – linked by cycle route and shuttle bus. **Road**: estate covers area north and south of A57 on Sheffield side of Snake Top, east of Hayfield and west of Castleton. **Parking**: many free car parks (not National Trust). Also pay and display (not National Trust) at Edale, Castleton, Bowden Bridge, Upper Derwent Valley and Hayfield. National Trust pay and display at Mam Nick (SK123833).

Duffield Castle

Milford Road, Duffield, Derbyshire

Map (3) C4   [icons]   1899

The remains of one of England's largest 13th-century castles. The foundations, the story and views are all that remain today. **Note**: unmanned site. No toilets. Steep steps – disabled access by arrangement.

Getting here: 128:SK343440. On the northern edge of Duffield village – A6 passes directly in front.

Finding out more: 01332 844052 or duffieldcastle@nationaltrust.org.uk. c/o Kedleston Hall, Kedleston, Derbyshire DE22 5JH

Duffield Castle	Open every day all year

Grantham House

Castlegate, Grantham, Lincolnshire NG31 6SS

Map ③ E4 1944

A handsome town house and one of the oldest buildings in Grantham. Architectural features from various eras; riverside walled garden. **Note**: the house is leased by the National Trust and the lessee is responsible for arrangements and facilities. Appointments may be needed on some dates.

Access for all: [D₂][WC][♿] House [♿][♿]
Grounds [♿]

Getting here: 130:SK916362. Immediately east of St Wulfram's church in the centre of Grantham.

Finding out more: 01476 564705 or granthamhouse@nationaltrust.org.uk

Grantham House		M	T	W	T	F	S	S
6 Apr–26 May*		·	·	**W**	**T**	·	·	·
1 Jun–30 Jun	2–5	·	·	**W**	**T**	·	·	·
6 Jul–27 Oct*		·	·	**W**	**T**	·	·	·

*By written appointment. The property is leased by the National Trust and the house and garden are open to visitors at various times, as advertised. The lessee is responsible for all arrangements and facilities. Entrance via gates opposite Church Street.

Gunby Hall

Gunby, near Spilsby, Lincolnshire PE23 5SS

Map ③ G3 1944

Fine red-brick house, dating from 1700, with Victorian walled gardens.

Access for all: [P₂][D₂][♿][••] Building [♿]
Grounds [♿]

Getting here: 122:TF467668. 2½ miles north-west of Burgh le Marsh, 7 miles west of Skegness on south side of A158 (access off roundabout).

The entrance hall at Gunby Hall, Lincolnshire

Finding out more: 01754 890212 or gunbyhall@nationaltrust.org.uk

Gunby Hall

The tenancy arrangements at Gunby Hall are changing in 2011. Please telephone 01526 342543 (Tattershall Castle) to confirm opening times.

Gunby Hall Estate: Monksthorpe Chapel

Monksthorpe, near Spilsby, Lincolnshire PE23 5PP

Map ③ G3 ✝ 2000

Remote late 17th-century Baptist chapel.

Access for all: [P₂][D₂] Building [♿][♿] Grounds [♿]

Getting here: 122:TF450654. From A158 in Candlesby, turn off main road opposite Royal Oak pub, following signs to Monksthorpe. Follow road for about 1½ miles and turn left. After 50 yards turn left at dead end sign. Parking is on the left at entrance to avenue.

Finding out more: 01526 342543 or monksthorpe@nationaltrust.org.uk

Monksthorpe Chapel		M	T	W	T	F	S	S
6 Apr–29 Sep	2–5	·	·	**W**	**T**	·	·	·

Chapel open and stewarded first Saturday of the month from April to September. Admission Wednesday and Thursday from April to September by key only, obtained from Gunby Hall (£10 deposit required). Services on Saturdays at 3: 16 April, 21 May, 18 June, 16 July, 20 August, 17 September (Harvest Festival), 15 October and 10 December (carol service at 2).

Hardwick Estate: Stainsby Mill

Doe Lea, Chesterfield, Derbyshire S44 5QJ

Map ③ D3　🏚 1976

Come and explore the workings of a fully operational watermill, which gives a vivid evocation of the workplace of a 19th-century miller. Flour is ground regularly and is for sale throughout the season. **Note**: nearest toilet at Hardwick Hall car park.

Exploring
- Discover the secrets of a 13th-century watermill.
- Children's trail and activity sheets available.
- Selected days: have a go at milling your own flour.

Eating and shopping: buy Stainsby freshly milled flour. Restaurant, kiosk, shop and toilets nearby at Hardwick Hall. Buy a souvenir guide about the history of the mill.

Checking the flour at Stainsby Mill, a working watermill on the Hardwick Hall Estate, Derbyshire

Making the most of your day: join us to celebrate National Mills weekend in May. **Dogs**: on leads in Hardwick Park only.

Access for all: 🚾♿📷🎧🔌·🖐🏠
Building 🏚 Grounds 🦽🏞

Getting here: 120:SK455653. **Foot**: Rowthorne Trail and Teversal Trail nearby. **Bus**: Stagecoach East Midlands 'Pronto' Chesterfield to Nottingham, alight Glapwell 'Young Vanish', 1½ miles. **Train**: Chesterfield 7 miles. **Road**: from M1 exit 29 take A6175 signposted to Clay Cross, first left and left again to Stainsby Mill. **Parking**: free (not National Trust). Limited car and coach parking.

Finding out more: 01246 850430 or stainsbymill@nationaltrust.org.uk

Hardwick Estate: Stainsby Mill		M	T	W	T	F	S	S
23 Feb–30 Oct	10–4			W	T	F	S	S
3 Dec–18 Dec	11–3						S	S

Open Bank Holiday Mondays and Good Friday 10 to 4.

Hardwick Hall

Doe Lea, Chesterfield, Derbyshire S44 5QJ

Map ③ D3　🏚🍴❄♿🌳　🏠🔔🍷 1959

'We come to Hardwick regularly, it is even better every time. Can't wait to see the new restaurant.'
Kerrie Burns, Staffordshire

One of the most splendid houses in England. Built by Bess of Hardwick in the 1590s, and unaltered since: yet its huge windows and high ceilings make it feel strikingly modern. Outside, stone gleams and glass glitters in the light. Its six towers make a dramatic skyline. Climbing up through the house, from one spectacular floor to the next, is a thrilling architectural experience. Rich tapestries, plaster friezes and alabaster fireplaces colour the rooms, culminating in the hauntingly atmospheric Long Gallery. **Note**: Old Hall is owned by the National Trust and administered by English Heritage (01246 850431).

The Long Gallery at Hardwick Hall, Derbyshire

Exploring
 — New: fascinating exhibition of Bess's letters.
 — Visit our new Discovery Room to investigate the deterioration agents.
 — Relax in the fragrant herb garden, orchards and lawns.
 — Take a tour of our historic stableyard and development project.
 — Explore the picturesque parkland on one of our circular walks.
 — Family fun: garden and park children's trails and Tracker Packs.

Eating and shopping: buy Hardwick souvenirs at the shop. Try meat reared on the estate at our restaurant. See our lovely collection of local gifts and produce. Get a snack, drink or ice-cream at the kiosk.

Making the most of your day: Hall tour available Wednesday to Sunday at 11 (£3 donation). Family activities and events, Elizabethan costume days, circular walks. **Dogs**: on leads and in the park and car park only.

Access for all: ⬚⬚⬚⬚⬚⬚⬚⬚⬚ ⬚⬚ **Building** ⬚⬚⬚ **Grounds** ⬚⬚

Getting here: 120:SK463638. **Foot**: Rowthorne Trail; Teversal Trail. **Bus**: Stagecoach East Midlands 'Pronto' Chesterfield to Nottingham, alight Glapwell 'Young Vanish', 1½ miles. **Train**: Chesterfield 8 miles. **Road**: 6½ miles west of Mansfield, 9½ miles south-east of Chesterfield; approach from M1 (exit 29) via A6175. A one-way traffic system operates in the park; access only via Stainsby Mill entrance (leave M1 exit 29, follow brown signs), exit only via Hardwick Inn. **Parking**: 100 yards, £2. Ponds parking, £2 (pay and display).

You may also enjoy: Hardwick Estate: Stainsby Mill.

Finding out more: 01246 850430 or hardwickhall@nationaltrust.org.uk

Hardwick Hall		M	T	W	T	F	S	S
Hall								
23 Feb–30 Oct*	12–4:30	·	·	W	T	F	S	S
3 Dec–18 Dec	11–3	·	·	·	·	·	S	S
Garden, shop, restaurant and kiosk								
23 Feb–24 Jul	11–5	·	·	W	T	F	S	S
25 Jul–4 Sep	11–5	M	T	W	T	F	S	S
7 Sep–30 Oct	11–5	·	·	W	T	F	S	S
3 Dec–18 Dec	11–3	·	·	·	·	·	S	S

Open Bank Holiday Mondays and Good Friday 12 to 4:30. *Hall entrance 11 to 12 is by guided tour only (limited availability). Additional heritage tours also available. Kiosk: open daily during main open season and between Christmas and New Year, but may close in bad weather. Stone Centre open daily all year. Hall, gardens and park close dusk during winter. Special winter tours and lunches for booked groups on Fridays in December (contact Estate Office).

High Peak Estate

See Dark Peak, page 211.

Ilam Park and South Peak Estate

See White Peak, page 223.

The spectacular north front of Kedleston Hall, Derbyshire: Robert Adam's Neo-classical masterpiece

Kedleston Hall

near Quarndon, Derby, Derbyshire DE22 5JH

Map ③ C4      1987

'**Wow! This house is amazing and there are so many interesting facts to find out!**'
Jessica Harvey, Derbyshire

Take a trip back in time to the 1760s at this spectacular Neo-classical mansion, framed by historic parkland. Designed for lavish entertaining and displaying an extensive collection of paintings, sculpture and original furnishings, Kedleston is a stunning example of the work of architect Robert Adam. The Curzon family have lived at the Hall since the 12th century and continue to live here. Lord Curzon's Eastern Museum is a treasure trove of fascinating objects acquired on his travels in Asia and while Viceroy of India (1899 to 1905). Used as a key location for *The Duchess*, the recent Hollywood blockbuster. **Note**: medieval All Saints church, containing many family monuments, is run by the Churches Conservation Trust.

Exploring
— Experience the stunning Adam interiors.
— Follow in the footsteps of *The Duchess*, using our trail.

Exploring
— Discover Britain's colonial connections in the Eastern Museum.
— Explore the parkland and see what wildlife you can spot.
— New: enjoy cozy sofas by warming fires in Caesar's Hall.
— New: children's Tracker Packs.

Eating and shopping: buy a Kedleston souvenir and local products. Peat-free plants for sale. Seasonal recipes made using local produce, including Kedleston Park lamb.

Making the most of your day: available most house open days at selected times – introductory talk, tours of fishing pavilion, great west stable or pleasure grounds, and brief talks by 18th-century housekeeper Mrs Garnett. **Dogs**: on leads in park and pleasure grounds.

Access for all: 🅿️♿🇩📶🚻🍴📷🎧💻📺♿
•• Ground floor ♿♿ State floor ♿♿
Grounds ➡️

Getting here: 128:SK312403. 5 miles north-west of Derby; 12 miles south-east of Ashbourne. **Cycle**: on parkland roads (not allowed on park walks and footpaths). **Bus**: Arriva 109 Derby to Ashbourne, calls at the Hall summer Saturdays only, otherwise alight the Smithy, 1 mile. **Train**: Duffield 3½ miles; Derby 5½ miles.

Road: all traffic should aim for intersection of A52/ A38, and follow A38 (north). Take first exit (by Derby University) and continue along Kedleston Road towards Quarndon. **Parking**: 200 yards, admission fees apply.

You may also enjoy: Calke Abbey, Sudbury Hall, White Peak and medieval Tattershall Castle.

Finding out more: 01332 842191 or kedlestonhall@nationaltrust.org.uk

Kedleston Hall		M	T	W	T	F	S	S
House								
19 Feb–30 Oct	12–5	M	T	W	·	·	S	S
Pleasure Grounds								
19 Feb–30 Oct	10–6	M	T	W	T	F	S	S
Park								
2 Jan–18 Feb	10–4	M	T	W	T	F	S	S
19 Feb–30 Oct	10–6	M	T	W	T	F	S	S
31 Oct–31 Dec	10–4	M	T	W	T	F	S	S
Restaurant and shop								
2 Jan–13 Feb	11–3	·	·	·	·	·	S	S
19 Feb–30 Oct	11–5	M	T	W	·	·	S	S
21 Jul–26 Aug	11–3	·	·	·	·	T	F	·
5 Nov–24 Dec	11–3	·	·	·	·	·	S	S
26 Dec–31 Dec	11–3	M	T	W	T	F	S	·

Last entry to house 4:15. Open Good Friday. Park occasional day closures November to February. Property closed 25 December. **19 February to 20 March: house will be shown by guided tour only.**

Longshaw Estate

Longshaw, near Sheffield, Derbyshire

Map ③ C2

A wonderful place to discover spectacular views of the Peak District, ancient woods, meadows, parkland and heather moorland. Explore the unusual sites of Longshaw's past, from millstone quarries to packhorse routes. The visitor centre, housed in the Shooting Lodge, is the ideal starting point for Longshaw and the Peak District. **Note**: Moorland Discovery Centre only open to the public for certain events and during school holidays.

Exploring
- Follow walking trails through the ancient woods and hay meadows.
- Enjoy spectacular views over the Derwent Valley and Peak District.
- Discover the hidden past with guidebook and family 'Ant' trail.
- New: restored kitchen garden – family events and taster days.

A panoramic view of the heathland and moorland of the Longshaw Estate, Derbyshire

Eating and shopping: browse in the shop for local and wildlife-themed products. Enjoy delicious home-baked local food, using produce from the estate and the Peak District. Daily specials created using produce from our new kitchen garden. All food comes with wonderful views.

Making the most of your day: year-round events programme, including special family events and trails in the autumn, Christmas, Easter and summer holidays. Circular, waymarked walks to explore the park and woodland. New wildlife webcams. **Dogs**: on estate on leads from early March to end of July.

Access for all: [icons] Building [icons] Grounds [icons]

Getting here: 110/119:SK266800. **Foot**: 2 miles by footpath from Grindleford, 3 miles from Hathersage and 7 miles from Sheffield. **Cycle**: connected to Sheffield (7 miles) by bridleway via Moss Road and Houndkirk. **Bus**: First 272 Sheffield to Castleton (passing Hathersage ≋), TM Travel 214 Sheffield to Matlock and 65 Sheffield to Buxton. All pass close Sheffield ≋. **Train**: Grindleford 2 miles (1 mile to visitor centre, 100 yards to Padley Gorge). **Road**: 7½ miles from Sheffield, next to A625 Sheffield to Hathersage road; Woodcroft car park is off B6055, 200 yards south of junction with A625. **Parking**: at Haywood (110/119: SK256778), Wooden Pole (110/119: SK267790) and Woodcroft (110/119: SK267802). Only Woodcroft accessible to coaches. All pay and display.

Finding out more: 01433 637904 or longshaw@nationaltrust.org.uk. Estate Office, Longshaw Estate, Longshaw, Sheffield, Derbyshire S11 7TZ

Longshaw Estate		M	T	W	T	F	S	S
Estate								
2 Jan–31 Dec	Dawn–dusk	**M**	**T**	**W**	**T**	**F**	**S**	**S**
Visitor centre								
2 Jan–20 Feb	10:30–4	·	·	·	·	·	**S**	**S**
21 Feb–30 Oct	10:30–5	**M**	**T**	**W**	**T**	**F**	**S**	**S**
5 Nov–18 Dec	10:30–4	·	·	·	·	·	**S**	**S**
27 Dec–31 Dec	10:30–4	·	**T**	**W**	**T**	**F**	**S**	·

Open Bank Holiday Mondays. Lodge is not open to the public. Telephone for extended Christmas opening. Closed 24 to 26 December.

Lyveden New Bield

near Oundle, Northamptonshire PE8 5AT

Map ③ E6 [icons] 1922

'**An amazing place to discover – the children loved the freedom to explore.**'
R. Harris, Kettering

Lyveden is a remarkable story of survival. One of England's oldest garden landscapes, Lyveden was abandoned in 1605 when its creator Sir Thomas Tresham died and his son became embroiled in the Catholic gunpowder plot. Today you can enjoy an experience of an Elizabethan garden with original moats, mounts, terracing and intriguing garden lodge. Period fruit trees recreate what was described as 'one of the fairest orchards in England', and the circular labyrinth reflects Tresham's original garden design. Lyveden is a place where you can relax in peace, explore with the new audio guide or venture further and discover Rockingham Forest.

Exploring
– Discover Lyveden through the new audio guide.
– Uncover the mysteries of Sir Thomas's symbolic garden lodge.
– Relax with a picnic in the peaceful setting of Lyveden.
– Enjoy stunning wildflower meadows between April and August.
– Explore the garden labyrinth.
– Enjoy the Lyveden Way – and discover Rockingham Forest.

Eating and shopping: enjoy an ice-cream sitting by the moated garden. Hot and cold drinks sold in the shop. Local honey (seasonal) and sale of wildflower plants and herbs.

Making the most of your day: free garden tours every Sunday from May to October. The freedom to explore makes Lyveden a great place for a family visit and an ideal setting for a picnic. **Dogs**: welcome on leads only.

Access for all: [icons] Building [icons] Grounds [icons]

Members may have to pay on special events days

The Old Manor

Norbury, Ashbourne, Derbyshire DE6 2ED

Map ③ B4 1987

Medieval hall featuring a rare king post, Tudor door and 17th-century Flemish glass. Gardens include a parterre herb garden. **Note**: limited parking (cars only).

Access for all: 🚻🚪◎ Building 🦽 Grounds 🦽🦽

Getting here: 128:SK125424. 4 miles from Ashbourne; 9 miles from Sudbury Hall.

Finding out more: 01283 585337 or oldmanor@nationaltrust.org.uk

The Old Manor		M	T	W	T	F	S	S
1 Apr–21 Oct	11–1					**F**		
2 Apr–22 Oct	2–4						**S**	

Property is tenanted and visits are only available during opening hours.

The Water Garden with Lyveden New Bield beyond, Northamptonshire

Getting here: 141:SP983853. **Bus**: Stagecoach in Northants X4 Northampton 🚉 to Peterborough 🚉, alight Lower Benefield, 2 miles by bridlepath; Judges minicoaches 8 Kettering to Corby, alight Brigstock, 2½ miles. Both pass close Kettering 🚉. **Train**: Kettering 10 miles. **Road**: 4 miles south-west of Oundle via A427, 3 miles east of Brigstock, off A6116. **Parking**: free, 100 yards.

You may also enjoy: another Elizabethan house and exciting garden project at Canons Ashby.

Finding out more: 01832 205358 or lyveden@nationaltrust.org.uk

Lyveden New Bield		M	T	W	T	F	S	S
5 Feb–13 Mar	11–4						**S**	**S**
16 Mar–30 Oct	10:30–5			**W**	**T**	**F**	**S**	**S**
1 Jul–4 Sep	10:30–5	**M**	**T**	**W**	**T**	**F**	**S**	**S**
30 Oct–27 Nov	11–4						**S**	**S**

Open Bank Holiday Mondays. Open Good Friday, 10:30 to 5.

Priest's House

Easton on the Hill, near Stamford, Northamptonshire PE9 3LS

Map ③ E5 1966

A delightful small late 15th-century building, with interesting local architecture and a museum exploring Easton's industrial past.

Access for all: Building 🦽🦽

Getting here: 141:TF009045. Approximately 2 miles south-west of Stamford off A43.

Finding out more: 01780 762619 or priestshouse2@nationaltrust.org.uk

Priest's House		M	T	W	T	F	S	S
3 Jul–28 Aug	2–4:30							**S**

Unmanned. Also open by appointment daily throughout year. Names of keyholders on property noticeboard. Appointments for groups may be made through local representative Mr Paul Way, 39 Church Street, Easton on the Hill, Stamford PE9 3LL.

Mr Straw's red-brick house at Worksop, Nottinghamshire

Staunton Harold Church

Staunton Harold, Ashby-de-la-Zouch,
Leicestershire LE65 1RW

Map ③ C4   🕂 1954

This is one of the few churches built between the outbreak of the English Civil War and the Restoration period. **Note**: toilets 500 yards (not National Trust). Staunton Harold Estate may ask for voluntary parking donation.

Access for all: 🅿️🔼 Building 🔼🔼

Getting here: 128:SK380209. 5 miles north-east of Ashby-de-la-Zouch, west of B587. Access from M42/A42 exit 13, follow Ferrers Centre brown signs – anvil symbol.

Finding out more: 01332 863822 (Calke Abbey) or stauntonharoldchurch@nationaltrust.org.uk

Staunton Harold Church	M	T	W	T	F	S	S
2 Apr–30 Oct	1–4:30						S	S
1 Jun–26 Aug	1–4:30			W	T	F	S	S

Church open Good Friday and Bank Holidays April to October. Services: Easter to December, second and fourth Sundays.

Mr Straw's House

5-7 Blyth Grove, Worksop,
Nottinghamshire S81 0JG

Map ③ D2   🏠❄️ 1990

'**We have thoroughly enjoyed this step back in time and history of two very different but splendid "gentlemen".'**
S. Woodcock, Bridlington

Step back in time to the early 20th century and find out how a grocer's family lived in this market town. This ordinary semi-detached house, with original interior decorations from 1923, was the home of the Straw family. For 60 years the family threw little away and chose to live without many of the modern comforts we take for granted. Be intrigued by stories of the family who made an extraordinary home in this ordinary house – hear about the times they lived in and see the everyday objects they treasured.

Exploring
  – Introductory video introduces the Straw family.
  – Explore three floors of Edwardian house with informative guides.
  – See annual exhibition of items not usually on display.
  – Visit the garden and replica greenhouse with cacti collection.
  – Children can follow a trail.
  – Occasional activity days and events.

Eating and shopping: small shop area with snacks and souvenirs.

Making the most of your day: tea and cakes, usually on first Saturday in month in orchard car park (provided by Friends group).

Access for all: 🅿️🔼🔼🔛🔼
No 5 🔼 No 7 🔼 Back garden 🔼

Getting here: 120:SK592802. In private road in suburbs north of Worksop town centre.
Cycle: NCN6, ¾ mile. **Bus**: Stagecoach 22 and 42 from Worksop. **Train**: Worksop ½ mile.

Road: follow signs for Bassetlaw Hospital and Blyth Road (B6045). Blyth Grove is a small private road off B6045, just south of Bassetlaw Hospital A&E entrance. House signposted with black and white sign at the entrance to Blyth Grove. **Parking**: free, across the road.

You may also enjoy: Clumber Park and The Workhouse.

Finding out more: 01909 482380 or mrstrawshouse@nationaltrust.org.uk

Mr Straw's House		M	T	W	T	F	S	S
12 Mar–29 Oct	11–5	·	**T**	**W**	**T**	**F**	**S**	·

Admission by timed ticket only for all visitors, including members – must be booked in advance by telephone or letter (with sae), not email, to Custodian. On quiet days a same-day telephone call is often sufficient. Last admission one hour before closing. Closed Good Friday. Due to its location in a residential area, the house is closed on Sundays as a courtesy to neighbours.

Sudbury Hall and the National Trust Museum of Childhood

Sudbury, Ashbourne, Derbyshire DE6 5HT

Map ③ B4    1967

'A great place to visit over and over again, as it will mean something different for children over the years.'
David Fletcher, Northampton

Two totally different experiences sitting side by side. The country home of the Lords Vernon, a delight of 17th-century craftsmanship, featuring exquisite plasterwork, wood carvings and classical story-based murals. Be amazed by the grandeur of the Great Staircase and Long Gallery. The Museum of Childhood is a delight for all ages with something for everyone. Explore the childhoods of times gone by, make stories, play with toys and share your childhood with others. You can be a chimney sweep, a scullion or a Victorian pupil, and be captivated by our archive film, interactives and displays.

Exploring
– Come and enjoy a morning tour of the Hall.
– Our coffee, cakes and cream teas are very popular.
– Meet and talk with our knowledgeable room guides.
– Treat your child to a museum birthday party.
– Enjoy our toys, interactives and displays.
– Have fun in the woodland play area.

Eating and shopping: fresh seasonal vegetables and delightful menus offer something new every day. Homemade scones, cakes and desserts are a real treat. Our gift and museum shops attract all ages with gifts, toys, games, books and homemade fudge.

Making the most of your day: family activities in the school holidays. Take a morning tour of the Hall. Explore our 'Have a go' area in the museum and woodland play area outdoors. Attend an event. **Dogs**: assistance dogs only.

Access for all: [icons] Sudbury Hall [icons]
Museum of Childhood [icons] Grounds [icons]

Getting here: 128:SK158322. 6 miles east of Uttoxeter. **Cycle**: cycleway from Uttoxeter to Doveridge, then road to property. **Bus**: Arriva 1 Burton on Trent to Uttoxeter (passing Tutbury ≋ and Hatton and close Burton on Trent ≋). **Train**: Tutbury and Hatton 5 miles. **Road**: 6 miles east of Uttoxeter at junction of A50 Derby to Stoke and A515 Ashbourne. **Parking**: free, 500 yards.

Toy car at the Museum of Childhood, Derbyshire

You may also enjoy: Kedleston Hall and Calke Abbey.

Finding out more: 01283 585305 (Infoline). 01283 585337 or sudburyhall@nationaltrust.org.uk

Sudbury Hall		M	T	W	T	F	S	S
Hall								
19 Feb–30 Oct	1–5	·	·	W	T	F	S	S
Museum, tea-room and shops								
19 Feb–3 Apr	11–5	·	·	W	T	F	S	S
4 Apr–30 Oct	11–5	M	T	W	T	F	S	S
5 Nov–11 Dec	11–4	·	·	·	·	·	S	S
Tours								
19 Feb–30 Oct	11–1	·	·	W	T	F	S	S
5 Apr–25 Oct	11–2	·	T	·	·	·	·	·
Christmas event								
3 Dec–11 Dec	11–4	M	T	W	T	F	S	S
Grounds								
19 Feb–11 Dec	10–5	M	T	W	T	F	S	S

Open Bank Holiday Mondays and Good Friday. Last entry 45 minutes before closing (Hall will close early if light level is poor). School visits and Hall tours available 11 to 1 (Tuesday, 'Hall tours only' every hour 11 to 2).

Children playing in the Outdoor Adventure Gallery at the National Trust Museum of Childhood, Derbyshire

Tattershall Castle

Sleaford Road, Tattershall, Lincolnshire LN4 4LR

Map ③ F3 1925

'The children could explore, pretend they were knights and hunt for dragons! The views are amazing from the battlements.' Sarah Dawson, Lincoln

Explore all six floors of this stunning red-brick medieval castle built by Ralph Cromwell, Lord Treasurer of England in 1434. Let the audio guide create a picture of what life was like at Tattershall Castle in the 15th century. Climb the 150 steps from the basement to the battlements and enjoy the magnificent views of the Lincolnshire countryside from the roof. Keep an eye out on summer weekends for a passing Spitfire, Hurricane or even a Lancaster Bomber! Then explore the grounds, moats, Guardhouse gift shop and neighbouring church, the largest parish church in the country!

Exploring
– Explore all six floors, from the basement to the battlements.
– Enjoy amazing views from the roof.
– Follow the audio tour.
– Picnic in the moated grounds.
– Explore the church.
– Visit the neighbouring RAF museum (weekdays only).

Eating and shopping: buy presents for all the family in our Guardhouse gift shop. Relax and enjoy light refreshments, also available from the shop.

Making the most of your day: major events, audio guides, family activities and 'have a go' sessions. **Dogs**: assistance dogs only.

Access for all: 🅿️ 🚻 💺 🪑 📷 💻 ♿
Building ♿ 🏛️ 🖐️ **Grounds** ♿ 🏛️

Getting here: 122:TF211575. **Cycle**: Hull to Harwich cycle route passes within 1 mile.

The Great Tower at Tattershall Castle, Lincolnshire

Ulverscroft Nature Reserve

Ulverscroft, Copt Oak, near Loughborough, Leicestershire

Map ③ D5   1945

Part of the ancient forest of Charnwood, Ulverscroft is especially beautiful during the spring bluebell season. Heathland and woodland habitats. **Note**: no toilet. Access by permit only from Leicestershire and Rutland Wildlife Trust, 0116 272 0444.

Access for all: Grounds 🦽

Getting here: 129:SK493118. 6 miles south-west of Loughborough.

Finding out more: 01332 863822 or ulverscroftnaturereserve@nationaltrust.org.uk

Ulverscroft Nature Reserve

Access by permit only from The Secretary, Leicestershire and Rutland Wildlife Trust, Brocks Hill Environment Centre, Washbrook Lane, Oadby, Leicestershire LE2 5JJ (0116 272 0444). Please allow a week to receive permit.

Bus: Brylaine 5 Lincoln to Boston (passing close Lincoln ≋). **Train**: Ruskington 10 miles. **Road**: on south side of A153, 15 miles north-east of Sleaford; 10 miles south-west of Horncastle. **Parking**: free, 150 yards. Coaches must reverse into parking area. Coaches must be booked in advance.

You may also enjoy: Belton House, Woolsthorpe Manor or the Gunby Hall Estate.

Finding out more: 01526 342543 or tattershallcastle@nationaltrust.org.uk

Tattershall Castle		M	T	W	T	F	S	S
5 Mar–13 Mar	11–4	·	·	·	·	·	S	S
14 Mar–30 Oct	11–5	M	T	W	·	·	S	S
5 Nov–18 Dec	11–4	·	·	·	·	·	S	S

Open Good Friday. Last audio guide issued one hour before closing. Opens 1 on some Saturdays if hosting a wedding. Please telephone to confirm in advance.

White Peak

White Peak Estate, Ilam, Ashbourne, Derbyshire and Peak District

Map ③ B3   🏠🏞🏊♣🏕 🛏🦮🏠 1906

White Peak Estate is situated in the spectacular setting of the Staffordshire and Derbyshire Peak District. Explore the rich daleside grasslands and ash woodlands in dramatic Dovedale. Enjoy Ilam Park's beautiful location beside the River Manifold, relax in the tea-room with amazing views of Dovedale, browse in the shop or discover the visitor centre with changing exhibitions. You can stay on our caravan site in Ilam Park, or our holiday cottages at Wetton Mill in the magnificent Manifold Valley. Use it as a

Bunster Hill, Dovedale, Peak District

base to explore the other parts of the White Peak Estate, such as Winster Market House. **Note**: Ilam Hall is let to the Youth Hostel Association.

Exploring
— Discover the dramatic limestone dalesides of Dovedale.
— Enjoy historic Ilam Park's gardens, park and walks.
— Manifold Valley – walks and cycling on the old railway line.
— Be reminded of local life in Winster Market House.
— Climb to the top of Thorpe Cloud for fantastic views.
— Explore the wide open spaces of the southern Peak District.

Eating and shopping: enjoy homemade dishes at Manifold tea-room in Ilam Park. Find great gifts in Ilam Park shop and the new mobile barn in Dovedale. Buy award-winning meat at the Peak District farm shop. Tea-room also at Wetton Mill (not National Trust).

Making the most of your day: varied programme of guided walks, talks and exhibitions. New downloadable walking trails, audio trails and podcasts from the Peak District website. **Dogs**: under close control and on leads in areas with livestock.

Access for all: 🅿️ 🅳 ♿ 🚻 💺 ⦿ ◎
Ilam Park stableyard ♿ ♿   Winster Market House ♿
Ilam Park grounds ♿ ♿ ♿ ➡️ ♿

Getting here: 119:SK132507 (Ilam Park) 119:SK152514 (Dovedale) 119:SK241606 (Winster Market House). Ilam Park and Dovedale are 4½ miles north-west of Ashbourne. Winster Market House is in Winster village, 4 miles west of Matlock. **Cycle**: NCN68, 2 miles. **Bus**: for Ilam and Dovedale: Bowers 442 Buxton ≋ to Ashbourne, daily, alight Thorpe, 2 miles Monday to Saturday, Ilam village Sunday and Bank Holidays. For Winster Market House Hulleys bus 172 Bakewell to Matlock ≋, daily. **Parking**: in Ilam Park, pay and display. Coaches by prior arrangement only.

You may also enjoy: Dark Peak and Longshaw Estate.

Finding out more: 01335 350503 or whitepeak@nationaltrust.org.uk.
White Peak Estate Office, Home Farm, Ilam, Ashbourne, Derbyshire DE6 2AZ

White Peak		M	T	W	T	F	S	S
Ilam Park								
2 Jan–31 Dec	Dawn–dusk	M	T	W	T	F	S	S
Ilam Park shop and tea-room								
2 Jan–20 Feb	11–4						S	S
Ilam Park shop								
21 Feb–30 Oct	11–5	M	T	W	T	F	S	S
4 Nov–18 Dec	11–4					F	S	S
Ilam Park tea-room								
21 Feb–30 Oct	11–5	M	T			F	S	S
9 Apr–30 Sep	11–5	M	T	W	T	F	S	S
5 Nov–18 Dec	11–4						S	S
Dovedale mobile barn								
22 Apr–30 Sep	11–5	M	T	W	T	F	S	S
Winster Market House								
2 Apr–30 Oct	11–5	M	T	W	T	F	S	S

For shop and tea-room Christmas opening telephone 01335 350503. Ilam Hall is available for overnight accommodation via the Youth Hostel Association (telephone 01335 350212). Ilam Park caravan site: open 1 April to 30 October, daily 8 to 8.

Winster Market House

See White Peak, page 223.

Woolsthorpe Manor

Water Lane, Woolsthorpe by Colsterworth,
near Grantham, Lincolnshire NG33 5PD

Map ③ E4 1943

Isaac Newton was born in this modest manor
house in 1642 and he made many of his most
important discoveries about light and gravity
here. A complex figure, Newton notched up
careers as diverse as Cambridge Professor and
Master of the Royal Mint, spent years studying
alchemy and the Bible as well as science, and
was President of the Royal Society. You can
still see the famous apple tree from Newton's
bedroom window and find your hidden
physicist in the interactive Science
Discovery Centre.

Exploring
- Experiment in the hands-on Discovery Centre.
- Be inspired by the house where a genius grew up.
- Contemplate the apple tree with a place in history.
- Summer exhibition – the history of the manor house.
- See the short film about Newton as a young man.
- Say hello to our rare breed sheep.

Eating and shopping: refuel with tea and cake
in our mini café. Visit the small shop in the
goat-free Goat House!

Making the most of your day: programme
of events, including regular 'Tales from
Woolsthorpe' and Conservation in Action.
National Science Week in March and summer
holiday workshops for children. Summer
exhibition and Apple Day.

Access for all: 🅿️🅿️🔥♿🚻🛗📷🗄🚪♿🅰
Building ♿♿♿ **Science Discovery Centre** ♿♿
Grounds ♿♿

Getting here: 130:SK924244. 8 miles south of
Grantham, ½ mile north-west of Colsterworth.
Foot: 1 mile by footpath from Colsterworth;

3 miles from the Viking Way, leaving Sewstern
Lane near Buckminster. **Bus**: Centrebus 608
Grantham to South Witham (passes close
Grantham ⇌). **Train**: Grantham 8 miles.
Road: at Woolsthorpe by Colsterworth, 8 miles
south of Grantham (not to be confused
with Woolsthorpe near Belvoir). Leave A1
southbound at B6403 Ancaster and Easton
turn, or A1 northbound at Woolsthorpe turn.
Follow brown signs then white National
Trust signs to car park in Water Lane. From
Melton follow B676 for Colsterworth and
Bourne; 1 mile after Stainby turn left at white
National Trust sign, then left into Water Lane.
Parking: free, 50 yards. Limited coach parking
(booking essential).

You may also enjoy: nearby Belton House,
17th-century Townend in the Lake District,
and Cragside's quirky technology.

Finding out more: 01476 860338 or
woolsthorpemanor@nationaltrust.org.uk.
23 Newton Way, Woolsthorpe by Colsterworth,
near Grantham, Lincolnshire NG33 5NR

Woolsthorpe Manor	M	T	W	T	F	S	S
5 Mar–13 Mar	11–5	.	.	.	.	.	S	S
16 Mar–30 Oct	11–5			W	T	F	S	S

Open Bank Holiday Mondays and Good Friday, 11 to 5.
A system of timed tickets may be in operation at busy times.

Newton's telescope at Woolsthorpe Manor, Lincolnshire

The Workhouse, Southwell

Upton Road, Southwell,
Nottinghamshire NG25 0PT

Map ③ D3 🏠 2002

Discover the most complete workhouse in existence. Find out about the Reverend Becher, the founder of The Workhouse and immerse yourself in the unique atmosphere of the building. Learn about the true stories of the 19th-century poor, brought to life by real archive evidence. Discover how society dealt with poverty through the centuries right up to the modern day. Explore the segregated work yards, day rooms, dormitories, master's quarters and cellars, then see the recreated working 19th-century garden and find out what food the paupers would have eaten.

Exploring
— Take a thought-provoking look at hidden histories of the poor.
— Share your thoughts and feelings with one of our volunteers.
— Enjoy the drama of our Living History events.
— Explore your own ancestry through our heritage hunter events.
— Discover the challenges of conserving an 'empty' property.
— Enjoy some quiet time in the recreated vegetable garden.

Eating and shopping: browse through the many specialist publications and items on sale. Buy our fresh, seasonal garden produce to eat at home.

Making the most of your day: programme of family activities, special events, tours and exhibitions. Children's trails and games to play.

Access for all: 🅿️🄳🄳🄴🄴🄻🄳🄸🄲🄴🄾🄳

Building 🄻🄴🄻🄳 Grounds 🄴🄳➡️

Getting here: 120:SK712543. **Foot**: Robin Hood Trail goes past The Workhouse. **Cycle**: National Byway (Heritage Cycle Route). **Bus**: Stagecoach 28/29 Newark to Southwell to Mansfield. Premier Travel 3 Newark to Southwell to Lowdham. Both pass Newark Castle ≋. Pathfinder 100 Nottingham to Southwell, alight Candle Meadow. **Train**: Fiskerton 2 miles; Newark Castle 7 miles; Newark North Gate 7½ miles. **Road**: 13 miles from Nottingham on A612 and 8 miles from Newark on A617 and A612. **Parking**: free, 200 yards.

You may also enjoy: Back to Backs, Birmingham, and Quarry Bank Mill, Cheshire.

Finding out more: 01636 817260 or theworkhouse@nationaltrust.org.uk

The Workhouse, Southwell		M	T	W	T	F	S	S
Guided tour*								
2 Mar–30 Oct	11–12	·	·	**W**	**T**	**F**	**S**	**S**
Workhouse								
2 Mar–30 Oct	12–5	·	·	**W**	**T**	**F**	**S**	**S**

*Guided tour (exterior) numbers limited. Open Bank Holiday Mondays and Good Friday. Last admission one hour before closing. Normal house admission from 12.

A volunteer explains about life at The Workhouse in Southwell, Nottinghamshire

West Midlands

From light to dark, a river god gazes down on visitors passing under Dry Arch Bridge at Croome

Map (4)

Outdoors
in the
West Midlands

In the West Midlands region there is a huge diversity of countryside to explore and enjoy. From the sweeping hills of Shropshire to the panoramic views afforded from the Clent Hills – just twelve miles from the Birmingham conurbation – there are miles of paths offering a family day out or simply a relaxing walk.

Below:
just one of the panoramic views from the head of Carding Mill Valley in Shropshire

The Clent Hills lie in the very heart of the region and are an ideal place to enjoy a gentle stroll. Or why not join one of the many guided walks which take place throughout the week? If you are more adventurous, try the increasingly popular pastime of geocaching or bring the family along for a volunteering day – where all ages can be part of caring for the countryside through our ongoing conservation work.

Kinver Edge, with its fascinating history and panoramic views towards Worcestershire and the Malvern Hills, is not too far away, and the nearby Rock Houses tea-room provides much-needed refreshments after a relaxing walk.

In the north of the region are the Staffordshire moorlands, including the lowland heath of Downs Banks, near Stone, where cattle graze the heathland.

Above:
**farmland at
Wilderhope
Manor Farm**
Right:
**Wenlock Edge
at Hill Top,
Shropshire**

Explore our parkland

There is an abundance of parkland in the West Midlands region. Discover 'Capability' Brown's designs at Berrington Hall, Charlecote Park and Croome Park, or wander through George London's restored parkland at Hanbury Hall (just a few miles from Birmingham) to see the recent planting undertaken to return the landscape to its 18th-century glory.

At Croome Park, take a gentle stroll to the outer eye-catchers, acquired and restored by the Trust in 2009, and see James Wyatt's and Robert Adam's designs for these follies in their former 18th-century splendour. On certain days you can climb to the top of the Panorama Tower and take in the stunning Worcestershire countryside.

Enjoy landscaped woodlands at the Dudmaston Estate, with miles of paths to explore, and discover the south Shropshire countryside. Alternatively, a little further north near Shrewsbury, enjoy a walk through the dappled woodland at Attingham Park.

Rare flowers, birds and fabulous views

The ancient woodland at Hawksmoor Nature Reserve in the Churnet Valley is an excellent place to spot green woodpeckers, spotted flycatchers and ravens. While the wild flowers and archaeology of Gibridding Wood at Hawksmoor have attracted artists and photographers for many years.

Whether you like a long ramble, a brisk walk or gentle stroll there are endless opportunities. The 'Long Mynd' (Long Mountain) in Shropshire, a Site of Special Scientific Interest, offers excellent walking, riding and cycling opportunities. An ancient track, the Portway, extends for ten miles and is home to a wide variety of flora and fauna, including an increasing number of ground-nesting birds – snipe, skylark, curlew and red grouse.

Nearby, Wenlock Edge is another rare and special landscape. Stretching nineteen miles through Shropshire, this thickly wooded limestone escarpment offers panoramic views, historic quarries, limekilns as well as rare flowers (such as several orchids, including the bee orchid), birds and insects, including the dingy skipper butterfly.

Above:
**the
Brockhampton
Estate,
Herefordshire**

Across in Herefordshire, tuck into the award-winning local food produced on the Brockhampton Estate after enjoying a walk through this traditionally farmed landscape – where there are miles of orchards, woodlands and pathways to explore.

The parkland at Croft Castle is open throughout the year. It offers a feast for the eyes as the seasons change and a feast for the senses in the tea-room, which serves a wide range of local produce (open all-year round and at weekends in the winter). You can literally walk through 1,000 years of history in one afternoon. Enjoy the new park walks at Baddesley Clinton and Packwood House, both close to Solihull.

Also follow in the footsteps of Queen Elizabeth I and William Shakespeare in the parkland at Charlecote Park. The bard was allegedly caught poaching here as a lad, and flogged. The parkland is open all-year round.

There are many events and activities in our countryside, from early morning bird walks to mini-beast hunts, guided tours and foraging walks. Ideal for everyone.

My favourite place

My favourite place is by the Brim Pool (on the Dudmaston Estate). This lovely spot is next to Comer Wood and accessible via public footpaths all-year round.

This a great place to spot buzzards, polecats and badgers. There are also signs that otters have used the pool.

Mike Annis
Head Forester,
Dudmaston Estate

Attingham Park

Atcham, Shrewsbury, Shropshire SY4 4TP

Map ④ H4   🏠✤♣ 1947

Attingham Park, built for the 1st Lord Berwick in 1785, was owned by the same family for more than 160 years. As their fortunes rose and fell, they proved themselves to be spenders, savers and saviours. Highlights include the atmospheric dining room, set for an evening banquet, and the contrasting decoration of the delicate feminine Boudoir with the rich, opulent textiles of the masculine Octagon Room. Outside, the walled garden and many park walks offer further delights. The mansion, set in beautiful parkland designed to impress, is at the heart of this great estate between Shrewsbury and the River Severn. **Note**: restoration and conservation in action ongoing in mansion and walled garden.

The dining room at Attingham Park, Shropshire

Exploring
- The mansion is open daily mid-March to end October.
- Attingham Re-discovered focus: laundry roof restoration.
- Watch the restoration of the walled garden throughout the seasons.
- Discover Attingham's story of love and neglect.
- Find out about the Berwick family and their changing fortunes.
- Enjoy peaceful walks through the deer park and grounds.

Eating and shopping: shop and Carriage House Café open daily all year. Take home seasonal fresh vegetables from the walled garden. Indulge in our home-baked cakes and scones. Browse in the new second-hand bookshop.

Making the most of your day: witness developments in the mansion and walled garden as we re-discover Attingham. Family trails and activities throughout local school holidays. Events programme throughout year. Waymarked walks. **Dogs**: welcome on leads in deer park and near the mansion. Identified off-lead areas.

Access for all: 🅿🚌♿🚻♿👜📷♪⬚👓
Mansion ♿♿♿ **Shop, bookshop and café** ♿♿
Grounds ♿➡♿♿

Getting here: 126:SJ550099. On the B4380 in Atcham. **Foot**: from main drive walk up the park road for approximately ½ mile to visitor reception at the stable courtyard. **Bus**: Arriva 96 Shrewsbury to Telford (passing close Shrewsbury ≋ and Telford Central). **Train**: Shrewsbury 5 miles. **Road**: 4 miles south-east of Shrewsbury, on north side of B4380 in Atcham village. **Parking**: free, approximately 25 yards from visitor reception.

You may also enjoy: Neo-classical Berrington Hall and also Sunnycroft, an Edwardian gentleman's suburban villa.

Finding out more: 01743 708123 (Infoline). 01743 708162 or attingham@nationaltrust.org.uk

Attingham Park		M	T	W	T	F	S	S
Park, walled garden, shop, café and bookshop								
Open all year	9–6	M	T	W	T	F	S	S
Mansion*								
12 Mar–30 Oct	11–5:30	M	T	W	T	F	S	S
Mansion winter tours								
8 Jan–6 Mar	11–2						S	S
5 Nov–27 Nov	11–2						S	S
Christmas in the Mansion								
10 Dec–23 Dec	11–4	M	T	W	T	F	S	S
Mansion tea-room								
1 Jan–6 Mar	10:30–4:30						S	S
12 Mar–30 Oct	11–5	M	T	W	T	F	S	S
5 Nov–4 Dec	10:30–4:30						S	S
10 Dec–31 Dec	10:30–4:30	M	T	W	T	F	S	S

***Tours only 11 to 1, then free-flow 1 to 5:30**. Last admission to Mansion one hour before closing. January, February, November and December: park, walled garden, shop, Carriage House Café and bookshop close at 5 or dusk if earlier. Bank Holiday weekends (Mansion): free-flow from 11. Mansion winter tours: 12 (book on 01743 708170 Monday to Friday). Mansion tea-room: open daily during February half-term (19 to 27 February, 10:30 to 4:30). Christmas Frost Fair 2 to 4 December. Whole site closed 25 December.

Attingham Park Estate: Cronkhill

near Atcham, Shrewsbury, Shropshire SY5 6JP

Map ④ H5   1947

Delightful Italianate villa designed by Regency architect John Nash. Stands proudly on a hillside with views across the Attingham Estate. **Note**: property contents belong to the tenants.

Access for all: [P] [access symbols] **Building** [symbols]
Grounds [symbols]

Getting here: 126:SJ535083. From Attingham Park take road to Cross Houses; Cronkhill is located on the right-hand side.

Finding out more: 01743 708162 or cronkhill@nationaltrust.org.uk

Attingham Park Estate: Cronkhill		M	T	W	T	F	S	S
25 Mar–27 Mar	11–4					F		S
10 Jun–12 Jun	11–4					F		S
7 Oct–9 Oct	11–4					F		S

Baddesley Clinton

Rising Lane, Baddesley Clinton, Warwickshire B93 0DQ

Map ④ K6  1980

This atmospheric house dates from the 15th century and was the home of the Ferrers family for 500 years. The house and interiors reflect its heyday in the Elizabethan era, when it was a haven for persecuted Catholics – there are three priest's holes. There is a delightful garden with stewponds and a romantic lake and nature walk.

Exploring
- Discover the priest's hole used in 1591.
- Relax and read in the Great Hall.
- Plot to plate – discover what's fresh in the vegetable garden.
- Murder most foul – investigate the evidence.
- Browse for bargains in the second-hand bookshop.
- Take a stroll, or bracing walk, across our extended parkland.

Eating and shopping: try our homemade bread – straight from the oven. Savour seasonal food, using produce from our own vegetable garden. Our varied menu will delight all diners. Locally sourced products and plants available in the shop.

Making the most of your day: set the scene with an introductory talk. Brunch lectures in the restaurant in spring and autumn. Easter trail for families. 'Hands on the Past' living history in the summer.

Access for all: [P] [access symbols]
Building [symbols] **Grounds** [symbols]

Getting here: 139:SP199723. **Foot**: Heart of England Way passes close by. **Train**: Lapworth, 2 miles; Birmingham International 9 miles. **Road**: ¾ miles west of A4141 Warwick to Birmingham road, at Chadwick End, 7½ miles north-west of Warwick, 6 miles south of

The courtyard at Baddesley Clinton, Warwickshire

M42 exit 5; 15 miles south-east of central Birmingham. **Parking**: free, 100 yards.

You may also enjoy: Packwood House – a mere two miles away.

Finding out more: 01564 783294 or baddesleyclinton@nationaltrust.org.uk

Baddesley Clinton		M	T	W	T	F	S	S
House, grounds, shop and restaurant								
1 Feb–31 Dec	11–5	·	T	W	T	F	S	S

Admission to house by timed ticket available from reception (not bookable). Open Bank Holiday Mondays. Closed 24 and 25 December.

Benthall Hall

Broseley, Shropshire TF12 5RX

Map (4) I5   1958

This fine stone house situated near the River Severn has mullioned and transomed windows, a stunning interior with carved oak staircase, decorated plaster ceilings and oak panelling. There is an intimate and carefully restored plantsman's garden, old kitchen garden and interesting Restoration church. **Note**: Benthall Hall is the home of Edward and Sally Benthall.

Exploring
- Discover the George Maw tiles hidden under the hall floor.
- Enjoy a walk along the woodland edge.
- Relax in the picturesque gardens.
- Find the priest's hole from the period of Charles II.

Making the most of your day: guided walks and tours of the Hall available by arrangement. There is a wonderful crocus display in the spring. **Dogs**: in the parkland and woodland only.

Access for all: ⬚⬚⬚⬚⬚
Building ⬚⬚ **Grounds** ⬚

Getting here: 127:SJ658025. **Bus**: Arriva 39 Telford/Wellington to Much Wenlock. **Train**: Telford Central 7½ miles. **Road**: 1 mile north-west of Broseley (B4375), 4 miles north-east of Much Wenlock, 1 mile south-west of Ironbridge. **Parking**: free, 100 yards. Space for one coach only.

Finding out more: 01952 882159 or benthall@nationaltrust.org.uk

Benthall Hall		M	T	W	T	F	S	S
House								
5 Apr–29 Jun	2–5:30	·	T	W	·	·	·	·
3 Jul–28 Sep	2–5:30	·	T	W	·	·	·	S
Garden								
5 Apr–29 Jun	1:30–5:30	·	T	W	·	·	·	·
3 Jul–28 Sep	1:30–5:30	·	T	W	·	·	·	S

Open Bank Holiday Sundays and Mondays, **including Easter Sunday and Monday**.

Berrington Hall

near Leominster, Herefordshire HR6 0DW

Map ④ H6 🏛️❋🌳🏠🍴 1957

'Well done to the tour guides for making it all very real. Thank you all so much!'
Mrs J. Buckley

Created as the perfect house in the perfect setting, Berrington Hall has many secrets for visitors to uncover. In this, one of Henry Holland's first houses, you can explore the family rooms and see how the servants moved around the house unseen by the family and guests. The interiors include Biaggio Rebecca ceilings, fine period furniture and there are some pieces on display from the Wade Collection (on loan from Snowshill Manor). The house is surrounded by one of Brown's final landscapes. Though it has a slightly austere exterior, the house has delicate interiors and a homely, welcoming feel.

Exploring
– Experience the arrival of the new Lady Rodney in 1891.
– Sympathise with a mother grieving after the First World War.
– See how the servants moved around the house unseen.
– Experience the life of William Kemp, the butler.
– Walk through one of Brown's final landscapes – explore Moreton Ride.
– Relax in the gardens, including traditional Herefordshire orchards.

Eating and shopping: browse in the shop for local products and gifts. Plant sales are inspired by the beautiful surrounding garden. Relax in the tea-room with a light lunch and home-baked cake.

Making the most of your day: family events throughout the year, as well as house quizzes and a play area. Guided tours of the house available. Costume collection on view by appointment. Waymarked estate walks.

Dogs: on leads in special dog walking area.

Access for all: 🅿️♿🚾🍴🛗📷 VT ••
Building 🅰️♿ Grounds ♿➡️♿

Getting here: 137:SO510637. **Bus**: Lugg Valley 492 Ludlow to Hereford (passing close Ludlow and Leominster), alight Luston, 2 miles. **Train**: Leominster 4 miles. **Road**: 3 miles north of Leominster, 7 miles south of Ludlow on west side of A49. **Parking**: free, 30 yards. Coaches: entry and exit via Luston/Eye Lane only (the B4361 off the A49). Tight turn into drive. No entry or exit for coaches directly from/to A49. Local area map on request.

You may also enjoy: learn whist or fan etiquette at Croft Castle and Parkland.

The sweeping staircase with bronzed balustrading at Berrington Hall, Herefordshire

Finding out more: 01568 615721 or berrington@nationaltrust.org.uk

Berrington Hall		M	T	W	T	F	S	S
Below stairs, gardens, park, tea-room and shop								
29 Jan–13 Feb	10–4	·	·	·	·	·	S	S
19 Feb–27 Feb	10–4:30	M	T	W	T	F	S	S
5 Mar–6 Nov	10–5:30	M	T	W	T	F	S	S
12 Nov–18 Dec	10–4:30	·	·	·	·	·	S	S
19 Dec–23 Dec	10–4:30	M	T	W	T	F	·	·
27 Dec–31 Dec	10–4	·	T	W	T	F	S	·
Mansion								
19 Feb–27 Feb	11–4	M	T	W	T	F	S	S
5 Mar–6 Nov	11–5	M	T	W	T	F	S	S
12 Nov–18 Dec	11–4	·	·	·	·	·	S	S
19 Dec–23 Dec	11–4	M	T	W	T	F	·	·

Parkland: restricted 28 February to 12 June (due to nesting birds). Below stairs, gardens, park, tea-room and shop open 1 to 3 January, 10 to 4. **House: 11 to 1 tours only. House ground floor only 12 November to 23 December.**

Biddulph Grange Garden

Grange Road, Biddulph, Staffordshire ST8 7SD

Map ④ J2   1988

Amazing Victorian garden created by Darwin contemporary James Bateman as an extension of his beliefs and scientific interests. His plant collection comes from all over the world – a visit takes you on a global journey from an Italian terrace to an Egyptian pyramid, via a Himalayan glen and Chinese-inspired garden. Discover the fabulous collection of rhododendrons, dahlia walk and oldest surviving golden larch in Britain, brought from China by the great plant hunter Robert Fortune. Explore the Geological Gallery: as you travel through time the biblical story of creation unfolds against a backdrop of science. A garden for all seasons. **Note:** many steps throughout the garden and from the car park to the entrance.

Exploring
- Take a tour of the new kitchen garden.
- Exhibition and audio-visual room tell the garden's story.
- Explore the hidden tunnels and pathways.

The parterre at Biddulph Grange Garden, Staffordshire

Exploring
- The unique Geological Gallery tells the story of creation.
- Play quoits on the quoits ground.
- Discover the newly restored arboretum pool.

Eating and shopping: taste local food, some of which is supplied by our onsite kitchen garden, in the tea-room and Acorn café. Browse the world-themed gift shop and plant centre.

Making the most of your day: talks, guided tours, events and children's trails throughout the year. Summer activities programme.

Access for all: 🅿️♿🚻♿🔄🔵
Building 🔾 Grounds 🔾

Getting here: 118:SJ895591. **Bus**: Baker Bus 99 from Congleton (passing Congleton ≋). **Train**: Congleton 2½ miles. **Road**: 1 mile north of Biddulph, 3½ miles south-east of Congleton, 7 miles north of Stoke-on-Trent. Access from A527 (Tunstall to Congleton road). Entrance on Grange Road. **Parking**: free, 50 yards.

You may also enjoy: Little Moreton Hall – a perfect Tudor gem.

Finding out more: 01782 517999 or biddulphgrange@nationaltrust.org.uk

Biddulph Grange Garden		M	T	W	T	F	S	S
21 Feb–27 Feb	10:30–3:30	M	T	W	T	F	S	S
3 Mar–31 Mar	10:30–5:30	M	·	·	T	F	S	S
1 Apr–31 Oct	10:30–5:30	M	T	W	T	F	S	S
4 Nov–19 Dec	10:30–3:30	M	·	·	·	F	S	S

Open Bank Holiday Mondays. Closes dusk if earlier. Tea-room: winter menu in February, March, October, November and December.

Birmingham Back to Backs

55-63 Hurst Street/50-54 Inge Street, Birmingham, West Midlands B5 4TE

Map ④ J5 🏢 ⬇️ 🏠 🍸 │2004│

An atmospheric glimpse into the lives of the ordinary people who helped make Birmingham an extraordinary city. On a fascinating guided tour, step back in time at Birmingham's last surviving court of back to backs; houses built literally back-to-back around a communal courtyard. Moving from the 1840s through to the 1970s, discover the lives of some of the former residents who crammed into these small houses to live and work. With fires alight in the grates, and sounds and smells from the past, experience an evocative and intimate insight into life at the Back to Backs. **Note**: visits by guided tour only (advance booking advised).

Exploring
– The guided tour brings the houses and characters to life.
– Make yourself at home, warm up by the fire.
– Learn more in the thought-provoking exhibition.
– Whose Story? events bring Birmingham's diverse heritage to life.
– Find out about life with communal privies and wash-houses.
– Discover stories about the people who lived and worked here.

Eating and shopping: buy mementoes of your visit in our reception. Traditional 1930s sweetshop (not National Trust).

Making the most of your day: exciting year-round events programme. Ground-floor tour also available.

Access for all: 🔲🦽🚾♿🖼️📖📺♿👁️🅿️
Building 🚶♿

The Back to Backs in Birmingham, West Midlands

Getting here: 139:SP071861. In the centre of Birmingham next to the Hippodrome Theatre. **Foot**: within easy walking distance of bus and railway stations (follow signs for Hippodrome Theatre). **Cycle**: NCN5. **Bus**: National Express West Midlands 35, 61/2/3 from Birmingham city centre. **Train**: Birmingham New Street ¼ mile. **Parking**: nearest in Arcadian Centre, Bromsgrove Street.

You may also enjoy: The Workhouse at Southwell.

Finding out more: 0121 666 7671 (booking line). 0121 622 2442 or backtobacks@nationaltrust.org.uk

Birmingham Back to Backs		M	T	W	T	F	S	S
8 Feb–23 Dec	10–5		T	W	T	F	S	
13 Feb–18 Dec	11–4							S

Admission by timed ticket and guided tour only. Booking is strongly recommended, especially at peak times. Open Bank Holiday Mondays. **Please note: during term time property is often closed 10 to 1 for schools on Tuesday, Wednesday and Thursday**. Booking line open Tuesday to Friday, 10:30 to 4, and weekends, 10 to 12. Last tour times vary due to light levels, please check with the property. **Closed September 5 to 11.**

We welcome dogs assisting visitors with disabilities

Brockhampton Estate

Greenfields, Bringsty, near Bromyard,
Herefordshire WR6 5TB

Map ④ I7

'A perfect day out. Woods, fields and
orchards enough to wander for hours – all
centred on an unbelievably beautiful house.'
Mr Ynys-Mons, Finchley, London

This beautiful medieval manor house,
surrounded by a moat, is entered via
a charming timber-framed gatehouse.
Experience the Great Hall where feasts and
celebrations have been held throughout
the centuries. Learn about the last owner
of Brockhampton, Colonel Lutley, who
bequeathed the entire 687-hectare (1,700-acre)
estate to the Trust in 1946. Enjoy the peace
and tranquillity as you sit by the moat in the
damson orchard. There are miles of walks
through the park and woodland, featuring
ancient trees and a rich variety of wildlife,
along with historic farming breeds such as
Hereford cattle and Ryeland sheep.

Exploring
- Experience life as lived in a medieval moated manor house.
- Cross the moat through the timber-framed gatehouse.
- Follow the nature trail and spot wildlife from our bird-hide.
- Enjoy the stunning views from the parkland.
- Step back in time with a Living History event.
- See the blossom in April, then pick damsons in September.

Eating and shopping: enjoy local produce
in the Old Apple Store tea-room and try our
delicious cakes made by estate tenants. Browse
for something unique in our Granary shop.
Award-winning jams and beef, honey and beer
from the Brockhampton Estate.

Making the most of your day: year-round
family activities. Explorer packs for children.
Living history re-enactments and medieval
Christmas event. Guided tours most weekends.
Woodland and estate walks leaflet available.
Picnicking. Nature trail with bird-hide.
Dogs: welcome on leads in grounds,
woods and parkland.

Access for all: [icons]
Building [icons] Grounds [icons]

Getting here: 149:SO682546.
Bus: First/Bromyard Omnibus 420 Worcester
to Hereford (passing Worcester Foregate Street
≅ and close Hereford ≅). **Road**: 2 miles east
of Bromyard on Worcester road (A44); house
reached by a narrow road through 1½ miles
of woods and park. **Parking**: 50 yards
and 1½ miles.

You may also enjoy: Croft Castle and Parkland,
a house with a story and a park to explore.

Finding out more: 01885 488099 (Infoline).
01885 482077 or
brockhampton@nationaltrust.org.uk

Brockhampton Estate		M	T	W	T	F	S	S
Estate								
Open all year	Dawn–dusk	M	T	W	T	F	S	S
Grounds, shop and tea-room								
1 Jan–3 Jan	10–4	M					S	S
19 Feb–27 Feb	10–4:30	M	T	W	T	F	S	S
5 Mar–6 Nov	10–5	M	T	W	T	F	S	S
12 Nov–18 Dec	10–4:30						S	S
27 Dec–31 Dec	10–4:30		T	W	T	F	S	
House								
19 Feb–27 Feb	11–4:30	M	T	W	T	F	S	S
5 Mar–6 Nov	11–5	M	T	W	T	F	S	S
12 Nov–18 Dec	11–4						S	S

Lower Brockhampton, Herefordshire

Stunning views over the Shropshire Hills: an Area of Outstanding Natural Beauty

Carding Mill Valley and the Shropshire Hills

Chalet Pavilion, Carding Mill Valley, Church Stretton, Shropshire SY6 6JG

Map ④ H5  1965

Covering as much as 2,000 hectares (4,942 acres) of heather-covered hills with stunning views of the Shropshire Hills Area of Outstanding Natural Beauty and the Welsh hills. An important place for wildlife, geology, landscape and archaeology, with excellent visitor facilities and information in Carding Mill Valley.

Exploring — Some of the best walking in the Marches.
— Take a picnic and sit, relax and enjoy Shropshire's food.
— Horse-riding and cycling routes across a variety of terrains.
— Join us for pond dipping, birdwatching, volunteering and much more.

Eating and shopping: Chalet Pavilion tea-room serves local food, including hot lunches. Shop next to tea-room sells maps, guides and gifts. Excellent cakes, teas, coffees, local drinks and snacks.

Making the most of your day: more than 50 walks and talks each year run by rangers. Use the shuttle bus to extend or enhance your walk. **Dogs**: under close control (grazing livestock).

Access for all: ⓟ🅳♿🚾♿♿♿
Building 🅰 Grounds ♿

Getting here: 137:SO443945. Main access from Church Stretton via Carding Mill Valley. **Foot**: many long-distance routes, including Jack Mytton Way and Shropshire Way. **Cycle**: 10 miles plus of off-road tracks and bridleways. **Bus**: Minsterley Motors 435 Shrewsbury to Ludlow, alight Church Stretton, ½ miles. Area of Outstanding Natural Beauty shuttle bus weekends and Bank Holidays (Easter to October), plus shuttle to Stiperstones. **Train**: Church Stretton 1 mile. **Road**: 15 miles south of Shrewsbury, west of Church Stretton Valley and A49; approached from Church Stretton and, on west side, from Ratlinghope or Asterton. **Parking**: 50 yards (pay and display). Open daily all year. Parking £4.20 (March to October), £2.50 (January, February, November and December), up to two hours £2. Minibus £10, coach £12. Top car park closes 7 (April to October), 4:15 (January, February, March and November to end December). Opens 9.

Finding out more: 01694 723068 or cardingmill@nationaltrust.org.uk

Carding Mill Valley	M	T	W	T	F	S	S
Countryside							
Open all year		M	T	W	T	F	S	S
Tea-room and shop							
1 Jan–3 Jan	11–4	M					S	S
8 Jan–13 Feb	11–4						S	S
19 Feb–30 Oct	11–5	M	T	W	T	F	S	S
31 Oct–23 Dec	11–4	M				F	S	S
26 Dec–31 Dec	11–4	M	T	W	T	F	S	

Toilet and information open 9 to 7 summer; 9 to 4:15 winter. **Shop closed Tuesday to Thursday 28 February to 31 March.** Shop opens 12 on weekdays, 20 March to 31 October and closes 4 until 19 March. Closes dusk if earlier.

Charlecote Park

Wellesbourne, Warwick,
Warwickshire CV35 9ER

Map ④ K7   🏠❀♠🏡🍴 1946

Charlecote Park has been home to the Lucy family since the 12th century. Their stories are told throughout the house by their portraits, the objects they collected from around the world and the design influence they had on the house and parkland. See how Mary Elizabeth Lucy remodelled the house in Victorian times. The gardens include a formal parterre, woodland walk and the wider parkland (inspired by 'Capability' Brown), which offer walks with picturesque views across the River Avon. A herd of fallow deer has been in the park since Tudor times.

Discovering Charlecote Park in Warwickshire

Exploring
- Seasonal access to previously closed areas of the parkland.
- Enjoy one of our guided walks or talks.
- Try your hand at a game of croquet.
- Experience the park and garden all year round.
- See the house festively decorated during weekends in December.

Eating and shopping: enjoy a range of hot meals and light snacks (light refreshments only on house closed days). We use home-grown produce whenever possible in the restaurant. Look out for our main shop and also our shop selling locally sourced produce.

Making the most of your day: year-round programme of events. Watch conservation in action. Plenty of outdoor space for children to enjoy. Please note that we do have gravel paths. **Dogs**: assistance dogs only.

Access for all: 🅿️🅳♿🚻🚼👶🛏️♿👁️
🅰️ Building 👣♿♿ Outbuildings ♿♿♿
Grounds 👣▶️🚫

Getting here: 151:SP263564. **Bus**: Stagecoach in Warwickshire X18 Leamington Spa ⇆ to Stratford-upon-Avon. **Train**: Stratford-upon-Avon, 5½ miles; Warwick 6 miles; Leamington Spa 8 miles. **Road**: 1 mile west of Wellesbourne, 5 miles east of Stratford-upon-Avon, 6 miles south of Warwick on north side of B4086. **Parking**: free, 300 yards.

You may also enjoy: one of 'Capability' Brown's final landscapes at Berrington Hall.

Finding out more: 01789 470277 or charlecotepark@nationaltrust.org.uk

Charlecote Park		M	T	W	T	F	S	S
Park, gardens and outbuildings								
Open all year	10–5:30	M	T	W	T	F	S	S
House								
4 Mar–30 Oct*	11–4:30	M	T	.	.	F	S	S
5 Nov–18 Dec	12–4	.	.	.	.	.	S	S
Restaurant								
1 Jan–3 Mar	11–4	M	T	W	T	F	S	S
4 Mar–30 Oct**	10:30–5	M	T	W	T	F	S	S
31 Oct–31 Dec	11–4	M	T	W	T	F	S	S
Shop								
1 Jan–27 Feb	11–4	.	.	.	.	.	S	S
4 Mar–30 Oct	10:30–5	M	T	.	.	F	S	S
5 Nov–18 Dec	11–4	.	.	.	.	.	S	S

Closed 23, 24, 25 December. House: *4 March to 30 April and 1 October to 30 October, 11 to 12 by conservation tour only. Additional opening Thursdays during Warwickshire school holidays (fall between March and October), limited access. Ground floor only in November and December. Park, garden, outbuildings: close 4 in January, February, November and December. Winter: May close at dusk if earlier than stated time. Restaurant: **Closes at 4 on Wednesdays and Thursdays. Shop: open daily during Warwickshire school holidays. Local produce shop: open as house 4 March to 30 October 12 to 5.

Clent Hills

Romsley, Worcestershire

Map (4) J6   1959

The Clent Hills, on the edge of Birmingham and the Black Country, offer a green oasis with panoramic views. **Note**: café (not National Trust) and toilets open Tuesday to Sunday (10 to 4) and Bank Holiday Mondays. Visit website for events programme.

Access for all:

Getting here: 139:SO938807 Nimmings Wood car park. South-west of Birmingham, close to M5 (junction 4).

Finding out more: 01562 712822 or clenthills@nationaltrust.org.uk. Waseley Hills Office, Gannow Green Lane, Birmingham, West Midlands B45 9AT

Clent Hills	Open every day all year

Nimmings car park gates close at dusk.

Clent Hills in the summer, Worcestershire

Coughton Court

near Alcester, Warwickshire B49 5JA

Map (4) K6   1946

Home to the Throckmorton family for 600 years, this finest of Tudor houses stands testament to a family's courage in maintaining their beliefs. From a position of high favour to one of fear and oppression post-Reformation, the Throckmortons were leaders in a dangerous age, helping to bring about Catholic emancipation in the 19th century. Explore this story of fascinating personalities through the 'family album' of portraits and Catholic treasures around the house. Coughton is still very much a family home with an intimate feel: the Throckmorton family live here, managing the stunning gardens which they have created. **Note**: charge for entrance to the walled garden, including members.

Exploring
- Escape into the glories of the Throckmortons' award-winning gardens.
- Marvel at the views from the Tudor tower.
- Discover the priest's hole, fascinating Catholic treasures and family portraits.
- Find out about Coughton's part in the Gunpowder Plot.
- Let our friendly guides share Coughton's secrets with you.
- Explore the bog garden, orchards, vegetable garden and lake.

Eating and shopping: sample delicious local ice-cream from the ice-cream parlour. Try home-baked cakes or hot lunches in the restaurant. Treat yourself to some local honey from the shop. Take home plants from the Throckmorton plant centre.

Making the most of your day: open-air theatre, concerts, school holiday activities. Children's play area, quizzes and house trails. Outdoor family adventure packs. 'Ten Highlights' guide. Conservation in action days. Second-hand bookshop.

Coughton Court, Warwickshire: still a family home

Access for all: ⬛⬛⬛⬛⬛⬛⬛⬛⬛
Building ⬛⬛⬛ Grounds ⬛➡⬛

Getting here: 150:SP080604. **Cycle:** NCN5, ½ mile. **Bus:** First 247 Redditch to Evesham (passing Redditch ☒ and close Evesham ☒), Stagecoach in Warwickshire 26 Redditch to Stratford-upon-Avon (passing close Stratford-upon-Avon ☒). **Train:** Redditch 6 miles. **Road:** 2 miles north of Alcester on A435. **Parking:** free, 150 yards. Offsite coach parking at Alcester Rugby Club.

You may also enjoy: more priest's holes and the moat at nearby Baddesley Clinton.

Finding out more: 01789 400777 or coughtoncourt@nationaltrust.org.uk

Coughton Court		M	T	W	T	F	S	S
House								
12 Mar–27 Mar	11–5						S	S
1 Apr–30 Jun	11–5			W	T	F	S	S
1 Jul–31 Aug	11–5		T	W	T	F	S	S
1 Sep–30 Sep	11–5			W	T	F	S	S
1 Oct–6 Nov	11–5				T	F	S	S
3 Dec–11 Dec*	12–6	M	T	W	T	F	S	S
Shop, restaurant and garden**								
As house	11–5:30	M	T	W	T	F	S	S
Walled garden**								
As house	11:30–4:45	M	T	W	T	F	S	S

Open Bank Holiday Mondays. **Closed Good Friday and 11 June and 9 July.** Admission by timed ticket at weekends and busy days. No hot food on Tuesdays. *Coughton Christmas Fair, find out more online. **Parts of the gardens may be closed March, October to December.

Croft Castle and Parkland

Yarpole, near Leominster,
Herefordshire HR6 9PW

Map ④ H6

Home of the Croft family for nearly 1,000 years Croft Castle, a place of power, politics and pleasure, nestles in peaceful Herefordshire countryside at the heart of a 607-hectare (1,500-acre) estate of woodlands, farm and parkland. Explore the miles of woodland trails, learn about the family who have made Croft so special. See the fine Georgian interiors and family portraits. Relax in the walled garden. Stroll through the woods to the Iron Age hill fort at Croft Ambrey. Croft has more than 300 veteran trees. Enjoy the 'atmosphere rooms', including the 18th-century Saloon. **Note:** parts of the property may close in high winds.

Exploring
 – Walk through miles of beautiful, tranquil woodland trails and glades.
 – Discover the 1,000-year history of the Croft family.
 – Explore the walled garden, its flowers, shrubs, apples and vines.
 – Experience Georgian life, play cards or read in the Saloon.
 – Enjoy the panoramic views from the Iron Age hill fort.
 – Relax in the silence and solitude of the surrounding parkland.

Eating and shopping: local food and drink freshly prepared in our own kitchen. Local beers, fruit juices, ciders, delicious homemade cakes and scones. Local gifts in shop, including the Heart of England range. Plant sales, second-hand bookshop, wildlife and gardening gifts.

Making the most of your day: castle-inspired play area, family room, events and activities. Waymarked walks across the estate.

Menu options to make the most of your day.
Dogs: on leads in parkland only.

Access for all:
Building ♿ Grounds ♿

Getting here: 137:SO455655. **Bus**: Lugg
Valley 492 Ludlow to Hereford (passing close
Ludlow ⬆ and Leominster), alight Gorbett
Bank, 2¼ miles. **Train**: Leominster 7 miles.
Road: 5 miles north-west of Leominster,
9 miles south-west of Ludlow; approach from
B4362, turning north at Cock Gate between
Bircher and Mortimer's Cross; signposted from
Ludlow to Leominster road (A49) and from
A4110 at Mortimer's Cross. **Sat Nav**: use HR6
0BL. **Parking**: 100 yards.

You may also enjoy: Berrington Hall just
five miles away, also a stunning riverside
garden, The Weir, near Hereford.

Finding out more: 01568 780246 or
croftcastle@nationaltrust.org.uk

Croft Castle and Parkland		M	T	W	T	F	S	S
Castle, garden, tea-room, shop and play area								
19 Feb–27 Feb	11–4	M	T	W	T	F	S	S
5 Mar–6 Nov	10–5:30*	M	T	W	T	F	S	S
12 Nov–18 Dec	10–4	·	·	·	·	·	S	S
19 Dec–23 Dec	10–4	M	T	W	T	F	·	·
Tea-room and play area								
1 Jan–20 Feb	11–4	·	·	·	·	·	S	S
27 Dec–31 Dec	10–4	·	T	W	T	F	S	·

Admission to castle between 11 and 1 by tour only.
*Castle closes 5. Shop opens 11, 5 March to 6 November.
Parkland: open daily 9 to 8:30, closes dusk if earlier; may
close in high winds.

The church and east front of Croft Castle, Herefordshire

Croome

near High Green, Worcester,
Worcestershire WR8 9DW

Map ④ J7 🏛 ✝ ❖ ♣ 🐾 1996

'**All staff unfailingly kind, patient and helpful.
Whole place is redolent of enthusiastic hope!**'
Felicity Butcher, Bath

Discover the beauty and space of Croome –
the ideal place to relax and unwind. The serene
landscape and lakeside are full of paths which
stretch for miles, taking you on a journey
through 18th-century pleasure gardens.
Wander with your family through the evocative
empty spaces of the magnificent mansion
house, and find out about the different
characters and communities which called
Croome their home from the 18th century to
the present day. Sounds, objects and images
bring the story of Croome to life, and there
are also plenty of exciting and fun events
throughout the year to enjoy. **Note**: Court
owned by Croome Heritage Trust and leased
by the National Trust.

Exploring
– Step inside the Court to
discover the characters
of Croome.
– Unwind with a stroll by the
relaxing river and lakeside.
– Venture out in the wider
parkland with our walks guide.
– Escape to the eye-catchers –
see Croome from a
different view.
– Watch birds and bats in roost
with our interactive batcam.
– Discover year-round events for
all the family.

Eating and shopping: enjoy a meal or light
snack in our 1940s-style canteen, which offers
ever-increasing locally sourced products.
You may even find our very own vegetables
in the homemade recipes from our
Dig for Victory plot.

Making the most of your day: new
RAF-themed children's play area and plenty of

Looking across South Park from the portico of the Court at Croome, Worcestershire

family events in school holidays. **Dogs**: allowed on leads – assistance dogs only inside the Court/canteen (dog waiting areas provided).

Access for all:
Court 🚶‍♀️🚶‍♂️♿🅿️ Grounds ♿➡️👁️♿

Getting here: 150:SO887452. **Bus**: Aston's 382 Worcester to Pershore, alight at Ladywood Road/Rebecca Road crossroads, walk 2 miles; 362 Worcester to Upton/Malvern, alight at Kinnersley, walk 2 miles. **Train**: Pershore 7 miles. **Road**: 9 miles south of Worcester and east of M5 off junction 7. Signposted off the A38 and B4084. **Parking**: free.

You may also enjoy: the timber-framed house and walled garden at The Greyfriars in the centre of Worcester.

Finding out more: 01905 371006 or croomepark@nationaltrust.org.uk. National Trust Estate Office, The Builders' Yard, High Green, Severn Stoke, Worcestershire WR8 9JS

Croome		M	T	W	T	F	S	S
Park, canteen and shop								
1 Jan–20 Feb	10–4:30						S	S
21 Feb–30 Oct	10–5:30	M	T	W	T	F	S	S
5 Nov–18 Dec	10–4:30						S	S
26 Dec–31 Dec	10–4:30	M	T	W	T	F	S	
Court								
1 Jan–20 Feb	11–4						S	S
21 Feb–30 Oct	11–4:30	M		W	T	F	S	S
5 Nov–18 Dec	11–4						S	S
26 Dec–31 Dec	11–4	M	T	W	T	F	S	

St Mary Magdalene church open in association with The Churches Conservation Trust. Park: last admission 45 minutes before closing time. Timed tickets for house on busy weekends and Bank Holiday Mondays.

Cwmmau Farmhouse

Brilley, Whitney-on-Wye, Herefordshire HR3 6JP

Map ④ G7   🏚️🏠 1965

Unique early 17th-century 'black and white' timbered farmhouse with many original features, including stone-tiled roofs and vernacular barns. **Note**: open eight afternoons a year. Available at other times as holiday cottage (telephone 0844 800 2070).

Access for all: 🏠 Building ♿♿

Getting here: 148:SO267514. 4 miles south-west of Kington between A4111 and A438. From Kington take Brilley road at junction opposite church, 3½ miles. Turn left at National Trust signpost. From A438 between Winforton and Whitney on Wye take Brilley road at junction opposite Stowe Farm, straight on for 2 miles. Turn right, approximately ¾ mile turn right at Trust signpost. Farmhouse is approximately ½ mile at end of 'no through road'.

Finding out more: 01981 590509 or cwmmaufarmhouse@nationaltrust.org.uk

Cwmmau Farmhouse		M	T	W	T	F	S	S
21 May–22 May	1–5						S	S
11 Jun–12 Jun	1–5						S	S
1 Oct–2 Oct	1–5						S	S
17 Dec–18 Dec	1–4						S	S

Dudmaston Estate

Quatt, near Bridgnorth, Shropshire WV15 6QN

Map (4) I5  1978

Dudmaston offers something unexpected in the Shropshire countryside, a house that provides a classical setting for a collection of modern and contemporary art. The modern art galleries were assembled by diplomat Sir George Labouchere, while his wife Rachel showed off her collections of botanical drawings and watercolours. Outside, the established gardens are a stunning backdrop to art sculptures. The Big Pool is the perfect setting for a short walk with stunning views of the house. The wider estate offers miles of walking routes and can be enjoyed year-round from the new car parks.

Exploring
- Explore the new kitchen garden.
- Enjoy our new children's play area.
- Discover one family's varied art collection.
- Explore the wider estate, including the dingle and Comer Wood.
- Enjoy the breathtaking gardens as the seasons change.
- Relax in the comfortable Oak Room and enjoy the view.

Eating and shopping: browse around our new shop selling hand-picked items – from elegant local craft work to our extending garden range, including Hanbury plants. Our tea-room offers a variety of home-baked cakes and hot meals.

Making the most of your day: garden games, guided tours around the gardens, a variety of events going on throughout the open season and in-depth booked tours in the house on Mondays. **Dogs**: on leads on footpaths only.

Access for all: 🅿️👪♿🚻♿📷🖥️🎫♿🅰️
Building 👣♿♿ Grounds ♿➡️

Getting here: 138:SO746887. **Foot**: walks from Hampton Loade car park to property. **Ferry**: from Severn Valley Railway via river ferry and walk from Hampton Loade (please check the ferry is running before setting off). **Bus**: Arriva Midlands 297 Bridgnorth to Kidderminster (passing close Kidderminster ☒). **Train**: Hampton Loade (Severn Valley Railway) 1½ miles; Kidderminster 10 miles. **Road**: 4 miles south-east of Bridgnorth on A442. **Parking**: at the house in the car park. Also parking at Hampton Loade and The Holt (both pay and display).

You may also enjoy: Upton House and Gardens and Nunnington Hall, Yorkshire.

Finding out more: 01746 780866 or dudmaston@nationaltrust.org.uk

Dudmaston Estate		M	T	W	T	F	S	S
Garden								
3 Apr–28 Sep	12–6	**M**	**T**	**W**	·	·	·	**S**
House								
3 Apr–28 Sep	2–5:30	·	**T**	**W**	·	·	·	**S**
Tea-room and shop*								
3 Apr–28 Sep	11:30–5:30	**M**	**T**	**W**	·	·	·	**S**

Open Easter Sunday and Bank Holiday Mondays. Snowdrop walks: 5, 6, 12 and 13 February. St Andrew's church, Quatt: open as house. *Shop opens at 12. Monday tours are available on specific dates, please contact the property for details.

Open-air entertainment at Dudmaston, Shropshire

Farnborough Hall

Farnborough, near Banbury,
Oxfordshire OX17 1DU

Map ④ L7 　🏠✿♣ 　1960

Honey-coloured stone house with exquisite
plasterwork and treasures collected during the
Grand Tour, surrounded by the fine landscaped
garden. **Note**: occupied and administered by
the Holbech family.

Access for all: P♿ Building ♿ Grounds ♿

Getting here: 151:SP430490. 6 miles north of
Banbury, ½ mile west of A423.

Finding out more: 01295 690002 or
farnboroughhall@nationaltrust.org.uk

Farnborough Hall		M	T	W	T	F	S	S
2 Apr-28 Sep	2-5:30	·	·	**W**	·	·	**S**	·
1 May-2 May	2-5:30	**M**	·	·	·	·	·	**S**
Terraced walk open as house.								

The Fleece Inn

Bretforton, near Evesham,
Worcestershire WR11 7JE

Map ④ K7 　🏛🍴🔔🍸 　1978

The Fleece Inn is a half-timbered medieval
farmhouse which originally sheltered a farmer
and his stock. The Inn was first licensed in 1848.
Fully restored to its former glory, with witches'
circles and precious pewter collection, it has
developed a reputation for traditional folk
music, morris dancing and asparagus.

Exploring — Annual Asparagus Auctions
and Festival Day – spring
Bank Holiday.
— Medieval thatched barn
licensed for civil weddings,
functions and events.
— Weekly folk session, regular
gigs and other events.

The Fleece Inn at Bretforton, Worcestershire

Exploring — Annual Apple and Ale Festival –
first weekend in October.

Eating and shopping: mouthwatering menu
using the finest local produce. Quality cask
ales, including landlord's own. Local ciders and
wines. Special asparagus menu between
23 April and 21 June.

Making the most of your day: traditional
folk music and morris dancing throughout
the year. Vintage and classic car events May
to September.

Access for all: P♿ 🚻♿🍴♿ Building ♿♿

Getting here: 150:SP093437. In the
village square in the centre of Bretforton.
Bus: Henshaws 554 from Evesham to
Chipping Campden. **Train**: Evesham 2½ miles.
Road: 4 miles east of Evesham, on B4035.
Parking: in village square only
(not National Trust).

Finding out more: 01386 831173 or
fleeceinn@nationaltrust.org.uk

The Fleece Inn		M	T	W	T	F	S	S
Open all year	12-10:30	·	·	·	·	·	·	**S**
Open all year	11-11	**M**	**T**	**W**	**T**	**F**	**S**	·
Closed Monday to Thursday, 3 to 6, January to May and September to December.								

The Greyfriars

Friar Street, Worcester,
Worcestershire WR1 2LZ

Map (4) J7　　1966

Built in 1480, with early 17th- and 18th-century additions, this fine timber-framed house was rescued from demolition after the Second World War and has been carefully restored and refurbished. An archway leads through to a delightful walled garden.

Exploring
　– A haven of tranquillity in the city centre.
　– Discover how The Greyfriars was saved from demolition.
　– See the collection of interesting textiles.
　– Explore the delightful walled garden.

Eating and shopping: enjoy afternoon tea in the garden. Buy plants grown at nearby Hanbury Hall.

Making the most of your day: family room with hands-on activities. Garden games in summer months.

Access for all: 🎨🖼️👁️ Building ♿🏠

Getting here: 150:SO852546. In centre of Worcester on Friar Street. **Bus**: from surrounding areas. **Train**: Worcester Foregate Street ½ mile. **Parking**: at Corn Market, Kings Street and Cathedral Plaza (pay and display). No onsite parking.

Finding out more: 01905 23571 or greyfriars@nationaltrust.org.uk

The Greyfriars			M	T	W	T	F	S	S
22 Feb–17 Dec	1–5		·		T	W	T	F	S	·

Admission by timed ticket on Bank Holidays. Open Bank Holiday Mondays. Closes dusk if earlier.

Hanbury Hall

School Road, Hanbury, Droitwich Spa,
Worcestershire WR9 7EA

Map (4) J6　　1953

'**We had a fantastic day – loads to see and do for all the family. Everyone is so friendly and welcoming**.'
Martha Eddy, March, Cambridgeshire

Hanbury Hall is a beautiful William and Mary-style house built in 1701 by Thomas Vernon, a lawyer and whig MP for Worcester. Inside a mix of interiors await to be discovered, from the restored Hercules rooms and recreated Gothic corridor, to the Smoking Room and magnificent recently restored staircase wall paintings by Sir James Thornhill. Surrounding the house are eight hectares (20 acres) of recreated early 18th-century gardens and 162 hectares (400 acres) of park. Features include the intricately laid out parterre, fruit garden, grove, orangery, orchard and bowling green. Park walks enable you to explore the surrounding countryside.

Exploring
　– Sit down in the house and admire the beautiful interiors.
　– Discover the story of the stunning wall paintings.
　– Stroll through the gardens and enjoy a game of bowls.
　– Relax and enjoy a picnic on the orangery lawn.
　– Have fun in our children's play area.
　– Enjoy the beautiful countryside on a park walk.

Eating and shopping: browse around our shop: discover our new extended gardening range. Buy a Hanbury-grown plant. Enjoy delicious meals in our tea-room overlooking the parterre. Relax and enjoy homemade cake in our open-air Stables Kiosk.

Making the most of your day: year-round varied events programme, including family activity days, concerts, open-air theatre productions, art exhibitions and themed

Hanbury Hall, Worcestershire: breathtaking wall paintings

Finding out more: 01527 821214 or hanburyhall@nationaltrust.org.uk

Hanbury Hall		M	T	W	T	F	S	S
House*, gardens, park, shop and tea-room								
8 Jan–13 Feb	11–4					·	S	S
House*, gardens, park, shop, tea-room and play area								
19 Feb–30 Oct	11–5	M	T	W	T	·	S	S
5 Nov–18 Dec	11–4				·	·	S	S
Gardens, park, shop and tea-room								
1 Jan–2 Jan	11–4	·	·	·	·	·	S	S
26 Dec–31 Dec	11–4	M	T	W	T	F	S	·

*19 February to 30 October: admission to house by guided tour from 11 to 1 (spaces limited), 1 to 5 free-flow. January to 13 February and November: house admission through tours 11:30 to 3:30 (limited access and spaces). December: limited free-flow access. Tour tickets are allocated on arrival and cannot be booked. Admission by timed ticket on busy days. Bank Holiday Mondays: free-flow access, 11 to 5. Whole property open Good Friday. Stables Kiosk open at busy times. Property closes dusk if earlier.

weekends. Park walks leaflet available.
Dogs: in car park and park only.

Access for all: 🅿 ♿ ⓘ ⓦ 🏛 ♨ ⋯ ⌽
Building ♿ ♿ ♿ Grounds ♿ ♿ ➡ ⋯

Getting here: 150:SO943637. **Foot**: number of public footpaths cross the park. **Bus**: First 144 Worcester to Birmingham (passing close Droitwich Spa ⟓), alight Wychbold, 2½ miles. **Train**: Droitwich Spa 4 miles. **Road**: from M5 exit 5 follow A38 to Droitwich; from Droitwich 4½ miles along B4090. **Parking**: free, 150 yards.

You may also enjoy: The Greyfriars: a 15th-century merchant's house in Worcester city centre.

Hawford Dovecote

Hawford, Worcestershire WR3 7SG

Map ④ J6   🏠 1973

The picturesque Hawford Dovecote has survived virtually unaltered since the late 16th century and retains many of its nesting boxes. **Note**: no toilet. Please park carefully to one side of the lane.

Access for all: Building ♿

Getting here: 150:SO846607. 3 miles north of Worcester, ½ miles east of A449.

Finding out more: 01527 821214 or hawforddovecote@nationaltrust.org.uk

Hawford Dovecote		M	T	W	T	F	S	S
27 Feb–30 Oct	9–6	M	T	W	T	F	S	S

Closes dusk if earlier. Other times by appointment.

Kinver Edge and the Rock Houses

Holy Austin Rock House, Compton Road, Kinver, near Stourbridge, Staffordshire DY7 6DL

Map (4) I5  1917

Kinver's woodland sandstone ridge offers dramatic views across surrounding counties and miles of heathland walking country. The famous Holy Austin Rock Houses, which were inhabited until the 1950s, are open to visitors at selected times.

Exploring
- Miles of woodland and heathland pathways to explore.
- Rare species of plants and insects to discover.
- Explore the Rock Houses and imagine living there.
- Pick up a walks leaflet and information guide.

Eating and shopping: don't miss our Rock House tea-room.

Access for all: ⏚ 🅿️ Dₐ 🖐 ⬇️ ⠿ Ⓐ
Building ♿ Grounds ♿

The Holy Austin Rock Houses at Kinver Edge, Staffordshire

Getting here: 138:SO836836. **Bus**: Hansons 228 ⊞ Merry Hill bus station to Kinver. **Train**: Stourbridge town 5 miles. **Road**: Kinver village is 4 miles west of Stourbridge, 4 miles north of Kidderminster. The Rock Houses are signposted from Kinver village High Street. **Parking**: at the Warden's lodge on Comber Road for the Edge and on Compton Road for the Rock Houses.

Finding out more: 01384 872553 or kinveredge@nationaltrust.org.uk

Kinver Edge and the Rock Houses		M	T	W	T	F	S	S
Countryside								
Open all year			M	T	W	T	F	S	S
House grounds								
Open all year	10–4		M	T	W	T	F	S	S
Kinver tea-room and upper terrace								
3 Mar–27 Nov	11–4		·	·	·	T	F	S	S
Lower Rock Houses								
3 Mar–27 Nov	2–4		·	·	·	T	F	S	S

Open Bank Holiday Mondays. Lower Rock Houses open for guided weekday tours (March to November), by prior arrangement (parties of ten or over). Rock Houses closed on Kinver Fête day in May (date to be confirmed).

Kinwarton Dovecote

Kinwarton, near Alcester, Warwickshire B49 6HB

Map (4) K7   1958

A lovely and rare 14th-century circular dovecote with metre-thick walls, hundreds of nesting holes and original rotating ladder. **Note**: farm stock may be grazing in field. No toilet.

Access for all: Building ♿

Getting here: 150:SP106585. 1½ miles north-east of Alcester, just south of B4089.

Finding out more: 01789 400777 or kinwartondovecote@nationaltrust.org.uk

Kinwarton Dovecote		M	T	W	T	F	S	S
1 Mar–31 Oct	11–6	M	T	W	T	F	S	S

Closes dusk if earlier. Other times by appointment.

Letocetum Roman Baths and Museum

Watling Street, Wall, near Lichfield,
Staffordshire WS14 0AW

Map (4) K5 1934

Explore the remains of this once-important
Roman staging post and settlement, including
mansio (Roman inn) and bathhouse.
Note: in the guardianship of English Heritage.

Access for all: Open-air site 🚶 Museum ♿

Getting here: 139:SK099067. Within the
village of Wall on the north side of A5, 3 miles
south of Lichfield.

Finding out more: 0121 625 6820
(English Heritage) or
letocetum@nationaltrust.org.uk

Letocetum Roman Baths and Museum

Open-air site is accessible at all reasonable times. Open-air
site and museum of Roman finds are manned by volunteers
on the last Saturday and Sunday of each month, from March
to end of October, 11 to 4. Site and museum also manned
by volunteers on Saturday, Sunday and Monday of Bank
Holiday weekends and every Sunday from 17 July to
4 September, 11 to 4. Guided walks some afternoons when
the site is manned by volunteers.

Roman remains at Letocetum Roman Baths, Staffordshire

Middle Littleton Tithe Barn

Middle Littleton, Evesham,
Worcestershire WR11 5LN

Map (4) K7 1975

One of the largest and finest 13th-century tithe
barns in the country. **Note**: no toilet.

Access for all: Building 🚶

Getting here: 150:SP080471. 3 miles
north-east of Evesham, east of B4085.

Finding out more: 01905 371006 or
middlelittleton@nationaltrust.org.uk

Middle Littleton Tithe Barn		M	T	W	T	F	S	S
1 Apr–31 Oct	2–5	**M**	**T**	**W**	**T**	**F**	**S**	**S**

Directions for access on the barn door.

Morville Hall

Morville, near Bridgnorth,
Shropshire WV16 5NB

Map (4) I5 1965

This beautiful stone-built house set in
attractive gardens is of Elizabethan origin
which was enlarged and expanded around 1750.
Note: Dower House garden also open
(not National Trust).

Access for all: 🏠 Building 🚶 Grounds ♿

Getting here: 138:SO668940. 3 miles west of
Bridgnorth, off A458.

Finding out more: 01746 780838 or
morvillehall@nationaltrust.org.uk

Morville Hall

Admission by guided tour. By written appointment only
with the tenants, Dr and Mrs C. Douglas.

Moseley Old Hall

Moseley Old Hall Lane, Fordhouses,
Wolverhampton, Staffordshire WV10 7HY

Map ④ J5 🏠 🏚 ✝ ✿ 🔔 1962

'**Fascinating and atmospheric, the history
brought brilliantly to life. A fantastic
experience and very welcoming. National
Trust at its best**.'
Mrs Weare, Hampton, Middlesex

This atmospheric Elizabethan farmhouse
conceals a priest's hole and hiding places, in
one of which Charles II hid while on the run
after being defeated at the Battle of Worcester
in 1651. You can also see the bed on which the
royal fugitive slept. Follow the story of the
King's dramatic escape from Cromwell's troops
and find out about 17th-century domestic life
in this friendly and fascinating historic home.
The Hall is an integral part of the Monarch's
Way Trail. The garden has plant varieties in
keeping with the period and has a striking knot
garden following a 17th-century design.

Exploring
  – Follow in the footsteps
    of a king.
  – Take a fascinating guided tour
    of the house.
  – Sit by the fire and immerse
    yourself in 17th-century life.
  – Discover the delights of the
    walled garden and the 'knot'.
  – Children will love to explore
    with our new Tracker Packs.
  – Come and see our new
    beehive and honey bees.

Eating and shopping: enjoy delicious light
lunches and homemade cakes in our very
popular tea-room. We regularly use locally
sourced ingredients. Browse for gifts and
plants in our National Trust shop. Find bargains
galore in the second-hand bookshop.

Making the most of your day: events and
activities throughout the year, including family
events, demonstrations and re-creations
of 17th-century life. Children's activities
on family event days and Mondays and

Tuesdays in August (events leaflet available).
Dogs: welcome on leads in the garden
and grounds.

Access for all: 🅿️ 🅿️ 🚻 🔧 🔧 📷 🔧 ✦ ⊙
House 🦽 🦽 **Shop and tea-room** 🦽 🦽
Grounds 🦽 🦽 ➡️ 🦽

Getting here: 127:SJ932044. 4 miles
north of Wolverhampton city centre.
Bus: National Express West Midlands 533 from
Wolverhampton; Arriva Midlands 70 from
Cannock, both ½ mile. **Train**: Wolverhampton
4 miles. **Road**: south of M54 between A449 and
A460; from north on M6 leave at exit 11, then
A460; from south on M6 and M54 take
exit 1; coaches must approach via A460 to
avoid low bridge. **Parking**: free, 50 yards. No
onsite coach parking (assigned dropping-off
place only). Information available on nearby
coach parking places. Narrow lanes and tight
corners. Turning point for large vehicles.

You may also enjoy: Baddesley Clinton, a
family home and refuge, and Packwood House,
a quiet country house.

Finding out more: 01902 782808 or
moseleyoldhall@nationaltrust.org.uk

Moseley Old Hall		M	T	W	T	F	S	S
5 Mar–3 Jul	12–5	·	·	**W**	·	·	**S**	**S**
4 Jul–18 Sep	12–5	**M**	**T**	**W**	·	·	**S**	**S**
21 Sep–30 Oct	12–5	·	·	**W**	·	·	**S**	**S**
5 Nov–18 Dec	12–4	·	·	·	·	·	**S**	**S**

Open Bank Holiday Mondays, 11 to 5. Entry 12 to 1 by guided
tour only (free-flow or guided tours from 1). **Open Saturday
to Wednesday during autumn half-term**. 5 November to
18 December: guided tour only. Christmas events.

17th-century life at Moseley Old Hall, Staffordshire

Packwood House

Packwood Lane, Lapworth,
Warwickshire B94 6AT

Map ④ K6 1941

The house is originally 16th-century, yet its interiors were extensively restored between the world wars by Graham Baron Ash to create a fascinating 20th-century evocation of domestic Tudor architecture. Packwood House contains a fine collection of 16th-century textiles and furniture, and the gardens have renowned herbaceous borders and a famous collection of yews.

Exploring
- Follow the spiral path to view the Yew Garden.
- Be inspired by the delicate stained-glass windows.
- Discover a fine collection of tapestries and furniture.
- Check your watch against the sundials.
- Experience a heady mix of fruit and flowers.
- Look out for homes for the workers – bee boles.

Eating and shopping: locally sourced products available in the shop. Garden plants for sale, many grown in our own nursery. Light refreshments available from our new kiosk.

Making the most of your day: set the scene with an introductory talk. Easter trail for families. Meet the Gardener evening tours. Open-air theatre. **Dogs**: welcome on leads in the car park and on public footpaths across estate.

Access for all: ⓟ♿♿♿🚻📷👓
Building 🏠♿ Grounds 🏠♿♿

Getting here: 139:SP174723.
Bus: Johnsons of Henley X20 Birmingham to Stratford-upon-Avon, alight Hockley Heath, 1¾ miles. **Train**: Lapworth 1½ miles; Birmingham International 8 miles.
Road: 2 miles east of Hockley Heath (on A3400), 11 miles south-east of central Birmingham. **Parking**: free, 100 yards.

The Yew Garden leading up to Packwood House, Warwickshire

You may also enjoy: Baddesley Clinton – a mere two miles away.

Finding out more: 01564 782024 or packwood@nationaltrust.org.uk

Packwood House		M	T	W	T	F	S	S
House, garden and shop								
1 Feb–30 Oct	11–5		T	W	T	F	S	S
Park								
Open all year	Dawn–dusk	M	T	W	T	F	S	S

Admission to the house by timed ticket available from reception (not bookable). Open Bank Holiday Mondays.

Rosedene

Victoria Road, Dodford, near Bromsgrove,
Worcestershire B61 9BU

Map ④ J6   🏠 ❄ 1997

Restored 1840s cottage, organic garden and
orchard illustrating the mid-19th-century
Chartist movement – a time of remarkable
British political change.

Access for all: ♿🚻 Building 📖 Grounds ♿

Getting here: 150:SO929730. Follow signs for
Dodford off A448, left into Priory Road, left
into Church Road, then left into Victoria Road.

Finding out more: 01527 821214 or
rosedene@nationaltrust.org.uk

Rosedene
Admission by guided tours, first Sunday of the month only, from 6 March to 4 December (booking essential). Tours available 10, 11:30, 1 and 2:30. Limited group visits at other times by arrangement (not in July and August).

Rosedene, Worcestershire: Chartist simplicity

Shugborough Estate

Milford, near Stafford, Staffordshire ST17 0XB

Map ④ J4    1966

The mysterious Shugborough Estate is the
ancestral home of the Earls of Lichfield. With
rumoured connections to the Holy Grail, the
364-hectare (900-acre) classical landscape is
peppered with unusual monuments. The fine
Georgian mansion house, with magnificent
views over riverside garden terraces, features
stunning collections of porcelain. Costumed
characters work in the servants' quarters and
farmstead: doing laundry, cheesemaking,
milling, brewing and baking. In these areas
the Staffordshire County Council Museum
collections are held including reconstructed
chemist shop, tailors' shop, Victorian
schoolroom and puppet collection. In
addition, the newly restored walled garden
grows historic varieties of fruit and vegetables.
Note: Shugborough is wholly financed,
administered and maintained by Staffordshire
County Council. Only the house and gardens
are free to members.

Exploring
 - Enjoy the whole estate: purchase a reduced estate ticket.
 - New: Patrick Lichfield's private apartments are now open.
 - Enjoy new museum galleries – toys, costumes, health, trades and wildlife.
 - Try out the beds in the new servants' bedroom.
 - Uncover the art of historic gardening in the walled garden.
 - Object of the month: see rare archived objects uncovered.

Eating and shopping: licensed tea-room
serving homemade, locally sourced food.
Seek out the perfect present in our gift shop.
Treat yourself in the ice-cream parlour.
Old-fashioned sweet shop and craft outlets
making and selling handmade goods.

Shugborough Estate, Staffordshire: the Georgian mansion house as seen from across the River Sow

Making the most of your day: year-round varied events programme, concerts, open-air theatre productions, themed weekends and family fun. **Dogs**: on leads in parkland and gardens only.

Access for all: ⟦icons⟧
Building ⟦icons⟧ Grounds ⟦icons⟧

Getting here: 127:SJ992225. 6 miles east of Stafford on A513. **Foot**: pedestrian access from east, from the canal/Great Haywood side of the estate. Estate walks link to towpaths along Trent & Mersey Canal and Staffordshire and Worcestershire Canal and to Cannock Chase trails. Lies on Staffordshire Way. **Bus**: Arriva 825 Stafford ⟦rail⟧ to Lichfield (passing close Lichfield City ⟦rail⟧). **Train**: Rugeley 5 miles; Rugeley Trent Valley 5 miles; Stafford 6 miles. **Road**: signposted from M6 exit 13; 6 miles east of Stafford on A513; entrance at Milford. **Parking**: £3 (pay and display, including members). Refunded on purchase of an all-sites ticket.

You may also enjoy: Attingham Park, Sudbury Hall and Biddulph Grange Garden.

Finding out more: 01889 881388 or shugborough@nationaltrust.org.uk

Shugborough Estate		M	T	W	T	F	S	S
House, farm, servants' quarters, grounds and tea-room								
18 Mar–28 Oct	11–5	M	T	W	T	F	S	S
Shop								
18 Mar–28 Oct	11–5	M	T	W	T	F	S	S
29 Oct–23 Dec	11–4	M	T	W	T	F	S	S

Open Bank Holiday Mondays. Opening times and admission prices may vary when special events held.

Sunnycroft

200 Holyhead Road, Wellington, Telford, Shropshire TF1 2DR

Map ④ I4   ⟦icons⟧ 1999

This substantial red-brick villa is typical of the many thousands that were built for the prosperous middle classes in the late Victorian period. Sunnycroft is one of the very few to have survived, with a mini estate and largely unaltered contents and decoration. **Note**: house, garden and tea-room now open from 11.

Exploring
– Enjoy wandering around this late-Victorian time capsule.
– Discover our collection of Leek embroidery.
– Explore and relax in the beautiful gardens and glasshouses.
– Enhance your visit by joining an introductory talk or tour.

Eating and shopping: take afternoon tea in the main house. Delicious cakes made in Shropshire. Browse in the second-hand bookshop.

Making the most of your day: our events programme reflects the heyday of the property, including traditional garden fête. **Dogs**: welcome on leads in grounds only.

Access for all: **Building** 🧑‍🦽
Grounds 🧑‍🦼➡️

Getting here: 127:SJ652109. In Wellington on the B5061. **Cycle**: NCN81, 1 mile. **Bus**: Arriva 66 from Telford (passing Wellington Telford West ≋). **Train**: Wellington Telford West ½ mile. **Road**: M54 exit 7, follow B5061 towards Wellington. **Sat Nav**: enter Sunnycroft's address rather than postcode. **Parking**: free, 150 yards in orchard. Not suitable for coaches. Additional free parking (not National Trust) in Wrekin Road car park.

Finding out more: 01952 242884 or sunnycroft@nationaltrust.org.uk

Sunnycroft		M	T	W	T	F	S	S
12 Mar–30 Oct	11–5	M				F	S	S
16 Dec–19 Dec	11–4	M				F	S	S

Timed tickets with introductory talk, then free-flow (not bookable). Two guided tours avaialble daily on a first-come first-served basis. Open free-flow throughout the house on Bank Holiday weekends and event days. Last admission one hour before closing.

Sunnycroft, Shropshire: a late-Victorian time capsule

Town Walls Tower

Shrewsbury, Shropshire SY1 1TN

Map ④ H4   🏠 1930

This last remaining 14th-century watchtower sits on what were once the medieval fortified, defensive walls of Shrewsbury. **Note**: no toilet or car parking and 40 extremely steep steps to top floor of property.

Access for all: **Building** 🧑‍🦽

Getting here: 126:SJ492122. Close to town centre near Welsh Bridge, on south of town wall.

Finding out more: 01743 708162 or townwallstower@nationaltrust.org.uk

Town Walls Tower		M	T	W	T	F	S	S
22 May	11–3							S
11 Jun	11–3						S	
31 Jul	11–3							S
20 Aug	11–3						S	

Tours between 11 and 3. Last admission 20 minutes before closing.

Immerse yourself in the 1930s at Upton House and Gardens, Warwickshire

Upton House and Gardens

near Banbury, Warwickshire OX15 6HT

Map (4) L7 1948

Join the guests of Lord and Lady Bearsted and experience a weekend house party of a 1930s millionaire. Surrounded by internationally important art and porcelain collections, hear and discover more about family life and soak up the atmosphere of the party. See the red and silver art deco bathroom and get close to art works by El Greco, Stubbs and Bosch. The stunning gardens – being returned to their 1930s heyday – consist of a sweeping lawn, which gives way to a series of terraces and herbaceous borders leading to a kitchen garden, tranquil water garden and spring bulb displays. **Note**: some areas of the gardens may be closed for ongoing maintenance.

Exploring
- Live the 1930s – listen to family stories and read papers.
- Discover more, with art and porcelain taster tours each day.
- Relax by the 1930s swimming pool overlooking the terraced garden.

Exploring
- Meander through the kitchen gardens, which supply the restaurant.
- New winter opening revealing more family stories and secrets.
- Free family activity packs for exploring the gardens.

Eating and shopping: visit the shop for a wide range of memorabilia, gifts and books, locally sourced food and plants inspired by Upton's beautiful garden. Enjoy homemade cakes and local produce in the restaurant. Book the restaurant or squash court for your function.

Making the most of your day: see the film, read family papers and magazines, play snooker or listen to 1930s broadcasts. Family events, jazz concerts and garden tours. National Collection of Asters in bloom in September.

Access for all: P♿ D♿ 📷 WC 🚻 🔑 💺 📷 VT ♫ ∴ 🅿 Building 🔩🔩🔩 Grounds 🔩🔩🔩

Getting here: 151:SP371461. On the edge of the Cotswolds, between Banbury and Stratford-upon-Avon. **Foot**: footpath SM177 runs adjacent to property, Centenary Way ½ mile, Macmillan Way 1 mile. **Cycle**: NCN5, 5 miles. Oxfordshire Cycle Way 1½ miles. **Train**: Banbury 7 miles. **Road**: on A422, 7 miles north of Banbury, 12 miles south-east of Stratford-upon-Avon. Signed from exit 12 of M40. **Parking**: free, 300 yards. Parking is on grass with hard-standing for coaches.

You may also enjoy: award-winning roses at nearby Coughton Court – a Tudor mansion with fascinating stories.

Finding out more: 01295 670266 or uptonhouse@nationaltrust.org.uk

Upton House and Gardens		M	T	W	T	F	S	S
Winter walk, servants exhibition, restaurant and shop*								
19 Feb–9 Mar	11–4	M	T	W	·	·	S	S
Garden, restaurant, shop and plant centre								
12 Mar–30 Oct	11–5	M	T	W	·	F	S	S
Taster tours**								
12 Mar–30 Oct	11–1	M	T	W	·	F	S	S
House***								
12 Mar–30 Oct	1–5	M	T	W	·	F	S	S
5 Nov–18 Dec	12–4	·	·	·	·	·	S	S
Exhibition, restaurant, winter walk and shop*								
31 Oct–21 Dec	12–4	M	T	W	·	·	S	S
26 Dec–31 Dec	12–4	M	T	W	T	F	S	·

25 July to 4 September: open every day. Winter walk, restaurant, shop and plant centre open 1 and 2 January.
*In addition short guided tours run during the day (timed tickets available on arrival only). **Tours last 35 minutes and focus on part of the collection (timed tickets available on arrival only). *** Open Thursday during summer holidays. House admission from 11 on Bank Holidays by timed ticket, but visitors may stay until 5. Ground floor open only in house November and December.

The Weir

Swainshill, Hereford, Herefordshire HR4 7QF

Map ④ H7 1959

A stunning riverside garden with sweeping views along the River Wye and Herefordshire countryside. The garden is spectacular all year round – drifts of spring bulbs give way to wild flowers, followed by autumn colour and the walled garden full of fruit and vegetables. Worth a visit any time of year. **Note**: sturdy footwear recommended.

Exploring
 — New: visit the walled garden.
 — Enjoy the carpets of spring flowers.
 — Summer wild flowers attract a range of wildlife.
 — The mature trees provide an array of autumn colour.

The Weir, Herefordshire, is glorious all year round

Help the Trust with Gift Aid on Entry for non-members

Eating and shopping: take a hamper to one of the riverside picnic sites.

Making the most of your day: children's days in August, with 'hands-on' activities and displays. Open-air theatre. **Dogs**: on leads in car park only.

Access for all: Grounds

Getting here: 149:SO438418. **Bus**: to Hereford and then taxi. **Train**: Hereford 5 miles. **Road**: 5 miles west of Hereford on A438. **Parking**: free.

Finding out more: 01981 590509 or theweir@nationaltrust.org.uk

The Weir		M	T	W	T	F	S	S
22 Jan–27 Feb	11–4	M	T	W	T	F	S	S
28 Feb–6 Nov	11–5	M	T	W	T	F	S	S
12 Nov–18 Dec	11–4						S	S

Last admission 45 minutes before closing.

Wichenford Dovecote

Wichenford, Worcestershire WR6 6XY

Map (4) I7   🏠 1965

A charming 17th-century half-timbered dovecote at Wichenford Court. The building, although small, is very striking. **Note**: no access to Wichenford Court (privately owned). No toilet.

Access for all: Building

Getting here: 150:SO788598. 5½ miles north-west of Worcester, north of B4204.

Finding out more: 01527 821214 or wichenforddovecote@nationaltrust.org.uk

Wichenford Dovecote		M	T	W	T	F	S	S
27 Feb–30 Oct	9–6	M	T	W	T	F	S	S

Open other times by appointment.

Wightwick Manor and Gardens

Wightwick Bank, Wolverhampton, West Midlands WV6 8EE

Map (4) J5   1937

Mander, Mawson & Morris – a suburban paradise. A stunning late Victorian manor house, built in the 'Old English' style by local industrialist Theodore Mander, Wightwick Manor is perhaps the best surviving example of a home furnished under the influence of the Arts and Crafts movement. The rich interiors feature many original wallpapers, fabrics and furnishings by William Morris, artwork by Rossetti and Burne-Jones, glass by Charles Kempe and ceramics by William de Morgan. The house sits in seven hectares (seventeen acres) of attractive Arts and Crafts gardens, designed by Thomas Mawson, which are Grade II listed in their own right.

Exploring
– Admire outstanding Arts and Crafts interiors and Pre-Raphaelite art.
– Impressive Arts and Crafts garden for all seasons.
– Edwardian kitchen garden and new Caribbean herb garden.
– Play a game of billiards and experience the year 1900.
– Brand new entrance and visitor reception pavilion.
– Exhibition to celebrate the founding of Morris and Co.

Eating and shopping: tea-room serving food grown in the Edwardian kitchen garden. Unique William Morris and Arts and Crafts-inspired gift shop. Plant sales to tempt your green fingers. Browse through the bargains in the second-hand bookshop.

Making the most of your day: guided tours of the house run most open days. Themed 20-minute Taster Tours run every day between 11 and 12:30. Extensive and varied calendar of events. **Dogs**: welcome on leads in garden.

Wightwick Manor and Gardens, West Midlands: a delight both inside and out

Access for all: [icons] Building [icons] Grounds [icons]

Getting here: 139:SO869985. **Bus**: National Express West Midlands 543 from Wolverhampton (passing close Wolverhampton [icon]). **Train**: Wolverhampton 3 miles. **Road**: 3 miles west of Wolverhampton on A454 to Bridgnorth. Please note new entrance directly on roadside of A454. **Parking**: extended car park. No coach parking.

You may also enjoy: Sunnycroft, a Victorian villa near Wellington, Shropshire.

Finding out more: 01902 761400 or wightwickmanor@nationaltrust.org.uk

Wightwick Manor and Gardens		M	T	W	T	F	S	S
16 Feb–30 Jun	11–5			W	T	F	S	S
1 Jul–31 Aug	11–5	M	T	W	T	F	S	S
1 Sep–30 Oct	11–5			W	T	F	S	S
4 Nov–18 Dec	11–5					F	S	S

House opens 12:30. Admission to house 11 to 12:30 is by 20-minute Taster Tour only. All house admission by timed ticket (only available from Visitor Reception on the day of visit). No guided tours on first Thursday and Saturday of the month – free-flow through house from 12:30. Open Bank Holiday Mondays (ground floor only). Tours vary as many of the contents are fragile, so some rooms cannot always be shown.

Wilderhope Manor

Longville, Much Wenlock, Shropshire TF13 6EG

Map (4) H5   [icons] 1936

Beautiful Elizabethan manor house restored by John Cadbury in 1936. Surrounding farmland managed for landscape and wildlife has permissive access. **Note**: manor is a popular youth hostel, so access to some rooms may be restricted.

Access for all: [icon] Building [icons] Grounds [icon]

Getting here: 138:SO545929. 7 miles south-west of Much Wenlock, 7 miles east of Church Stretton, ½ mile south of B4371.

Finding out more: 01694 771363 (Hostel Warden YHA) or wilderhope@nationaltrust.org.uk

Wilderhope Manor		M	T	W	T	F	S	S
9 Jan–27 Mar	2–4							S
3 Apr–25 Sep	2–4			W				S
2 Oct–18 Dec	2–4							S

North West

**Making an entrance, Neptune perches
precipitously at the summit
of Lyme Park's grand portico**

Outdoors in the North West

Discover some of Britain's finest landscapes, wildlife and fascinating industrial heritage while enjoying amazing hospitality, great food and drink.

Top right:
**Rosebay,
Sandscale Haws**
Below:
**Wasdale,
Cumbria, with
a striking and
dramatic view
of Wastwater in
the distance**

The Lake District

For pure drama and internationally-renowned beauty, the Lake District is unbeatable. Thousands come here searching for spiritual refreshment and, of course, there are endless physical challenges to enjoy – for this is the birthplace of climbing and the natural home to so many outdoor activities.

The Trust looks after one quarter of the Lake District National Park, encouraging access and enjoyment of this magnificent place. We care for England's highest mountain, Scafell Pike, and our deepest lake, Wastwater, and most of the central fells and major valley heads are owned or leased by the Trust, together with 24 lakes and tarns.

Beatrix Potter, whose love of the area is legendary, left us 1,600 hectares (4,000 acres) and fourteen farms when she died in 1943. This great estate had already begun to be purchased piece by piece – beginning in 1902 with Brandelhow on the shore of Derwentwater, funded by local people who wanted to save it from development by wealthy Victorian merchants.

Coniston Water, which inspired Arthur Ransome and Donald Campbell, is home to many varieties of plants, including meadow flowers and the rare small-leaved lime. Look out for our walk and tree trail through Monk Coniston grounds to the iconic landscape of Tarn Hows.

In Borrowdale, enjoy rugged crags and dramatic fells. Fine sessile oak woodlands and internationally important lichens, mosses and insects all thrive here, as do wildfowl and waders, which nest along the shores of Derwentwater. A great viewpoint is Friar's Crag, at the north end of the lake, near Keswick.

There is wheelchair access to Friar's Crag, as well as at Tarn Hows and Harrowslack, near Hawkshead – just across Windermere and easily reached by ferry.

Fix the Fells project is an upland footpath scheme which repairs dozens of footpaths on the fells which are being eroded by the sheer number of walkers and, of course, the weather. You could help us in many ways, so visit **www.fixthefells.co.uk** to see what you can do.

Our website offers many downloadable walks – also available at our information centres or shops.

Mouthwatering dishes for every season

We love food! All our tea-rooms, restaurants, farm tea-rooms and pubs use local, seasonal produce to create mouthwatering dishes. Whatever the season you'll find something scrumptious, be it spring lamb and fresh peas; a strawberry cream tea at the height of summer; a warming soup or stew to take away the autumn chill; or mince pies and mulled wine with the smell of cloves in the air to get you into the Christmas spirit.

Regional specialities include damson dishes at Sizergh, venison from the parks at Lyme, Dunham and Tatton, and Herdwick lamb from Trust farms in Cumbria. Acorn Bank's lovely garden gives us home-grown herbs and lots of rhubarb varieties.

Of course, there are endless delicious cheeses to savour in Cheshire, but did you know this is also the gooseberry centre of Britain?

Fare from the farm

Taste Herdwick stew and other traditional Cumbrian fare at walkers' tea-rooms at Yew Tree Farm in Rosthwaite, Borrowdale, or try award-winning Kendal Crumbly cheese at Low Sizergh Barn. Many of our tenants now also supply Booths supermarkets in the region with National Trust meat, so look out for it while shopping. In addition it is well worth going out of your way to visit our farms on the Dunham Massey Estate which have opened tea-rooms and ice-cream parlours.

Getting around

Enjoy leaving your car behind and catch the local bus, train or boat. Just sit back and enjoy the view. Or try a bike trail and feel at one with nature. Visit our website to be inspired.

Ancient woodland and stunning views

In West Cheshire explore the very special Sandstone Ridge, with splendid views of the Cheshire Plain and Welsh Mountains from Alderley Edge, Bickerton Hill and nearby Bulkeley Hill Wood; while Helsby Hill has views across the Mersey Estuary to Liverpool.

Both Bickerton and Helsby have Bronze Age forts at their summits, while Bulkeley, part of the Peckforton range of hills, has acres of ancient woodland and the Sandstone Trail running its length.

Views of the Peak District and Welsh Mountains, with wide expanses of the great Cheshire Plain, can be seen from The Cloud, a great rocky heathland near Timbersbrook in Cheshire.

Romantic ruins

Further south lies the folly of Mow Cop; built in 1754 it is famed as the birthplace of Primitive Methodism and stands in romantic ruin. To the west of the county is the site of Lewis Carroll's birthplace near Daresbury – kindly donated to the Trust by the Lewis Carroll Birthplace Trust. Here you can find the 'footprint' of Daresbury Parsonage, in which Carroll was born in 1832, while nearby Daresbury Church has a stained glass window featuring Carroll and his Wonderland characters.

Rolling coastline, wildlife and flowers in South Cumbria and Lancashire

Arnside Knott on the Cumbrian coast and Eaves and Waterslack Woods in Lancashire are home to a fantastic variety of wild flowers and butterflies. There are many lovely walks with so much to spot (our website offers a downloadable map to aid your hunt).

Holme Park Fell, on the other side of the M6 as you approach Junction 36, is covered with heather and wild flowers and home to numerous birds and bees, all thriving in its craggy and majestic limestone nooks and crannies.

Outdoors in the North West

Natterjack toads, a nationally rare species, live happily at Sandscale Haws in Cumbria, and at Formby in Lancashire you can hear their extraordinary mating calls on May and June evenings. Sandscale is also home to a rich variety of birds, including shelducks, eider ducks, goldeneyes and plovers, and the high, grass-covered sand dunes are perfect for a day's exploring. Formby also has one of the last remaining colonies of red squirrels.

Manchester, Liverpool and Lancashire's 'green lungs'

To the south, Manchester and Liverpool rely on the Trust's 'green lung', in the form of open countryside and parkland, with the Stubbins Estate and Holcombe Moor providing the same service north of Bury, Lancashire. Dunham Massey, Lyme Park, Quarry Bank Mill and Little Moreton Hall all have outdoor spaces, large and small, some with vast estates and walking trails for you to get away from the urban sprawl. Speke Hall in Liverpool offers greenery and space for children to play, while Rufford Old Hall and Gawthorpe Hall in Lancashire are set in tranquil gardens.

Car parks in the Lake District

Lanthwaite Wood	NY 149 215
Buttermere	NY 172 173
Honister Pass	NY 225 135
Seatoller	NY 246 137
Rosthwaite	NY 257 148
Bowderstone	NY 254 167
Watendlath	NY 276 164
Kettlewell	NY 269 196
Great Wood	NY 272 213
Aira Force	NY 401 201
Glencoyne Bay	NY 387 188
Wasdale Head	NY 182 074
Old Dungeon Ghyll	NY 285 062
Stickle Ghyll	NY 295 064
Elterwater	NY 329 047
Tarn Hows	SD 326 995
Ash Landing	SD 388 955
Sandscale Haws	SD 199 758
Blea Tarn	NY 296 044
Harrowslack	SD 388 960
Red Nab	SD 385 995
Glen Mary	SD 321 998

Camp in the Lake District with the Trust

Get back to nature by camping at one of our campsites, the perfect base for a holiday.

Low Wray Campsite

Lying on the quiet western shore of Windermere, this site has spectacular lake and fell views. There is lake access for non-powered boating activities.

Set in the heart of 'Beatrix Potter' country, you can enjoy beautiful walks to Hill Top at Near Sawrey, Potter's home, as well as to the Beatrix Potter Gallery at Hawkshead and in the grounds of Wray Castle.

Great Langdale Campsite

In the heart of the Lake District mountains, this is an ideal location for climbing and fell walking.

Just a few miles from Ambleside and convenient for the other Lakes' attractions, this is a great base from which to climb Scafell Pike, England's highest mountain, after which you should reward yourself with a pint in one of the nearby traditional Lakeland hostelries.

Wasdale Campsite

This site is a mere stone's throw from beautiful Wastwater, the deepest lake in England and one which has a distinctive Nordic character. The pyramidal peak of Great Gable is reflected in its waters.

Arguably, the most dramatic location in England, Scafell Pike and numerous high fell walking routes are within striking distance. This is a remote place where peace and tranquillity reign.

Camping pods

For those who prefer something a little bit more luxurious than a tent...

Telephone 015394 63862 or visit **www.ntlakescampsites.org.uk** for further information and terms and conditions.

Acorn Bank Garden and Watermill

Temple Sowerby, near Penrith,
Cumbria CA10 1SP

Map (6) E7   🏛️🚼✿🏠 1950

'My visit to Acorn Bank was sheer bliss! An idyllic and peaceful oasis with aromas to calm the senses.'
V. Dawson, Knutsford

Acorn Bank Garden and Watermill, Cumbria

Best known for its collection of 250 herbs and traditional fruit orchards. Sample the tea-room menu, where culinary herbs from the garden are used daily in soups and salads, and fruit from the orchards are used in delicious puddings and cakes. Wander along the Crowdundle Beck to the partially restored watermill, spotting wildlife in the woods on the way, then enjoy the views across the Eden Valley to the Lake District from the magnificent backdrop of the sandstone house (which, although not open to the public, adds to the wonderful setting). Stay a while longer in a holiday cottage. **Note**: access to fragile grass paths in the garden may be restricted after wet weather.

Exploring
— Relax in the tranquil and sheltered walled gardens.
— Discover fascinating stories behind the plants in the herb garden.
— Find great crested newts in the garden pond.
— Spot red squirrels in Acorn Bank's woodland.
— Watch the waterwheel turning at the mill (most weekend afternoons).
— Listen to birdsong as you stroll beside Crowdundle Beck.

Eating and shopping: enjoy locally sourced produce as well as herbs and fruit from the garden in the tea-room. Plants for sale in the garden courtyard. Browse in the shop, housed in an 18th-century dovecote.

Making the most of your day: Apple Day, 16 October, is a great day out for the whole family (charge, including members). **Dogs**: welcome on leads on the woodland walk and in the garden courtyard.

Access for all: 🅿️🅳♿🚻👶🖐️📷🏠🚶♿
Watermill ♿🚶 shop and admission point ♿🚶
Grounds 🚶♿🚶➡️🚶

Getting here: 91:NY612281. **Foot**: public footpath from Temple Sowerby. **Cycle**: NCN7, 6 miles. **Bus**: Grand Prix 563 Penrith to Kirkby Stephen, to within 1 mile (passes close Penrith ≋ and Appleby ≋). **Train**: Langwathby 5 miles; Penrith 6 miles. **Road**: just north of Temple Sowerby, 6 miles east of Penrith, 1 mile from A66. **Parking**: free, 80 yards. Tight access for coaches (recommended route map available when booking).

You may also enjoy: Townend, a Lakeland farmhouse at Troutbeck, or Wordsworth House at Cockermouth.

Finding out more: 017683 61893 or acornbank@nationaltrust.org.uk

Acorn Bank Garden and Watermill		M	T	W	T	F	S	S
Garden, watermill, woodland walks and shop								
26 Feb–6 Mar	10–5	·	·	·	·	·	S	S
12 Mar–30 Oct	10–5	·	·	W	T	F	S	S
Tea-room								
26 Feb–6 Mar	11–4:30	·	·	·	·	·	S	S
12 Mar–30 Oct	11–4:30	·	·	W	T	F	S	S

Open Bank Holiday Mondays, 10 to 5, tea-room 11 to 4:30.

Alderley Edge

Nether Alderley, Macclesfield, Cheshire

Map (5) D8 1946

Walk the dramatic red sandstone escarpment of Alderley Edge, with views over the Cheshire Plain and to the Peak District. Explore woodland paths or walk to Hare Hill Garden. Bickerton Hill and Bulkely Hill Wood; Mow Cop, the Cloud and Helsby Hill offer a variety of landscapes with stunning views.

Exploring
- Alderley Edge is designated an SSSI for its geological interest.
- A history of copper mining since the Bronze Age.
- Derbyshire Caving Club opens the mines twice a year.
- Bickerton Hill is an SSSI for its flora and fauna.

Eating and shopping: Wizard Country Inn, Alderley Edge (not National Trust). Wizard tea-room, Alderley Edge (not National Trust – weekends only).

Making the most of your day: series of guided walks takes place at Alderley Edge through the summer. **Dogs**: under close control and on leads in fields (particularly during lambing/bird nesting season).

Access for all: Grounds

Getting here: Alderley Edge 118:SJ860776; The Cloud 118:SJ905637; Mow Cop 118:SJ857573; Bickerton Hill 117:SJ498529; Bulkely Hill 117:SJ527553; Helsby Hill 117:SJ492754; Lewis Carroll's Birthplace 118:SJ593805; Maggoty Wood 118:SJ889702; Burton Wood SJ317743; Caldy Hill SJ223855; Heswall Fields SJ245824; Thurstaston Common SJ248845. **Parking**: at some properties (roadside elsewhere); pay and display at Alderley Edge (closing time displayed at entrance).

Finding out more: 01625 584412 or alderleyedge@nationaltrust.org.uk. c/o Cheshire Countryside Office, Nether Alderley, Macclesfield, Cheshire SK10 4UB

Alderley Edge		M	T	W	T	F	S	S
Open all year	8–5:30*	**M**	**T**	**W**	**T**	**F**	**S**	**S**

*Closes 6, 31 May to 26 September and 5, 1 November to 31 December. Tea-room also open Bank Holidays but closed 24 and 25 December.

The sun shines down on a path through trees on the top of Alderley Edge in Cheshire

The Beatles' Childhood Homes

Woolton and Allerton, Liverpool

Map (5) C8 🏠 2002

'Simply the best Beatles tour I have ever been on!'
J. Mansfield, New York, USA

A combined tour to Mendips and 20 Forthlin Road, the childhood homes of John Lennon and Paul McCartney, is your only opportunity to see inside the houses where the Beatles met, composed and rehearsed many of their earliest songs. Walk through the back door into the kitchen and imagine John's Aunt Mimi cooking him his tea, or stand in the spot where Lennon and McCartney composed 'I Saw Her Standing There'. Join our custodians on a fascinating trip down memory lane in these two atmospheric period houses, so typical of Liverpool life in the 1950s. **Note**: access to these houses is by National Trust minibus tour only (charge including members).

Exploring
– Original family photographs by Mike McCartney on display.
– Visit the bedroom where John Lennon did his dreaming.
– Walk in the footsteps of these musical legends.
– Listen to original audio commentary by Mike and Paul McCartney.
– Experience two very different 1950s houses.

Eating and shopping: guidebooks and postcards for sale at both houses and Speke Hall shop. Local produce served at Speke Hall's Home Farm restaurant.

Making the most of your day: departures from convenient pick-up points (city centre and Speke Hall). Our comfortable minibus and easy online booking service allow you to relax, as we take the strain out of visiting.

Access for all: 👨‍🦽 🚾 📷 🖥️ 🎧 ⠿ 🅰️ **Building** ♿

A view out from 20 Forthlin Road in Liverpool, Merseyside, the childhood home of Paul McCartney

Getting here: 108:SJ422855. No direct access by car or on foot to either house. Access is via minibus tour (advance booking essential) from Liverpool city centre or Speke Hall.
Parking: for morning tours numerous public pay and display car parks in city centre. For afternoon tours, parking at Speke Hall.

You may also enjoy: Speke Hall, a rare Tudor mansion, or The Hardmans' House, a post-war time capsule.

Finding out more: 0844 800 4791 (Infoline). 0151 427 7231 (booking line) or thebeatleshomes@nationaltrust.org.uk

The Beatles' Childhood Homes	M	T	W	T	F	S	S
26 Feb–27 Nov	*		·	·	W	T	F	S	S

Open Bank Holiday Mondays. *Admission by guided tour only, times vary, visit www.nationaltrust.org.uk/beatles for bookings. 26 February to 13 March and 2 November to 27 November: all tours depart from Liverpool city centre. 16 March to 30 October: morning tours depart from Liverpool city centre, afternoon tours depart from Speke Hall. To guarantee a place visitors are advised to book in advance. Any photography or duplication of audio tour material is strictly prohibited. You will be asked to deposit all handbags, cameras and recording equipment at the entrance to both houses.

Beatrix Potter Gallery

Main Street, Hawkshead, Cumbria LA22 0NS

Map (6) D8   🏠 1944

'**Lovely to see original illustrations**.'
Mrs J. McVay, Loughborough

Step inside this charming 17th-century building to enjoy a new exhibition of Beatrix Potter's original watercolour paintings and sketches. This gallery has an interesting history, as previously it was the office of Beatrix's husband, William Heelis. Many of these pictures are only displayed at this location. Learn more about Beatrix as a farmer and early supporter of the National Trust. **Note**: nearest toilet 300 yards in main village car park (not National Trust). Timed ticket entry.

Exploring
– New exhibition: 'Little friends all over the world'.
– *The Tale of Timmy Tiptoes* celebrates its centenary.
– Children will love the trail based on the displays.
– Imagine working life before computers when visiting Mr Heelis's office.

Exploring
– Discover the picturesque and historic Hawkshead village.
– Visit website to download local walks.

Eating and shopping: visit our Trust shop at Hawkshead, only 50 yards from the Gallery, or shop online (www.shop.nationaltrust.org.uk/beatrixpotter). Enjoy the meals and refreshments available in Hawkshead village (not National Trust).

Making the most of your day: visit Hill Top House to find out more about the amazing life of Beatrix Potter.

Access for all: 🅿️♿🚐📷 ∷ 🔄 Building ♿

Getting here: 96:SD352982. In Main Street, Hawkshead village, next to Red Lion pub.
Bus: Stagecoach in Cumbria 505 Windermere 🚆 to Coniston. Cross Lakes Shuttle from Bowness to Hawkshead. **Train**: Windermere 6½ miles via ferry. **Road**: B5286 from Ambleside (4 miles); B5285 from Coniston (5 miles). **Parking**: 300 yards (pay and display), not National Trust.

You may also enjoy: Hill Top House, Townend, *Gondola*, Wordsworth House, or a walk around Tarn Hows, Coniston.

Beatrix Potter Gallery, Cumbria: once the office of Potter's husband William Heelis

Finding out more: 015394 36355. 015394 36471 (shop) or beatrixpottergallery@nationaltrust.org.uk

Beatrix Potter Gallery		M	T	W	T	F	S	S
Gallery								
12 Feb–31 Mar	11–3:30	M	T	W	T	.	S	S
2 Apr–26 May	11–5	M	T	W	T	.	S	S
28 May–1 Sep	10:30–5	M	T	W	T	.	S	S
3 Sep–30 Oct	11–5	M	T	W	T	.	S	S
Shop								
12 Feb–1 Apr	10–4	M	T	W	T	F	S	S
2 Apr–30 Oct	10–5	M	T	W	T	F	S	S
2 Nov–31 Dec	10–4	.	.	W	T	F	S	S

Open 25 February, Good Friday (22 April), 3 June and 28 October. Limited number of timed tickets available daily. Shop closes at 1 on 24 and 31 December. Shop closed 25, 26 and 27 December.

Borrowdale

near Keswick, Cumbria

Map D7  1902

Spectacular landscape around Derwentwater, where the Trust cares for much of the valley, including Derwentwater – its island and Georgian Manor, Watendlath hamlet, Bowder Stone, Friar's Crag, Ashness Bridge and Castlerigg Stone Circle. Explore Brandelhow Park, the first piece of the Lake District to be safeguarded from development by the Trust.

Exploring
— Amble from Keswick to Friar's Crag for breathtaking views.
— Float in a boat across Derwentwater, then walk up Catbells.
— Wander at Watendlath, location of Walpole's *Herries Chronicles*.
— Explore the mined landscape of the Coledale Valley.

Eating and shopping: visit our lakeside shop for inspired local souvenirs. Enjoy refreshment at one of the Trust tenant cafés: Rosthwaite, Watendlath, Seathwaite, Stonethwaite. Taste local Herdwick lamb at the Flock Inn, Rosthwaite, or purchase free-range eggs at Ashness or Stonethwaite farm.

Rowing and fishing on Derwentwater, Cumbria

Making the most of your day: tours and events throughout the season. Family Discovery Days on Derwent Island five times a year, unique opportunity to meet those who live on and care for this fascinating island. **Dogs**: grazing livestock, so please keep your dogs under close control (particularly at lambing time).

Access for all: 🚾 Grounds ♿

Getting here: 90:NY250160. **Cycle**: NCN71 (C2C). **Ferry**: Keswick Launch Company boat service to various National Trust sites around Derwentwater, 017687 72263. **Bus**: to information centre: Stagecoach in Cumbria X4/5 Penrith ≋ to Workington, 555 Lancaster to Keswick (passing close Lancaster ≋, Kendal and Windermere). **Train**: nearest station Penrith. **Road**: B5289 runs south from Keswick along Borrowdale. **Parking**: car parks (pay and display) at Great Wood GR273214, Watendlath GR274163, Kettlewell GR266196, Bowderstone GR253167 , Rosthwaite GR257148, Seatoller GR246138, Honister GR225135. Coach parking by prior arrangement at Seatoller car park only. Limited parking at Catbells; park at Keswick and take boat or bus.

Finding out more: 017687 74649 or borrowdale@nationaltrust.org.uk. Bowe Barn, Borrowdale Road, near Keswick, Cumbria CA12 5UP

Borrowdale		M	T	W	T	F	S	S
Countryside								
Open all year		M	T	W	T	F	S	S
Shop and information centre								
19 Feb–31 Oct	10–5	M	T	W	T	F	S	S

May close later on some summer evenings.

Borrowdale: Force Crag Mine

Coledale Valley, Keswick, Cumbria

Map ⑥ D7   1979

Last mineral mine to be worked in the Lake District. Explore the processing mill and landscape with a guide. **Note**: Charges apply to members. Children over ten years only.

Access for all: Building Grounds 🦽

Getting here: NY200217. 2¾ miles west of Braithwaite near Keswick.

Finding out more: 017687 74649 or forcecragmine@nationaltrust.org.uk. Bowe Barn, Borrowdale Road, Keswick, Cumbria CA12 5UP

Borrowdale: Force Crag Mine
Entry by guided tour during open days. Contact National Trust Borrowdale for dates.

Bridge House

Rydal Road, Ambleside, Cumbria LA22 9AN

Map ⑥ D8   1926

This tiny but iconic building has 400 years of fascinating history: from an apple store to a family home.

Getting here: NY:374047. Bridge House Information Centre is located in Ambleside, adjacent to Rydal Road car park.

Finding out more: 015394 32617 or bridgehouse@nationaltrust.org.uk

Bridge House
Telephone for opening arrangements.

Buttermere and Ennerdale

near Cockermouth, Cumbria

Map ⑥ C7   1935

The beautiful lakes of Buttermere, Crummock Water and Loweswater are surrounded by dramatic high fells, in some of Lakeland's most stunning scenery. Over the fells to the south lies 'Wild Ennerdale', where the National Trust and our partners are working to allow a wilder landscape to evolve. **Note**: nearest toilet in Buttermere village.

Exploring
- Walk and picnic around all the lakes.
- Go boating: available to hire on Crummock Water and Loweswater.
- Fishing on Crummock Water, Buttermere and Loweswater by permit.
- Enjoy the extensive off-road cycling in Ennerdale.

Crummock Water in the Buttermere Valley, Cumbria

Eating and shopping: pubs and cafés in Buttermere, Loweswater and Ennerdale village.

Making the most of your day: there is a wide variety of lowland and high fell walks from Buttermere and Ennerdale Water (walking guides available from shops in Keswick and Cockermouth). **Dogs**: on leads near stock grazing.

Access for all: Grounds

Getting here: 89:NY180150. 8 miles south of Cockermouth. **Bus**: Stagecoach in Cumbria 77/77A from Keswick and Cockermouth to Buttermere; 17/22 from Whitehaven to Ennerdale, then 219F. **Parking**: at Honister Pass, Buttermere village, Lanthwaite Wood to Crummock Water (pay and display) and by Ennerdale Water (not National Trust).

Finding out more: 017687 74649 or buttermere@nationaltrust.org.uk. Bowe Barn, Borrowdale, Keswick, Cumbria CA12 5UP

Buttermere and Ennerdale	Open every day all year

Cartmel Priory Gatehouse

The Square, Cartmel, Grange-over-Sands, Cumbria LA11 6QB

Map (6) D9   1946

Interesting 14th-century gatehouse of medieval priory. **Note**: mainly in private residential use. The Great Room is open several days a year.

Access for all: ⬛🅰 Building 🔾

Getting here: 96:SD378788. In the square in village centre.

Finding out more: 01524 701178 or cartpriorygatehouse@nationaltrust.org.uk

Cartmel Priory Gatehouse	

Visit website, email or telephone the property for opening times.

Coniston and Tarn Hows

near Coniston, Cumbria

Map (6) D8    1930

Coniston covers a large area of some of the Lake District's most scenic woodland, water and fells. One of many lovely places is the iconic Tarn Hows beauty spot, with its magnificent mountain views. The readily accessible Blea Tarn in Little Langdale also has superb views and fine walking.

Exploring
- Explore the Norse settlement site at Fell Foot.
- Visit Blea Tarn for spectacular views of the Langdale Pikes.
- There is access to much of Coniston Water shoreline.
- Visit the restored Monk Coniston walled garden.

Eating and shopping: ice-cream van at Tarn Hows during peak season.

Making the most of your day: superb network of paths and bridleways at Coniston. Cruise on steam-powered yacht *Gondola*, disembarking at Monk Coniston jetty for a walk through Monk Coniston grounds to Tarn Hows. **Dogs**: on leads (stock grazing).

Access for all: 🅿 🚽 Grounds 🔾 ➡

Getting here: OL7:SD326995. Tarn Hows 2 miles north-east of Coniston. OL6:SD295 043, Blea Tarn in Little Langdale, 5 miles north of Coniston. **Bus**: Stagecoach in Cumbria 505 'Coniston Rambler' Windermere to Coniston. Cross Lakes Experience to Hawkshead. **Parking**: pay and display, at Tarn Hows OL7:326995, Glen Mary OL7:321998 and Blea Tarn OL6:295043. Not suitable for coaches.

Finding out more: 015394 41456 or coniston@nationaltrust.org.uk. Boon Crag, Coniston, Cumbria LA21 8AQ

Coniston and Tarn Hows	Open every day all year

Dunham Massey, Cheshire, offers stunning grounds and salacious scandals

Dalton Castle

Market Place, Dalton-in-Furness,
Cumbria LA15 8AX

Map (6) D9   1965

14th-century tower built to assert the authority
of the Abbot of Furness Abbey. **Note**: opened
on behalf of the National Trust by the Friends
of Dalton Castle.

Access for all: [icons] **Building** [icon]

Getting here: 96:SD226739. In market place at
top of main street of Dalton.

Finding out more: 01524 701178 or
daltoncastle@nationaltrust.org.uk

Dalton Castle
Visit the website, email or telephone the property for
opening times.

Dunham Massey

Altrincham, Cheshire WA14 4SJ

Map (5) D8    1976

'**Absolutely brilliant! We can beat you at
cricket but we have nothing like Dunham.
It made our holiday.**'
Tim Lovegrove, Perth, Australia

Set in a magnificent 121-hectare (300-acre)
deer park, this Georgian house tells the story
of the owners and the servants who lived here.
Discover the salacious scandals of the 7th Earl
of Stamford, who married Catherine Cocks, a
former bare-back circus rider, and the 2nd Earl
of Warrington, who was so enamoured with
his wife that he wrote a book anonymously on
the desirability of divorce! Uncover these and
other fascinating stories when you explore
this treasure-packed house, then take a stroll

in one of the North's great gardens, including Britain's largest winter garden. **Note**: visitors (including members) require a white entry ticket – available from visitor reception.

Exploring
– Britain's largest and best winter garden awaits you.
– Truly now a garden for all seasons.
– Play our piano or Edwardian games in the Gallery.
– Enjoy a game of croquet on a summer's afternoon.
– Wine coolers to potties – the Trust's greatest silver collection.
– House, park and garden tours available at no extra charge.

Eating and shopping: go local. Sample a beer from the award-winning brewery or honey from our own hives. Spring, summer, autumn or winter – our menu reflects the season. Something for every budget in our shop.

Making the most of your day: year-round events programme for all the family, including Boredom Busters during school holidays. Free children's quizzes/trails. Extensive picnic lawns. Walks leaflet. Cycling for under fives. **Dogs**: welcome on leads in deer park and walks around the estate.

Access for all: 🅿️🐕♿🚻👶🔊📷🖼️📹♿
:·🅰️ House 🔊♿♿ Restaurant 🔊♿♿
Park and garden 🔊➡️♿♿

Getting here: 109:SJ735874. **Foot**: close to Trans-Pennine Trail and Bridgewater Canal. **Cycle**: NCN62, 1 mile. **Bus**: Warrington Coachways 38 Altrincham Interchange ⭐ to Warrington; Warrington Borough Transport 5. **Train**: Altrincham 3 miles; Hale 3 miles. **Road**: 3 miles south-west of Altrincham off A56: M6 exit 19; M56 exit 7. **Sat Nav**: coaches please avoid Sat Nav route – low bridge. **Parking**: 200 yards approximately. March to November shuttle buggy service operates most days between car park and visitor facilities.

You may also enjoy: Europe's most powerful working waterwheel, at the awe-inspiring Quarry Bank Mill.

Finding out more: 0161 941 1025 or dunhammassey@nationaltrust.org.uk

Dunham Massey		M	T	W	T	F	S	S
House*								
26 Feb–30 Oct	11–5	M	T	W	.	.	S	S
Garden*								
1 Jan–25 Feb	11–4	M	T	W	T	F	S	S
26 Feb–30 Oct	11–5:30	M	T	W	T	F	S	S
31 Oct–31 Dec	11–4	M	T	W	T	F	S	S
Restaurant and shop								
1 Jan–25 Feb	10:30–4	M	T	W	T	F	S	S
26 Feb–30 Oct	10:30–5	M	T	W	T	F	S	S
31 Oct–31 Dec	10:30–4	M	T	W	T	F	S	S
Park*								
Open all year	9–5	M	T	W	T	F	S	S
Mill								
26 Feb–30 Oct	12–4	M	T	W	.	.	S	S
White Cottage****								
27 Feb–30 Oct	2–5	.	.	.	.	.	.	S

*11 to 12 visit to house by guided taster tour only (restricted numbers, allocated upon arrival). Open Good Friday. **Winter closure at 4 or dusk if earlier. *** March to October gates remain open until 7:30. Property closed 23 November for staff training and 25 December (including park). ****Open last Sunday of the month only – all visits must be booked by email or on 0161 928 0075.

Fell Foot Park

Newby Bridge, Windermere, Cumbria LA12 8NN

Map ⑥ D9   🏠🌳♿🔔🍴 1948

The views of Lake Windermere beyond the park are breathtaking. The Victorian lawns and garden sweep away to fine picnic areas and lakeshore. Enjoy a lunch on the boathouse patio, where you can enjoy watching the boats and soaking in the atmosphere. Bring your own boat to explore the lake. **Note**: launching and slipway facilities available for a wide variety of craft.

Exploring
– Hire a rowing boat for a couple of hours.
– Stroll around the grounds and enjoy the magnificent views.
– Let the children loose on our adventure playground.

Eating and shopping: savour our hearty, warming soup, made with fresh seasonal ingredients. We use local Cumbrian produce to create great Cumbrian food. A delicious picnic in the park – what could be better!

Making the most of your day: rowing boats available for hire April to October (weather permitting). **Dogs**: on leads welcome.

Access for all: ⟦Pᵈ⟧⟦Dᵈ⟧⟦👥⟧⟦wc⟧⟦🚻⟧ Grounds ⟦♿⟧

Lake Windermere by Fell Foot Park, Cumbria

Getting here: 96/97:SD381869. **Ferry**: seasonal ferry links Fell Foot to Lakeside (southern terminus of main Windermere cruise ferries). **Bus**: Travellers Choice 618 Ambleside to Barrow-in-Furness (connections from Windermere ≋). **Train**: Grange-over-Sands 6 miles; Windermere 8 miles. **Road**: at the southern tip of Lake Windermere, entrance from A592. **Parking**: admission charge includes car parking. Parking charges for non-members apply. Coach access difficult (booking essential).

Finding out more: 015395 31273 or fellfootpark@nationaltrust.org.uk

Fell Foot Park		M	T	W	T	F	S	S
Park								
1 Jan–31 Dec	Dawn–dusk	M	T	W	T	F	S	S
Catering facilities								
12 Feb–1 Apr	11–3	M	T	W	T	F	S	S
2 Apr–31 Oct	10–4	M	T	W	T	F	S	S

During advertised events, later closing. Facilities (such as rowing boat hire): 3 April to 31 October, daily, 11 to 4 (last boat must be returned by 4:30). Weather permitting.

Formby

near Freshfield, Liverpool

Map ⑤ B7   ⟦🏛⟧⟦🏖⟧⟦🏞⟧⟦🐾⟧ ⟦1967⟧

This ever-changing sandy coastline set between the sea and Formby town offers miles of walks through the woods and dunes. Glimpse a rare red squirrel or see a historic landscape levelled for asparagus. Prehistoric animal and human footprints can sometimes be found in silt beds on the shoreline. **Note**: toilets close at 5:30 in summer, 4 in winter.

Exploring
– Enjoy a bracing walk on the sandy beaches.
– Explore Formby's historic asparagus landscape.
– Follow the fascinating Formby Point audio guide trail.
– Search for secretive red squirrels in the pine woods.

Eating and shopping: refresh yourself with ice-creams, soft drinks and coffee from mobile van.

Making the most of your day: guided walks and awareness days. Circular walks and longer walks linked to the Sefton Coastal Path. Formby Point audio guide trail. **Dogs**: under close control (vulnerable wildlife).

Access for all: ⟦Pᵈ⟧⟦wc⟧⟦🚻⟧⟦•• ⟧⟦⌖⟧
Accessible toilet ⟦♿⟧ Grounds ⟦♿⟧⟦▶⟧

Getting here: 108:SD275080. **Foot**: Sefton Coastal Footpath traverses the property. **Cycle**: NCN62, 3 miles. **Train**: Freshfield 1 mile. **Road**: 15 miles north of Liverpool, 2 miles west of Formby, 2 miles off A565. 6 miles south of Southport. Follow brown signs from roundabout at north end of Formby bypass. **Sat Nav**: entrance at grid reference SD281082: use postcode L37 1LJ. **Parking**: cars £4.50, minibuses £10, coaches £25 (booking essential for coaches). Dune car park closes 5.30, April to October and 4, November to March. Width restriction 3 yards.

Enjoying a walk on Formby Beach, Liverpool

Finding out more: 01704 878591 or formby@nationaltrust.org.uk. Victoria Road, Freshfield, Formby, Liverpool L37 1LJ

Formby		M	T	W	T	F	S	S
1 Jan–27 Mar	9–4	M	T	W	T	F	S	S
28 Mar–30 Oct	9–5:30	M	T	W	T	F	S	S
31 Oct–31 Dec	9–4	M	T	W	T	F	S	S

Closed 25 December. Car parks may be very full in peak season, with long queues. Group bookings: 01704 874949.

Gawthorpe Hall

Burnley Road, Padiham, near Burnley, Lancashire BB12 8UA

Map (5) D6   1972

This imposing house, set in tranquil grounds, resembles the great Hardwick Hall. In the 19th century Sir Charles Barry created the opulent interiors we see today. Several rooms display part of an international collection of needlework, lace and costume. The wooded park offers wonderful walks. **Note**: financed and run in partnership with Lancashire County Council.

Exploring
- Admire the fantastic interiors and furniture in the house.
- Enjoy displays from the nationally important textile collection.
- Observe treecreepers and woodpeckers in the woods.
- Explore the woodland and pond.

Eating and shopping: enjoy light snacks in the tea-room after your walk.

Making the most of your day: events throughout the year, including motorcycle show in June and open-air theatre in July. **Dogs**: under close control in grounds only.

Access for all: 🅿♿🚻♿📖📷♿
Building 🔲 Grounds 🔲

Getting here: 103:SD806340. **Foot**: via driveway from Burnley Road. **Bus**: frequent Transdev Lancashire United and Burnley and Pendle buses from Burnley bus station. **Train**: Rose Grove 2 miles. Also Burnley Barracks and Burnley Manchester Road stations, nearby bus links. **Road**: on east outskirts of Padiham; ¾-mile drive to house on north of A671; M65 exit 8 towards Clitheroe, then signposted from second traffic light junction to Padiham. **Parking**: 150 yards (places limited). Tight access and turning.

Finding out more: 01282 771004 or gawthorpehall@nationaltrust.org.uk

Gawthorpe Hall		M	T	W	T	F	S	S
House								
2 Apr–30 Oct	1–5	·	T	W	T	·	S	S
Tea-room								
2 Apr–30 Oct	12:30–4:30	·	T	W	T	·	S	S
Grounds								
Open all year	10–6	M	T	W	T	F	S	S

Open Bank Holidays and Good Friday. Opening times and prices are controlled by Lancashire County Council and subject to change.

The south front of Gawthorpe Hall, Lancashire

'Gondola'

Coniston Pier, Lake Road, Coniston,
Cumbria LA21 8AN

Map (6) D8   [icons] 1980

'A ride on the "Gondola" was like going out
with friends who were so proud of their boat.'
Mrs Lockwood, Nottinghamshire

The original Victorian *Gondola* was first
launched in 1859 and now, completely rebuilt
by the National Trust, gives passengers the
chance to sail in her sumptuous, upholstered
saloons. This is the perfect way to view
Coniston's spectacular scenery. Sail to Monk
Coniston jetty at the north of the lake, then
walk through the Monk Coniston garden on to
Tarn Hows. Circular walk four miles.
All sailings are subject to weather conditions.
Note: charge (including members). No toilet.

Exploring   – Explorer cruises – hear about
Coniston's
famous connections!
– For a grand Victorian
day out, disembark at
Brantwood House.
– Enjoy *Swallows and Amazons*-
type adventure.
– Combine your cruise with a
circular walk to Tarn Hows.

Eating and shopping: local, freshly prepared
food at the Bluebird Café, Coniston Pier.
Disembark at Brantwood jetty for Jumping
Jenny's tea-room. Catering provided for private
hires. *Gondola* souvenirs available on board.

Making the most of your day: look out for
cruises and guided walks, evening Campbell
and *Bluebird* talks and more. **Dogs**: in outside
areas only.

Access for all: [icons] Gangway [icons]

Getting here: 96:SD307970. Sails from
Coniston Pier (½ mile from Coniston village).
Bus: Stagecoach in Cumbria 505 from
Windermere ➡. **Train**: Foxfield, not Sunday,
10 miles; Windermere 10 miles via vehicle ferry.

The elegant 'Gondola' on Coniston Water, Cumbria

Road: A593 from Ambleside. Pier is at end of
Lake Road, turn immediately left after petrol
station if travelling south from centre of
Coniston village. **Parking**: 50 yards, pay and
display, at Coniston Pier (not National Trust).

You may also enjoy: Hill Top, Beatrix Potter
Gallery and Townend.

Finding out more: 015394 41288 or
gondola@nationaltrust.org.uk. Low
Wray Campsite, Low Wray, Ambleside,
Cumbria LA22 0JA

'Gondola'		M	T	W	T	F	S	S
1 Apr–30 Oct	Times vary	**M**	**T**	**W**	**T**	**F**	**S**	**S**

For sailing timetable and fares, visit www.nationaltrust.org.
uk/gondola or telephone 015394 41288. We reserve the right
to cancel sailings and charters in the event of high winds. In
the event of cancellation due to adverse weather conditions,
private charters or unforeseen operational difficulties,
every reasonable effort will be made to inform the public.
Piers at Coniston, Monk Coniston, Parkamoor and
Brantwood (not National Trust).

Grasmere and Great Langdale

near Ambleside, Cumbria

Map (6) D8  1925

The iconic Langdale Pikes stand majestic in the landscape. The Trust owns most of the valley farms, Trust campsite, the glaciated valley of Mickleden, a Victorian garden at High Close and the dramatic Dungeon Ghyll. In and around Grasmere the Trust owns the lake bed and parts of Rydal Water.

Exploring
- A wonderful opportunity to walk up to the Langdale Pikes.
- Wide range of low-level circular routes in both valleys.
- Breathtaking scenery.
- Old Dungeon Ghyll is a popular area for rock climbing.

Eating and shopping: the Old Dungeon Ghyll hotel at head of Great Langdale. Numerous cafés, restaurants and hotels in Grasmere.

Making the most of your day: annual Langdale Gala (usually held in July), and Grasmere Lakeland Sports and Show (August Bank Holiday). All non-National Trust events. **Dogs**: allowed under close control.

Access for all: [P][WC] Grounds [access icon]

Getting here: 89/90:NY290060. Great Langdale valley starts 4 miles west of Ambleside. Grasmere is 4 miles to the north of Ambleside. **Foot**: Coast to Coast footpath runs through both valleys. There is also a network of footpaths which runs through both valleys. **Cycle**: NCN37, then links from Skelwith Bridge to Elterwater. NCN6 is planned to come to Grasmere. **Bus**: to Grasmere village: Stagecoach in Cumbria 555/6, 599 from Windermere ≥. To Langdale Campsite: Stagecoach in Cumbria 516 from Ambleside. **Train**: Windermere 8 miles. **Road**: junction 36 M6. A591 to Ambleside. A591 continues to Grasmere. A593 to Skelwith Bridge, then B543 to Great Langdale.

Parking: three National Trust car parks in the Langdale valley. Three non-National Trust car parks in Grasmere village (pay and display).

Finding out more: 015394 63823 or grasmere@nationaltrust.org.uk. Central and East Lakes Property Office, The Annex, The Hollens, Grasmere, Cumbria LA22 9QZ

Grasmere and Great Langdale	Open every day all year

The Hardmans' House

59 Rodney Street, Liverpool, Merseyside L1 9EX

Map (5) B8 2003

Step back in time and experience the 1950s. In this time capsule of post-war years, you will glimpse the life of an extraordinary couple. Renowned photographer E. Chambré Hardman and his gifted wife Margaret lived and worked together in this remarkable Georgian house for 40 years, keeping everything, changing nothing. **Note**: admission by guided tour – booking not required but advised to avoid disappointment.

Exploring
- Spot the unopened food rations and admire glamorous period clothing.
- Listen to the reminiscences of former members of staff.
- Enjoy evocative original photographs taken by this talented couple.
- Explore Liverpool through the lens of a remarkable photographic partnership.

Eating and shopping: unique photographic prints and postcards available from our shop, along with property guidebooks.

Making the most of your day: book your place on a tour in advance to avoid disappointment. Virtual tour of the house available. Children's quiz trail. Series of evening talks planned, contact property for details.

Access for all: [P][D][WC][icons] Building [access icons]

A photograph of the wedding of Edward Chambré Hardman and Margaret Mills

Hare Hill

Over Alderley, Macclesfield, Cheshire SK10 4QB

Map ⑤ D8   ❖ ♣ 1978

This tranquil woodland garden, especially spectacular in early summer, includes more than 70 varieties of rhododendrons, plus azaleas, hollies and hostas. At its heart is a delightful walled area, with a pergola and wire sculptures. The surrounding parkland has an attractive permitted path to nearby Alderley Edge. **Note**: car park closes at 5.

Exploring
– Walk through landscaped parkland to Alderley Edge.
– Bring your binoculars and spot the prolific birdlife.
– Relax in the beautiful setting of the walled garden.

Making the most of your day: enjoy glorious walks. **Dogs**: under close control on the estate only.

Access for all: 🚹 👓 📷 Grounds 🦽 🚻

Getting here: 108:SJ355895. ¾ mile north of Liverpool city centre. Rodney Street is off Hardman Street and Upper Duke Street. Follow fingerposts '59 Rodney Street'. Visitor entrance on Pilgrim Street. **Bus**: frequent Arriva services from surrounding area. **Train**: Liverpool Lime Street ½ mile. **Parking**: no onsite parking. Offsite parking most days at Anglican Cathedral (pay and display). Slater Street NCP.

Finding out more: 0151 709 6261 or thehardmanshouse@nationaltrust.org.uk

The Hardmans' House		M	T	W	T	F	S	S
16 Mar–30 Oct	11–3:30			W	T	F	S	S

Open Bank Holiday Mondays. Admission by timed ticket only, including members. Visitors are advised to book in advance (by telephone or email to property) to avoid disappointment, as tickets on the day are subject to availability.

Getting here: 118:SJ873763. **Train**: Alderley Edge 2½ miles; Prestbury 2½ miles. **Road**: between Alderley Edge and Macclesfield (B5087). Turn off north on to Prestbury Road. Left at T junction after 200 yards, continue ¾ mile, entrance on left. From Prestbury take Chelford Road 1½ miles, entrance on right. **Parking**: not suitable for coaches.

Finding out more: 01625 584412 or harehill@nationaltrust.org.uk

Hare Hill		M	T	W	T	F	S	S
2 Apr–1 May	10–5			W	T		S	S
2 May–29 May	10–5	M	T	W	T	F	S	S
1 Jun–27 Oct	10–5			W	T		S	S

Open Bank Holiday Mondays and Good Friday.
Last admission one hour before closing.

Hawkshead and Claife

near Hawkshead, Cumbria

Map (6) D8 1929

Hawkshead village, home to the Beatrix Potter Gallery, is surrounded by beautiful countryside, which includes Windermere lakeshore. North of the village is the 15th-century Courthouse, all that remains of the estate once held by Furness Abbey. The grounds of Wray Castle are open all year for you to explore.

Exploring
- Enjoy wonderful low-level walks with great views.
- Discover amazing historical buildings in countryside settings.
- Leave the car behind – visit by boat, bus and boot.
- Visit website to download local walks and for event details.

Eating and shopping: there are plenty of catering options and shopping opportunities available in Hawkshead village, including the Hawkshead National Trust gift shop. Visit our internet shop at www.shop.nationaltrust.org.uk/beatrixpotter.

Making the most of your day: experience the wonderful countryside that inspired Beatrix Potter; why not visit Hawkshead and the gallery there? National Trust campsite on lakeshore at Low Wray (90:NY372012). Visit website for details. **Dogs**: allowed in countryside, under close control. Assistance dogs only on guided walks and tours.

Access for all: 🅰️

Getting here: 96/97:SD352982. Hawkshead is 6 miles south-west of Ambleside.
Foot: off-road path from Windermere ferry to Sawrey; many footpaths in the area.
Ferry: Windermere car ferry; also passenger ferry from Bowness. **Bus**: Stagecoach in Cumbria 505 Windermere ⊟ to Coniston.
Train: Windermere 6 miles via vehicle ferry.
Parking: pay and display parking at Ash Landing (close to ferry) and Harrowslack; free car park at Red Nab. All close to Lake Windermere. Car parks (not National Trust) in Hawkshead village (pay and display).

Finding out more: 015394 41456 or hawkshead@nationaltrust.org.uk. Boon Crag, Coniston, Cumbria LA21 8AQ

Hawkshead and Claife		M	T	W	T	F	S	S
Countryside								
Open all year		M	T	W	T	F	S	S
Courthouse								
2 Apr–30 Oct	11–4	M	T	W	T	F	S	S

Hawkshead Courthouse: access by key from the National Trust shop, The Square, Hawkshead, or the Beatrix Potter Gallery ticket office in Hawkshead. Free admission but no parking facilities. Many steps with handrail to entrance. ½-mile walk approximately from the village.

The village of Hawkshead in the Lake District, where Beatrix Potter acquired farms and cottages

Hill Top

Near Sawrey, Hawkshead, Ambleside,
Cumbria LA22 OLF

Map (6) D8 1944

Enjoy the tale of Beatrix Potter – Hill Top is a time capsule of this amazing woman's life. Full of her favourite things, the house appears as if Beatrix had just stepped out for a walk. Every room contains a reference to a picture in a 'tale'. The lovely cottage garden is a haphazard mix of flowers, herbs, fruit and vegetables. Hill Top is a small house and a timed-ticket system is in operation to avoid overcrowding and to protect the interior. Hill Top can be very busy and visitors may sometimes have to wait to enter the house. **Note**: tickets cannot be booked and **early sell-outs** are possible, especially during school holiday periods.

Exploring
- Don't miss the children's garden trail (during holiday periods).
- Explore a traditional English country garden, throughout the seasons.
- Enjoy the views which inspired Beatrix's tales and illustrations.
- See website for details of Beatrix Potter walks and events.
- Leave the car behind and use boat, bus and boot.
- Downloadable local walks available from website.

Eating and shopping: visit our internet shop www.shop.nationaltrust.org.uk/beatrixpotter or use our mail-order service, contact hilltop.shop@nationaltrust.org.uk or 01539 436801. Treats available in the shop. Sawrey House Hotel and Tower Bank Arms serve meals and refreshments.

Making the most of your day: leave the car behind and visit us by boat, bus, boot or bike – see 'Windermere Cross Lakes Experience' website (not National Trust); include a visit to the Beatrix Potter Gallery.

Hill Top, Cumbria: Beatrix Potter's house

Access for all: 🕵️ 💻 ♿ •• 📷 **Building** ♿ ♿
Garden ♿ ➡️

Getting here: 96/97:SD370955. 2 miles south of Hawkshead, in Near Sawrey hamlet; 3 miles from Bowness via ferry. **Foot**: off-road path from ferry (2 miles), marked. **Bus**: Cross Lakes Experience from Bowness Pier 3 across Lake Windermere on to Stagecoach in Cumbria 525; also 505 from Windermere 🚉 changing at Hawkshead (April to September only, plus weekends in October). Telephone 01539 445161 for complete ferry and bus timetable. **Train**: Windermere 4½ miles via vehicle ferry. **Road**: B5286 and B5285 from Ambleside (6 miles), B5285 from Coniston (7 miles). **Parking**: limited car parking.

You may also enjoy: the Beatrix Potter Gallery, Townend and Wordsworth House, or a walk around Tarn Hows, Coniston.

Finding out more: 015394 36269 or hilltop@nationaltrust.org.uk

Hill Top		M	T	W	T	F	S	S
House								
12 Feb–31 Mar	10:30–3:30	M	T	W	T	.	S	S
2 Apr–26 May	10:30–4:30	M	T	W	T	.	S	S
28 May–1 Sep	10–5	M	T	W	T	.	S	S
3 Sep–30 Oct	10:30–4:30	M	T	W	T	.	S	S
Shop and garden								
12 Feb–1 Apr	10:15–4	M	T	W	T	F	S	S
2 Apr–27 May	10–5	M	T	W	T	F	S	S
28 May–2 Sep	9:45–5:30	M	T	W	T	F	S	S
3 Sep–30 Oct	10–5	M	T	W	T	F	S	S
31 Oct–23 Dec	10–4	M	T	W	T	F	S	S

House open Good Friday and also Fridays 25 February, 3 June and 28 October. Limited number of timed tickets available daily, early sell-outs possible. Small car park. Access to garden and shop free during opening hours. Shop closes 4 on 23 December.

Little Moreton Hall

Congleton, Cheshire CW12 4SD

Map ⑤ D9   1938

Gaze at the drunkenly reeling South Range, cross the moat and marvel at the cobbled courtyard before you enter a Hall full of surprises. The skill of the craftsmen fascinates as you climb the stairs to the Long Gallery – imagine life here in Tudor times. The various delights of this unique property include some remarkable wall-paintings and a pretty Knot Garden. Colourful tales of both the Moreton family and this iconic building are revealed to you by our tour guides. Delicious home-baked local food and a visit to the shop complete your day.

Exploring
- Learn about the fascinating history on a free guided tour.
- Soak up the atmosphere in the Great Hall.
- Enjoy the Knot Garden and relax in the tranquil orchard.
- Experience a Tudor Yuletide during December.
- Discover the writing on the walls of the chancel.
- Follow the discovery trail on our short estate walk.

Eating and shopping: delicious home-cooked food in the Brewhouse Restaurant. Sample puddings, cakes and scones baked in our kitchen. Treat yourself to a souvenir from our friendly, welcoming shop. Our shop and restaurant are pleased to support local producers.

Making the most of your day: regular living history and musical events bring the Hall to life. Short talks (Bank Holidays) offer a quick historical insight. Exhibitions, displays, open-air theatre, family activities throughout year. Yuletide celebrations. **Dogs**: on leads in car park and estate walk only.

Access for all: 🅿️ 🄳 🔧 🚻 ⬆️ 🏠 📷 🎒 💻 [VT] 🎫
⬤⬤ 📶 Building ♿ 👨‍🦽 👨‍🦽 Grounds ♿ 👨‍🦽 ➡️

Getting here: 118:SJ832589. **Bus**: infrequent service. Stanways 315 Alsager 🚋 to Congleton (passing close Kidsgrove 🚆). **Train**: Kidsgrove 3 miles; Congleton 4½ miles. **Road**: 4 miles south-west of Congleton, on east side of A34. From M6 exit 17 follow signs for Congleton and join A34 southbound (signed Newcastle) from Congleton. **Parking**: 100 yards.

You may also enjoy: Hare Hill Garden and Biddulph Grange Garden – both within a short drive.

Finding out more: 01260 272018 or littlemoretonhall@nationaltrust.org.uk

Little Moreton Hall		M	T	W	T	F	S	S
26 Feb–13 Mar	11–4						S	S
16 Mar–30 Oct	11–5			W	T	F	S	S
5 Nov–18 Dec	11–4						S	S

Open Bank Holiday Mondays. Closes dusk if earlier. Access during Yuletide celebrations restricted to ground floor, garden, shop and restaurant. Special openings at other times for booked groups.

The exquisite Little Moreton Hall, Cheshire

Lyme Park

Disley, Stockport, Cheshire SK12 2NR

Map ⑤ E8 🏛🏚✝♣♠♨ 🏠▲🔔🍸 1947

'**Spectacular, I love it here. Beautiful day, beautiful everything. Would love to come back!'**
Carla Unkefer, Louisville, Ohio

On the edge of the Peak District, nestling within sweeping moorland, Lyme Park is a magnificent estate. Its wild remoteness and powerful beauty contrast with one of the most famous country-house images in England – the backdrop to where Darcy meets Elizabeth in *Pride and Prejudice*. Discover a colourful family history – from rescuing the Black Prince, sailing into exile with the Duke of Windsor, to the writing of the hit series *Upstairs Downstairs*. Enjoy hearing visitors play the piano as you discover impressive tapestries, clocks and beautifully furnished rooms, or escape to the park and feel miles from anywhere. **Note**: owned and managed by the National Trust but partly financed by Stockport Metropolitan Borough Council.

Exploring
- Welcome CD to listen to as you drive to house.
- Stroll among luxurious borders and sweeping lawns.
- Relax and take a seat in the restored library.
- Let off steam in Crow Wood playscape.
- Play with the toys in the nursery bedroom.
- Enjoy the new exhibition.

Eating and shopping: try a seasonal special in the restaurant or treat yourself to afternoon tea. Why not grow your own souvenir from the plant shop or browse in our well-stocked bookshop?

Making the most of your day: programme of events all year. School holiday and family activities. Family quizzes in house and garden. Walk leaflets available for park.

An autumnal view of Lyme Park in Cheshire

Dogs: under close control and in park only (on leads in some areas).

Access for all: 🅿♿🚽♿♿🔍📷📹👓🅰
Building ♿♿ Grounds 🚶

Getting here: 109:SJ965825. **Foot**: at the northern end of Gritstone Trail; paths to Macclesfield Canal, Poynton Marina 1 mile and Peak Forest Canal 2½ miles. **Bus**: TrentBarton 199 Buxton to Manchester Airport, to park entrance. **Train**: Disley, ½ mile from park entrance. National Trust courtesy shuttle service from park admission kiosk to house for pedestrians on days house is open.

Road: entrance on A6, 6½ miles south-east of Stockport (M60 exit 1), 12 miles north-west of Buxton (house and car park 1 mile from entrance). **Parking**: coaches £20 unless bringing booked groups to house and garden.

You may also enjoy: Little Moreton Hall.

Finding out more: 01663 762023 or lymepark@nationaltrust.org.uk

Lyme Park		M	T	W	T	F	S	S
House, garden and Mary Queen of Scots exhibition								
26 Feb–30 Oct	11*–5	M	T	.	.	F	S	S
Garden and Beatrix Potter exhibition								
5 Nov–31 Dec	11–3	.	.	.	.	.	S	S
Restaurant and shop								
26 Feb–30 Oct	11–5	M	T	.	.	F	S	S
3 Dec–17 Dec	11–4	.	.	.	.	.	S	S
Park								
Open all year	8–6	M	T	W	T	F	S	S
Timber Yard plant sales and shop								
1 Jan–20 Feb	11–4	.	.	.	.	.	S	S
26 Feb–30 Oct	10:30–5	M	T	W	T	F	S	S
Timber Yard coffee shop								
Open all year	11–4	M	T	W	T	F	S	S

*Between 11 and 12 entry to house is by guided tour only (numbers restricted). Closed 25 December.

Nether Alderley Mill

Congleton Road, Nether Alderley, Macclesfield, Cheshire SK10 4TW

Map (5) D8 1950

This charming rustic mill is one of only four virtually complete corn mills in Cheshire. **Note**: only open for booked groups. No toilet.

Access for all: Building [♿]

Getting here: 118:SJ844763. 1½ miles south of Alderley Edge, on east side of A34.

Finding out more: 01625 445853 or netheralderleymill@nationaltrust.org.uk

Nether Alderley Mill
Open for group visits only by prior arrangement.

Quarry Bank Mill and Styal Estate

Styal, Wilmslow, Cheshire SK9 4LA

Map (5) D8  1939

Visit Quarry Bank at Styal and discover the compelling story of mill workers, entrepreneurs and the Industrial Revolution. Watch hand-spinners at work, experience the clatter of machinery and the hiss of steam engines, and marvel at Europe's most powerful working waterwheel. Take a guided tour of the Apprentice House, which housed the pauper children who worked in the mill.
Visit the stunning garden – the Greg family's picturesque valley retreat adjoining the mill. Stroll to Styal village, built by the Gregs to house the mill workers and still a thriving community, or walk through beech woods along the beautiful River Bollin.

Exploring
- Experience demonstrations on how cotton was processed into cloth.
- See how water power was supplemented by steam power.
- Enjoy the garden, its terraced paths, spectacular views and cave.
- See how apprentices lived and worked and visit Styal village.

Exploring Quarry Bank Mill and Styal Estate, Cheshire

Exploring – Follow a choice of family trails.
– Enjoy a family picnic near the play area.

Eating and shopping: browse in the shop for gifts, mementos and glass cloths produced in the mill. Plants for sale in the mill yard. Enjoy lunch or afternoon tea in our Mill café, and fresh coffee or delicious ice-cream from the Pantry.

Making the most of your day: programme of events and guided walks throughout the year. School holiday activities for all the family. Children's play area. Picnic facilities. Trails and Tracker Packs. Cycle route. **Dogs**: under close control on estate. On lead only in mill yard.

Access for all: P♿️🚻♿️♿️📷 VT ••🅰️
Building 🏛️🏛️♿️ Grounds ♿️➡️♿️

Getting here: 109:SJ835835. **Cycle**: NCN6, 1½ miles. RCR85 ½ mile. **Bus**: Swans Travel 200 Manchester Airport ☒ to Wilmslow. **Train**: Styal ½ mile; Manchester Airport 2 miles; Wilmslow 2½ miles. **Road**: 1½ miles north of Wilmslow off B5166, 2 miles from M56, exit 5, 10 miles south of Manchester. Heritage signs from A34 and M56. **Parking**: 200 yards. Coaches £15, unless booked.

You may also enjoy: Alderley Edge, Dunham Massey, Lyme Park, Tatton Park, Little Moreton Hall.

Finding out more: 01625 445896 (Infoline). 01625 527468 or quarrybankmill@nationaltrust.org.uk

Quarry Bank Mill and Styal Estate		M	T	W	T	F	S	S
Mill and Apprentice House								
1 Jan–11 Mar	11–3:30	·	·	W	T	F	S	S
12 Mar–30 Oct	11–5	M	T	W	T	F	S	S
2 Nov–31 Dec	11–3:30	·	·	W	T	F	S	S
Shop, café and ticket/information office								
1 Jan–11 Mar	10:30–4	·	·	W	T	F	S	S
12 Mar–30 Oct	10:30–5	M	T	W	T	F	S	S
2 Nov–31 Dec	10:30–4	·	·	W	T	F	S	S
Garden								
12 Mar–30 Oct	11–5	M	T	W	T	F	S	S

Open seven days a week in all school holiday periods. Property closed 4 to 7 January for essential maintenance and 24, 25 December. Mill: last admission one hour before closing. Apprentice House guided tours: limited availability – timed tickets only (available from Mill on early arrival). Popular school visit destination during term time, so may be busy then.

Rufford Old Hall

200 Liverpool Road, Rufford, near Ormskirk, Lancashire L40 1SG

Map ⑤ C6   🏠❄️🔔⛱️ 1936

Step back in time at one of Lancashire's finest 16th-century Tudor buildings, where a young Will Shakespeare once performed. His stage, the Great Hall, is as spectacular today as when the Bard was performing for the owner, Sir Thomas Hesketh, and his raucous guests. Wander around the house and marvel over the fine collections of furniture, arms, armour and tapestries. Then step outside and enjoy the gardens, topiary and sculpture and a walk in the woodlands, alongside the canal.

Exploring – Stand behind the giant screen, where Shakespeare made costume changes.
– Imagine the feasts that took place in the Great Hall.
– Enjoy a family picnic in the grounds.

Eating and shopping: complete your visit with delicious local food in the tea-room. Browse in the shop and our peat-free plant centre.

View of the Great Hall at Rufford Old Hall, Lancashire

The Solar Tower, which dates from the middle of the 14th century, at Sizergh Castle and Garden, Cumbria

Making the most of your day: discover fascinating facts from room guides and see conservation in action. Family events programme, outdoor and house quizzes for children. **Dogs**: on leads in grounds only, not formal gardens.

Access for all: 🅿🚻♿🔊📷🖼📶∷🄰
Building 🏠♿👶 **Grounds** ♿➡

Getting here: 108:SD462161. **Foot**: adjoins towpath of Rufford extension of Leeds to Liverpool Canal. **Bus**: J&S 347 Southport to Chorley, Stagecoach in Lancashire 2B Preston to Ormskirk, Sundays only. **Train**: Rufford, not Sunday, ½ mile; Burscough Bridge 2½ miles. **Road**: 7 miles north of Ormskirk, in village of Rufford on east side of A59. From M6 exit 27, follow signs for Parbold then Rufford. **Parking**: 10 yards. Car park can be very busy on summer days. Limited coach parking.

You may also enjoy: Elizabethan Gawthorpe Hall, with its nationally important textile collection.

Finding out more: 01704 821254 or ruffordoldhall@nationaltrust.org.uk

Rufford Old Hall		M	T	W	T	F	S	S
House, garden, shop and tea-room*								
26 Feb–6 Mar	11–4						S	S
12 Mar–30 Oct	11–5	M	T	W			S	S
Garden, shop and tea-room								
5 Nov–18 Dec	11–4						S	S

*Access to Hall may be from 1 occasionally. Open 14 to 16 February and 21 to 23 February for half-term (house closed). Also opens Thursdays during August.

Sizergh Castle and Garden

Sizergh, near Kendal, Cumbria LA8 8AE

Map ⑥ E8 🏬🏛🎐🌳🛶🍴🏠 1950

'**Excellent, well preserved and presented, very friendly staff and volunteers, excellent facilities**.'
Allison Clough, Sunderland

This imposing house, at the gateway to the Lake District, stands proud in a rich and beautiful garden, which includes a pond, lake, National Collection of Hardy Ferns and a superb limestone rock garden. Still lived in by the Strickland family, Sizergh has many tales to tell and certainly feels lived in, with centuries-old portraits and fine furniture sitting alongside modern family photographs. The exceptional wood panelling culminates in the Inlaid Chamber, returned here in 1999 from the Victoria & Albert Museum. The 647-hectare (1,600-acre) estate includes limestone pasture, orchards and ancient, semi-natural woodland.

Exploring
– Admire some of England's finest Elizabethan wood carving and panelling.
– Relax in the National Trust's largest limestone rock garden.
– See the kitchen garden, orchard and herbaceous border.

Exploring
- Follow footpaths to stunning viewpoints of Morecambe Bay/Lakeland hills.
- Visit the Strickland Arms pub and Low Sizergh farm shop.

Eating and shopping: savour local, seasonal food in our contemporary licensed café. Buy a picnic to enjoy while relaxing in the garden. Plants and local products from our shop. Sample the food at the pub and farm tea-room.

Making the most of your day: varied programme of events throughout the year. Explore the estate with a walks leaflet. Garden trail and house quizzes for children. **Dogs**: welcome in the car park and on the estate footpaths only.

Access for all: ♿🅿️ 🅳♿ ♿ 🔼 💺 📷 🖥️ ᏉᎢ 🚻
👓 🅰️ Building 🔼♿♿ Grounds 🔼▶️♿♿

Getting here: 97:SD498878. 3½ miles south of Kendal. **Foot**: footpaths 530002 and 530003 pass by Sizergh Castle. **Cycle**: NCN6, 1½ miles. RCR20 passes main gate. **Bus**: Stagecoach in Cumbria 555 Keswick to Kendal/Lancaster (passing close Lancaster ➔), 552 Kendal to Arnside (passing close Arnside ➔). All pass Kendal ➔. **Train**: Oxenholme 3 miles. **Road**: M6 exit 36 then A590 towards Kendal, take Barrow-in-Furness turning and follow brown signs. From Lake District take A591 south then A590 towards Barrow-in-Furness. **Sat Nav**: enter LA8 8DZ. **Parking**: 250 yards.

You may also enjoy: Fell Foot Park, Arnside and Silverdale, as well as Townend.

Finding out more: 015395 60951 or sizergh@nationaltrust.org.uk

Sizergh Castle and Garden		M	T	W	T	F	S	S
House								
13 Mar–30 Oct	12*–5	M	T	W	T	.	.	S
Garden								
13 Mar–30 Oct	11–5	M	T	W	T	F	S	S
31 Oct–31 Dec	11–4	M	T	W	T	F	S	S
Café and shop								
1 Feb–12 Mar	11–4	M	T	W	T	F	S	S
13 Mar–30 Oct	11–5	M	T	W	T	F	S	S
31 Oct–31 Dec	11–4	M	T	W	T	F	S	S

*Access to house, 12 to 1, by guided tour only (limited places – can be booked or taken on the day, if available). Free-flow from 1. Timed ticket system may be in operation at busy times. Café and shop closed 25 December.

Speke Hall, Garden and Estate

The Walk, Liverpool L24 1XD

Map ⑤ C8 🏠 🏘️ 🔼 💥 🐾 🔔 1944

'Guides had great knowledge and made the visit the best ever, an ideal family day out.'
Mr and Mrs Kynaston, Chester

Speke Hall is a rare example of a Tudor manor house with restored Victorian interiors and William Morris wallpaper. Situated in a most unusual setting, it is surrounded by attractive gardens protected by a collar of woodland. Constructed by a devout Catholic family, who were keen to impress visitors with their home's grandeur (the Great Hall, in particular, is spectacular), this beautiful building has witnessed more than 400 years of turbulent history. Uncover the hidden Tudor secrets, play billiards or enjoy a bracing walk with stunning views of the Welsh hills. A perfect oasis from modern life. **Note**: administered and financed by the National Trust, assisted by a grant from National Museums Liverpool.

Exploring
- Join a Victorian costumed guided tour.
- Take your cue from us – have a go at billiards.
- Explore the gardens and woodland walks.
- Children can burn off energy in the playground and maze.
- Families can discover more with our free Tracker Packs.

Eating and shopping: browse in our well-stocked shop for local gifts, products and plants. Why not use our free plant babysitting service? Relax in the Home Farm restaurant and enjoy freshly made regional specialities, such as Scouse Pie and Wet Nelly.

Making the most of your day: highlights of our year include Easter, Hallowe'en, the Christmas season, open-air theatre and themed Tudor and Victorian events. Families will enjoy our all-weather play areas and special activities.

Dogs: on leads in woodland and on signed estate walks.

Access for all:  ⬚⬚⬚⬚⬚⬚⬚⬚⬚ ⬚⬚ Hall ⬚⬚⬚⬚ Grounds ⬚⬚⬚⬚

Getting here: 108:SJ419825. 8 miles south of Liverpool City Centre on the banks of the River Mersey; follow brown road signs. Adjacent to Liverpool John Lennon Airport. **Foot**: linked to Mersey Way footpath. **Cycle**: NCN62, 1¾ miles. **Bus**: Arriva 80A, Paradise Street interchange to Liverpool Airport (passing Liverpool South Parkway ⊞) and close Liverpool Lime Street); 500 Liverpool Lime Street ⊞ to Liverpool Airport. All to within 1 mile of main gates (additional half mile walk to main reception). Additional service planned, please telephone property for details. **Train**: Liverpool South Parkway 2 miles; Hunt's Cross 2 miles. Taxi and bus services available from South Parkway. **Road**: on north bank of Mersey, adjacent to Liverpool John Lennon Airport. 1 mile off A561. Follow airport signs from M62 exit 6, A5300; M56 exit 12. **Parking**: large car park next to Home Farm visitor centre.

You may also enjoy: a tour of The Beatles' Childhood Homes and The Hardmans' House.

Finding out more: 0844 800 4799 (Infoline). 0151 427 7231 or spekehall@nationaltrust.org.uk

Speke Hall, Garden and Estate		M	T	W	T	F	S	S
House								
26 Feb–13 Mar*	11–4:30	·	·	·	·	·	S	S
16 Mar–30 Oct	11–5	·	·	W	T	F	S	S
5 Nov–11 Dec	11–4:30	·	·	·	·	·	S	S
Grounds**								
2 Jan–31 Dec	11–4:30	·	T	W	T	F	S	S
Home Farm – reception, restaurant and shop*								
26 Feb–13 Mar	11–4	·	·	·	·	·	S	S
16 Mar–24 Jul	11–5	·	·	W	T	F	S	S
26 Jul–6 Sep	11–5	·	T	W	T	F	S	S
7 Sep–30 Oct	11–5	·	·	W	T	F	S	S
5 Nov–11 Dec	11–4	·	·	·	·	·	S	S

Open Bank Holiday Mondays. *11 to 1, entry to house by guided tour only, restricted numbers, tickets issued on first-come, first-served basis (at peak times tickets for these tours may run out). Unguided viewing of the house from 1 onwards. 26 February to 13 March, some rooms still under case covers, conservation cleaning demonstrations take place during this period. **Grounds (garden and estate) closed 1 January, 24 to 26 December and 31 December. Grounds (garden and estate) open until 5:30 16 March to 30 October. *** Shop closes 30 minutes after reception.

The Library at Speke Hall in Liverpool

Stagshaw Garden

Ambleside, Cumbria LA22 0HE

Map ⑥ D8 ✿ 1957

A fine collection of shrubs, including rhododendrons, azaleas and camellias. Adjacent to the garden are Skelghyll Woods. **Note**: no toilet.

Access for all: Grounds ⬚⬚

Getting here: 90:NY380029. ½ mile south of Ambleside on A591.

Finding out more: 015394 46027 or stagshaw@nationaltrust.org.uk

Stagshaw Garden		M	T	W	T	F	S	S
1 Apr–30 Jun	10–6:30	M	T	W	T	F	S	S

July to end October: by appointment, send sae to Property Office, St Catherine's, Patterdale Road, Windermere LA23 1NH.

The Japanese garden at Tatton Park, Cheshire: just one of the delights on offer

Tatton Park

Knutsford, Cheshire WA16 6QN

Map ⑤ D8 1960

This is one of the most complete historic estates open to visitors. The early 19th-century Wyatt house sits amid a landscaped deer park and is opulently decorated, providing a fine setting for the Egerton family's collections of pictures, books, china, glass, silver and specially commissioned Gillows furniture. The theme of Victorian grandeur extends into the garden, with its Fernery, Orangery, Rose Garden, Tower Garden, Pinetum, Walled Garden with its glasshouses, Italian and Japanese gardens. Other features include a 1930s working rare breeds farm, a children's play area, speciality shops and 400-hectare (1,000-acre) deer park.

Note: managed and financed by Cheshire East Council. RHS show, Christmas and other events – supplementary charge.

Exploring
- The mansion has one of the finest Gillows furniture collections.
- A new nature trail features plants and wildlife to spot.
- The gardens contain 250 years of garden design and history.
- Explore 500 years of history at the Old Hall.
- Visit one of over 100 events held throughout the year.
- Feed rare breed animals at the 1930s working farm.

Eating and shopping: The Stables restaurant offers quality hot and cold local produce. The Housekeeper's Store sells regional produce including estate-reared meat. Hampers are tailored to include local cheeses, wine and preserves. Visit Tatton Gifts or the garden shop for historical unique gifts.

We welcome dogs assisting visitors with disabilities

Making the most of your day: visit www.tattonpark.org.uk for events. Members – free admission to house and gardens only, half-price entry to farm, car entry charge. Old Hall special openings. **Dogs**: on leads at farm and under close control in park only.

Access for all: [icons]
Building [icons] Grounds [icons]

Getting here: 109/118:SJ745815.
Cycle: Cheshire Cycleway passes property.
Bus: buses from Knutsford in high season Sundays and Bank Holiday Mondays Easter to end August; otherwise from surrounding areas to Knutsford, then 2 miles. **Train**: Knutsford 2 miles. **Road**: 2 miles north of Knutsford, 4 miles south of Altrincham, 5 miles from M6, exit 19; 3 miles from M56, exit 7, well signposted on A556; entrance on Ashley Road, 1½ miles north-east of junction A5034 with A50. **Sat Nav**: follow directional signs to Tatton Park rather than using satellite navigation systems. **Parking**: charge, including Trust members.

You may also enjoy: Lyme Park, Quarry Bank Mill or Dunham Massey.

Finding out more: 01625 374435 (Infoline). 01625 374400 or tatton@cheshireeast.gov.uk. www.tattonpark.org.uk

Tatton Park		M	T	W	T	F	S	S
Parkland								
26 Mar–2 Oct	10–7	M	T	W	T	F	S	S
Mansion								
26 Mar–2 Oct	1–5		T	W	T	F	S	S
Gardens								
26 Mar–2 Oct	10–6	M	T	W	T	F	S	S
Farm								
26 Mar–2 Oct	12–5		T	W	T	F	S	S
Shops								
26 Mar–2 Oct	10:30–5	M	T	W	T	F	S	S

Open Bank Holiday Mondays. Last admission one hour before closing. Restaurant open every day 10 to 6, except low season. Guided mansion tours Tuesday to Sunday at 12 by timed ticket (available from garden entrance after 10:30) on first-come, first-served basis, small charge including members. Old Hall special openings, telephone for details and prices. **1 January to 25 March and 3 October to 31 December: parkland open Tuesday to Sunday 11 to 5; mansion open for Christmas events and October half-term; gardens open Tuesday to Sunday 11 to 4; farm Saturday and Sunday 11 to 4. Shops and restaurant open Tuesday to Sunday 11 to 4.** Closed 25 December.

Townend

Troutbeck, Windermere, Cumbria LA23 1LB

Map (6) D8   1948

The Brownes of Townend were just an ordinary farming family, but their home and belongings bring to life more than 400 years of extraordinary stories. You will understand why Beatrix Potter described Troutbeck Valley as her favourite as you approach this traditional stone and slate farmhouse. Once inside, you are welcomed into the farmhouse kitchen, which has a real fire burning most days and a quirky collection of domestic tools. Exploring further, you can marvel at the intricately carved furniture and discover why the collection of books belonging to a farming family is of international importance.

Exploring
– Discover more about life as a Lake District farmer.
– Have a go at making a rag rug.
– Relax in the pretty cottage garden.
– Find out more on a guided tour in the mornings.
– Download a circular walk taking in Townend from our website.

Eating and shopping: look through our small selection of postcards and souvenirs. Warm up with a hot drink from our vending machine. Treat yourself to a second-hand book. Buy a plant from our selection, grown in the garden.

Visitors at Townend, Cumbria

Making the most of your day: have a go at making a rag rug or enjoy our live interpretation. Our children's trail helps to bring the house to life.

Access for all: ♿ ♿ 🖥 📷 📷 Building 🏠
Grounds 🏠♿

Getting here: 90:NY407023. 3 miles south-east of Ambleside at south end of Troutbeck village. **Bus**: Stagecoach in Cumbria 555, 599 from Windermere ▣, alight Troutbeck Bridge, 1½ miles. **Train**: Windermere 2½ miles. **Road**: off A591 or A592. **Parking**: free, 300 yards. Not suitable for coaches or campervans.

You may also enjoy: another Cumbrian farmhouse: Hill Top, Beatrix Potter's house at Near Sawrey.

Finding out more: 015394 32628 or townend@nationaltrust.org.uk

Townend		M	T	W	T	F	S	S
House tours*								
12 Mar–30 Oct	11–1		·	·	W	T	F	S	S
House								
12 Mar–30 Oct	1–5		·	·	W	T	F	S	S

*11 to 1 entry by hourly guided tour only (tours at 11 and 12), 1 to 5 free-flow. Places on guided tours are limited and available on a first-come first-served basis. Open Bank Holiday Mondays. May close early due to poor light. Please note: property less busy at weekends.

Ullswater and Aira Force

near Watermillock, Penrith, Cumbria

Map ⑥ D7   1906

Dramatic walks around Aira Force waterfall and picturesque pleasure grounds, renowned in Victorian times as a beauty spot. Beyond Aira Force there are four farms, beautiful woodlands and acres of wild fell. Wordsworth's famous daffodils can be found on the shores of the lake.

Exploring   – Enjoy the breathtaking waterfalls at Aira Force.

Looking towards Ullswater in Cumbria

Exploring   – Relax among Wordsworth's daffodils on the shore of Ullswater.
– Enjoy the new level path around Brotherswater.
– Take in stunning views from the summit of Gowbarrow.

Eating and shopping: Aira Force tea-room (not National Trust) by car park. Walk from Glenridding to Side Farm tea-room (Trust farm).

Making the most of your day: delight in the stunning scenery. **Dogs**: under close control (stock grazing).

Access for all: ♿ ♿ Grounds 🏠➡

Getting here: 90:NY401203. 7 miles south of Penrith. **Cycle**: NCN71, 2 miles. **Bus**: Stagecoach in Cumbria 108 Penrith ▣ to Patterdale. **Train**: Penrith 10 miles. **Parking**: two car parks at Aira Force and Glencoyne Bay (pay and display). Coaches must book in advance.

Finding out more: 017684 82067 or ullswater@nationaltrust.org.uk. Tower Buildings, Watermillock, Penrith, Cumbria CA11 0JS

Ullswater and Aira Force	Open every day all year

Wasdale, Eskdale and Duddon

near Wasdale, Cumbria

Map (6) C8 1929

From Scafell Pike, England's highest mountain, look down on Wastwater, England's deepest lake, with its majestic screes. The National Trust owns the valley farms, campsite, lake, surrounding mountains and the nearby Nether Wasdale Estate. Walk the delightful paths of Upper Eskdale or explore the ever-changing Duddon Valley.

Exploring
— Visit Hardknott Roman fort.
— Camp at the head of Wasdale at our Trust site.
— Admire the amazing stone walls at Wasdale Head.

Making the most of your day: explore the many paths in these spectacular valleys.
Dogs: under close control (stock grazing).

Access for all: Grounds 🏔

Getting here: NY152055. **Train**: Drigg 8 miles; Dalegarth (Ravenglass & Eskdale Railway) ¼ mile from Eskdale; Foxfield 8 miles from Duddon; Seascale 8 miles from Wasdale.
Road: Wasdale to Wastwater: 5 miles east of A595 Cumbrian coast road from Barrow to Whitehaven, turning at Gosforth. Also from Santon Bridge. Eskdale (NY177013) to Boot: 6 miles east of A595, turning at Eskdale Green. Also from Santon Bridge. Duddon (NY196932) to Ulpha: 3 miles north of A595, turning at Duddon Bridge near Broughton-in-Furness.
Parking: at Wasdale Head (pay and display).

Finding out more: 019467 26064 or wasdale@nationaltrust.org.uk. The Lodge, Wasdale Hall, Wasdale, Cumbria CA20 1ET

Wasdale, Eskdale and Duddon	Open every day all year

Windermere and Troutbeck

near Windermere, Cumbria

Map (6) D8 1927

Take a footpath from Ambleside over Wansfell to the Troutbeck Valley, admire tiny Bridge House or visit the Roman fort in Ambleside. Stroll through Cockshott Point on the lake at Bowness-on-Windermere or walk to Orrest Head, Adelaide Hill or Miller Ground, just some of our sites around Windermere.
Note: no toilet.

Exploring
— Enjoy breathtaking views from the summit of Wansfell.
— Relax by the lake on Cockshott Point.
— Visit Bridge House, Ambleside's smallest building.
— Follow in the footsteps of Romans at Galava Roman Fort.

Making the most of your day: exciting events around Windermere. Make a day of it and visit nearby Fell Foot and Townend.
Dogs: under close control (stock grazing).

Access for all: Bridge House 🏔

Getting here: 90:NY407023. **Bus**: Stagecoach in Cumbria 555/6, 599 from Windermere ≋, alight Troutbeck Bridge, then 1½ miles. **Train**: Windermere 2½ miles. **Road**: Troutbeck is signposted east of A591 Windermere to Ambleside road. **Sat Nav**: postcode directs to Property Office (not open to public).
Parking: car parks (not National Trust).

Finding out more: 015394 46027 or windermere@nationaltrust.org.uk. St Catherine's, Patterdale Road, Windermere, Cumbria LA23 1NH

Windermere and Troutbeck	Open every day all year

Wordsworth House and Garden

Main Street, Cockermouth, Cumbria CA13 9RX

Map (6) C7   🏠 ❄ 1938

Step back to the 1770s and experience life as William and his sister Dorothy might have at this beautiful, homely property. Enjoy a warm welcome from the Wordsworths' servants and find out more about the restoration of the house and garden. William's beloved garden inspired many of his poems and contains 18th-century flowers, fruit and vegetables – all used in the house. Visit the cellars, and learn about what happened to the house, garden and Cockermouth as a whole in 2009's devastating flood. The Discovery Room has fascinating research material and touchscreens, and there are daily recipe tastings and children's trails.

Exploring
- Explore our hands-on rooms with toys, costumes and books.
- Meet the servants and enjoy a gossip.
- Come along for a talk, tour or special event.
- Listen to music from the harpsichord.
- Write with quill pen and ink, or do some baking.
- Sample an 18th-century Cumberland recipe.

Eating and shopping: browse for Wordsworth and local souvenirs in our shop. Enjoyed the garden? Buy a plant to take home. Tasty local food available from the shop.

Making the most of your day: costumed servants, family activities every school holiday, talks, harpsichord music, garden tours, cooking demonstrations, original Wordsworth items, Georgian tastings and games, plus craft activities. **Dogs**: on leads in front garden only.

Access for all: 🅿️♿🚻🔆📷🏛️📺♿👁️🄰
Building ♿⬆♿ **Grounds** ♿

A maid of all work makes tea in the Georgian kitchen at Wordsworth House and Garden, Cumbria

Getting here: 89:NY118307. In the centre of Cockermouth. **Foot**: close to all town car parks and bus stop. **Cycle**: NCN71 (C2C) and NCN10 (Reivers) pass door. **Bus**: Stagecoach in Cumbria X4/5 Penrith ☒ to Workington; AA/Hoban/Reay's 35/6 Workington to Cockermouth. **Train**: Workington 8 miles; Maryport 6½ miles. **Road**: off A66, on Cockermouth Main Street. **Sat Nav**: note: entrance on Main Street, not side gate on Low Sand Lane. **Parking**: nearest parking in town centre car parks. Long stay car park signposted as coach park (not National Trust), 300 yards on Wakefield Road, walk back over footbridge to house.

You may also enjoy: beautiful Buttermere, or a walk along the Whitehaven coast.

Finding out more: 01900 820884 (Infoline). 01900 824805 or wordsworthhouse@nationaltrust.org.uk

Wordsworth House and Garden		M	T	W	T	F	S	S
House and garden								
12 Mar–30 Oct	11–5	M	T	W	T	.	S	S
Shop								
4 Jan–15 Jan	10–4	.	T	W	T	F	S	.
12 Mar–30 Oct	10–5	M	T	W	T	F	S	S
31 Oct–23 Dec	10–4:30	M	T	W	T	F	S	.

Last entry 4. Timed tickets may operate on busy days.

Yorkshire

The serpentine Half Moon Pond at Studley
Royal Water Garden twists and turns,
pointing the way towards Fountains Abbey

Map (5)

Outdoors
in Yorkshire

Famed for its moorland
heaths, Yorkshire also
boasts acres of green fields,
surrounded by drystone
walls. It is a haven for wildlife
and perfect for walkers.

The National Trust owns
land in the Yorkshire Dales,
North York Moors, Marsden
Moor and the Yorkshire
coast, including part of
the Cleveland Way. There
are also hidden gems, such
as Brimham Rocks and
Hardcastle Crags.

Below:
**Ravenscar,
as seen from
the beach at
Boggle Hole**

Discover ancient landscapes

On the North York Moors, the Bridestones is a wonderful
place to visit, with views to be enjoyed over open moorland,
woodland and sheltered valleys.

The Bridestones were formed more than 150 million years ago,
with one being affectionately named The Pepper Pot, due to its
unusual shape.

Three types of heather can be found here, and these create a
carpet of colour throughout the summer. First to bloom are
the striking magenta flowers of the bell heather in June,
together with the pale pink cross-leaved heather on the
wetter soils, leading to the finale, the soft purple haze and
honey scent of ling.

At Brimham Rocks, you'll come across more than 26 hectares
(64 acres) of fabulous rock formations, with equally imaginative
names such as The Dancing Bear, Castle Rock, The Anvil and
The Eagle. A site that is more than 320 million years old, it has
been created as a result of geological movement, ice ages and
the erosive effects of the weather. For centuries, visitors have
marvelled at the Idol Rock, which, at 200 tonnes, stands on a
plinth just 12 inches across.

The past beckons at Marsden Moor

If you love the open air and want to get out into the countryside, then take a walk on Marsden Moor. This windswept landscape appears bleak and inhospitable, but provides grazing for cattle and sheep and is home to numerous birds, such as golden plover, red grouse, curlew, snipe and the diminutive twite – in fact the estate is designated as an international Special Protection Area for birds. Footpaths across the moor sometimes follow ancient pack-horse routes, from where it is possible to glimpse evidence of the estate's industrial past.

Meadows as far as the eye can see

Centuries of farming have created a landscape in the Yorkshire Dales that is utterly stunning. With drystone walls, green fields and meadows stretching as far as the eye can see, everyone should take the opportunity to discover this wonderful corner of Yorkshire.

The estates at Malham Tarn and Upper Wharfedale contain some of the finest upland landscapes in the Yorkshire Dales, with limestone pavements, waterfalls and flower-rich hay meadows criss-crossed with stone walls and studded with traditional field barns. Caring for nearly 3,000 hectares (7,500 acres) in Malhamdale, the Trust has waymarked walks and trails throughout the Dales, from Malham Cove to Fountains Fell. So go for a ramble, a circular walk or follow a trail across the ancient limestone pavements. Take a route around Malham Tarn, which with adjacent areas of raised bog, fen and woodland, is protected as a National Nature Reserve.

This special area is home to a unique community of rare plants and animals, as well as being the focal point of an outstanding region of classic upland limestone country. The limestone pavements in the Dales are a unique and irreplaceable habitat that has formed as a result of erosion by water over the centuries. Today it supports unusual and diverse plant communities. Visitors can discover more by joining one of the summer wildflower walks in Malhamdale or Upper Wharfedale hosted by the Trust.

Above:
ancient field enclosures at Cray, in the Upper Wharfedale Valley

It is easy to imagine mesolithic hunters sitting around a campfire, or you may fancy that you hear the chink of Roman centurions' armour as they march from Chester to York, or even – from our more recent industrial past – the rattle of pack horses' harnesses and clatter of workers' clogs. Walking at Marsden is not always for the faint-hearted – so why not join one of many guided walks with our volunteers and discover stunning views, inspiring history and a rich variety of moorland?

Below:
Buckstones Moss in the north of the Marsden Moor Estate

Explore the Yorkshire coast
Discover the Yorkshire coastline, taking in the Ravenscar Coastal Centre and Peak Alum Works and the Old Coastguard Station at Robin Hood's Bay.

Above:
picturesque Runswick Bay in North Yorkshire

Nestling on the edge of the North Sea, at the foot of Robin Hood's Bay is the Old Coastguard Station – now an interpretive visitor centre, with panoramic views across the bay from Ness Point in the north to Ravenscar in the south. Find out about the hidden history of an ancient landscape and hear how the building has been an important focus of village life.

At Ravenscar, take in commanding views across the bay at a height of 200 metres. The Trust cares for a wealth of features in and around the village, including the remains of a Second World War radar station, a reinstated rocket post – once used by local coastguards – flower-rich meadows, farmland and bluebell woods.

My favourite hidden view
On a clear day, admittedly rare in Marsden, if you are brave enough to step off the Pennine Way and wander across Black Moss you will get a fantastic view over the whole of our moorland estate.

Standing here, surrounded by 2,500 hectares (6,177 acres) of bog, you really feel you are in the midst of a remote wilderness – yet to the east and west civilisation is surprisingly close.

It never ceases to amaze me how the wild open expanse of the moors along the South Pennines and the Peak District National Park always remains peaceful and still, even though they are crowded in by towns and villages.

This is a place to come and enjoy the wild open spaces created by man over thousands of years, and now being managed as a haven for wildlife.

Don't forget to listen out for the rare twite and the call of the grouse, curlew and golden plover breaking the silence with their song.

Gemma Wren
Countryside Manager, Marsden Moor Estate

Beningbrough Hall and Gardens

Beningbrough, York,
North Yorkshire YO30 1DD

Map ⑤ G4  1958

'**Excellent, interesting and varied, we enjoyed making a portrait!**'
Mr and Mrs Alexander, Yorkshire

This is a family friendly house and garden. The grand 1716 Georgian mansion is set in a park and gardens and there are more than 100 18th-century portraits and seven interpretation galleries, run in partnership with the National Portrait Gallery. There is also a fully equipped Victorian laundry, with wet and dry rooms, and a working walled garden, which supplies the Walled Garden Restaurant. Children will love the wilderness play area and there are many family activities to enjoy. Journey through Beningbrough and explore our Artrageous spaces, the changing faces, then discover some unexpected places.

Exploring
- Find out about Georgian life in the 18th-century mansion.
- Discover the 'Making Faces' galleries and commission your own portrait.
- Working walled garden supplying produce to the Walled Garden Restaurant.

Exploring
- Explore acres of gardens and wilderness play area – new activities.
- Get Artrageous!: join in our free family art workshops.
- Fully equipped Victorian laundry, with wet and dry rooms.

Eating and shopping: enjoy restaurant hot lunches and snacks made with local, seasonal produce. Snack kiosk serves ice-cream, sandwiches and hot drinks. Ice-cream kiosk and BBQ in summer. The shop and plant centre stocks a selection of quality goods.

Making the most of your day: living history and family activities, including Artrageous!, plus family garden interpretation. 'Victorian Below Stairs' tours on Tuesdays. Guided garden walks (including weekends). Annual Food and Craft Festival. **Dogs**: on leads in parkland only (assistance dogs only in garden and grounds).

Access for all: 🅿♿♿🚾♿♿📷👓🅰
Georgian mansion ♿♿♿♿ Stable block ♿♿
Grounds ♿♿➡♿

Getting here: 105:SE516586. **Foot**: footpath from York, along River Ouse, 10 miles. **Cycle**: NCN65. **Bus**: Stephensons 29 York to Easingwold, alight Shipton, 1 mile. **Train**: York 8 miles. **Road**: 8 miles north-west of York, 2 miles west of Shipton, 2 miles south-east of Linton-on-Ouse (A19). **Parking**: free, 100 yards. Coaches must come via A19 and use coach entrance. No coach access from the west via Aldwark toll bridge.

View of the Georgian mansion from the walled garden at Beningbrough in the north of the county

You may also enjoy: Treasurer's House, in the centre of York, Fountains Abbey and Studley Royal, near Ripon.

Finding out more: 01904 472027 or beningbrough@nationaltrust.org.uk

Beningbrough Hall and Gardens		M	T	W	T	F	S	S
House, galleries, gardens, shop and restaurant								
1 Mar–6 Apr	11–5:30	M	T	W	.	.	S	S
9 Apr–24 Apr	11–5:30	M	T	W	T	F	S	S
25 Apr–29 May	11–5:30	M	T	W	.	.	S	S
30 May–5 Jun	11–5:30	M	T	W	T	F	S	S
6 Jun–24 Jul	11–5:30	M	T	W	.	.	S	S
25 Jul–4 Sep	11–5:30	M	T	W	T	F	S	S
5 Sep–23 Oct	11–5:30	M	T	W	.	.	S	S
24 Oct–30 Oct	11–5:30	M	T	W	T	F	S	S
Galleries, gardens, shop and restaurant								
19 Feb–27 Feb	11–3:30	M	T	W	T	F	S	S
5 Nov–18 Dec	11–3:30	.	.	.	.	.	S	S

Last admission to house 4:30. House and restaurant closes 5. Whole property open 26 and 27 December. Open 1 January to 18 February Saturday and Sunday, 11 to 3:30 (excluding house).

Braithwaite Hall

East Witton, Leyburn, North Yorkshire DL8 4SY

Map (5) E3

A 17th-century tenanted farmhouse in beautiful Coverdale. The hall, sitting room and carved staircase are on show to visitors. **Note**: no toilet.

Access for all: Building 🏠

Getting here: 99:SE117857. 1½ miles south-west of Middleham, 2 miles west of East Witton (A6108). Narrow approach road.

Finding out more: 01969 640287 or braithwaitehall@nationaltrust.org.uk

Braithwaite Hall	
June to September by arrangement in advance with the tenant, Mrs Duffus. Please contact well in advance to arrange a mutually convenient time for your visit.	

Bridestones, Crosscliff and Blakey Topping

Staindale, Dalby, Pickering, North Yorkshire YO18 7LR

Map (5) I3

The Bridestones has peculiar shaped rocks, heather moorland, ancient woodland, herb-rich meadows. Blakey Topping has superb all-round views. **Note**: Dalby Forest drive – toll charges apply, including members. Nearest toilet at Staindale Lake car park.

Access for all: 🅿️🖼️📱 Grounds 🏠

Getting here: 94:SE877906. In North York Moors National Park.

Finding out more: 01723 870423 or bridestones@nationaltrust.org.uk. c/o Peakside, Ravenscar, Scarborough, North Yorkshire YO13 0NE

Bridestones	Open every day all year

Brimham Rocks

Summerbridge, Harrogate, North Yorkshire HG3 4DW

Map (5) F4

An amazing collection of weird and wonderful rock formations which makes a great day out for families, climbers and those wanting to enjoy the simple pleasures of fresh air and magnificent views over Nidderdale. Let your imagination run wild as you explore the labyrinth of paths through this unique landscape. **Note**: beware of changes in height and cliff edges.

Fantastical shapes at Brimham Rocks, North Yorkshire

off B6265. **Sat Nav**: only gives approximate location. **Parking**: pay and display (coins only), charge applies to non-members £4 up to four hours, then £5. Motorcycles free; minibuses £8 all day; coaches £15 all day. Coaches/groups welcome but must book.

Finding out more: 01423 780688 or brimhamrocks@nationaltrust.org.uk

Brimham Rocks		M	T	W	T	F	S	S
Open all year	8 to dusk	M	T	W	T	F	S	S
Visitor centre, shop and kiosk								
19 Feb–27 Feb	11–5	M	T	W	T	F	S	S
5 Mar–3 Apr	11–5	.	.	.	.	.	S	S
9 Apr–25 Apr	11–5	.	M	T	W	T	F	S	S
30 Apr–22 May	11–5	.	.	.	.	.	S	S
28 May–2 Oct	11–5	M	T	W	T	F	S	S
8 Oct–16 Oct	11–5	.	.	.	.	.	S	S
22 Oct–30 Oct	11–5	M	T	W	T	F	S	S
5 Nov–18 Dec	11–4	.	.	.	.	.	S	S

Visitor centre, shop and kiosk open Bank Holiday 2 May. Also open 26 and 27 December, 11 to dusk. Facilities may close in bad weather.

Exploring — Marvel at the fantastically shaped rock formations.
— Let children explore this natural playground.
— Enjoy magnificent views over Nidderdale and beyond.
— Great for walking over moorland and through woodland.

Eating and shopping: excellent range of Yorkshire products for sale in our shop. Great value picnic food from our refreshment kiosk. Why not treat yourself to a hot chocolate or ice-cream?

Making the most of your day: discover the rocks' geological and social history and how we conserve this special place in the visitor centre. Regular guided walks. Tracker Packs available for five to eleven year olds. **Dogs**: under control and on leads on moorland April to June (ground-nesting birds).

Access for all: [icons]
Building [icons] Grounds [icon]

Getting here: 99:SE206650. 10 miles south-west of Ripon. **Foot**: Nidderdale Way passes through. **Cycle**: cyclists welcome on main track only. **Bus**: Harrogate & District 24 Harrogate ≋ to Pateley Bridge, alight Summerbridge, 2 miles. Sundays and Bank Holidays May to October AS Coaches 'Nidderdale Rambler' 825 Harrogate to Brimham Rocks circular. **Road**: 11 miles north-west of Harrogate off B6165, 10 miles south-west of Ripon, 4 miles east of Pateley Bridge

East Riddlesden Hall

Bradford Road, Riddlesden, Keighley, West Yorkshire BD20 5EL

Map (5) E5 [icons] 1934

'**Very enjoyable, beautiful grounds and the staff were exceptionally friendly and well informed.**'
Ms F. Sanford

Every time that you stand in the gardens of East Riddlesden you will experience something new. The pink cherry trees, clematis, borders, daffodils and soothing lavender beds all create a sense of tranquillity far removed from the bustle of modern life. This peace is very different from the Hall's tumultuous past, which includes tales of ghosts and dastardly deeds. Going into the Hall feels like walking through someone's home; it has a cosy lived-in feel, and creates a relaxing atmosphere where visitors can feel at ease examining the exquisite embroideries and blackwork, oak furniture and pewter.

Exploring

— Savour the tranquillity of our romantic award-winning gardens.
— Visit one of the finest 17th-century barns in northern England.
— Go wild in our children's natural play areas.
— Seek out the ghostly grey lady among our exquisite embroideries.
— Spy on local birdlife in our bird-feeding area.
— Step into the shoes of a 17th-century merchant.

The Great Chamber at East Riddlesden Hall, in the west of Yorkshire

Eating and shopping: indulge yourself with homemade soups, made using herbs from the garden, and our delicious locally sourced cakes. Get horticultural inspiration from our plant sales area and shop.

Making the most of your day: explore our herb interpretation area and discover our new composting area. Follow one of our fun trails to find out more. **Dogs**: sorry no dogs in the house or garden.

Access for all: ♿🅿️♿🚹🖼️🏠🎨👓📷
Building 🚶♿♿ Grounds ♿

Getting here: 104:SE079421. **Cycle**: cycle racks available. **Bus**: Keighley & District 662 Bradford Interchange ➯ to Keighley, alight Granby Lane. **Train**: Keighley 1½ miles. **Road**: 1 mile north-east of Keighley on south side of the Bradford Road in Riddlesden, close to Leeds & Liverpool Canal. A629 relief road

from Shipley and Skipton signed for East Riddlesden Hall. **Parking**: free, 100 yards. Parking for one coach (no double-deckers). Narrow entrance to property.

You may also enjoy: Hardcastle Crags and Gibson Mill.

Finding out more: 01535 607075 or eastriddlesden@nationaltrust.org.uk

East Riddlesden Hall		M	T	W	T	F	S	S
House, shop and tea-room								
19 Feb–30 Oct	10:30–4:30	M	T	W	.	.	S	S
Shop and tea-room								
5 Nov–18 Dec	11–4	.	.	.	.	.	S	S

Open Good Friday. At certain times, entry to the house may be by guided tour.

Fountains Abbey and Studley Royal Water Garden

Fountains, Ripon, North Yorkshire HG4 3DY

Map ⑤ F4   🏛️🏠✝️🔭↕️❄️🌳
🏠♦️🍷 1983

'A fantastic visit – the abbey really came alive for us through the passion and knowledge of our guide.'
P. Cummins, Leeds

A World Heritage Site, set in 323 hectares (800 acres) of beautiful countryside, offering an unparalleled opportunity to appreciate the range of England's heritage. Discover the magnificent 12th-century abbey ruins and the only surviving Cistercian corn mill. Amble through the beautiful landscaped Georgian water garden of Studley Royal, complete with Neo-classical statues, follies and breathtaking views. Spot the differences between the three breeds of wild deer as you explore the medieval deer park. Delight in the richly decorated Victorian St Mary's church and take time out to relax in the Reading Room in Elizabethan Fountains Hall. **Note**: cared for in partnership with English Heritage.

Entry is still possible at most places up to 30 minutes before closing

Stunning vaulting in the Cellarium at Fountains Abbey, North Yorkshire

Exploring
- Discover the Abbey's story at the Porter's Lodge exhibition.
- Enjoy climbing, swinging and jumping in the children's play area.
- Search for the hermit's grotto in the Georgian water garden.
- Spot the species of bats that live in the Abbey.
- Look for centuries-old graffiti at Fountains Mill.
- Visit the Banqueting House to see wild flowers in summer.

Eating and shopping: tempt your taste-buds with our local and seasonal menu, including our estate-reared venison, and buy local produce in the shop. Enjoy the lakeside view from our Victorian tea-room. Find the perfect gift in our shop and new plant area.

Making the most of your day: find out more on guided tours and wildlife walks throughout the year. Enjoy open-air theatre, Christmas entertainment, medieval re-enactments and changing exhibitions. School holiday children's trails and craft workshops. **Dogs**: on short leads only.

Access for all:
Building **Grounds**

Getting here: 99:SE271683. **Foot**: 4 miles from Ripon via public footpaths and bridleways. **Cycle**: signed on-road cycle loop. **Bus**: Harrogate District Community Transport (Ripon Roweller 139) Ripon to Markington (connections with Harrogate and District 36 from Harrogate). **Road**: 4 miles west of Ripon off B6265 to Pateley Bridge, signposted from A1, 12 miles north of Harrogate (A61). **Parking**: at visitor centre car park, free, and Studley Royal deer park (pay and display). Coach parking at visitor centre only. Access off B6265.

You may also enjoy: the dramatic rock formations and views at nearby Brimham Rocks.

Finding out more: 01765 608888 or fountainsabbey@nationaltrust.org.uk

Fountains Abbey		M	T	W	T	F	S	S
1 Jan–31 Jan	10–4	**M**	**T**	**W**	**T**	·	**S**	**S**
1 Feb–31 Mar	10–4	**M**	**T**	**W**	**T**	**F**	**S**	**S**
1 Apr–30 Sep	10–5	**M**	**T**	**W**	**T**	**F**	**S**	**S**
1 Oct–31 Oct	10–4	**M**	**T**	**W**	**T**	**F**	**S**	**S**
1 Nov–31 Dec	10–4	**M**	**T**	**W**	**T**	·	**S**	**S**
St Mary's Church								
1 Apr–30 Sep	12–4	**M**	**T**	**W**	**T**	**F**	**S**	**S**
Deer park								
Open all year	7–9	**M**	**T**	**W**	**T**	**F**	**S**	**S**

Estate closes dusk if earlier. Whole estate closed 24 and 25 December. Studley Royal shop opening times vary.

Goddards Garden

27 Tadcaster Road, York,
North Yorkshire YO24 1GG

Map (5) H5 ❖ 1984

Visit the former gardens of Noel Goddard
Terry, of the famous York chocolate-making
firm. Designed by George Dillistone, the
garden complements the house's Arts and
Craft style. With yew-hedged garden rooms,
bowling green, wilderness gardens and plants
for every season, it is also an oasis for wildlife.
Note: house not open to public (offices).

Exploring	– An excellent example of a late Arts and Crafts garden.
	– Formal terraces, gardens and herbaceous borders enclosed by yew hedges.
	– Explore the garden and see the restored greenhouse.

Making the most of your day: enjoy a picnic
in this tranquil garden, surrounded by lovely
scenery and the sound of one of the few British
colonies of midwife toads. **Dogs**: on leads only.

Access for all: Grounds 🧑‍🦽➡️

Getting here: 105:SE589497. **Bus**: First York
4, 12, 13; Yorkshire Coastliner 840, 842, 843,
845, X44 from York 🚉. **Train**: York 1½ miles.
Road: follow York outer ring road (A1237/A64),
turn on to A1036 Tadcaster Road, signed to
York city centre, then turn right after
St Edward's church, through brick gatehouse
arch. **Parking**: free. Not suitable for coaches.

Finding out more: 01904 702021 or
goddardsgarden@nationaltrust.org.uk

Goddards Garden		M	T	W	T	F	S	S
1 Mar–28 Oct	11–4:30	**M**	**T**	**W**	**T**	**F**	·	·

Closed Bank Holidays. Last admission one hour
before closing.

Hardcastle Crags

near Hebden Bridge, West Yorkshire

Map (5) E6  1950

Explore this beautiful wooded valley with its
deep ravines, tumbling streams and glorious
waterfalls. Walk through woodland rich in
wildlife with over 25 miles of footpaths and
see the striking seasonal changes in the plants
and trees. At its heart is Gibson Mill, a former
cotton mill and entertainment emporium, now
a visitor centre using sustainable energy, where
you can discover more about the valley's
200-year history with dressing up and
exhibitions. There are also themed walks,
and guided tours of Gibson Mill to enjoy.
Note: steep paths throughout.

Exploring	– Enjoy 25 miles of walks through spectacular changing scenery.
	– Stunning autumn colours, springtime bluebells and ever-changing birdsong.
	– Visit our flagship sustainable property, Gibson Mill.
	– Discover 200 years of industrial and social history.
	– Guided walks, family trails and events throughout the year.

Eating and shopping: Muddy Boots Café
offers a selection of locally produced snacks
and delicious locally baked cakes, hot and cold
drinks and ice-cream.

Waterfall at Hardcastle Crags, West Yorkshire

Our small shop offers a selection of interesting books, gifts, cards and prints.

Making the most of your day: four circular walks, ranging from three to seven miles; downloadable walks on the website. Staff and volunteer-led themed walks, events and guided tours. **Dogs**: under control at all times.

Access for all: [icons] **Building** [icons] **Grounds** [icon]

Getting here: 103:SD988291. 2 miles north-east of Hebden Bridge. **Foot**: access on foot via riverside walk from Hebden Bridge. Pennine way and Bridleway both pass close to the property. **Cycle**: NCN68 passes close by. **Bus**: for local buses visit www.wymetro.com or call 0113 245 7676. **Train**: for local trains www.wymetro.com or call 0113 245 7676. **Road**: at end of Midgehole Road, 1½ miles north-east of Hebden Bridge, off the A6033 Keighley Road. **Sat Nav**: use HX7 7AA for Midgehole car park, HX7 7AZ for Clough Hole car park and look out for National Trust sign. **Parking**: pay and display. Weekdays and up to three hours at weekends £3.50; over three hours at weekends £5; motorcycle £1; minibus £5. Please note: visitors are encouraged to come on foot, by cycle or public transport.

You may also enjoy: East Riddlesden Hall and Quarry Bank Mill.

Finding out more: 01422 844518. 01422 846236 (weekends) or hardcastlecrags@nationaltrust.org.uk. Hollin Hall, Crimsworth Dean, Hebden Bridge, West Yorkshire HX7 7AP

Hardcastle Crags		M	T	W	T	F	S	S
1 Jan–31 Dec		M	T	W	T	F	S	S
Gibson Mill								
2 Jan–27 Feb	11–3	·	·	·	·	·	S	S
1 Mar–30 Oct	11–4	·	T	W	T	·	S	S
5 Nov–24 Dec	11–3	·	·	·	·	·	S	S
Muddy Boots Café								
2 Jan–27 Feb	11–3	·	·	·	·	·	S	S
1 Mar–30 Oct	11–4	·	T	W	T	·	S	S
5 Nov–24 Dec	11–3	·	·	·	·	·	S	S

Local school holidays Muddy Boots Café open daily, Gibson Mill open Saturday to Thursday. Also open Good Friday, Boxing Day and all Bank Holiday Mondays 1 May to 29 September. Café open until 5 on Saturday and Sunday.

Maister House

160 High Street, Hull, East Yorkshire HU1 1NL

Map (5) J6 | 1966 |

Rebuilt in 1743 after a fire, this merchant's house survives from Hull's international trading heyday. **Note**: staircase and entrance hall only on show. No toilet.

Access for all: Building [icon]

Getting here: 107:TA102287. In Hull city centre.

Finding out more: 01723 879900 or maisterhouse@nationaltrust.org.uk. c/o Peakside, Ravenscar, Scarborough, North Yorkshire YO13 0NE

Maister House		M	T	W	T	F	S	S
4 Jan–30 Dec	10–4	M	T	W	T	F	·	·
Closed Bank Holidays.								

Malham Tarn Estate

Waterhouses, Settle,
North Yorkshire BD24 9PT

Map (5) D4    | 1946 |

This stunning area of limestone pavements, upland hill farms and flower-rich hay meadows provides a marvellous setting for walking, cycling or just enjoying the great outdoors. The National Nature Reserve is home to a unique community of rare plants and animals, with a glorious display of flowers in summer. **Note**: nearest toilet at National Park car park in Malham, or Orchid House exhibition.

Exploring
 – Excellent walking and cycling opportunities around the tarn.
 – Stroll from Malham to the beautiful Janet's Foss waterfall.
 – Awe-inspiring, far-reaching views around the estate.
 – Walk-in exhibition and group classroom at the Orchid House.

Eating and shopping: tea-rooms and facilities in Malham village.

Making the most of your day: guided walks and events throughout the year; summer holiday activities for the kids. **Dogs**: on leads only.

Access for all: Town Head Barn 🐾 Grounds 🐾

Getting here: 98:SD890660. Estate extends from Malham village, 19 miles north-west of Skipton, north past Malham Tarn. **Foot**: 6 miles of Pennine Way and ¾ mile of Pennine Bridleway on property. **Bus**: Pennine 210 Skipton to Malham (passing Skipton ≋), limited service, 1 mile. Contact the estate office to confirm whether the Malham Tarn shuttle bus is running from Settle. **Train**: Settle 7 miles. **Parking**: in Malham village, not National Trust (pay and display). Free parking at Watersinks car park on south side of Malham Tarn.

Finding out more: 01729 830416 or malhamtarn@nationaltrust.org.uk

'Janet's Foss' on the Malham Tarn Estate, North Yorkshire

Malham Tarn Estate		M	T	W	T	F	S	S
Open all year		M	T	W	T	F	S	S
Town Head Barn								
19 Feb–31 Oct	10–4	M	T	W	T	F	S	S

Marsden Moor Estate

Marsden, Huddersfield, West Yorkshire

Map ⑤ E7　🏛️🚻♿ 1955

The estate, covering nearly 2,248 hectares (5,553 acres) of unenclosed common moorland, takes in the northern part of the Peak District National Park. The landscape supports large numbers of moorland birds. The estate is an SSSI, International Special Protection Area and a candidate Special Area of Conservation. **Note**: nearest toilet in Marsden village.

Exploring	– Miles of footpaths for serious walkers.
	– A place to be alone with your thoughts.
	– Dramatic scenery and visible industrial heritage.

Making the most of your day: Marsden Heritage Trail with defined walks of four, eight or ten miles to help you explore this dramatic countryside. **Dogs**: on leads only.

Access for all: Exhibition 🐾 Grounds 🐾

Getting here: 109:SE025100. Around Marsden village. **Foot**: Kirklees Way and Pennine Way pass through. Huddersfield Narrow Canal towpath nearby. **Bus**: First 185 from Huddersfield. **Train**: Marsden (adjacent to estate office). **Road**: between A640 and A635. **Parking**: around the estate, free, including in Marsden village (not National Trust) and at Buckstones and Wessenden Head (National Trust).

Finding out more: 01484 847016 or marsdenmoor@nationaltrust.org.uk. Estate Office, The Old Goods Yard, Station Road, Marsden, Huddersfield, West Yorkshire HD7 6DH

Marsden Moor Estate		M	T	W	T	F	S	S
Open all year		M	T	W	T	F	S	S
Exhibition Centre								
Open all year	9–5	M	T	W	T	F	S	S

Middlethorpe Hall Hotel, Restaurant and Spa

Bishopthorpe Road, York,
North Yorkshire YO23 2GB

Map (5) H5    2008

Built in 1699, this quintessentially William and Mary house next to York Racecourse was once the home of the 18th-century diarist Lady Mary Wortley Montagu. Furnished with antiques and fine paintings and set in eight hectares (twenty acres) with manicured gardens and parkland beyond, Middlethorpe Hall's country-house character remains unspoilt.

The house and gardens are already accessible to the public as a hotel, and welcome guests to stay, to dine in the restaurant and to have afternoon tea (booking strongly advised). Contact hotel direct for best available offers. **Note**: all paying guests to the hotel are welcome to walk in the garden and park. Children above the age of six are welcome.

Finding out more: 01904 641241.
01904 620176 (fax) or
info@middlethorpe.com.
www.middlethorpe.com

The gracious Middlethorpe Hall Hotel, North Yorkshire

Moulton Hall

Moulton, Richmond,
North Yorkshire DL10 6QH

Map (5) F2   1966

Elegant 17th-century manor house with a beautiful carved staircase. **Note**: no toilet.

Access for all: 🅿 Building 🦽 Grounds 🦽

Getting here: 99:NZ235035. 5 miles east of Richmond; turn off A1, ½ mile south of Scotch Corner.

Finding out more: 01325 377227 or
moultonhall@nationaltrust.org.uk

Moulton Hall

By arrangement in advance with the tenant, Viscount Eccles. Please give as much notice as possible in order to arrange a mutually convenient time for your visit.

Mount Grace Priory

Staddle Bridge, Northallerton,
North Yorkshire DL6 3JG

Map (5) G3   ✛ 1953

England's most important Carthusian ruin. The individual cells reflect the hermit-like isolation of the monks. **Note**: operated by English Heritage; members free, except on event days. Visit website for directions.

Access for all: 🅳 🚾 🦽 🖼 🦽
Building 🦽🦽 Grounds 🦽

Getting here: 99:SE449985. 6 miles north-east of Northallerton, ½ mile off A19 ½ mile south of its junction with A172.

Mount Grace Priory		M	T	W	T	F	S	S
2 Jan–31 Mar	10–4	·	·	·	T	F	S	S
1 Apr–30 Sep	10–6	·	·	·	T	F	S	S
1 Oct–23 Dec	10–4	·	·	·	T	F	S	S
29 Dec–31 Dec	10–4	·	·	·	T	F	S	·

Closed 1 January and 24 to 26 December.

Statues of Flora and Zephyr by R. J. Wyatt at
Nostell Priory in West Yorkshire

Nostell Priory and Parkland

Doncaster Road, Nostell, near Wakefield,
West Yorkshire WF4 1QE

Map (5) G6 1954

'One of the best historic houses we have
ever had the pleasure of visiting. With the
friendliest volunteers too!'
Miss L. Bewley, Hexham

Built on the site of a medieval priory, Nostell
has been the home of the Winn family for
300 years. Commissioned by Sir Rowland Winn
in 1733, James Paine built the house. Later
additions by Robert Adam created exceptional
interiors. Visitors can explore the large park
with a range of walks and views. Gardens
include lakeside walks, a newly planted
orchard, vegetable beds and an adventure
playground. Inside the house, see a collection
of Chippendale furniture made specially
for Nostell. Paintings by Brueghel, Hogarth
and Kauffmann. A John Harrison (*Longitude*)
longcase clock and an 18th-century doll's
house. **Note**: conservation work on stables
due to be completed by summer.

Exploring
– 18th-century doll's house in
the Museum Room.
– See the wooden workings of
the John Harrison clock.
– Discover the grounds by
following the gardens'
sensory trails.
– Explore the adventure
playground in Low Wood.

Exploring
– Visit the stables and see how
important horses were.
– Take a guided walk through
the park, Wednesdays
and Saturdays.

Eating and shopping: new courtyard restaurant
and simple food outlet, serving hot and cold
food. New shop stocking larger range of
interesting gifts and souvenirs. Weekend
barbecue in the garden, weather permitting. Ice-
cream bicycle around the grounds in summer.

Making the most of your day: family activities,
craft fairs, theatre, concerts, upstairs-
downstairs tours (booking essential). Guided
parkland walks Wednesday and Saturday, house
trails. House tours 11:15, 11:45, 12:15, Wednesday
to Sunday. **Dogs**: on leads in park only.

Access for all: ♿ 🚻 ♿ ♿ ♿ ♿ 📷 🚻 ⋯ 🅿
House ♿ ♿ ♿ **Stable Block** ♿
Grounds ♿ ♿ ➡ ♿ ♿

Getting here: 111:SE407172. 5 miles south of
Wakefield within easy reach of A1, M1 and M62.
Foot: via pedestrian entrance on the A638.
Cycle: NCN67, 3 miles. **Bus**: Arriva 495 and
496 Wakefield to Doncaster; Arriva 185, B Line
123, 223 from Wakefield. **Train**: Fitzwilliam
1½ miles. **Road**: on A638 5 miles south-east
of Wakefield towards Doncaster. **Sat Nav**: use
WF4 1QD. **Parking**: £2 for non-members.

You may also enjoy: Kedleston Hall and
Clumber Park.

Finding out more: 01924 863892 or nostellpriory@nationaltrust.org.uk

Nostell Priory and Parkland		M	T	W	T	F	S	S
Parkland								
1 Jan–31 Dec	9–7	M	T	W	T	F	S	S
House*								
26 Feb–30 Oct	1–5			W	T	F	S	S
3 Dec–4 Dec	1–4						S	S
7 Dec–11 Dec	1–4			W	T	F	S	S
7 Dec–8 Dec	5–8			W	T			
Shop and tea-room								
26 Feb–30 Oct	10–5:30	M	T	W	T	F	S	S
31 Oct–31 Dec	10–4	M	T	W	T	F	S	S
7 Dec–8 Dec	5–8			W	T			
Gardens**								
26 Feb–30 Oct	11–5:30			W	T	F	S	S
5 Nov–31 Dec	11–4						S	S

*House open 11 to 1 for guided tours at 11:15, 11:45, 12:15, normal opening 1 to 5. **Gardens open Monday to Sunday 11 to 4:30 during local school holidays. Open Bank Holiday Mondays: house, 11 to 5, gardens, shop and tea-room, 10 to 5:30. Parkland closes dusk if earlier. Rose garden may be closed on occasions for private functions. Closed 25 December.

Nunnington Hall

Nunnington, near York,
North Yorkshire YO62 5UY

Map (5) H4   🏠 ❄ 1953

The sheltered walled garden, with spring-flowering organic meadows, orchards and flamboyant peacocks, complements this beautiful Yorkshire house, nestling on the quiet banks of the River Rye. Enjoy the atmosphere of this former family home. Explore period rooms while hearing the Hall's many tales, and then discover one of the world's finest collections of miniature rooms in the attic. The Hall also holds a series of important art and photography exhibitions during the year. Why not make a day of it? Its proximity to Rievaulx Terrace makes it an ideal double visit in one day.

Exploring
– Visit our art and photography exhibitions.
– Discover the amazing Carlisle Collection of miniature rooms.
– Enjoy a stroll in the organic walled garden.

Eating and shopping: waitress service in tea-room, serving local and seasonal produce. Special diets catered for, including gluten-free options. Lovely picnic spots and tea-garden. Look for the local ranges in the shop.

Making the most of your day: full events programme throughout the year, including temporary exhibitions, family activities, food events, concerts and many more.
Dogs: welcome in the car park only.

Access for all: 🅿 ♿ 🚻 ♿ 🔊 ∷
Building 🔥 ♿ 🕯 Grounds ♿ 🕯

Getting here: 100:SE670795.
Bus: Stephensons 195 Hovingham to Helmsley.
Road: in Ryedale, 4½ miles south-east of Helmsley (A170) Helmsley to Pickering road; 1½ miles north of B1257 Malton to Helmsley road; 21 miles north of York, B1363. Nunnington Hall is 7½ miles south-east of the National Trust Rievaulx Terrace and Temples.
Parking: free, 50 yards.

You may also enjoy: Rievaulx Terrace, Beningbrough Hall and Gardens, Treasurer's House and The Bridestones.

Finding out more: 01439 748283 or nunningtonhall@nationaltrust.org.uk

Nunnington Hall		M	T	W	T	F	S	S
19 Feb–30 Oct	11–5		T	W	T	F	S	S
5 Nov–18 Dec	11–4						S	S

Open Bank Holiday Mondays.

Roses in the garden of Nunnington Hall, North Yorkshire

The Old Coastguard Station

The Dock, Robin Hood's Bay,
North Yorkshire YO22 4SJ

Map (5) I2 1998

The Old Coastguard Station, North Yorkshire

Discover how the elements have formed and are still changing the landscape with the help of our interactive exhibition. Find out about the coastal creatures and their habitat and see the shoreline inhabitants in our rock-pool tank. Learn more about the village, its people and its history. **Note**: steep walk from car park.

Exploring – Be fascinated by our interactive exhibition.
– See shoreline creatures up close in the rock-pool aquarium.
– Explore the Dinosaur Coast.
– Don't miss our historic village trail.

Eating and shopping: the shop sells a range of gifts and books, as well as providing local information.

Making the most of your day: follow the village trail, join a guided walk or go rockpooling. Arts and crafts exhibitions. **Dogs**: allowed in building if carried.

Access for all: [icons]
Old Coastguard Station [icons]

Getting here: 94: NZ953049. On slipway at bottom of village. **Foot**: Cleveland Way passes alongside the building. Coast-to-Coast Path finishes at building. **Cycle**: NCN1 nearby. **Bus**: Arriva 93 from Middlesbrough, Guisborough, Whitby and Scarborough. **Train**: Whitby 5 miles. **Road**: off A171 Whitby to Scarborough, signposted Robin Hood's Bay. No access for cars down the steep hill to the old village. **Parking**: Scarborough Borough Council car parks 546 yards (charge including members).

Finding out more: 01947 885900 or oldcoastguardstation@nationaltrust.org.uk

The Old Coastguard Station		M	T	W	T	F	S	S
1 Jan–20 Feb	10–4						S	S
21 Feb–27 Feb	10–4	M	T	W	T	F	S	S
5 Mar–3 Apr	10–4						S	S
9 Apr–30 Oct	10–5	M	T	W	T	F	S	S
5 Nov–18 Dec	10–4						S	S
19 Dec–23 Dec	10–4	M	T	W	T	F		
27 Dec–31 Dec	10–4		T	W	T	F	S	

Planned refit in January, please telephone to check opening times.

Ormesby Hall

Church Lane, Ormesby, near Middlesbrough, Redcar & Cleveland TS7 9AS

Map (5) G2  1962

'**A day full of adventure and fun. Great for children to hear how life was for parents and grandparents.**'
Tim Fletcher, Durham

Home of the Pennyman family for nearly 400 years, this classic Georgian mansion, with its Victorian kitchen and laundry, attractive gardens and estate walks, provides lively resources for local schools and community groups, and a unique venue for wedding ceremonies and corporate events. Weekend visitors can experience the spirit of the intimate home of Colonel Jim Pennyman, the last of the Pennyman line, and his arts-loving wife Ruth, as well as the stylish legacy of the 18th-century character 'Wicked' Sir James Pennyman – so named due to his extravagant lifestyle and his gambling with the family fortune.

The Victorian laundry at Ormesby Hall,
Redcar & Cleveland

Exploring
- Enjoy beautiful gardens in an 18th-century landscape setting.
- Follow our family trails, indoors and out.
- Sit and relax awhile in the Reading Room.
- Admire the working stables, home to Cleveland Mounted Police horses.
- Discover more in the 'Cache in the Attic' stores.

Eating and shopping: enjoy tea in the servants' hall or on the terrace. Taste scones and cakes hand-baked at the hall. Pick up a souvenir from our reception or tea-room.

Making the most of your day: ask about our weekday programme of special-interest activities and events, including lunchtime lectures and conservation tours. Enjoy the only model railway layouts owned by the National Trust. **Dogs**: on leads in park only.

Access for all: 🅿️🐕‍🦺♿🚻🍴📷🖼️🎨👶🅰️
Building 🏠♿ Grounds ➡️♿

Getting here: 93:NZ530167. **Cycle**: NCN65, 2¼ miles. **Bus**: Arriva 5/9/63/69 from Middlesbrough (passing close Middlesbrough 🚂). **Train**: Marton 1½ miles; Middlesbrough 3 miles. **Road**: 3 miles south-east of Middlesbrough, west of A19. From A19 take A174 to A172. Follow signs for Ormesby Hall. Car entrance on Ladgate Lane (B1380). **Sat Nav**: use TS3 0SR for main entrance. **Parking**: free, 100 yards.

You may also enjoy: a coastal contrast at Souter Lighthouse, or the intimate Jacobean feel of Washington Old Hall.

Finding out more: 01642 324188 or ormesbyhall@nationaltrust.org.uk

Ormesby Hall		M	T	W	T	F	S	S
12 Mar–30 Oct	1:30–5						**S**	**S**

Open Bank Holiday Mondays and Good Friday. Closed 2 and 3 July for concert (contact property for information).

Rievaulx Terrace

Rievaulx, Helmsley, North Yorkshire YO62 5LJ

Map ⑤ H3   🏠♿♿ 1972

Discover one of Ryedale's true gems – the 18th-century landscape of Rievaulx Terrace. Stroll through woods, then out on to the terrace, with its stunning views down over the Cistercian ruin of Rievaulx Abbey. In spring the bank between the temples is awash with wild flowers, in summer the lawns are the perfect spot for picnics, while in autumn the beech woods are a mass of rich hues. Rievaulx Terrace's close proximity to Nunnington Hall makes it an ideal double visit in one day. **Note**: no access to Rievaulx Abbey from terrace.

Exploring
- Take your time and enjoy the scenic walk.
- Bring a hamper and have a picnic.
- Join in the family activities.
- Find out more by joining a guided tour.
- Spot the fascinating flora and fauna.

Eating and shopping: treat yourself to an ice-cream, drinks and snacks. Don't miss the shop selling National Trust ranges.

Making the most of your day: events programme throughout year, including family activities in school holidays and programme of guided tours. Free batricars available to book at specific times. **Dogs**: welcome on leads.

Access for all: ⬛⬛⬛⬛⬛⬛⬛⬛
Visitor centre ⬛ Temples ⬛ Grounds ⬛⬛⬛⬛

Getting here: 100:SE579848. **Foot:** Cleveland Way within ¾ mile. **Bus:** Moorsbus M9 from Helmsley Sunday and Bank Holidays April to October, daily August. Discounted entry for visitors using the Moorsbus. **Road:** 2½ miles north-west of Helmsley on B1257. **Parking:** free, 100 yards. Unsuitable for trailer caravans. Tight corners and no turning space beyond coach park.

You may also enjoy: Nunnington Hall, Beningbrough Hall and Gardens, Treasurer's House and The Bridestones.

Finding out more: 01439 798340 (summer). 01439 748283 (winter) or rievaulxterrace@nationaltrust.org.uk

Rievaulx Terrace		M	T	W	T	F	S	S
19 Feb–30 Oct	11–5	M	T	W	T	F	S	S
Open Bank Holidays.								

The Ionic Temple at Rievaulx Terrace, North Yorkshire

Roseberry Topping

Newton-under-Roseberry, North Yorkshire

Map ⑤ G2 ⬛⬛⬛⬛ 1985

Layers of human and geological history have shaped this distinctive and iconic landmark, with its bluebell woods and heather moorland. **Note:** nearest toilet at Newton-under-Roseberry car park (not National Trust).

Access for all: ⬛

Getting here: 93:NZ575126. 1 mile from Great Ayton, next to Newton-under-Roseberry village on A173 Great Ayton to Guisborough.

Finding out more: 01723 870423 or roseberrytopping@nationaltrust.org.uk. c/o Peakside, Ravenscar, Scarborough, North Yorkshire YO13 0NE

Roseberry Topping	Open every day all year

Treasurer's House

Minster Yard, York, North Yorkshire YO1 7JL

Map ⑤ H5 ⬛⬛⬛⬛ 1930

Only a few metres from York Minster, this was the first house ever given to the National Trust complete with a collection – and it is not all that it first seems! It has a history spanning 2,000 years, from the Roman road in the cellar to the Edwardian servants' quarters in the attics, and thirteen period rooms in between. These house one man's remarkable collection of antique furniture, ceramics, textiles and paintings from a 300-year period. Infamous ghost stories are another of the many quirky attributes of this property. Outside is an attractive formal sunken garden.

Exploring
– Take the attic tour and learn about Edwardian servant life.
– Join the cellar tour – hear about Roman ghostly sightings.

Treasurer's House in York, North Yorkshire

Exploring
- Relax in the quiet walled garden.
- Enjoy refreshment in the table service tea-room.
- Trails for children available daily.
- Engaging room guides.

Eating and shopping: your favourite National Trust photographic images are for sale. Small selection of local artists' and craft work for sale. Range of homemade bakes, cakes, soups and special dietary dishes. Themed food events, including Christmas lunches and Edwardian breakfasts.

Making the most of your day: attic and cellar tours of Edwardian social history and archaeology of Roman road. Themed tours. Family trails and activities every school holiday. Vegetable plant sales. Food events. Workshops. **Dogs**: on leads in formal garden only.

Access for all: 🅳♿🂠🖼🍴👶🎧🅰
Building 🔼🏠 Grounds ♿➡

Getting here: 105:SE604523. In city centre adjacent to Minster (north side, at rear). **Cycle**: NCN65, ⅓ mile. Close to city cycle routes. **Bus**: from surrounding areas. **Train**: York ½ mile. **Parking**: nearest in Lord Mayor's Walk. Park and ride service from city outskirts.

You may also enjoy: Beningbrough Hall and Gardens.

Finding out more: 01904 624247 or treasurershouse@nationaltrust.org.uk

Treasurer's House		M	T	W	T	F	S	S
19 Feb–27 Feb	11–3	M	T	W	T	·	S	S
28 Feb–31 Oct	11–4:30	M	T	W	T	·	S	S
1 Nov–30 Nov	11–3	M	T	W	T	·	S	S
Tea-room								
19 Feb–27 Feb	11–3	M	T	W	T	·	S	S
1 Dec–19 Dec	11–3	M	T	W	T	·	S	S

1 March to 31 October: free-flow. February and November: entry by Ghostly Myths or Fascinating Frank guided tour to selected rooms. Herb garden openings limited, check before visiting.

Upper Wharfedale

North Yorkshire BD23 5JA

Map ⑤ E4   🔽🚻🅿🏠 [1989]

Along the Upper Wharfe Valley the characteristic drystone walls and barns of the Dales, important flower-rich hay meadows, beautiful riverside and valleyside woodland combine to create a wonderful place to relax and explore the great outdoors.

Exploring
- Spectacular scenery to explore and enjoy.
- Excellent walking and cycling opportunities.
- Beautiful picnic spots along the banks of the River Wharfe.
- Picturesque villages and hamlets to stroll around.

Eating and shopping: village tea-rooms, shops and pubs, farm shops.

Making the most of your day: guided walks and events throughout the year; summer holiday activities for the kids. **Dogs**: on leads only.

Access for all: 🅿♿ Town Head Barn ♿
Grounds ➡

Getting here: 98:SD935765. Upper Wharfedale extends from Kettlewell village (12 miles north of Skipton) north to Beckermonds and Cray. **Foot**: the Dales Way runs through Upper Wharfedale following the scenic route of the

River Wharfe on its way from Ilkley to Bowness in Windermere. **Cycle**: Kettlewell lies on the Yorkshire Dales Cycleway (Sustrans regional route 10) between Coverdale and Skipton. **Bus**: Pride of the Dales 72 Skipton ⊞ to Buckden. **Train**: Skipton, 12 miles. **Road**: B6160 runs the length of Upper Wharfedale through Cray, Buckden and Kettlewell, towards Grassington (7 miles) and Ilkley in the south. **Parking**: in Kettlewell and Buckden, not National Trust (pay and display).

Finding out more: 01729 830416 or upperwharfedale@nationaltrust.org.uk. Yorkshire Dales Estate Office, Waterhouses, Settle, North Yorkshire BD24 9PT

Upper Wharfedale		M	T	W	T	F	S	S
Estate								
Open all year		M	T	W	T	F	S	S
Town Head Barn								
19 Feb–31 Oct	10–4	M	T	W	T	F	S	S

Yorkshire Coast

near Ravenscar, North Yorkshire

Map ⑤ 12  1976

Along the Cleveland Way National Trail is a diverse collection of coastal properties stretching south from Saltburn to Newbiggin Cliffs at Filey. Discover breathtaking cliff views and a wide variety of coastal wildlife. Visit the Ravenscar Visitor Centre to discover more about man's industrial footprint on the landscape.

Exploring
— See how the elements have created this stunning landscape.
— Discover more about Britain's first chemical industry.
— Spot wildlife in bluebell woods and clifftop meadows.
— Explore your very own Jurassic Park.

Eating and shopping: enjoy the exhibition at the Ravenscar Visitor Centre and shop for all your walking/cycling requirements, local gifts and light refreshments.

Making the most of your day: wildlife activities and guided walks at Ravenscar, Boggle Hole and Saltburn. Boat trips from Whitby. Industrial heritage exhibition at Ravenscar Visitor Centre. **Dogs**: on leads allowed.

Access for all: 🚻♿🏷️🗺️🅿️
Ravenscar Visitor Centre ♿ Grounds ♿

Getting here: 94:NZ980016. **Foot**: Cleveland Way passes through property. **Cycle**: NCN1. **Bus**: To Ravenscar, Esk Valley Coaches 115 from Scarborough or Whitby Monday to Saturday. **Train**: Saltburn, Whitby, Scarborough and Filey for access to various parts of the coast. Scarborough 12 miles from Ravenscar Visitor Centre. **Road**: visitor centre in Ravenscar village, signposted off A171 Scarborough to Whitby. **Parking**: free roadside parking at Ravenscar.

Finding out more: 01723 870423 or yorkshirecoast@nationaltrust.org.uk. Peakside, Ravenscar, Scarborough, North Yorkshire YO13 0NE

Yorkshire Coast		M	T	W	T	F	S	S
Countryside	Open every day all year							
Coastal Centre								
8 Apr–2 Oct	10–4:30	M	T	W	T	F	S	S
8 Oct–30 Oct	10–4:30	.	.	.	.	.	S	S

Ravenscar visitor centre open Bank Holiday Mondays.

Wild flowers on the Yorkshire Coast, North Yorkshire

Left:
puffins on Staple Island, Inner Farne, Northumberland

Heaven for walkers

Inland Northumberland offers the natural beauty and tranquillity of Allen Banks and Staward Gorge – a walking heaven with many miles of footpaths – while both Ros Castle and the World Heritage Site of Hadrian's Wall boast breathtaking views. There are also numerous beautiful woodland walks, including one along the banks of the River Wear at Moorhouse Woods, north of Durham City, and another beside the Derwent at Ebchester.

An island treasure

Accessible by a causeway at low tide, Holy Island is a treasure that has as its centrepiece Lindisfarne Castle. Once a Tudor fort, the castle sits on a rocky crag that can be seen for miles along the sweeping coastline. Converted into a holiday home in 1903, this enchanting place, with its small rooms full of intimate decoration and design, is totally charming. Don't miss the lovely walled garden just below the castle. This was planned by Gertrude Jekyll and dates back to 1922.

Also be sure to stroll along the headland and explore the village – just remember to keep an eye on the tides which cover the causeway.

A legacy from Roman times

One of the most rugged stretches of countryside in the North East is home to Hadrian's Wall. Snaking across the landscape, the wall was built around AD122 when the Roman Empire was at its height. A World Heritage Site, it remains one of Britain's most impressive ruins.

The Trust protects six miles of Hadrian's Wall, including Housesteads Fort, one of the best preserved sections of the frontier and a place which conjures an evocative picture of Roman military life.

My favourite view

My favourite view is from Greenleighton Hill, towards the northern end of the Wallington Estate.

It's a classic viewpoint. To the north you can see Simonside and the dark mass of Harwood Forest, look east and you can glimpse the sea, while to the west and south the farmland and woodlands of the estate are spread out, with the eye-catcher on Rothley Crags drawing your attention.

The hill, which is grazed mainly by sheep, lies at about 900 feet, and can be quite exposed in winter. Evidence of the past is everywhere – the walk from the car park follows old workings along the limestone outcrop, and the spoil heaps overlie a much older prehistoric enclosure and the ridge and furrow of past arable cultivation.

Close to the hilltop there is a well-preserved prehistoric hut circle where a quarryman has carved his name on a large boulder – perhaps it was his favourite view too?

Harry Beamish
North East Regional Archaeologist

Allen Banks and Staward Gorge

Bardon Mill, Hexham,
Northumberland NE47 7BU

Map 6 F5 🏠 🏛 🏊 🐕 1942

This extensive area of spectacular gorge and river scenery forms the largest area of ancient woodland in the county, with miles of waymarked walks to explore. Look out for the remains of a medieval pele tower and a reconstructed Victorian summerhouse. All sits within the North Pennines AONB.

Exploring
– Explore miles of tranquil and beautiful walks.
– See spectacular views from the medieval pele tower.
– Home to red squirrels, dormice and woodland birds and plants.

Eating and shopping: you'll find plenty of opportunities for a picnic either at Allen Banks car park, in the woodland or river bank settings.

Making the most of your day: enjoy the peaceful surroundings of Allen Banks and Staward Gorge. Guided walks and family activities including Forest Schools, tree trail and workshops on fungi and woodland birds. **Dogs**: welcome under close control.

Access for all: 🚾 ♿ Grounds 🦽

Getting here: 86:NY799640. **Foot**: numerous public and permitted rights of way give access to walkers. **Cycle**: NCN72, 2½ mile. **Bus**: Arriva/Stagecoach in Cumbria 685 Carlisle to Newcastle upon Tyne, to within ½ mile. **Train**: Bardon Mill 1½ mile. **Road**: 5½ miles east of Haltwhistle, 3 miles west of Haydon Bridge, ½ miles south of A69, near meeting point of Tyne and Allen rivers. **Sat Nav**: avoid using. **Parking**: at Allen Banks (pay and display), members free. Cars £3. Two coaches at a time maximum (all coaches must book). 3.3-metre height restriction on approach road. Coaches £10 full day.

Finding out more: 01434 344218 or allenbanks@nationaltrust.org.uk. Housesteads Farm, Haydon Bridge, Hexham, Northumberland NE47 6NN

Allen Banks and Staward Gorge	Open every day all year

A flight of steps leading up from the River Allen into Morales Wood, an area of dense woodland at Allen Banks, Northumberland

Cherryburn

Station Bank, Mickley, Stocksfield,
Northumberland NE43 7DD

Map ⑥ G5  1991

The Chillingham Bull, **engraved by Thomas Bewick in 1789**

Thomas Bewick (1753–1828), Northumberland's
greatest artist, wood engraver and naturalist,
was born in the cottage here. The nearby
19th-century farmhouse, the later home
of the Bewick family, houses an exhibition
on Bewick's life and work and a small shop
selling books, gifts and prints from his
original wood engravings. Occasional printing
demonstrations take place in the adjoining
barn. There are splendid views over the
Tyne Valley.

Exploring
- View the exhibition, dedicated to the work of Thomas Bewick.
- Enjoy seeing the donkeys in the farmyard.
- Take a stroll around the Paddock Walk.
- Bring a picnic and enjoy one of our many events.

Eating and shopping: browse through the
bargain books in the shop. Buy prints from
the original Bewick engravings. Sample
Northumbrian biscuits with your coffee.
Try our fantastic picnic area.

Making the most of your day: full events
programme, with printing demonstrations

most Sunday afternoons. Folk in the Farmyard
first Sunday of the month, May to October.

Access for all: 🅿️ ♿ 🚻 💺 👁️ 📷 ♿ ⠿
Building ♿♿♿ Grounds ♿

Getting here: 88:NZ075627. Close to
south bank of River Tyne. **Bus**: Go North
East 10 Newcastle to Hexham (passes
Newcastle ≥), alight Mickley Square, ¼ mile.
Train: Stocksfield 1½ miles; Prudhoe 1½ miles.
Road: 11 miles west of Newcastle, 11 miles east
of Hexham; ¼ mile north of Mickley Square
(leave A695 at Mickley Square onto Riding
Terrace leading to Station Bank).
Parking: free, 100 yards.

You may also enjoy: the live interpretation
at the nearby birthplace of pioneering railway
engineer George Stephenson.

Finding out more: 01661 843276 or
cherryburn@nationaltrust.org.uk

Cherryburn		M	T	W	T	F	S	S
12 Mar–30 Oct	11–5	M	T		T	F	S	S

**Detail of printing equipment in Thomas Bewick's Press
Room at Cherryburn, Northumberland**

Cragside

Rothbury, Morpeth, Northumberland NE65 7PX

Map (6) G3 🏠🏠⬆✚♠🏠 1977

'**Fascinating house, stunning grounds. We enjoyed a lovely walk around the lakes. Food in the tea-room was lovely – home cooked!**'
Mrs Gregory, Blackburn, Lancashire

Discover the world of Lord Armstrong – Victorian inventor, innovator and landscape genius. Cragside house was a wonder of its age. Built on a rocky crag, it is crammed full of ingenious gadgets and was the first house in the world to be lit by hydro-electricity. The gardens are incredible. One of the largest rock gardens in Europe leads down to the Iron Bridge, which in turn leads across to the formal garden. Children will love our adventure play area and exploring Nelly's Labryrinth, a network of paths and tunnels cut out of a vast area of rhododendron forest. **Note:** challenging terrain and distances. Stout footwear essential.

Exploring
- The first house to be lit by hydro-electricity.
- Marvel at the many ingenious gadgets in the house.
- Escape to the tranquillity of the woodland and lakes.
- Get lost in the labyrinth.
- Take a peek from our wildlife hide.
- Lift a Mini in our exhibition!

Eating and shopping: enjoy locally sourced food and drink in our Stables tea-room. Treat yourself to a sweet indulgence: cream teas, home bakes, ice-cream. Extensive range of plants for sale in visitor centre courtyard. Northumbrian products and gifts in shop.

The elegant formal garden at Cragside, Northumberland

Making the most of your day: free minibus shuttle service between key features. Introductory talks at front of house. Spot birds and local wildlife from our hide. Family activities in school holidays. Numerous self-guided walks. **Dogs**: welcome on estate, on leads at all times.

Access for all: ⓟ ⓓ ♨ ⓦ🄲 🅗 🄿 📷 🅙
⦂⦂ Ⓐ House 🄿 🄳 Visitor centre 🄿 🄳 🄳
Estate 🄻 ➡

Getting here: 81:NU073022. **Bus**: Arriva 508 Newcastle to Rothbury (passes Morpeth ≋), Sundays only, June to October. Go North East 144 Morpeth to Thropton with connections from Newcastle. **Road**: 13 miles south-west of Alnwick (B6341) and 15 miles north-west of Morpeth on Wooler road (A697), turn left on to B6341 at Moorhouse Crossroads, entrance 1 mile north of Rothbury. **Parking**: free, nine car parks throughout estate. Coach parking 350 yards from house, 150 yards from visitor centre. Coaches cannot proceed beyond the coach park or tour estate as drive is too narrow.

You may also enjoy: Wallington, Lindisfarne Castle and Souter Lighthouse.

Finding out more: 01669 620333 or cragside@nationaltrust.org.uk

Cragside		M	T	W	T	F	S	S
House*								
12 Mar–15 Apr	1–5	·	T	W	T	F	S	S
16 Apr–1 May	11–5	·	T	W	T	F	S	S
3 May–27 May	1–5	·	T	W	T	F	S	S
28 May–5 Jun	11–5	·	T	W	T	F	S	S
7 Jun–22 Jul	1–5	·	T	W	T	F	S	S
23 Jul–11 Sep	11–5	·	T	W	T	F	S	S
13 Sep–21 Oct	1–5	·	T	W	T	F	S	S
22 Oct–30 Oct	11–5	·	T	W	T	F	S	S
Gardens, estate, shop and tea-room								
12 Mar–30 Oct	10–7	·	T	W	T	F	S	S
2 Nov–18 Dec	11–4	·	T	W	T	F	S	S

*House open 11 to 5 on Saturdays, Sundays and local school holidays. Also open Bank Holiday Mondays. Open 19 to 27 February (except Mondays): house (ground floor only) 12 to 4; grounds, 11 to 4. Also open 5 to 6 March: house ground floor only, 12 to 4, grounds 11 to 4. On Bank Holiday weekends the property is very crowded. Last admission to house one hour before closing. House may open late or close early if light or temperature levels are too low. Occasionally entry to house from 11 to 1 may be by guided tour only, on a first-come, first-served basis (places limited).

The iconic Dunstanburgh Castle, Northumberland

Dunstanburgh Castle

Craster, Alnwick, Northumberland NE66 3TT

Map ⑥ H3 🄷 🏰 1961

An iconic castle ruin, on one of the most beautiful stretches of Northumberland coastline. An exhilarating walk from Craster. **Note**: managed by English Heritage.

Getting here: 75:NU258220. 9 miles north-east of Alnwick, approached from Craster to the south or Embleton to the north (on foot only).

Finding out more: 01665 576231 or dunstanburghcastle@nationaltrust.org.uk

Dunstanburgh Castle		M	T	W	T	F	S	S
2 Jan–8 Mar	10–4	M	·	·	T	F	S	S
1 Apr–30 Sep	10–5	M	T	W	T	F	S	S
1 Oct–31 Oct	10–4	M	T	W	T	F	S	S
3 Nov–31 Dec	10–4	M	·	·	T	F	S	S

Closed 1 January and 24 to 26 December.

Farne Islands

Northumberland

Map (6) H2 ✝ 🏛 🦜 1925

Possibly the most exciting seabird colony in England with unrivalled views of 23 species – including 37,000 pairs of puffins. Large grey seal colony with more than 1,000 pups born every autumn. Strong links with Celtic Christianity and St Cuthbert. A short boat journey to a different world! **Note**: access by boat from Seahouses (charge including members). Toilet on Inner Farne only.

Exploring — Opportunity to view seabirds at unbelievably close range.
— Excellent photographic opportunities.
— Chapel of St Cuthbert with fine stained-glass windows.
— Unrivalled views of the Northumberland hinterland.

Eating and shopping: visit our shop in Seahouses for beautiful local crafts.

Fantastic puffin range, with fleeces, socks, mugs and coasters.

Access for all: 🚻 📷 ♿ •• Grounds 🦽

Getting here: 75:NU230370. 2 to 5 miles off the Northumberland coast, opposite Bamburgh. Trips every day from Seahouses harbour, weather permitting. **Cycle**: NCN1, ¾ mile. From Seahouses harbour. **Bus**: Arriva 501 Newcastle ⇔ to Alnwick ⇔ to Berwick, alight Seahouses, 1½ miles. **Train**: Chathill, not Sunday, 4 miles. **Parking**: in Seahouses opposite harbour (pay and display), not National Trust.

Finding out more: 01665 721099 (Infoline). 01665 720651 or farneislands@nationaltrust.org.uk

Farne Islands		M	T	W	T	F	S	S
Staple Island								
1 May–31 Jul	10:30–1:30	M	T	W	T	F	S	S
Inner Farne Island								
1 May–31 Jul	1:30–5	M	T	W	T	F	S	S
Both islands								
1 Apr–30 Apr	10:30–6	M	T	W	T	F	S	S
1 Aug–31 Oct	10:30–6	M	T	W	T	F	S	S

Only Inner Farne and Staple Islands can be visited. Information centre and shop in Seahouses open all year, 10 to 5.

Visitors arrive at the Farne Islands, off Northumberland's coast

For enquiries contact 0844 800 1895

George Stephenson's Birthplace, Northumberland: his whole family lived in one room

George Stephenson's Birthplace

Wylam, Northumberland NE41 8BP

Map (6) G5   1949

This quaint small stone cottage was built *circa* 1760 to accommodate mining families. The furnishings reflect the year the great rail pioneer, George Stephenson, was born here (1781), when his whole family lived in the one room.

Exploring
- Tread the same flagstones as young George did.
- Listen to the live interpretation.
- Learn about the pioneering steam locomotive *Rocket*.

Eating and shopping: enjoy a light snack in the cosy Stephenson tea-room.

Buy a souvenir book on the Stephenson family. Look out for the Geordie Food day in June.

Making the most of your day: extend your visit by strolling along the banks of the River Tyne.

Access for all: ♿ 🚻 ♿ 🅿 ·· ⓐ
Building 🔾

Getting here: 88:NZ126650. **Foot**: access on foot (and cycle) through country park, ½ mile east of Wylam. **Cycle**: NCN72. Level ride beside River Tyne (approximately 5 miles). **Bus**: Go North East 684 Newcastle to Ovington, alight Wylam, 1 mile. **Train**: Wylam ½ miles. **Road**: 8 miles west of Newcastle, 1½ miles south of A69 at Wylam. **Parking**: by war memorial in Wylam village, ½ mile, not National Trust (pay and display).

Finding out more: 01661 853457 or georgestephensons@nationaltrust.org.uk

George Stephenson's Birthplace	M	T	W	T	F	S	S
19 Mar–30 Oct 11–5				**T**	**F**	**S**	**S**
Open Bank Holiday Mondays.							

Gibside

near Rowlands Gill, Burnopfield, Gateshead,
Tyne & Wear NE16 6BG

Map ⑥ H5

Escape to this tranquil nature reserve: a grand
forest garden and landscape park created by
one of the richest men in Georgian England.
Gibside offers miles of woodland and riverside
walks with views across the Derwent Valley.
Explore an architectural gem of a chapel, see red
kites soar above the famous tree-lined avenue,
discover our ever-changing walled garden and
our vibrant stables discovery centre, with lots
of eating and shopping temptation on the
way. Bring the family for wildlife spotting and
outdoor adventures, including nature playscape
and rope-climbing challenge, or indoor fun with
our milkable cow and Gibside Hall playhouse.

Exploring
— See walled garden and
Victorian shrubbery come
back to life.
— Look for nature at our wildlife
hide and viewing cameras.
— Reach the Column of Liberty
for a fantastic panorama.
— Uncover Mary Eleanor Bowes'
dramatic story of torture
and abduction.
— Enjoy changing exhibitions
at the Stables.

Eating and shopping: savour breakfast
butties, homemade lunches and afternoon
teas inspired by our kitchen garden in the
Potting Shed tea-room and Renwick's Coffee
and Bookshop. Make a picnic with food from
Gibside Larder food shop. Treat yourself to
gifts and plants.

Making the most of your day: events every
weekend all year round. Monthly farmers'
market. Family trails and orienteering pack.
Dogs: welcome on leads.

Access for all: [icons]
Chapel [icons] Landscape garden [icons]

Column to liberty at Gibside, Tyne & Wear

Getting here: 88:NZ172583. **Foot**: ½ mile from
Derwent Walk, footpath/cycle track linking
Gateshead and Consett. **Cycle**: NCN14, ½ mile.
Bus: Go North East 'The Red Kite' 45, 46, 47
from Newcastle (passing Newcastle ≋ and
Metrocentre), alight Rowlands Gill, ½ mile.
Train: Blaydon 5 miles; Metrocentre 5 miles.
Road: 6 miles south-west of Gateshead,
20 miles north-west of Durham; entrance on
B6314 between Burnopfield and Rowlands Gill;
from A1 take exit north of Metrocentre and
follow brown signs. **Parking**: free, 100 yards.
Limited coach parking.

Finding out more: 01207 541820 or
gibside@nationaltrust.org.uk

Gibside		M	T	W	T	F	S	S
Landscape garden, walks and stables								
1 Jan–28 Feb	10–4	M	T	W	T	F	S	S
1 Mar–31 Oct	10–6	M	T	W	T	F	S	S
1 Nov–31 Dec	10–4	M	T	W	T	F	S	S
Chapel								
1 Jan–27 Feb	10–3.30	·	·	·	·	·	S	S
1 Mar–31 Oct	10–5	M	T	W	T	F	S	S
5 Nov–31 Dec	10–3.30	·	·	·	·	·	S	S
Tea-room, gift shop and food shop								
2 Jan–28 Feb	10–4	M	T	W	T	F	S	S
1 Mar–31 Oct	10–5	M	T	W	T	F	S	S
1 Nov–31 Dec	10–4	M	T	W	T	F	S	S

Estate closed 24 and 25 December. Tea-room last orders 30
minutes before closing.

Hadrian's Wall and Housesteads Fort

Bardon Mill, Hexham,
Northumberland NE47 6NN

Map (6) F5  1930

Running through an often wild landscape with vast panoramic views, the wall was one of the Roman Empire's most northerly outposts. Built around AD122, it has sixteen permanent bases, of which Housesteads Fort is one of the best preserved, conjuring up an evocative picture of Roman military life. **Note**: fort is owned by the National Trust and maintained and managed by English Heritage.

Exploring
- Enjoy walking alongside the wall.
- Wander through the extensive archaeological remains.
- Take in panoramic views of Hadrian's Wall country.
- Look out for different flora and fauna.

Eating and shopping: small shop selling local and 'Roman' souvenirs. Refreshment kiosk with limited indoor seating.

Making the most of your day: family trail available, and main events organised by English Heritage at Housesteads. **Dogs**: welcome on leads.

Access for all: ♿🚻♿👁 Visitor centre ♿
English Heritage museum ♿ Fort ♿♿

Getting here: 87:NY790688. **Foot**: Hadrian's Wall Path and Pennine Way. **Cycle**: NCN72. **Bus**: Stagecoach in Cumbria/Classic Coaches AD122 Hadrian's Wall service, April to November daily, Newcastle ≋ to Hexham to Carlisle (passing Haltwhistle ≋). Check before journey. **Train**: Hexham or Haltwhistle connect with AD122 bus. **Road**: 6 miles north-east of Haltwhistle, best access from car parks at Housesteads, Cawfields and Steel Rigg. **Parking**: pay and display (not National Trust), charge including members. Car and coach parks operated by National Park Authority at Housesteads (½-mile walk to the Fort), Steel Rigg and Cawfields.

Finding out more: 01434 344525 (visitor centre). 01434 344363 (English Heritage museum) or housesteads@nationaltrust.org.uk

Housesteads Fort		M	T	W	T	F	S	S
2 Jan–31 Mar	10–4	M	T	W	T	F	S	S
1 Apr–30 Sep	10–6	M	T	W	T	F	S	S
1 Oct–31 Dec	10–4	M	T	W	T	F	S	S

Closed 1 January and 24 to 26 December. Telephone for details or visit www.english-heritage.org.uk.

Hadrian's Wall runs through wild country at Hotbank Cragg, Northumberland

Holy Jesus Hospital

City Road, Newcastle upon Tyne,
Tyne & Wear NE1 2AS

Map (6) H5

Holy Jesus Hospital survives amid 1960s city-centre developments, displaying features from all periods of its 700-year existence. The National Trust's Inner City Project is now based here, working to provide opportunities for inner-city dwellers to gain access to and enjoy the countryside on their doorstep.
Note: owned by Newcastle City Council but managed by the National Trust.

Exploring
— Visit our exhibition room during the week.
— Listen to voices from the past on our interactive displays.
— Get a guided tour on first Saturday of every month.
— Don't miss the plant fair on the June open day.

Eating and shopping: tea, coffee and biscuits available on Saturday open days.

Making the most of your day: discover the site's fascinating history and learn about the remains of the 14th-century Augustinian friary, Tudor tower, 17th-century almshouse and Victorian soup kitchen.

Access for all: 🅿 🅿 ♿ 📷 🎞 Building ♿ ♿ ⬆

Getting here: 88:NZ253642. In centre of Newcastle upon Tyne. **Cycle**: close to riverside routes. **Bus**: Stagecoach buses from city centre. **Train**: Newcastle ½ mile. **Underground**: Tyne and Wear Metro to Monument, ¼ mile. **Road**: close to Tyne Bridge and A167. **Parking**: nearest in city centre car parks, 30 yards (pay and display).

Finding out more: 0191 255 7610 or holyjesushospital@nationaltrust.org.uk

Holy Jesus Hospital		M	T	W	T	F	S	S
11 Jan–30 Jun	12–4		T	W	T			
4 Jul–26 Aug	12–4	M	T	W	T	F		
30 Aug–15 Dec	12–4		T	W	T			

Closed Bank Holiday Mondays and Good Friday. Guided tours first Saturday of every month (except January), 10 to 4 (last tour 3:30).

Lindisfarne Castle

Holy Island, Berwick-upon-Tweed,
Northumberland TD15 2SH

Map (6) G1

Dramatically perched on a rocky crag and accessible via a three-mile causeway at low tide only, the island castle presents an exciting and alluring aspect. Originally a Tudor fort, it was converted into a private house in 1903 by the young Edwin Lutyens. The small rooms are full of intimate decoration and design, with windows looking down upon the charming walled garden planned by Gertrude Jekyll. The property also has several extremely well-preserved 19th-century lime kilns.
Note: emergency toilet only.

Exploring
— Decide how old the castle is – Elizabethan or Edwardian?
— Specialist Gertrude Jekyll garden, explore the 1911 planting plan.
— See the castle's internal wind indicator.
— Do not miss the 19th-century headland lime kilns.
— Invigorating seaside walks, with rock pools to explore.
— Search for wild flowers and spot the seabirds.

Eating and shopping: visit the National Trust shop in Holy Island village for delicious honey and mustard products from Chainbridge border honey farm. Flavoursome jams and preserves from nearby Oxford Farm. Mouth-watering Heterslaw bakery cakes and biscuits. Tasty Loopy Lisa homemade flavoured fudge.

Lindisfarne Castle, Northumberland, was converted into a private home in 1903

Making the most of your day: children's quizzes make family visits more memorable. Specialist Gertrude Jekyll garden talks, monthly May to August. **Dogs**: assistance dogs only.

Access for all: ▢▢▢▢▢▢▢▢▢
Castle ▢ Shop ▢ Grounds ▢▢

Getting here: 75:NU136417. Tidal island off the north Northumberland coast.
Foot: approached on foot from main Holy Island village and car park, 1 mile from entrance.
Cycle: NCN1. Coast and Castles cycle route.
Bus: Perryman's 477 from Berwick-upon-Tweed ➤, with connecting buses at Beal to and from Newcastle. Times vary with season and tides. Also private island minibus service from Holy Island car park to castle. **Train**: Berwick-upon-Tweed 10 miles from causeway. **Road**: on Holy Island, 5 miles east of A1 across a tidal

causeway. **Parking**: 1 mile (pay and display), not National Trust, charge including members.

You may also enjoy: a visit to the Farne Islands to wonder at the abundance and variety of seabirds.

Finding out more: 01289 389244 or lindisfarne@nationaltrust.org.uk

Lindisfarne Castle		M	T	W	T	F	S	S
12 Mar–30 Oct	Times vary	·	T	W	T	F	S	S
Garden								
Open all year	Dawn–dusk		T	W	T	F	S	S

Open Bank Holiday Mondays (including Scottish Bank Holidays) and seven days a week during August. National Trust flag flies only when the castle is open. Castle winter opening: two weekends a month from 10 to 3, depending on tidal access. For tide tables and detailed opening times send sae to Lindisfarne Castle stating which month you wish to visit or visit www.lindisfarne.org.uk.

Seaton Delaval Hall

The Avenue, Seaton Sluice,
Northumberland NE26 4QR

Map (6) H4

Play a part in the unfolding story of the National Trust's recent acquisition. Seaton Delaval Hall, built between 1719 and 1732, is a great English baroque villa designed by Sir John Vanbrugh for Admiral George Delaval. It has formal gardens with colourful borders and is much more than an architectural masterpiece. For 900 years, the estate has been a stage for drama, intrigue and romance, while the surrounding landscape has fuelled industrial revolution. The Hall has survived terrible fires, military occupation and potential ruin. It now provides an amazing space for arts, heritage and the community to come together. **Note**: new property, so may be busy. Ongoing building works. Parking/toilet facilities may be limited.

Exploring
- Marvel at Vanbrugh's central hall, gutted by fire in 1822.
- Imagine horses Admiral, Julius and Peacock in the magnificent stables.
- Relax in Lady Hastings' captivating gardens with striking sculptures.
- Enjoy great portraits and furniture in the family collection.
- Delve into the atmospheric cellars.
- Discover how industry shaped the Delavals' fortunes.

Eating and shopping: visit the East Wing café and taste the famous Seaton Delaval ice-cream. Why not buy a souvenir in the West Wing pavilion?

Making the most of your day: explore the grand central hall, cellars, stables, gardens and estate. **Dogs**: assistance dogs only.

Access for all: 🅿️♿🔊📖♿ Central Hall ♿ Stables ♿ Garden ♿ ➡️

The Trust's most recent large acquisition: Seaton Delaval Hall, Northumberland

Members may have to pay on special events days

Seaton Delaval Hall, Northumberland

Getting here: NZ321766. 2 miles south of Blyth and 2 miles north of Whitley Bay, between villages of Seaton Delaval and Seaton Sluice. **Foot**: at the heart of a network of footpaths: Seaton Sluice (¾mile), Seaton Delaval (1 mile), Blyth and North Tyneside. **Cycle**: NCN1, cycle paths to all local towns and villages, old mining wagon way to Monkseaton, 'Coast and Castles' trail along coast. **Ferry**: North Shields Ferry Terminal 8 miles. **Bus**: Arriva 363/4 (Newcastle city centre to Blyth route), every 30 minutes, stopping at Seaton Delaval, New Hartley, Seaton Sluice and the coast (connects with 308/9 bus to Whitley Bay and North Tyneside). **Train**: West Monkseaton Metro 3 miles (cycle path); Cramlington 7 miles (buses), Newcastle upon Tyne 13 miles (buses). **Road**: A190 passes through estate, linking to A193 coast road and A19; 5 miles from A1. **Parking**: free.

You may also enjoy: Cragside – another palace built on the profits of the North East's industrial prowess.

Finding out more: 0191 237 9100 or seatondelavalhall@nationaltrust.org.uk

Seaton Delaval Hall		M	T	W	T	F	S	S
2 Jan–28 Mar	11–3	M				F	S	S
1 Apr–31 Oct	11–5	M				F	S	S
4 Nov–31 Dec	11–3	M				F	S	S

Closed 23 to 26 December.

Souter Lighthouse and The Leas

Coast Road, Whitburn, Sunderland, Tyne & Wear SR6 7NH

Map (6) I5   🏠🚻♿👶🏠🍽 1990

'**Spectacular scenery with room for children to play and learn. Everyone's so friendly – a great day out!**'
Zoë Stokes, Newcastle

Souter is an iconic clifftop beacon, offering a great family-friendly visit. When opened in 1871, it was a technological marvel, being the first lighthouse built to use electricity. Decommissioned in 1988, the machinery remains in working order today. To the north, The Leas has two and a half miles of beach, cliff and grassland with soaring seabirds and, to the south, Whitburn Coastal Park provides walks and family trails. This year the spectacular glass optic from nearby Coquet Island Lighthouse is on display in Souter's Engine Room – offering a unique chance to see the inside and outside of this vital machinery. **Note**: steep stairs (ground-floor CCTV shows views from the top for those unable to climb).

Exploring
– Climb the 76 steps to the top for spectacular views.
– Clamber on *Neptune*, our open-air play-area boat.
– Explore the engine room's fantastic examples of engineering and technology.
– Discover the Victorian keeper's cottage, returned to its former glory.
– Become a pirate or princess using the dressing-up box.
– Take a bracing walk along the clifftop.

Eating and shopping: relish the seasonal menu, which uses homegrown and local produce. Enjoy the waitress-service tea-room or The Galley's assisted-service catering in relaxed surroundings (variety of dietary needs satisfied). Invest in our guidebook as a souvenir of your visit.

Children playing in a rock pool at the Wherry, to the south of Souter Lighthouse, Tyne & Wear

Making the most of your day: enjoy hands-on family activities, foghorn demonstrations, open-air play area and trails, and the picnic area. Ask about our full programme of events and activities, including rock-pool rambles. **Dogs**: on leads in grounds only.

Access for all:
Building **Grounds**

Getting here: 88:NZ408641. On the north-east coast south of South Shields on the River Tyne. **Foot**: South Tyneside Heritage Trail; 'Walking Works Wonders' local trail. **Cycle**: NCN1, adjacent to property. **Ferry**: Shields Ferry operated by Nexus, crossing River Tyne from North Shields to South Shields, crossing time 7 minutes, runs twice hourly in season. **Bus**: Stagecoach North East E1, E2, E6 Sunderland to South Shields (passes Sunderland and Metro South Shields). E1 passes lighthouse, other services pass close by. **Train**: East Boldon and South Shields (Tyne & Wear Metro) both 3 miles. **Road**: 2½ miles south of South Shields and 5 miles north of Sunderland on A183 coast road. **Parking**: free, 100 yards. Car park barrier locked at set times in evening (see notices at entrance).

You may also enjoy: contrasting intimate homes at Washington Old Hall and Ormesby Hall, and technology at Cragside.

Finding out more: 0191 529 3161 or souter@nationaltrust.org.uk

Souter Lighthouse and The Leas		M	T	W	T	F	S	S
12 Mar–30 Oct	11–5	**M**	**T**	**W**	**T**	·	**S**	**S**

Open Good Friday. Please telephone for details of winter opening arrangements. Open Fridays 1 July to 26 August for lighthouse tours and refreshments from The Galley.

Wallington

Cambo, Morpeth, Northumberland NE61 4AR

Map (6) G4 1941

'An unexpected gem.'
Mr Harris, Sheffield

Dating from 1688, Wallington was home to many generations of the Blackett and Trevelyan families, who all left their mark. The result is an impressive, yet friendly, house with a magnificent interior and fine collections. The remarkable Pre-Raphaelite central hall was decorated to look like an Italian courtyard and features a series of paintings of Northumbrian history by William Bell Scott. The formality of the house is offset by the tranquil beauty of the surrounding landscape – with lawns, lakes, parkland and woodland. The beautiful walled garden, with its varied plant collection and charming conservatory, is an enchanting must-see.

Exploring —
- Relax, picnic or play in the grassy courtyard.
- Marvel at Lady Wilson's Cabinet of Curiosities.
- Look out for red squirrels at the wildlife hide.
- See our fascinating collection of dolls' houses.
- Stretch your legs with a walk on the extensive estate.
- Let off steam in the adventure playground.

Eating and shopping: browse for gifts and treats in the shop. Tuck into local produce in the clocktower café, grab a Wallington burger from the farm shop kitchen or a 'cuppa' in the garden kiosk. Visit our farm shop for a tasty souvenir.

Making the most of your day: year-round programme of events for all ages, including open-air theatre, food and craft festival, guided walks, music, dancing and hands-on activities. Adventure playground and children's trail. **Dogs**: on leads in grounds and walled garden only.

Access for all: 🅿️🐕♿🚻🔔🏠📷💻🚶‍♀️👁️
House ♿🚶‍♀️🔔♿ Café ♿🚶‍♀️
Grounds ♿➡️♿♿

Getting here: 81:NZ030843. **Bus**: Arriva 419 from Morpeth, Wednesday, Friday only (passing close Morpeth ⭍). **Road**: A1 north to Newcastle then 20 miles north-west (A696, airport/Ponteland road), and turn off on B6342 to Cambo. A1 south to Morpeth (A192) then 12 miles west (B6343). **Parking**: free, 200 yards.

You may also enjoy: escaping to another 18th-century landscape garden at Gibside.

Finding out more: 01670 773967 (Infoline). 01670 773600 or wallington@nationaltrust.org.uk

Wallington		M	T	W	T	F	S	S
House								
5 Mar–30 Oct	11–5						S	S
7 Mar–28 Oct*	1–5	M		W	T	F		
Walled garden**								
Open all year	10–7	M	T	W	T	F	S	S
Gift shop and café								
1 Jan–18 Feb	10:30–4:30	M	T	W	T	F	S	S
19 Feb–25 Sep	10:30–5:30	M	T	W	T	F	S	S
26 Sep–31 Dec	10:30–4:30	M	T	W	T	F	S	S
Farm shop (outside turnstile)								
1 Jan–18 Feb	10:30–4	M	T	W	T	F	S	S
19 Feb–25 Sep	10:30–5	M	T	W	T	F	S	S
26 Sep–31 Dec	10:30–4	M	T	W	T	F	S	S

*House also open 11 to 5 during school holidays, daily except Tuesday (16 April to 2 May, 28 May to 5 June, 23 July to 5 September and 22 to 30 October). Last admission one hour before closing. **Garden closes 4 in January, February, November and December and 6 in March and October, or dusk if earlier. Gift shop, café and farm shop closed some days over Christmas. Café last orders 30 minutes before closing.

The Central Hall at Wallington, Northumberland

Washington Old Hall

The Avenue, Washington Village, Washington,
Tyne & Wear NE38 7LE

Map ⑥ H5 1956

At the heart of historic Washington village
this picturesque stone manor house and its
gardens provide a tranquil oasis, reflecting
gentry life following the turbulence of the
English Civil War. The building incorporates
parts of the original medieval home of
George Washington's direct ancestors, and it
is from here that the family took their surname
of 'Washington'. Much-used and loved by local
schools and community groups, including a
hugely supportive Friends organisation, the
Old Hall is also popular with couples wanting
intimate wedding ceremonies and companies
organising corporate events. **Note**: steep steps
in garden (lift available).

Exploring
- Stroll through the Jacobean garden to the wildflower nut orchard.
- See authentic oak furniture in 17th-century room settings.
- Admire pictures showing the life and times of George Washington.
- Find out about the time when nine families lived here.
- Admire the vegetables – lovingly tended by staff, volunteers and schoolchildren.

Eating and shopping: refresh yourself in
the tea-room, run by our Friends. Pick up a
souvenir of your visit from our reception.
Seek out bargains from our Friends'
bric-a-brac display.

Making the most of your day: picnic anywhere
in the gardens, and enjoy a game of croquet.
Seasonal garden trails, events and activities,
including Fourth of July Independence Day
ceremony. **Dogs**: on leads in garden only.

Access for all: 🅿️♿🚻♿📷♿:.🅰️
Building ♿♿♿ **Grounds** ♿♿➡️♿

Getting here: 88:NZ312566. In Washington
village next to church on the hill. **Cycle**: NCN7,
1 mile. **Bus**: Go North East W6 from
Washington Galleries bus station to Concord,
connections from Gateshead, Heworth and
Newcastle. Bus routes are changing, contact
travelline, 0871 200 2233. **Train**: Heworth
(Tyne & Wear Metro) 4 miles; Newcastle
7 miles. **Road**: 7 miles south of Newcastle,
5 miles from The Angel of the North. From A1
exit junction 64 stay in lane and continue on
and straight over Princess Anne Interchange
roundabout. Take your next left at Biddick
Lane roundabout and continue on until you
pick up brown signs. From A19 and any other
route head for Washington then join the A1231:
stay on this road until you pick up brown signs
to Washington Old Hall. **Parking**: small car park
beside Old Hall, free. Unrestricted parking
on The Avenue (coaches must park on
The Avenue).

You may also enjoy: the intimate Pennyman
family home at Ormesby Hall or a coastal
contrast at Souter Lighthouse.

Finding out more: 0191 416 6879 or
washingtonoldhall@nationaltrust.org.uk

Washington Old Hall		M	T	W	T	F	S	S
House								
13 Mar–30 Oct	11–5	M	T	W	.	.	.	S
Gardens								
13 Mar–30 Oct	10–5	M	T	W	.	.	.	S

Open Good Friday and Easter Saturday.

Visitor with a trained diabetic hypo-alert dog in the
garden at Washington Old Hall, Tyne & Wear

Wales

Sweeping views and the wild majesty
of the Brecon Beacons

Outdoors in Wales

With miles of rugged coastline and some of the highest peaks in Britain, the National Trust cares for many dramatic and iconic landscapes in Wales, offering a huge variety of places to visit and explore.

Inspirational scenery

More than 60 miles of Pembrokeshire's coastline is looked after by the Trust.

With traditional cattle and sheep grazing restored to Pembrokeshire's coastal heaths and inland commons, spectacular improvements to the flora and fauna can be seen in these special places. Star of the Pembrokeshire coast is the chough, with more than 60 breeding pairs. In early autumn seal pups can be seen on a number of beaches, and the guillemots that nest on the cliffs at Stackpole are a sight not to be missed.

Explorers are very well catered for, with hundreds of miles of coastal and inland footpaths. Fine circular walks can be found at Stackpole (lakes and cliffs), Marloes, St David's Head, Dinas Island, near Fishguard, Little Milford and Lawrenny Woods on the secluded River Cleddau. Most areas of coast can be reached by one of the coastal shuttle buses – part of an excellent network (**www.pembrokeshiregreenways.co.uk**) – and guides can be bought at St David's shop and most car parks. **National Trust parking is available at: Broadhaven, Bosherton, Marloes, Martin's Haven and Stackpole.**

Above:
Llŷn Peninsula, North Wales

Unspoilt charm

The Llŷn Peninsula is a Welsh jewel. Multicoloured beach huts (available for hire) provide a vibrant backdrop to the long, sweeping beach at Llanbedrog, while in the sheltered bay at Porthor the sand famously whistles underfoot, due to the unique shape of the grains. The fishing village of Porthdinllaen is picture-postcard perfect, and adults can enjoy a drink at the pub on the beach, while children build sandcastles. Or for one of the best views in Wales stroll to the Coastguards' Hut on top of Mynydd Mawr, from where you can see Ireland on a clear day. Look out for the rare chough flying overhead, dolphins swimming in the bay and seals basking in the sun. A coastal path has recently been opened around the whole peninsula.

Left:
Brecon Beacons National Park, South Wales
Far right:
countryside at Hafod y Llan, with the Nantgwynant Valley beyond, Snowdonia, Wales

Further south, Llandanwg is not to be missed. Its beautiful, sandy beach has views across to the Llŷn Peninsula and a medieval church half buried in the sand. Above Barmouth is Dinas Oleu, a coastal hillside and the very first property passed to the Trust, in 1895. From here walkers can enjoy spectacular views over the surrounding area. Nearby, Egryn has been continually inhabited for more than 5,000 years and the medieval hall house and outbuildings are newly restored. The award-winning house is now available as an unique holiday cottage (**www.nationaltrustcottages.co.uk**). **National Trust parking is available at: Aberdaron, Llanbedrog, Porthdinllaen, Porthor and Uwchmynydd.**

Majestic beauty

In Snowdonia, a land of legend, majesty and breathtaking beauty, the Trust cares for eleven of the peaks and many miles of footpaths. These include a wheelchair-accessible, riverside path in the village of Beddgelert.

At Craflwyn there are woodland walks meandering past waterfalls and streams. For the more adventurous, the Watkin path is a spectacular route from Hafod y Llan farm to the top of Snowdon. Along the route you will see where the Trust is grazing Welsh black cattle to conserve the flora and fauna of this world-famous landscape. With the towering Tryfan, the dramatic Carneddau mountain range and the tranquil waters of Llyn Ogwen, there is always something new to explore among the peaks and valleys of Eryri. **National Trust parking is available at: Craflwyn, Cregennan, near Dolgellau, and Namor, near Aberglaslyn.**

A haven for wildlife

The lagoon at Cemlyn is a haven for wildlife and nesting birds. During the winter it is a great place to come and watch the winter wildfowl, while in late spring a colony of Arctic and common terns return to nest. The rocky sea cliffs here are among the oldest in Britain, with some being more than 1,000 million years old.

Dramatic landscape

With its spectacular combination of sensational valleys and distinctive flat-topped summits, the Brecon Beacons is a haven for those in search of a place to unwind, relax and feast on fresh air – in fact about 250,000 pairs of walking boots trudge along the slopes each year. Some of its most popular gems – Pen-y-Fan, Sugar Loaf, Skirrid and Henrhyd Falls – are cared for by the Trust.

Look out for ancient features as you explore this wonderful landscape. For example, fossils of some of the first land plants can be found on the Beacons. These appear as dark smudges in the rocks, however once under a microscope the intricate cell structure can clearly be seen. These fossils are of *Gosslinga breconensis*, which emerged about 417 million years ago when the land that we now call the Brecon Beacons was being laid down in a vast shallow sea somewhere near the equator.

Mae'r wybodaeth sydd yn y llawlyfr hwn am feddiannau'r Ymddiriedolaeth Genedlaethol yng Nghymru ar gael yn Gymraeg o Swyddfa'r Ymddiriedolaeth Genedlaethol, Sgwar y Drindod, Llandudno LL30 2DE, ffôn 01492 860123.

White water

The picturesque beauty spot of Henrhyd Falls on the Nant Llech boasts the impressive title of the highest waterfall in South Wales. It is only one of a series of beautiful waterfalls produced by the narrow, steep-sided gorges at the head of the Neath and Tawe rivers.

Historic parkland

The Dinefwr Parkland is a designated National Nature Reserve. Why not enjoy a historic walk with stunning views towards the castle, house and along the Tywi Valley? You may even spot some of the resident fallow deer or the stunning White Park cattle that have been in Dinefwr for more than a thousand years.

There are three walks in the upland 1,000-hectare (2,500-acre) Dolaucothi Estate, all with glorious views across the Cothi Valley. Another view which is hard to beat is the one from Paxton's Tower, which was built in 1811 by Sir William Paxton as a memorial to Lord Nelson.

Sweeping bays, fabulous walks and history

Gower is home to sandy bays, secluded coves, sand dunes, salt marsh, grassy clifftops and commons. With miles of paths, walking is a great way to explore the great variety of habitats and wildlife.

Breathtaking Rhossili Bay is overlooked by the Old Rectory, the most popular Trust holiday cottage. Walk to the top of Rhossili Down for panoramic views, or for a level walk head from the Trust shop and Visitor Centre in Rhossili to the Old Coastguard Lookout. When the tide is out, the adventurous can cross the rocky causeway to the tidal island of Worm's Head, where grey seals laze on the rocks.

Gower's landscape has been shaped by farming since the Stone Age. With many archaeological features, including neolithic burial chambers, Iron Age forts and the Vile at Rhossili (a medieval open-field strip system), Gower is an ideal place to discover these remnants of our ancestors.
National Trust parking is available at: Pennard.

Rolling coastline

The coast of Ceredigion has an unspoilt and intimate charm, and is nationally important as a conservation resource. The gently rolling coastline, with occasional striking rocky outcrops and steep wooded river valleys running inland, is a valuable example of mankind's long-term relationship with the local environment.

Mwnt, a small horseshoe-shaped bay, is probably the best place to spot a bottlenose dolphin in Ceredigion, while the sandy beach at Penbryn is a popular magnet for families.
National Trust parking is available at: Mwnt and Penbryn.

Left:
**St David's Head,
Pembrokeshire**

My favourite place

After spending a day in St David's and its surrounding coast and countryside, the world always feels to me a much better place. The attractive architecture of Britain's smallest city perfectly reflects its rural setting, and the majestic cathedral, concealed in the valley, is always uplifting. The Trust information centre in the city is a good place to plan your day.

For me though, it is the unspoilt, natural grandeur of the coastal fringes that I head for – leaving the raw open appeal of ecologically rich commons such as Waun Fawr, Tretio and Dowrog inland.

Porthclais' historic harbour, with its limekilns and boulder-built sea defences, offers a glimpse of the recent past and the influence of the sea on everyday life on the peninsula. The walk from here round Treginnis – the westernmost tip of Wales – offers expansive views across St Bride's Bay and over the turbulent waters of 'The Bitches' to Ramsey Island. The chance of seeing choughs, peregrines or porpoises adds to the excitement.

But it is St David's Head that has the strongest draw. Standing on top of the extinct volcano of Carn Llidi you can see, if you look carefully, 3,000 years of agricultural endeavour laid out below you. Peer through the heather and semi-natural vegetation and you can even make out prehistoric boundaries, shelters and dwellings. The even older neolithic burial chamber of Coetan Arthur does its best to blend into the background.

Jonathan Hughes
General Manager, Pembrokeshire

Aberconwy House

Castle Street, Conwy LL32 8AY

Map ④ E2 　　🏠 | 1934

This is the only medieval merchant's house in Conwy to have survived the turbulent history of the walled town over nearly six centuries. Furnished rooms and an audio-visual presentation show daily life from different periods in its history. **Note**: nearest toilet 50 yards on quay.

Exploring
— Explore how people lived from Tudor to Victorian times.
— Follow the stories of centuries from room to room.
— Discover what the walls are made of.
— Let the introductory footage bring old Conwy to life.

Eating and shopping: stock up on souvenirs in the shop. Conwy is full of great places to eat.

Making the most of your day: live music in the house. Ghost stories. Children's trail. Easter and Hallowe'en activities. Lace demonstrations. Guided tours. **Dogs**: assistance dogs only allowed.

Access for all: 📖 ♿ Building ♿

Getting here: 115:SH781777. At junction of Castle Street and High Street. **Cycle**: NCN5. **Bus**: from surrounding areas. **Train**: Conwy railway station 300 yards. **Parking**: no onsite parking.

Finding out more: 01492 592246 or aberconwyhouse@nationaltrust.org.uk

Aberconwy House			M	T	W	T	F	S	S
House									
19 Feb–27 Feb	11–5		M	T	W	T	F	S	S
5 Mar–6 Mar	11–5							S	S
12 Mar–30 Jun	11–5		M		W	T	F	S	S
1 Jul–31 Aug	11–5		M	T	W	T	F	S	S
1 Sep–30 Oct	11–5		M		W	T	F	S	S
Shop									
4 Jan–12 Mar	11–5			T	W	T	F	S	
13 Mar–30 Oct	11–5:30		M	T	W	T	F	S	S
31 Oct–31 Dec	11–5		M	T	W	T	F	S	S

Closed 25 and 26 December.

Aberconwy House, the oldest building in Conwy

Aberdeunant

Taliaris, Llandeilo, Carmarthenshire SA19 6DL

Map ④ E8 　　🏠 📷 🛏 | 1996

Traditional Carmarthenshire farmhouse in an unspoilt setting. **Note**: administered on the National Trust's behalf by a resident tenant. No toilet.

Access for all: 🅿 Building ♿ Grounds ♿

Getting here: 146:SN672308. Full details are sent on booking.

Finding out more: 01558 650177 (Dolaucothi Gold Mines) or aberdeunant@nationaltrust.org.uk

Aberdeunant
Admission by guided tour and appointment only. Tours take place April to September: first Saturday and Sunday of each month, 12 to 5. Telephone Dolaucothi Gold Mines to book. Last booking taken at 5 on Thursday prior to opening.

Aberdulais Falls

Aberdulais, near Neath,
Neath Port Talbot SA10 8EU

Map ④ E9 🏛🏚⬆🛗🎨🍽 1980

Set in a steep gorge, this property demonstrates the power of water and its impact on industry. Our film, *Reflections on Tin*, shows its 400-year-old history, from 1584, including a visit by the famous artist Turner. An early water-powered tin works was the last industry. Today the waters of the River Dulais are used to make Aberdulais Falls self-sufficient in environmentally friendly energy, with its waterwheel – the largest in Europe generating electricity. Lifts enable visitors to access the upper levels for excellent views of the falls. **Note**: waterwheel and turbine subject to water levels and maintenance.

Exploring
- 'The Tin Exhibition' – about adults and children who worked here.
- Check out our summer guided tours.
- Watch the waterwheel generating electricity.
- Wonder at the spectacular waterfall – best when it rains!

Eating and shopping: don't miss the National Trust shop. Enjoy Welsh cakes and bara brith in the tea-room. Experience our famous welcome and savour our lemon drizzle cake.

Making the most of your day: activity days, demonstrations and family quiz trails. Painting and archaeology days. **Dogs**: on leads only.

Access for all: 🅿♿🚻♿♿♿♿♿
Stable and Tin Exhibition ♿♿♿
Turbine House ♿♿♿♿♿
Grounds ♿♿♿➡♿

Getting here: 170:SS772995. **Foot**: via Neath to Aberdulais Canal footpath. **Cycle**: NCN47 passes property. Access near B&Q Neath to Neath Canal towpath and Aberdulais Canal Basin. **Bus**: Veolia X63 Swansea to Brecon, First Cymru X55 Swansea to Aberdare, First Cymru 154 Neath to Aberdulais, First Cymru 158 Swansea to Banwen, Silverline 775 Neath ➔ to Aberdulais. **Train**: Neath 3 miles. **Road**: on A4109, 3 miles north-east of Neath. 4 miles from M4 exit 43 at Llandarcy, take A465 signposted Vale of Neath. **Sat Nav**: follow brown signs, not Sat Nav. **Parking**: outside and on opposite side of road.

You may also enjoy: Dinefwr Park and Castle.

Finding out more: 01639 636674 or aberdulais@nationaltrust.org.uk

Aberdulais Falls		M	T	W	T	F	S	S
8 Jan–20 Feb	11–4						S	S
21 Feb–27 Feb	11–4	M	T	W	T	F	S	S
5 Mar–6 Mar	11–4						S	S
12 Mar–30 Oct	10–5	M	T	W	T	F	S	S
4 Nov–18 Dec	11–4					F	S	S

Open Bank Holidays (excluding 1 January, plus 25 and 26 December).

Aberdulais Falls, Neath Port Talbot, seen from the lower level

Bodnant Garden

Tal-y-Cafn, Colwyn Bay, Conwy LL28 5RE

Map ④ F2   🏠 ✿ 🔔 1949

Bodnant Garden, Conwy: so much to discover

'Variety on a grand scale, with beauty to behold around every corner.'
Mrs S. Jackson, Durham

Marvel at plants from all over the world grown from seed and cuttings collected over a century ago on plant-hunting expeditions. Created by five generations of one family, this 32-hectare (80-acre) garden is superbly located, with spectacular views across Snowdonia. With expansive lawns and intimate corners, grand ponds and impressive terraces, a steep wooded valley and stream, awe-inspiring plant collections and continually changing glorious displays of colour, there is always something to enjoy. Paths throughout allow you to explore, discover and delight in the garden's beauty – enjoy the clean, fresh fragrances of nature.
Note: garden and tea-rooms managed on behalf of National Trust by Michael McLaren.

Exploring
– Spectacular displays of daffodils, magnolias and camellias in early spring.
– 180-foot long laburnum arch flowers in late May.
– Discover the magical Dell, with towering 200-year-old trees.
– See the tallest coastal redwood in the UK.
– Learn the history of our heliochronometer, and how it works.
– Superb summer colours melt into an explosion of autumnal tints.

Eating and shopping: sample the delicious home-baked cakes in the tea-rooms. In the Pavilion tea-room try locally produced wine and beer. Bodnant-raised plants in the garden centre (not National Trust). Find that special bespoke gift in the craft shops (not Trust).

Making the most of your day: varied programme of family events, open-air theatre, evening plays. Family trails and Explorer Backpacks. Waymarked route for wheelchairs and pushchairs. Peek inside The Poem, last Tuesday of each month. **Dogs**: assistance dogs only allowed.

Access for all: 🅿️ 🚻 ♿ 🍴 📷 🔍 ♿ :•:
Grounds ♿ ♿ ➡ ♿

Getting here: 115/116:SH801723. **Bus**: Arriva 25, from Llandudno (passing Llandudno Junction ➤). **Train**: Tal-y-Cafn unmanned station, 2-mile walk along main road, no footpath. Alternatively Llandudno Junction ➤ then bus. **Road**: 8 miles south of Llandudno and Colwyn Bay off A470, entrance 1½ miles along the Eglwysbach road. Signposted from A55, exit 19. **Parking**: 150 yards from garden entrance. Tight turning circle for coach access. Limited disabled parking.

You may also enjoy: the Victorian walled garden at Penrhyn Castle.

Finding out more: 01492 650460 or bodnantgarden@nationaltrust.org.uk

Bodnant Garden		M	T	W	T	F	S	S
Garden								
26 Feb–31 Oct	10–5	M	T	W	T	F	S	S
1 Nov–13 Nov	10–4	M	T	W	T	F	S	S
Pavilion tea-room								
26 Feb–31 Oct	10–5	M	T	W	T	F	S	S
1 Nov–13 Nov	10–4	M	T	W	T	F	S	S
14 Nov–17 Dec	11–3:30	M	T	W	T	F	S	S
Magnolia tea-room								
1 Apr–31 Oct	11–4	M	T	W	T	F	S	S

Bodysgallen Hall Hotel, Restaurant and Spa

Llandudno, Conwy LL30 1RS

Map ④ F2  2008

This Grade I-listed 17th-century house has the most spectacular views towards Conwy Castle and Snowdonia. It is set in 89 hectares (220 acres) of award-winning romantic gardens, highlights of which include a rare parterre – filled with sweet-smelling herbs – several follies, a cascade, walled garden and formal rose gardens. Beyond, the hotel's parkland offers miles of stunning walks.

The house and gardens are already accessible to the public as a hotel and welcome guests to stay, to dine in the restaurants and to have afternoon tea (booking strongly advised). Contact hotel direct for best available offer. **Note**: all paying guests to the hotel are welcome to walk in the garden and park. Children above the age of six are welcome.

Finding out more: 01492 584466. 01492 582519 (fax) or info@bodysgallen.com. www.bodysgallen.com

Bodysgallen Hall, Conwy, as seen from the gardens

Chirk Castle

Chirk, Wrexham LL14 5AF

Map ④ G3   1981

'**Absolutely excellent! A great day out – much more here than I had expected, all very well informed and friendly**.'
Mrs Stanion, Stockport

Completed in 1310, Chirk is the last Welsh castle from the reign of Edward I still lived in today. Features from its 700 years include the medieval tower and dungeon, 17th-century Long Gallery, grand 18th-century state apartments, servants' hall and historic laundry. The award-winning gardens contain clipped yews, herbaceous borders, shrub and rock gardens. A terrace with stunning views looks out over the Cheshire and Shropshire plains. The parkland provides a habitat for rare invertebrates, wild flowers and contains many mature trees and also some splendid wrought-iron gates, made in 1719 by the Davies brothers. **Note**: major redevelopment work underway. Some items removed from display until May. Temporary tea-room.

Exploring
- Meet the medieval guards and discover life 700 years ago.
- Explore the stark medieval Adam Tower and dungeon.
- Try on armour and join in guard duty.
- Be awestruck by over 400 years of elegant family living.
- Encounter Berkshire pigs, ancient trees and bluebells in the woods.
- Savour peace and quiet in the award-winning gardens.

Eating and shopping: be tempted by local fresh food from the farm shop and sample seasonal menus in the tea-room (temporary tea-room facilities only until new restaurant at Home Farm opens in September). Browse the gift shop, plant sales and second-hand books.

Discovering the 700-year-old Chirk Castle, Wrexham

You may also enjoy: the magnificent architecture and gardens of Powis Castle.

Finding out more: 01691 777701 or chirkcastle@nationaltrust.org.uk

Chirk Castle		M	T	W	T	F	S	S
Estate*								
2 Jan–31 Dec	7–6:30	M	T	W	T	F	S	S
Garden, tower, shops and tea-rooms								
5 Feb–27 Feb	10–4						S	S
21 Feb–25 Feb	10–4	M	T	W	T	F		
2 Mar–30 Jun	10–5			W	T	F	S	S
1 Jul–30 Oct	10–5	M	T	W	T	F	S	S
5 Nov–18 Dec	10–4						S	S
State rooms **								
9 Mar–30 Jun	11–5			W	T	F	S	S
1 Jul–30 Oct	11–5	M	T	W	T	F	S	S
State rooms* *								
10 Dec–18 Dec	11–4						S	S

Open Bank Holiday Mondays. *Closes dusk if earlier. **State rooms by guided tour only 11 to 12, free-flow 12 to closing. ***Part open for Christmas event. Garden and tower close at 5 in March and October. State rooms close at 4 in March and October.

Cilgerran Castle

near Cardigan, Pembrokeshire SA43 2SF

Map ④ C7 🏛 1938

This striking 13th-century castle is in a stunning location overlooking the Teifi Gorge and has inspired many artists, including Turner. **Note**: in the guardianship of Cadw – Welsh Assembly Government's historic environment service. Dogs on leads allowed.

Access for all: 🚾♿🅿

Getting here: 145:SN195431. On rock above left bank of the Teifi, 3 miles south-east of Cardigan, 1½ miles east of A478.

Finding out more: 01443 336104 or cilgerrancastle@nationaltrust.org.uk

Cilgerran Castle		M	T	W	T	F	S	S
2 Jan–31 Mar	10–4	M	T	W	T	F	S	S
1 Apr–31 Oct	10–5	M	T	W	T	F	S	S
1 Nov–31 Dec	10–4	M	T	W	T	F	S	S

Closed 1 January and 24 to 26 December.

Making the most of your day: our new leaflets tell you all about the many places to explore (including the fortress, tranquil gardens and woods), plus fascinating stories about servants' life and the Myddelton family home. **Dogs**: on leads welcome everywhere outdoors except formal gardens. Please note, no shady parking.

Access for all: 🅿♿🚾🎧📷♿:·:
State rooms ♿♿ Adam Tower ♿
Gardens ♿♿➡♿

Getting here: 126:SJ275388. **Foot**: permitted footpaths from Chirk and Offa's Dyke Path, open April to September. Entrance and exit drives during season 1½ miles to visitor centre and castle. 1½ miles from Llangollen Canal to moor near Chirk Tunnel. **Bus**: Arriva 2/A Wrexham to Oswestry. **Train**: Chirk ⇌ ¼ mile to gates, 1½ miles to castle. **Road**: entrance 1 mile off A5, 2 miles west of Chirk village; 7 miles south of Wrexham, 5 miles from Llangollen, signposted off A483. **Parking**: free, 50 yards to visitor centre, 200 yards to castle. Steep hill from visitor centre to castle and garden. One-way system on driveway, follow signs to entrance.

Colby Woodland Garden

near Amroth, Pembrokeshire SA67 8PP

Map ④ C8 ⬛⬛⬛⬛⬛⬛ 1980

Admiring a sculpture at Colby Woodland Garden, Pembrokeshire

'**A wonderful hidden treasure that's a delight to wander around.**'
Mr Williams, Shoreham-by-Sea

Set in a tranquil and secluded valley, this glorious informal woodland garden with a fascinating industrial past is always bursting with colour and wildlife. Whatever the season, there's something to delight. Spring brings carpets of bluebells and an abundance of camellias, rhododendrons and azaleas. Enjoy shady woodland walks, the wildflower meadow and colourful walled garden in summer followed by the marvellous colours of autumn. Explore the meadow with its meandering stream and abundance of dragonflies, butterflies and other insects. Discover more about the garden's wildlife and its history and take a virtual tour of Pembrokeshire in the Bothy exhibition. **Note**: the house is not open.

Exploring — Wander the woodland walks and spot the carved benches.
— Discover the tallest *Cryptomeria japonica* tree in the UK.
— Climb up to the summerhouse and glimpse the sea.
— Be amazed by the *trompe l'oeil* paintings in the gazebo.
— Explore the wider Colby Estate, with its network of footpaths.
— Walk down to the beach at Amroth (¾ mile).

Eating and shopping: buy a souvenir of your visit at the Trust shop. Visit the Bothy tea-room for a freshly prepared treat. Browse in the gallery, full of local art and crafts. Visit Summerhill Farm Shop for award-winning lamb and beef.

Making the most of your day: full events programme, including Easter trails, twilight wildlife and bat walks, family fun days, children's quiz, wildlife events, summer holiday activities, guided walks and cream teas with the Head Gardener. **Dogs**: on leads in woodland garden only.

Access for all: 🅿️🔲🔲🔲🔲🔲🔲🔲🔲🔲
Grounds 🔲🔲🔲

Getting here: 158:SN155080. **Foot**: from beach via public footpath in Amroth (beside Amroth Arms). **Bus**: Silcox 350/1 from Tenby (passing Kilgetty ≋). **Train**: Kilgetty 2½ miles. **Road**: 1½ miles inland from Amroth beside Carmarthen Bay. Follow brown signs from A477 Tenby to Carmarthen road or off coast road at Amroth Castle caravan park. **Parking**: free, 50 yards. Please note 31 October to 31 December car park is pay and display. Contact property for route map for coaches and cars.

You may also enjoy: Tudor Merchant's House and the Stackpole Estate.

Finding out more: 01834 811885 or
colby@nationaltrust.org.uk

Colby Woodland Garden		M	T	W	T	F	S	S
Woodland garden, walled garden and shop								
19 Feb–30 Oct	10–5	M	T	W	T	F	S	S
Tea-room								
19 Feb–3 Apr	10–4						S	S
4 Apr–30 Oct	10–5	M	T	W	T	F	S	S
Gallery								
4 Apr–30 Oct	11–5	M	T	W	T	F	S	S
Woodland garden, walled garden, bothy and car park								
31 Oct–31 Dec	10–4	M	T	W	T	F	S	S

Closed 25 and 26 December.

Conwy Suspension Bridge

Conwy LL32 8LD

Map ④ E2   🏠 🚂 1965

See how trade and travel brought Conwy to
life and discover how a husband and wife kept
Thomas Telford's bridge open every day of the
year, whatever the weather. **Note**: no toilet.

Exploring – Marvel at Thomas Telford's
graceful bridge design.
– Enjoy the stunning views over
the Conwy estuary.
– Visit the beautifully restored
tiny toll house.

Eating and shopping: bring your own picnic to
enjoy on the grassed area.

Making the most of your day: guided talks on
Thomas Telford. **Dogs**: allowed.

Access for all: Building 🏛 Grounds 👣

Getting here: 115:SH785775. 100 yards from
town centre, adjacent to Conwy Castle.
Cycle: NCN5. **Bus**: Arriva buses from
surrounding areas. **Train**: Conwy ¼ mile;
Llandudno Junction ½ mile. **Parking**: no
onsite parking.

Finding out more: 01492 573282 or
conwybridge@nationaltrust.org.uk

Conwy Suspension Bridge		M	T	W	T	F	S	S
12 Mar–30 Oct	11–5	M	T	W	T	F	S	S

Thomas Telford's graceful Conwy Suspension Bridge, Conwy

Dinefwr Park and Castle

Llandeilo, Carmarthenshire SA19 6RT

Map ④ E8  1990

'**A fantastic landscape, a striking house and strong feel of Welsh history. So much for us all to do!**'
Greg Guile, Carmarthenshire

Newton House, in the landscape park at Dinefwr, Carmarthenshire

A magical land of power and influence for more than 2,000 years, Dinefwr Park and Castle is an iconic place in the history of Wales. Two forts are evidence of a dominant Roman presence. The powerful Lord Rhys held court at Dinefwr and influenced decisions in Wales. The visionaries of George and Cecil Rice designed the superb 18th-century landscape that you see today. The 'hands-on' Newton House gives visitors an atmospheric *circa* 1912 experience. Exhibitions on the first floor tell Dinefwr's story and inspire visitors to explore the castle and park.

Exploring — Experience Dinefwr's magic on waymarked walks through the park.

Exploring —
- Be thrilled by views from the top of the castle.
- Let off steam in the children's play area.
- Get close to the rare and historic White Park cattle.
- Help with servants' tasks in the brushing room.
- Listen to the servants chatting about their daily work.

Eating and shopping: buy local Welsh produce in the atmospheric shop. Eat our local fare in the Billiard Room tea-room. Taste local wines and beers overlooking the croquet lawn. Stay at one of our two holiday cottages.

Making the most of your day: regular hidden history and deer park tours (charge including members), school holiday and family activities. Edwardian-themed days and Christmas events. Varied programme of events. Waymarked walks around the park. **Dogs**: welcome on leads, in outer park only.

Access for all: ⬚⬚⬚⬚⬚⬚
Building ⬚⬚⬚⬚⬚ **Grounds** ⬚

Getting here: 159:SN625225. **Bus**: from surrounding areas to Llandeilo, then 1 mile. **Train**: Llandeilo 1 mile. **Road**: on west outskirts of Llandeilo A40(T); from Swansea take M4 to Pont Abraham, then A48(T) to Cross Hands and A476 to Llandeilo; entrance by police station. **Sat Nav**: problems, do not use. **Parking**: 50 yards. Narrow access.

You may also enjoy: Dolaucothi Gold Mines and Llanerchaeron.

Finding out more: 01558 824512 (visitor centre) or dinefwr@nationaltrust.org.uk

Dinefwr Park and Castle		M	T	W	T	F	S	S
3 Jan–18 Feb	11:30–4	M	T	W	T	F	S	S
19 Feb–30 Jun	11–5	M	T	W	T	F	S	S
1 Jul–31 Aug	10–6	M	T	W	T	F	S	S
1 Sep–30 Oct	11–5	M	T	W	T	F	S	S
31 Oct–20 Dec	11:30–4	M	T	W	T	F	S	S
Park, house and shop								
1 Jan–2 Jan	12–4						S	S
21 Dec–31 Dec*	12–4	M	T	W	T	F	S	S

Boardwalk, deer park and play area close 3:30 during winter, 4:30 at other times, except July and August, when they close at 5:30. *Closed 24 and 25 December. Tea-room open all year (apart from 1 and 2 January and 21 to 31 December).

Dolaucothi Gold Mines

Pumsaint, Llanwrda,
Carmarthenshire SA19 8US

Map ④ E7   1941

These unique gold mines are set amid wooded hillsides overlooking the beautiful Cothi Valley. 2,000 years ago, the powerful Romans left behind a glimpse of gold-mining methods. The harsh mining environment continued in the 19th and 20th centuries, ending in 1938. Guided tours take you back to experience the conditions of the Roman, Victorian and 1930s underground workings. See and hear the 1930s mine and mine machinery. Have a go at gold panning and take the opportunity to experience the frustrations of searching for real gold. Stay on our caravan site opposite the Gold Mines. **Note**: underground tours involve steep slopes, stout footwear essential.

Exploring
 – Experience the thrill of an underground guided tour.
 – Sift the panning troughs and keep what you find.
 – Get to grips with gold in the gold exhibition.
 – Enjoy the walks around this beautiful upland estate.

Eating and shopping: buy rare Welsh gold jewellery in the shop. Taste local cooking in our mine tea-room.

Making the most of your day: frequent underground tours (charge including members, please note younger children may not be carried). Regular school holiday and family activities. Self-guided walks around the estate. **Dogs**: on leads only.

Access for all: 🅿️♿️🔄👓 **Building** ♿️♿️

Getting here: 146:SN662403. **Bus**: Morris 289 from Lampeter. **Train**: Llanwrda, 8 miles. **Road**: between Lampeter and Llanwrda on A482. **Parking**: free. Overflow car park opposite main entrance.

Experiencing the thrill of Dolaucothi Gold Mines, Carmarthenshire

You may also enjoy: Dinefwr Park and Castle, as well as Llanerchaeron.

Finding out more: 01558 650177 or dolaucothi@nationaltrust.org.uk

Dolaucothi Gold Mines		M	T	W	T	F	S	S
Mines, shop and tea-room								
12 Mar–30 Jun	11–5	M	T	W	T	F	S	S
1 Jul–31 Aug	10–6	M	T	W	T	F	S	S
1 Sep–30 Oct	11–5	M	T	W	T	F	S	S
Caravan site								
31 Mar–30 Oct	12–5	M	T	W	T	F	S	S
Christmas shop (Coach House Pumsaint)								
9 Nov–18 Dec	11–4	·	·	W	T	F	S	S

Pumsaint Information Centre and estate walks open all year. Underground tours last one hour approximately (helmets with lights provided). Smaller children will only be allowed on tours at the discretion of staff (telephone for advice). Groups can be booked out of hours/season.

Erddig

Wrexham LL13 0YT

Map ④ H3  1973

Described as 'the jewel in the crown of Welsh country houses', Erddig is a fascinating yet unpretentious early 18th-century country house which reflects a gentry family's 250 years of upstairs-downstairs life. The extensive downstairs area contains Erddig's unique collection of servants' portraits, while the upstairs rooms are an amazing treasure trove of fine furniture, textiles and wallpapers. Outside, an impressive range of outbuildings includes stables, a smithy, joiners' shop and sawmill. It is set within a superb 18th-century formal garden and romantic landscape park – which are the starting points for walks, bicycle and carriage rides through the estate.

Exploring
- Gain a fascinating insight into life below stairs.
- An amazing miscellany of treasures and trivia within the house.
- Enjoy the outstanding formal gardens and country estate.
- Look out for the themed country walking routes.

Visitors enjoying a horse-drawn coach ride in the gardens at Erddig, Wrexham

Exploring
- Take a horse and carriage ride around the grounds.
- Hire a bicycle: tracks criss-cross the estate.

Eating and shopping: pick up gifts in the shop. Take home a selection of peat-free plants. Enjoy refreshments in the restaurant, ice-cream parlour and tea garden. Try a bottle of our own cider.

Making the most of your day: full events programme, including open-air theatre, festivals, craft fairs, Christmas markets and family fun days. Guided walks, tree trails and discovery tours. **Dogs**: on leads in country park only.

Access for all: ⬚⬚⬚⬚⬚⬚⬚⬚⬚⬚⬚⬚⬚
Building ⬚⬚ Exhibition Room ⬚⬚
Grounds ⬚⬚⬚⬚

Getting here: 117:SJ326482. 2 miles from Wrexham. **Bus**: Arriva 2 from Wrexham, alight Felin Puleston, 1 mile walk through Erddig Country Park. **Train**: Wrexham Central 2½ miles; Wrexham General 3½ miles via Erddig Road and footpath. **Road**: 2 miles south of Wrexham. Signposted A525 Whitchurch road. A483 exit 3. **Parking**: free, 200 yards. Accessible drop-off point. Parking for three coaches.

You may also enjoy: Chirk Castle, as well as Powis Castle and Garden.

Finding out more: 01978 355314 or erddig@nationaltrust.org.uk

Erddig		M	T	W	T	F	S	S
House								
12 Mar–30 Oct*	12:30–4:30	M	T	W	T	F	S	S
31 Oct–31 Dec**	11–3:30	M	T	W	T	F	S	S
Garden, restaurant and shop								
2 Jan–20 Feb	11–4						S	S
21 Feb–27 Feb	11–4	M	T	W	T	F	S	S
5 Mar–30 Oct	11–5:30	M	T	W	T	F	S	S
31 Oct–31 Dec	11–4	M	T	W	T	F	S	S

*Themed tours at 11:30 and 12; free-flow from 12:30. **Bakery, kitchen and laundry rooms only. Last admission to house one hour before closing. House and gardens closed 25 December. No electric light in the house; for close study of pictures and textiles avoid dull days, especially in March and October.

Gower: Rhossili Shop and Visitor Centre

Coastguard Cottages, Rhossili, Gower,
Swansea SA3 1PR

Map (4) D9  1933

Overlooking Rhossili Bay, the popular National
Trust shop boasts a range of gifts, souvenirs
and confectionery. It is a great place to start
exploring this beautiful area. The Visitor Centre,
on the first floor, provides local information.
Note: nearest toilet at Rhossili car park
(not National Trust).

Exploring   – Pick up a National Trust walks
                leaflet and go exploring.
           – Families come and discover
                Rhossili with a Tracker Pack.
           – Relax on one of the sandy
                beaches around Gower's coast.

Eating and shopping: try our tenant farmer's
saltmarsh lamb (01792 391421). Treat yourself
to locally made food and gifts, or a souvenir.

Making the most of your day: events
held throughout the year, contact
gower.admin@nationaltrust.org.uk for details.

Access for all: **Building**
Grounds

Getting here: 159:SS414881. **Bus**: Veolia
Gower Explorer 118 Swansea to Rhossili.
Road: south-west tip of Gower Peninsula,
approached from Swansea via A4118 and then
B4247. **Parking**: 50 yards (not National Trust),
charge including members.

Finding out more: 01792 390707 or
rhossili.shop@nationaltrust.org.uk

Rhossili Visitor Centre		M	T	W	T	F	S	S
7 Jan–27 Feb	11–4					F	S	S
28 Feb–31 Mar	10:30–4:30	M	T	W	T	F	S	S
1 Apr–31 Oct	10:30–5	M	T	W	T	F	S	S
1 Nov–23 Dec	11–4	M	T	W	T	F	S	S

1 April to 31 October: closes 6 weekends during
school holidays.

Looking out across breathtaking Rhossili Bay, Gower

The Kymin

The Round House, The Kymin, Monmouth,
Monmouthshire NP25 3SF

Map (4) H8  1902

Picnic spot amongst woods and pleasure
grounds, visited by Nelson. Spectacular views
across Wales. Attractive Georgian banqueting
house and temple.

Access for all: **Building**
Grounds

Getting here: 162:SO528125. 2 miles east of
Monmouth and signposted off A4136.

Finding out more: 01600 719241 or
kymin@nationaltrust.org.uk

The Kymin		M	T	W	T	F	S	S
Round House								
26 Mar–31 Oct	11–4	M					S	S
Grounds								
Open all year	7–9	M	T	W	T	F	S	S

Open Good Friday. Round House: last admission 15 minutes
before closing (croquet set and other games for hire
and toilet available when open). Car park open during
daylight hours only.

Llanerchaeron

Ciliau Aeron, near Aberaeron,
Ceredigion SA48 8DG

Map ④ D6 1989

This rare example of a self-sufficient 18th-century Welsh minor gentry estate has survived virtually unaltered. The villa, designed in the 1790s, is the most complete example of the early work of John Nash. It has its own service courtyard with dairy, laundry, brewery and salting house, and walled kitchen gardens (with all its produce for sale when in season). The pleasure grounds and ornamental lake and parkland provide peaceful walks. The Home Farm complex has an impressive range of traditional, atmospheric outbuildings and is a working organic farm with Welsh Black cattle, Llanwenog sheep and rare Welsh pigs.

Exploring
— Discover and experience the main residence and staff quarters.
— Wander through the pleasure grounds and ornamental lake.
— Explore the working walled gardens.
— Learn about the farm – the buildings and inhabitants.
— Don't miss the special events days throughout the year.
— Experience self-sufficiency at its best.

Eating and shopping: enjoy light meals and cakes, or bring a picnic. Shop in reception area sells local beer, jams and cider. Property farm and garden produce is on sale in reception. Cards, gifts, second-hand bookshop and locally made produce available.

Making the most of your day: seasonal gardening and nature activities. Visit the website for the full events list. **Dogs**: river and parkland walks for dogs on leads.

Access for all: ⓟ Ⓓ 🅼 🅼 🅻 🖼 🆅🆃 👓
Building 🏠♿🅻 Grounds ♿

You may also enjoy: Dolaucothi Gold Mines, Dinefwr Park and Castle and Colby Woodland Gardens.

Finding out more: 01545 570200 or llanerchaeron@nationaltrust.org.uk

Llanerchaeron			M	T	W	T	F	S	S
21 Feb–27 Feb	11:30–4		M	T	W	T	F	S	S
2 Mar–3 Apr	11:30–3:30		·	·	W	T	F	S	S
4 Apr–30 Oct	11–5		M	T	W	T	F	S	S
2 Nov–11 Dec	11:30–3:30		·	·	W	T	F	S	S
Farm and garden only									
7 Mar–29 Mar	11:30–3:30		M	T					
31 Oct–6 Dec	11:30–3:30		M	T					
12 Dec–31 Dec	11:30–3:30		M	T	W	T	F	S	S
Evening opening									
1 Jun–29 Jun	5–8		·	·	W	·	·	·	·

Café and shop open as whole property. 3 and 4 December, 11 to 4: Christmas Food and Craft Fair. 31 October to 11 December: ground floor of house only open. Whole property closed 25 December.

Pigs on the farm at Llanerchaeron, near Aberaeron, Ceredigion

Penrhyn Castle

Bangor, Gwynedd LL57 4HN

Map ④ E2 🏠 ✝ 🛗 ❄ 🍴 | 1951

This enormous 19th-century neo-Norman castle sits between Snowdonia and the Menai Strait. It is crammed with fascinating items, such as a one-ton slate bed made for Queen Victoria, elaborate carvings, plasterwork and mock-Norman furniture, in addition it has an outstanding collection of paintings. The restored kitchens are a delight and the stable block houses a fascinating industrial railway museum, a model railway museum and a superb dolls' museum. The 24.3 hectares (60 acres) of grounds include parkland, an exotic tree and shrub collection as well as a Victorian walled garden.

Admiring the view of the keep at Penrhyn Castle, Gwynedd

Exploring	– Wander through lavishly furnished state rooms.
	– Enjoy one of the finest art collections in Wales.
	– Explore the warren of workrooms in the servants' area.
	– Explore our open parkland and glorious gardens.
	– Marvel at the stunning views over mountains and sea.

Eating and shopping: enjoy freshly prepared locally sourced food in our self-service licensed tea-room. Indulge in our home-baked cakes and scones; the Penrhyn cream tea is a great favourite. Treat yourself to many traditional treats, such as Anglesey eggs and Teisen Berffro.

Making the most of your day: find out more about our Victorian kitchen or join in the many events throughout the season, including summer fun days (packed with children's activities) and our Victorian Christmas. **Dogs**: on leads in grounds only.

Access for all: 🅿️🚻♿🔔👜📷💻📠📶🅰️ Building 🔾🔾♿♿ Grounds 🔾🔾

Getting here: 115:SH602720. **Cycle**: NCN5, 1¼ miles. **Bus**: Arriva 5/5X Caernarfon to Llandudno, Padarn 76 from Bangor, both to castle driveway. **Train**: Bangor 3 miles. **Road**: 1 mile east of Bangor, at Llandygai on A5122. Signposted from junction 11 of A55 and A5. **Parking**: free, 500 yards.

You may also enjoy: Plas Newydd, Aberconwy House, Conwy Suspension Bridge, Plas yn Rhiw and Tŷ Mawr Wybrnant.

Finding out more: 01248 363219 (Infoline). 01248 353084 or penrhyncastle@nationaltrust.org.uk

Penrhyn Castle		M	T	W	T	F	S	S
Castle								
12 Mar–30 Oct	12–5	M	·	W	T	F	S	S
1 Jul–31 Aug	11–5	M	·	W	T	F	S	S
Stable block, shop and museums								
19 Feb–27 Feb	11–4	M	·	W	T	F	S	S
5 Mar–6 Mar	11–4	·	·	·	·	·	S	S
12 Mar–30 Oct	11–5	M	·	W	T	F	S	S
1 Jul–31 Aug	10–5	M	·	W	T	F	S	S
3 Dec–4 Dec	11–4	·	·	·	·	·	S	S
10 Dec–11 Dec	11–4	·	·	·	·	·	S	S

Grounds and tea-room: as castle but open one hour earlier. Victorian kitchen: as castle but last admission 4:45. Last audio tour 4.

Plas Newydd Country House and Gardens

Llanfairpwll, Anglesey LL61 6DQ

Map ④ D2 🏯🏛️✿🍃🖼️ 🏠🔔🍷 1976

Plas Newydd, the ancestral home of the Marquess of Anglesey, bears witness to a turbulent history: noble beginnings during Henry VIII's reign, triumphant success at Waterloo, bankruptcy at the turn of the 20th century and the revival of the family fortunes in the 1930s. The house is famous for its association with Rex Whistler, and contains his exquisite romantic mural and the largest exhibition of his works. Located on the Menai Straits, with glorious views across Snowdonia, you can stroll through an Australasian arboretum, Italianate summer terrace or follow a woodland path leading to the marine walk along the Straits.

Exploring
– Discover portraits and landscapes in the Angleseys' home.
– Enjoy crafted timber shelters, bird hides and Menai boat trips.
– Wander in the landscaped grounds and along the marine walk.
– Find the rhododendron garden – spectacular in April, May and June.
– Children: enjoy playing in the family room and adventure playground.
– Learn about the links with HMS *Conway*.

Eating and shopping: Whistlers at Plas Newydd serves a varied selection of food and drinks. Our gift shop includes great ideas and inspiring offers. There is also a second-hand bookshop in our specialist coffee shop, located inside the house.

Children join in a Family Fun event in the garden at Plas Newydd, Anglesey

Making the most of your day: take a stroll through the rhododendron garden and the marine walk. Also why not join us at weekends in December for our Christmas Craft and Food Fair? **Dogs**: in the car park only.

Access for all: 🅿️🅿️♿🚾♿🖼️💻 ♿
Building 🔁♿♿ Grounds ♿

Getting here: 114/115:SH521696. 2 miles south-west of Llanfairpwll. **Cycle**: NCN8, ¼ mile. **Bus**: Arriva 42 Bangor to Llangefni (passing Bangor ≋ and close Llanfairpwll ≋). **Train**: Llanfairpwll 1¾ miles. **Road**: 2 miles south-west of Llanfairpwll A55 junctions 7 and 8a, or A4080 to Brynsiencyn; turn off A5 at west end of Britannia Bridge. **Parking**: free, 400 yards.

You may also enjoy: Penrhyn Castle, Glan Faenol, Aberconwy House, Swtan and Plas yn Rhiw.

Finding out more: 01248 715272 (Infoline). 01248 714795 or plasnewydd@nationaltrust.org.uk

Plas Newydd		M	T	W	T	F	S	S
House*								
19 Mar–2 Nov	11:15–5	M	T	W	·	·	S	S
Shop, tea-room, woodland and adventure playground**								
2 Jan–19 Mar	11–4	·	·	·	·	·	S	S
20 Mar–2 Nov	10–5:30	M	T	W	T	F	S	S
3 Nov–31 Dec	11–4	M	T	W	T	F	S	S
Garden and coffee shop								
19 Mar–2 Nov	10–5:30	M	T	W	·	·	S	S
Rhododendron garden					·			
2 Apr–8 Jun	11–5:30	M	T	W	·	·	S	S

*House open for **tours only** until 1; free-flow from 1 until close. **Closed 25 December. Picnics allowed in area by the car park only. Please note house is accessible to manual wheelchairs only.

Plas yn Rhiw

Rhiw, Pwllheli, Gwynedd LL53 8AB

Map ④ C4 🏚 ❀ 🏞 🏠 1952

The house was rescued from neglect and lovingly restored by the three Keating sisters, who bought it in 1938. The views from the grounds and gardens across Cardigan Bay are among the most spectacular in Britain. The house is 16th-century with Georgian additions, and the garden contains many beautiful flowering trees and shrubs, with beds framed by box hedges and grass paths. It is stunning whatever the season.

Exploring	– Find out how the Keating sisters lived in the 1930s.
	– Explore the meandering paths and enjoy the stunning views.
	– Discover the two-seater garden privy!
	– See for yourself what inspired Honora Keating's delightful landscape paintings.

Eating and shopping: enjoy a hot or cold drink and ice-cream from the shop. Plant sales and gifts.

Making the most of your day: plant sales. Guided tours by arrangement. Easter Egg hunt. **Dogs**: on leads and only on the woodland walk below car park.

Access for all: 🅿️ 🚻 ♿ 📷 🚶 ⣿
Building ♿ 🔼 Grounds ♿ 🔼

Getting here: 123:SH237282. **Bus**: Nefyn 17b Pwllheli to Aberdaron (passing Pwllheli ≋), stops outside Plas yn Rhiw gate. **Train**: Pwllheli 10 miles. **Road**: 12 miles south-west of Pwllheli. Follow signs to Plas yn Rhiw. B4413 to Aberdaron (drive gates at bottom Rhiw Hill). **Parking**: small car park, 80 yards. Not suitable for large vehicles. Narrow lanes.

You may also enjoy: on the grand scale – Penrhyn Castle, Bangor.

Finding out more: 01758 780219 or plasynrhiw@nationaltrust.org.uk

Plas yn Rhiw		M	T	W	T	F	S	S
24 Mar–1 May	12–5	·	·	·	T	F	S	S
2 May–29 Aug	12–5	M	·	W	T	F	S	S
1 Sep–30 Sep	12–5	M	·	·	T	F	S	S
1 Oct–30 Oct	12–4	·	·	·	T	F	S	S

Open Bank Holidays. Garden and snowdrop wood open occasionally at weekends in January and February.

The library at Plas yn Rhiw, Pwllheli, Gwynedd

Powis Castle and Garden

Welshpool, Powys SY21 8RF

Map (4) G5  1952

The world-famous garden, overhung with clipped yews, shelters rare and tender plants. Laid out under the influence of Italian and French styles, it retains its original lead statues and an orangery on the terraces. High on a rock above the terraces, the castle, originally built *circa* 1200, began life as a medieval fortress. Remodelled and embellished over more than 400 years, it reflects the changing needs and ambitions of the Herbert family – each generation adding to the magnificent collection of paintings, sculpture, furniture and tapestries. A superb collection of treasures from India is displayed in the Clive Museum. **Note**: visitors (including members) need a ticket from visitor reception.

Exploring
- Relax in the sumptuous 10.5-hectare (26-acre) garden.
- Delight in the grandeur of the Elizabethan Long Gallery.
- Be amazed by the exquisite collection of Indian treasures.
- Go behind the scenes with castle and garden tours.
- Travel back in time with our themed events.

Eating and shopping: locally sourced seasonal produce served in the restaurant. Try our bara brith, made with our own secret recipe. Take home your own Powis plant, propagated in our nursery. Gifts and products from Wales on sale in the shop.

Making the most of your day: children's activities during school holidays, tours and lectures about the castle and garden during autumn and winter. Weekly talks and tours about caring for the collection.

Access for all: ⃞⃞⃞⃞⃞⃞⃞⃞⃞⃞⃞⃞
Building ⃞ Grounds ⃞⃞▶⃞⃞

Visitors admiring the view from the terraced gardens at Powis Castle and Garden, Powys

Getting here: 126:SJ216064. **Foot**: 1-mile walk from Park Lane, off Broad Street in Welshpool. Access from High Street (A490). **Bus**: Tanant Valley D71 Oswestry to Welshpool; X75 Shrewsbury to Llanidloes. On both alight High Street, 1 mile. **Train**: Welshpool 1¼ miles from town on footpath. **Road**: 1 mile south of Welshpool; signed from main road to Newtown (A483); enter by first drive gate on right. **Parking**: free. Telephone for advice on coach parking.

You may also enjoy: another medieval castle, Chirk Castle in Wrexham.

Finding out more: 01938 551944 (Infoline). 01938 551929 or powiscastle@nationaltrust.org.uk

Powis Castle and Garden		M	T	W	T	F	S	S
Castle and Clive Museum								
2 Mar–31 Mar	1–4	M	·	W	T	F	S	S
1 Apr–30 Sep	1–5	M	·	W	T	F	S	S
1 Oct–30 Oct	1–4	M	·	W	T	F	S	S
Castle								
4 Nov–31 Dec	12–4	·	·	·	·	F	S	S
Garden, restaurant and shop								
2 Mar–31 Mar	11–4:30	M	·	W	T	F	S	S
1 Apr–30 Sep	11–5:30	M	·	W	T	F	S	S
1 Oct–30 Oct	11–4:30	M	·	W	T	F	S	S
4 Nov–31 Dec	11–4	·	·	·	·	F	S	S

Last admission to castle 45 minutes before closing. Closed 24 and 25 December. Garden, restaurant and shop open 26 December, weather permitting.

St David's Visitor Centre and Shop

Captain's House, High Street, St David's, Pembrokeshire SA62 6SD

Map (4) A8   1974

Opposite The Cross in the centre of St David's, Wales's smallest historic city, the Visitor Centre and Shop is open all year. Try out our new interactive technology for a complete guide to the National Trust in Pembrokeshire – places to visit, beaches and walks – and browse in the well-stocked shop. **Note**: no toilet.

St David's Head, Pembrokeshire, seen from Penberry

Exploring — Take a virtual tour of Pembrokeshire.
— Pick up a leaflet and plan where to visit next.
— Discover more about the coast and countryside in our care.

Eating and shopping: comprehensive range of merchandise, including books, cards and maps. Treat yourself to locally made gifts and produce.

Making the most of your day: walks and evening talks throughout the year (ask staff for information).

Access for all: Building 🏠

Getting here: 115:SM753253. In the centre of St David's. **Foot**: Pembrokeshire Coast Path within 1 mile. **Bus**: Richards 411 from Haverfordwest ☰. Celtic Coaster and Puffin Shuttle during main holiday season. **Parking**: no onsite parking.

Finding out more: 01437 720385 or stdavids@nationaltrust.org.uk

St David's Visitor Centre and Shop		M	T	W	T	F	S	S
3 Jan–19 Mar	10–4	M	T	W	T	F	S	·
20 Mar–31 Dec	10–5:30	M	T	W	T	F	S	S

Closes 4 on Sunday. Closed 25, 26 and 27 December.

Segontium

Caernarfon, Gwynedd

Map ④ D2   1937

Fort built to defend the Roman Empire against rebellious tribes. **Note**: in the guardianship of Cadw – Welsh Assembly Government's historic enviroment service. Museum not National Trust.

Access for all: Grounds

Getting here: 115:SH485624. On Beddgelert road, A4085, on south-east outskirts of Caernarfon, 500 yards from town centre.

Finding out more: 01286 675625 or segontium@nationaltrust.org.uk

Segontium	
Museum (not National Trust) open Tuesday to Sunday, 12:30 to 4:30 (open Bank Holiday Mondays). Closes end of November.	

Stackpole Estate

Stackpole, near Pembroke, Pembrokeshire

Map ④ B9

Once owned by the Cawdor family, who transformed much of the natural landscape, this beautiful and varied stretch of coastline is famous for its award-winning sandy beaches, wooded valleys, dramatic cliffs and lily ponds. The Bosherston Lakes and Stackpole Warren are part of Stackpole National Nature Reserve, managed in partnership with the Countryside Council for Wales. Wildlife includes otters, herons, wintering wildfowl and dragonflies, as well as breeding seabirds and choughs. Also on the estate is Stackpole for Outdoor Learning, a residential eco-centre for schools and families, and the Stackpole Centre, a multipurpose venue offering group accommodation. **Note**: Stackpole Centre is being refurbished.

Skenfrith Castle

Skenfrith, near Abergavenny, Monmouthshire NP7 8UH

Map ④ H8   1936

Remains of early 13th-century castle, built beside the River Monnow to command one of the main routes from England. **Note**: in the guardianship of Cadw – Welsh Assembly Government's historic enviroment service.

Access for all: Building

Getting here: 161:SO456203. 6 miles north-west of Monmouth, 12 miles north-east of Abergavenny, on north side of the B4521.

Finding out more: 01874 625515 or skenfrithcastle@nationaltrust.org.uk

Skenfrith Castle		M	T	W	T	F	S	S
Open all year	Dawn–dusk	M	T	W	T	F	S	S

View towards the Eight Arch Bridge from where Stackpole Court, Pembrokeshire, once stood

Exploring
- Relax on excellent sandy beaches at Broadhaven South and Barafundle.
- Enjoy the spectacular clifftop scenery – look out for choughs.
- Visit Bosherston Lily Ponds, home to otters, wildfowl and dragonflies.
- Walk miles of footpaths – linking lakes, woods, cliffs and beaches.
- See where Stackpole Court once stood and admire the views.
- Coarse fishing – permits available. Conditions apply.

Eating and shopping: the Boathouse café at Stackpole Quay serves local, seasonal food. Mencap Walled Garden produces and sells plants, fruit and vegetables. Stay in one of our holiday cottages at Stackpole Quay.

Making the most of your day: theatre and music concerts at the Stackpole Centre. Guided walks and activities. **Dogs**: under control on the estate.

Access for all: ⃞⃞⃞⃞ Building ⃞
Grounds ⃞⃞

Getting here: 158:SR992958. 6 miles south of Pembroke. **Foot**: via Pembrokeshire Coast Path. **Bus**: Silcox 388 Pembroke ⃟ to Angle. **Train**: Pembroke 5 miles. **Road**: B4319 from Pembroke to Stackpole and Bosherston (various entry points onto estate). **Parking**: at Stackpole Quay, Broadhaven South and Bosherston Lily Ponds (charge applies). Access via narrow lanes with passing places.

You may also enjoy: Colby Woodland Garden and Tudor Merchant's House.

Finding out more: 01646 661359 or stackpole@nationaltrust.org.uk. Old Home Farm Yard, Stackpole, near Pembroke, Pembrokeshire SA71 5DQ

Stackpole Estate	Open every day all year

Late 15th-century exterior of the Tudor Merchant's House, Tenby, Pembrokeshire

Tudor Merchant's House

Quay Hill, Tenby, Pembrokeshire SA70 7BX

Map ④ C9 ⃞ 1937

Step back 500 years and discover how the Tudor merchant and his family would have lived in this fascinating three-storey house, situated close to the harbour within the historic walled town of Tenby. Features of the house include a fine 'Flemish' round chimney and the original scarfed roof trusses. **Note**: no toilet.

Exploring
- Ask the staff about how the Tudors lived.
- Don't miss the latrine tower or the Flemish chimney.
- Small herb garden open, weather permitting.

Eating and shopping: house information and Tudor replica items for sale.

Making the most of your day: children can try on Tudor costumes and play with replica toys. See the staff wearing Tudor costumes on Bank Holidays. Easter and Hallowe'en family events. Children's quiz.

Access for all: 🖼️⬛️🖥️♿️👁️ Building ♿️

Getting here: 158:SN135004. In the centre of Tenby off Tudor Square. **Foot**: Pembrokeshire Coast Path within ¼ mile. **Bus**: local services from surrounding areas, drop off at town walls, ¼ mile. **Train**: Tenby ½ mile. **Parking**: very limited parking on streets within town walls apart from July and August, when parking is in pay and display car parks only or via park and ride.

Finding out more: 01834 842279 or tudormerchantshouse@nationaltrust.org.uk

Tudor Merchant's House		M	T	W	T	F	S	S
19 Feb–27 Feb	11–3	M	T	W	T	F	S	S
5 Mar–13 Mar	11–3	·	·	·	·	·	S	S
14 Mar–17 Jul	11–5	M	T	W	T	F	·	S
18 Jul–28 Aug	11–5	M	T	W	T	F	S	S
29 Aug–30 Oct	11–5	M	T	W	T	F	·	S

Open Saturdays on Bank Holiday weekends, 11 to 5.

Eating and shopping: bring your own picnic and relax by the stream.

Making the most of your day: introductory talks. Woodland walks. Exhibition room. Families will enjoy the children's art packs, family activity sheet and woodland animal trail. **Dogs**: under close control.

Access for all: 🅿️♿️🚻🖼️ Building ♿️♿️ Grounds ♿️

Getting here: 115:SH770524. **Bus**: Jones 64 Llanrwst to Cwm Penmachno (passing Betws-y-Coed 🚆), alight Penmachno, then 2-mile walk. **Train**: Pont-y-pant 2½ miles. **Road**: at the head of the Wybrnant Valley. From A5 6 miles south of Betws-y-Coed, take B4406 to Penmachno. House is 2½ miles north-west of Penmachno by forest road. **Parking**: free, 500 yards. No access for coaches (33-seater minibuses welcome). Telephone to arrange access.

Finding out more: 01690 760213 or tymawrwybrnant@nationaltrust.org.uk

Tŷ Mawr Wybrnant		M	T	W	T	F	S	S
24 Mar–30 Oct	12–5	·	·	·	T	F	S	S

Open Bank Holiday Mondays.

Tŷ Mawr Wybrnant

Penmachno, Betws-y-Coed, Conwy LL25 0HJ

Map ④ E3   🏠🖼️ 1951

Explore centuries of Welsh living in this traditional stone-built upland farmhouse. Set in the heart of the beautiful Conwy Valley, Tŷ Mawr was the birthplace of Bishop William Morgan, the first translator of the Bible into Welsh. Walks lead from the house through woodland and traditionally managed landscape.

Exploring
- View the impressive Bible collection in nearly 100 languages.
- Discover how people survived without electricity or other creature comforts.
- New: explore the woodland animal trail.

Tŷ Mawr Wybrnant, Conwy, birthplace of Bishop William Morgan, first translator of the Bible into Welsh

Northern Ireland

A feast for the eyes: Venus and Eurydice stand sentinel at opposite ends of the vast octagonal hall at Mount Stewart House

Outdoors in Northern Ireland

For enticing open spaces, exhilarating challenges and serenely tranquil getaways, Northern Ireland, with more than 120 miles of coastline and 40 square miles of scenic countryside in the Trust's care, cannot be beaten.

The mild climate and diverse landscape, with its ever-changing vistas, make it a wonderful place to explore. Why not try one of our wide range of walks? There is an enormous choice for all levels, whether you are someone who simply wants to take a stroll or a serious rambler. Alternatively try pedal or paddle power, and see the countryside from a bicycle or canoe!

Let the north coast amaze you

Some of the region's best-loved visitor attractions are dotted along the stunning coast of North Antrim. Explore the iconic Giant's Causeway, discover the historic ruins of Dunseverick Castle, or stroll along the majestic sweeping arc of White Park Bay. Brave the elements and cross Carrick-a-Rede rope bridge, or marvel at the bustling seabird colonies at Larrybane, with its views beyond to Rathlin Island and the west coast of Scotland.

There are few better places to experience this diverse coastline than the distinctive headland of Fair Head, which rises 190 metres and gives dramatic views of nearby Murlough Bay. On unspoilt Rathlin Island inspirational views across to the Scottish Islands and Mull of Kintyre can be seen from the waymarked path through Ballyconagan.

Above: **curious rock formations at the Giant's Causeway, County Antrim**

Other coastal treasures include the tiny village of Glenoe near Larne, with its spectacular waterfall, while the footpath along Skernaghan Point on the northern tip of Islandmagee leads to open headland, cliffs, coves and beautiful beaches. Along the geologically rich coastline to the north-east lies the delightful seaside village of Cushendun and the ecologically important raised blanket peat bog at Cushleake Mountain.

A haven for wildlife

The coastline of County Down has much for walkers and naturalists alike, with rocky shore and heathland at Ballymacormick Point and wildfowl, wading birds and gulls at Orlock Point.

Strangford Lough, Britain's largest sea lough and one of Europe's key wildlife habitats, offers bracing coastal walks among delicate wild flowers and butterflies. There are also rock pools bursting with marine life and opportunities for spectacular birdwatching. Visitors to Ballyquintin Farm, on the Ards Peninsula, can enjoy stunning views of Strangford Lough and learn how this critical site is managed for wildlife and conservation.

Further south, the fragile 6,000-year-old sand dunes of Murlough National Nature Reserve, near Newcastle, form an extraordinarily beautiful dune landscape with a network of paths and boardwalks – perfect for walking.

Above: cattle wander through White Park Bay on the North Antrim coast

Below: wide open spaces at Murlough National Nature Reserve, County Down

Wild and beautiful

Escape the hustle and bustle of the city and go off the beaten track. Within fifteen minutes of Belfast you can find yourself meandering along the Lagan river bank at Minnowburn, climbing Cregagh Glen in the Castlereagh Hills, exploring the woodland paths of Collin Glen or tramping the upland heath to the summit of Divis Mountain for spectacular views over the city.

To the west of the region, idyllic County Fermanagh boasts a kaleidoscope of tranquil landscapes to discover – including the woodland and wetlands of Crom on the serene shores of Lough Erne.

Or for a real walk on the wild side, the Trust's Mourne Mountain paths allow hikers to enjoy the dramatic scenery of Northern Ireland's highest mountain, the majestic Slieve Donard, as well as neighbouring Slieve Commedagh.

Have paddle, will travel

The National Trust has links to Northern Ireland's five canoe trails, all along exciting stretches of water with public access for canoeists. Each trail allows you to see an abundance of wildlife while exploring a different part of Northern Ireland's interesting countryside – from the picturesque islands in Strangford Lough, to the calming countryside along the Blackwater River and the lakeland paradise on Lough Erne. For more information on the canoe trails visit **www.canoeni.com**

Outdoors in Northern Ireland

Further information

Euro notes are accepted by the Trust's Northern Ireland properties.

Under the National Trust Ulster Gardens Scheme, a number of private gardens are generously opened to the public in order to provide income for Trust gardens in Northern Ireland. For the 2011 programme telephone 028 9751 0721.

To find out what is happening in Northern Ireland this year, see our 2011 *Events Guide*.

Below:
crisp snow on the eastern slope of Divis Mountain, overlooking Belfast

My favourite time of year

As Divis and the Black Mountain warden I am extremely fortunate to be able to enjoy the mountains in all weathers, but my favourite month is February. The sky is clean, clear and crisp and you can see for miles and miles. This is the best time to experience the unique pleasure of solitude. Few venture out, only hardy walkers who appreciate the snow-dusted mountain ridges. These reveal many secrets. Ancient field patterns emerge etched out on the mountainside, reminders of forgotten dwellings and the people that once lived there.

Hovering kestrels are a familiar sight. They hang motionless in the cold breeze, steadily watching their ground-dwelling prey before dropping like stones – they benefit from patience. Small flocks of a Scandinavian winter bird visitor, the fieldfare, can be seen foraging for winter berries, worms and insects. This is a truly lovely bird – plump, with a slate-grey nape and rump, speckled chest, chestnut back and a distinctive black tail.

Last year I tracked a hare's footprints through the snow as it covered more than one mile without, unlike me, sinking once into the snow drifts. I never even got close to seeing the hare – it must have known where it was going.

Easy to get to and bracing in the February wind, the view over Belfast from the Black Mountain is stunning. This area is the noisiest place on the mountains, as the city's traffic is no longer shielded by the escarpment front of the hills. It is amusing to sit in the snow at the summit and hear the jingle of ice-cream vans selling their 99s far below.

With spectacular panoramic views of Strangford Lough, the Mournes and the Sperrins, as well as Scotland and Donegal, a bracing walk in February is a great day out for visitors who want to feel the wind in their hair.

Dermot McCann
Divis and the Black Mountain Warden

Ardress House

64 Ardress Road, Annaghmore, Portadown,
County Armagh BT62 1SQ

Map (7) D7   1959

This charming 17th-century farmhouse,
elegantly remodelled in Georgian times, offers
fun and relaxation for all the family. Set in 40
hectares (100 acres) of countryside, there
are apple orchards, beautiful woodland and
riverside walks. The atmosphere of a working
farmyard has been rekindled with the return
of small animals.

Ardress House, County Armagh: 17th-century charm

Exploring
- Enjoy 'The Ladies' Mile' walk through trees and shrubs.
- Children will love feeding the chickens in the farmyard.
- Attractive garden, with scenic woodland and riverside walks.
- Elegant Neo-classical drawing room, with plasterwork by Michael Stapleton.

Eating and shopping: drinks and ice-cream
available. Picnic in the attractive garden and
charming woodlands.

Making the most of your day: see miniature
Shetland ponies, pygmy goats, Soay sheep,
ducks and chickens. Events include Country
Capers and Ghostly Hallowe'en. Children's play
area. **Dogs**: on leads in garden only.

Access for all: Building Grounds

Getting here: H914561. **Bus**: Ulsterbus 678
Portadown to Tullyroan Bridge (passing
close Portadown) to within ¼ mile.
Train: Portadown 7 miles. **Parking**: free, 10 yards.

Finding out more: 028 8778 4753 or
ardress@nationaltrust.org.uk

Ardress House		M	T	W	T	F	S	S
12 Feb–13 Feb	12–5						S	S
12 Mar–26 Jun	1–6						S	S
22 Apr–1 May	1–6	M	T	W	T	F	S	S
2 Jul–28 Aug	1–6				T	F	S	S
3 Sep–25 Sep	1–6						S	S
27 Oct–30 Oct	12–5				T	F	S	S

Admission by guided tour (last admission one hour before
closing). Open Bank Holiday Mondays and all other public
holidays in Northern Ireland **including 17 March**. Grounds
('The Lady's Mile') open daily all year, dawn to dusk.

The Argory

144 Derrycaw Road, Moy, Dungannon,
County Armagh BT71 6NA

Map (7) C7   1979

Built in the 1820s, this handsome Irish gentry
house is surrounded by its 130-hectare
(320-acre) wooded riverside estate. The former
home of the MacGeough Bond family, a tour
of this Neo-classical masterpiece reveals it is
unchanged since 1900 – the eclectic interior
still evoking the family's tastes and interests.
Outside there are sweeping vistas, superb
spring bulbs, scenic walks and fascinating
courtyard displays. A second-hand bookshop,
adventure playground and Lady Ada's
award-winning tea-room provide retreats
for children and adults alike.

The Argory, County Armagh, was built in the 1820s

Exploring
- Garden, woodland and riverside walks with wonderful sweeping views.
- Snowdrop walks and superb spring bulbs.

Exploring – Fascinating courtyard displays and sundial in the rose garden.
– Children's adventure playground and environmental sculpture trail.
– Mansion is a treasure trove of Victorian and Edwardian interests.
– Four generations of MacGeough Bond family lived in the mansion.

Eating and shopping: enjoy afternoon tea in Lady Ada's tea-room. Light lunches and snacks available. Browse the gift shop and second-hand bookshop.

Making the most of your day: lively programme of events – craft fairs, poultry fairs, musical events. The mansion is a particular delight at Christmas, when it comes alive with music. **Dogs**: on leads in grounds and garden only.

Access for all: ⬛ ⬛ ⬛ ⬛ Grounds ⬛ ➡

Getting here: H871577. **Cycle**: NCN95, 7 miles. **Bus**: Ulsterbus 67 Portadown to Dungannon (both pass close Portadown ➤), alight Charlemont, 2½-mile walk. **Road**: 4 miles from Charlemont, 3 miles from M1, exit 13 or 14 (signposted). Coaches must use exit 13; weight restrictions at Bond's Bridge. **Parking**: 100 yards.

You may also enjoy: Ardress House – a charming 17th-century farmhouse nearby.

Finding out more: 028 8778 4753 or argory@nationaltrust.org.uk

The Argory		M	T	W	T	F	S	S
Grounds								
1 Jan–30 Apr	10–5	M	T	W	T	F	S	S
1 May–30 Sep	10–6	M	T	W	T	F	S	S
1 Oct–31 Dec	10–5	M	T	W	T	F	S	S
House								
12 Mar–30 Jun	11–5	M	·	·	T	F	S	S
1 Jul–31 Aug	11–5	M	T	W	T	F	S	S
1 Sep–30 Sep	11–5	M	·	·	T	F	S	S
1 Oct–30 Oct	11–4	M	·	·	T	F	S	S

Admission to house by guided tour (last admission one hour before closing). Open Bank Holiday Mondays and all other public holidays in Northern Ireland, **including 17 March**. Tea-room, shop and second-hand bookshop open as house, and also 27 to 31 December.

Carrick-a-Rede

119a Whitepark Road, Ballintoy, County Antrim BT54 6LS

Map ⑦ D3 1967

Take the exhilarating rope bridge to Carrick-a-Rede island and enjoy a truly clifftop experience. This 30-metre deep and 20-metre wide chasm is traversed by a rope bridge traditionally erected by salmon fishermen. Visitors bold enough to cross to the rocky island are rewarded with fantastic views. **Note**: maximum of eight people on bridge at once. Suitable clothing and footwear recommended.

Exploring – Fantastic birdwatching and unrivalled coastal scenery.
– Uninterrupted views of Rathlin and the Scottish islands.
– Site of Special Scientific Interest: unique geology, flora and fauna.
– Stay in Carrick-a-Rede holiday cottage.

Eating and shopping: new National Trust tea-room facilities now open. Delicious array of light lunches and snacks available.

Making the most of your day: guided tours (by prior arrangement). Breathtaking coastal path experience – part of the Causeway Coast Way from Portstewart to Ballycastle and the Ulster Way. **Dogs**: on leads (not permitted to cross bridge).

Access for all: ⬛ ⬛ ⬛ ⬛ ⬛ Grounds ⬛ ⬛ ➡

Getting here: D049446. **Foot**: on North Antrim Coastal Path and road, 7 miles from Giant's Causeway, ½ mile from Ballintoy village and 1½ miles from Ballintoy Church on Harbour Road. **Cycle**: NCN93, 5 miles. **Bus**: Ulsterbus 172 from Coleraine, Ulsterbus 252 and 256 from Belfast. **Road**: on B15, 7 miles east of Bushmills, 5 miles west of Ballycastle. Giant's Causeway 7 miles. **Parking**: free.

Finding out more: 028 2076 9839 or carrickarede@nationaltrust.org.uk

Carrick-a-Rede		M	T	W	T	F	S	S
Bridge								
1 Jan–27 Feb	10:30–3:30	M	T	W	T	F	S	S
28 Feb–26 May	10–6	M	T	W	T	F	S	S
27 May–31 Aug	10–7	M	T	W	T	F	S	S
1 Sep–31 Oct	10–6	M	T	W	T	F	S	S
1 Nov–31 Dec	10:30–3:30	M	T	W	T	F	S	S

Last entry to rope bridge 45 minutes before closing. Car park and North Antrim Coastal Path open all year. Bridge open weather permitting. Closed 25 and 26 December.

Castle Coole

Enniskillen, County Fermanagh BT74 6JY

Map (7) A7  1951

'**Our tour guide was excellent, loved contrast of the opulent decoration upstairs and lived-in feel of the servants' quarters**.'
Mr and Mrs Murphy, Glengormley

Experience the stately grandeur of this stunning 18th-century mansion set in a beautiful wooded landscape park – which is ideal for family walks. Castle Coole is one of Ireland's finest Neo-classical houses: the sumptuous Regency interior and the State Bedroom prepared for George IV provide a rare treat for visitors, allowing them to glimpse what life was like in the home of the Earls of Belmore. Discover the story of the people who lived and worked below stairs as you explore the splendid suite of servants' rooms and service quarters of this magnificent property.

Exploring
- Tour one of Ireland's finest Neo-classical houses.
- Take a guided tour of the historic basement.
- Enjoy a walk in the historic landscape and woodlands.
- Explore the Grand Yard and see the Belmore Coach.
- Discover the wildlife that live in and around Lough Coole.
- Cycle along part of the Castle to Castle Cycle Trail.

Eating and shopping: relax and unwind over lunch in the Tallow tea-room. Souvenirs and gifts can be purchased in the shop.

Making the most of your day: enjoy a walk around the Lake Walk, with breathtaking views and the opportunity to catch a glimpse of the tremendous variety of wildlife. Musical events throughout the year. **Dogs**: on leads in grounds only.

Access for all: 🅿️🔲🔲🔲🔲🔲🔲
Building 🔲🔲🔲 Grounds 🔲➡️

Getting here: H245431. **Cycle**: NCN91. **Bus**: Ulsterbus 95, Enniskillen to Clones (connections from Belfast). **Road**: 1½ miles south-east of Enniskillen on Belfast to Enniskillen road (A4). **Parking**: walkers' car park. Main car park, 150 yards.

You may also enjoy: Castle Coole is within driving distance of Florence Court and Crom.

Finding out more: 028 6632 2690 or castlecoole@nationaltrust.org.uk

Castle Coole		M	T	W	T	F	S	S
Grounds								
1 Jan–28 Feb	10–4	M	T	W	T	F	S	S
1 Mar–31 Oct	10–7	M	T	W	T	F	S	S
1 Nov–31 Dec	10–4	M	T	W	T	F	S	S
House, tea-room and shop								
12 Mar–29 May	11–5	.	.	.	.	.	S	S
22 Apr–2 May	11–5	M	T	W	T	F	S	S
1 Jun–29 Jun	11–5	M	T	W	.	F	S	S
1 Jul–31 Aug	11–5	M	T	W	T	F	S	S
3 Sep–25 Sep	11–5	.	.	.	.	.	S	S

House: admission by guided tour (last tour one hour before closing). Open Bank Holiday Mondays and all other public holidays in Northern Ireland **including 17 March**.

The Saloon at Castle Coole, County Fermanagh

Castle Ward

Strangford, Downpatrick,
County Down BT30 7LS

Map (7) F7

The classical side of Castle Ward, County Down

Castle Ward will take you on a journey of discovery. The 18th-century eccentric house with two distinctly different styles, classical and Gothic, will entice you to explore further. This truly beautiful 332-hectare (820-acre) walled demesne, with walking trails, exotic garden, stunning vistas and picturesque farmyard, will unlock your imagination through family history, leisure pursuits, events and industrial heritage. A children's pastimes centre and laundry room are a short walk from the house in the stableyard, alongside a gift shop, second-hand bookshop and tea-room.

Exploring
- Relax and enjoy the new Stableyard visitor reception.
- Visit The Barn, a fabulous new interactive children's play area.
- Indulge in cream teas in Lord Bangor's sitting room.
- Walk for miles on scenic trails through atmospheric woodlands.
- Attempt the 'mega slide' in the adventure playground.
- Picnic in the Victorian garden or by the Lough shore.

Eating and shopping: shop for local produce in the delightful gift shop. Pick up a bargain book from the second-hand bookshop. Organic soup, sandwiches and traybakes from the stableyard tea-room. Stay overnight in the caravan park to complete your visit.

Making the most of your day: extensive programme of events throughout the year, including Pirate's Picnic, Pumpkinfest, book fair and Santa's house. Children can explore with new interactive Tracker Packs and activity sheets. Guided house tours. **Dogs**: on leads in grounds only.

Access for all:

Building Grounds

Getting here: J573484. **Foot**: on Lecale Way. **Ferry**: from Portaferry. **Bus**: Ulsterbus 16E Downpatrick to Strangford, with connections from Belfast (passing close Belfast Great Victoria Street ■); bus stop at gates. Ulsterbus Lecale Rambler (Saturday, Sunday only) in summer. **Road**: 7 miles north-east of Downpatrick, 1½ miles west of Strangford village on A25, on south shore of Strangford Lough, entrance by Ballyculter Lodge. **Sat Nav**: is incorrect, once on the Strangford Road follow signs for Castle Ward only. **Parking**: free, 250 yards.

You may also enjoy: discovering exotic rhododendron species and viewing hand-fired pottery at nearby Rowallane Garden.

Finding out more: 028 4488 1204 or castleward@nationaltrust.org.uk

Castle Ward		M	T	W	T	F	S	S
Grounds								
1 Jan–31 Mar	10–4	M	T	W	T	F	S	S
1 Apr–30 Sep	10–8	M	T	W	T	F	S	S
1 Oct–31 Oct	10–5	M	T	W	T	F	S	S
1 Nov–31 Dec	10–4	M	T	W	T	F	S	S
House, tea-room and shop								
12 Mar–30 Oct	11–5	M	T	W	T	F	S	S

Last admission to house one hour before closing. Timed tickets apply to guided house tours. Open Bank Holiday Mondays and all other public holidays in Northern Ireland **including 17 March**. April to September: cornmill operates on Sundays. Barn opens daily, 12 to 5. Second-hand bookshop opens daily, 1 to 5.

Crom

Upper Lough Erne, Newtownbutler,
County Fermanagh BT92 8AP

Map (7) A8  1987

Escape to this breathtaking 810-hectare
(2,000-acre) demesne, set amid the romantic
and tranquil landscape of Upper Lough
Erne. One of Ireland's most important nature
conservation areas, Crom's ancient woodland
and picturesque islands are home to many rare
species. Stay for longer in our holiday cottages
or campsite. **Note**: the 19th-century castle is
private and not open to the public.

Exploring
- Hire a boat and explore the islands.
- Have a go at coarse angling or pike fishing.
- Enjoy woodland walks and nature trails.
- Stay at one of our holiday cottages or campsite.

Eating and shopping: afternoon tea available
in the visitor centre. Gifts and souvenirs
available to buy.

Making the most of your day: regular guided
walks by our conservation warden. Visit the
historic castle ruins. Enjoy a Cot Trip on Bank
Holiday Mondays. **Dogs**: on leads only.

**Crichton Tower on Gad Island in Lough Erne at Crom,
County Fermanagh**

Getting here: H380255. **Cycle**: NCN91.
Ferry: from Derryvore church (must be
booked 24 hours in advance). **Bus**: Ulsterbus
95 Enniskillen to Clones (connections from
Belfast), alight Newtownbutler, 3 miles.
Road: 3 miles west of Newtownbutler, on
Newtownbutler to Crom road, or follow signs
from Lisnaskea (7 miles). Crom is next to the
Shannon to Erne waterway. Public jetty at
visitor centre. **Parking**: 100 yards.

Finding out more: 028 6773 8118 or
crom@nationaltrust.org.uk

Crom		M	T	W	T	F	S	S
Grounds								
12 Mar–31 May	10–6	M	T	W	T	F	S	S
1 Jun–31 Aug	10–7	M	T	W	T	F	S	S
1 Sep–31 Oct	10–6	M	T	W	T	F	S	S
Visitor centre								
12 Mar–30 Sep	11–5	M	T	W	T	F	S	S
1 Oct–30 Oct	11–5	·	·	·	·	·	S	S

Open Bank Holiday Mondays and all other public holidays
in Northern Ireland **including 17 March**. Last admission one
hour before closing. Tea-room open as visitor centre (closed
October).

The Crown Bar

46 Great Victoria Street, Belfast,
County Antrim BT2 7BA

Map (7) E6 [♿] [🍺] 1978

Wonderful atmospheric setting, with period
gas lighting and cosy snugs. Ornate interior of
brightly coloured tiles, carvings and glass.

Getting here: J336737. In the centre of Belfast,
on Great Victoria Street.

Finding out more: 028 9024 3187 or
info@crownbar.com

The Crown Bar		M	T	W	T	F	S	S
Open all year	11:30–11	M	T	W	T	F	S	·
2 Jan–25 Dec	12:30–10	·	·	·	·	·	·	S

Closed 25 and 26 April, 2 May, 12 and 13 July, 25 and
26 December.

Derrymore House

Bessbrook, Newry, County Armagh BT35 7EF

Map (7) D8 1953

An elegant 18th-century thatched cottage with its peculiar gentrified vernacular style. A rich history and delightful walks. **Note**: no toilet.

Access for all: [P] Grounds [access icons]

Getting here: J057275. 1½ miles from Newry, on A25 off the Newry to Camlough road at Bessbrook.

Finding out more: 028 8778 4753 or derrymore@nationaltrust.org.uk

Derrymore House	M	T	W	T	F	S	S
Grounds							
Open all year	M	T	W	T	F	S	S

Treaty Room only open 2 and 30 May, 12 and 13 July, plus 29 August, 2 to 5:30.

Divis and the Black Mountain

Divis Road, Hannahstown, near Belfast, County Antrim BT17 0NG

Map (7) E6 [icons] 2004

The mountains rest in the heart of the Belfast Hills, which provide the backdrop to the city's skyline, while the rich, varied archaeological landscape is home to a host of wildlife. There are walking trails along a variety of terrain – through heath, on stone tracks, along boardwalks and road surface. **Note**: cattle roam freely during summer months.

Exploring
– Panoramic views across Northern Ireland, Donegal and Scotland.
– Home to a wealth of flora, fauna and archaeological remains.
– Fantastic viewpoint for Hallowe'en firework displays.
– New six-mile trail – Divis Mountain to Lady Dixon Park.

Eating and shopping: tea and coffee machine in the Long Barn.

Making the most of your day: a haven for those seeking the wild countryside experience. Programme of guided walks to discover the wealth of biodiversity and archaeological remains. 'Changing Places' toilet and accessible toilets available. **Dogs**: welcome but please note cattle roam freely during summer.

Access for all: [icons] Visitor centre [icon] Mountain [icon]

Getting here: J266741. 1 mile west of Belfast. **Bus**: Ulsterbus 106 – alight at Divis Road. **Road**: minor road west of A55. **Parking**: free.

Finding out more: 028 9082 5434 or divis@nationaltrust.org.uk

Divis and the Black Mountain	Open every day all year
Car park open 9 to 8.	

View from Divis Mountain, County Antrim, towards Belfast city

Downhill Demesne and Hezlett House

Mussenden Road, Castlerock,
County Londonderry BT51 4RP

Map (7) C3 🏛️🏠🏚️⛓️🌸🎡
🎢🔔🍷 1949

Visit the stunning landscape of Downhill Demesne, with its beautiful gardens and magnificent clifftop walks, affording rugged headland views across the awe-inspiring north coast. Discover the striking 18th-century mansion of the eccentric Earl Bishop that now lies in ruin, then explore Mussenden Temple, perched on the cliff edge. As an extra treat you can learn about the reality of life in the rural 17th-century cottage of Hezlett House, told through the people who once lived in one of Northern Ireland's oldest surviving buildings.

Exploring
- Enjoy a stroll around the inspiring gardens.
- Take in the panoramic views from Mussenden Temple.
- Children's Tracker Packs – include binoculars, compass and bird identification cards.
- Visit the garden restoration project at the Bishop's Gate.
- Take part in the archaeology project at Downhill Demesne.
- Hezlett House is also home to the Downhill Marbles Collection.

Eating and shopping: tea and coffee facilities offered at reception of Hezlett House. Perfect for a picnic in the sheltered gardens.

Making the most of your day: programme of events available. Beautiful orchard to explore at Hezlett House. **Dogs**: on leads only.

Access for all: 📷🚻 Building ♿ Grounds ♿

Getting here: C757357. **Cycle**: NCN93 borders property. **Ferry**: Magilligan to Greencastle ferry (8 miles). **Bus**: Ulsterbus 234 Coleraine to

Mussenden Temple on the Downhill Demesne, County Londonderry

Londonderry, alight crossroads, few minutes walk. **Train**: Castlerock ½ mile. **Road**: 1 mile, west of Castlerock and 5 miles west of Coleraine on Coleraine to Downhill coast road (A2). **Parking**: at Lion's Gate. Not suitable for 50-seater coaches. Alternative parking for coaches at Bishop's Gate entrance or Hezlett House, ½ mile from Temple.

You may also enjoy: Portstewart Strand, Giant's Causeway and Carrick-a-Rede rope bridge.

Finding out more: 028 70 848728 or downhilldemesne@nationaltrust.org.uk. 107 Sea Road, Castlerock, County Londonderry BT51 4TW

Downhill and Hezlett		M	T	W	T	F	S	S
Downhill Demesne grounds								
Open all year		M	T	W	T	F	S	S
Hezlett House and facilities								
26 Mar–2 Oct	10–5	M	T	W	T	F	S	S

Florence Court

Enniskillen, County Fermanagh BT92 1DB

Map (7) A7 🏠🔭✳♣♠🏠🔔🍸 1954

The charming Georgian mansion of Florence Court, County Fermanagh

'We really enjoyed our visit. The guided tour was brilliant and our lunch was delicious.'
Mrs Noon, Herefordshire

There is something for all the family at this warm and welcoming 18th-century property, the former home of the Earls of Enniskillen. The house enjoys a peaceful setting in West Fermanagh, with a dramatic backdrop of mountains and forests. There are glorious walks to enjoy, as well as fine vistas and play areas. There is even a charming walled garden. Every aspect of life in this classical Irish house, with its fine interiors and exquisite decoration, are brought to life on fascinating guided tours. Outside there are numerous places to explore, including sawmill, ice house and thatched summerhouse.

Exploring
- Take a guided tour of this fine 18th-century house.
- Enjoy spectacular views and discover flora and fauna.
- Visit the mother Irish yew tree.
- Visit Nelly Woolly's grave.
- Listen to the birdsong in the walled garden.
- Explore the atmospheric pleasure grounds.

Eating and shopping: enjoy homemade delights in the Stables restaurant. The Coach House shop offers a range of gifts.

Making the most of your day: range of events throughout the year. Tracker Packs available for children. Licensed civil wedding venue, with a number of historic rooms to hire for that special occasion. **Dogs**: on leads in garden and grounds only.

Access for all: 🅿🄳🚾🏢🛗📖👓🅰
Building 🏢🏢♿ Grounds 🏢➡🚶

Getting here: H176349. **Cycle**: NCN91. Entrance on Kingfisher Trail. **Bus**: Ulsterbus 192 Enniskillen to Swanlinbar, alight Creamery Cross, 2-mile walk. **Road**: 8 miles south-west of Enniskillen via A4 Sligo road and A32 Swanlinbar road, 4 miles from Marble Arch Caves. **Parking**: 200 yards.

You may also enjoy: Castle Coole and Crom – within easy driving distance.

Finding out more: 028 6634 8249 or florencecourt@nationaltrust.org.uk

Florence Court		M	T	W	T	F	S	S
Gardens and park								
1 Jan–28 Feb	10–4	M	T	W	T	F	S	S
1 Mar–31 Oct	10–7	M	T	W	T	F	S	S
1 Nov–31 Dec	10–4	M	T	W	T	F	S	S
House, tea-room and shop								
12 Mar–17 Apr	11–5						S	S
22 Apr–1 May	11–5	M	T	W	T	F	S	S
2 May–30 Jun	11–5	M		W	T	F	S	S
1 Jul–31 Aug	11–5	M	T	W	T	F	S	S
1 Sep–29 Sep	11–5	M	T	W	T		S	S
1 Oct–30 Oct	11–5						S	S
31 Oct	11–5	M						

House: admission by guided tour (last admission one hour before closing). Open Bank Holiday Mondays and all other public holidays in Northern Ireland, **including 17 March**. Tea-room and gift shop also open 27 to 31 December.

Giant's Causeway

44a Causeway Road, Bushmills,
County Antrim BT57 8SU

Map (7) D3   1962

Northern Ireland's iconic World Heritage Site and Area of Outstanding Natural Beauty is home to a wealth of local history and legend. Explore the basalt stone columns left by volcanic eruptions 60 million years ago and search for distinctive stone formations fancifully named the Camel, Harp and Organ. **Note**: construction of new visitor centre may cause disruption.

Exploring
— Beautiful coastal path extends 11 miles to Carrick-a-Rede.
— Geology, flora and fauna of international importance.
— Runkerry Head provides a spectacular two-mile walk.
— Some of Europe's finest cliff scenery, with fantastic birdwatching.

Eating and shopping: during building work temporary facilities are available at the Causeway Hotel.

Making the most of your day: Finn MacCool's Causeway steeped in legend and folklore. Open for walking all year, with stunning coast and cliff paths for exploration. Guided tours for groups (fifteen plus). **Dogs**: on leads only.

Access for all: 🚽 Grounds 👤♿👤 ➡

Visitors on Giant's Causeway, County Antrim

Getting here: C944439. **Foot**: path from Portballintrae alongside steam railway and from Dunseverick Castle (4½ miles). **Cycle**: NCN93. **Bus**: Ulsterbus 172, 177 from Coleraine. Ulsterbus 252 is a circular route from Belfast via the Antrim Glens. **Train**: Coleraine 10 miles or Portrush 8 miles. Giant's Causeway and Bushmills Steam Railway, 200 yards (028 2073 2844). **Road**: on B146 Causeway to Dunseverick road 2 miles east of Bushmills. **Parking**: limited. Park and ride from Dundarave.

Finding out more: 028 2073 1582 or giantscauseway@nationaltrust.org.uk

Giant's Causeway		M	T	W	T	F	S	S
Stones and coastal path								
Open all year		M	T	W	T	F	S	S
Visitor information and shop								
1 Jan–28 Feb	9:30–4	M	T	W	T	F	S	S
1 Mar–31 May	9:30–5	M	T	W	T	F	S	S
1 Jun–30 Jun	9:30–6	M	T	W	T	F	S	S
1 Jul–31 Aug	9:30–7	M	T	W	T	F	S	S
1 Sep–30 Sep	9:30–6	M	T	W	T	F	S	S
1 Oct–31 Oct	9:30–5	M	T	W	T	F	S	S
1 Nov–31 Dec	9:30–4	M	T	W	T	F	S	S

Due to construction work there are limited Trust facilities (including visitor information, shop and toilets) available at adjoining Causeway Hotel. Telephone 028 2073 1855 for further information. Closed 25 and 26 December.

Gray's Printing Press

49 Main Street, Strabane,
County Tyrone BT82 8AU

Map (7) B5 🏠↕ 1966

A treasure trove of galleys, ink and presses hidden behind an 18th-century shop front in the heart of Strabane.

Access for all: 🚽♿ Building 👤♿

Getting here: H345976. On Main Street, Strabane.

Finding out more: 028 8674 8210 or grays@nationaltrust.org.uk

Gray's Printing Press

Admission by guided tour. Last admission 45 minutes before closing. Telephone for opening dates and times.

Mount Stewart House, Garden and Temple of the Winds

Portaferry Road, Newtownards,
County Down BT22 2AD

Map (7) F6 [icons] 1976

Mount Stewart is one of the most unique and unusual gardens in the National Trust's ownership. The garden reflects a rich tapestry of design and great planting artistry that was the hallmark of Edith, Lady Londonderry. The mild climate of Strangford Lough allows astonishing levels of planting experimentation. The formal areas exude a strong Mediterranean feel and resemble an Italian villa landscape; the wooded areas support a range of plants from all corners of the world, ensuring something to see whatever the season. Engaging tours of the opulent house reveal its fascinating heritage and historic world-famous artefacts and artwork.

Exploring
- Explore one of the finest gardens in Europe.
- Discover the fascinating history of Mount Stewart mansion.
- Magnificent views of Strangford Lough from Temple of the Winds.
- Follow in footsteps of kings, queens, Prime Ministers and poets.
- Picturesque lake surrounded by beautiful swathes of woodland.
- Dinosaurs and duck-billed platypuses jostle on Dodo Terrace.

Eating and shopping: buy the best of local craft products in our shop. Try our unique Mount Stewart ice-cream. Visit the recently opened plant centre – a haven for gardeners. Enjoy a meal in the award-winning Bay Restaurant.

Making the most of your day: busy programme of events throughout the year – jazz in the garden, craft fairs, guided walks, garden tours, children's events and Santa's Grotto. Family activity packs also available. **Dogs**: on leads in grounds and garden only.

Access for all: [icons]
Building [icons] Grounds [icons]

Getting here: J555694. **Bus**: Ulsterbus 10 Belfast to Portaferry, bus stop at gates. **Train**: Bangor 10 miles. **Road**: 15 miles south-east of Belfast on Newtownards to Portaferry road, A20, 5 miles south-east of Newtownards. **Parking**: free, 100 yards.

You may also enjoy: Strangford Lough – an Area of Outstanding Natural Beauty and of unique importance for nature conservation.

Finding out more: 028 4278 8387 or mountstewart@nationaltrust.org.uk

Mount Stewart		M	T	W	T	F	S	S
Lakeside gardens								
Open all year	10–6	M	T	W	T	F	S	S
Formal gardens								
12 Mar–31 Oct	10–6	M	T	W	T	F	S	S
House								
12 Mar–31 Oct	12–6	M	T	W	T	F	S	S
Temple of the Winds								
13 Mar–30 Oct	2–5	·	·	·	·	·	·	S

Open Bank Holiday Mondays and all other public holidays in Northern Ireland, **including 17 March**. House: admission by guided tour (timed tickets only); last admission one hour before closing. Lakeside gardens closed 25 December. Telephone for shop and restaurant opening times.

Tir Nan Og in Mount Stewart gardens, County Down

Murlough National Nature Reserve

Keel Point, Dundrum, County Down BT33 0NQ

Map (7) E8    1967

Murlough is an extraordinarily beautiful dune landscape, fringing one of Northern Ireland's most popular beaches and overlooked by the rounded peaks of the Mourne Mountains to the south. The fragile 6,000-year-old sand dunes, Ireland's first nature reserve, are an excellent area for walking and wildlife. **Note**: limited toilet facilities.

Exploring
- Most extensive example of dune heath within Ireland.
- Over 330 species of butterflies and moths, including marsh fritillary.
- Dune flowers, common and grey seals, wintering wildfowl and waders.
- Evidence of human habitation from neolithic times to present day.

Eating and shopping: enjoy a latte in the beach café. Picnics in the car park or on the beach.

Making the most of your day: explore the network of paths and boardwalks through the dunes, woodland and heath. Self-guided nature walk, series of guided walks, volunteer events and family activities throughout the year. **Dogs**: welcome, restrictions apply when ground-nesting birds are breeding or cattle are grazing.

Access for all:

Getting here: J401350. Belfast is 25 miles approximately north on the A24. Newry is 25 miles west and Downpatrick is 10 miles to the east, both on the A25. **Foot**: 1 mile from south side of Dundrum village (follow Keel Point Road). From Newcastle is a longer walk

Tall grasses on the beach at Murlough National Nature Reserve, County Down

(but includes beautiful 2-mile stretch along beach). **Cycle**: NCN99 (Belfast to Newry) passes entrance. **Bus**: Ulsterbus 20 Belfast to Newcastle, alight at Lazy BJ Caravan Park after Dundrum. **Road**: signposted off the A2, between Dundrum and Newcastle. **Parking**: J394338. Open all year, pay and display (members free). Admission charge when facilities open. Suitable for coaches.

Finding out more: 028 4375 1467 or murlough@nationaltrust.org.uk

Murlough		M	T	W	T	F	S	S
Nature reserve								
Open all year	Dawn–dusk	M	T	W	T	F	S	S
Facilities								
19 Mar–17 Apr	10–6						S	S
22 Apr–2 May	10–6	M	T	W	T	F	S	S
7 May–12 Jun	10–6						S	S
18 Jun–18 Sep	10–6	M	T	W	T	F	S	S
24 Sep–9 Oct	10–6						S	S

Open Bank Holiday Mondays and all other public holidays in Northern Ireland, **including 17 March**.

Patterson's Spade Mill

751 Antrim Road, Templepatrick, County Antrim BT39 0AP

Map (7) E6  1991

Hear the hammers, smell the grit and feel the heat of traditional spade-making. Guided tours vividly capture life during the Industrial Revolution and dig up the history and culture of the humble spade. Find the origin of the phrase 'a face as long as a Lurgan spade'.

Spade-maker at work at Patterson's Spade Mill, County Antrim

Exploring
- Last working water-driven spade mill in the British Isles.
- See red-hot billets of steel fashioned into spades.
- Listen to the thunder of the massive water-powered trip hammer.
- Travel back in time to a bygone industrial era.

Eating and shopping: handcrafted spades on sale and made to specification. Tea and coffee available from drinks machine.

Making the most of your day: enjoy a 'Slippery feast' on St Patrick's Day and full steam ahead at the fascinating Stationary Engine Day. Guided tours and demonstrations for all the family with the Spade Maker. **Dogs**: on leads only.

Access for all: ⊞ ⊞ ⊞ ⊞ Building ⊞ ⊞ Grounds ⊞

Getting here: J261854. **Bus**: Ulsterbus 110, 120 Belfast to Cookstown, bus stop at gates. **Train**: Antrim 8 miles. **Road**: 2 miles north-east of Templepatrick on Antrim to Belfast road, A6; M2 exit 4. **Parking**: free, 50 yards.

Finding out more: 028 9443 3619 or pattersons@nationaltrust.org.uk

Patterson's Spade Mill		M	T	W	T	F	S	S
2 Apr–17 Apr	2–6						S	S
22 Apr–2 May	2–6	M	T	W	T	F	S	S
7 May–29 May	2–6						S	S
1 Jun–31 Aug	2–6	M	T	W	T		S	S
3 Sep–25 Sep	2–6						S	S

Admission by guided tour. Open Bank Holiday Mondays and all other public holidays in Northern Ireland **including 17 March**. Last admission one hour before closing.

Portstewart Strand

118 Strand Road, Portstewart, County Londonderry BT55 7PG

Map (7) C3   1981

The magnificent two-mile strand of glistening golden sand is one of Northern Ireland's finest and most popular beaches with all ages. It is the perfect spot to spend lazy summer days and take long walks into the sand dunes, which are a haven for wild flowers and butterflies.

Exploring
- Explore the sand dunes and waymarked nature trail.
- Many species of butterflies and moths, and colourful wild flowers.
- Visit the newly restored Grangemore birdhide for fantastic birdwatching.
- Enjoy lazy summer days, family picnics and sandcastles.

Paddling at Portstewart Strand, County Londonderry

Eating and shopping: light refreshments available at the environmentally friendly visitor centre, which also houses a beach shop.

Making the most of your day: relax and enjoy the sea and sand. Or meander through the dunes to see the wildlife – look out for the common blue butterfly, six-spot burnet moths and rare orchids. **Dogs**: on leads only.

Access for all: ⊞ ⊞ Beach ➡

Getting here: C811366. Just outside the centre of Portstewart. **Cycle**: NCN 93 runs nearby. **Bus**: Ulsterbus 140 from Coleraine (connections from Belfast route 218). **Train**: Coleraine. **Parking**: on beach.

Members may have to pay on special events days

Finding out more: 028 7083 6396 or portstewart@nationaltrust.org.uk

Portstewart Strand		M	T	W	T	F	S	S
Beach								
Open all year		M	T	W	T	F	S	S
Facilities								
26 Feb–27 Mar	10–4	M	T	W	T	F	S	S
28 Mar–24 Apr	10–5	M	T	W	T	F	S	S
25 Apr–29 May	10–6	M	T	W	T	F	S	S
30 May–31 Aug	10–7	M	T	W	T	F	S	S
1 Sep–30 Sep	10–5	M	T	W	T	F	S	S
1 Oct–30 Oct	10–4	M	T	W	T	F	S	S

Facilities close two hours before the barrier.

Rowallane Garden

Saintfield, County Down BT24 7JA

Map ⑦ E7   1956

Be inspired by this enchanting garden's dazzling array of exotic species from the four corners of the globe. Created in the mid-1860s by the Reverend John Moore, this informal plantsman's garden reflects the beautiful natural landscape of the surrounding area. There are spectacular displays of shrubs, including a large collection of rhododendron species and several areas managed as wildflower meadows. It is also home to a notable natural Rock Garden Wood, with shade-loving plants. The outstanding walled garden includes spectacular displays of herbaceous plants, shrubs and bulbs.

The walled garden at Rowallane, County Down

Exploring
- Browse for gardening ideas in the newly opened garden shop.
- Watch the master potter at work in the Secret Garden.
- Take a tranquil walk around the famous Rock Garden Wood.
- Book a gardening tour with the Head Gardener.
- Discover exotic and rare species of rhododendron.
- Follow the farmland trail to the summit of Trio Hill.

Eating and shopping: try delicious homemade soup from the Garden Kitchen tea-room. Pick up a bargain book from the second-hand bookshop. Purchase a unique Rowallane Garden glazed stoneware pot. Explore the garden shop for inspirational ideas.

Making the most of your day: wide range of events, such as Hot Jazz, spring and autumn plant fair, Ghosts and Gourds and Yuletide market. Children's activity sheets available. **Dogs**: on leads in garden only.

Access for all: 🅿️🚻♿🚽🎨 Grounds 🏛♿

Getting here: J412581. **Foot**: ¾ mile from Saintfield village centre. **Bus**: Ulsterbus 15 Belfast to Downpatrick (passing Belfast Great Victoria Street 🚉). **Road**: 11 miles south-east of Belfast, 1 mile south of Saintfield, on road to Downpatrick (A7). **Parking**: free.

You may also enjoy: touring Castle Ward, an eccentric house with two entirely different styles of architecture.

Finding out more: 028 9751 0131 or rowallane@nationaltrust.org.uk

Rowallane Garden		M	T	W	T	F	S	S
2 Jan–28 Feb	10–4	M	T	W	T	F	S	S
1 Mar–30 Apr	10–6	M	T	W	T	F	S	S
1 May–31 Aug	10–8	M	T	W	T	F	S	S
1 Sep–31 Oct	10–6	M	T	W	T	F	S	S
1 Nov–31 Dec	10–4	M	T	W	T	F	S	S

Closed 1 January plus 25 and 26 December. Gift shop and tea-room open daily spring and summer, Thursday to Sunday in winter. Please telephone for details.

The rear of 17th-century 'Plantation' house, Springhill, County Londonderry, with the Sperrin Mountains beyond

Springhill

20 Springhill Road, Moneymore, Magherafelt, County Londonderry BT45 7NQ

Map (7) C6  1957

Experience the beguiling spirit of this inimitable 17th-century 'Plantation' home, with its walled gardens and parkland, full of tempting waymarked paths. Informative Sunday afternoon Living History tours breathe life into the fascinating past of this welcoming family home. There are ten generations of Lenox-Conyngham family tales to enthrall you, as well as numerous portraits and much furniture to admire – not forgetting Ireland's best-documented ghost, Olivia. The old laundry houses the celebrated Costume Collection, which features some fine 18th- to 20th-century pieces that highlight its great charm and enthralling past.

Exploring
– Fun for all the family, with new trails for children.
– Fascinating new costume exhibition every year.
– Enjoy short walks around the charming estate.
– Relax in the herb garden with a chamomile lawn.
– Admire the 1,000-year-old yew tree.

Eating and shopping: delicious cream teas in the Servants' Hall tea-room. Look for presents in our little gift shop. Select a book in our 'Well Read' bookshop. Enjoy a picnic in the garden.

Making the most of your day: meet the family from long ago, enjoy the walks and then relax in the Servants' Hall tea-room with a delicious cream tea of homemade scones and raspberry jam. **Dogs**: on leads in grounds only.

Access for all:
Building

Getting here: H866828. **Foot**: from Moneymore village, 1 mile. **Cycle**: NCN94/95, 5 miles. **Bus**: Ulsterbus 210 and 110 Belfast to Cookstown, alight Moneymore village, 1 mile. **Road**: 1 mile from Moneymore on Moneymore to Coagh road, B18. **Parking**: 50 yards.

You may also enjoy: Wellbrook Beetling Mill, with its water-powered mill wheel.

Finding out more: 028 8674 8210 or springhill@nationaltrust.org.uk

Springhill		M	T	W	T	F	S	S
House and costume collection								
12 Mar–26 Jun	12–5	·	·	·	T	F	S	S
22 Apr–2 May	12–5	M	T	W	T	F	S	S
1 Jul–31 Aug	12–5	M	T	W	T	F	S	S
3 Sep–25 Sep	12–5	·	·	·	·	·	S	S
Grounds								
Open all year	10–7	M	T	W	T	F	S	S

House: admission by guided tour. Open Bank Holiday Mondays and all other public holidays in Northern Ireland, **including 17 March**. Last admission one hour before closing.

Wellbrook Beetling Mill

20 Wellbrook Road, Corkhill, Cookstown, County Tyrone BT80 9RY

Map (7) C6   1968

Nestling in an idyllic wooded glen that offers lovely walks and picnic spots, this, the last working water-powered linen beetling mill, offers a unique experience for all the family. Try some scutching, hackling and weaving as you take part in hands-on demonstrations, set against the thundering cacophony of beetling engines.

Exploring
— Follow the head-race to the source of the power.
— Lovely walks and picnic opportunities by the Ballinderry River.
— Watch the massive water-powered wheel as it turns.
— Look out for pearl mussels in the mill race.

Eating and shopping: tea and coffee are available on request. Delicious afternoon teas on Living History days. Irish linen and gifts are for sale in the small cottage shop. Picnic tables near the river.

Making the most of your day: tour the mill and find out about its history and historic linen-making processes. Experience Living History days. Walk up the head-race and then relax with a picnic on the lawn. **Dogs**: on leads in grounds only.

Access for all: ☒ ☒ ☒ ☒
Building ☒ ☒ Grounds ☒ ☒

Getting here: H750792. **Cycle**: NCN95. **Bus**: Ulsterbus 80 from Cookstown, with connections from Belfast, ½ mile. **Road**: 4 miles west of Cookstown, ½ mile off Cookstown to Omagh road (A505): from Cookstown turn right at Kildress Parish Church or follow Orritor Road (A53) to avoid the town centre. **Parking**: free, 10 yards.

Finding out more: 028 8675 1735 or wellbrook@nationaltrust.org.uk

Wellbrook Beetling Mill		M	T	W	T	F	S	S
12 Mar–26 Jun	2–6	·	·	·	·	·	S	S
22 Apr–1 May	1–6	M	T	·	·	F	S	S
1 Jul–30 Aug	2–6	M	T	·	T	F	S	S
3 Sep–25 Sep	2–6	·	·	·	·	·	S	S

Admission by guided tour. Open Bank Holiday Mondays and all other public holidays in Northern Ireland **including 17 March**. Last admission one hour before closing. Telephone for shop opening arrangements.

The Wellbrook Beetling Mill in County Tyrone

Pride of Britain Hotels

Privately owned luxury hotels in 40 locations around the UK reflecting a mix of traditional and contemporary styles, all offering excellent cuisine, comfortable accommodation and outstanding service. Many have spa facilities too.

Pride of Britain Hotels is the official hotel partner to the National Trust.

For your 2011 directory please telephone 0800 089 3929. To book, telephone the same number or visit **www. nationaltrust.org.uk/hotels**

Pride of Britain will donate 5 per cent of the value of each booking to the National Trust. This does not affect the price you pay.

National Trust Working Holidays

The National Trust Working Holidays programme provides great opportunities to make new friends, socialise and work together in a team. You can get away from the day-to-day distractions of modern living to achieve a worthwhile objective and make a significant difference to the preservation of our coast, countryside and historic houses. They are a real learning experience, with activities ranging from hedge laying or drystone walling to growing vegetables and repairing footpaths.

For those of you who like your home comforts, premium holidays offer more comfortable bedrooms which may be ensuite. Also included are Youth Discovery holidays for sixteen to eighteen year olds. Young people wanting to know more about this or other opportunities should email youth@nationaltrust.org.uk. There are also opportunities for whole families to enjoy a holiday together.

Each holiday is run by Trust staff and trained volunteer leaders, so experience is not necessary – just plenty of energy and enthusiasm!

For a brochure telephone 0844 800 3099, email working.holidays@ nationaltrust.org.uk or to book online visit **www. nationaltrust.org.uk/ workingholidays**

Bed and Breakfast on National Trust Farms, Camping and Caravan Sites

Enjoy some of the best of our countryside and coastal areas and a warm welcome by staying with National Trust tenant farmers or at one of our camping and caravan sites. For details visit **www.nationaltrust.org.uk/ holidays** or telephone for a B&B leaflet (0844 800 1895).

Historic House Hotels

Treat yourself to a break at Hartwell House Hotel, Restaurant and Spa near Aylesbury (page 121), Middlethorpe Hall Hotel, Restaurant and Spa in York (page 303) or Bodysgallen Hall Hotel, Restaurant and Spa in North Wales (page 336) – all generously given to the National Trust in 2008. Please note all paying guests to the hotels are welcome to walk in the garden and park.

Bodysgallen Hall Hotel, Restaurant and Spa in North Wales

Your visit

This section of the *Handbook* provides information that will help you make the most of your visits to our places. Please also see the questions and answers on page 380, as these contain important information.

Admission fees and opening arrangements

Members of the National Trust are admitted free to virtually all places (see information about membership, page 387). Admission fees include VAT and are liable to change if the VAT rate is altered. The prices for most places include a voluntary ten per cent donation under the Gift Aid on Entry scheme, see below. Current admission prices are given in full on our website **www.nationaltrust.org.uk** or are available from the Membership Department on 0844 800 1895. Please note that prices may vary during off-peak or busy times; our website always offers the definitive information.

Gift Aid on Entry: the Gift Aid on Entry scheme gives non-members a choice between paying the standard admission price or paying the Gift Aid Admission, which includes a 10 per cent voluntary donation. Gift Aid Admissions enable the Trust to reclaim tax on the whole amount – currently an extra 25 per cent – potentially a very significant boost to a place's funds.

Gift Aid donations must be supported by a valid Gift Aid declaration, and a Gift Aid declaration can only cover donations made by an individual for him/herself or for him/herself and members of his/her family.

The admission prices shown on the National Trust's website, or which are available on request from the Trust's Membership Department, are inclusive of the ten per cent voluntary donation where places are operating the Gift Aid on Entry scheme, but both the standard admission price and the Gift Aid Admission will be displayed onsite and on our website.

Most Trust members already pay their subscriptions using Gift Aid, helping the Trust to the tune of many millions of pounds every year at no extra cost to themselves. If you would like to know more about Gift Aid, please contact the Membership Department on 0844 800 1895.

Children: under-fives are free. Children aged five to sixteen usually pay half the adult price. Seventeens and over pay the adult price. Children not accompanied by an adult are admitted at the Trust's discretion. Most places offer discounted family tickets (usually covering one or two adults and up to three children, unless stated otherwise).

Concessions: as a registered charity which has to raise all its own funds, the National Trust cannot afford to offer concessions on admission fees. We do, however, offer free entry on Heritage Open Days (visit website for details) and very occasionally for other special events, such as Bonus Time.

Educational visits: we welcome visits from schools, colleges and special interest groups (see page 387). Many places have an onsite learning officer and a programme of learning activities, which provide a stimulating opportunity for learning outside the classroom. We encourage schools and groups to get more involved by building partnerships with their local Trust site. Contact the place you wish to visit directly for details of fees, programmes and to discuss requirements.

It is advisable for teachers to make a preliminary visit before they bring their group. This can be arranged free of charge. Frequent visitors will find it worthwhile to consider educational group membership (see page 387).

Group visits: groups are always welcome. All group visitors are required to book in advance and arrangements should be made direct with the property. Admission discounts are usually available for groups of more than fifteen people, although this can vary and needs to be confirmed when booking. The Travel Trade Office at the Trust's Central Office (see page 388) can also provide general groups information and details on special interest tours and activities for groups. For further information visit **www.nationaltrust.org.uk/groups**

National Gardens Scheme open days: each year many of the National Trust's gardens are opened in support of the National Gardens Scheme (NGS). If this is on a day when the garden is not usually open, National Trust members will have to pay for entry. All money raised is donated by the NGS to support nurses' and garden charities, including the Trust garden careership training scheme. The Trust acknowledges with gratitude the generous and continuing support of the National Gardens Scheme Charitable Trust.

Busy days: Bank Holidays and summer weekends, as you'd expect, are our busiest days. There's always plenty of space to explore the outdoors, but houses can be crowded. That's why some places use timed tickets to smooth the flow of people entering. It may mean a wait before you can enter the house (a chance to explore the garden or park, perhaps), but it's very rare for houses to be so full that people have to be turned away disappointed. Nonetheless, it may be worth telephoning in advance if you are planning a long journey – and at some very small houses, booking is essential (for example, Mr Straw's House).

Toilets
There is always one available, either onsite, when we are open, or nearby, unless the individual entry specifically indicates 'no toilet'.

Handling collections
In some houses visitors are invited to handle robust items, many of which have been brought in for this purpose. Other objects will be too fragile or important to be handled without the possibility of irreparable damage and loss. Volunteer room guides and staff are available to guide you on what can be handled, and we hope you will enjoy interacting with our collections where this is possible. At an increasing number of places we positively encourage your involvement and you will be welcome to play a piano or even try your hand at snooker! Just ask what's available.

Access information
Entries for each place are shown using an extensive range of symbols, many devised uniquely for the National Trust. The key to these symbols is on the inside front cover.

It is our policy to admit an essential companion or carer of a disabled visitor free of charge, on request, while the normal membership charge or admission fee applies to the disabled visitor. To save having to 'request' a companion's free entry, we can issue an Access for All Admit One Card in the name of the disabled person. To obtain an Admit One Card please telephone 01793 817634 or email **enquiries@nationaltrust.org.uk**

If you have a specific access requirement, we do suggest you contact the property direct, and they will be pleased to advise you.

At some of our larger gardens and parks we have powered vehicles (PMVs) available to borrow, variously self-drive and/or volunteer-driven. Details are listed under each entry. Some of our places have only one PMV, so it is advisable to telephone to check availability and whether they operate a booking system, before visiting. Wherever possible, we admit users of powered wheelchairs and similar small vehicles to our buildings. This is subject to the physical limitations of the place and any other temporary constraints. Again, it is advisable to check in advance.

Our virtual tour project has continued to grow and more than 30 National Trust places now offer these tours (which will be made available on our website). Some virtual tours include British Sign Language interpretation.

We continue to work with local and national disability groups, as well as with our disabled volunteers, to improve access at our places. Roger, one of our volunteer wardens at Sheringham Park, was diagnosed with multiple sclerosis nearly four years ago. Despite this he has continued to volunteer and is convinced that it has helped him to adjust to his new way of life.

We welcome assistance dogs inside our houses, gardens, restaurants and shops.

The *Handbook* provides just a brief indication of the access facilities at our places. More detailed information regarding access provision is available in our *Access Guide*, which you can obtain free of charge from the Membership Department; simply telephone 0844 800 1895 or write to FREEPOST NAT9775, Warrington WA5 7WD. This book is also available in large print, and can be downloaded from **www.nationaltrust.org.uk/accessforall**

Both the *Access Guide* and *National Trust Magazine* are available free on CD or tape. If you wish to receive these regularly, please contact SoundTalking direct by emailing admin@soundtalking.co.uk or telephoning 01435 862737.

Guided tours

Many places now offer 'taster' tours between 11 and 1, before opening for free-flow visiting. These tours of particular rooms provide specialist insights into curatorial and conservation issues. Other places offer guided tours only for groups, so to avoid disappointment please telephone in advance or check the website.

Events

We offer a variety of events at National Trust places throughout the year, from wildflower walks, to family fun at Easter and Hallowe'en. There are live summer concerts, living history events, countryside open days and open-air theatre productions. Our lecture lunches and 'behind-the-scenes' tours, which run throughout the year, explain the work of our gardeners and house staff, while our 'Conservation in Action' events provide opportunities for you to see conservation specialists at work and talk to them about their techniques. The year ends with Christmas craft fairs, carol concerts and winter walks. For details telephone 0844 800 1895 or visit **www. nationaltrust.org.uk/events**

Enjoying the outdoors

We're more than pretty houses. We're sea and spray, boulders and moors, hills and dales. We own so much spectacular coastline and countryside. We are most famous for spectacular landscapes and coastline, such as the dramatic fells of the Lake District, the peaks of Snowdonia or the white Cliffs of Dover, but the chances are that there's one of our beautiful green spaces within easy reach of where you live – complete with footpaths and trails to make it easy for you to get out and enjoy them.

Dogs

We always try to provide facilities for dogs, such as water for drinking bowls, areas where they can be exercised and shady spaces in car parks (though dogs should not be left alone in cars). Sometimes gardens or areas within gardens may be open for dogs on leads, at the discretion of the local manager (assistance dogs are always welcome).

These facilities vary from place to place and according to how busy it is on a particular day. The primary responsibility for the welfare of dogs remains, of course, with their owners. Any specific restrictions, such as needing to be kept on a lead, are listed in the 'Making the most of your day' section of each entry.

Dogs are welcome at most countryside places, where they should be kept under close control at all times. Please observe local notices on the need to keep dogs on leads, particularly at sensitive times of year, such as during the breeding season for ground-nesting birds, at lambing time or when deer are calving. Dogs should be kept on a short lead on access land between 1 March and 31 July, and at any other time when near livestock.

In some areas we have found it necessary to introduce restrictions, usually seasonal, and particularly on beaches, due to conflicts with other users. Where access for dogs is restricted, we attempt to identify suitable alternative locations nearby.

Please clear up dog mess and dispose of it responsibly. Where dog-waste bins are not provided, please take the waste away with you.

Eating and shopping

Every purchase made from Trust shops, restaurants, tea-rooms and coffee shops makes a vital contribution to our work.

Shops: many places have shops offering a wide range of relevant merchandise, much of which is exclusive to the National Trust. These shops' times are given in the opening arrangements table. Many are open for Christmas shopping. We also operate a number of shops in towns and cities, which are open during normal trading hours (see below). We also offer many National Trust gifts for sale online at **www. nationaltrust.org.uk/shop**

Restaurants and tea-rooms: the 150 tea-rooms and cafés operated by the Trust are often located in very special buildings, such as stable blocks or hothouses. We aim to offer a sincere welcome and to showcase the best local and seasonal produce, cooking and baking. At all cafés we offer facilities for families with children, either to warm baby food or provide children's portions. There are also many autumn, winter and Christmas events.

National Trust recommends: our trading company National Trust Enterprises collaborates with leading British designers and manufacturers to create inspiring collections based on the Trust's historical places, land and archives. Partners include Fired Earth, Hi-Tec, Duresta, Stevensons of Norwich, Alitex, Scotts of Thrapston, Vale Garden Houses and Caspari.

For further details visit **www.nationaltrust.org.uk/ werecommend**

Welcoming families

As well as organising a wealth of activities and events to make your day with us truly memorable, we offer various facilities to help your visit run smoothly. Our places are relaxing and inspiring, giving a sense of freedom and fun and the opportunity to reconnect as a family. We are determined to recognise and promote the uniqueness of each place and we encourage everyone, from local communities to young people and families, to discover their intriguing stories with us.

Facilities: on your arrival, parking is made easy, and we offer family tickets at most places. You can find baby-

---

Town shops: opening times vary, so please telephone for details if you are making a special journey.

Bath Marshall Wade's House, Abbey Churchyard, BA1 1LY (01225 460249)

Cambridge 9 King's Parade, CB2 1SJ (01223 311894)

Canterbury 24 Burgate, CT1 2HA (01227 457120)

Chichester 92a East Street, PO19 1HA (01243 773125)

Conwy Aberconwy House, 2 Castle Street, LL32 8AY (01492 592246)

Dartmouth 8 The Quay, TQ6 9PS (01803 833694)

Hereford 7 Gomond Street, HR1 2DP (01432 342297)

Hexham 25/26 Market Place, NE46 3PB (01434 607654)

Isle of Wight Brighstone shop and museum, North Street, Brighstone, PO30 4AX (01983 740689)

Kendal 16–20 Stricklandgate, LA9 4ND (01539 736190)

London Blewcoat School, 23 Caxton Street, Victoria, SW1H 0PY (020 7222 2877)

Monmouth 5 Church Street, NP25 3BX (01600 713270)

St David's Visitor Centre and Shop, Captain's House, 6 High Street, SA62 6SD (01437 720385)

Salisbury 41 High Street, SP1 2PB (01722 331884)

Seahouses information centre and shop, 16 Main Street, NE68 7RQ (01665 721099)

Sidmouth Cosmopolitan House, Old Fore Street, EX10 8LS (01395 578107)

Skipton 6 Sheep Street, BD23 1JH (01756 799378)

Stratford-upon-Avon 45 Wood Street, CV37 6JG (01789 262197)

Street Clark's Village, Farm Road, BA16 0BB (01458 440578)

Swindon Heelis café and shop, Kemble Drive, SN2 2NA (shop 01793 817600; café 01793 817474)

Truro 9 River Street, TR1 2SQ (01872 241464)

Wells 16 Market Place, BA5 2RB (01749 677735)

York shop and tea-room, 32 Goodramgate, YO1 7LG (shop 01904 659050; tea-room 01904 659282)

changing and baby-feeding areas at many places – and some have purpose-designed parent and baby rooms. Our restaurants have highchairs, children's menus, colouring sheets, and some also have play areas.

To make it easier for families to visit our historic buildings, front slings for smaller babies and hip-seat carriers or reins for toddlers are often available to borrow. There are usually arrangements for storing prams and pushchairs at the entrance, as regrettably it is not possible to take these inside. We welcome baby back-carriers wherever we can, although at some houses where space is limited (and at very busy times) it's not always possible.

Activities: many National Trust places have guides, trails or quizzes for children and families, and increasingly we are trying to find ways to tell the stories of our places through activities that are more hands-on. Tracker Packs are one example – these bags are packed with activities to do as you explore together as a family. They are free to borrow, although some places will require you to leave a deposit. Many sites have discovery activity rooms and play areas too. Visit **www.nationaltrust. org.uk/familyactivities** for inspiring ideas, and we would love to hear how these places have helped you rekindle your childhood memories.

Learning and discovery – when places come to life
The National Trust is committed to placing learning at the heart of the organisation. We encourage everyone – local communities, young people, families – to engage with us to develop their sense of discovery and their enthusiasm for sharing it.

We welcome visitors from across the educational sector and from special interest groups. It is advisable for teachers to make a preliminary visit before they bring their group. This can be arranged free of charge. Frequent visitors will find it worthwhile to consider educational group membership (see page 387).

Weddings and private functions
The bell and glass symbols at the top of entries in this *Handbook* indicate that the place is licensed for civil weddings (bell symbol) and/or available for private functions (glass symbol) such as wedding receptions, anniversaries, family celebrations and so on. For more information, contact the place, the Membership Department on 0844 800 1895 or visit **www.nationaltrust. org.uk/hiring**

Your safety
We aim to provide a safe and healthy environment for visitors to our places, and we ensure that the work of our staff, volunteers and contractors does not jeopardise visitors' safety or health. You can help us by:

– observing all notices and signs during your visit;

– following any instructions and advice given by Trust staff;

– ensuring that children are properly supervised at all times;

– wearing appropriate clothing and footwear in built places, the countryside and gardens.

At all our sites the responsibility for visitor safety should be seen as one that is shared between the Trust and the visitor. The Trust takes reasonable measures to minimise risks in ways that are compatible with our conservation objectives – but not to eliminate all risks. This is especially the case at our coastal and countryside sites, where we aim to avoid measures that might restrict access or affect people's sense of freedom and adventure.

As the landscape becomes more rugged or remote, the balance of responsibility between the landowner/ manager and the visitor shifts. There will be fewer safety measures and warning signs, and visitors will need to rely more on their own skills, knowledge, equipment and preparation. To help ensure your safety:

– take note of weather conditions and forecasts and be properly equipped for changes in the weather. Please note that some places (or parts of) may close in severe weather. It is always advisable to check opening arrangements before setting out on your journey;

– make sure you are properly prepared, equipped and clothed for the terrain and the activity in which you are participating;

– tell others of your intended route and estimated time of return;

– make sure you have the necessary skills and abilities for the location and activity and are aware of your own limitations.

Your questions answered

Where can I picnic? Very many places welcome picnics and some have a designated picnic area. A few cannot accommodate them. Fires and barbecues are generally not allowed. If you are planning a picnic at a National Trust place for the first time, a quick phone call is all that is needed to check that all will be well.

Is there somewhere to leave large or bulky bags? In historic buildings you will be asked to leave behind large items of hand luggage during your visit. This is to prevent accidental damage and to improve security. The restriction includes rucksacks, large handbags, carrier (including open-topped) bags, bulky shoulder bags and camera/camcorder bags. In most houses where the restriction applies (principally historic houses with vulnerable contents, fragile decorative surfaces or narrow visitor routes), it is possible to leave such items safely at the entrance; this policy reflects standard practice at museums and galleries worldwide. See the Welcoming families section on page 378 for additional information on back-carriers and pushchairs.

What types of footwear are restricted? Any heel which covers an area smaller than a postage stamp can cause irreparable damage to floors, carpets and rush matting. We regret, therefore, that sharp-heeled shoes are not permitted. Plastic slippers are provided for visitors with unsuitable or muddy footwear,

or alternative footwear is available for purchase. Please remember that ridged soles trap grit and gravel, which scratch fine floors. Boot-scrapers and brushes are readily available and overshoes may be provided at properties with particularly vulnerable floors.

Where can I sit down? Seats for you to use are provided at various points in all the Trust's historic houses and gardens. They will be clearly indicated and will make it easy for you to take a rest, confident that you are not sitting on a fragile historic chair.

Why is it dark inside some historic rooms? This is to prevent – or at least slow down – the deterioration of light-sensitive contents, especially textiles and watercolour paintings. Light levels are regularly monitored and carefully controlled using blinds and sun-curtains. We recommend that you allow time for your eyes to adapt to these darker conditions in rooms where light levels are reduced to preserve vulnerable material.

Some historic houses offer special tours during the winter months, when house staff share with you the secrets of their traditional housekeeping practices. Guided tours explain why we need generally low light levels inside houses and why we have to close many of our houses during at least part of the winter. Events showing the process of 'Putting the House to Bed' are advertised in the

local press and in regional newsletters, or details can be obtained from the Membership Department (see page 388), or **www.nationaltrust.org. uk/events**

Why is it so cold inside some houses in winter? The heating systems in National Trust houses are not designed for the levels of domestic heating that we have become used to in our own homes. You are advised to dress warmly – just like our hardy staff and volunteers! – when you visit Trust houses in the winter.

May I use my mobile telephone? The use of mobile telephones disturbs the tranquillity of visits to historic places and interferes with radio control of conservation heating systems. Before entering historic buildings, visitors are asked to silence mobile phones and divert calls to voicemail. See Where can I take photographs? below, for advice on use of mobile phones with built-in cameras.

Where can I take photographs? We welcome amateur photography out of doors at our places. Amateur photography without flash or tripods is permitted indoors when houses are open, at the discretion of the Property/ General Manager and where owners of loan items have granted permission.
The use of mobile phones with built-in cameras is similarly permitted indoors (again, no

flash please). At most places special arrangements can be made for interested amateurs (as well as voluntary National Trust speakers, research students and academics) to take interior photographs by appointment outside normal opening hours. Requests to arrange a mutually convenient appointment must be made in writing to the place concerned. Please note that not all places are able to offer this facility and those that do may make an admission charge (including National Trust members).

All requests for commercial, non-editorial photography go through the Broadcast Media Liaison Officer (020 7799 4547).

How are measurements shown?

Area is shown in hectares (with the acre equivalent in brackets); and distances are shown in yards and miles. Heights where mentioned are shown in metres, except where a structure may have been built to achieve a very specific height in imperial measurements (such as Leith Hill Tower in Surrey).

Biking at Black Down in West Sussex

Your journey

Each entry includes its OS Landranger (or OSNI) series map number and grid reference, an indicator of its location and public transport/ road access.

Car-free days out

Travelling on foot, by bike, bus, train or boat to National Trust places can be an enjoyable and environmentally friendly way of visiting. In support of car-free travel, a growing number of places offer incentives for visitors arriving without a car – from a discount on entry to a tea-room voucher. Visit **www.nationaltrust.org.uk/ carfreedaysout**

Public transport

Details of access by public transport were correct as of July 2010. No indication of service frequency is provided.

You are strongly advised to check services and timetables before setting out, with **www.traveline.info** or **www.transportdirect.info** – both provide multi-modal journey planning services. The National Trust is grateful to Journey Solutions – a partnership of Britain's bus and train operators – for checking and updating the public transport information. Journey Solutions manages PLUSBUS, Britain's integrated train and bus ticketing system.

For details visit **www.plusbus.info**

Ferry: some places are best reached (Greenway for example) – or can only be reached (Orford Ness) – by a short but enjoyable boat trip.

Bus: unless otherwise stated, bus services pass the site entrance (although there may be a walk from the bus stop). Many bus services connect properties with local train stations – 'passing ⊠' indicates that the bus service passes the station entrance or approach road and 'passing close ⊠' indicates that a walk is necessary.

Train/London Underground: the distance from each place to nearest railway stations is given.

Cycling

More than 200 National Trust places are within 1¼ miles or 2km of the UK's 12,600-miles National Cycle Network (NCN). Combined with bridleways, byways and quiet roads, this network provides opportunities for cycling to your favourite places. We work closely with Sustrans, the sustainable transport charity, to promote cycling as a healthy, enjoyable and environmentally-friendly way of reaching our places.

- *Handbook* entries give information on the nearest NCN route. For example 'NCN4, 2 miles' denotes the property is 2 miles from NCN route number 4.

- Unless otherwise stated, most Trust places have cycle parking onsite or nearby.

Walking

There is no better way to appreciate the variety of places cared for by the National Trust than by exploring on foot. Long-distance walking routes, including thirteen National Trails, link many Trust places, on top of a scenic web of local paths and access land. We have promoted the freedom to roam over open country, coast and woods for more than a century and continue to work to improve access for all today.

- Hundreds of guided walks take place at our places each year. They are a great way to find out more about our conservation work, wildlife, history, farming and so much more, while enjoying a healthy stroll. Many places also offer waymarked trails, leaflets and maps.

- Hundreds of walks sheets are available free on the Trust website to download, print and take on your day out.

Before setting out visit **www. nationaltrust.org.uk/walks** for a route map and description of our interesting walks.

Handbook entries give information on pedestrian access from the nearest town or railway station and details of routes passing through or nearby.

Car parks

Visitors use car parks at Trust places entirely at their own risk. You are advised to secure your car and not to leave any valuable items in it during your visit. Parking in Trust car parks is free for members displaying current stickers, although a valid membership card should always be shown to a member of staff on request. Individual members' stickers cannot be used to gain free parking for coaches.

Car-parking sticker

This year your car-parking sticker can be found on the inside front cover of this *Handbook*, lightly glued to a bookmark which can also be easily removed.

If you need a replacement or additional sticker, please ask a member of staff at the visitor reception at your next visit.

You will need to show your current membership card, which should continue to be shown to staff on request whenever you enter Trust places and pay and display car parks.

The sticker is not a substitute or alternative to a current membership card – it's just for use in pay and display car parks.

Further information to help plan your journey

Transport Direct: plan how to get there by public transport or car from any UK location or postcode using **www.transportdirect.info**

Sustrans: for NCN routes and cycling maps visit **www.sustrans.org.uk** or telephone 0117 929 0888.

National Rail Enquiries: for train times visit **www.nationalrail.co.uk** or telephone 0845 748 4950.

Traveline: for bus routes and times for England, Wales and Scotland visit **www.traveline.info** or telephone 0871 200 2233.

Taxis from railway stations: **www.traintaxi.co.uk**

Public transport in Northern Ireland (train and bus): **www.translink.co.uk** or telephone 028 9066 6630.

Joining in with the Trust

As a charity we rely greatly upon additional support, beyond membership fees, to help us to protect and manage the coastline, countryside, historic buildings and gardens in our care. You can help us in several ways, such as making a donation or leaving a gift to us in your will… or by volunteering.

Volunteer with us

During 2009 we were fortunate enough to enjoy the support of 61,000 volunteers, who together contributed during the year a truly remarkable 3.5 million hours of combined effort – worth tens of millions of pounds if we had had to pay for these supremely generous gifts of time, which we could never have afforded.

So if you'd like to get involved we'd love to hear from you.

There are many roles available, from welcoming visitors to a historic house to tackling countryside conservation tasks. You could also take part in a working holiday (see page 374), join a supporter group (see page 384) or take part in our employee volunteering programme. Come and talk with us about your interests and how we could involve you.

We also have a number of opportunities specifically designed for young people, and we are developing volunteering roles which families can take on together – so there really is something for everyone.

By volunteering you will make new friends, gain work experience, use and develop your skills and see behind the scenes of our beautiful places – and with your help

we'll make a real difference to them.

To find out more, contact your local place, telephone 01793 817632 or visit **www.nationaltrust.org.uk/volunteering** or **www.nationaltrust.org.uk/youth**

Voluntary talks service

The National Trust has a group of enthusiastic and knowledgeable volunteer speakers available to give illustrated talks to groups of all sizes. Talks cover many aspects of the Trust's work, from the Neptune Coastline Campaign to garden history, conservation, individual places and regional round-ups. Talks can also be tailored to meet your group's particular interests. To find out more, contact the Talks Service Co-ordinator at your local National Trust regional or country office (see page 388).

There are numerous roles for volunteers, from welcoming visitors to tackling countryside conservation tasks

Join your local Trust supporter group

Join your local National Trust supporter group and experience the fresh air, hidden depths and new views of the National Trust while helping to conserve our heritage for ever, for everyone.

Getting together with people who feel passionate about the same things as you do is priceless. Sharing experiences together and finding out more about the places you visit is just part of the pleasure of joining a local National Trust association. You'll also enjoy learning from expert speakers, going on behind-the-scenes tours and taking relaxing holidays. Our associations promote the National Trust within their local area and raise money for conservation and development projects through all kinds of events. Join an association and be part of something amazing.

You could also join one of our local friends or advisory groups; imagine getting to see what really goes on behind the scenes at your favourite Trust place – understanding the history and the stories that make it what it is – not to mention ensuring its healthy future. As a part of a friends group, you'll have a unique relationship with the place which is most special to you. You can get involved with their volunteering team, learn about conservation, organise events and fundraising and work on ideas for the future.

If you can see yourself in the great outdoors (or sometimes the great indoors), building, creating and conserving – a National Trust Volunteer Group could be the perfect choice for you. You'll help conserve our special places – both locally and further afield. You might be constructing a footpath, building a fence or helping to restore natural habitats on the coast, but whatever you're doing, you'll be in the company of a great bunch of like-minded people.

Supporter groups play a vital role in bringing our places to life and opening them up for everyone to enjoy. Get involved with your local supporter group today and enjoy a deeper and more rewarding experience with the National Trust.

To find out more telephone 01793 817636, email sglo@nationaltrust.org.uk, or visit **www.nationaltrust.org.uk/supportergroups**

Donations
You can help us protect the special places in our care by donating to appeals, such as the work to reunite Croome Landscape Garden with Croome Court. Or perhaps you would like to give to the ongoing work in the Lake District, or the appeal to save and protect the coastline – the Neptune Coastline Campaign. You will find all of these appeals and more at **www.nationaltrust.org.uk/donations** You could support your favourite place by giving a donation and by buying a raffle ticket when you visit.

We also organise several programmes to give donors the opportunity to see at first hand the work they support, such as the Benefactor, Patron and Quercus programmes. These include special behind-the-scenes events and the opportunity to talk to our experts. To find out more email enquiries@nationaltrust.org.uk or telephone 0844 800 1895.

Art Fund
The National Trust is grateful to the Art Fund (**www.artfund.org**) for its continuing generous support in the acquisition of historic contents (Seaton Delaval Hall and Red House are recent examples). We warmly welcome Art Fund members, who may visit places which benefited directly, free of charge.

Legacies
By making provision for the National Trust with a legacy in your will, you would be providing a lasting gift for future generations. Every sum, whatever the size, will make a positive difference to our work across England, Wales and Northern Ireland in permanently safeguarding our natural and built heritage. We guarantee never to use a single penny on administration costs or overheads. Choose too where you would like your gift to be directed – the project, place or region which means most to you.

Find out more by requesting your free colour guide to making and updating a Will, available from our

Membership Department, or visit us today at **www. nationaltrust.org.uk/legacies**

Your gift is as special to us as the unique places it helps to protect.

The Trust welcomes offers of chattels: works of art, furniture and other objects that may be displayed in a historical setting.

Please contact your nearest regional office with details of the objects and, if possible, with a photograph. Please be aware that many of our places restrict their acquisitions to objects that have a historical connection with the house in question, in order to maintain the authenticity of the displays. Regrettably, therefore, we may not always be able to accept your offer, regardless of the intrinsic value and interest of the objects.

How you can support the National Trust in the US – join The Royal Oak Foundation

More than 40,000 Americans, including members and donors, belong to The Royal Oak Foundation, the National Trust's membership affiliate in the US. A not-for-profit organisation, The Royal Oak Foundation helps the National Trust, through the generous tax-deductible support of members and friends, by making grants towards its work. Member benefits include National Trust *Handbook*, three editions of *National Trust Magazine* and *The Royal Oak Newsletter*, and free admission to places of the National Trust and of the National Trust for Scotland.

The Royal Oak sponsors lectures, tours and events in the US, designed to inform Americans of the Trust's work, on topics related to UK gardens, country house interior design, art, architecture and social history.

The Royal Oak Foundation
35 West 35th Street,
Suite 1200, New York,
NY 10001-2205, USA.

Telephone 001 212 480 2889,
fax 001 212 785 7234
email general@royal-oak.org
website **www.royal-oak.org**

National Trust books, guidebooks, electronic newsletter and prints

We publish a range of books and guidebooks that promotes our work and the great variety of places and collections in our care. To buy any of these books or other titles about Trust places, please visit the National Trust Bookshop. Details of selected new titles can be found in the members' magazine or online. Visit **www.nationaltrustbooks.co.uk** or telephone 0845 672 0012.

To subscribe to the Trust's free quarterly electronic newsletter, *ABC* (Arts, Building and Conservation), email abc@nationaltrust. org.uk. Past copies of this critically acclaimed publication – full of fascinating material and news – are posted on the Trust's website.

The official decorative print sales website of the National Trust is **www.ntprints.com**. The collection of images available to purchase vividly illustrates the rich diversity and historical range of properties and collections in the Trust's care, and includes works of fine art, sumptuous interiors and exteriors, gardens and landscapes by some of the country's leading photographers. A range of print sizes and finishes is available, including art paper and canvas, with prices starting at as little as £12.

Have your say

Governance
A guide to the Trust's governance arrangements is available on our website www. nationaltrust.org.uk A paper copy is also available on request from the Secretary. Copies of our Annual Report and Accounts are also available; contact our Membership Department for more information or to request a copy.

Annual General Meeting
We believe that it is a crucial part of the governance of any large organisation, such as the Trust, that once a year the members have the chance to meet the officers and senior staff of the organisation at the Annual General Meeting (AGM). It is an opportunity for you to comment and make suggestions, to make your views known to the Trustees and the staff both through questions and through putting forward and debating resolutions of real interest to the organisation.

You will receive the formal papers for our AGM – including voting papers – with the autumn magazine. We hope you will consider attending this year's AGM. However you don't need to come to the meeting to take part. You can listen to the meeting and take part in the debates on our webcast. You can also let us know your views by returning your voting papers – or voting online – ahead of the meeting.

In addition, you have the opportunity to elect members of our Council. The Council is made up of 52 members, 26 elected by you and 26 elected by organisations whose interests coincide in some way with those of the National Trust. This mix of elected and appointed members ensures that the Trust takes full account of the wider interests of the nation for whose benefit it exists. The breadth of experience and perspective which this brings also enables the Council to act as the Trust's conscience in delivering its statutory purposes.

Privacy Policy
The National Trust's Privacy Policy sets out the ways in which the Trust processes personal data. This Privacy Policy only relates to personal data collected by the National Trust via our website, membership forms, fundraising responses, emails and telephone calls.

The full Privacy Policy is available on our website www.nationaltrust.org.uk

The Data Protection Act 1998
The National Trust makes every effort to comply with the principles of the Data Protection Act 1998.

Use made of personal information
Personal information provided to the National Trust via our website, membership forms, fundraising responses, emails and telephone calls will be used for the purposes outlined at the time of collection or registration in accordance with the preferences you express.

Consent
By providing personal data to the National Trust you consent to the processing of such data by the National Trust as described in the full Privacy Policy. You can alter your preferences as follows.

Verifying, updating and amending your personal information
If, at any time, you want to verify, update or amend your personal data or preferences please write to:

National Trust,
Membership Department,
PO Box 39,
Warrington WA5 7WD.

Verification, updating or amendment of personal data will take place within 28 days of receipt of your request.

If subsequently you make a data protection instruction to the National Trust which contradicts a previous instruction (or instructions), then the Trust will follow your most recent instruction.

Subject access requests
You have the right to ask the National Trust, in writing, for a copy of all the personal data held about you (a 'subject access request') upon payment of a fee of £10.

To access your personal data held by the National Trust, please apply in writing to:

The Data Controller,
National Trust,
Heelis, Kemble Drive,
Swindon SN2 2NA.

Your membership

- Membership of the National Trust allows you free parking in Trust car parks and free entry to most Trust places open to the public during normal opening times and under normal opening arrangements, provided you can present a current membership card.

- **Remember to display your car-parking sticker.**

- **Please check that you have your card with you before you set out on your journey. Without it, we regret that you may not be admitted free of charge, nor will we subsequently be able to refund any admission charges.**

- Membership cards are **not transferable**.

- If your card is lost or stolen, please contact the Membership Department (address on page 388), telephone 0844 800 1895.

- A temporary card can be sent quickly to a holiday address.

- In some instances an entry fee may apply. Additional charges may be made:

  - when a special event is in progress;

  - when we open specially for a National Gardens Scheme open day;

  - where the management of a place is not under the National Trust's direct control, for example Tatton Park, Cheshire;

  - where special attractions are additional and/or separate elements of the property, for example steam yacht *Gondola* in Cumbria, Dunster Watermill in Somerset, the model farm and museum at Shugborough in Staffordshire and the Tudor Old Hall and farm at Tatton Park in Cheshire;

  - where special access conditions apply, for example The Beatles' Childhood Homes in Liverpool, where access is only by minibus from Speke Hall and Liverpool city centre, and all visitors (including Trust members) pay a fare for the minibus journey.

- The National Trust welcomes educational use of its properties. Our Educational Group membership is open to all charitable status education groups whose members are in full-time education. Membership entitles you to free entry to our places providing you book your visit in advance. For full benefits and terms and conditions telephone 0844 800 1895.

- Members wishing to change from one category of life membership to another, or requiring information on pensioner membership should contact the Membership Department for the scale of charges.

- Entry to places owned by the Trust but maintained and administered by English Heritage or Cadw (Welsh Historic Monuments) is free to members of the Trust, English Heritage and Cadw.

- Members of the National Trust are also admitted free of charge to properties of the National Trust for Scotland (NTS), a separate charity with similar responsibilities. NTS places include the famous Inverewe Garden, Bannockburn, Culloden and Robert Adam's masterpiece, Culzean Castle. Full details are contained in *The National Trust for Scotland Guide to Properties* (priced £5, including post and packaging), which can be obtained by contacting the NTS Customer Service Centre, telephone 0844 493 2100. Information is also available at **www.nts.org.uk**

- Reciprocal visiting arrangements also currently exist with certain overseas National Trusts, including Australia, New Zealand, Barbados, Bermuda, Canada, Italy and – closer to home – Jersey and Guernsey. There is also a reciprocal visiting arrangement in place with the Manx Museum and National Trust on the Isle of Man (**your current membership card is always needed**). A full list is on our website and may be obtained from the Membership Department.

Getting in touch

The National Trust supports the National Code of Practice for Visitor Attractions.

We are very willing to answer questions and keen to receive comments from members and visitors. Please speak to a member of staff in the first instance.

Many National Trust places provide their own comment cards and boxes. All your comments will be read, considered and action taken where necessary, but it is not possible to answer every comment or suggestion individually.

National Trust Membership Department
PO Box 39, Warrington WA5 7WD.
0844 800 1895
0844 800 4410 (minicom)

Email **enquiries@nationaltrust.org.uk** for all general enquiries, including membership and requests for information.

National Trust Holiday Cottages
0844 800 2072 (brochures)
0844 800 2070 (reservations)

Central Office
The National Trust and National Trust (Enterprises) Ltd, Heelis, Kemble Drive, Swindon, Wiltshire SN2 2NA.
01793 817400
01793 817401 (fax)

Enquiries by telephone, email or in writing should be made to the Trust's Membership Department (see above), open seven days a week (9 to 5:30 weekdays, 9 to 4 weekends and Bank Holidays).

(Our 0844 numbers are charged at 5p per minute from BT landlines, charges from mobiles and other operators may vary.) You can also obtain information from our website **www.nationaltrust.org.uk**

Regional/country contacts

South West

(*Cornwall*)
Lanhydrock, Bodmin, Cornwall PL30 4DE
01208 265200
sw.customerenquiries@nationaltrust.org.uk

(*Devon*)
Killerton House, Broadclyst, Exeter, Devon EX5 3LE
01392 881691
sw.customerenquiries@nationaltrust.org.uk

(*Bristol/Bath, Dorset, Gloucestershire, Somerset and Wiltshire*)
Wiltshire Office, Eastleigh Court, Bishopstrow, Warminster, Wiltshire BA12 9HW
01985 843600
sw.customerenquiries@nationaltrust.org.uk

Regional/country contacts

London and South East

(*Berkshire, Buckinghamshire, Hampshire, part of Hertfordshire, Isle of Wight, Greater London and Oxfordshire*)
Hughenden Manor, High Wycombe, Buckinghamshire HP14 4LA
01494 755500
lse.customerenquiries@nationaltrust.org.uk

(*Kent, Surrey, East Sussex and West Sussex*)
Polesden Lacey, Dorking, Surrey RH5 6BD
01372 453401
lse.customerenquiries@nationaltrust.org.uk

East of England

(*Bedfordshire, Cambridgeshire, Essex, part of Hertfordshire, Norfolk and Suffolk*)
Westley Bottom, Bury St Edmunds, Suffolk IP33 3WD
01284 747500.
ee.customerenquiries@nationaltrust.org.uk

Midlands

East
(*Derbyshire, Leicestershire, Lincolnshire, Northamptonshire and Nottinghamshire*)
Clumber Park Stableyard, Worksop, Nottinghamshire S80 3BE
01909 486411
mi.customerenquiries@nationaltrust.org.uk

West
(*Birmingham, Herefordshire, Shropshire, Staffordshire, Warwickshire and Worcestershire*)
Attingham Park, Shrewsbury, Shropshire SY4 4TP
01743 708100
mi.customerenquiries@nationaltrust.org.uk

North West

(*Cumbria and Lancashire*)
The Hollens, Grasmere, Ambleside, Cumbria LA22 9QZ
015394 35599
nw.customerenquiries@nationaltrust.org.uk

(*Cheshire, Greater Manchester and Merseyside*)
18 High Street, Altrincham, Cheshire WA14 1PH
0161 928 0075
nw.customerenquiries@nationaltrust.org.uk

Yorkshire and North East

(*Yorkshire, Teesside, North Lincolnshire*)
Goddards, 27 Tadcaster Road, York YO24 1GG
01904 702021
yne.customerenquiries@nationaltrust.org.uk

(*County Durham, Newcastle and Tyneside, Northumberland*)
Scots' Gap, Morpeth, Northumberland NE61 4EG
01670 774691
yne.customerenquiries@nationaltrust.org.uk

Wales
Trinity Square, Llandudno LL30 2DE
01492 860123
wa.customerenquiries@nationaltrust.org.uk

Northern Ireland
Rowallane House, Saintfield, Ballynahinch, County Down BT24 7JA
028 9751 0721
ni.customerenquiries@nationaltrust.org.uk

National Trust for Scotland
Hermiston Quay, 5 Cultins Road, Edinburgh EH11 4DF
0844 493 2100
information@nts.org.uk

Heritage Lottery Fund

Using money raised through the National Lottery, the Heritage Lottery Fund (HLF) sustains and transforms a wide range of heritage for present and future generations to take part in, learn from and enjoy. From museums, parks and historic places to archaeology, natural environment and cultural traditions, we invest in every part of our diverse heritage. The HLF has supported 33,900 projects, allocating £4.4 billion across the UK. We have supported the following National Trust projects:

Beningbrough Hall and Gardens, North Yorkshire
Biddulph Grange Garden, Staffordshire
Birmingham Back to Backs, West Midlands
Chedworth Roman Villa, Gloucestershire
Clumber Park, Nottinghamshire
Dinefwr Park and Castle, Carmarthenshire
Divis and the Black Mountain, Belfast
Giant's Causeway, County Antrim
Gibside, Newcastle upon Tyne
Greenway, Devon
Hardcastle Crags, West Yorkshire
The Hardmans' House, Liverpool
Hardwick Hall, Derbyshire
Ickworth, Suffolk

Holy Jesus Hospital, Newcastle
Llanerchaeron, Ceredigion
Lyme Park, Cheshire
Morden Hall Park, London
Nostell Priory and Parkland, West Yorkshire
Prior Park Landscape Garden, Bath
Springhill, County Londonderry
Stowe Landscape Gardens, Buckinghamshire
Sudbury Hall and the National Trust Museum of Childhood, Derbyshire
Tyntesfield, North Somerset
Wordsworth House and Garden, Cumbria
The Workhouse, Southwell, Nottinghamshire

heritage lottery fund
LOTTERY FUNDED

Awarding funds from
The National Lottery®

If you would like to find out more please visit **www.hlf.org.uk**

Area maps

This key shows how England, Wales and Northern Ireland are divided into eleven areas for the purposes of this *Handbook*, and displayed on seven maps. The maps show those places which have individual entries as well as many additional coast and countryside sites in the care of the National Trust.

In order to help with general orientation, the maps show main roads and population centres. However, the plotting of each site serves only as a guide to its location. (Large-scale maps can be purchased from National Trust shops.) Please note that some countryside places, for example those in the Lake District, cover many thousands of hectares. In such cases the symbol is placed centrally as an indication of general location.

KEY:

Map 1	South West
Map 2	London and South East
Map 3	East of England East Midlands
Map 4	Wales West Midlands
Map 5	Yorkshire North West (S)
Map 6	North West (N) North East
Map 7	Northern Ireland

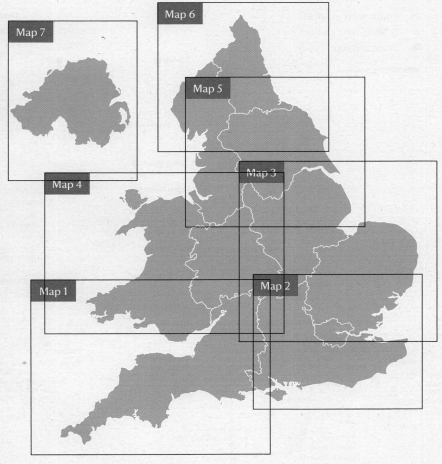

Map 1

■ **South West** (page 9)
▲ Buildings and gardens
■ Coast and countryside

0   10   20 miles
0   10   20   30 Km

South West

Grid references (row labels)
A B C D E F

1 2 3 4 5 6 7 8 9 10

Locations

Pen Anglas
Dina Island
Cilgerran Castle
Ynys Barri
Newcastle Emlyn
Fishguard
Cardigan
Dol Gold
St David's Head
St David's
Aberdeunant
Dinefwr and Castle
Llandeilo
St Bride's Bay
Haverfordwest
Carmarthen
St Clears
Paxton's Tower
Ammanford
Henr
Martin's Haven
Marloes Deer Park
Milford Haven
Neyland
Colby Woodland Garden
Narberth
Kidwelly
Llanelli
M4
Marloes Sands
Freshwater West
Pembroke
Tenby
Ragwen Point
Burry Port
Swansea
Stackpole Estate
Tudor Merchant's House
Gower Peninsula
Port Talbot
Broadhaven
Lydstep Headland
Rhossili
Port Einon
Barafundle Bay
Pennard Cliffs
Po

Countisbury
Watermeet
Lundy
Ilfracombe
Heddon Valley
Lynmouth
Morte Point
Woolacombe
Baggy Point
Braunton
Arlington Court
Barnstaple
South Molton
East Titchberry
Bideford
South Hole
Buck's Mills
Great Torrington
Sandy Mouth
Dunsland
Bude
Crackington Haven
Holsworthy
Okehampton
Boscastle
Finch Foundry
Castle Drogo
Barras Nose
Tintagel Old Post Office
Launceston
Teigr Valley
Port Quin
Lydford Gorge
The Rumps and Pentire Point
Camelford
Lawrence House
Widecombe in the Moor
Rough Tor
The Church House
Padstow
Wadebridge
Tavistock
Holne Woo
Park Head
Trowlesworthy
Carnewas and Bedruthan Steps
Bodmin
Liskeard
Buckland Abbey
Hembury Woods
Newquay
Lanhydrock
Cotehele
Plym Bridge Woods
Crantock and Holywell Bay
Saltash
Antony
PLYMOUTH
Trerice
Saltram
Chapel Porth and Wheal Coates
St Austell
Fowey
Looe
Bodigga Cliff
Wembury
Zennor Head
Truro
The Gribbin
South Milton Sands
Godrevy
St Ives
East Pool Mine
The Dodman
Overbeck's
Bosigran
Camborne
Trelissick Garden
Nare Head
Bolt Tail
Levant Mine
Botallack Count House
Trengwainton Garden
Falmouth
St Anthony Head
Bolberry Down
Soar Mill Cove
Cape Cornwall
Godolphin
Glendurgan Garden
Bolt Head
Mayon Cliff
Penzance
Helston
Helford
Portlemouth Down
St Michael's Mount
Porthcurno
Poldhu
Penrose Estate: Gunwalloe and Loe Pool
Mullion Cove
Kynance Cove
Lizard Point

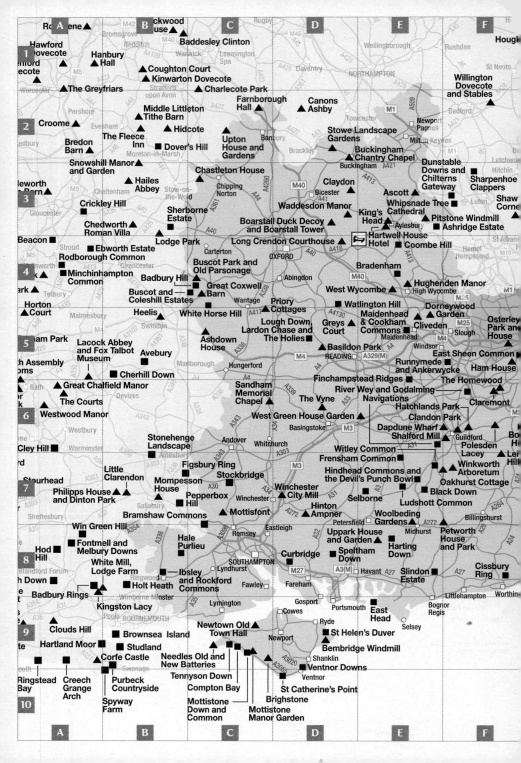

G **H** **I** **J** **K** **L**

Mill

Dunwich Heath
Coast Centre
and Beach

1

Waterbeach
Histon
Burwell
Newmarket
Bury St Edmunds
Saxmundham
Leiston
CAMBRIDGE
Aldeburgh

▲ Theatre Royal

■ Anglesey Abbey,
Gardens and
Lode Mill
Stowmarket
Ickworth
Woodbridge
Kyson
Hill
Orford Ness
Sutton Hoo

2

▲ Wimpole
Estate
Haverhill
▲ Melford Hall
Long
Melford
Lavenham
Guildhall
IPSWICH
Sudbury
Flatford:
Bridge
Cottage
■ Pin Mill

Saffron
Walden
Halstead
Felixstowe

Coggeshall:
Paycocke's and
Grange Barn ▲
Colchester
■ Dedham
Vale
Harwich

3

Bishop's
Stortford
Braintree
Bourne Mill

Hatfield
Forest
Witham
West
Mersea
Clacton-on-Sea

Ware
Hertford
Harlow
Blakes Wood
Copt Hall
Marshes
Chelmsford
Maldon

4

■ Danbury and
Lingwood
Commons
Northey Island
Burnham-on-Crouch

London

Fenton House
2 Willow Rd
Brentwood
Rayleigh
Rayleigh
Mount

Sutton House
Basildon
Southend-on-Sea

▲ Eastbury Manor House

Roman Bath
▲ Rainham Hall
Canvey Island

5

George Inn
Red House
Blewcoat School
St John's Jerusalem
Sheerness
Carlyle's House
Rochester
■ Morden Hall Park
Whitstable
Herne Bay
Margate

Owletts
Cobham Wood
and Mausoleum
Coldrum Long Barrow
Faversham
Ramsgate

■ Selsdon Wood
Canterbury
A257

Quebec
House
Knole
Old Soar
Manor
Maidstone

6

Chartwell
Ightham Mote
Stoneacre
South East
Deal

Emmetts
Garden
South Foreland
Lighthouse

Toys Hill
Ashford
White Cliffs
Dover

Chiddingstone
Sprivers
Garden
Sissinghurst
Castle
Folkestone

7

Standen
Tunbridge Wells
Scotney
Castle
Tenterden
Hythe

▲ Wakehurst Place
Smallhythe Place
Royal Military Canal

Nymans
Sheffield Park
and Garden
Bodiam Castle
New Romney

Haywards
Heath
Bateman's
Rye
Lamb House

8

Saddlescombe Farm
and Newtimber Hill
Battle
Hastings

Devil's Dyke
Lewes
Hailsham
Bexhill-on-Sea

Monk's House
Brighton

Alfriston Clergy House
Eastbourne

9

Newhaven
Frog Firle
Farm
Birling Gap and
the Seven Sisters
Chyngton Farm
Crowlink

Map 2

■ **South and South East**
(page 95)

■ **London** (page 161)

▲ Buildings and gardens

■ Coast and countryside

⌂ Historic House Hotel

0   10   20 miles
0   10   20   30 km

10

G **H** **I** **J** **K** **L**

Map 3

- **East of England** (page 171)
- **East Midlands** (page 203)
- ▲ Buildings and gardens
- ■ Coast and countryside

0   10   20 miles
0 10   20   30 km

East of England

Gunby Hall
Monksthorpe Chapel
Skegness

Louth
Mablethorpe

Brancaster Estate and Millennium Activity Centre
Stiffkey Marshes
Blakeney National Nature Reserve
Sheringham Park
West Runton and Beeston Regis Heath
Hunstanton
Wells-next-the-Sea
Blakeney
Morston Marshes
Cromer
Felbrigg Hall Gardens and Estate
North Walsham
Blickling Estate
Aylsham
Fakenham

Boston
Holbeach
King's Lynn
St George's Guildhall
East Dereham
Horsey Mere
Horsey Windpump
Heigham Holmes
Great Yarmouth
Elizabethan House Museum

Wisbech
Peckover House and Garden
Downham Market
Swaffham
NORWICH
A146
A143
Lowestoft

March
Oxburgh Hall
Watton
Wymondham
Attleborough
Darrow Wood
Bungay
Beccles

Chatteris
Littleport
Ely
Brandon
Thetford
Diss
A1143
Halesworth
Southwold
Dunwich Heath Coastal Centre and Beach

St Ives
Wicken Fen
Mildenhall
Eye
A1120

Waterbeach
Histon
Burwell
Newmarket
Bury St Edmunds
Theatre Royal
Stowmarket
Saxmundham
Leiston
Aldeburgh

CAMBRIDGE
Anglesey Abbey, Gardens and Lode Mill
Ickworth
Woodbridge
Orford Ness

Wimpole Estate
Haverhill
Melford Hall
Lavenham Guildhall
IPSWICH
Kyson Hill
Sutton Hoo

Royston
Saffron Walden
Long Melford
Sudbury
Flatford: Bridge Cottage
Pin Mill
Felixstowe
Harwich

Halstead
Coggeshall: Paycocke's and Grange Barn
Colchester
Dedham Vale

Bishop's Stortford
Braintree
Bourne Hill

Ware
Hatfield Forest
Witham
Copt Hall Marshes
West Mersea
Clacton-on-Sea

Harlow
Blakes Wood
Maldon

Hoddesdon
Chelmsford
Danbury and Lingwood Commons
Northey Island

Burnham-on-Crouch

Brentwood
Rayleigh
Rayleigh Mount
Sutton House
Basildon
Southend-on-Sea
Roman Bath
Eastbury Manor House
Rainham Hall
Canvey Island

George Inn
Red House
St John's Jerusalem
Sheerness
Margate
Whitstable
Herne

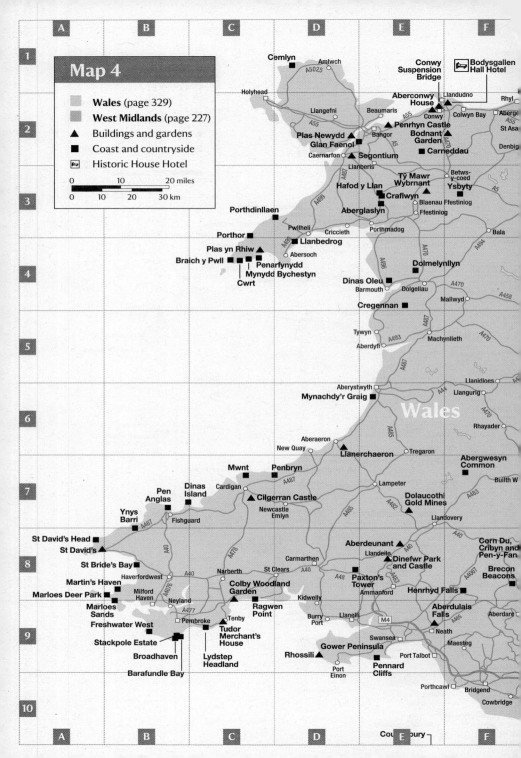

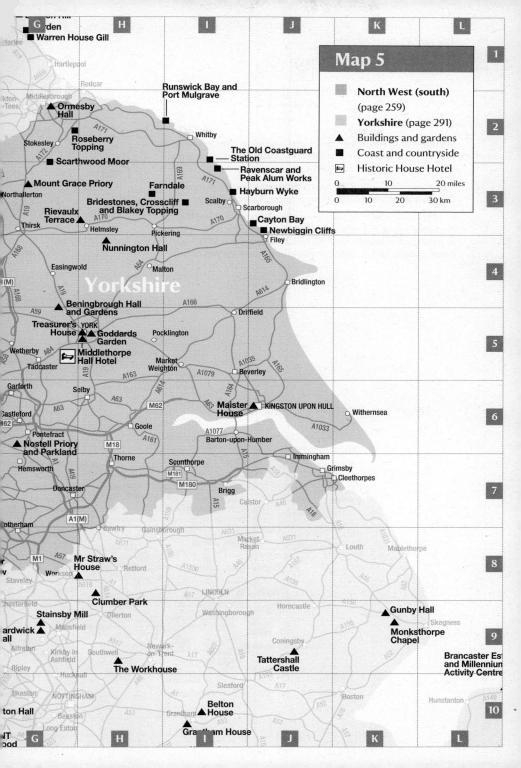

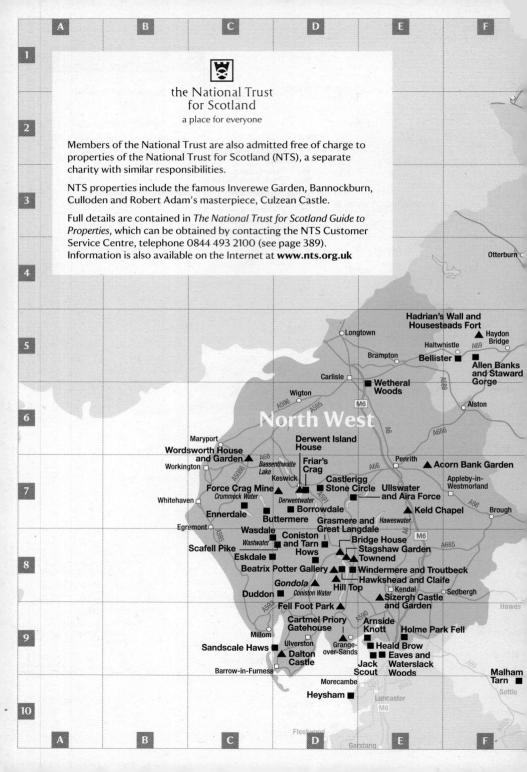

the National Trust
for Scotland
a place for everyone

Members of the National Trust are also admitted free of charge to properties of the National Trust for Scotland (NTS), a separate charity with similar responsibilities.

NTS properties include the famous Inverewe Garden, Bannockburn, Culloden and Robert Adam's masterpiece, Culzean Castle.

Full details are contained in *The National Trust for Scotland Guide to Properties*, which can be obtained by contacting the NTS Customer Service Centre, telephone 0844 493 2100 (see page 389). Information is also available on the Internet at **www.nts.org.uk**

North West

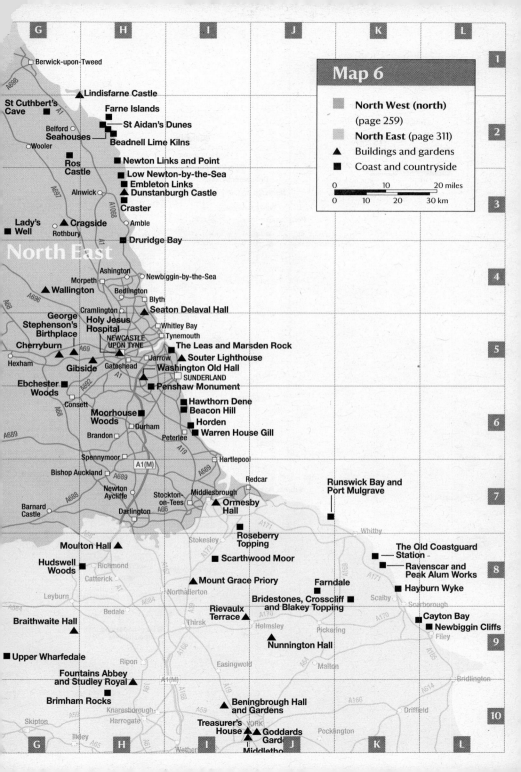

Index of properties by county/administrative area

Properties with no individual entries are shown in italics.
* Denotes properties shown only on maps.

Northern Ireland

County Antrim

Ballyconagan (7:E3) *404
Carrick-a-Rede (7:D3) 354, 358
Cushendun (7:E4) 354
Cushleake Mountain (7:E4) 354
Dunseverick Castle (7:D3) 354
Fair Head (7:E3) 354
Giant's Causeway (7:D3) 354, 365
Glenoe (7:E5) 354
The Gobbins (7:F5) *404
Larrybane (7:D3) 354
The Manor House,
  Rathlin Island (7:E3) *404
Mullaghdoo and Ballykeel (7:F5) *404
North Antrim Cliff Path (7:D3) *404
Patterson's Spade Mill (7:E6) 367
Portmuck (7:E5) *404
Rathlin Island (7:E3) 354, 356
Skernaghan Point (7:E5) 354
White Park Bay (7:D3) 354

County Armagh

Ardress House (7:D7) 357
The Argory (7:C7) 357
Ballymoyer (7:C8) *404
Derrymore House (7:D8) 362

Belfast

Collin Glen (7:E6) 355
The Crown Bar (7:E6) 361
Divis and the Black
  Mountain (7:E6) 355, 356, 362
Lisnabreeny (7:E6) *404
Minnowburn (7:E6) 355

County Down

Ballymacormick Point (7:F6) 355
Ballyquintin Farrn (7:F7) 355
Blockhouse Island (7:E9) *404
Castle Ward (7:F7) 360
Green Island (7:E9) *404
Kearney (7:F7) *404
Knockinelder (7:F7) *404
Lighthouse Island (7:F6) *404
Mount Stewart House, Garden and
  Temple of the Winds (7:F6) 366
Mourne Coastal Path (7:E8) *404
Murlough Bay (7:E3) 354, 367
Murlough National Nature
  Reserve (7:E8) 355, 367
Orlock Point (7:F6) 355
Rowallane Garden (7:E7) 369
Slieve Donard (7:E8) 355
Strangford Lough Wildlife
  Centre (7:F7) 355

County Fermanagh

Castle Coole (7:A7) 359
Crom (7:A8) 355, 361
Florence Court (7:A7) 364

County Londonderry

Barmouth (7:C4) *404
Downhill Demesne
  and Hezlett House (7:C3) 8, 363
Grangemore Dunes (7:C4) *404
Portstewart Strand (7:C3) 368
Springhill (7:C6) 8, 370

County Tyrone

Gray's Printing Press (7:B5) 365
Wellbrook Beetling Mill (7:C6) 371

Northern Ireland's North Coast

Carrick-a-Rede (7:D3) 354, 358
Downhill Demesne
  and Hezlett House (7:C3) 363
Dunseverick Castle (7:D3) 354
Giant's Causeway (7:D3) 354, 365
Murlough Bay
  and Fair Head (7:E3) 354, 367
Portstewart Strand and
  the Bann Estuary (7:C3) 368
Rathlin Island (7:E3) 354
White Park Bay (7:D3) 354

Tourist areas

For information on the properties
below, please visit
www.nationaltrust.org.uk and
follow links to the new website.

Isle of Wight

Bembridge and Culver Downs
Borthwood Copse
Chillerton Down
Compton Bay and Downs
Newtown National Nature Reserve
St Catherine's Down
  and Knowles Farm
St Helens Duver
The Needles Headland
  and Tennyson Down
Ventnor Downs

North Devon

Arlington Court and the National
  Trust Carriage Museum
Bideford Bay and Hartland
Dunsland
Heddon Valley
Lundy
Morte Point
Watersmeet

The Lake District

Borrowdale
Arnside and Silverdale
Buttermere Valley
Coniston and Tarn Hows
Derwent Water
Duddon Valley
Ennerdale
Eskdale
Friar's Crag
Grasmere
Great Langdale
Hawkshead and Claife
Little Langdale
Nether Wasdale
Sizergh Castle and Garden
Ullswater and Aira Force
Wasdale
Windermere and Ambleside

Northern Ireland's North Coast

Carrick-a-Rede
Downhill Demense
  and Hezlett House
Dunseverick Castle
Giant's Causeway
Murlough Bay and Fair Head
Portstewart Strand and the Bann
  Estuary
Rathlin Island
Rough Fort
White Park Bay

Peak District

Derwent Valley
Dovedale National Nature Reserve
Edale Valley
Hope Valley
Ilam Park
Kinder Scout
Longshaw
Marsden Moor
Miller's Dale and Ravenstor
Stanton Moor Edge
The Manifold Valley

Suffolk Coast and Heath

Dunwich Heath: Coastal Centre
  and Beach
Kyson Hill
Orford Ness National
  Nature Reserve
Pin Mill
Sutton Hoo

Mid and South East Wales

Abergwesyn Common
Berthlwyd
Brecon Beacons
Clytha Park
Henryhd Falls
Lanlay Meadows
Skirrid
Sugar Loaf
The Kymin
Upper Tarell Valley

Property and general index

Properties with no individual entries are shown in italics.
* Denotes properties shown only on maps.

Index   415

National Trust

© 2011 National Trust

Editor
Lucy Peel

Editorial assistance
Anthony Lambert
Penny Shapland
Wendy Smith

Production
Graham Prichard

Art direction
Craig Robson
Wolff Olins

Supporter relations
and sponsor
Alex Youel

Design
LEVEL Partnership

Database developers
Roger Shapland
Dave Buchanan

Maps
© Blacker Design,
Maps in Minutes™/
Collins Bartholomew
2010

Origination
Zebra
Printed
St Ives, Peterborough

Printed on Charisma Silk
and Cocoon Silk, both
made from 100 per cent
post-consumer waste

NT LDS stock no: 73801/11
ISBN 978-0-7078-0415-6

Image acknowledgements

*National Trust
Photographic
Library photographers:*

Matthew Antrobus
Steve Atkins
Cristian Barnett
Bill Batten
Don Bishop
Alex Black
Mark Bolton
Daniel Bosworth
Clive Boursnell
Andrew Butler
Michael Caldwell
Joe Cornish
Derek Croucher
Nick Daly
David Dixon
Rod Edwards
Andreas von Einsiedel
Philip Fenton/
  Lightwork
Geoffrey Frosh
Dennis Gilbert
Nick Guttridge
John Hammond
E. Chambré Hardman
Jerry Harpur
Paul Harris
Catherine Hayburn
Andrea Jones
Chris King
Andrew Lawson
Andrew Leighton
David Levenson
Nadia Mackenzie
Andy Marshall
Leo Mason
Nick Meers
John Millar
Paul Mogford
Geoff Morgan
Robert Morris
David Noton
Alasdair Ogilvie
Phil Ripley
Stephen Robson
David Sellman
Ben Selway
Arnhel de Serra
Ian Shaw
William Shaw
Rupert Truman
Penny Tweedie
Colin Varndell
Charlie Waite
Paul Wakefield
David Watson

*Additional
images
supplied by:*

Janet Baxter
Karen Birch (staff)
John Bigelow Taylor
Heather Bradshaw
Nick Brooks
Bernie Brown
Mike Cable
CAMS
John Crowe
Jonathan Cummins
  (staff)
Richard Daniel
Geoff Durrant
Gavin Duthie
Phil Evans
Zoe Frank
Jason Friend
Rika Gordon
David Hardman
Guy Harrop
Mike Henton
Chris Hill
Steve Hughes
Malcolm Jarvis
Robert Jordan
Andy Keen
David Kirkham
Keith Morris
Dave Morton
Alan Novelli
Erik Pelham
P. Preston
Seamus Rogers
Jonathan Sargant
Norfolk Museums and
  Archaeology Service
Haidee Sheahan
David Slade
Peter Spooner and
  George Littler
Richard Todd
Paul Watson
Tony West

Welcome to the National Trust

All about us

- the Trust is a registered charity. We were founded in 1895 to look after places of historic interest or natural beauty in England, Wales and Northern Ireland permanently for the nation.

- we are completely independent of the Government and receive no direct state grant or subsidy for our core work.

- we are one of Europe's leading conservation bodies, protecting through ownership, management and covenants 255,000 hectares (630,000 acres) of land of special importance and 709 miles (1,141 kilometres) of coastline.

- the support of our 3.8 million members, as well as visitors, volunteers, tenants, partners and benefactors is vital to us.

- historic buildings in our care date from the Middle Ages to modern times. We are also responsible for ancient monuments, gardens, landscape parks and farmland leased to more than 1,500 tenant farmers.

- the Trust has the unique statutory power to declare land inalienable. Such land cannot be voluntarily sold, mortgaged or compulsorily purchased against our wishes without special parliamentary procedure. This special power means that Trust protection is for ever.

- all our income is spent on the care and maintenance of the land and buildings in our protection, however we are always in need of financial support as we cannot meet the cost of all our obligations.

Our strategic aims are

- engaging supporters;

- improving our conservation and environmental performance;

- investing in our people;

- financing our future.

Join us and enjoy

- free entry and parking at more more than 350 historic houses and gardens, ancient monuments, nature reserves and parks;

- free parking at our many countryside and coastline locations;

- this *Handbook* – the complete guide to all the places you can visit;

- regional newsletters packed with details of special events at locations near you;

- three editions of our magazine exclusively for members – featuring news, views, gardening and letters;

- information on your local supporter groups and details on how you can get involved;

- membership also entitles you to free admission to properties cared for by the National Trust for Scotland.

Best of all, you will know that you are helping to protect the places you enjoy for ever, for everyone.

The Trust online

You can find information about all the places in this *Handbook* on our website at **www.nationaltrust.org.uk** (online information is updated daily). To help you make the most of your visit, most places show additional information about their history and features. The website also includes regional news and events, information about volunteering and learning opportunities, as well as hiring a venue for corporate or private functions. In addition we have a dedicated holiday cottages website at **www.nationaltrustcottages.co.uk** and an online gift shop at **www.nationaltrust.org.uk/shop**

For monthly news, events information, details of things to do and places to visit, updates on our work and suggestions of how you might get involved, sign up for your free email newsletter via **www.nationaltrust.org.uk/email**

This *Handbook* contains email addresses for those places which can be contacted direct. General email enquiries should be sent to enquiries@nationaltrust.org.uk

Feel free

Make the most of the great outdoors with the National Trust this year. Whether you want to walk, cycle, camp, surf or just take a gentle stroll, there are endless special places to explore. With 709 miles of coastline and many thousands of hectares of countryside in our care, there is so much to see and do – from a picnic by the sea on a beautiful summer's day, to an exhilarating winter walk in one of our wonderful gardens.

For more information – and inspiration – visit www.nationaltrust.org.uk/feelfree

www.nationaltrust.org.uk

ISBN 978-0-7078-0415-6

9 780707 804156

Also by Peternelle van Arsdale

The Beast Is an Animal